Management

Management

Jerry Kinard
Western Kentucky University

D. C. HEATH AND COMPANY
Lexington, Massachusetts   Toronto

Dedicated to my wife, Linda,
and my children, Amy, Carole, Brian, and Holly,
whose love and devotion make life
worth living

Cover Design: Dustin Graphics, based on a photograph by Jan Halaska/Photo Researchers, Inc.

Illustration Credits

19 © Punch/Rothco; **33** The Bettmann Archive; **35** Historical Pictures Service; **36** The Bettmann Archive; **38** © Punch/Rothco; **41** Historical Pictures Service; **155** © Punch/Rothco; **190** © Punch/Rothco; **264** Rothco; **284** Rothco; **357** © Punch/Rothco; **408** Biotec Systems, a division of Hamilton Sorter Co., Inc.; **410** Rothco; **499** UPI/Bettmann Newsphotos; **500** The Bettmann Archive; **539** Rothco.

Published simultaneously in Canada.

Printed in the United States of America.

International Standard Book Number: 0-669-09223-1

Library of Congress Catalog Card Number: 87-81817

10   9   8   7   6   5   4   3   2   1

Preface

I had four goals in writing *Management*:

1. To give students a sound understanding of the nature and practice of management
2. To describe the environment of management and the various decision-making situations that managers face
3. To show how to apply management theories in these day-to-day work situations
4. To stimulate interest in the discipline of management.

To meet these goals, I have integrated theory and practice through text examples, boxed features, real-world cases, and action-oriented exercises. Organized by the management functions, the text systematically develops a fundamental understanding of the responsibilities and challenges confronting managers. It is specifically designed for introductory management students and assumes no previous course work in management.

Thorough coverage of the basic functions of management—planning, organizing, staffing, leading, and controlling—makes this text a comprehensive one. Students are exposed to the full scope of management theory as specified by AACSB guidelines with chapters on the management of production and information, social responsibility and ethics, international management, labor-management relations, and careers in management. Reports on up-to-date topics such as robotics, ergonomics, technostress, just-in-time planning, stock market scandals, entrepreneurship, career paths, women in management, and personal computer use by managers familiarize students with the exciting business world of today.

Organization

Management is made up of six interrelated parts corresponding to the traditional functions of management. Part One introduces the field of management and describes managers' tasks and responsibilities. It also provides a brief history of management thought and describes the environment in which managers work. Part Two analyzes managers' planning and decision-making functions, explaining the planning process, strategic planning, and how managers choose among alternative courses of action. Part Three presents various ways to organize human and physical resources to accomplish organizational goals in all kinds of businesses. Part Four discusses managers and motivation, communicating with organizational members, minimizing conflict within the organization, and being an effective leader. Part Five examines the process of control and various types of controlling, including production and information control tools. Part Six addresses special concerns beyond the management functions—social responsibility and ethics, the international dimension of management, and labor-management relations. A concluding chapter highlights women in management and focuses on today's career opportunities in management for both men and women.

Teaching and Learning Aids

Teachers and students need a textbook that is both fundamentally sound and stimulating. Special care was taken to cover all pertinent topics in *Management*. Various features are incorporated throughout the text to interest students and aid effective learning.

Part openers. A part opener begins each major section, explaining the section's purpose and relating it to previous sections. Separate paragraphs establish each chapter's place in that section.

Chapter outline. An outline of topics covered appears on the first page of the chapter, so that students can effectively preview and review what they read.

Management in Action. A real-world *Management in Action* incident opens each chapter, dramatically depicting a management situation related to the chapter's major themes. For example, "The 'Un-Manager' of Gore-Tex" illustrates the Chapter 1 discussion of management styles and "Motivating the Creative Employee" shows how the motivation theories presented in Chapter 10 are used by managers.

Chapter Preview. A brief introduction links the opening incident with chapter topics and lists learning objectives.

Marginal notes. Marginal annotations throughout the chapter highlight each important management concept.

Real-world examples. Sears, K mart, IBM, and General Motors are among the many real companies featured whose experiences provide a practical, true-to-life view of management.

Boxed features. A wealth of boxed material, directly related to chapter topics, enlivens each chapter, providing real-world examples of managers at work, practical tips on day-to-day problems, and the most current computer applications. *On the Job* describes how managers at companies like Pillsbury and Continental Airlines make decisions and cope with stress. Students can contrast leadership styles, personalities, and decision-making approaches. *The*

Manager's Notebook gives practical advice on handling specific problems and improving managerial skills, from "Managing for Maternity" to "How to Disagree with Your Boss." *On-Line Management* features managers using personal computers, robots, management information systems, and decision support systems. General interest topics in *The In-Box* include employee fitness programs and "bossless" systems.

Chapter Review. A chapter summary repeating the chapter's learning objectives works as a guide for meaningful review.

The Manager's Dictionary. At the end of each chapter, important terms explained in the chapter are listed as an additional review. Page numbers indicate where in the chapter each term is boldfaced and defined. The end-of-book *Glossary* contains a comprehensive list of these terms.

Review Questions. Review questions at the end of each chapter are tied to the chapter's learning objectives.

Management Challenge. Students can connect theory and practice by solving business problems in these end-of-chapter exercises.

Cases. Two real-world cases reflect the major themes of the chapter and help students refine their decision-making skills.

Acknowledgments

Like all textbooks, *Management* is the culmination of the efforts of many great people. To these people, whose tireless efforts went into reviewing the project at various stages, I am genuinely appreciative:

John R. Beem
College of Du Page

Michael Cicero
Highline Community College

Harris Dean
Lansing Community College

Richard Deane
Georgia State University

Phyllis Fowler
Macomb Community College

Gary Gage
Pensacola Junior College

Robert D. Goddard
Appalachian State University

Stanley D. Guzell
Youngstown State University

Dan Hoyt
Arkansas State University

Bruce H. Johnson
Gustavus Adolphus College

Candida Ann Johnson
Holyoke Community College

B. Wayne Kemp
University of Tennessee at Martin

Timothy A. Matherly
Florida State University

Elizabeth Redstone
Cuyahoga Community College

Charles W. Roe
Nicholls State University

Edward Stead
East Tennessee State University

H. Ralph Todd
American River College

Ted Valvoda
Lakeland Community College

Alan Vogel
Cuyahoga Community College

John Warner
University of New Mexico

Special thanks go to Peter Wright and Linda Kinard, whose thoughtful insights, numerous contributions, and probing inquiries greatly strengthened the book. I also extend sincere appreciation to Roy Carpenter and Joseph Miller, who supported my efforts throughout the writing of the manuscript.

I am grateful to a number of people who provided research and word processing assistance. Linda Buras, my graduate assistant, was an invaluable asset. Frances Landry and Rhonda Smith were equally valuable. These people have my heartfelt thanks.

The staff of D. C. Heath and Company worked long and hard to see this project through to its completion, and I thank them. I am especially indebted to Susan Gleason, developmental editor, who provided overall guidance for the project; Ann Hall, who did a masterful job of editing the manuscript; and Cathy Brooks, production editor, who piloted the manuscript through the production process.

Finally, I wish to thank my wife and children, who unselfishly allowed this text to encroach on their time. For their understanding and patience, I am truly grateful.

J. L. K.

Contents

CHAPTER 6
Managerial Decision
Making   136

PART FOUR

Leading 258

P A R T   F I V E
Controlling   368

CHAPTER 16
Quantitative Control
Tools   418

PART SIX

Beyond the Management Functions   444

CHAPTER 17
Management's Social
Responsibility   446

Management

PLAN

CONTROL

ORGANIZE

LEAD

STAFF

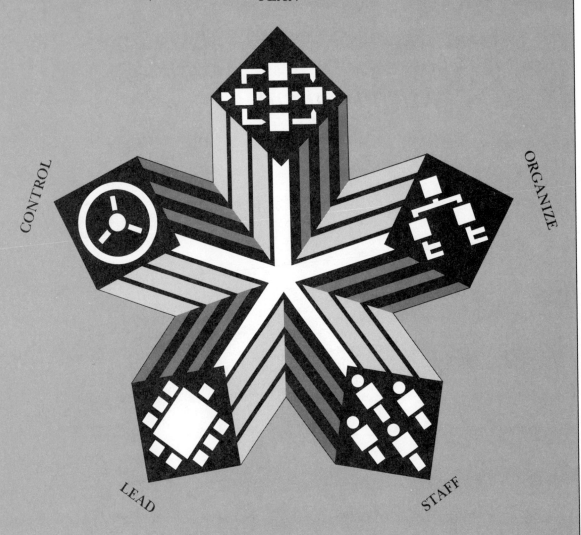

Introduction: The Essence of Management

This section has four objectives: (1) to acquaint undergraduate students with the tasks and responsibilities of managers in all types of organizations; (2) to give a brief history of the development of management thought; (3) to describe the setting in which managers work; and (4) to provide a framework for the remainder of this text. You will gain insight into the dynamic, challenging field of management and discover how important management is to the efficient operation of both profit-making and nonprofit-making organizations.

Chapter 1, "The Nature of Management," describes the functions that all managers perform—the daily activities that consume their time and energy. The various levels of management, the skills managers need at different levels, and the roles they play are also discussed.

Chapter 2, "Schools of Management Thought," focuses on major contributions to management theory from the nineteenth century to the present. Three schools of thought are presented—classical, behavioral, and quantitative. The classical, or traditional, school of management at first emphasized using scientific principles of management to find the "one best way" of performing any task. Later, as people began to recognize the importance of management at all organizational levels, this school expanded to include administrative processes and organizational theory. The behavioral school of management analyzes the human element in organizational settings. The quantitative school advocates managers' using mathematical models and quantitative tools in making decisions. Specific quantitative tools discussed in this chapter are illustrated in later chapters.

Chapter 3, "The Environment of Management," presents the internal and external forces shaping the environment of a business. Political and legal, economic, social, and technological forces are external factors affecting a firm. Organizational resources and the value systems of a firm's managers are internal forces. All these forces create both problems and opportunities for organizations; you will see how some businesses adapt or fail to adapt to these forces.

CHAPTER OUTLINE

Management Defined

A Formal View of the Manager's Job
    Planning
    Organizing
    Staffing
    Leading
    Controlling

An Informal View of the Manager's Job

Management Roles
    Interpersonal Roles
    Informational Roles
    Decisional Roles

The Management Hierarchy
    Top Management
    Middle Management
    Supervisory Management

Management Skills

Management as a Discipline

Managerial Styles: Contrasting Profiles

The Nature of Management

The "Un-Manager" of Gore-Tex

When Bill Gore resigned from Du Pont to start his own business in 1958, he was forty-five years old and had a wife and five children to support. He left behind a seventeen-year career, a good salary, and lots of job security—but he took with him valuable knowledge gained from his work and a management philosophy that was a world apart from that of most managers.

Gore's approach to running W. L. Gore & Associates was so different, in fact, that he was called an "un-manager."[1] For instance, his company's structure was more like a lattice than like the traditional pyramid. Everyone dealt directly with everyone else in relationships that were a crosshatching of horizontal and vertical lines. There were no managers or subordinates—only associates. Gore even said, "We don't manage people here. They manage themselves."[2] No one had a job title at W. L. Gore & Associates and little attention was paid to where people were on the organization chart. Everyone determined where in the organization he or she best fit. Tasks were performed by work teams of individuals who developed technologically advanced products sold throughout the world.[3]

How did the company do? In 1985, W. L. Gore & Associates was comprised of thirty plants and three thousand associates. Sales exceeded $225 million annually, and both revenue and earnings were growing at a compounded annual rate of 25%.[4] More than a half-million people had received Gore-Tex artificial blood vessels, and the company's waterproof sportswear, filter bag, and wire-coating businesses were highly profitable.

3

Preview

What worked for W. L. Gore & Associates may not work for other companies. Many variables affect the management philosophy and leadership style that combine to create the atmosphere of the workplace. These variables include the personalities and backgrounds of the people involved, the nature of the work, and the size and complexity of the organization. Because Bill Gore trusted employees so much and believed so strongly in a task-force approach to problem solving in technical areas, he just about dispensed with any management structure. But most firms are organized and managed differently: jobs are more structured, authority-reporting relationships are more sharply delineated, and management is recognized as important to the efficient operation of the firm.

Some people would call Gore a leader; others would call him a manager. Still others would argue that he was a hybrid of both. What is the difference between the two? *Is* there a difference? Professor Abraham Zaleznik of Harvard Business School distinguishes between leaders and managers this way:

> Leaders . . . are often dramatic and unpredictable in style. They tend to create an atmosphere of change, ferment, even chaos. They are often obsessed by their ideas, which appear visionary and consequently excite, stimulate, and drive other people to work hard and create reality out of fantasy.
>
> Managers are typically hard-working, analytical, tolerant, and fair-minded. They have a strong sense of belonging to the organization and take great pride in perpetuating and improving upon the status quo. But managerial executives focus predominantly on process, whereas leaders focus on substance.[5]

Given these distinctions, Gore probably should be classified as a combination leader-manager. As a leader, he motivated and inspired his people to work diligently and to be creative. As a manager, he systematically coordinated the organization's resources and tasks to achieve organizational goals.

This introductory chapter will discuss the nature of managerial activity and explain how managers, as leaders, help accomplish organizational goals. While studying this chapter, you will learn:

✓ Why managers are essential to the efficient operation of all types of organizations

✓ The basic functions all managers perform

✓ The different roles played by managers

✓ The three levels of management that constitute the management hierarchy

✓ The skills and abilities needed by managers at different levels

✓ How managers differ in management style and decision-making behavior

Management Defined

Managers use resources to attain goals

Organizations establish a variety of goals

What do you think of when the term *manager* is mentioned? Like some people, you might envision Billy Martin kicking dirt on an umpire's shoes, or Lee Iacocca explaining how Chrysler Corporation repaid its debt to the federal government. These are the kinds of images some of us conjure up when the word *manager* is used. Martin and Iacocca are managers. Their objectives are basically the same as that of Bill Gore—to maximize the potential of their people and coordinate their efforts to attain some predetermined goal. This gives us a good working definition of **management.** For Martin, the goal was the World Series Championship; for Iacocca, it is to become the most successful auto maker in the United States; and for Gore, it was to produce and market his company's products profitably. Martin, Iacocca, and Gore, like thousands of other people, practice management. Their job is to achieve organizational goals through the combined efforts of people.

All organizations establish a variety of goals and direct their energies and resources to achieving them. A profit-oriented business firm, for example, might have a return-on-investment goal; a hospital would have goals centered around patient care; and an educational institution would establish goals for teaching, research, and community service. All organizations also have resources that can be used to meet these objectives. Such resources can be classified into two categories: human and nonhuman. Nonhuman resources include plants and equipment, land, and financial resources. Human resources are employees' skills and knowledge. As shown in Figure 1.1, management is the force

FIGURE 1.1
Management as a
unifying force

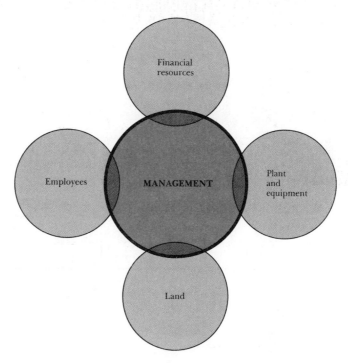

that unifies these resources. It is the process of bringing them together and coordinating them to help accomplish organizational goals.

The importance of management in the production of goods and services has been recognized for a long time. For instance, a manager:

- Puts together the factors of production—including land, labor, and capital—to produce goods and services

- Makes business decisions

- Takes risks for which the reward is profit

- Acts as an innovator by introducing new products, new technology, and new ways of organizing business[6]

example of industry which uses all raw material is pary. obvious success.

Influence from internal and external groups

Without management, virtually no business could survive. While land, labor, and capital usually are considered the factors of production, proper management increases their value to a business.

In much the same way that they bring together different resources, managers also are accountable to a number of different groups of people. Certainly they must answer to the owners of the business and to its employees, customers, and creditors. Many people also contend that a business's obligations extend to society as a whole—a situation that was certainly true of Union Carbide in the toxic leak disaster at Bhopal. We can say that business managers must be responsible to everyone who is either involved in a business's operations or affected by its activities. Figure 1.2 depicts a manager's interactions with other groups of people.

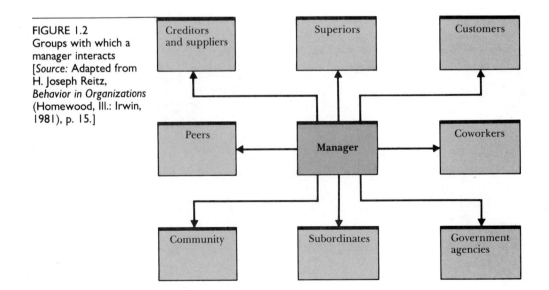

FIGURE 1.2
Groups with which a manager interacts
[*Source:* Adapted from H. Joseph Reitz, *Behavior in Organizations* (Homewood, Ill.: Irwin, 1981), p. 15.]

Creditors and suppliers · Superiors · Customers · Peers · Manager · Coworkers · Community · Subordinates · Government agencies

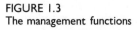

A firm's goals and responsibilities are not separate concerns. For example, the management of any private corporation has an obligation to invest the owners' funds prudently to assure an adequate return on the owners' investment. This responsibility dictates the firm's profit objectives. A pharmaceutical company like Johnson & Johnson, after the Tylenol poisoning scare, might have a goal of developing effective, risk-free drugs—an objective that would result from the firm's responsibilities to its customers. A chemical company like Union Carbide might want to eliminate its sources of pollution because of its obligations to society. And Du Pont might emphasize its safety program for the benefit of its employees.

In private enterprise, managers can best meet their many obligations by operating effectively and efficiently. A firm's profits are a measure of its success. With adequate profit, owners receive a favorable return on their investment, and employees are assured that the company won't go out of business. Adequate profit also lets managers invest in product research and development, pollution abatement, employee benefits, and other areas. A manager is responsible to many groups. The manager's effectiveness depends on whether he or she can fulfill responsibilities to all these groups.

A Formal View of the Manager's Job

Regardless of the type of firm, all managers have certain basic functions—planning, organizing, staffing, leading, and controlling. The scope and nature of these functions differ from manager to manager and from firm to firm. And the order in which they are performed is rarely as orderly as is shown in Figure 1.3. Even so, all managers must be concerned with these activities.

Planning

The function of **planning,** covered in more depth in Part Two of this book, encompasses determining specific objectives and how to accomplish them. Top-level managers set plans for the entire company; lower-level managers prepare plans for their immediate areas of responsibility. For example, top-

---

FIGURE 1.3
The management functions

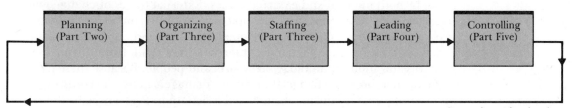

Corrective action is taken

Levels of planning

level managers of a bank plan ways to increase its deposits and to enlarge its share of the market. These plans may require opening new branch banks, modifying interest rates, or offering additional services. Branch managers, on the other hand, plan for taking care of walk-in customers. Their plans may call for adequate staffing at peak periods, procedures for opening and closing accounts, and periodic teller balancing.

Planning doesn't occur in a vacuum. It is done in light of budgetary constraints, personnel requirements, competition, and other factors. For example, a bank's plans to modify its interest rates would be influenced by what other financial institutions do and by how such actions would affect earnings. Similarly, the branch manager's plan to take care of customers efficiently would be affected by staffing limitations and other events beyond his or her control.

Organizing

When goals have been established, a manager must create a way to accomplish them. In other words, through **organizing,** he or she must develop a system in which people can perform tasks that lead to the desired results. Initially, organizing by top-level executives includes the following activities:

- Creating job positions with defined duties, responsibilities, requirements, and salary ranges based on job requirements

- Arranging positions into a hierarchy by establishing authority-reporting relationships

- Determining the number of subordinates each manager should have reporting to him or her (called *span of control* or *span of management*), the number of hierarchical levels in the organization, and the most appropriate way to set up departments *(departmentation)*

Developing a structure like this ensures that duties are well-defined and coordinated. Each position in the organization is accountable for identifiable tasks that contribute to its overall purpose.

Organizing is an ongoing process

Of course, most organizations also undergo continual change. Jobs may be enlarged, diminished, or eliminated; additional positions may be created; new production methods may be instituted; new management skills may be required; or reporting relationships may be altered. Such change is brought about by both internal and external forces. External forces of change may be social, political, economic, and technological. More technologically advanced production methods might be developed, new laws and regulations might be enacted, and values might change. Internal forces result from the interaction of an organization's technology, structure, and people. Because these internal and external forces of change always exist, managers must constantly organize and reorganize. Organizing is discussed at length in Part Three of this book.

Staffing

As we have pointed out, organizing involves creating job positions with assigned duties and responsibilities. **Staffing,** also covered in Part Three, involves the recruitment, selection, development, and retention of employees with appropriate qualifications for positions created by the manager. Staffing is one of the manager's most important duties because the success of any organization depends on the quality of its employees. Most managers therefore choose their new employees very carefully. Staffing usually is systematic and includes many of the following activities:

Matching jobs and people (margin note)

- Human resource planning

- Announcing and advertising vacant positions

- Receiving applications

- Preliminary and final interviewing

- Testing

- Medical examination

- Final selection and orientation

Staffing is influenced by laws (margin note)

Staffing has undergone remarkable change in recent years. Human resource planning, equal employment opportunity, affirmative action, equal pay for equal work, and similar terms were rarely mentioned twenty-five years ago. Today, managers involved in staffing are tremendously aware of the importance of these concepts. For the most part, the changes have benefited employers and employees alike because they have resulted in a better matching of people and jobs. But they also have created problems that managers of the past could not have imagined.

Leading

Leadership requires good interpersonal skills (margin note)

As we saw at the beginning of this chapter, leadership is the heart and soul of management. **Leading** involves influencing others in order to accomplish specific objectives. To be effective leaders, managers need to understand individual and group behavior, techniques of motivation, and effective styles of leadership. Managers must develop relationships that ensure adequate communication with their subordinates. Leading also includes managing personal conflict, helping employees deal with changing conditions, and, in some cases, disciplining employees.

Even in the most freewheeling of companies, leading is more than creating a "one big, happy family" atmosphere. It involves developing a climate of individual integrity, corporate honesty, and high productivity. A climate like this can best be created by making decisions with a question in mind: What is right, just, and equitable? Effective leadership is built on a foundation of mutual trust and respect.

A manager must do a number of things to be an effective leader. For instance, he or she must make certain that everyone in the unit knows exactly what is expected in terms of performance. Objectives must be identifiable, measurable, and individually attainable. The manager also must recognize and reward outstanding performance. This involves setting up an appraisal-reward system that rewards superior performance and does not reward mediocrity. To be effective, managers also must surround themselves with competent employees and ask their advice when making decisions that affect them. In other words, a manager should use all the organizational resources available— especially people.

Many managers lack leadership

Of the five basic functions of management, leading is perhaps the one area where most managers are weakest. Lawrence Appley, chairman emeritus of the American Management Association (AMA), contends that American businesses are suffering from the greatest leadership vacuum this nation has ever seen. This void, he says, stems from managers' failure to recognize human development and the demands this places on managers in the workplace.[7] Because effective leadership is at the core of effective management, Part Four of this book addresses this topic at length.

Controlling

In **controlling,** a manager continually compares the performance of the organization with its goals and takes corrective action, if needed. Actual results may differ from desired results in any area, but the three that require the most attention are product quality, worker performance, and cost control. Controlling is discussed further in Part Five.

The quality of the company's product may not measure up for a number of reasons. For instance, raw materials used in the manufacturing process may be inferior, or their blending or mixing may be improper. Product quality also will suffer if the manufacturing process malfunctions. For example, a machine breakdown may cause the quality of the final product to be unacceptable.

Setting standards

Control also is required when employees fail to meet desired performance standards. Controlling people follows the same procedure as controlling product quality: establishing standards, measuring worker output and comparing it with standards, and taking corrective action when necessary. Employee performance standards are formulated through experience, judgment, and observation. Once standards are determined, some method for measuring worker performance must be developed. Typically, each employee is formally evaluated annually on all critical job elements. In an appraisal interview, the employee is told which areas need improvement and how to bring it about. In some cases, additional training and instruction are needed; in other cases, disciplinary action is required.

The third major area requiring significant attention, cost control, involves comparing expenditures with budgeted funds. Actual costs are compared with standards set before actual production for such items as materials, labor, and overhead. Variation from the standards helps managers find problem areas and can lead to cost-reduction programs.

An Informal View of the Manager's Job

Managers react as well as act

The functions just discussed tell us what managers *should* do. In James Cribbin's opinion, these functions depict managers of ideal firms under ideal conditions, where they are masters of their fate and captains of their souls.[8] What do managers *actually* do? In reality, managers do perform these functions, but their duties are much more complicated.

Managers spend as much—and perhaps more—time reacting as they do acting. They are entangled in many relationships and situations, some over which they have little control. A more realistic description of what managers do is provided by Leonard Sayles:

1. Managers strive to implement their personal career plans, using the firm as a vehicle. In so doing, they seek to satisfy the requirements of the organization.

2. Managers seek to be sensitive and responsive to the needs of their superiors. They try to keep abreast of new pressures, new developments, and new requirements that may affect the way they do their work.

3. Managers negotiate with peers in other interdependent departments in an effort to get their jobs done effectively.

4. Managers cultivate good personal relations with staff and service groups whose actions can impact their jobs for better or worse.

5. Managers respond to the requests, demands, and requirements of various individuals and groups in order to retain their goodwill. Thus, they must be flexible in adjusting to a variety of personalities, cliques, and eccentricities.

6. Managers oversee the flow of work into, within, and out of their departments to assure that it goes smoothly.

7. Managers are alert to the work output, needs, wants, and morale of their subordinates, and they interact with their subordinates while maintaining a managerial perspective.

8. Managers represent their subordinates and their subordinates' views to higher-level managers and to individuals in other departments.

9. Managers try to retain control over their own lives while accommodating the needs of the firm. Thus, they set priorities and engage in those activities that satisfy the demands of their families, the firm, and themselves.

10. Managers attempt to cope with stress so as to receive psychic as well as economic income from their work.

11. Managers strive to attain organizational rewards which they use to secure more important off-the-job goals.[9]

Management Roles

Carrying out the management functions requires a manager to behave in a certain way—to fill certain roles. Mintzberg identified ten managerial roles related to the interpersonal, informational, and decisional aspects (see Table 1.1), which are part of all management jobs.[10]

Interpersonal Roles

Managers interact with other people

The most basic of a manager's **interpersonal roles**—those in which the manager interacts with others—is that of *figurehead*. Some figurehead duties are largely ceremonial and others relatively important, but none involves significant decision making. Signing documents or presiding at a ceremonial event are examples of figurehead duties. The *leader* role is evident in the interpersonal relationship between manager and subordinates. As a leader, the manager hires, trains, evaluates, motivates, and promotes subordinates. The manager also serves as a *liaison* between the company and the external community. He or she fulfills this role through community service, conferences, social events, and so forth.

Informational Roles

Managers gather and disseminate information

A second set of managerial activities relates to receiving and transmitting information. These **informational roles** require managers to serve as *monitors, disseminators,* and *spokespersons*. As a *monitor,* the manager tries to keep informed about what is happening in the organization or group. He or she gathers information from news reports, trade publications, magazines, clients, asso-

TABLE 1.1 Management roles	INTERPERSONAL ROLES	INFORMATIONAL ROLES	DECISIONAL ROLES
	Figurehead	Monitor	Entrepreneur
	Leader	Disseminator	Disturbance handler
	Liaison	Spokesperson	Resource allocator
			Negotiator

ciates, and a host of similar sources. As a *disseminator*, a manager sends outside information into the organization and internal information from one subordinate to another. A manager serves as a *spokesperson* whenever he or she represents the company or its position to other groups, including the press, government agencies, customers, and trade organizations.

Decisional Roles

The third set of managerial activities involves decision making, or **decisional roles.** As decision maker, the manager becomes an *entrepreneur, disturbance handler, resource allocator,* and *negotiator.*

Managers make a variety of decisions

The manager acting as an *entrepreneur* recognizes problems and opportunities and initiates action that will move the organization in the desired direction. Often he or she may create new projects, change organizational structure, and institute other important programs for improving the company's performance. As a *disturbance handler,* the manager deals with situations over which he or she has little control. These may involve conflict between people or groups, or unexpected events outside the company may affect the firm's operations. In either case, immediate attention usually is needed, and the manager must rearrange his or her schedule to take care of the emergency. As a *resource allocator,* the manager must divide the company's resources as well as personal time among the various demands on them. This involves assigning work to subordinates, scheduling meetings, approving budgets, deciding on pay increases, making purchasing decisions, and other matters related to the firm's human, financial, and material resources. The manager acting as *negotiator* represents the firm in financial matters. For example, the manager is a negotiator when the company tries to buy another firm, when meeting with a union seeking a new contract, or with members of the financial community to negotiate a new stock issue.

The Management Hierarchy

Three distinct levels of management

Although all managers may perform the same basic duties and play similar roles, the nature and scope of their activities differ. As we have said, planning performed by top-level managers differs significantly from that performed by lower-level managers. In fact, all of the functions—organizing, staffing, leading, and controlling—vary from one level of management to the next. Broadly speaking, three levels of management form the management hierarchy, as shown in Figure 1.4.

Top Management

A company's **top management** is made up of individuals who have the responsibility for making the decisions and formulating the policies that affect all aspects of the firm's operations. In a small company, top management may be

FIGURE 1.4
The management
hierarchy

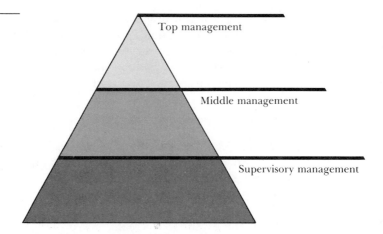

limited to one or two persons. In a giant corporation, top management can include a dozen or more people who make decisions affecting the entire firm. For example, the owner-manager of a small, independent retail store may make all the decisions affecting the operations of the business. On the other hand, top management of a large firm, such as Apple Computer or General Motors, will consist of everyone responsible for divisional operations.

Job titles can be confusing

In most cases, a job title indicates management level. For instance, the titles of president, chief executive officer, executive vice president, and vice president usually indicate top-management positions. In other instances job titles can be misleading. For example, a vice president may have limited authority and only minor impact on the overall operations of the firm. This is why it is sometimes impossible to classify positions according to job titles. Consider the following job titles commonly used in the banking industry: vice president, assistant vice president, senior vice president, and executive vice president. Other managerial titles also are used, such as operations manager, cashier, and personnel manager. To further complicate the situation, some managers are officers of the firm while others are not. Clearly, job title does not indicate management level in every case, as the bank titles show. A manager's assigned job duties and the authority needed to fulfill those duties are what determine management level.

Middle Management

Middle managers manage supervisors

Middle management includes all managers above the supervisory level but below the level where overall company policy is determined. In a manufacturing firm, the positions of regional sales manager and production superintendent would fall into this category. In a university, academic deans are middle managers. And in a hospital, the director of nursing is a middle manager.

In all instances, these managers have authority over other managers. For example, a regional sales manager has authority over sales managers, and a production superintendent has authority over production supervisors. An academic dean has authority over academic department chairpersons, and a director of nursing has authority over nursing supervisors.

Supervisory Management

At the base of the pyramid is **supervisory management.** Supervisors manage workers who perform the most basic job duties required in the business. Examples of supervisory personnel are production supervisors, sales managers, warehouse supervisors, service managers, and loan officers.

Technically, supervisors are managers. As such, they must reflect the company's point of view to their subordinates. At the same time, however, supervisors usually feel a great deal of empathy for their subordinates. These feelings stem from close personal contact and the fact that most supervisors have come up from the ranks of labor. Consequently, supervisors often feel they are neither fish nor fowl—neither management nor labor. This is why supervisors usually are called the "people in the middle." That is especially true when the distinction between management and labor is blurred by the use of job titles such as lead person or set-up person. Because of the expectations placed on supervisors from above and below, many people contend that the person on the firing line—the supervisor—has the toughest job in management.

The "people in the middle"

The three levels of management are illustrated in the organizational chart of Spring Valley Nursing Home, shown in Figure 1.5. And a different way of distinguishing the levels is discussed in the Manager's Notebook on page 17.

Management Skills

Effective managers are essential to the performance of all organizations. Whether they have the ability to plan, organize, staff, lead, and control business operations effectively can determine a firm's ultimate success or failure. But, more important, good management practices can be *learned* and *applied.* Management success depends both on a fundamental understanding of the principles of management and on the application of technical, human, and conceptual skills.

For instance, here are several common myths about management:

- Leaders are born, not made.

- Management is nothing more than common sense.

- Management is a "hit or miss" proposition.

- Businesses often succeed in spite of managers, not because of managers.

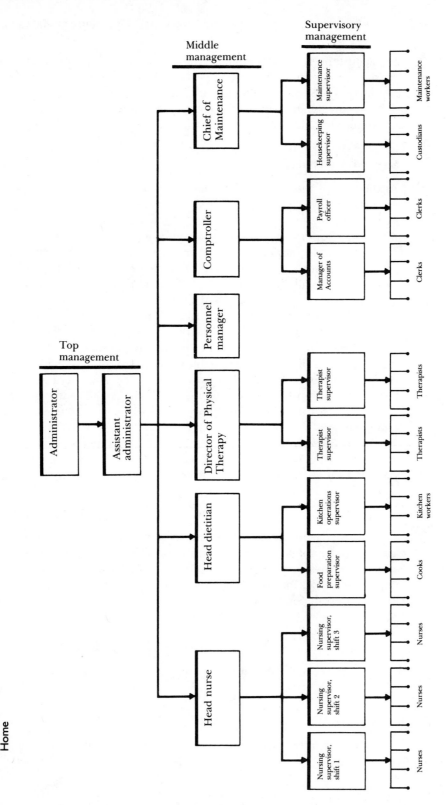

FIGURE 1.5
Organization chart of
Spring Valley Nursing
Home

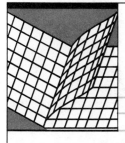

THE MANAGER'S NOTEBOOK

What's Your Managerial Time Frame?

After years of study, certain behavioral scientists have come to the conclusion that there really is something unique about the way managers think, something that makes them different from the rest of us. Foremost among these scientists is Elliott Jaques, director of the Institute of Organization and Social Studies at England's Brunel University. Jaques's contribution revolves around a concept called the "time frame of the individual."

At the heart of the managerial difference is the fact that, according to Jaques's studies, managers can see a long way into the future. They seem to be able to identify the steps necessary for major organizational change, envision how each step will work out, even years in the future, and take action to set the machinery in motion.

According to Jaques, only one person in several million is capable of a twenty-year time frame, although he does note that Konosuke Matsushita has laid down a two-hundred-and-fifty-year plan for his giant Japanese company!

What this all amounts to in organizational terms is that a sort of natural structure can be found in most organizations, in which most jobs can be classified according to the time frame of the people holding them. An unskilled worker can function within a one-day time frame, but his or her supervisor must be able to see at least three months into the future. The supervisor's boss, in turn, can plan a year or more ahead; he or she then reports to a general manager with perhaps a five-year time frame. And at the very top sits a chief executive officer who can plan as far as twenty years into the future.

Source: Walter Kiechel, III, "How Executives Think," *Fortune,* February 4, 1985, pp. 127–128.

FIGURE 1.6
Managerial skills needed by managers at different organizational levels (*Source:* Reprinted by permission of the *Harvard Business Review.* An exhibit from "Skills of an Effective Administrator" by Robert L. Katz (September-October 1974). Copyright © 1974 by the President and Fellows of Harvard College; all rights reserved.)

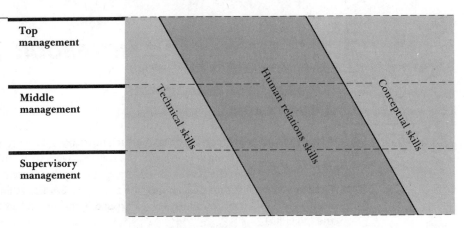

Management does require common sense. But it also requires a great deal more. It isn't merely a "hit or miss" proposition. In addition to the solid background knowledge that a manager must have, certain principles of management should always be followed, regardless of the type of organization or the particular position a manager holds. A principle can be defined as a comprehensive, fundamental law, doctrine, or assumption.[11] Principles are so basic that the efficient management of any organization depends on whether they are followed. But they must be learned. Common sense does not guarantee their application. Several of the most important principles of management are discussed in detail in Chapter 2.

Management principles have universal application

Modern business organizations are dynamic and complex, and competition in the marketplace is fierce. Consequently, managers must be highly skilled to succeed. The skills managers need can be classified as *technical, human relations,* and *conceptual.* Figure 1.6 shows the relative importance of these skills at various levels of management.

Supervisors use technical skills extensively

Technical skills are the specialized knowledge and abilities that can be applied to specific tasks. Normally, technical skills are most important at lower levels of management and much less important at upper levels. A production supervisor in a manufacturing plant, for example, must know the processes used and be able to physically perform the tasks he or she supervises. A word processing supervisor must have specialized knowledge about the computer software used in the department. In most cases, technical skills are important at this level because supervisory managers must train their subordinates in the proper use of work-related tools, machines, and equipment.

Managers need human relations skills

Human relations skills are the abilities needed to resolve conflict, motivate, lead, and communicate effectively with other workers. Because all work is done when people work together, human relations skills are equally important at all levels of management. Chapters 10 through 13 emphasize the importance of human relations skills and discuss in detail the methods of improving those skills.

"Arthur was a good man but he never learned how to establish goals, define priorities, delegate responsibilities, or free himself from the tyranny of organization charts." © Punch ROTHCO

Conceptual skills are the abilities needed to view the organization from a broad perspective and to see the interrelations among its components. Conceptual skills are most important in strategic (long-range) planning; therefore, they are more important to top-level executives than to middle managers and supervisors.

Top-level managers use conceptual skills

Management as a Discipline

Management is a relatively new academic discipline. Before World War II, all the books on management filled only a modest shelf. Today, management texts are read not only by students who want to climb the corporate ladder, they're on the best seller lists as well. Before World War II, very few colleges taught management.[12] Today, hundreds of colleges and universities offer degrees in the field, and advanced management seminars and courses are common all over the industrialized world.

The performance of the American manufacturing industry during the war drew attention to management and the study of management. But interest in management was really sparked by an Englishman—Sir Stafford Cripps,

Management after World War II

chancellor of the exchequer in Britain's first postwar Labour government. Cripps believed management was the force that could restore Britain's postwar economy. He created productivity teams of British businesspeople who were sent to the United States to study management.[13] Largely because of his actions, the United States became world-famous as the place to learn management techniques. Today, virtually all countries have adopted sound management practices. Japanese management has become so efficient, in fact, that many American companies are adopting techniques developed in Japan. For instance, several American corporations, including Martin Marietta, Hughes Aircraft, Sperry-Vickers, Honeywell, and Solar Turbines, have instituted quality control circles, a method of achieving quality developed by the Japanese Union of Scientists and Engineers (JUSE) under the guidance of Dr. Kaoru Ishikawa in 1962.

Management is practiced as a profession, just like law or medicine, and, like attorneys and physicians, managers use a variety of tools. The manager's tools include economics, mathematics, psychology, accounting, and computer science. Managers draw on other disciplines to minimize the risks of making difficult decisions. But even the most disciplined, scientific managers can't totally eliminate risk in their decision making. They try to make the best possible decisions in light of all the information they have gathered.

Managerial Styles: Contrasting Profiles

We've told you what managers have in common. What we haven't mentioned, though, is the unique style or approach each manager brings to the job. Whether based on formal management training or on years of experience, each manager's style is his or her own. To fully appreciate how managers' styles differ, consider the approaches of some well-known leaders.

Managers' styles differ

The personalities and approaches to management of Franklin Delano Roosevelt and Adolf Hitler offer stunning contrasts. Both came into power in 1933 and were leaders of powerful nations. But their objectives and methods made them enemies. First, consider their physical characteristics and personalities. Roosevelt was paralyzed; Hitler was a fiery orator who mesmerized his audiences in prewar Germany. Their socioeconomic backgrounds and rise to power were just as different. One of their greatest contrasts, however, was in their managerial leadership style. Although it comes from a work of fiction, the following description by Herman Wouk is perhaps the most striking possible comparison:

> The contrast of Franklin Delano Roosevelt and Adolf Hitler in their warmaking is altogether Plutarchian. Spidery calculation versus all-out gambling; steadfast planning versus impulsive improvising; careful use of limited armed strength versus prodigal dissipation of overwhelming strength; prudent reliance on generals versus reckless overruling of them; anxious concern for troops versus impetuous outpouring of their lives; a timid dip

ON THE JOB

The Toughest Bosses in the United States

In 1980 and 1984, *Fortune* magazine published lists of the toughest bosses in America, as perceived by the people who work for them. The 1984 list of the most demanding senior-level executives to be found in major U.S. corporations is presented below. Keep in mind, too, that these are some of the nation's most *effective* managers.

Name	Title/Company	Selected Comments
John Welsh, Jr.	Chairman, General Electric	abrasive; creative; extraordinarily bright
Richard Snyder	President, Simon and Schuster	brilliant; a quick temper; difficult to work for
Andrew Grove	President, Intel Corporation	blunt; merciless with people who aren't honest
Robert Malott	Chairman, FMC Corporation	a bully; bright; moody; obnoxious
Fred Ackman	Chairman, Superior Oil	throws his weight around; can't tolerate disagreement
William Klopman	Chairman, Burlington Industries	smart; cold; poor interpersonal skills; autocratic
Richard Rosenthal	Chairman, Citizens Utilities	egomaniac; cold; a self-proclaimed genius
Martin Davis	CEO, Gulf and Western	a master of intimidation
Joel Smilow	Senior Executive, Beatrice Companies	fires people arbitrarily; no trust in people
John Johnson	President, Johnson Publishing Company	runs his firm like a plantation

Source: Steven Flax, "The Toughest Bosses in America," *Fortune,* August 6, 1984, pp. 18–23. © 1984, Time, Inc. All rights reserved.

of a toe in combat versus total war with the last reserves thrown in; such was the contrast between the two world opponents as they at last came to grips in 1942, nine years after they both took power.[14]

The owners of two professional athletic teams are also strikingly different in their managerial approaches. New York Yankees owner George Steinbrenner, often is described as an impatient, goal-oriented man who replaces managers more often than do owners of other clubs. Steinbrenner is a "celebrity" whose face appears in television ads and whose tirades make newspaper headlines.

Clint Murchison, Jr.'s approach to managerial leadership is totally different. Murchison is the former owner of the Dallas Cowboys football team; and from when the franchise began in 1960 until he sold the team in 1984, he had only one general manager and one coach. He quietly managed the Cowboys behind the scenes. By any standards, both organizations are successful. But that success was achieved by vastly different approaches to management.

The contrasting approaches to management by Robert E. Wood, former president of Sears (1928–1956), and Sewell Avery, former president and board chairman of Montgomery Ward (1931–1955), have become legendary. Wood was a far-sighted, risk-taking entrepreneur willing to put into practice new ideas and merchandising methods.[15] Avery, on the other hand, was a highly conservative man who hated taking risks. His myopic vision of merchandising and inept management practices made Montgomery Ward lose a significant market share to its competitors.[16]

Risk takers and conservatives

No two people are exactly alike. Consequently, no two people manage the same way. A manager's style reflects his or her personality, philosophy, the influence of other people and groups, the nature and tradition of the organization, and other variables. It's not surprising, then, that managers' approaches differ so greatly. On the Job, page 21, discusses one approach to getting the job done. Chapter 12, "Leadership," discusses at length the various approaches to leadership and decision making.

Review

✓ *Why managers are essential to the efficient operation of all types of organizations.* Management is the process of maximizing the potential of an organization's people and coordinating their efforts to attain predetermined goals. Essentially, the practice of management involves coordinating and utilizing human and nonhuman resources in the pursuit of such goals. Because business managers are accountable to a number of different groups (owners, customers, employees, creditors, and society in general), the goals that they establish are in direct response to their responsibilities. Typically, a private enterprise establishes profit, service, and survival objectives.

✔ *The basic functions all managers perform.* All managers, regardless of their position, perform certain basic functions—planning, organizing, staffing, leading, and controlling. Planning, perhaps the most important of all managerial functions, is the establishing of goals and objectives. Organizing involves developing a structure and assigning tasks necessary to attain these goals. Staffing, as the name suggests, is the selection of people who have appropriate qualifications. The fourth function, leading, is the heart of management activity. It involves providing necessary guidance for people who work for the firm. Finally, controlling involves comparing performance with established standards and taking corrective action when necessary.

✔ *The different roles played by managers.* Managers play ten roles that fall into three areas: interpersonal (figurehead, leader, and liaison roles), informational (monitor, disseminator, and spokesperson roles), and decisional (entrepreneur, disturbance handler, resource allocator, and negotiator roles).

✔ *The three levels of management that constitute the management hierarchy.* Managers are commonly classified as top-level, middle-level, and supervisory, depending on their organizational position and the authority inherent in their jobs.

✔ *The skills and abilities needed by managers at different levels.* Basic skills needed by managers include technical, human relations, and conceptual skills. Technical skills are most important for supervisory management. Human relations skills are used equally by all levels of managers. Conceptual skills are most important to top-level managers.

✔ *How managers differ in management style and decision-making behavior.* Management "styles" differ from individual to individual. Some managers are autocratic; others involve their subordinates extensively in decision making. Some are production-oriented; others are people-centered. The approach taken by a manager depends, to a great extent, on his or her personality, the type of organization for which he or she works, and relationships with a number of other people including superiors and subordinates.

THE MANAGER'S DICTIONARY

As an extra review of the chapter, try defining the following terms. If you have trouble with any of them, refer to the page numbers listed.

management (5)	controlling (13)	middle management (14)
planning (7)	interpersonal roles (13)	supervisory management (15)
organizing (8)	informational roles (10)	technical skills (18)
staffing (9)	decisional roles (12)	human relations skills (18)
leading (9)	top management (12)	conceptual skills (19)

REVIEW QUESTIONS

1. What kinds of goals do organizations establish? Why do they differ from one organization to another?

2. Why are managers necessary in business organizations?

3. Discuss the various responsibilities of business managers. How do they meet these obligations?

4. List and describe the functions of managers.

5. In what capacities or "roles" do managers serve? Give an example of each.

6. Describe the three levels of management.

7. What is the relationship between job title and level of management?

8. Describe the skills that managers must possess.

9. Which skills are most important for top-level managers? for middle managers? for supervisors?

10. Can management be learned? Why or why not?

11. Is there one best "style" of management? Justify your answer.

12. Why do managers' approaches differ? Explain.

13. Cite several factors that determine a manager's "style."

MANAGEMENT CHALLENGE

1. Think of a manager you know personally—perhaps your present boss, an administrator at your university, or a friend who holds a management position in a company in your hometown. Make a list of specific activities that you have observed this person perform.

2. From this list of activities, categorize each under the following functions: planning, organizing, staffing, leading, and controlling.

3. Next, see if you can identify the managerial role represented by each activity. For example, if you have observed this manager reading a newspaper or magazine, he or she is *monitoring* information. Similarly, presiding at a ceremonial event would be classified as a *figurehead* role.

4. Which management hierarchical level does this manager fall into? To whom does he/she report? Who reports to him/her?

5. Of the three skills needed by managers—technical, human relations, and conceptual—in which are you strongest? In which are you weakest?

6. Describe the personality traits and managerial approaches of a manager whom you greatly admire. Do you believe he or she would exhibit the same traits in another setting, or would the situation dictate the style used? Explain.

7. If you were appointed sales manager of a newly established automobile dealership, what type of salespeople would you employ? Why?

8. What kinds of knowledge would you expect these automobile salespeople to possess? What methods would you use to provide them with the training they need?

9. How would the skills needed by the service manager of an automobile dealership differ from those needed by a sales manager? As a service manager, what qualifications would you look for in a mechanic?

CASE 1.1

GM's Leaner Management Style[17]

General Motors Corp. is considering doing without middle management in its Orion Township assembly plant north of Detroit in what may be the beginning of a leaner plant management style, a spokesman says.

If approved "sometime in the next few weeks," the plan to eliminate jobs for 26 general foremen would make the Orion plant, set to open next summer, the second GM facility to cut out the middle foremen, spokesman John Grix said.

The Shreveport, La., assembly plant, opened last July, was the first GM plant successfully to eliminate the middle foremen, who act as liaison between the foremen on the shop floor and the superintendent of the department, Grix said. About 20 general foremen were eliminated there, GM said.

"We're talking about a complete elimination of middle management," he said.

GM has about 600 general foremen at 25 U.S. assembly plants, Grix estimated. He would not disclose how much they are paid.

"The advantages are the elimination of a tremendous amount of busy work by the middle management," and it also aids worker-management cooperation, he said. The money savings "isn't an awful lot," he said.

If successful at Orion, the plan could be used at GM's Detroit-Poletown plant, which is under construction, and may be the wave of the future, he said. Ford Motor Co. has contacted GM for more information on the management system, GM said.

The cuts are being made in newly built plants because of resistance at established plants, Grix said.

The jobs evolved as plant procedures grew up, "just so the superintendent would not have

to deal directly with 10 or 12 foremen," Grix said. "This way, he or she would have to deal with only two general foremen."

Management consultants for years have criticized the usefulness of the middlemen, saying they just add red tape. The Japanese have largely eliminated them, Grix said.

Chrysler Corp. still has general foremen, spokesman Bob Heath said.

Questions

1. Discuss the pros and cons of eliminating middle management in these automobile assembly plants.

2. Why do you think the Japanese auto makers have taken this approach? What other forms of management have we adopted from other countries?

CASE 1.2

Marriott's Management Savvy[18]

At the end of each year, *Dun's Business Month* chooses what it considers to be the five best-managed companies in America. In 1984, one of the firms selected to the elite list was Marriott Corporation, the well-known hotelier that is big and getting bigger.

When the accomplishments of Marriott are compared to those of other firms in the lodging business, they do appear remarkable. For instance, Marriott initiated construction on the first luxury convention hotel to be built in Manhattan in more than twenty years. Since 1970, the company has spent more than $4 billion in hotel development; today its name can be seen

at the top of nearly one hundred and fifty hotels throughout the country. Marriott's financial growth has been impressive, too. Between 1980 and 1984, its earnings grew at an annual rate of 24%, and its gross receipts reached nearly $3.5 billion. These figures are even more impressive when you consider that the industry as a whole has been stagnant in recent years.

Although Marriott is best known for its hotels, about half of its profits comes from two other businesses—food catering services and fast-food restaurants. Today, Marriott serves more in-flight meals on airlines than any other catering firm does. And its fast-food restaurants—Roy Rogers, Bob's Big Boy, and Host—qualify it as the third-largest restaurateur in the country.

Much of Marriott's success can be credited to financial savvy. For example, Marriott began selling some of its hotels in the mid-1970s but continued to operate them under management contracts. The revenue generated enabled the company to expand quickly and, at the same time, lessened the burden of being capital-intensive. Marriott also raises billions of dollars through tax-shelter partnerships that sell groups of hotels to private investors. Every piece of property sold during the past twenty years has been sold at a profit.

The management savvy of Marriott's managers is noteworthy, too. Marriott President J. Willard "Bill" Marriott contends that much of the company's success is due to its concern over expenses and its attention to detail. For instance, Marriott and the four executive vice presidents who report to him spend half their time visiting Marriott facilities. They concern themselves with everything from the sixty-six steps that maids follow in cleaning a room to the portions of food that are served. They even learn to cook in the company kitchen.

Questions

1. In your opinion, do Marriott's visits to Marriott facilities reflect a distrust of lower-level managers? Explain.

2. Which of the basic management functions do you think Bill Marriott is most concerned with? Why?

CHAPTER OUTLINE

Schools of Management Thought

The Classical School

Early Management Theorists
Robert Owen • Charles Babbage
Scientific Management Theorists
Frederick Winslow Taylor • Henry L. Gantt • The Gilbreths • Harrington Emerson
Classical Administrative and Organization Theorists
Henri Fayol • Chester I. Barnard • Mary Parker Follett
Other Contributors to the Classical School

The Behavioral School

Elton Mayo and the Hawthorne Experiments
Criticisms of the Hawthorne Experiments
Other Hawthorne Experiments
Other Behaviorists

The Quantitative School

More Recent Theories

Schools of Management Thought

M A N A G E M E N T   I N   A C T I O N

Iron-Fist Management in Japan

Most people believe that three things are behind Japan's remarkable productivity and spiraling economic growth over the past twenty years: scientific management, computers and technology, and management style.

It's evident that the Japanese have adopted and refined scientific management, which generally was born in the United States. They've also become a recognized world leader in manufacturing robots and computers. But, contrary to a widespread myth, Japanese management is not highly participative. In fact, many prominent Japanese business leaders admire and emulate autocratic leadership, an approach they consider decidedly American.[1]

In August 1984, Japan's leading business newspaper, *Nihon Keizai Shimbun,* published its list of Japan's best-managed companies. First and second place went to two firms run much like a dictatorship—Kyocera, a ceramics manufacturer, and Fanuc, a company making robots and machinery. Japanese refer to the kind of leadership in these companies as "one man," because the person at the organization's top is the one who charts its direction and rules with an iron fist. Ichiro Isoda, chairman of Sumitomo Bank, says that the "one man" companies are both aggressive and successful. They tend to be pacesetters in their industry, and they usually succeed overseas.[2]

Isoda is considered one of Japan's most autocratic managers. When he became president of Sumitomo Bank in 1977, he ended committee management, reorganized the bank, and gave each division head unlimited authority. Other large, autocratically run Japanese companies are Suntory Ltd., a distiller and manufacturer of soft drinks; Kurushimadock Group, shipbuilders; Daiei,

Inc., Japan's largest retailing chain; Seibu Railway Group; Minebea Company, which manufactures ball bearings, measuring instruments, and computer keyboards; Secom Company, a police protection service; and Seibu Group of Retail Enterprises.[3] Although these companies are uniquely Japanese, the leadership style of their top managers is quite American.

Preview

Perhaps more than any other industrialized nation, Japan relied on American ingenuity to revitalize its economy after World War II. The Japanese have not only adopted American manufacturing methods but also, in many cases, have actually improved on them. Their concern for efficiency and their use of computer-augmented quantitative techniques also have contributed to high productivity.

Japanese business leaders have successfully adopted many American theories, such as the "one man" concept with its powerful leadership, as well as the Japanese and American hybrid—Theory Z. This system stresses the importance of the worker to the productivity and growth of the company. But the Japanese and the Americans aren't the only ones who have added to the development of management. German, English, and French writers have also contributed greatly.

Our knowledge of production methods and administrative practices has evolved over time. Early theorists believed that scientific management was the key to improving worker efficiency. Their contributions are embodied in the classical, or traditional, school of management thought. Later, the classical school broadened to include administrative and organization theory. In the early 1900s, when industrial psychologists began studying the human side of production, the behavioral school of management thought was born. The quantitative school, which uses mathematical models and quantitative tools developed mostly since World War II, is the newest school of management thought. Advances in computer hardware and software are behind this field's unprecedented growth.

Chapter 2 discusses the major contributions to each school of management thought. New theories also will be presented. After studying the chapter, you will understand:

✔ Why the study of management has been approached from different perspectives

✔ The development of the classical, or traditional, school of management theory

✔ The foundations of the behavioral school of management

✔ How mathematical models have shaped the quantitative school of management thought

✔ Recent contributions to management theory

Schools of Management Thought

For centuries, scholars and businesspeople alike have tried to understand the practice of management. But, like all social sciences, management is inexact. No single approach to its understanding has been totally satisfactory. Some researchers have focused on what individual workers and managers do, to gain insight into the process. Other researchers have concentrated on how people work with one another in organizations, and still others have analyzed the type and nature of decisions managers make. The schools of management thought that resulted from these and other inquiries can be classified as *classical, behavioral,* and *quantitative.* Other theories also have been proposed in recent years.

Three schools of management thought

The Classical School

The **classical,** or **traditional, school** at first focused on scientific principles of management. The management process was analyzed in terms of the methods used by the workers at the lower levels of the organization. Later, when the importance of management at all organizational levels became apparent, the school's theories expanded to consider what managers do and the forces that shape what they do, focusing on management functions as well as principles of scientific management in order to understand the practice of management. Using the principles of scientific management, traditional managers stress the methodology of performing tasks in order to enhance worker efficiency and productivity.

Scientific management emphasized first

Some writers believe that the classical school of management considers the human element in an organization to be relatively unimportant. Some even suggest that managers think workers are only cogs in a production machine or extensions of their tools and equipment. But, as you will see, concern for the human element is at the core of classical theory.

Early Management Theorists

Mechanical power transformed craft guilds into factories where goods could be mass-produced. Eli Whitney's cotton gin, James Watts's steam engine, and other early inventions of the Industrial Revolution changed the lives of working men and women. But new production methods and new problems for managers came with the new factory system. Very little is known about the philosophies of early managers, but the writings of two early British theorists, Robert Owen and Charles Babbage, contain some insights into how managers coped with the Industrial Revolution.

Owen was a social reformer

Robert Owen   Robert Owen (1771–1858) can best be described as a social reformer. Although he owned a successful business, he warned of the evils of industrialism, which would attack the moral fiber of society. Owen credited his business success to his understanding of human nature and to his "habits of exactness." He paid particular attention to plant layout and machine maintenance in his cotton mills, but his overriding concern was for the workers. In fact, he chided other employers for failing to improve conditions for workers and for refusing to eliminate human misery. He was labeled a radical because of his attempts to set a minimum-age law to protect children against the abuses of employers. In his later years, Owen worked to help the poor and to solve employment problems. Unfortunately, he was unable to apply what he had learned in his factories to society as a whole.

Charles Babbage   Charles Babbage (1792–1871) made his contributions to management long before scientific management became popular in America. Although Babbage's contemporaries thought he was an eccentric screwball, his genius is evident in his inventions. He developed the first mechanical calculator, for example, and formulated the basic computer concepts that were incorporated in IBM's first large-scale electronic computer.

Babbage advocated systematic study

When developing his computer, Babbage became interested in management. Faced with the problem of getting workers to perform their tasks more efficiently, he visited many British factories to observe their operations. During these visits, he examined manufacturing processes, tools, skills, and machinery. Like Frederick W. Taylor, a later management theorist, Babbage believed that a manager could study the operations of a factory systematically and find ways to improve its efficiency. He was an avid proponent of division of labor, economies of scale in manufacturing, incentive pay, and profit sharing. Babbage advocated many of the same concepts voiced by Taylor, Gantt, the Gilbreths, and others who were not prominent until several years later.

Scientific Management Theorists

Scientific management is a systematic, analytical study of work, which originated in the United States around 1900. Its objective was to find the most efficient method for performing any task and to train workers in that method. The most important contributors to scientific management were Frederick W. Taylor, Henry Gantt, Frank and Lillian Gilbreth, and Harrington Emerson.

Father of scientific management

Frederick Winslow Taylor   Called the "father of scientific management," Frederick W. Taylor (1856–1915) is an important contributor to the classical school of management theory. Taylor wanted to find the most effective way to use people and resources in the workplace. He believed that there was one best way of performing every process and task in industry. He thought that, to find

Frederick W. Taylor entered the work force as an apprentice patternmaker and machinist in 1875. After earning a degree in engineering, he joined Enterprise Hydraulic Works of Philadelphia in 1878. In 1901, Taylor retired to spend his remaining years as a consultant to Bethlehem Steel on scientific management.

the best way, workers' performance of a task should be examined scientifically, objectively, and in great detail, using an empirical and experimental approach. Only then could a more productive way of doing the job be found. After finding the "one best way" of performing a job, the manager should then teach it to the workers. Taylor thought that an incentive system rewarding fast workers and penalizing slow workers would encourage them to adopt the new system quicker. He believed that scientific methods would eventually replace intuition and rule-of-thumb, which had been used in organizations up until then. Taylor's principles of management are listed in Table 2.1.

Taylor's book *Shop Management* was published in 1903, and his *Principles of Scientific Management* in 1911. His writings pointed out that scientific management covered more than just tools and work methods—it was a revolutionary way of thinking. Taylor's testimony before a Special House Committee in 1912 explains this idea of scientific management:

> Scientific management is not any efficiency device, not a device of any kind for securing efficiency; nor is it any bunch or group of efficiency devices. It is not a new system of figuring costs; it is not a new scheme of paying men; it is not a piecework system; it is not a bonus system; it is not a premium system; it is no scheme for paying men; it is not holding a stop watch on a man and writing things down about him; it is not time study; it is not motion study nor an analysis of the movements of men; it is not

TABLE 2.1 Taylor's scientific principles of management	1. Develop a science for each element of an individual's work; this replaces the old rule-of-thumb method.
	2. Scientifically select and then train, teach, and develop the worker. In the past, workers chose their own work and trained themselves as best they could.
	3. Heartily cooperate with the workers to ensure that all the work is being done in accordance with the new methods.
	4. Work is divided almost equally between management and workers. Management takes over all work for which it is better fitted than the workers are. In the past, almost all the work and the greater part of the responsibility were thrown upon the workers.

the printing and ruling and unloading of a ton or two of blanks on a set of men and saying, "Here's your system; go use it." It is not divided foremanship or functional foremanship; it is not any of the devices which the average man calls to mind when scientific management is spoken of. . . .

Now, in its essence, scientific management involves a complete mental revolution on the part of the workingman engaged in any particular establishment or industry—a complete mental revolution on the part of these men as to their duties toward their work, toward their fellow men, and toward their employers. And it involves the equally complete mental revolution on the part of those on management's side—the foremen, the superintendent, the owner of the business, the board of directors—complete mental revolution on their part as to their duties toward their fellow workers in the management, toward their workmen, and toward all of their daily problems. And without this complete mental revolution on both sides, scientific management does not exist.

This is the essence of scientific management, this great mental revolution.[4]

Although Taylor was concerned with spreading the methods of scientific management throughout the organization, the workshop remained his primary field of investigation. His philosophy was accepted largely because it provided a response to current labor unrest.

Henry L. Gantt   The place of Henry Gantt (1861–1919) in history was carved during his fourteen-year association with Frederick Taylor, first as an engineer at the Midvale Steel Works and later at Simonds Rolling Machine Company and Bethlehem Steel. Although their approach to problems often differed and their points of view often clashed, Gantt became an important disciple of Taylor.

In 1901 Gantt devised his task-and-bonus wage plan, which paid workers a bonus besides their regular pay if they completed their assigned tasks in the time allowed. Unlike Taylor's plan, Gantt's system did not penalize workers who failed to complete their work in the allotted time. Gantt's plan also provided bonuses for supervisors. Each supervisor was given a bonus for every worker who met the standard, plus an extra bonus if all workers did so. This

Henry Gantt is best known for developing the Gantt chart, a bar chart used by managers to compare actual with planned performance.

plan was the first financial reward for supervisors who taught workers proper work methods.

    Although his task-and-bonus wage plan was well known because of his writings, Gantt is best known for developing a bar chart for planning and

The Gantt chart

controlling work activities. This "daily balance chart"—now known as the Gantt chart—schedules work on the basis of time rather than on quantities. This chart, the forerunner of the program evaluation and review technique (PERT), is illustrated in Chapter 16, "Quantitative Control Tools."

The Gilbreths   Frank Bunker Gilbreth (1868–1924) and his wife, Lillian Moller Gilbreth (1878–1972), made their greatest contribution in the area of time

Gilbreths pioneered time and motion study

and motion study. Their work led to today's job simplification, meaningful work standards, and incentive pay plans. The story of their lives as theorists and inventors and parents of twelve children is immortalized in a book and motion picture, *Cheaper by the Dozen.*

    Although Frank had qualified for admission to Massachusetts Institute of Technology, he chose to become a bricklayer for Whidden Company. There he developed an improved method for laying bricks that required significantly fewer body motions and increased threefold the number of bricks a person could lay in a day. He also found a better method for stacking bricks, eliminating unnecessary body movements, and he developed an adjustable stand to eliminate the bending normally required to pick up a brick. He insisted on a precise consistency for mortar; this minimized tapping with the trowel.

    In 1904, Frank married Lillian Moller, whose background was in management and psychology. They spent their lives searching for the "one best

Pioneers of time and motion study, Frank and Lillian Gilbreth spent a lifetime searching for the "one best way" to perform tasks.

way" to perform tasks. Although they invented many devices, one of the most important was the microchronometer, a clock with a large sweeping hand capable of recording time to 1/2000 of a second. Using this device, they could analyze work to determine how much time each body movement took. (Because motion picture cameras did not run at a constant speed in those days, the microchronometer was especially valuable.) The Gilbreths were particularly concerned with minimizing hand movements in physical tasks. For example, they broke down hand motions into seventeen separate movements (called therbligs—Gilbreth spelled backwards with the *th* transposed). Each of these movements was analyzed on film to determine if effort was wasted.

In areas other than time and motion study, the Gilbreths developed the "white list" personnel card system that was the forerunner of today's merit-rating systems. They also tried to simplify the English alphabet, the typewriter keyboard, and spelling. Their investigation into worker fatigue and its effect on productivity was the start of today's research on ergonomics. After Frank's death in 1924, Lillian continued to show how scientific management could help—rather than hurt—the individual worker by helping him or her improve work methods; reduced motion was for the worker's sake as well as for management's.

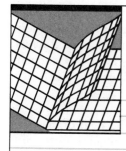

THE MANAGER'S NOTEBOOK

Emerson's Twelve Principles of Efficiency

1. Clearly defined ideal (objectives). Eliminate the vagueness, uncertainty, and aim-lessness characteristic of a great many undertakings.
2. Common sense. This is common sense that strives for knowledge and seeks advice from every quarter, unconfined in any position yet maintaining dignity of balance.
3. Competent counsel. Seek advice from competent individuals.
4. Discipline. Adhere to rules. This is designed to bring about allegiance to and observance of the other eleven principles.
5. Fair deal. Manage with justice and fairness.
6. Reliable, immediate, adequate, and permanent records. Maintain factual records on which to base decisions.
7. Dispatching. Plan work scientifically.
8. Standards and schedules. Develop methods and time for performing tasks.
9. Standardized conditions. Create a uniform environment.
10. Standardized operations. Establish uniform work methods.
11. Written standard-practice instructions. Reduce practice to writing.
12. Efficiency reward. Reward workers for successfully completing tasks.

Source: Daniel A. Wren, *The Evolution of Management Thought* (New York: John Wiley & Sons, 1979), pp. 183–185.

Emerson's scientific management of railroads

Harrington Emerson   Harrington Emerson (1853–1931), who coined the term *efficiency engineering,* applied scientific principles of management to the railroad industry in the early 1900s. Waste and inefficiency, he said, cost the railroad industry a million dollars every day—money that could be saved through proper organization. As you can see in the Manager's Notebook on this page, Emerson's twelve principles of efficiency cover good human relations as well as work methods. When viewed as a whole, these principles form a basis for building a sound management system even today.

Classical Administrative and Organization Theorists

Classical school expanded

Scientific management was aimed at improving the efficiency and productivity of workers; consequently, it provided little guidance for managers above the supervisory level. But, realizing the importance of efficient operations at all organizational levels, theorists began to focus on organizations as a whole. While some writers concentrated on managers' administrative practices, others examined organizational structure, the functioning of formal and informal organizations, and the social environment of management. Of particular importance are the contributions of Henri Fayol, Chester Barnard, and Mary Parker Follett.

Father of modern management theory

Henri Fayol   Perhaps the single greatest contributor to the field of classical administrative theory was Henri Fayol (1841–1925), the French industrialist now considered the "father of modern management theory." Fayol's management philosophy first appeared in print in 1900.

Fayol classified business activities into six functional groups:

1. Technical (production, manufacture, adaptation)
2. Commercial (buying, selling, exchange)
3. Financial (finding the best use of capital)
4. Security (protection of people and property)
5. Accounting
6. Managerial

Fayol considered managerial activities the least understood but often the most crucial of the six functions. Management, he said, is "neither an exclusive privilege nor a particular responsibility of the head or senior members of the

"No, J.R., you were supposed to bring the management efficiency study."   © Punch
ROTHCO

business; it is an activity spread, like all other activities, between head and members of the body corporate."[5] He identified five basic managerial functions: planning, organizing, commanding, coordinating, and controlling. His concept of what each function entails is evident in the following quotation:

> To manage is to forecast and plan, to organize, to command, to coordinate and to control. To foresee and provide means examining the future and drawing up the plan of action. To organize means building up the dual structure, material and human, of the undertaking. To command means maintaining activity among the personnel. To coordinate means binding together, unifying and harmonizing all activity and effort. To control means seeing that everything occurs in conformity with established rule and expressed command.[6]

Functions of management

Managerial activities require special qualities. The qualities are (1) physical, (2) mental, (3) moral, (4) general education, (5) specialized knowledge, and (6) experience. The importance of each ability depends on the manager's position in the organization and its size. In large organizations, for example, Fayol regarded technical ability as the single most important ability at the worker level. At the highest level in a large organization, managerial ability is the most important, whereas technical ability is significantly less important. In a small firm, though, technical ability is the single most important quality for the top person, but managerial ability is significantly important, too.

Principles of management

Although Fayol's assessment of the importance of management has considerable merit, his greatest contribution to management theory is his fourteen principles of management. It's important to note that Fayol considered principles to be flexible and adaptable—not rigid rules. Moreover, he pointed out that there is no limit to the number of management principles that can improve an organization's operation.

1. *Division of work.* Division of work (labor) encompasses three basic concepts: (1) breaking down a task into its components, (2) training workers to become specialists in specific duties, and (3) putting activities in sequence so one person's efforts build on another's. Specialization is the key to division of work because it assures greater efficiency and productivity.

2. *Authority and responsibility.* Authority is the right to give directives or to command action. This right rests in the job the manager holds in an organization. Responsibility, on the other hand, is a sense of obligation that goes with authority. Authority should be delegated only to subordinates who are willing to assume commensurate responsibility.

3. *Discipline.* Fayol defined discipline as "obedience, application, energy, behavior, and outward marks of respect" observed in accordance with agreements between the firm and its employees.[7] In other words, discipline means adhering to all plans that govern business operations. These agreements are enforced through judiciously applied penalties.

4. *Unity of command.* An employee should receive directives from only one superior. Violating this principle undermines authority and jeopardizes discipline and stability.

5. *Unity of direction.* All activities geared toward achieving the same objective should be directed and controlled by one person. This improves coordination and ensures that energies are channeled in the proper direction.

6. *Subordination of individual to general interest.* The overall interest of the firm is more important than the interest of any person or group of people who work for it.

7. *Remuneration of personnel.* Wages should be fair and equitable to both the workers and the company.

8. *Centralization.* Centralization and its counterpart, decentralization, mean how much authority is concentrated at the top of an organization or dispersed throughout the management hierarchy. The question of centralization or decentralization is a question of proportion. It is important to find the optimal degree of each in an organization.

9. *Scalar chain.* Often called the chain of command, this is the line of managers from highest to lowest in an organization. All organizational requests and directives must follow this chain. The only time a departure from the chain of command can be tolerated is when the welfare of the organization is at stake.

10. *Order.* Order is best defined by the adage "a place for everything (or everyone) and everything in its place."

11. *Equity.* In dealing with employees, equity and kindness are most important.

12. *Stability of tenure of personnel.* Experienced, well-trained managers and workers are crucial to the success of a business, so a stable work force should be maintained. Some turnover, however, is expected and desirable. Retirement, death, illness, and job promotions lead to turnover.

13. *Initiative.* Fayol defined initiative as the ability to think through and develop a plan of action. He believed that the most capable managers instill this attribute in their subordinates.

14. *Esprit de corps.* In union, there is strength. All members of an organization should work together harmoniously to achieve a common goal. The job of the manager is to "coordinate effort, encourage keenness, use each man's abilities, and reward each one's merit without arousing possible jealousies and disturbing harmonious relations."[8]

Chester I. Barnard   Sometimes called the originator of the management systems concept, Chester I. Barnard (1886–1961) is best known for his analysis

Born in Malden, Massachusetts, Chester I. Barnard attended Harvard University from 1906 to 1909 but never received a degree. He began working for New Jersey Bell in 1909 and became the company's president in 1927.

of how formal and informal organizations operate and for his "acceptance" theory of authority. Barnard said that "formal" organizations are created when several people agree to work together because of the limitations of working separately. Thus, whenever two or more people agree to work together for some purpose, they are a formal organization. Such cooperation requires communication among group members, a desire to contribute to the group, and a common goal. The executive in a formal organization has several duties: planning, maintaining communication flow, and making sure that other members of the organization work together.[9]

Originator of management systems concept

Barnard rejected the idea that authority is inherent in an organizational position. He felt that authority is not in "persons of authority" but rather in subordinates' acceptance of orders. A subordinate who refuses to obey an order is rejecting the authority. Yet, Barnard recognized the need for individuals to assent to authority. Subordinates will accept and submit to authority, Barnard contended, if the following conditions are satisfied:

1. They understand the directive,

2. They feel that the directive is consistent with the purpose of the organization,

3. The directive does not conflict with their personal beliefs, and

4. They are able to perform the task as directed.[10]

Mary Parker Follett   A philosopher and social scientist, Mary Parker Follett (1868–1933) bridged the gap between the classical and behavioral schools of management. Stressing the importance of harmony and cooperation among group members, she disapproved the use of authority to dominate others and command actions. This, she said, offended the worker emotionally. Follett argued that every problem could be resolved in a way to benefit all concerned. Effective leadership depended on the consent of the group. In her opinion, cooperation, group consent, and effective problem solving would be the foundation for our future industrial system.

Follett stressed group consent

Follett believed business objectives should not be achieved at the expense of the worker. Instead, workers should be made to feel they are cooperating partners with managers in pursuit of objectives. Follett strongly believed in the competence theory of authority. The right to exercise authority depended on the situation; it was not vested in an organizational position. She argued that workers should not feel that they work for someone. Instead, they should feel that they work to satisfy some common goal. She asserted that cooperation, rather than coercion, was the key to effective leadership.

Other Contributors to the Classical School

Most scholars agree that the most significant contributions to the classical school of management thought were made by Taylor, Gantt, the Gilbreths, Emerson, Fayol, Barnard, and Follett. The contributions made by several others are noteworthy, too. Alexander Church (1866–1936) is generally regarded as the first American to conceptualize the functions of managers and to show the interrelationships of the components. Oliver Sheldon (1894–1951) was perhaps the first to recognize management's social responsibility. James Mooney (1884–1957) is known for his analysis of organizational structure and for the importance he attached to the scalar and functional processes, one of the "pillars" of organization theory. Max Weber (1864–1920) contributed to our understanding of bureaucracy, and Lyndall Urwick (1891–1983) synthesized the philosophies of other writers.

The Behavioral School

The **behavioral school** of management has its origins in industrial psychology and sociology. It emphasizes the interactions of people in an organization in order to understand the practice of management. Particularly important was the work of Hugo Münsterberg (1863–1916), a German psychologist who studied the application of behavioral science in a manufacturing environ-

Father of industrial psychology

ment.[11] Now recognized as the father of industrial psychology, Münsterberg was especially interested in matching jobs with people and in structuring the work environment so that workers would produce up to their potential, much as Digital Equipment Corporation is doing in its Enfield, Connecticut, plant. Digital's plan is explained in the In-Box on page 44. The most extensive research on the impact of environmental factors on worker productivity, however, were the now-famous Hawthorne experiments.

Elton Mayo and the Hawthorne Experiments

The Hawthorne experiments

Elton Mayo (1880–1949), an Australian who emigrated to the United States in 1922, is credited with conducting the studies that created the behavioral school of management. His **Hawthorne experiments,** which were conducted at Western Electric's Hawthorne, Illinois, plant, were begun in 1924 and concluded in 1932.[12] Of all the various experiments in this period, it was the relay assembly experiments (1927–1932) that captured the attention of people concerned with human relations in industry. Recent studies have cast doubt on the conclusions drawn from these studies. The methods used by Mayo and the team of researchers from Harvard University have been criticized. Let's look at the commonly reported version of the experiments before we turn our attention to the criticisms.

The relay assembly experiments were designed to determine the effect of rest pauses, lunch breaks, working hours, and other conditions on worker productivity. To assess this impact, six female workers were selected from a relay assembly department of 100 people and placed in a separate experimental room; there, conditions such as piecework incentives, rest breaks, and snacks were modified periodically. Throughout, researchers noted their behavior, attitudes, and productivity, and from these recordings Mayo interpreted the results of the studies.

Hawthorne effect explained

Output reached an all-time high of 3,000 relays per worker per week in the final phase of the experiments. Because that phase had the same control conditions as the beginning, the researchers concluded that the rest breaks, pay, and changes in work schedules could not have caused the recorded changes in output. Their only explanations for increased productivity were psychological and sociological; that is, the participants worked harder and produced more simply because they knew they were being observed. The workers' reaction has since come to be called the **Hawthorne effect.** A more detailed description of the Hawthorne test results can be found in Table 2.2.

Criticisms of the Hawthorne Experiments

Both the Hawthorne effect and the researchers' methods in the relay assembly experiments have been criticized harshly in recent years.[13] First, let's look at the criticisms of the methodology and then examine recent comments of the participants in the relay assembly test room.

THE IN-BOX

Digital Equipment Goes "Bossless"

Digital Equipment Corporation is trying something new and different at its Enfield, Connecticut, plant—team management. Instead of producing computer circuit board modules on an assembly line, each board is made from start to finish by a team of eighteen persons. Each team member is expected to be able to perform any of the twenty tasks involved in constructing a module, whereas on the typical assembly line, each person performs the same task repetitiously. In addition, workers establish their own hours of work at the Enfield plant. There are no time clocks. Each team also serves as its own quality control inspector.

This so-called bossless system is not revolutionary. It has been tried dozens of times over the past few years, but it is new for Digital. Such an approach assumes that workers who are given greater control over their jobs will be more productive. Digital's workers are helping to validate that assumption: the time required to produce a circuit board has been reduced by 40%, scrap has been cut in half, and product quality has improved substantially.

Because Digital's management believes that workers' social needs should be partially satisfied at the work place, it designed the physical environment at Enfield to encourage social interaction. Desks are situated to increase eye contact, a portable conference room can be moved about for meetings, and a volleyball net and exercise equipment have been installed at one end of the building. Instead of investing heavily in robotics and automation, Digital is trying to increase productivity through personal involvement and job enrichment.

Source: Wendy Fox, "Digital Trying the Bossless System," *Boston Globe*, October 14, 1984, pp. A88–A92.

Critics say that these were some of the flaws in the research design and execution:

1. Participants were not chosen randomly from the relay assembly department.

Problems with research methods

2. After eight months, two of the original participants were removed from the experiment for excessive talking, low productivity, and insubordination.

3. Replacements for the two dismissed participants produced at a higher level than the others even though, unlike the others, they had not experienced eight months of the so-called motivating effects of warm and friendly supervision.

TABLE 2.2
Relay assembly test room—Hawthorne experiments

PHASE	MODIFICATION IN WORKING CONDITIONS	RESULTS
1	None; two-week period prior to selecting participants	
2	Workers moved to experimental room; no other changes were made; output was approximately 2,400 per worker per week	
3	Piecework incentive-pay plan introduced	
4	Two five-minute rest pauses introduced	Output increased
5	Two ten-minute rest pauses introduced	Output increased
6	Six five-minute rest pauses introduced	Output dropped slightly
7	Return to two rest breaks, participants given hot snack provided by company	Output increased
8	Workday reduced a half-hour, snacks and rest breaks remained intact	Output increased
9	Workday reduced another half-hour	No effect
10	Workday increased one hour	Output increased
11	Saturday morning shift eliminated	No change
12	Work schedule arrangements returned to original conditions (no breaks or snacks, Saturday morning shift reinstated, etc.)	Output reached an all-time high
13	Conditions same as when experiment began	

4. Workers in the main assembly department worked under a less-preferred incentive system.

5. Workers in the main assembly room were sent home when they ran out of parts. Hence, there was an incentive to stretch out the work. In the experimental room, the participants were paid for waiting or were given other chores.

6. There was a wider variety of relays to be assembled in the main assembly room than in the experimental room.

7. Assembly job runs were much longer in the experimental room, thereby reducing set-up time for any given period of production.

8. In the main assembly room, workers had housekeeping chores around their benches; in the experimental room, this was not the case.

9. In the main room, workers were required to stack the relays in boxes. In the experimental room, they pushed each relay off their benches into a chute.

10. The insulating material used in the experimental room was different from that used in the main room.

11. When five workers in the main assembly room were placed on the incentive system used in the experimental room, their productivity increased 12.5% immediately. This incentive system was eliminated in the main room when other workers wanted to be in on it, resulting in a 16% decline in productivity among the five workers.

12. When variations in the workday were made, the workers in the experimental room did not suffer an economic penalty. They were paid for the time removed from their shift.

13. Threats to eliminate free lunches were used to motivate the workers.[14]

**Participants
interviewed years later**

Perhaps the most enlightening explanation for the increased output was provided in 1981 by three of the participants in the experiments—Theresa Layman, Wanda Blazejak, and Donald Chipman, who was one of the room observers. Researchers who interviewed them concluded that pay was definitely an important factor in increased productivity. In addition, the improved working conditions in the experimental room (pleasant supervision, freedom to communicate with coworkers, and a more relaxed, "family" atmosphere) were credited for the improved performance.[15] This evidence overwhelmingly suggests that productivity increased with incentive pay and better working conditions. The workers were not motivated to work harder because they were singled out and observed, as many writers had concluded over the years.

Other Hawthorne Experiments

**Other studies at
Western Electric**

Two other studies that were part of the Hawthorne experiments, the mica-splitting test and the bank-wiring observation room experiment, suggest that productivity increases were a result of factors other than the Hawthorne effect. Researchers in the mica-splitting test monitored the output of five experienced workers at their regular department work stations, where they split, measured, and trimmed mica chips used for insulation. Then the workers were moved to a special test room and given rest breaks. After a brief decline in productivity, their output increased by an average of 15% and remained at that level for the rest of the experiment. When they returned to their regular department, their output dropped to its original level. Since no other conditions had changed, the researchers attributed the increase in output to the beneficial effects of rest pauses, not to the effect of the experiment itself.

In the bank-wiring observation room, fourteen workers who assembled telephone terminals were put into an experimental room. Their output was measured over an extended period and compared to their output before being moved. Pay and working conditions were unchanged. Despite the move to the experimental room, the workers' output did not change, which it would have if the Hawthorne effect had occurred. Throughout the one-year experiment, the group maintained the steady rate of production informally agreed on by the group members. Peer pressure slowed down the fast workers and prompted slower workers to keep up. If the team got ahead of its normal rate in the morning, the members tended to ease up in the afternoon. Thus, in these studies, there was no increase in output to be explained by the Hawthorne effect.[16]

Other Behaviorists

The list of researchers who have followed in Mayo's footsteps is lengthy. Researchers have studied leadership styles, motivational techniques, behavior modification approaches, and other human and organizational behavioral concepts for more than fifty years. A variety of theories has emerged. Among the most important contributors are Douglas McGregor (Theory X and Theory Y attitudes toward human behavior), Rensis Likert (leadership), Abraham Maslow (motivation), Chris Argyris (leadership and motivation), Frederick Herzberg (motivation), Edwin Ghiselli (human relations and leadership), Kurt Lewin (group dynamics), Jacob Moreno (group behavior), B. F. Skinner (motivation), Victor Vroom (leadership and motivation), and Ralph Stogdill (leadership). Their works are discussed in more depth in Parts Three and Four.

The Quantitative School

Although quantitative methods for solving problems have existed since ancient times, it was Frederick W. Taylor who pioneered a more scientific approach to management. During World War II, many new quantitative tools were developed to aid the military. Because of the success of these techniques, businesses began using them in planning and decision making.[17]

The **quantitative school** of management uses sophisticated mathematical models to simulate business problems. Simulation lets managers thoroughly analyze existing and potential problems and make decisions based on predictable outcomes. Some of the more useful quantitative tools are linear programming, network analysis, and queuing theory. These and other quantitative tools used in industry will be explained in more depth in Chapter 16.

Quantitative tools

Recent advances in computer technology generally have been behind the development and use of quantitative techniques by business. Because of the computer, managers now are able to manipulate vast amounts of data quickly and accurately. Moreover, new computer software designed to solve specific problems has improved planning and is giving business better control over many operations that had been handled by people. Managers have found computer-augmented quantitative methods particularly useful in planning, scheduling work assignments, and controlling inventory.

Quantitative tools are computer-aided

The quantitative approach to decision making consists of the seven basic steps (similar to the scientific method) shown in Figure 2.1.

Defining the problem precisely is often the most difficult step in the procedure. But it is the most important aspect, since the outcome depends on a clearly and accurately stated problem. The second step is developing a real-life situation. Mathematical models typically show the mathematical relationships of the variables that affect the problem. These relationships generally

FIGURE 2.1
The quantitative
management approach
to decision making

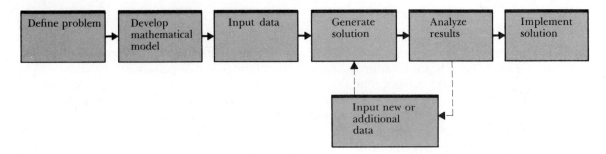

are expressed in terms of equations and inequalities.[18] Since the model represents a real-life situation, the data must be accurate to obtain correct results. Data can be compiled from records, company reports, industry publications, individuals who are familiar with the problem, and many other sources. With these data, the model can be manipulated to arrive at the most satisfactory solution. Sometimes the solution can be found merely by solving the equations. Other times, trial-and-error must be used. In still other cases, certain steps must be repeated with new or additional data to arrive at the best solution. Once the solution has been generated, implementing it is the final step.

The various quantitative tools developed over the years are too numerous to describe. Moreover, their development and refinement usually cannot be attributed to any one person. Some of the most widely used tools, major contributors to their development, and their areas of application are presented in Table 2.3.

More Recent Theories

Many new theories explaining the behavior of managers and organizations have emerged in recent years. Three of the more prominent are *contingency theory, systems theory,* and *Theory Z.*

Contingency theory is based on the premise that situations dictate managerial action; that is, different situations call for different approaches. No single way of solving problems is best for all situations. This type of thinking challenges the concept of "universality" proposed by Fayol and other classical writers who believed that managerial principles and practices should be applied consistently in all situations.

Contingency theory is integrative, meshing the ideas and concepts of the other schools of management thought. Drawing from a wide range of disci-

TABLE 2.3
Summary of quantitative techniques

TOOL	DEVELOPED BY	APPLICATIONS
Game Theory	J. von Neumann O. Morgenstern M. Shubik	Timing and pricing in a competitive market; military strategy
Information Theory	C. Shannon S. Goldman W. Weaver	Data processing system design; organization analysis; advertising effectiveness in market research
Inventory Control	F. W. Harris T. W. Whitin J. F. Magee K. Arrow T. Harris J. Marschak	Economic lot size and economic order point
Linear Programming	L. V. Kantorovich T. C. Koopmans W. Leontieff G. B. Dantzig R. Dorfman P. A. Samuelson	Assignment of equipment and personnel; scheduling; product mix; scheduling transportation routing; allocation processes
Probability Theory	R. A. Fisher T. C. Fry W. Feller H. Cramer	Application in all areas
Queuing Theory	A. K. Erlang L. C. Edie P. M. Morse M. G. Kendall	Inventory control; traffic control; scheduling
Replacement Theory	G. Terborgh J. Dean	Replacement of equipment through failure and deterioration
Sampling Theory	W. E. Deming H. F. Dodge R. G. Romig	Quality control; marketing research
Simulation (including Monte Carlo method)	C. J. Thomas W. L. Deemer R. E. Zimmer-man N. H. Jennings	System reliability evaluation; profit planning; logistic system studies; inventory control; manpower needs
Statistical Decision Making	A. Wald E. C. Molina O. L. Davies W. A. Shewhart R. Schlaiffer	Estimation of model parameters in probabilistic models

Source: Claude S. George, Jr., *The History of Management Thought,* 2/e, © 1972, pp. 165–166. Adapted by permission of Prentice-Hall, Inc., Englewood Cliffs, New Jersey.

plines, it applies the concepts as appropriate to individual situations. Contingency theory focuses on identifying and understanding the forces that shape an organization's environment and on applying the management approach known to work best under those conditions.

The **systems theory** holds that a manager must be able to see the interrelationships of the different parts of his or her organization and must understand how the organization fits into its larger environment. Today's organizations are generally considered open systems; that is, they are affected by environmental forces. A manager must be aware of those forces and must adapt the organization to them. By viewing a firm as a single unit and as part of a larger system, managers will have better perspective when it comes to planning, organizing, staffing, leading, and controlling.

The Japanese approach **Theory Z** is the term coined by William G. Ouchi to characterize the Japanese approach to managing a business. Though some American firms have adopted it, it is a nontraditional approach in this country. This philosophy, based on several ideas that are uniquely Japanese, emphasizes the workers as the key to increased productivity and economic growth.[18] For instance, some workers have the security of employment without the threat of being fired or laid off until mandatory retirement at age fifty-five. Workers are trained to perform a variety of tasks and are rotated from job to job to reduce excessive boredom. Promotions are from within the company, and progression through the ranks is slow and deliberate. The most significant aspect of Theory Z, however, is the importance it places on the traditional Japanese collective decision making and control mechanisms. In Japan, the Theory Z approach is supported by social custom and cultural pressure.

Review

✓ *Why the study of management has been approached from different perspectives.* Management is a broad and intricate field of study, yet if we are to see what makes organizations successful, we must understand management thoroughly. Vast and complex, management is an exciting area of investigation. Researchers' findings on management practices fall into three separate categories: classical, behavioral, and quantitative.

✓ *The development of the classical, or traditional, school of management theory.* Scientific management emphasized finding the "one best way" of performing tasks, which would minimize inefficiency and improve productivity. In its infancy, the classical school focused more on the supervisory level of management and on workers themselves. Later, as the importance of management became apparent at all levels, the classical school expanded to include the activities of all managers. Contrary to common belief, the classical school placed tremendous importance on the individual worker and on his or her social environment. Major contributors to this field of study include Robert Owen, Charles Babbage, Frederick W. Taylor, Henry L. Gantt, Frank and Lillian Gilbreth, Harrington Emerson, Henri Fayol, Chester I. Barnard, and Mary Parker Follett.

✔ *The foundations of the behavioral school of management.* The behavioral school of management originated with the work of Hugo Münsterberg, the father of industrial psychology. His pioneering work in applying psychological concepts to industry blazed the trail for others who would study human behavior in business organizations. Modern theorists, however, trace their roots to a series of studies conducted at Western Electric's Hawthorne, Illinois, plant from 1924 to 1932. These studies, conducted by Elton Mayo and a team of researchers from Harvard University, led to conclusions that increased productivity by workers was a result of the fact that they work more diligently and produce more under observation. This phenomenon, called the Hawthorne effect, has come under sharp attack in recent years. Additional study of the research methods and new information from personal interviews with the participants have prompted some researchers to call the Hawthorne effect a myth.

✔ *How mathematical models have shaped the quantitative school of management thought.* The quantitative school is a continuation and refinement of scientific management. The basis of this approach is the development and use of mathematical models that simulate real-life situations. Quantitative tools in decision making became important in World War II. Following the war, their use spread rapidly throughout industry. The application of quantitative techniques aided by the computer is virtually limitless today.

✔ *Recent contributions to management theory.* New approaches to management have been developed recently. Among the more important are contingency theory, systems theory, and Theory Z. Contingency theory is based on the belief that situations determine managerial action. Systems theory stresses the importance of the organization as a system of interrelated parts and the organization as a component of a larger system. Theory Z refers to the Japanese management practices that emphasize secure employment, participative decision making, group harmony and group action, and control through culturally based peer pressure.

THE MANAGER'S DICTIONARY

As an extra review of the chapter, try defining the following terms. If you have trouble with any of them, refer to the page numbers listed.

classical (traditional) school (31)
scientific management (32)
behavioral school (42)

Hawthorne experiments (43)
Hawthorne effect (43)
quantitative school (47)

contingency theory (48)
systems theory (50)
Theory Z (50)

REVIEW QUESTIONS

1. Why has the study of management been approached from different perspectives?

2. Name the "schools of management thought." Briefly describe the foundation of each school.

3. Why was the classical school expanded to include administrative practices and organization theory? Explain.

4. Name two early British management theorists. What were their major contributions to management thought?

5. Who were some early American theorists? Cite one major contribution of each.

6. How did Gantt's incentive pay plan differ from Taylor's?

7. Why did Gantt's incentive pay system provide bonuses for foremen? Why didn't it penalize workers who failed to produce up to standard?

8. Were the Gilbreths interested in improving efficiency beyond the scope of manufacturing? Explain.

9. What was Henri Fayol's greatest contribution to management theory? Why is he called the father of modern management theory?

10. Which business activity did Fayol consider most important? Why?

11. How did Barnard and Follett's contributions to classical management theory differ from those of other classical theorists?

12. Who originated the behavioral school of management thought? How does the behavioral school differ from the classical school?

13. When did the quantitative management school originate? List some quantitative tools that are widely used in industry.

14. How has the computer aided in the development and application of quantitative management tools?

15. How does a Theory Z approach to management differ from the approach used by most American managers? In your opinion, does Theory Z work in the United States? Why or why not?

MANAGEMENT CHALLENGE

1. In your opinion, did the classical school of management thought really emphasize the human element, or did it view workers as mere extensions of tools and work methods used in the manufacturing process?

2. Frederick W. Taylor described scientific management as a "complete mental revolution" on the part of managers and workers. Explain what he meant by this phrase.

3. Assume that you are the owner-manager of a small manufacturing firm producing paper bags used by retailers throughout a region of the country. What abilities would you need to manage the plant efficiently? Discuss.

4. Is the Hawthorne effect a fact or a myth? Justify your answer.

5. What relationships do you see between the classical and quantitative schools of management thought?

6. As the owner-manager of a business, would you implement a Theory Z management approach? Why or why not?

CASE 2.1

Applying Management to Baseball: The Dodger Tradition[19]

The late Phil Wrigley, former owner of the Chicago Cubs, once said, "Baseball is too much of a sport to be a business and too much of a business to be a sport." Recently, baseball appears to be suffering many of the problems that have afflicted other organizations: strikes, demands for higher salaries, arbitration, alcohol and drug abuse, requests for tax subsidies, and the airing of management-player differences on national television. George Steinbrenner, owner of the New York Yankees, even apologized to the city of New York for the performance of his team on national television in the fall of 1981.

The Los Angeles Dodgers organization is managed differently. Peter O'Malley, who holds a business-law degree from the University of Pennsylvania, treats baseball more like a business than a circus. The club is financed

solely on the money it takes in. This includes player salaries, ballpark maintenance, scouting expenses, equipment and supplies, and other related expenses.

O'Malley believes that winning is not the only goal in running a profitable sports franchise, even though the Los Angeles Dodgers have the third best won-lost percentage in baseball over the past decade. Dodger Stadium is clean and beautifully landscaped, and Dodger training camps are considered the best in the world. O'Malley also is aware of the risks of overexposure. Each year, the team forgoes millions of dollars in revenue because televising the games would have an adverse effect on game attendance. (The Dodgers consistently draw more people to the home games than does any other professional baseball club.) But the most important part of the club's success is its stability. Many of its front-office personnel have been with the club for more than thirty years. Some, in fact, have been around for more than forty years. Turnover is almost nil, even among secretaries. The same holds true on the ballfield: for example, Walter Alston managed the team for twenty-three years without fearing the loss of his job over one or two poor seasons. In contrast, other clubs seem to change managers with the change of seasons.

The Dodgers approach scouting differently, too. Other clubs rely on a scouting pool, headquartered in Newport Beach, California, to provide them with information on young prospective ballplayers. The Dodgers, on the other hand, have twenty-four full-time and twenty-two part-time scouts who travel across the United States and Latin America looking for talent.

Instead of trying to outbid other teams for players in the free-agent market, O'Malley puts his money in developing minor league players. To indoctrinate young minor league players into the Dodger tradition and to give them a chance to interact with former successful big-league stars, the club became the first to bring major and minor leaguers together in one camp. Interacting with retired long-time Dodgers like Sandy Koufax or Don Drysdale, for example, demonstrates to young players that the Dodger organization is built on loyalty.

The Dodger organization also looks after its ballplayers' wives and children. The club flies the families to its training camp; there they enjoy such things as free tennis lessons, dancing, golf, and trips to the Bahamas.

The Dodgers have their own private jet, allowing the Dodger players to board immediately after a game and depart for their next destination, rather than wasting time and losing sleep in airports. Some players say this gives them the edge in a close pennant race.

While these amenities represent somewhat unconventional ways of conducting business, the Dodger organization also uses traditional methods. For instance, manager Tom Lasorda has banned beards and long hair. And when it comes to making a cost-effective decision, personal feelings are set aside. Former player personnel vice president Al Campanis traded his son, a Dodger player, to another ball club because he didn't think his son was good enough to make the team. And when Steve Garvey became a free agent, O'Malley refused to get into a bidding war with other teams. As a result, Garvey, who had become a legend in Los Angeles, signed with the San Diego Padres.

Questions

1. Characterize the management philosophy of Peter O'Malley.

2. What principles of management are evident in O'Malley's approach to managing the Los Angeles Dodgers? Discuss.

CASE 2.2

Volvo Eliminates the Assembly Line[20]

In 1971, the top management of Volvo, Sweden's largest employer, chose to try something radically different in designing its new Kalmar plant. It eliminated the traditional assembly line, replacing it with self-managed work groups. As soon as the plans were unveiled, critics called the approach ludicrous. Some even accused the company of engaging in public relations gimmicks.

When Volvo was founded in 1927, production was based on groups of skilled workers who worked on a single car until it was driven out the door. But by the 1940s, the work group approach had eroded and technology was taking over. During the 1950s, like other automobile manufacturers, Volvo was turning out cars on an assembly line. And, like other companies that utilized assembly line technology, Volvo was experiencing problems with its employees. By the 1960s, employee turnover had reached 52% and absenteeism was on the upswing.

When Pehr Gyllenhammar joined Volvo as CEO in 1971, the company was in shambles. Labor shortages, coupled with all types of work force problems, were hindering productivity. Plans to build the company's new Kalmar plant were muddled. Gyllenhammar responded by creating a task force to develop an alternative plan for its proposed Kalmar plant. The resulting plan called for work groups instead of assembly lines.

Gyllenhammar's rationale for eliminating the assembly line is evident in his statement:

> We invent machines to eliminate work and then we find that psychological tensions cause even more health and behavior problems. People don't want to be subservient to machines and systems. They react to inhuman conditions in very human ways: by job hopping, absenteeism, apathetic attitudes, antagonism, and even malicious mischief.

Gyllenhammar objected also to the assembly line's focus on materials instead of people: people continually had to run after their work as it moved along in front of them. Moreover, the assembly line fostered an antisocial atmosphere, virtually eliminating personal contact. When people did talk, they had to yell above the noise of the line.

The Kalmar plant began operations in 1974 under its new system. The plan called for twenty-five work groups of approximately twenty workers each. Each group was to be accountable for a particular, identifiable portion of the car—electrical systems, interiors, doors, and so forth. Within each group, the members organized themselves the way they saw fit. No longer were foremen responsible for keeping the line moving: the role of the foreman was that of consultant and teacher. Each group decided when the car was ready to move to the next production stage, and any worker could override the computer that controlled the carrier moving the car from one stage to the next.

Each group was accountable for quality inspection, but, if an error did slip through, someone at another work station could catch it. For example, a worker noticing a scratch in the paint could return the car to the painting station. Then, under computer control, the car would return to where the production process left off.

Since the Kalmar plant began operations in 1974, behavioral scientists from all over the world have traveled to Sweden to see Volvo's manufacturing process. Most have been favorably impressed. Volvo is also pleased. In fact, the production process has proved so successful that Volvo has designed all its new plants on the same concept.

According to Gyllenhammar, Volvo is willing to give up increased productivity to attain some sort of worker happiness. Volvo's workers are more satisfied with their jobs than are many of their contemporaries who work on assembly lines. But one final point should be made: Sweden's labor costs are the highest in the world, a tradeoff for improved job satisfaction and lower absenteeism and turnover.

Questions

1. Evaluate the pros and cons of abolishing the assembly line at Kalmar. Was this a wise decision?

2. Do you see a conflict between methods for improving productivity and concerns over human behavior? Explain.

CHAPTER OUTLINE

Environment Defined

Organization *or* Environment?

Organization *and* Environment

External Environmental Forces

Political and Legal Forces

The Political Climate • *The Rationale for Government Intervention* •
Business Reactions

Economic Forces

National Trends • *Company and Industry Considerations*

Social Forces

Technological Forces

Examples of Technological Breakthroughs • *Requirements for*
Technological Innovation • *Obstacles to Technological Innovation* •
Business Responses

International Influences

Internal Environmental Forces

Physical Resources

Financial Resources

Human Resources

Managerial Values and Ethics

The Environment of Management

M A N A G E M E N T   I N   A C T I O N

Small Is Beautiful

General Electric, AT&T, and a host of other companies have a new philosophy that would have been considered economic heresy a few years ago: they are advocating small plants instead of giant manufacturing complexes. Conventional wisdom stresses economies of scale; that is, producing goods in huge factories at relatively low per-unit costs. Today, however, huge manufacturing complexes are being replaced with smaller facilities, giant bureaucracies are being dismantled, and managers are talking about "diseconomies of scale."

Beginning with the Industrial Revolution, managers operated as though bigness brought efficiency. The idea worked for a long time, and for decades American business dominated world markets with low-cost goods through longer and longer production runs in larger and larger factories. But when America's manufacturing productivity rate began declining, managers took a new look at this philosophy. The result was a shift to smaller plants. S. C. Johnson & Sons split its 1,200-person work force at its Racine, Wisconsin, plant into four separate units. General Electric now produces airline engines at eight satellite plants instead of at two giant complexes. AT&T opted for smaller, automated facilities at its subsidiary, AT&T Technologies.[1]

Several things signaled the need for change. By the mid-1970s, American managers began realizing that economy of scale was not enough to give them an advantage in world markets. Foreign competition was so great that American steel mills and other large manufacturing firms were unable to produce at capacity. In addition, technology was advancing so fast in some industries that plants were becoming obsolete sooner than expected. When managers realized what was happening, they decided to invest in less costly, smaller facilities. At about the same time, the development of computer-assisted design and manufacturing made producing goods in small, customized batches economically feasible.[2]

In switching to smaller plants, manufacturers found other benefits besides lower cost. They can turn out customized products efficiently, eliminate several layers of management, and improve communication because there are fewer organizational levels. As a result, labor relations are better, and workers feel that they have more effect on plant operations; also, companies can respond to their customers' needs more quickly.

Preview

Not all companies are opting for small plants. IBM, for example, is still stressing economies of scale with a vengeance, turning out its personal computers at a fairly low cost per unit. Furthermore, some industries such as aircraft manufacturing will always require large factories. But for a growing number of firms, small is now beautiful. The movement from large manufacturing complexes to smaller plants has been prompted by economic and technological forces that affect a firm's operations by shaping its environment. Other variables also come into play. Political, legal, and social forces are other external variables that affect a firm's operations. Internal forces include organizational resources and the managers' value systems. Each of these forces is discussed at length in this chapter. After studying Chapter 3, you will be able to explain:

✔ What a firm's environment is

✔ The diverse external forces that affect a firm's operation

✔ The opportunities and constraints posed by the internal forces that affect a company

Environment Defined

As we pointed out in Chapter 1, organizations are accountable to a number of different groups, including customers, suppliers, creditors, government agencies, and the public. They must be responsive to these groups and operate within the boundaries they establish.

Forces shape the environment

Managers don't have the luxury of being able to do whatever they choose. They must make decisions within a framework of external and internal forces. That framework defines the environment of management. These forces can be constraints or opportunities for a company. The external environment, as shown in Figure 3.1, generally consists of political and legal, economic, social, and technological forces. The internal environment is made up of a company's resources and the managers' value systems.

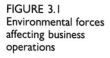

FIGURE 3.1
Environmental forces
affecting business
operations

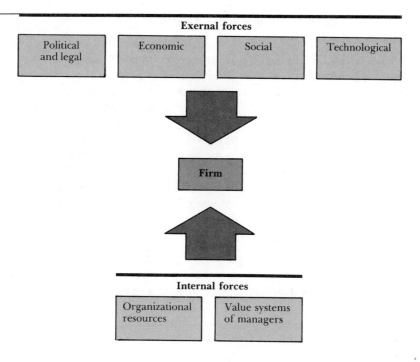

Organization *or* Environment?

Since we know without a doubt that environmental forces surround organizations, the question becomes: What determines successful business performance? Two schools of thought attempt to answer this question from diametrically different viewpoints: those of environmental determinism and organizational determinism.

Environment affects the firm

In support of **environmental determinism,** scholars in the field of industrial organization argue that business performance fundamentally is affected only by competition in the industry, and that the firm cannot influence its environment. Those in organizational theory and behavior maintain that a business's success depends largely on how an organization fits with its environment. Environmental determinism has its roots in Darwin's theory of natural selection, that is, nature ultimately selects which species will survive and which will become extinct.

In support of **organizational determinism,** scholars in sociology, economics, and, more recently, strategic management have different arguments. They believe that an organization not only adapts to its environment but that the success of the business depends on how well it can influence the environmental forces in its favor. The issue is close to the hotly debated question of whether individuals affect their environment or whether the environment affects the individual. The answer is "a little of both."

Organization *and* Environment

Firms influence their environment

We can assume that organizations are influenced by environmental forces, as you will see in the following sections. We also can accept the idea that firms can use the external environment to their own advantage. It's safe to assume that large, powerful organizations with greater resources can have more influence on external environmental forces than small, less-powerful organizations can. For example, consider the auto industry's success in persuading lawmakers to relax gasoline mileage standards in 1985. Chrysler Corporation was the only American auto maker that met the overall 26 MPG average set by the federal government. But General Motors, Ford Motor Company, and American Motors managed to avoid the huge fines called for by the enforcement legislation because of their influence. Now, let's look at each of the environmental forces more thoroughly.

External Environmental Forces

External environmental forces are those that operate beyond a firm's boundaries and affect its operations. They include political and legal, economic, social, and technological influences. Each of these forces, working independently or in combination with others, imposes constraints or creates opportunities for the firm.

Political and Legal Forces

Government influences

Congress was given substantial economic power by the U.S. Constitution. Among other things, Congress is empowered to collect taxes, print currency, form armies, establish patents and copyrights, and regulate interstate commerce and commercial transactions with foreign nations. State and local governments also are given the power to enact laws that regulate economic activity. Together, these government units define the political and legal environment of private economic activity.

Government intervention occurs whenever government policies affect the allocation of society's resources. Such intervention and allocation can be direct or indirect. *Direct* intervention and allocation of resources occurs when the government acts as a consumer and purchases goods and services, or when it employs people. *Indirect* intervention comes through legislation.[3]

The Political Climate   Government administrations generally can be considered either probusiness or antibusiness. A probusiness stance encourages new business ventures and expansion. An antibusiness attitude imposes obstacles and curtails growth. For example, reducing or eliminating the depletion allowance for oil and gas exploration firms will curtail exploration. Similarly, a decision to lengthen the period for depreciation write-offs on investment property will hurt commercial investors. In these instances, government action

Positive and negative impact

will hurt companies financially because of tax considerations. On the other hand, a government body's decision to subsidize low-interest home loans will revitalize the home construction industry and generate new growth. Likewise, a decision to allow American firms to trade with countries with different political views—Cuba, for example—would result in economic expansion for many businesses.

Historically, Americans have characterized the Republican party as the friend of big business and the Democratic party as its foe. Much of this can be traced to the Great Depression and later to Franklin D. Roosevelt's administration, which supported the right of people to form and join unions. Even today, the Democratic party carries the antibusiness stigma and the Republican party the antiworker scar in the minds of millions of workers.

Government regulation of private economic activity is neither new nor uniquely American. The Babylonians had usury laws limiting the interest that could be charged on loans. Queen Elizabeth I of England granted monopoly privileges to favored businesspeople until her power to do so was removed by the courts and given to Parliament. What is new, however, is the recent expansion of government intervention in the American economy. Government intervention has expanded at a rate reminiscent of the depression-dominated 1930s. Of fifty-three major federal regulatory agencies, twenty were established in the 1970s and six in the 1960s.[4]

Nowhere is government intervention more evident than in the recent breakup of AT&T. In an effort to promote competition in the phone-service industry, the courts ordered AT&T into divestiture, effective January 1, 1984. This ruling, which resulted from a lawsuit brought by the Department of Justice in 1974, dissolved one of the nation's largest and most successful corporate giants. Government intervention also is evident in the banking and transportation industries, where deregulation has resulted in numerous new financial firms, airlines, and trucking companies.

The Rationale for Government Intervention   The market economy responds to three questions:

1. What goods should be produced?

2. How should they be produced?

3. Who should produce them?

Each member of society pursues his or her own self-interest when making private purchases. Added together, these purchases influence allocation, production, and distribution. That is, consumers purchase goods and services that give them the greatest satisfaction, firms manufacture goods in ways that minimize their costs and maximize their profits, and goods are distributed among consumers according to their preferences and incomes. Thus, when individuals pursue their personal self-interest, society's interest as a whole is served.

THE IN-BOX

Are Managers Liable?

On May 2, 1985, E. F. Hutton pleaded guilty to 2,000 counts of fraud, which stemmed from its cash-management practices. Essentially, Hutton was guilty of drawing checks on more than $1 billion in uncollected funds. Although the giant brokerage firm was fined $2 million and was ordered to make restitution amounting to additional millions, there is still a lingering question in the minds of legal analysts: Should the Department of Justice have charged E. F. Hutton or its managers with criminal conduct?

This question focuses on individual accountability. Many analysts believe that a corporate executive should not be charged with a crime unless he or she personally profits from a scheme to defraud clients, creditors, or others. The opposing argument holds that companies obey the law—or disobey it—only through people. Advocates of this philosophy argue that only people, not companies, can be deterred by the penalties that the criminal system imposes. They say that a fine levied on a corporation is treated like any other cost of doing business. They feel that people, rather than corporations, should bear the burden of any penalty imposed by the courts.

The failure of the Justice Department to bring charges against E. F. Hutton employees smacks of a "deal" between Hutton and the government prosecutors, according to some observers. But for now, the case clearly shows that companies and their managers are not one and the same.

Source: William B. Glaberson, "The Punishment of Hutton Doesn't Fit the Crime," *Business Week,* June 3, 1985, p. 40.

The duties of government

Government intervention is minimal as long as a market economy makes these decisions automatically. Essentially, government has three duties: (1) to maintain law and order, (2) to enforce contracts, and (3) to define property rights.[5] As long as the market takes society's best interests into account, government intervention is unnecessary. But when there is a breakdown in the market mechanism, such as in the E. F. Hutton case in the In-Box on this page, government regulation is necessary. Such intervention generally takes four forms: antitrust enforcement, economic regulation (such as regulating prices charged by a monopoly), social regulation (such as imposing air- and water-quality standards), and direct participation in the market as a buyer or a producer of goods or services.

The political and legal sector includes legislation, decrees of regulatory agencies, court decisions, foreign policy, and tariffs, all of which provide opportunities and constraints to business. For example, consider Ford Motor

TABLE 3.1 Selected federal laws affecting business operations	FEDERAL LEGISLATION	MAJOR PROVISIONS
	Sherman Antitrust Act of 1890	Outlaws combinations of businesses and other practices restricting competition
	Federal Trade Commission Act, 1914	Prevents unfair methods of competition
	National Labor Relations Act of 1935	Gives most workers the right to form and join unions and to engage in collective bargaining
	Robinson-Patman Act, 1936	Prohibits price discrimination
	Fair Labor Standards Act of 1938, as amended	Regulates minimum wages and overtime pay
	Civil Rights Act of 1964, as amended	Prohibits employers from discriminating against workers on the basis of age, race, sex, and national origin
	Age Discrimination in Employment Act, 1967	Protects workers against arbitrary age discrimination in hiring, compensation, and other conditions of employment
	Occupational Safety and Health Act, 1970	Protects workers from hazards in the workplace
	Air Quality Act of 1967, as amended	Regulates particulates emitted into the air
	Federal Water Pollution Control Act of 1972, as amended	Regulates discharge of pollutants into navigable waterways
	Consumer Goods Pricing Act, 1975	Prohibits price maintenance agreements among producers and resellers in interstate commerce

Opportunities and constraints

Company. Can you think of a constraint and an opportunity in Ford's political and legal environment? Such federal safety requirements as head rests and sturdy bumpers are constraints on auto makers because they increase the cost of car production. On the positive side, the government's insistence that Japanese car makers limit their exports to the United States is an opportunity for Ford Motor Company and other American car manufacturers.

As another example, cigarette manufacturers also face constraints and opportunities. On one hand, the U.S. government subsidizes the growing of tobacco. This is a "plus" for cigarette manufacturers because it lowers cigarette production costs. On the other hand, the government stipulates that all cigarette advertising and packaging must have visible health warnings. This stipulation is obviously a "minus" for cigarette firms. Some of the more significant federal laws that impact business operations, and the major provisions of each, are shown in Table 3.1.

Business Reactions Organizations try to influence political and legal trends because they are so important to business operations. Among the lobbyists that business uses to influence government policies are the U.S. Chamber of Commerce, the Committee for Economic Development, the National Association of Manufacturers, and the Business Roundtable.

The U.S. Chamber of Commerce, a federation of several thousand chambers of commerce and trade associations, was created in 1912 to promote a unified voice for business opinion. It is a powerful proponent of legislation that favors the business community and an opponent of government interference in the business sector.

The Committee for Economic Development is a group of business leaders who try to educate the public about business's attempts to increase productivity, maintain high employment, and achieve higher living standards. This group was formed in 1942 and has become more active in recent years.

The National Association of Manufacturers was begun in 1895. Its main objective is legislation promoting entrepreneurship, trade, and commerce. Members of the Business Roundtable, formed in 1972, are the top managers of the largest and most powerful American corporations. They are most concerned with matters relating to energy, taxes, pollution control, import quotas, and tariffs.

Economic Forces

The economic environment includes trends in the gross national product (GNP), disposable personal income, consumer spending, industrial investment, employment, population growth, money markets, capital markets, the structure of industry, the nature of competition, demand for products, and similar variables. Trends in some of these forces are shown in Figures 3.2–3.5.

Positive and negative impact

National Trends Economic trends, like political and legal forces, can positively or negatively affect business performance. Some economic forces affect all businesses, while others influence only select industries. A higher GNP and higher consumer spending levels generally benefit most businesses. But recessions, which usually are bad for most firms, tend to be beneficial for movie makers. The assumption is that during recessions, when many people are unemployed, they try to avoid harsh reality by going to the movies or by taking part in other escapist activities.

Let's look at two more industries that are directly affected by economic variables—housing and recreational products. Higher interest (mortgage) rates mean higher mortgage payments for people who buy houses. When interest rates and mortgage rates continue to rise, many potential home buyers put off their purchases. This severely constrains firms in home construction and related industries, such as lumber, roofing, and cement. But manufacturers of recreational products like boats and snowmobiles are affected positively as

FIGURE 3.2
U.S. unemployment
rate, 1960–1985
[*Source:* Robert J.
Gordon,
Macroeconomics
(Boston: Little, Brown,
1987), p. 21.]

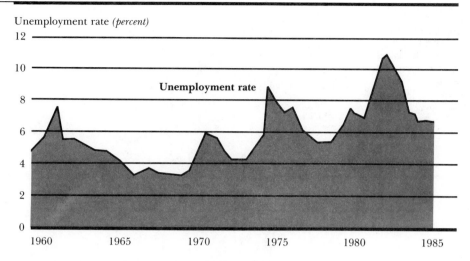

Unemployment rate *(percent)*

FIGURE 3.3
U.S. inflation rate,
1900–1986 [*Source:*
Robert J. Gordon,
Macroeconomics
(Boston: Little, Brown,
1987), p. 19.]

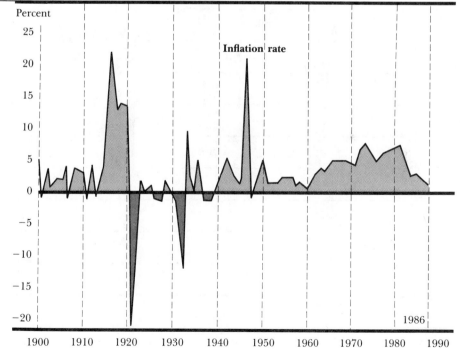

Percent

FIGURE 3.4
Changes in growth rate
of real GNP,
1910–1985 [*Source:*
Ralph T. Byrns and
Gerald W. Stone,
Economics (Glenview,
Ill.: Scott Foresman,
1987), p. 158.]

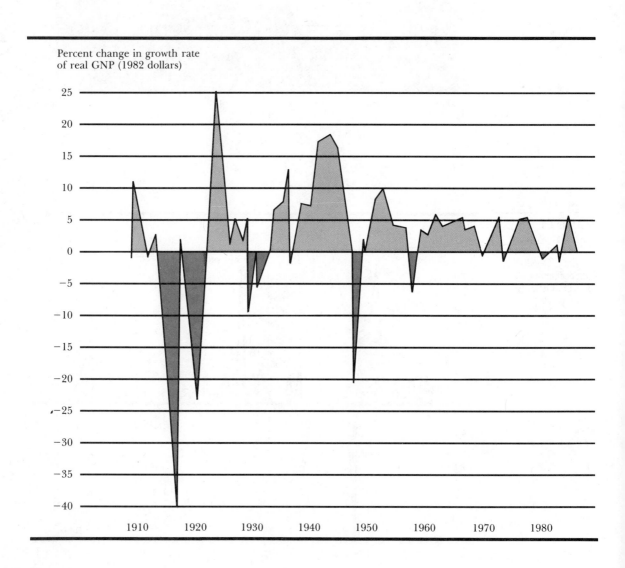

Percent change in growth rate
of real GNP (1982 dollars)

FIGURE 3.5
Projected growth of various work groups through 1990 (*Source:* Bureau of Labor Statistics.)

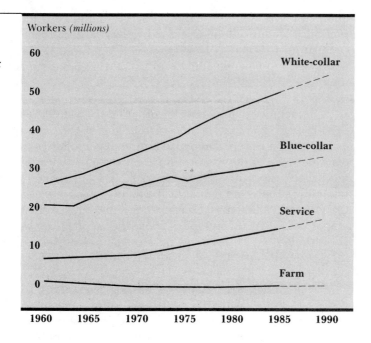

Workers *(millions)*

60	White-collar
50	
40	Blue-collar
30	
20	Service
10	
0	Farm

1960   1965   1970   1975   1980   1985   1990

disposable personal income rises. With more money in their pockets, consumers are better able to afford leisure products.

Firms stimulate the economy

It is important to remember that business can influence economic forces to its advantage just as it can political and legal forces. For example, a firm or an industry can stimulate the economy by infusing money into it or by inducing people to spend more. Consider, for example, the impact of lower-than-market interest rates and rebates offered by automobile manufacturers in recent years. Ford Motor Credit Corporation, General Motors Acceptance Corporation (GMAC), and Chrysler Credit Corporation offered lower-than-market rate financing. Car sales soared. This depleted large inventories, stimulated production, and generally caused an upswing in the industry. There was also a ripple effect. Firms that manufactured component parts called back workers who had been laid off, extra shifts were added, and overtime became common. Other industries can affect the economy in a similar way. Low mortgage rates, for instance, can stimulate home construction, and discount air fares can attract more passengers for the airline industry.

Company and Industry Considerations   The type of industry and the nature of the competition are primary economic forces affecting business operations. For instance, there is intense price competition among firms in some industries, while firms in other industries may tend to compete in service, product quality or availability, or other areas. While price is important to most customers, it is only one of several considerations. For example, an Amtrak rail ticket from Chicago to New Orleans is significantly cheaper than an airline ticket, but most people choose to fly. In this situation, cost is less important than time. Airlines compete in price as well as in service in their unregulated industry.

Market structure determines price

Remember that a manager often has very little control over the price of the product. The market structure largely determines the selling price. For example, in a purely **competitive industry** a seller has absolutely no control over the price of the product. Such a market is characterized by many buyers and sellers, easy entry into the market, and a prevailing "market price" determined by supply and demand. It would be foolish to sell the product for less than the prevailing market price, since all of the product could be sold at the market price. An attempt to sell above the market price would be futile because the product is readily available at the market price. The production and marketing of agricultural products is close to being a purely competitive market.

Limited pricing freedom

In a **monopoly,** a firm sells a product or service for which there are no good substitutes. Without regulation, a monopolist would price the product at a level that would give him or her the greatest profits. AT&T, Consolidated Edison, or other monopolies that operate in the public interest do not price their service at a level that will assure the maximum profit because they are regulated by public agencies. Their rates are governed by regulatory bodies that grant or deny requests for rate increases. In practice, their rates are relatively low and the quantity demanded is relatively high.

An **oligopolistic industry** is characterized by a few sellers, generally huge capital investments, and by "interdependency." The pricing policies of one or more firms prompt reactions from other firms in the industry. A firm may cut its price to that of its competitors or may even set it below the competition. The result often is a price war in which every company loses. This market structure has a price leader who usually has a larger market share and more influence on price than other firms do. USX, R. J. Reynolds, and General Motors are the leaders in their industries. Even the industry leader, though, cannot determine the exact quantity of the product that will be demanded at any given price, because demand is a function not only of the product's price but of the price of competing products as well.

Firms have some flexibility

The market structure that allows each firm considerable discretion in its pricing policies is **monopolistic competition.** Since there are many sellers and buyers in this market, the seller who wishes to charge a higher price must make the product different or offer it with other incentives, such as convenience or additional service. Of course, a seller who wants to capture a low-income segment or one who appeals to a cost-conscious buyer may purposely underprice competitors. But the pricing policies must reflect the image that the seller wishes to project and the expectations of the targeted market segment.

Social Forces

Ultimately, all organizations are affected by the social forces of their environments. These forces include national traditions, values, customs, consumer psychology, and social responsibility. Social trends have presented both opportunities and threats to the business sector over the years.

Social trends affect business

First, let's take a look at the general population. Americans are living longer, their disposable income has increased tremendously over the past twenty years, two-income families are now the norm, and the average level of education has risen steadily. These and other factors have affected business significantly.

With more leisure time on their hands and more money in their pockets, older Americans are enjoying comforts and pleasures of life that their grandfathers never imagined. Affluent retirees today buy Winnebagos and other motor homes in unprecedented numbers. They are also some of the most important clients of stock brokerages, banks, and other financial institutions. Because of their economic and political clout, older Americans influence the way we do business.

The typical American family has changed, too. It has become smaller and better educated, and its per capita income has risen substantially. During the mid-1980s, a majority of households had two incomes for the first time in our history. In general, wives and mothers have decided to pursue careers outside the home for two reasons—the need for additional family income and the desire for the stimulation of the workplace.

There also are more single-parent households today than ever before. Consequently, there is a greater need for low-income housing, more child care facilities, and quick, nutritious meals. Swanson, Stouffer, and other food companies have profited by catering to working parents who don't have the time to spend on food preparation.

Social forces determine product offerings

Attitudes, interests, and concerns have evolved. For example, the national physical fitness trend has meant greater income for fitness businesses, such as gymnasiums, health spas, and handball and tennis courts. Weight consciousness and concern for good health have prompted numerous food and beverage firms to diversify their products. Weight Watchers' pizza, Carnation's Coffee-Mate, Coca Cola's Tab, General Foods' Sanka, and Nabisco's salt-free crackers are examples of products marketed in response to concerns over hypertension, obesity, and other health problems. Even breweries have capitalized on people's concern with their physical appearance. Anheuser-Busch, Coors, Miller Brewing Company, and most other major breweries have seen sales of their lower calorie (light) beers grow significantly.

Social forces can hurt business too. Increased awareness of pollution has resulted in laws that severely restrict the operations of many chemical, steel, textile, and paper companies. Pollution-control devices, modifications in manufacturing processes, and pollution-abatement equipment have escalated operating costs. As pointed out in the In-Box on page 71, USX, Ciba Geigy Corporation, 3M, and other companies affected by pollution laws are spending huge sums of money to reduce hazardous waste and find solutions to solid-waste disposal problems.

Business affects social trends

Remember that business acts as well as reacts to social forces. By trying to sway social forces in its favor, business can enhance its environment and reap financial rewards. The entertainment industry is a prime example of how an industry can alter social trends. Capitalizing on technological innovations in video equipment, movie makers began marketing films in the form of video discs and cassette tapes. Video rental firms have prospered while theaters have suffered declining patronage as a result. Home viewing is a social trend that caught on quickly.

Business also can use the social environment to its advantage by creating new customs and by expanding existing customs. At the prompting of greeting-card companies, for example, Americans began celebrating Grandparents' Day recently. Like Mother's Day, Valentine's Day, and other holidays, Grandparents' Day proved to be a boon for florists, long-distance communication companies, and manufacturers of candy and greeting cards.

Technological Forces

Often, technological variables are breakthroughs that result in improved products, services, and production methods. Because of the now-dizzying pace of technological change, top-level managers face the future with increasing apprehension. Today's well-thought-out corporate decisions may prove disastrous in the future if there are technological innovations by competitors or suppliers. For instance, capital expenditures may provide little benefit if the resources they purchase today become obsolete tomorrow. This is especially true with investments in computer hardware. Because of the speed of innovations in computer technology, companies are reluctant to invest millions of dollars in mainframe computers. An alternative is to lease mainframes or use microcomputers if possible. Because of technological breakthroughs by Apple Computer, IBM, and other firms, microcomputers are a very attractive alternative to mainframes. Their lower price tag, combined with their expanded capabilities and versatility, can satisfy most users. Improvements in microcomputer technology have meant greater precision and speed in banking, insurance, and investment firms. In addition, small and large manufacturing firms alike now use microcomputers to solve their inventory, scheduling, and cash-flow problems.

Technology affects management decisions

Examples of Technological Breakthroughs   Technological change has provided many benefits. Improvements in health care, logistics, and customer service, for example, are a direct result of technological innovations. To appreciate fully the impact of technology on business operations, consider the following developments.

THE IN-BOX

Polluting Firms React to Environmental Forces

Faced with spiraling costs of solid-waste disposal, firms are searching for ways to prevent pollution rather than dispose of pollution-causing waste.

Ciba Geigy Corporation has switched from zinc to a process using hydrogen in the manufacture of a plastic additive. USX now recycles acidic waste used to clean steel and iron oxide used to make magnetic tape. These firms, along with dozens of other companies faced with pollution problems, are searching for better ways of solving their waste disposal problems.

Traditionally, companies producing hazardous waste as a by-product of their manufacturing processes used landfills for disposal because they were the least expensive alternative. But when government regulations placed tighter restrictions on the use of landfills, companies were forced to use other, more expensive methods. Besides the costs of disposal, some companies have the additional cost of cleaning up dump sites. Taken together, these costs are becoming prohibitive for a growing number of companies. Consequently, waste prevention has been given a higher priority than waste disposal.

Waste reduction programs focus on four specific areas: raw materials, manufacturing processes, equipment, and reuse. By pursuing all these alternatives, USX has cut its waste in half and its use of landfills by 80%; 3M has changed its sandpaper-manufacturing process and redesigned equipment used in the process, resulting in a reduction of 400 tons of hazardous waste each year; and Ciba Geigy has modified its dye-making technology, thereby increasing product yield while reducing waste. While these approaches are partial solutions to waste-disposal problems, the key to further reduction is research and development to design products that minimize waste.

Source: Alix Freedman, "Firms Curb Hazardous Waste to Avoid Expensive Disposal," *Wall Street Journal,* May 31, 1985, pp. 25–26.

- *Masers and lasers.* Amplified electromagnetic radiation that produces coherent beams of microwaves and light—now known as masers and lasers—has become a multibillion dollar industry whose greatest impact is in land-based and satellite communications.

- *Platinum-based antitumor drugs.* In 1978, Bristol Laboratories marketed its first cancer-suppressing drugs used to treat many forms of intractable cancers.

• *Robots.* Robots are used routinely in jobs that are tedious, hot, or hazardous. They are especially useful in die casting, welding, spray painting, stamping and forging, and operating lathes, grinders, and drill presses. Advantages of using robots in the workplace include greater flexibility, increased productivity, lower costs, higher quality, and greater work reliability.[6]

Requirements for Technological Innovation   Practically all technological innovations rest on a scientific base. Even innovations in service industries depend on scientific principles: cable television depends on functioning space satellites, electronic banking requires computers, automobiles are built at lower cost by using robots. A basic knowledge of scientific principles is essential for innovation in any industry. And, with it, innovative ideas mushroom.

The United Nations Office of Economic and Commercial Development has summarized the conditions that are important to technological innovation:

1. Technologically oriented universities nearby that can cooperate in new ventures with business

2. Successful entrepreneurs as role models

3. Institutions and venture-capital sources that are comfortable with technological innovators and that possess the rare business-appraisal abilities needed to turn inventions into profits

4. Good communication (proximity and frequent consultation) among all the essential people in the innovation process[7]

Obstacles to Technological Innovation   On the other hand, innovation is hindered by any number of circumstances—some internal, but most external. Internal obstacles to innovation typically are unrelated to the product's technical merit. Instead, they arise from the inadequacies of the people involved. These inadequacies include (1) lack of scientific and technical knowledge, (2) resistance to change, and (3) poor management. External hindrances to innovation include fears of technology's effect on society and government restrictions on research and development.

Internal and external barriers to innovation

Business Responses   Business also attempts to influence technological forces to its advantage. IBM and Xerox, for example, struggle to be the first on the market with revolutionary new equipment and processes to maintain their strong market positions and their progressive image. Other firms also invest heavily in research and development. Nearly one-fourth of 3M's sales revenues in the early 1980s, for example, were from products developed in the previous five-year period.[8] Other companies seek the competitive edge with an abundant supply of bright, capable, technically trained employees. Sometimes a firm even keeps on more employees than it needs in periods of recession so that it will be adequately staffed when prosperity returns. For example, a company like Martin Marietta can't wait to get a government contract before hiring engineers and other technically trained workers who are in short supply. Their services must be maintained continually.

Competing in the high technology market

There is another method of effectively competing in a market dominated by new technology: enter into agreements with the foreign companies that developed the technology. RCA, Motorola, Zenith, and other companies that sell electronic equipment took advantage of Japanese video recorder technology by marketing the products under American brand names. General Motors used a similar tactic when it installed the Japanese Isuzu diesel engine in its Luv trucks.

International Influences

International influences on a company's external environment pose constraints and opportunities for businesses. Because of the growing impact of international trade on domestic firms, we will examine these influences.

Opportunities and problems abroad

The political and legal climate surrounding international trade sometimes inhibits business, sometimes encourages it. Political sanctions, tariffs, subsidies, import quotas, and the like constrain some firms but create opportunities for others. The forces of popular culture in international markets are also important. Changes in tastes for clothes, music, and food, for example, have created a strong market for American jeans, fast-food restaurants, and Western music in the Far East. Social customs, legal restrictions, and social problems create obstacles to successful competition in some countries. For example, some American firms conducting business in South Africa are being boycotted by opponents of South Africa's apartheid policies.

Effect of economic and technological forces

International economic and technological forces also affect American business. Foreign investors are choosing to invest heavily in the United States because of its political stability. Hotels, land, financial institutions, and high-tech firms attract foreign investors, especially those from the Middle East. The international monetary-exchange rate also affects American business. When the dollar is strong relative to foreign currencies, foreign-made products become relatively inexpensive and Americans can buy them at "bargain" prices. This hurts American manufacturers, who then demand protection. A strong dollar also makes American-made goods relatively expensive in foreign markets; consequently, sales overseas are adversely affected. These and other economic forces affecting international trade are discussed at length in Chapter 18, "International Management."

Exporting and importing technology

As we have pointed out, American firms import foreign technology and export American technology. Electronics, automotive and computer technology, and robots are examples of goods and services that are both imported and exported. We import robots from Japan and sell computers to the Soviet Union. We import automobiles from West Germany and export farm equipment to China. Such transactions occur because all countries have certain products that they can produce at an economic advantage and other products that they must import at an economic disadvantage. International trade provides opportunities for greater profits and helps stabilize prices. But there is a technological advantage as well. When a country sells its technologically advanced products, production capacity is more fully used and per-unit manufacturing costs lowered.

Internal Environmental Forces

A business's environment is affected not only by external forces but also by internal forces. These include (1) the physical, financial, and human resources of the firm, and (2) the value systems of managers. Like external forces, these internal influences provide both problems and opportunities for the firm.

Physical Resources

Physical resources aid or hinder success

Every firm has physical resources that either aid or hinder its performance. They include the physical plant and its location, manufacturing equipment, raw materials, transportation and distribution facilities, and other resources vital to its operations. Dow Chemical's research and development center in Midland, Michigan, for example, is considered one of the finest toxic-testing facilities in the world. This resource clearly helps Dow develop new, safe products in a timely manner. Dallas–Fort Worth (DFW) International Airport is another example of how the physical plant affects a firm's environment and enhances its efficiency. Although DFW takes up more space than other airports, its ability to move people and aircraft efficiently is widely recognized. Kennedy Airport in New York City, on the other hand, is considered inefficient and overcrowded. Both its location and its layout hinder Kennedy International's operations.

Access to a dependable supply of raw materials and component parts gives a firm a competitive edge in the marketplace. International Paper Company and Crown Zellerbach Corporation, for example, benefit from owning sources of raw materials. Other firms, particularly giant manufacturing companies, own factories that produce component parts for their products. Still others protect themselves with long-term contracts that ensure an uninterrupted supply of raw materials. Firms that are subject to supply interruptions operate under less-favorable conditions because of the uncertainty surrounding future operations.

A firm's environment is also influenced by its manufacturing equipment. Japan's steel producers, for instance, have made significant inroads into world markets because their modern equipment and processes enable them to produce steel more efficiently than do American steel mills that rely on older, less-efficient equipment. American auto makers also are at a competitive disadvantage when they produce cars in inefficient plants. This is why Lee Iacocca closed several Chrysler plants when he took over as Chrysler chairman a few years ago.

Perhaps the best example of how physical resources affect an organization is the health care industry. Hospitals that offer state-of-the-art diagnostic services, complete surgical facilities, and modern postoperative care have an advantage over those that don't provide complete health services. Because of their resources, they are better able to attract health-care personnel and generate capital.

Financial Resources

A firm's financial resources include the assets that enable it to meet its operating costs, expand, conduct research and development, borrow additional funds, and so on. A business's financial position affects its stock price, its ability to raise additional capital, and its ability to take advantage of profitable opportunities when they arise. The financially sound firm can borrow money at lower interest rates, insist on special services as a highly valued customer, and maintain the goodwill of suppliers, stockholders, creditors, and others. The financially unstable company, on the other hand, most likely will find it difficult to raise capital, maintain a highly competitive position, or take advantage of income-producing opportunities.

Inadequate financial resources

To appreciate the difficulties created by inadequate financial resources, consider the enormous problems faced by Chrysler Corporation when it was in danger of going bankrupt in the early 1980s. Suppliers demanded cash payment, borrowing money became increasingly difficult, interest rates charged Chrysler escalated because of the greater likelihood of default, and the price of its stock plummeted. But when the Chrysler management convinced Congress that the federal government should bail it out with a government-backed loan, its environment improved. Armed with enough money to continue operating and finding itself in an improving economy, Chrysler turned from a firm in dismal condition into a highly profitable one within two years.

Another company that found itself in trouble because of financial problems is USX. In 1982, the giant steel producer was losing more than $200 million each quarter on its basic steel business and was paying out $1 billion a year in interest on $7.9 billion of debt. To reduce its bank debt, the firm began selling some of its choice assets, including its headquarters building in Pittsburgh, timberland, and other real estate holdings. Many of the company's problems stemmed from its decision to pry itself away from relying on basic steel by purchasing Marathon Oil Company for $6.6 billion. Because of depressed oil prices and a bleak outlook for the oil industry, many observers questioned the company's decision to put so much money in one giant acquisition.[9]

Now let's look at a firm that was able to survive even though it filed for reorganization under Chapter 11 of United States bankruptcy laws. Wickes Companies, a huge retailer of building materials, apparel, food, and drugs, succumbed to high interest rates and operational problems and sought protection under Chapter 11 guidelines in 1982. Less than three years later the company was slimmer and healthier and had a future considerably brighter than its past. Company divisions were reduced from twenty-nine to twelve, more than 1,400 outlets were closed, and the number of employees was cut nearly in half. Wickes was able to get back on its feet because of a reorganization plan approved by its creditors. Basically, company officials persuaded creditors to approve the reorganization quickly—before the company became "too healthy." In this way the company met creditors' demands without selling its most promising divisions. By 1985 the company's debt had been reduced 50%, and it reported an operating profit of $296 million.[10] By using its limited financial resources wisely, Wickes was able to improve its condition and to remain a viable retailing conglomerate.

Human Resources

The third resource that shapes a firm's character and differentiates it from other companies is its people. Although a company's investment in its human resources is not reflected on the balance sheet, people are just as important—perhaps more important—than its physical and financial resources.

Investments in people   Human resources include blue-collar workers, technical and professional employees, staff-support personnel, and managers. Especially important are people whose technical and professional expertise set the firm apart from its competition. One of the most important human resources, however, is the company's management. Experienced managers who have the necessary technical, human, and conceptual skills are a firm's single most important asset. Many companies have grown from very modest operations to giant economic powers because of effective management. Among the best-managed companies in the country, as shown in the In-Box on page 77, are Marriott Corporation, Melville Corporation, Texas Commerce Bancshares, Times Mirror Company, and Wang Laboratories. Managers of these companies possess foresight and an unwavering commitment to excellence.

Managerial Values and Ethics

Human values are basic convictions about what is right and wrong. Managers, like all other people, operate within the scope and limitations of their moral convictions. Their value systems help define the firm's internal environment.

THE IN-BOX

Dun's List of the Five Best-Managed Companies

Each year, *Dun's Business Month* chooses what it considers the best-managed companies in the United States. The 1984 list was comprised of ambitious, innovative companies that began small and propelled themselves into positions of leadership in their respective fields. In every case, these firms benefited from dynamic leadership, prudent risk taking, and unrelenting dedication to a goal.

Name of Company	President/CEO
1. Marriott Corporation	J. Willard Marriott
2. Melville Corporation	Francis J. Rooney, Jr.
3. Texas Commerce Bancshares	Ben F. Love
4. Times Mirror Company	Robert F. Erburu
5. Wang Laboratories	An Wang

Source: "The Five Best-Managed Companies," *Dun's Business Month,* December 1984, pp. 35–49.

Every manager has needs, ambitions, preferences, and desires. And every manager must make decisions that fulfill or detract from these needs and wants. Thus, a manager's decision making is shaped by his or her needs, desires, and moral beliefs, and by the expectations of the organization, as shown in Figure 3.6. Each of these forces, working independently or with others, is reflected in what the manager does.

Basically, a manager's value system can be broken down into six separate categories:

1. Theoretical values: desire for truth and knowledge

2. Aesthetic values: concern for beauty and art

3. Economic values: concern for wealth

4. Social values: interest in friendships and people

5. Political values: orientation toward power

6. Religious values: belief in supernatural power[11]

FIGURE 3.6
Forces that influence
managerial action

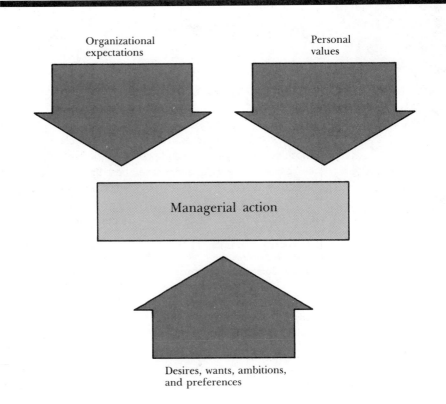

Because these are learned values—developed through years of interaction with others—different people have different values and, thus, behaviors. What seems unethical to one person may seem perfectly ethical to another. This is especially true of people who live in countries with cultures different from ours. A kickback or political bribe may be an accepted way of conducting business in one culture but unethical or even unlawful in another. Thus, the manager working in an international market must constantly struggle to balance personal values with his or her employer's expectations. Consider, for example, the dilemma of a sales representative competing against sales representatives for Middle East or Far East companies. The sales representative's personal values or legal constraints, such as those imposed by the Foreign Corrupt Practices Act, may not allow him or her to compete effectively. But the employer still depends on him or her to "get the business."

**Culture influences
business values**

For the most part, American businesspeople operate on a high moral level. But occasionally they involve themselves in highly questionable or, in some cases, downright unlawful activities. Table 3.2, excerpted from a comprehensive list, shows unethical or unlawful activities of some American businesses.

TABLE 3.2
Questionable/unlawful
activities of American
businesses

COMPANY	ACTIVITY
Allied Chemical	Fixing prices; tax fraud
Amerada Hess	Fixing prices
American Airlines	Illegal campaign contributions
American Beef Packers	Charged with defrauding creditor
American Brands	Charged with bribery
American Can	Charged with fixing prices
American Cyanamid	Fixing prices
Archer-Daniels-Midland	Defrauding grain buyers
Ashland Oil	Illegal campaign contributions
Beatrice Foods	Fixing prices
Bethlehem Steel	Fixing prices
Boise Cascade	Fixing prices
Borden	Fixing prices
Borg-Warner	Fixing prices
Carnation	Fixing prices
Celanese	Fixing prices
Consolidated Foods	Fixing prices
Cook Industries	Defrauding customers
Diamond International	Illegal campaign contributions
Du Pont	Fixing prices
Firestone	False tax-return charges
Fruehauf	Criminal tax evasion
General Dynamics	Improper accounting
Genesco	Fixing prices
B. F. Goodrich	Tax evasion
Goodyear	Illegal political contributions
Greyhound	Illegal campaign contributions
Gulf Oil	Illegal political contributions
Heublein	Bribery
International Paper	Fixing prices
3M	Illegal campaign contributions
J. Ray McDermott	Wire fraud; racketeering charges
Pan American	Unlawful fare-cutting
Jos. Schlitz Brewing	Illegal rebates to customers
Tenneco	Mail fraud

Source: Irwin Ross, "How Lawless Are Big Companies?" *Fortune,* December 1, 1980, pp.
57–61. © 1980, Time Inc. All rights reserved.

Review

✓ *What a firm's environment is.* Management must make decisions within a framework of internal and external forces. These forces, which can constrain or
present opportunities for a business, define its environment. Proponents of
the environmental determinism theory believe that a business's success depends

largely on the fit between the organization and its environment. Organizational determinism scholars argue that an organization can not only adapt to its environment but can also influence the environmental forces in its favor.

✓ *The diverse external forces that affect a firm's operation.* External variables that affect a firm can be broadly classified as political and legal, economic, social, and technological. The political and legal forces are the laws, rulings, decrees, and policies of legislative bodies and government agencies that regulate business transactions. Economic forces consist of trends in the gross national product, disposable income, consumer spending patterns, business cycles, money markets, and similar influences. The social environment encompasses social values, customs, and traditions that provide both opportunities and constraints for business. Technology refers to scientific breakthroughs that permit better, more efficient products and processes.

International influences also pose constraints and present opportunities for business. Companies are affected by the legal climate surrounding international trade, political sanctions, tariffs, subsidies, and import quotas, as well as social customs and popular culture in other countries.

✓ *The opportunities and constraints posed by the internal forces that affect a company.* Internal variables are a company's physical, financial, and human resources, along with the value systems of managers who control those resources. Competitive advantages and disadvantages result from the resources a firm can use. Firms that invest in modern, technologically advanced manufacturing equipment have an advantage over those with inefficient or obsolete production methods. Similarly, financially strong firms are in a better position to take advantage of business opportunities than are the financially weak.

A firm's human resources clearly set it apart from the competition. People with extensive technical and scientific knowledge and those who demonstrate outstanding managerial abilities are especially important to a company's success.

THE MANAGER'S DICTIONARY

As an extra review of the chapter, try defining the following terms. If you have trouble with any of them, refer to the page numbers listed.

environmental determinism (59)

organizational determinism (59)

competitive industry (68)

monopoly (68)

oligopolistic industry (68)

monopolistic competition (68)

REVIEW QUESTIONS

1. What forces shape the environment of management? Differentiate between these forces.

2. Give an example of an external force that affects the environment of management. Why is this force considered external to the firm?

3. Cite an example of an internal force. How does this force present both an opportunity and a constraint for a firm? Explain.

4. Why does government involve itself in the affairs of private business?

5. How does government intervention affect management? Be specific.

6. Name three federal laws that affect business operations. Which of these do you consider most significant? Why?

7. What are the four basic market structures? How is a firm's pricing freedom affected by market forces?

8. Explain how our society has changed in recent years. Show how these changes have been a plus for some firms and a minus for others.

9. Give an example of a technological innovation that has created a positive situation for management.

10. Name the internal forces that shape a firm's environment. Which of these is the most important? Why?

MANAGEMENT CHALLENGE

1. Think of an organization with which you are fairly familiar. How has this organization changed its operations in recent years (new products, plant closings, employee layoffs, different marketing strategies, new manufacturing processes, bankruptcy, major personnel changes, plant expansions, and so on)?

2. What forces have led to these changes? Have they affected the firm negatively or positively? Explain.

3. In your opinion, which external forces are likely to have the greatest impact on this firm in the future? Why?

4. Based on your knowledge of this organization, how would you rate its organizational resources—physical, financial, and human?

5. When a firm violates the law, should criminal charges be brought against it or against its managers? Justify your answer fully.

CASE 3.1

Defying the Laws at Dixon Corporation[12]

"You can't do it, you fool! It's against the second law of thermodynamics," Spike snapped at Bob, a businessman trying to revive an old and faltering family business. From that negative beginning was born a collaboration that, in retrospect, is almost a classic example of innovation. Spike and Bob eventually produced a new, low-friction, long-wearing material that needs no lubrication—something even Du Pont said couldn't be made. Motivated by past failures, when Dixon Corporation had tried to use nylon in the manufacture of low-friction bearings, Bob believed that the material could be made and that he was the one who could do it. And the family business, Dixon Corporation, was back on its feet.

Bob's bachelor's degree was in English, Spike's in physical chemistry. As a chemist, Spike had spent three years researching underwater explosives involving sophisticated experiments. He drew on this experience when helping Bob develop the new plastic bearing material. The resulting product grew out of necessity and Bob's unrelenting efforts. The customers wanted it, the time was right, and Bob believed he had the know-how to succeed.

With Spike's advice, a specially created apparatus, and an experimental design, the new, dry-bearing material was developed for Dixon's textile industry customers within eight months. The product, Rulon, was a thousand times more wearable than Teflon. The bearings made from the material were widely adopted by the textile industry and also used in such products as television tuners, appliances, audio cassettes, and (with modification) missile nose cones.

Dixon Corporation grew from a handful of employees to several hundred, and annual sales increased from $75,000 to $1 million within a few years. An entirely new industry had been founded as well.

Questions

1. Describe the external and internal variables that affected the development of Rulon.

2. Which of these variables do you feel was most important? Why?

CASE 3.2

Apartheid in South Africa Affects American Firms[13]

American businesses' $2.3 billion investment in South Africa is being jeopardized by the political and economic climate caused by racial strife. Even if no revolution results from the government's apartheid policies, violence and social unrest pose problems for American firms.

American business faces a dilemma. South Africa's resources and cheap labor make it an attractive alternative to other countries. But the repression of blacks, who make up 70% of South Africa's population, is causing labor problems. Business leaders are afraid that political upheaval will undermine their companies' investments. American businesspeople are also feeling pressure at home. Groups opposing apartheid are demanding that U.S. businesses get out of South

Africa or sell off their investments there. Many of these groups are pressuring Congress to impose sanctions on the South African government. As a result of these lobbying efforts, a number of influential politicians have announced their support of government sanctions. In December 1984, thirty-five Republican members of Congress sent a letter to the South African ambassador threatening to restrict U.S. business there and impose other sanctions if apartheid wasn't ended. One bill introduced in Congress would prohibit new U.S. investments in South Africa and ban the sale of gold South African Krugerrand coins here.

Opponents of apartheid plan to use economic pressures to end racial discrimination in South Africa. Companies that continue to operate there will be characterized as supporters of apartheid. Thirty-one of the fifty largest U.S. corporations conduct business in South Africa.

Half of South Africa's petroleum industry, 70% of its computer industry, and nearly one-third of its automobile industry are American-owned. Many of America's most respected corporations will be caught between principles and economics.

Already, many of America's largest and most prestigious firms are ending their operations in South Africa. IBM, General Motors, and Burroughs, for example, have divested themselves of their subsidiaries there.

Questions

1. What arguments can you give against divestment or withdrawal of U.S. firms from South Africa?

2. Identify the forces that shape the South African environment in which U.S. firms operate. Which of these appear to be the most significant?

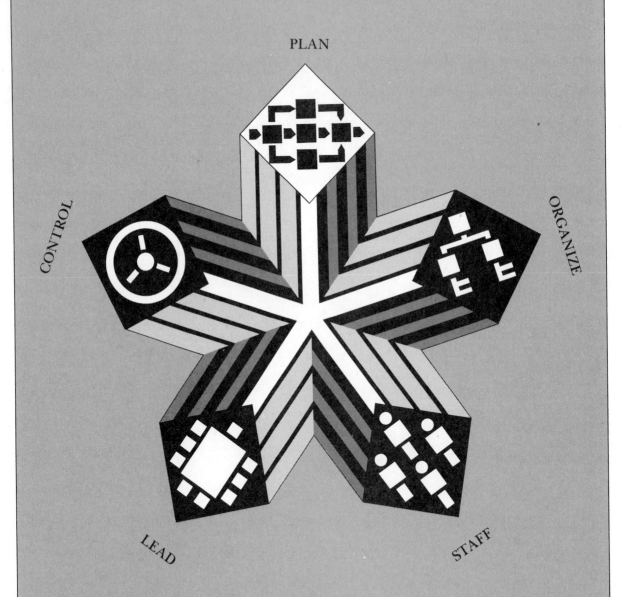

Planning and Decision Making

Organizations are created to accomplish objectives that could not be attained otherwise. These objectives generally take two forms: providing a service and making a profit. To achieve an organization's objectives, managers must develop plans for ensuring that all required activities are systematic and timely. Such plans provide direction for the organization and create a framework for decision making. Thus, the planning and decision making that managers do are interrelated. Part Two is designed to illustrate the relationship between planning and decision making; this is a foundation for the study of other functions of management.

Chapter 4, "Managerial Planning," describes the sequential steps in the planning process and explains the various types of business plans. The chapter also discusses the many ways that planning benefits managers and shows how planning differs at various organizational levels. Finally, the chapter pinpoints the relationship between planning and forecasting and describes a number of methods for analyzing the present and predicting the future.

Chapter 5, "Strategic Planning," stresses the importance of long-range planning by top-level managers. The steps in the strategic planning process are examined. This chapter also gives special attention to the role of strategic planning in small businesses.

Chapter 6, "Managerial Decision Making," focuses on the steps in the decision-making process. Three types of decisions are described and illustrated: decisions under certainty, decisions under risk, and decisions under uncertainty. The chapter also discusses the advantages and drawbacks of various types of group decision making. Finally, the chapter suggests methods for generating creative ideas for solving difficult problems and explains why managers often make poor decisions.

CHAPTER OUTLINE

The Planning Process

Planning: Successes and Failures
Penn Central
The Great Atlantic & Pacific Tea Company
Sears, Roebuck and Company
K mart
General Motors

Benefits of Planning

Characteristics of a Good Plan

Classifying Plans
Duration of Plans
Specificity of Plans
Level of Plans
Strategic Planning • Administrative Planning • Tactical Planning • Tactical versus Strategic Planning

Forecasting: A Critical Element
Product Life Cycle
Statistical Projections
Simple Growth Pattern • Moving Average • Exponential Smoothing • Trend Lines
Market Research Methods
Comparative Studies • Leading Indicators • Experimental Research • Intention-to-Buy Surveys • Judgmental Methods
Analytical Models
Technological Forecasting Methods
Delphi Technique • Scenarios • Impact Analysis

Management by Objectives
Purpose of MBO
What Makes a Successful MBO Program?
Pitfalls of MBO

Managerial Planning

Coca-Cola's Plans Fizzle

It was supposed to be the most significant soft-drink development in Coca-Cola Company's history—one that would boost sales and tickle the fickle palates of young consumers.

Coca-Cola changed its ninety-nine-year-old, world-famous formula for two reasons: Pepsi had been cutting into Coke's market share, and market research revealed that younger consumers preferred a sweeter taste to Coke's crisp taste. Fifty-five percent of the people surveyed under test market conditions favored the new formula over the old Coke. When both beverages were identified, the margin became greater.[1] The company spent four-and-a-half years in planning and market research.

So Coke changed. On April 23, 1985, company chairman Roberto Goizueta introduced the "new" Coke to the world, saying "the best has been made even better." But the new formula met widespread resistance within hours of its introduction. Prompted by public demonstrations, a deluge of angry phone calls, and a write-in protest over the next few months, Goizueta knuckled under. On July 10, the company announced its plans to bring back old Coca-Cola under a new name, Coca-Cola Classic, and to sell it alongside the new Coke.

The company had failed to consider the ingrained, almost patriotic feelings that Americans have for Coke. As company president Donald Keough pointed out, "We did not understand the deep emotions of so many of our customers for Coca-Cola."[2] All the time, money, and effort poured into consumer research failed to measure the depth of emotional attachment people felt toward the original Coke. In an uncertain world, Coke had been a rock of stability for millions of people.

What could have been a disaster may, however, turn out to be a coup for Coca-Cola. Although the initial plan didn't call for two Cokes to compete with Pepsi, that is precisely what happened. One even tastes like Pepsi. And since the company will continue selling new Coke, none of the money spent to launch it was wasted. If anything, the furor created by the formula change has made Coke more of a household word than it was before 1985.

Some critics contend that Coca-Cola made a herculean mistake by introducing new Coke. Others say that it was part of a deliberate, Machiavellian plan to create support for the old Coke. In truth, it was a plan based on incomplete information.

Preview

Planning is an activity we perform before taking action. It is anticipatory decision making—a process of deciding what to do and how to do it before action is required. Its purpose is to facilitate progress and improve performance. Planning allows integrated, consistent, and purposeful action. Mistakes can be avoided and problems can be anticipated and overcome before crises arise. But planning must be based on prudent forecasts and reasonable premises. It cannot be done in an atmosphere of blind optimism and disregard for competitive and environmental realities.

Coca-Cola's decision to replace Coke with a new, sweeter-tasting formula was based on a plan for improving sales. The plan, which took into account competition, consumer preferences, existing products, and other crucial factors, was designed to anticipate problems and eliminate them before they occurred. Based on all available information, Coca-Cola's decision appeared to be prudent. But the future is uncertain, and Coca-Cola's research failed to measure one important factor—the emotional impact of eliminating a long-standing product. Simply put, Coca-Cola's plan did not reflect the deep-rooted feelings of American consumers. The plan had to be modified.

Almost every manager recognizes the virtues of sound business planning, yet it remains one of the most neglected aspects of management. The importance of planning to the overall performance of the firm will be explained in Chapter 4. After studying this chapter, you will understand:

✔ The steps and levels in the planning process

✔ Why some businesses' plans have succeeded and some have failed

✔ The benefits of planning

✔ The characteristics of a good plan

✔ How plans are classified

✔ The critical element of forecasting

✔ How management by objectives improves the effectiveness of the individual and the organization

The Planning Process

It is universally accepted that managers plan. In fact, planning is the most important thing managers do because everything a company does depends on the adequacy of its plans. One common question asked by managers is, "How much time should be devoted to planning?" Certainly, every manager should devote some time to planning, but precisely how much is probably indefinable. It varies according to the manager's duties, level, company, and industry. Generally speaking, the higher the management level, the more time should be devoted to planning. The nature of planning differs, too. The president of a company is more concerned with long-term decisions; the plant supervisor with planning today's jobs.

Time spent in planning varies

Theoretically, there are three levels of planning—strategic, administrative, and operational. But in practice the distinctions become blurred because all types of planning are part of a single, dynamic planning process. The sequential steps in the planning process, shown in Figure 4.1, are as follows:

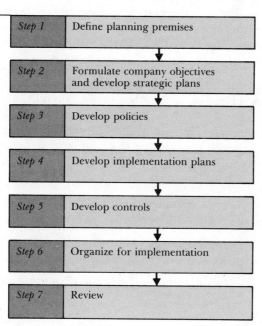

FIGURE 4.1
The planning process
[*Source:* Adapted from Robert J. Mockler, *Business Planning and Policy Formulation* (New York: Appleton-Century-Crofts, 1972), pp. 6–8.]

Step 1	Define planning premises
Step 2	Formulate company objectives and develop strategic plans
Step 3	Develop policies
Step 4	Develop implementation plans
Step 5	Develop controls
Step 6	Organize for implementation
Step 7	Review

1. *Define planning premises.* The first step is determining what will have a major impact on planning through a study of pertinent environmental factors (the economy, society, public policy, the industry, and the market), available company resources, past and current company operations, and profitability.

2. *Formulate company objectives and develop strategic plans.* In the light of the planning premises, the manager must develop and appraise alternative long-term objectives for the company. These objectives are commonly referred to as the company's *mission* or purpose. For example, the mission of a nuclear power plant is to provide an adequate supply of electrical energy, whereas the mission of an airline is to provide public air transportation. The manager selects the objective that will most profitably exploit the market opportunities that were identified during the first step. The general philosophy and overall strategy that will guide and control all phases of planning are also formulated now. For the nuclear power plant, safety might be the overriding concern, whereas the airline may strive to be the industry's low-cost carrier. The In-Box on page 91 shows how the Wharton Applied Research Center is encouraging managers to identify their company's direction.

3. *Develop policies.* After developing and evaluating objectives, the manager selects the overall policies that will fulfill the company objective and still satisfy market, industry, and company criteria. Such policies are general statements that provide a sense of direction for subordinates. While they are flexible enough to permit some discretion in decision making, they serve as guidelines that channel managerial action. For instance, a company may make a concerted effort to employ the physically handicapped whenever possible to meet its objective of staffing with the best people available. Another firm may strive to increase its market share through a policy of selling its products at the lowest price in a particular geographic region.

4. *Develop implementation plans.* The manager next selects operating plans for all areas of the business. They should be consistent with the overall planning premises, objectives, and policies established in the preceding steps and within the capabilities of the company. Derivative policies, rules, and procedures in all planning areas also should be specified. The sales forecast is one of the most important aspects of this planning stage because it defines the budgetary limits for all plans.

5. *Develop controls.* After the operating plans are completed, methods for measuring performance against the plans must be developed. These controls usually are in the form of budgets.

6. *Organize for implementation.* The manager next must establish adequate administrative procedures for implementing the plan.

7. *Review.* Reviewing and modifying the plan as needed is the final step in the planning process.

Steps in the planning process

THE IN-BOX

Planning and Sketching

Since 1979, the Wharton Applied Research Center at the University of Pennsylvania has offered management development seminars for hundreds of executives who want to improve their planning skills. To help them assess where their companies are and the direction they are taking, the seminar leaders ask each participant to depict his or her company in the form of a drawing. Examples are shown below:

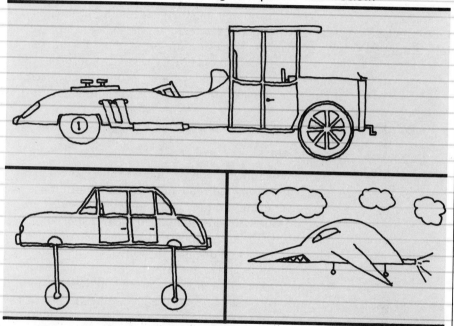

The top drawing says a lot about where this company is heading. The front of the vehicle is a race car and the rear is a Model T. More important, they are headed in opposite directions. This vehicle was drawn by an executive of a firm that is struggling to get into another field. Obviously, the old is a hindrance to the new.

The car in the lower left drawing suggests a highly conservative company. Built high off the road, the car can withstand bumps and potholes. The drawing in the lower right—a sleek aircraft—reflects a ruthless, aggressive banking firm.

Source: Sanford L. Jacobs, "Wharton Course Teaches Planning Using Managers' Drawings of Firms," *Wall Street Journal,* October 31, 1984, p. 33. Reprinted by permission of *The Wall Street Journal,* © Dow Jones & Company, Inc., 1984. All rights reserved.

Operating managers understand the process

Every departmental manager should understand the planning process as a whole because his or her annual operating plans are an integral part. That is, the goals of each operating unit contribute to the overall objectives of the company. Operating managers need to know how their objectives grow out of the overall company objectives and to understand how overall company directions dictate operating policies.

Corporate success depends on maintaining this perspective, because operating managers are vital in achieving the company's overall objective. The operating managers translate company strategy into action, see that plans are carried out, and take corrective action when necessary.

Planning: Successes and Failures

Successful economic performance is the primary purpose of business. How well a firm operates determines its ability to survive and grow. However, too many managers focus on the present and are unconcerned about controlling future events. Business history is filled with stories of companies whose managers concentrated on day-to-day profits and neglected to plan for the future. The following examples illustrate the consequences of failing to plan for the future.[3]

Penn Central

Lack of planning is disastrous

At the beginning of the twentieth century, the nation's railroads had little or no competition. Railroad management had built a nationwide distribution network during the previous half-century, and there was no competition on the horizon. Railroads dominated the transportation industry. Because of lack of foresight, it was inconceivable to railroad managers that another transportation system could displace the railroad. Consequently, they failed to develop complementary forms of transportation, such as trucking, air freight, and shipping, even though they were in the best position to do so. Instead, the demise of railroads began. Today, we need only review the history of Penn Central's collapse and the financial disasters of most of the other railroads to comprehend the significance of their error.

The Great Atlantic & Pacific Tea Company

A&P is another example of a dominant firm experiencing a decline. For years, A&P dominated the retail food industry. Its success was based on establishing retail outlets serving the major markets across the United States. This strategy worked well when cities were loose federations of local communities grouped around an economic hub. However, the A&P management failed to recognize the market change after World War II. During this period, more affluent people began moving away from inner cities. A&P perceived neither the change in its type of customers nor its weakening market position. Within twenty years, A&P's survival was in question. Faced with obsolete and unprofitable stores, limited access to suburban markets, the changing customer base of its store locations, and customers' diminished purchasing power, A&P was no longer the dominant force that it once was in food retailing.

Sears, Roebuck and Company

Many companies have focused on short-term profits, have neglected strategic (long-term) planning, and have fallen victim to short-term difficulties. Some have been able to reverse this course. Probably the best example is Sears, Roebuck and Company. Sears traditionally measured performance on the basis of the profitability of individual stores and managers. All stores and managers were evaluated on the basis of their weekly profits rather than on growth or other measures of performance. This short-term measurement of performance is commonly called **bottom-line management.** During the rapid economic growth of the 1950s and 1960s, increasing profitability was an easily attainable strategy. Obvious tactics called for raising prices, emphasizing upgraded and higher-quality merchandise, and accenting private-label goods that carried a higher markup. Although charging higher prices meant surrendering entire market segments of lower-priced merchandise to discount stores, the Sears strategy of "Trade Up America" worked well; profits increased dramatically.

Sears emphasized short-term profits

However, history shows that economic expansions are followed by periods of economic contraction. Sears and other consumer-oriented companies ignored early warning signs. For instance, per capita disposable income moved up steadily between 1940 and 1972 but started to decline in the fourth quarter of 1973. The era of affluence and rising living standards ended in the United States in September 1973, shortly before the Arab oil embargo.

Sears failed to recognize what was happening and continued upgrading. Its customers' loyalty thinned along with their pocketbooks, but Sears kept increasing its inventories. In September 1974, a year after the standard of living began declining, Sears projected a strong rebound in the fourth quarter. But as the nation's economic growth leveled off and then turned down, it became more difficult for store managers to increase profits. Sears's 1974 profits slumped for the first time in thirteen years. Customers turned to lower-priced merchandise offered by K mart, J. C. Penney, and Montgomery Ward.

Sears changes strategies

Recognizing its error, Sears once again became customer oriented. It began to reemphasize its lower-price lines, to reduce inventories, and to abandon its upgrading efforts. Today, profits remain important, but Sears recognizes that short-term success is not the only measure of performance.

As Sears learned the hard way, planning helps managers foresee potential hazards as well as new opportunities. Moreover, planning lets managers avoid pitfalls and exploit opportunities. Good planning is reflected in profitability. Because of the complexity of the business environment, most executives recognize the importance of planning to both long-term growth and current performance. Now let's turn our attention to two companies that have prospered because their managers consider strategic planning so important.

K mart

Example of sound planning

Strategic planning changed the direction of the S. S. Kresge Company. In the early 1960s, Kresge management believed that the future was limited for variety stores. It felt that customers wanted a no-frills, mass-merchandising approach emphasizing low prices on national brands in freestanding, suburban department stores that offered adequate parking. This was entirely different from its own outlets—small, antiquated stores, poorly stocked, overstaffed, and located in central cities. S. S. Kresge transformed into K mart.

Today K mart is one of the largest retailers in the United States and is considered the pacesetter in merchandising. Even Sears has emulated some of K mart's tactics. The success of this strategy is even more apparent when you consider that W. T. Grant, S. S. Kresge, and F. W. Woolworth were companies of similar size with identical approaches to marketing in the early 1960s. K mart has seen its profits surge dramatically since 1962, when its profits were less than $10 million. During the same time, Woolworth has maintained its position and Grant has gone out of business.

General Motors

Even before the 1973 oil embargo and the world energy crisis, GM had evaluated its line of vehicles and determined that they were too heavy and too large. In the summer of 1973, GM engineers gave management their first automobile weight-reduction program, which was based on redirecting the company's product lines. GM considered the energy crisis a challenge to its dominant position in the industry and to its entire marketing strategy. Company management considered this change in its environment a threat to its market position and called for a total break with the previous corporate strategy of "trading up" developed by Alfred Sloan in the 1920s.

Planning pays off

GM recognized that the environment of the 1970s and 1980s dictated the need for a new approach. Management believed that government safety, emissions, and fuel economy regulations, along with ever-present inflation, would throw the marketplace into turmoil. Confronted by this threat to its profitable operation, management looked for a new strategy. GM believed that its customers were interested in comfort, performance, styling, and economy—all rolled into a smaller package. The company therefore adopted a strategy of down-sizing its vehicles before profits began falling. Short-term performance setbacks did not prevent management from investing in the future. To support the strategy, GM went into debt for the first time in years;

but profits in the years afterward proved that this new strategy, based on sound business planning, was successful.

| **Benefits of Planning** | There is hardly a manager alive who would deny the value of planning. Still, many managers give too much lip service and devote too little effort to planning. Many managers would avoid planning altogether if they could find a substitute for achieving the same ends. Some of the spoken and unspoken planning-related fears that managers often express include these: |

- Planning is difficult (and I might not do a good job).

- It limits my actions. (If it's not in the plan, I can't do it.)

- It forces me to make decisions (and that makes me vulnerable).

- Making a plan provides a yardstick for evaluation (and I might not measure up).

- Planning brings direction and organization out of chaos (and removes a very good excuse).

- Planning brings its own chaos and disruption (when managers resist or choose not to follow the plan).[4]

Perhaps the best method for overcoming the fear of planning is to recognize the rewards of planning. Benefits are both immediate and pervasive. Some of the more obvious benefits are:

1. *Planning facilitates professional growth.* Planning is one of the key skills for any manager who wishes to grow in capability and status. Managers rarely fall short of their potential because they lack technical knowledge. Rather, their shortcomings usually result from failing to plan logically and consistently so that limited resources are distributed where they are needed most.

2. *Plans provide the framework for the organization.* Plans establish desired results and identify the work necessary to accomplish them. When managers organize, they determine what tasks are needed to accomplish their plans, who should do them, and how people can work together most effectively. The organizational arrangement must relate to the work to be done. In addition, if a logical hierarchy of plans is established, it becomes the basis for the organizational hierarchy.

3. *Plans aid in delegating authority.* Most managers have difficulty delegating authority. They feel that allowing other people to perform a task will be less efficient than doing it themselves. This reluctance is partly caused by the frustration of observing others clumsily performing jobs at which the managers are proficient. Planning can help here. A plan forces the manager to determine in advance who will be accountable for various tasks.

4. *Plans help motivate people.* People work harder when they know what is expected of them. Planning provides an objective to focus on and, when coupled with performance standards and a reward system, helps integrate personal objectives with those of the organization.

Advantages of planning

5. *Planning aids communication flow.* Employees need information to help them solve work-related problems. Most communication systems fail to provide proper information because they do not pinpoint individual responsibilities. Good plans, however, provide a framework, giving people the information they need and want. Plans that specify individuals' exact areas of accountability convey messages much more forcefully than do messages directed to entire groups.

6. *Planning helps shape the future.* Unless managers know what they want to accomplish, they go through their daily activities without a sense of direction. Plans help them envision the future. When managers clarify their goals, they are more likely to accomplish them.

7. *Plans help monitor work.* Work is too often evaluated after it has been completed. If costly mistakes were made, the causes can be identified and prevented from happening again. For control to be most effective, however, work must be assessed while it is going on as well as after it has been completed. Consequently, programs and schedules must be developed to accompany objectives. This way, plans have a dual capacity—to determine what to do and whether it is being done properly.[5]

8. *Planning builds confidence.* A good planning process that allows all levels of management to participate builds confidence in an organization because it gives everyone a long-term perspective. It indicates that management has a direction, that decision making is under control, and that the whole organization is striving to achieve the same objectives.[6]

Planning also yields some tangible financial rewards. Here are summaries of some of the more significant research findings:

Financial rewards

- Thune and House compared the financial results of seventeen manufacturing firms that engaged in formal planning over a period of at least three years with nineteen firms that did not. Firms that planned outperformed nonplanners in earnings per share, earnings on common stock, and earnings on employed capital.[7]

- Fulmer and Rue studied 386 manufacturing and service firms to determine if planning yielded financial rewards. Their study revealed that manufacturers of durable goods that engaged in formal planning outperformed similar companies that did not practice formal planning. Moreover, they found that the differences were much more pronounced in large firms than in small companies.[8]

- Karger and Malik studied the effects of planning on financial success in three industries—drugs, electronics, and machinery. In the machinery industry, sales of planners increased at an annual rate of 19.6% compared to 8.6% for nonplanners. Earnings per share for planners grew at a 10.1% average annual rate and only 2.4% for nonplanners. The net income of planners nearly tripled (on the average) in ten years, while nonplanners' net income remained the same, and the average annual return on equity for planners was 13.2% versus 7.1% for nonplanners. Similar differences were found for the sample as a whole.[9]

Characteristics of a Good Plan

Every sound business plan must have these characteristics: objectivity, futurity, flexibility, stability, comprehensiveness, clarity, and simplicity.[10]

Planning should, first of all, be based on *objective* thinking. It should be factual, logical, and realistic. It also should be directed to achieving organizational goals rather than personal objectives.

Since a plan is a forecast of some future action, it must have the quality of *futurity*; otherwise, it has little value as a basis for action. If a plan is to be effective, it must foresee with reasonable accuracy the nature of future events affecting the industry and the firm. The inability to foresee future events, a human limitation that we cannot overcome, is the weak link in the planning process. As we move from the level of operating manager to top management, predictions become less accurate because upper levels deal with longer time spans. It is usually necessary, therefore, to decentralize detailed planning.

Uncertain future creates problems for planners

Because no one can foresee the future, plans must have *flexibility*. They must adjust smoothly and quickly to changing conditions without seriously losing their effectiveness. The more difficult it is to predict the future, the more flexible the plans must be.

Stability is related to flexibility. A stable plan will not have to be abandoned because of long-term changes in the company's situation. It may be affected by long-range developments, but it should not be changed materially from day to day.

A business plan must be *comprehensive* enough to provide adequate guidance, but not so detailed as to be unduly restrictive. It should cover everything required of people, but not in such detail that it inhibits initiative.

Although a good plan must be comprehensive, it should also be *simple*. A simple plan seeks to attain its objective with the fewest components, forces, effects, and relationships. A plan should not be ambiguous. Lack of clarity makes understanding and implementation difficult.

Classifying Plans

Some organizations, particularly giant American corporations, use literally hundreds of plans. Some are of paramount importance; others are not. Some are in effect for long periods; others are short-lived. In studying these plans, we will find it helpful to classify the various types of plans that a company may use. Basically, plans may be classified on three bases: duration, specificity, and organizational level.

Duration of Plans

Long-range planning

Some plans are in effect for short periods, whereas others stretch decades into the future. The planning horizon for Georgia-Pacific Corporation, for instance, reaches into the twenty-first century. Managers of Georgia-Pacific know that it takes ninety-nine years to grow Douglas firs in the northwestern region of the United States.[11] Seedlings must be planted today to assure adequate lumber supplies in the future.

Short-range planning

On the other hand, some plans are hardly completed before they expire. Temporary, or single-use, plans governing a course of action are common in all organizations. As illustrated in Figure 4.2, short-range plans cover a period of one year or less, medium-range plans last from one to five years, and long-range plans are in effect for five years or more.

Specificity of Plans

Plans also can be classified according to how general or specific they are. **Single-use plans** are predetermined courses of action developed for unique, nonrecurring situations. By contrast, **standing plans** are predetermined courses

FIGURE 4.2
Duration of business plans

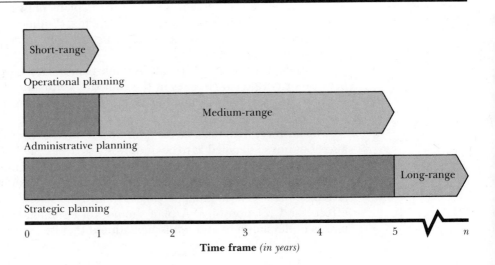

Operational planning

Short-range

Administrative planning

Medium-range

Strategic planning

Long-range

Time frame *(in years)*
0   1   2   3   4   5   *n*

of action developed for repetitive situations. A budget, for example, is a single-use plan. It becomes obsolete whenever the time period for which it was prepared expires. Rules, policies, and procedures, on the other hand, are standing plans. They continuously govern the operations of a company until they are modified or eliminated. The various types of single-use and standing plans are:

Budget: A *budget* is a single-use plan that commits resources to an activity over a given period. It may be expressed in dollars, worker-hours, units of product, machine-hours, or any other numerically measurable term.

Objective: An *objective,* or goal, is the end toward which business activity is directed. It is a statement of what the organization seeks to accomplish and, as such, is a single-use plan.

Policy: A *policy* is a general guideline that channels the decision making of subordinates. A policy is narrow enough to provide managers with a sense of direction but flexible enough to permit considerable discretion in day-to-day decision making. It is a standing plan.

Procedure: A *procedure* is a standing plan that establishes a specific method for handling activities. It details the exact manner or chronological sequence in which action must be taken.

Program: A *program* is a composite of policies, procedures, rules, and task assignments necessary to carry out capital and operating budgets. In general, it is a standing plan.

Rule: A *rule* is the simplest type of standing plan. It dictates action that must or must not be taken in a given situation.

Schedule: A *schedule* is a single-use plan that commits resources (worker-hours and machine-hours) to a given activity.

Strategy: A *strategy* is a single-use plan formulated in contemplation of actions that competitors may undertake.

Level of Plans

Perhaps the most useful method for classifying plans is based on where they are formulated in an organization. In this system of classification, plans are strategic, administrative, and tactical. Table 4.1 illustrates these three planning levels.

Strategic Planning   Unlike short- and medium-range plans, **strategic planning,** or top management planning, includes the development of overall com-

TABLE 4.1
The three levels of
business planning

TYPE OF PLANNING	ORGANIZATIONAL LEVEL	NATURE OF PLANNING
Strategic	Top management	Includes the development of overall company objectives, taking into consideration external environmental factors that affect operations on a long-term basis
Administrative	Middle management/ major functional units	Focuses on policies that govern the activities of major functional departments of a firm (manufacturing, finance, marketing, personnel, etc.)
Tactical	Lower-level/supervisory management	Planning at this level is directed toward the fulfillment of departmental goals under budgetary constraints

pany objectives and is primarily concerned with solving long-term problems associated with external, environmental influences. It addresses these questions: What business are we in? What business should we be in? Where will we be in ten years if we continue doing what we are now doing?

Firms have four alternatives to help them answer these questions:

1. Expansion within the existing industry

2. Diversification into another industry

3. Divestment of existing assets

4. A strategy of wait and see

Top-level planning

Selecting any of these requires that a company engage in strategic planning. How far into the future a firm projects depends on the industry and the anticipated business environment. It is not unreasonable for firms that manufacture aerospace hardware to plan twenty years in the future, for example. Companies in the garment industry cannot plan much beyond four or five years, however. After a firm has developed a vision for its future, it compares where it would like to be with where it is now and where it will be if it does nothing. The difference between where a firm would like to be and where it will be if it does nothing is called the **planning gap.** Strategic planning is primarily concerned with closing that gap.[12]

Planning by major functional units

Administrative Planning   In contrast to strategic planning, which establishes the mission of the organization, **administrative planning** is the process that structures a firm's resources to achieve maximum performance. Administrative plans do not involve such matters as plant layout, merchandise display, and servicing customers. They concentrate on product market aims, selection of geographic areas, and policies dealing with the major functions of the organization (production, marketing, finance, research, personnel, etc.). Some practical planning tools are presented in the Manager's Notebook on page 102.

Lower-level planning

Tactical Planning   **Tactical planning** is concerned with the efficient, day-to-day use of resources allocated to a department manager's area of responsibility. These managers typically work with a one-year operating budget. For example, a sales manager may be required to develop an operational plan to sell a certain number of items within a specific period.

Tactical versus Strategic Planning   The distinction between tactical and strategic planning can be confusing because it is relative rather than absolute. For this reason, decisions that appear to be strategic to one person may seem tactical to another. According to Ackoff, tactical planning differs from strategic planning in three ways:

1. The longer the effect of a plan and the more difficult it is to reverse, the more strategic it is. Therefore, strategic planning is concerned with decisions that have long-lasting effects that are difficult to reverse. For example, next week's production planning is more tactical and less strategic than planning a new plant. In general, strategic planning is concerned with the longest time period worth considering; tactical planning is concerned with the shortest worth considering. Both types of planning are essential; in fact, they are complementary. Like the head and tail of a coin, they can be looked at separately but cannot be separated.

Tactical planning is short-term

2. Strategic planning is broad in scope. Tactical planning is narrower. A strategic plan for a department may be a tactical plan from the viewpoint of a division. Other things being equal, planning at the corporate level is generally more strategic than is planning at any organizational level below it.

3. Tactical planning selects the means to pursue specified goals. The goals are normally supplied by a higher level of management in the organization. Strategic planning is concerned with both determining the goals and selecting the means to attain them. Thus, strategic planning is concerned with ends as well as means.[13]

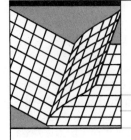

THE MANAGER'S NOTEBOOK

The Hidden Tools of Planning

There are planning tools all around you—that desk calendar, the clock on the wall, your telephone, that slip of paper in your pocket. A manager who learns how to use them and the other simple tools of planning will get the job done better and faster.

First, make a checklist of the resources available and the resources needed. Divide the list into people, money, time, and materials. Ask who is available, what skills they have, and who would benefit from being involved in the project. A mistake most managers make is to try to do everything themselves.

Next, plan the order of events or procedures and when they will take place. Find the critical points and set up a follow-up system to see whether everything is going according to schedule. Project a completion date.

Prepare for the unforeseen by gathering people with practical experience in the project and having them write down a contingency. Have them share their answers and discuss them. Then vote on the most likely contingency and plan for it.

Keep communication lines open. Ask for information, ideas, and feedback; negotiate options; tell others about progress and about changes in the plan.

Source: Rich Tewell, "Some Simple Action Planning Tools," *Supervisory Management,* The American Management Association, August 1985, pp. 6–9.

It should be apparent that certain types of tactical plans have characteristics that are typical of strategic plans. For instance, a division of a major corporation trying to capture a larger market share may use the same planning elements as those used in higher level, strategic planning. The basic differences between the two types of plans are presented in Table 4.2.

Forecasting: A Critical Element

Planning and forecasting are not the same thing, although they are closely related. **Forecasting** predicts or projects what will happen under a given set of circumstances in the future; planning specifies the steps that will be taken to achieve an objective. Economic and marketing forecasting provides specific quantitative premises for use in formulating plans.

TABLE 4.2
Differences between strategic and tactical plans

	STRATEGIC PLANS	TACTICAL PLANS
Uncertainty	High	Low
Nature of problems	Unstructured	Structured
Time frame	Long, continuous	Short, fixed
Details	Few	Many
Data sources	External	Internal
Organizational level	Top	Lower
Point of view	Corporate	Functional

Source: Leon Reinharth, H. Jack Shapiro, and Ernest A. Kallman, *The Practice of Planning* (New York: Van Nostrand Reinhold, 1981), pp. 135–136.

Overall economic forecasts—projections of what will happen in the economy—are made first in comprehensive planning. Then come forecasts of trends within the industry, including what the total market for a firm's products will be and what share of the market the company can realistically expect to capture. Forecasts within specific market segments are also made when possible. These environmental forecasts then are combined with internal company factors, such as promotional budgets and pricing strategies, to develop a sales forecast.

Forecasts based on economic data

Some of the more commonly used long-term economic forecasts include projections of the gross national product, disposable personal income, the economy, and full employment. Short-term forecasts include industrial production models, statistical models of the economy, and short-range predictions of the GNP.[14] These economic indicators provide managers with information regarding the short- and long-term economic outlook for the nation as a whole and for specific industries. Thus, the long-term economic forecasts form the bases for more specific industry and market forecasts. For most companies, these specific industry and market forecasts have more relevance to planning than long-term economic projections do because sales forecasts are developed around them.

Various statistical and nonstatistical techniques can be used in forecasting. Some of the more popular forecasting methods are:

1. Use of the product life cycle to project future sales

2. Statistical projections

3. Market research methods

4. Analytical models

5. Technological forecasting methods.[15]

Product Life Cycle

One concept that is often of value in forecasting is the **product life cycle,** which suggests that all products pass through a series of growth curves until they reach a point where demand either levels out or begins to decline. Figure 4.3 illustrates this concept.

The curve begins with a period of low sales and low profits as the new product is introduced to the market. This is followed by a phase of growth in which sales increase rapidly, profits are relatively high, and unit costs are low because of economies of scale. In the third stage—maturity—growth slows as competitors enter the market, and the profit per unit diminishes because of the additional expenditures necessary to increase sales. In the final stage—decline—sales decrease. Consider, for example, the product life cycle of two different products—microwave ovens and black-and-white television sets. Microwave ovens are now in the early maturity stage, where sales are increasing and profits remain relatively high. Black-and-white television sets, on the other hand, are in the decline phase, where sales and profits are low. Therefore, plans for marketing these products differ significantly.

One obvious forecasting problem is evident from looking at Figure 4.3. A purely statistical projection made at any of the early stages of the life-cycle curve would have resulted in a totally inaccurate forecast. Another forecasting problem is that the time span for each phase differs. Still another complication is the fact that the life cycle can be accidentally or deliberately extended, which distorts the expected pattern.

Statistical Projections

Many statistical techniques are available for projecting the future. All are based on the assumption that past performance is the best indicator of future per-

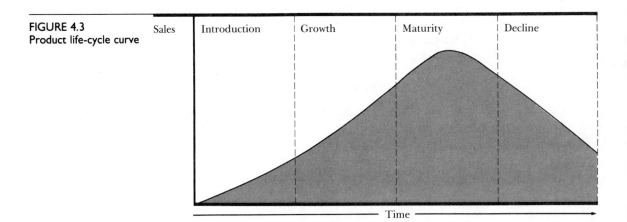

FIGURE 4.3
Product life-cycle curve

formance. Whether this is a valid assumption depends on a number of considerations, including the age of the product and the phase of its life cycle. Four statistical techniques used to project the future are (1) simple growth pattern, (2) moving average, (3) exponential smoothing, and (4) mathematical trends.

Simple Growth Pattern   This method of forecasting is based on the average *annual rate of growth* calculated over a past period. For example, bank deposits are typically projected on the basis of past data.

Statistically based forecasts

Moving Average   A **moving average** is a method of eliminating regular seasonal or cyclical patterns from the data to indicate the underlying trend. After the trend is calculated, it can then be eliminated statistically so that the seasonal factors can be studied. Each point in the moving average is the mean of a number of consecutive points of the series. The demand for automobile tires, for instance, can be projected this way.

Exponential Smoothing   Another technique for short-term forecasting is **exponential smoothing.** This method is based on a moving average that is exponentially weighted so that the more recent data is given greater importance, and the past forecasting error is taken into account in each successive forecast. Sales for air-conditioning units can be projected this way, for example.

Trend Lines   A number of mathematical techniques are available for calculating a **trend line,** which is a hypothetical projection of a previous pattern of events into the future. The simplest method is to fit a line on a graph by eye, using a straightedge. Or the trend line can be calculated mathematically by the method of least squares. Projections of college enrollments, for example, are normally based on trend line analysis.

Market Research Methods

Market-based forecasts

Market research methods to forecast the future include comparative studies, surveys of leading indicators, experimental research, intention-to-buy surveys, judgmental methods, and others.

Comparative Studies   One method of forecasting is to examine the performance of some item similar to the item being studied. For example, a company introducing a new pain reliever might analyze the price, promotion, and progress of similar products introduced in the preceding five years.

Leading Indicators   A **leading indicator** is an event that always precedes another event, thereby giving advance warning of change. For instance, an economic output figure for the building industry might be used as an indicator for other economic activity.

Experimental Research   This category includes numerous marketing tests designed to provide information for assessing a product's profitability. Probably the most widely used method of gaining insight into a new product's potential is test-marketing. Projected sales of consumer products such as cigarettes and soft drinks are often based on test-marketing.

Intention-to-Buy Surveys   As its name suggests, an **intention-to-buy survey** is designed to gather information on what the consumer will buy. A company frequently bases on intention-to-buy survey data its projected sales of major household appliances, automobiles, and industrial products.

Judgmental Methods   When little or no data exist on which to base a forecast, the knowledge and experience of company employees can be helpful. Key executives, sales managers, or salespersons may be asked what quantity of an item will sell at various prices. A demand schedule is developed from the feedback.

Analytical Models

Regression analysis

Some of the more sophisticated methods for forecasting involve the use of mathematical models. The most widely used analytical method is **regression analysis,** a technique that measures the mathematical relationship of one or more variables to the item under study. If a statistical relationship can be found, this relationship becomes the basis of the forecast; for example, it is possible to project gasoline sales based on automobile registrations. Similarly, tax revenues can be projected based on census data.

Technological Forecasting Methods

The term **technological forecasting** applies to a number of forecasting tools that have been developed in recent years. The term is somewhat misleading because the techniques are just as useful in forecasting economic activity as they are in projecting future technological advances.

Forecasts based on technology

Delphi Technique   In the **Delphi technique,** a panel of experts forecasts the future by answering a series of questionnaires. Initially, each expert is asked to predict the future of the variable under study. Responses are distributed to all participants, who are allowed to modify their own when they learn the other experts' forecasts. With the modified predictions distributed to all participants, the process is repeated over and over. The result is a prediction based on the participants' shared knowledge. Chapter 6, "Managerial Decision Making," presents a complete description of the Delphi technique.

Scenarios   A **scenario** is an attempt to describe a series of happenings that demonstrate how to attain a particular goal. As with the Delphi technique, experts who predict the implications of postulated technological developments typically are used.

Impact Analysis   **Impact analysis** is designed to predict the effect of technological breakthroughs on specific industries. It differs from scenarios in that scenarios depict a procedure for attaining a goal whereas impact analysis focuses on the effect of technological developments. The impact of synthetic lubricants on the petroleum industry can be predicted in this manner.

Management by Objectives

If overall corporate goals are to be attained, each organizational unit and employee must work toward that end. Management by objectives has been widely acclaimed in recent years as the best way to integrate each worker into the overall company strategy.

The phrase "management by objectives" or "MBO" has become part of the language of managers throughout the world. In virtually every type of organization—from churches to the military, and from multinational corporations to the family-owned grocery store—managers are familiar with the term. It has appeared under several names: results-oriented management, management by objectives and results, "planagement," and management by agreement, to name a few.[16] **Management by objectives (MBO)** has been defined by George Odiorne as

MBO defined

> a management process whereby the supervisor and the subordinate, operating under a clear definition of the common goals and priorities of the organization established by top management, jointly identify the individual's major areas of responsibility in terms of the results expected of him or her, and use these measures as guides for operating the unit and assessing the contributions of each of its members.[17]

As Figure 4.4 shows, MBO involves setting specific, measurable goals with subordinates and then periodically discussing their progress. In some firms, MBO is the only method used for appraising the performance of supervisory personnel. MBO can be used with any employee to make certain that objectives are established and agreed on and to ensure that each employee gets timely feedback on his or her performance. Management by objectives essentially has four basic steps.

FIGURE 4.4
The MBO process
(*Source:* Ricky W.
Griffin, *Management*,
1984, p. 121. Reprinted
with permission from
Houghton Mifflin
Company.)

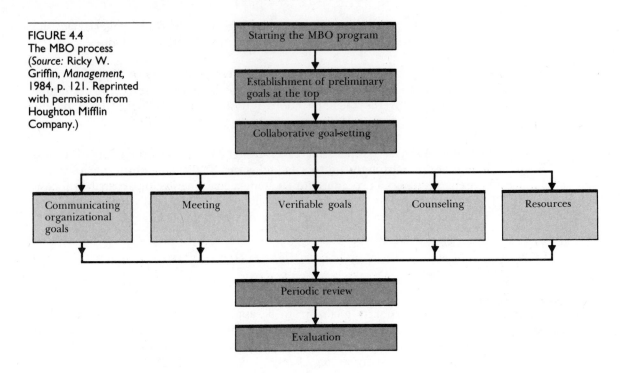

1. *Precisely defining the job that needs to be done.* Overall goals are usually set by top-level management; supervisors usually set more specific departmental goals.

2. *Establishing goals.* Supervisors and workers *together* set attainable, specific objectives to be achieved over a set period of time.

3. *Evaluating results.* At the end of the time period, supervisors evaluate how well objectives have been met.

4. *Providing feedback to the subordinate.* Subordinates are informed of their progress, and the process of setting objectives begins again.[18]

Purpose of MBO

Reasons for using MBO

The primary purpose of MBO is to improve the effectiveness of the individual and of the organization as a whole. It also guides the management process itself. As a framework for organizing thought and activity, MBO forces managers to answer the question posed by Peter Drucker: "What are the purposes and nature of our organization, and what should they be?" After that question has been answered, clear objectives are established, along with priorities and measures of performance. Then an environment is created in which employees exercise self-direction and self-control by monitoring their results and taking corrective action as needed.[19]

What Makes a Successful MBO Program?

Setting up an MBO program does not assure that individual employees will be integrated automatically into the overall company plan. A successful MBO requires several steps. First, top management must openly support the program and must establish overall organizational goals. These goals must take into consideration the future economic outlook, the firm's strengths and weaknesses, and its opportunities and problems. Finally, statements of goals should be clear, concise, and consistent with policies, procedures, and other plans adopted by the company.

MBO requires management support

Management by objectives is unlikely to be successful if managers and workers have negative attitudes toward it. Like most other programs designed to improve the effectiveness of individuals in an organization, it requires supportive supervisors, honest and mature subordinates, and high mutual trust. Some researchers feel that MBO is inappropriate in companies undergoing rapid change. Introducing a total MBO program, they contend, causes too many shock waves. They argue instead for a mini-MBO program that takes less time to work out, costs less, and minimizes employee anxiety in these situations.[20]

Pitfalls of MBO

The secret of success in implementing and utilizing an MBO program is recognizing the pitfalls that can trap a manager. The most common mistakes that managers make in attempting to institute MBO are these:

1. Managers fail to support the program fully.

2. Subordinates are not given an equal voice in the setting of objectives.

3. Managers fail to prepare adequately for evaluation and feedback.

4. Managers fail to recognize that a subordinate can meet an objective and still have unsatisfactory performance.

5. Too much paperwork is required.

6. Too many objectives are set.

7. A system of rewards is omitted.

8. Supervisors are not trained properly in the process and the mechanics involved.

9. Objectives are never modified.[21]

Review

✔ *The steps and levels in the planning process.* Planning is management's attempt to anticipate, and take advantage of, future events. The planning process has several steps: (1) defining the planning premises, (2) setting company objectives and formulating strategic plans, (3) developing policies, (4) developing implementation plans, (5) developing controls, (6) establishing administrative procedures for implementing the plan, and (7) reviewing and modifying the plan as needed.

✔ *Why some businesses' plans have succeeded and some have failed.* Business history is filled with stories of companies whose managers concentrated on the present and failed to plan for the future. Managers looking at the successes and failures of the Penn Central railroad, A&P, Sears, Roebuck, K mart, and General Motors will gain valuable insight into the benefits of planning.

✔ *The benefits of planning.* Planning benefits an organization in numerous ways. Planning helps managers grow professionally, aids communication flow, and provides a sense of direction for the organization. Plans help motivate workers, monitor work, and identify tasks necessary to accomplish organizational goals.

✔ *The characteristics of a good plan.* Business plans can be classified in a number of different ways, three of which are according to their (1) duration, (2) specificity, and (3) organizational level. Plans classified according to duration fall into three groups: short-range (one year or less), medium-range (one to five years), and long-range (five years or more). Specificity refers to the type of situation that plans cover. Policies, for example, govern recurring situations. Budgets, on the other hand, are single-use plans that expire when the time period for which they were developed is up.

✔ *How plans are classified.* Perhaps the most useful method for classifying plans is on the basis of organizational level. Overall company planning carried out by top management is called strategic planning, planning at the major department level is administrative planning, and that done at the supervisory level is tactical planning.

✔ *The critical element of forecasting.* Since plans are made in anticipation of future events, it is important to project the future accurately. Various forecasting methods are available to the manager. Some managers rely heavily on the product life cycle as a basis for projecting a product's future. Others use statistical techniques or rely on less quantitative methods such as intention-to-buy surveys and test-marketing.

✔ *How management by objectives improves the effectiveness of the individual and the organization.* Management by objectives is a widely acclaimed method for integrating each employee's efforts into the overall company plan. The system has three purposes: (1) to permit subordinates to participate in setting their individual goals, (2) to provide a sense of direction for all employees so that they see the relationship between their jobs and the objectives of the company, and (3) to provide management with a system for evaluating each individual's performance. The success of an MBO program requires top management's total support, positive attitudes by all organizational members, and precisely defined corporate objectives.

THE MANAGER'S DICTIONARY

As an extra review of the chapter, try defining the following terms. If you have trouble with any of them, refer to the page number listed.

bottom-line management (93)
single-use plans (98)
standing plans (98)
budget (99)
objective (99)
policy (99)
procedure (99)
program (99)
rule (99)

schedule (99)
strategy (99)
strategic planning (99)
planning gap (101)
administrative planning (101)
tactical planning (101)
forecasting (102)
product life cycle (104)
moving average (105)
exponential smoothing (105)

trend line (105)
leading indicator (105)
intention-to-buy survey (106)
regression analysis (106)
technological forecasting (106)
Delphi technique (106)
scenario (107)
impact analysis (107)
management by objectives
   (MBO) (107)

REVIEW QUESTIONS

1. What does the planning process entail?

2. Cite examples of companies that experienced financial difficulties because they failed to plan.

3. List some of the benefits of good business planning.

4. What are the characteristics of a good plan?

5. How can plans be classified?

6. Distinguish plans by duration. Distinguish plans by specificity.

7. How does strategic planning differ from other levels of planning?

8. Explain the relationship between planning and forecasting.

9. Cite several forecasting methods that can be used by business managers to forecast the future.

10. What are the components of an MBO program?

11. Can you think of any reasons why an MBO program might fail? Explain.

MANAGEMENT CHALLENGE

1. Assume that you have recently been employed as the managing director of a public art museum located in a major metropolitan area. What type of planning, if any, would you do?

2. As the managing director of the museum, with what specific types of plans would you be most concerned? Why?

3. How would your planning differ from that performed by a top-level manager of a manufacturing firm? Explain.

4. How would you measure the performance of the museum? Be specific.

5. What methods would you use to project the number of visitors to the museum? Why?

CASE 4.1

Planning by Hunch[22]

Too many British executives are convinced that they don't need to plan because they already know where their companies are headed.

It's "staggering" how little planning British companies do, according to Dean Berry, chairperson of the business strategy center at the London Business School. Their planning is little more than an extended budgetary exercise, he said.

Why is British business turning away from planning when it is so popular in the United States and Japan? Because strategic planning techniques are too rigid in these uncertain times, says Kaya Napstrek, the head of corporate planning at Imperial Chemical Industries, one of Britain's biggest industrial companies. "They are no good for the 1980s," he believes.

Many large British companies consider other matters to be more important than predicting future growth. These include increasing efficiency, developing and improving the product, marketing, and finding small, profitable corners of the market. Planners make educated guesses called scenarios—that's all.

The British firm Shell International was stung by this reliance on scenarios to foresee the future. The company was involved in a disastrous nuclear energy venture with Gulf Oil and also found itself burdened with too many supertankers. At first, company planners reacted by spewing out too many scenarios—up to twenty, in fact—for something as unpredictable as oil prices.

Company planners now try to anticipate only three things: how much money should be invested and what people will be needed, what the competition will do, and what changes will occur in the business climate, such as oil prices and recessions. Instead of planning one year, five years, or ten years ahead, the company changes its plans regularly and stretches only three to five years into the future, according to Guy de Wouters, Shell International's strategic planning director. The plans contain no figures.

Shell International decisions are the result of no more than two to four scenarios. These guesses are checked to see how right or wrong they are, but company planners don't expect to be right all the time. "We have abandoned any idea of forecast planning," de Wouters said. "The risks have become higher and higher."

Planners at Dunlop, a major British tire maker, agree. The company's one-year budgeting and five-year strategic plans had become increasingly mechanistic and numerical, said company planning director Roy Marsh. Dunlop planners are now more open-ended in their guesses about company growth, protectionism, and fluctuations in the currency exchange rate.

Questions

1. Shell International changed its planning process after its two disastrous ventures. In your opinion, could the company have modified the existing planning system instead? How?

2. What pitfalls could Shell and Dunlop encounter under their current planning methods?

CASE 4.2

A Cigarette by Any Other Name . . . May Not Sell[23]

In the mid-1980s, the management of Liggett & Myers Tobacco Company faced major decisions about increasing its share of the cigarette market. Should it develop a new cigarette for the Hispanic market or just translate ads for its existing brands into Spanish? If a new cigarette were introduced, what brand name would appeal to Hispanics? The Hispanic market was attractive—more than twenty million people with purchasing power of $60 billion a year.

Liggett & Myers quickly rejected translating its ads. Management decided it was a token gesture that might only alienate Hispanics. The other alternative—a new product—raised a crucial question. What name would have a slight Latin sound but not become too closely identified with Hispanics? Following consumer testing and door-to-door interviews with nearly five hundred Hispanic families in five major U.S. cities on their smoking habits, the names "Dorado" and "Superior" appeared the most popular. As a result, Liggett & Myers came out with two brands. The only differences between the two are their packaging and advertising slogans. Dorado is "crafted for pleasure" while Superior is "created to satisfy," according to company advertising.

After the two were manufactured, test-marketing began. Dorado captured a .68% share of the cigarette market in Albuquerque and Santa Fe, New Mexico, while L&M Superior garnered a .45% market share in Corpus Christi and Brownsville, Texas. Considering the brand loyalty traditionally exhibited by Hispanics, both brands were considered highly successful.

Liggett & Myers naturally wants the cigarette to appeal to Anglos as well as to Hispanics, so they designed the advertising campaign to be homogeneous. There are no Hispanic people or Spanish themes, only pictures of the cigarette pack—a tobacco leaf and a wood carving. Such an approach, management believed, would enable Liggett & Myers to introduce the brands into other markets more easily.

Questions

1. In your opinion, what was Liggett & Myers's overall strategy in introducing the new products?

2. Hispanics rely more on television than on newspapers and magazines for information. Yet, cigarette advertising on television is prohibited in America. Would the plans formulated by Liggett & Myers have taken this into account? How?

3. Evaluate the planning that preceded the decision to introduce the new cigarettes. At what organizational level were plans made? How specific were the plans? Discuss.

CHAPTER OUTLINE

Strategic Planning Today

The Strategic Planning Process

Levels of Strategic Planning

Step 1: Formulate Corporate Mission

Step 2: Establish Specific Objectives

Step 3: Analyze the Environment
  Political and Legal Forces
  Social Forces
  Economic Forces
  Technological Forces
  Other Considerations

Step 4: Assess Opportunities and Problems
  Other Considerations
  Management Expertise

Step 5: Evaluate Alternatives
  Alternative Strategies for Retailers and Service Firms
  Other Aspects of Competition

Step 6: Implement the Strategy

Step 7: Evaluate and Control

Strategic Planning in Small Businesses

Strategic Planning

Family Dollar Has Unique Strategy

When the top management of Family Dollar looks for sites to build new stores, they look for oil spots and cheap shoes. So says company president Lewis Levine, who proudly acknowledges that Family Dollar stores cater to low-income customers who drive old cars and wear inexpensive shoes.[1]

By refusing to budge from its low-income sales strategy, Family Dollar has become one of the most profitable discount retailers in the country. Its strategy is simple: offer merchandise of reasonable quality at low prices. Most items sell for less than twenty dollars, and all sales are cash. The typical customer spends around six dollars per trip. The stores are almost identical in size and layout, built from a plan developed at the home office in Charlotte, N.C. Well lighted, air-conditioned, and clean, each store occupies eight thousand square feet or less. About 30% of the merchandise carries a brand name, but seconds and irregulars constitute less than 4% of total sales.

By carefully identifying its market and then serving the needs of that market, Family Dollar has compiled an enviable record. Sales are growing at 21% annually, earnings are growing even faster, and the book value of its common stock has increased steadily. It has found a niche between its two main rivals: Dollar General at the low end of the market, and Wal-Mart at the high end. Dollar General undersells Family Dollar by selling closeouts and irregulars. Wal-Mart has upgraded its offerings to compete with K mart.

Family Dollar's strategy is to keep the costs of operations low. It offers only five thousand items, inventory is tightly controlled, merchandise is shipped from a single warehouse, and pricing for all stores is done at headquarters.

How profitable has this formula been? Very profitable—the company has accumulated thirty-nine consecutive quarters of record sales and earnings.[2]

Family Dollar's management is convinced that continued success depends on keeping steadfastly to its strategy. As Wal-Mart and Kmart upgrade their merchandise, Family Dollar is left with a bigger niche to itself.

Preview

During the scientific management era, Henri Fayol, Frederick W. Taylor, and other authorities emphasized the importance of managerial planning. Unlike the planning at Family Dollar however, near-term production goals were stressed, rather than long-term business objectives. For the most part, plans were mere extensions of past practices. Since then, business planning has gone through several phases.

In the 1950s, budgeting and strategic planning were synonymous. Myopic managers focused on their day-to-day operations and paid little attention to their businesses' changing environment. Managers in the 1960s seemed to have financial and legal considerations foremost in planning. Beginning in the 1970s, managers were forced to pay more attention to long-term planning. Environmental upheavals, such as the 1973 oil embargo and the proliferation of international competitors in the world marketplace, forced American businesspeople to develop a systematic means of analyzing their environment, assessing their opportunities and problems, and identifying niches where they have a competitive advantage. Strategic planning as we know it today was born.

This chapter shows the importance of strategic planning for all types of organizations and analyzes the procedure for developing a strategic plan. The following important ideas are presented in this chapter:

✔ What strategic planning is today

✔ Steps in the strategic planning process

✔ Why strategic planning is carried out at two different levels

✔ The importance of the corporate mission

✔ How a company's objectives affect its mission

✔ The importance of analyzing the environment

✔ What affects a firm's opportunities and problems

✔ How to choose the right strategic plan

✔ The importance of properly implementing a strategy

✔ Why evaluation and control are necessary

✔ The importance of strategic planning for small businesses

Strategic Planning Today

Present-day strategies

Strategic planning generally answers three crucial questions: "What business are we in? What business should we be in? Where will we be in ten years if we continue doing what we are now doing?" It focuses on defining the firm's mission, analyzing its environment, evaluating its strengths and weaknesses, and identifying a niche in the market where the firm has a competitive advantage.

Strategic planning often is confused with extended budgeting. There also is confusion on the difference between strategic planning and tactical planning. As we said in Chapter 4, "Managerial Planning," a strategic plan is pertinent to the whole organization, and is carried out on the corporate level, whereas a tactical plan is directed toward the fulfillment of departmental goals. **Operational planning** is for the purpose of carrying out a tactical plan. Operational plans are specific departmental plans. The various types and levels of planning are illustrated in Table 5.1.

The Strategic Planning Process

The strategic planning process, illustrated in Figure 5.1, is made up of seven sequential steps: (1) formulating the corporate mission; (2) establishing concrete specific objectives; (3) analyzing the environment; (4) pinpointing opportunities and problems based on the environmental analysis; (5) evaluating alternatives; (6) implementing the strategic plan that will give the firm a competitive advantage; and (7) evaluating the success of the strategy.

Levels of Strategic Planning

Business-level strategy

An organization that produces a single product or provides a single service can develop a single strategy that encompasses its entire operation. Such a strategy is referred to as a **business-level strategy.** But many organizations offer diverse product lines or, in some cases, are made up of several unrelated operations. Westinghouse, for example, manufactures several unrelated lines of products, ranging from industrial robots to home washing machines and refrigerators. Organizations such as Westinghouse need to develop different strategies for different levels of operations. That is, they need to develop business-level strategies for each diverse operation as well as a corporate-level strategy for the company as a whole.

TABLE 5.1
Types and levels of
business planning

LEVELS	TYPES			
Corporate Level (Strategic)	Strategic Planning			
Departmental (Tactical)	Marketing Plan	Financial Plan	Production Plan	Human Resources Plan
Specific Departmental (Operational)	New Product	Profit Plan	Production Capacity Plan	Recruitment and Selection Plan
	Promotion Plan	Investment Plan	Incentives Plan	Training Plan
	Sales Plan	Purchase Plan	Labor Utilization Plan	Promotion Plan
	Public Relations Plan	Cash Flow	Quality Control Plan	Retirement Plan
	Marketing Research Plan	Capital Budget	Order Filling Plan	Union Relations Plan

Source: Adapted from Paulo De Vasconcellos Filho, "Strategic Planning: A New Approach," *Managerial Planning*, March/April 1982, p. 14. Reprinted with permission of Planning Executive Institute.

**Corporate-level
strategy**

The **corporate-level,** or **grand, strategy** is a long-term, comprehensive strategy of firms that offer diverse product lines or are comprised of several unrelated operations. It focuses on two questions: "What business should we be in?" and "How shall we conduct that business?" Failure to answer the first question can be critical, because being in the wrong business can be fatal. For example, railroad executives years ago saw themselves as being in the railroad business, not in the transportation business, so they stayed out of the airline and automobile industries. This narrow view proved to be a critical mistake for the railroads. On the other hand, Xerox took a broader view of its operations. Xerox executives considered their company to be in the information business, rather than in the photocopying business. By moving into new business areas, Xerox has been able to prosper despite fierce competition in its primary line of activity, photocopying.[3]

Determining how business should be conducted is important, because the basic actions set forth in the corporate-level strategy position a firm in its industry. A firm that is poorly positioned has little or no chance for long-term

FIGURE 5.1
Sequential steps in
strategic planning

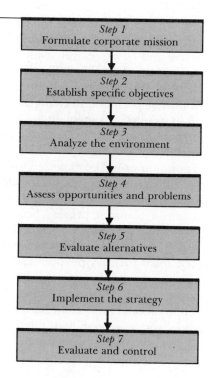

success. Strategic planning at the corporate level, then, provides direction for the organization as a whole. Essentially, the corporate-level, or grand, strategy determines the role that each business in the organization will play. At a company like Raytheon, for example, top management integrates the business-level strategies for its aircraft, publishing, and other divisions into a comprehensive, overall master plan.

The business-level strategy for each division (or for the whole company if it is not diversified) answers the question: "How will we compete in the market?" This strategy has several components, including the products or services that will be offered, the market segment that will be focused on, the firm's relationship with an array of other organizations and individuals, and other factors.

**Step 1:
Formulate
Corporate
Mission**

An organization's objectives, policies, and strategy are primarily based on its **mission.** According to Lloyd L. Byars, an organization's mission has two parts: its philosophy and its purpose.[4] A company's **organizational philosophy** establishes its values, beliefs, and guidelines, which channel its business conduct. Its **organizational purpose** defines the activities it intends to perform and the kind of organization it intends to be.

Importance of philosophy

Thomas J. Watson, Jr., former chairman of the board of IBM, emphasized the importance of having an organizational philosophy. Watson said that, for an organization to survive and be successful, it must have a sound set of beliefs and values on which to base its policies. The organization must completely and faithfully adhere to those beliefs, while remaining flexible in a changing environment. It must be prepared to change everything about itself except the beliefs set forth in its mission statement.[5]

Organizational purpose

An organization's purpose defines its present and potential customers, and asks the question, "Are we in the right business?" For example, Delta Airlines and Chrysler Corporation would be expected to define their purpose in the same way—to provide transportation for customers now and in the future. As we have already pointed out, formulating the corporate mission is an important step in the strategic planning process, because defining the purpose too narrowly sometimes can be disastrous. Petroleum companies, for instance, should consider themselves in the energy business rather than in the exploration and refining of fossil fuels. A purpose should take a wide perspective and be consistent with successful corporate strategy.

An organization's mission is, thus, the foundation in the planning process. Ideally, a company's philosophy should remain unchanged. Its purpose should be analyzed periodically, however, to determine if modifications are needed.

Step 2: Establish Specific Objectives

Examples of objectives

As Chapter 4 pointed out, objectives are the ends toward which business activity is aimed. They are statements that identify what the organization hopes to accomplish. Objectives make the company's mission tangible and measurable. For example, a utility company may consider its mission to be providing an abundant energy source to a community. Specific objectives associated with the mission might include generating 20% of its energy in nuclear reactors or reducing the consumption of natural gas by 15% over the following three years. Such objectives clearly set forth the goals with which progress can be measured.

Most businesses have profit, survival, and growth objectives. These objectives can be achieved only if the firm positions itself properly in the market and fills a need that other businesses cannot satisfy. In some cases, the need can be satisfied by introducing a new product; in other instances, a *niche* can be developed by offering lower prices or something else that appeals to the consumer. Du Pont shifted its strategy to be more responsive to its customers' needs, as the In-Box on page 121 shows.

Satisfying different needs

The marketplace is heterogeneous. It is made up of people of different races, sexes, income levels, educational backgrounds, religions, political beliefs, and so on. These differences make it virtually impossible to appeal to the entire marketplace. A cosmetics manufacturer, for example, cannot succeed by manufacturing identical products for all races. A men's clothing retailer

THE IN-BOX

Du Pont Shifts Its Strategy

What does a company do when it loses its competitive edge?

Du Pont faced this problem. The technological innovation on which the company's reputation had been built had slowed to a virtual standstill. The heat from the competition was intense. Its traditional businesses were declining.

Du Pont met the challenge by shifting its strategy away from its long-standing base in plastics and fibers into newer technologies, including specialty agricultural chemicals, biomedical products, and electronic goods.

Today, Du Pont is more decentralized, with fewer levels of management. Self-management, an emphasis on individual decision making, is the new force. Lower-level managers exercise considerable decision-making authority. The new corporate culture is more relaxed and informal.

Du Pont's goal is to become more responsive to customers' needs. Every employee now is expected to be a salesperson, to be a positive force for the company. Researchers and marketing specialists are expected to work together, not separately.

In the past, the company operated on the assumption that it could invent its way to success, virtually ignoring its customer needs and the changes taking place in the market. Today, Du Pont realizes that it has to change both its business and the way it does business. So sweeping are the changes that company executives now refer to their employer as the "new" Du Pont.

Source: Alix M. Freedman, "Du Pont Trims Costs, Bureaucracy to Bolster Competitive Position," *Wall Street Journal,* September 25, 1985, pp. 1 +.

most likely will not prosper by appealing to all income levels or age groups. Gillette's Right Guard deodorant was not the "perfect family deodorant," as its ads once suggested. The needs and wants of each segment are different. The astute manager must recognize that different products satisfy different needs. One of the keys to success is to identify which homogeneous market segment the product or service will be directed to and to formulate objectives related to that market segment.

Step 3: Analyze the Environment

Probably the most important determinant of an organization's success is its ability to cope with a changing environment. Chapter 3 examined four external forces that shape an organization's environment: political and legal, social, economic, and technological. Because of their profound impact on the success or failure of a firm, they warrant additional discussion here.

Political and Legal Forces

Political and legal forces

These forces deal with executive decrees, legislation, government regulations, foreign policy, court decisions, and the like. They are probably the easiest external forces to monitor because they are routinely reported in the news media. Although little can be done to offset these forces, just knowing about them can be important. For example, AT&T was unhappy with the court divestiture decision, but AT&T management could plan accordingly because they could guess the probable outcome.

Government regulations certainly affect competition. Tariffs, subsidies, price controls, and import quotas bear directly on a firm's success. In most cases, these regulations protect industries; in other cases, they stifle growth and prosperity.

Today, the trend is toward deregulation, especially in financial, telecommunications, and transportation industries. Deregulation is having positive and negative effects in the marketplace. Phasing out government-mandated interest-rate ceilings has totally changed the nature of competition in the banking industry. Critics argue that the deregulation legislation was directly responsible for forty-five bank failures in 1983 and the dwindling number of banks nationwide.[6] In the telecommunications industry, more than one hundred firms now compete in manufacturing telephones, an area that once was considered the exclusive domain of AT&T's Western Electric. Deregulation in the trucking industry has resulted in more carriers and lower shipping costs per truck load. In the airline industry, both the carrier and the consumer have been affected. Major airlines are limiting or abandoning less profitable routes, while the nation's twenty-two major markets show an increase in the number of daily departures.[7] The rural routes abandoned by the large carriers are being snatched up by new, small airlines that can operate more inexpensively.

Consumers can earn higher interest rates on their savings, choose from a wider range of products, and take advantage of discounted fares for travel. On the other hand, deregulation may force some businesses—particularly the weaker firms—to file for bankruptcy or to discontinue marginally profitable services.

Social Forces

Social forces

These forces affect the way people live, including what they value. Strategists who are analyzing the environment should monitor past and present trends. Management must be able to see trends correctly and take appropriate action when trends appear unfavorable. The management of Philip Morris realized that the trend in cigarette sales was unfavorable, for example, so it bought

Miller Brewing Company. The move was consistent with Philip Morris's mission—to provide customers with pleasurable products made from agricultural commodities. Philip Morris also was able to capitalize on its existing strengths: production and advertising. Cigarettes and beer are both advertised the same way to many of the same customers and sold through similar distribution outlets.[8]

The corporate strategy also must address several important questions related to timing: What does the future hold in store for this industry? Is this a growth industry, or a mature one? Is this the right time to develop and market a new product or to expand into new markets? At what stage in their life cycles are our existing products? These questions must be considered to make the strategy meaningful.

Importance of timing

Introducing a product at the proper time is instrumental to its success. Ford Motor Company made a big mistake with the introduction of its Edsel. Its appearance was drastically different from cars already on the market. Consumers simply didn't approve of its styling. Years later, Ford introduced the sporty Mustang, a car directed to the right audience, at the right price, with styling that appealed to large numbers of consumers.

Economic Forces

Economic forces

Recessions, inflation, interest rates, the value of currencies, and similar economic variables are all economic forces. The appropriateness of a strategy depends partly on the present and future state of the economy. If a recession is anticipated, a cost-cutting strategy may be best. On the other hand, favorable economic forecasts may signal the need for a strategy based on expansion.

Technological Forces

Technological forces

Managers who are formulating a firm's strategy also must take into account technological innovations and their impact on consumer preferences. The wise manager not only will assess the existing demand for a product or service but also will project it into the future. Such projections are crucial because of rapidly developing technology. American consumers are known for volatile changes in their buying habits. In their choice of clothes, for example, American shoppers shifted from cotton and other natural fibers to polyester and then back to cotton in a relatively short period. Their taste for small cars drastically changed within a few short months when gas prices began to decline.

Other Considerations

Other variables in addition to the forces we have just discussed affect an organization's environment. Particularly important are the availability of labor and labor and energy costs.

For most organizations, the availability of labor and its costs are crucial. In recent years, small towns and communities throughout the country have established industrial development boards whose primary function is to attract new industry to their areas. In a vast majority of cases, firms discover that an inadequately trained labor force is the greatest obstacle they have to overcome.

Labor costs and availability

Labor costs can be staggering. For many firms, labor costs are the largest single category of operations costs. For example, consider the impact that a reduction in hourly wage rates and benefits had on Chrysler Corporation's earnings in 1981. During this recessionary period, Chrysler was on the brink of bankruptcy, faced with high interest rates, a high level of unemployment nationwide, and escalating labor costs. Perhaps more than any other factor, concessions granted by the United Auto Workers contributed to the revitalization of Chrysler.

Energy considerations

Energy costs also affect an organization's environment. Whether a firm will relocate, build another plant, expand operations, or enter a new venture altogether depends on the availability of energy at a reasonable cost. Energy-intensive industries, such as aluminum manufacturing and chlorine-caustic soda manufacturing, are the most severely affected whenever energy costs rise or energy supplies are threatened. Trying to moderate these costs and uncertainties, firms such as Dow Chemical and BASF Wyandotte have invested heavily in new technology (new chlorine cell design) and cogeneration capabilities.

It is evident that the environment is a source of both opportunities and threats for every organization. In the strategic planning process, all environmental forces should be closely monitored. Studies have shown that successful firms change their strategy as the environment around them changes.[9] The key to success lies in developing a strategy that will give the company a competitive advantage and then putting it into effect at exactly the right time.[10]

Step 4: Assess Opportunities and Problems

Many companies fail to take their competition seriously. Normally, firms implicitly assume that the most serious competitors are those with the greatest resources.[11] This is not always the case. Many businesses also fail to analyze their own weaknesses. The strategic purpose for gathering information on internal strengths and weaknesses is to compare this information with perceived environmental threats and opportunities and to make decisions based on the comparisons.[12]

Internal strengths and weaknesses

Harvard Professor Michael Porter suggests that an organization should analyze five major areas in its environment. Each industry's strengths and weaknesses apply to each organization within it, he contends.[13] The five areas are:

1. *Threat of new entrants.* Firms in a particular industry have an advantage if additional competitors are kept from entering the market. *Economies of scale*

exist in industries in which large firms can produce goods at lower costs than small firms can. New firms find it difficult to enter the field because of the competitive advantage enjoyed by large firms. Another barrier to entering a market involves *access to distribution channels.* Most manufacturers devote considerable time and effort to developing efficient distribution channels for their products. For years, the U.S. automobile industry maintained a tremendous advantage over foreign car makers because the importers did not have enough dealerships and service centers throughout the country. *Excessive capital requirements,* including investments in plants, equipment, and working capital, also may impede a firm's entry into a market. The costs can be particularly prohibitive for manufacturing firms.

2. *Bargaining power of buyers.* Buyers can have a tremendous impact on a firm's environment in a particular industry. Customers may be able to force down prices, bargain for higher quality, or pit one competitor against another.

Environmental strengths and weaknesses

3. *Bargaining power of suppliers.* Suppliers affect an industry through their ability to control prices and product quality.

4. *Threat of substitute products.* Substitute products satisfy the consumer's needs but may not appear to be substitutes. For example, electronic security-alarm systems are substitutes for security guards. They are less expensive to operate, and their advantage increases as labor costs rise. Whenever substitute products are available, the industry's environment is threatened.

5. *Intensity of rivalry among existing firms.* The first step in analyzing the rivalry among firms is to identify competitors. Next, their tactics must be evaluated. Intense rivalry is caused by slow growth periods, the existence of numerous, diverse competitors, and other factors. Managers must be aware of the forces that cause intense rivalry and be able to defend themselves against it.

Other Considerations

Several other variables can affect a firm's competitive advantage or disadvantage. Close proximity to an uninterruptable supply of raw materials gives a firm an advantage over its competition. Locating a manufacturing facility near a source of raw materials or near the market served will most likely result in lower transportation costs and fewer delivery delays as well. International Paper Company, for example, locates its paper-products plants near timberland, Kaiser Aluminum situates its facilities near sources of bauxite, and Dow Chemical operates several of its chlorine plants near salt domes.

Other factors affecting success

Opportunities for vertical and horizontal integration also can affect a firm's competitive position. **Vertical integration** typically involves ownership of sources of raw materials or component parts, or the distribution outlets. General Motors, for instance, owns AC-Delco, a supplier of component parts for its automobiles. Exxon distributes a significant portion of its refined products through company-owned stations. Such an arrangement lets a firm make a profit at different levels. Other companies expand horizontally. Companies using **horizontal integration** create or purchase facilities in similar lines. A retailer located in one city might open a second store in another location, for example. Or a firm engaged in coal mining might move into oil and gas exploration.

Management Expertise

Another variable that affects a firm's competitive position is its management expertise. A firm can assess its competitive strengths and weaknesses by answering the following questions: What are the ages of our key executives? Are they likely to remain with the firm for the foreseeable future? When they retire or leave the company, can they be replaced with equally competent successors? Regardless of the quality of the strategy or the amount of time and effort that goes into its development, a strategy is only as valuable as the people who implement it.

Step 5: Evaluate Alternatives

Internal and external strategies

The right strategy creates a viable fit between the firm and its environment. Six internal strategies are worth considering: (1) holding on to the status quo; (2) concentrating on one market or one product; (3) **retrenchment** (a significant change in strategy brought about by poor performance); (4) **divestiture** (strategy in which a firm sells one of its major divisions); (5) **liquidation** (strategy in which a business is sold to avoid bankruptcy); and (6) innovation. External strategic options include (1) horizontal and vertical integration (discussed in Step 4), (2) **joint ventures** (a company created by merging two or more firms in order to take advantage of each firm's strengths); and (3) diversification. Diversification strategies are either internal or external. If the diversification strategy's focus is to extend the product line, then the strategy is internal. For example, Gillette offset its loss of market share in razor blades by diversifying into toiletry products, hair coloring, and disposable lighters. External diversification is an expansion into unrelated markets. This kind of diversification occurred when Dart Corporation, a fast-growing company in the houseware and battery business, merged with Kraft Corporation, a slow-growing company in the food industry.[14]

While the strategies just mentioned are viable options, it is important to remember that the objective is to select the *one* strategy that will give the firm a competitive advantage, as in the case of Wang Laboratories, detailed in On-Line Management on page 127. Porter identified three generic-competitive strategies that are particularly useful to single business units or separate product divisions within a corporation:

ON-LINE MANAGEMENT

Changes at Wang

Wang Laboratories built its phenomenal success on a very profitable niche in the computer industry—word processing. But today Wang's customers want more.

Clients are no longer satisfied with simple word processing. They want unified office computer systems that handle graphics and manipulate numbers as well as words. And they want these systems to interact smoothly with other computers.

In response, Wang did a strategic about-face to meet the challenge of the present and the future. It began producing IBM-compatible equipment and formed technological alliances with other companies. This reversed Wang's operating premise that all research and development should be done in-house and that Wang would rather beat the competition than join it.

These changes represent a way of thinking different from that of An Wang, who founded the company in 1951. The changeover is largely due to the realization that Wang must coexist with IBM in the office. Had the market remained static, Wang Laboratories probably would have maintained its "go it alone" strategy. The results could have been disastrous.

Source: David Wessel, "In a Volatile Industry, Wang Laboratories Is Consistent but Flexible," *Wall Street Journal*, Nov. 6, 1984, p. 1.

Selecting one strategy

1. **Least-Cost Strategy.** This emphasizes producing a standardized product at a low cost.

2. **Differentiation.** This strategy focuses on providing a product or service that customers consider unique.

3. **Niche.** In this approach, the product is targeted to a particular group of customers.[15]

A number of firms, including RCA, Coca-Cola, and Rockford Headed Products, Inc., have successfully implemented Porter's plans. After analyzing the industry environment and finding that its competitors were producing uniform products, RCA chose the least-cost strategy. In this way, it capitalized on its strengths: good access to resources and high levels of experience and

Examples of generic-competitive strategies

expertise within the firm. On the other hand, Coca-Cola adopted a differentiation strategy when its market share began to erode. By combining its marketing and manufacturing efforts, Coke was able to modify its product line and regain its customer base by producing caffeine-free and diet soft drinks. Rockford Headed Products, Inc., a company that traditionally manufactured fasteners for industrial users, adopted a niche strategy when it began producing custom-made, self-threading screws for a specific market. This improved the company's profitability.[16]

Alternative Strategies for Retailers and Service Firms

Managers too often assume that price is the only basis for competing effectively. While price can be important, it is only one of several determinants of success. To many customers, a product's price is secondary to service, its reputation, availability, and other factors. For instance, the rates charged by major motel chains typically are higher than those of independent motels. But on any given day, a Howard Johnson or Holiday Inn on a major thoroughfare is likely to be at or near capacity, while the occupancy rates of independent motels further away from the highway most likely will be lower. Location and services justify a higher room rate.

Bases for competing

Merchants must offer items that are desirable for the market segment they wish to capture. The choice of products can either enhance or diminish the company's overall reputation. For example, Nieman-Marcus has built a reputation by offering one-of-a-kind items, especially designed for high-income buyers who are more concerned with availability than with price. Even quality-conscious department stores recognize the need to separate lower-quality, lower-priced merchandise from high-quality, high-priced merchandise. Like many other such retailers, Cain-Sloan of Nashville, Tennessee maintains a bargain basement for cost-conscious shoppers.

Remember that the image of any product cannot be separated from the environment it's sold in or from the buyer's self-image. We all think we are unique. Our decisions are tied to some image of what we are or what we hope to become. The consumer considers products, brands, and the conditions of purchase important to his or her self-image. The environment in which the merchandise is presented also is significant. Sterling silverware sold only in high-quality jewelry and department stores may present a product image that fits the important self-image of most consumers. But if the same merchandise also is offered in a less fashionable setting—a discount house—the product image may not match the consumer's self-image.[17]

Other Aspects of Competition

A retailer often will carry competing lines of merchandise. A merchant, for example, may sell three well-known brands of cameras—Canon, Olympus, and Minolta—and a lesser-known brand. Although the quality and features of all four brands may be comparable, the lesser-known probably would carry a lower price tag simply because the public has not given it the "stamp of approval" that justifies a higher price. To a great extent, national advertisements create a quality image for products. The retailer does not carry the burden of convincing the public that the well-known product is of superior quality. Product differentiation exists whenever the consumer believes that there is a difference in two products; physical differences are not necessary.

Options for the retailer
The retailer who must select a generic-competitive strategy must keep one additional consideration in mind. Just after going into business many businesspeople learn that they cannot effectively compete on the basis of price or product image. This is particularly true of the small retailer competing with well-established, giant chain stores that purchase in large quantities. The newcomer's alternative is to compete on some other basis, such as location, convenience, or service. Consumers who demand special services are willing to pay for them. Delivery, credit, personal selling, alterations, installation, and repair are a few of the service areas that may provide a merchant with an advantage over competitors.

Step 6: Implement the Strategy

A strategic plan that is compatible with an organization's strengths is virtually useless unless it is implemented properly. Among the most important considerations when implementing a strategy is how well it matches the organization's culture, employee skills, and the commitment that top management has to it.

Organizational culture
Organizational culture differs from one organization to the next. For example, some organizations take risks whereas others are risk averse; some are innovative whereas others have a "wait and see" attitude. If the firm takes risks, management is likely to favor a bold and active strategy. A risk-averse firm, on the other hand, will favor a strategy that minimizes its chance of financial loss. A business that highly values research and development probably will favor a strategy based on technological competitive advantage. A firm that places little importance on research and development most likely will support a strategy that emphasizes promotion and sales.

Managers implementing a strategic plan also should look at the skills of the people in the organization. Does the existing work force have the abilities to implement the strategy, or will additional people be needed? Will some people have to be trained before the strategy can be implemented? Managers who examine these questions can help assure the success of the chosen strategy.

Commitment to the strategy
Finally, top management must agree that the chosen strategy is the best way to accomplish the organization's objectives. They must thoroughly understand all facets of the strategy as well as the resources required to implement it.

Step 7: Evaluate and Control

When developing a strategic plan, managers must not only look at the firm's existing environment but also must predict its future conditions. Managers must be ready to recognize departures from predictions and to modify the plan accordingly. For example, technological innovations may radically alter the products demanded by consumers. Or changes in the law may affect the nature of competition or create new markets altogether. Political forces, especially those in foreign countries, may create new opportunities or may eliminate existing markets. Social and economic forces also are subject to change. These kinds of changes may call for modifications in the strategic plan.

Modifying the strategy

A firm's existing strengths may decline because of a curtailment in a raw material supply, the untimely death or departure of key executives, significant changes in the financial market, or other circumstances. Both internal and external forces can bring about the need for strategy modifications.

The strategy may not need major surgery. Slight adjustments most likely can be made periodically to reflect unforeseen happenings. Minor modifications do not radically alter the direction of the firm; they merely refine the plan. In fact, modifications that anticipate change are particularly helpful. Such adjustments are possible, though, only if managers gather new information regularly and if they continually evaluate new opportunities.

Return on investment, growth rates, changes in market share, and other control measurements help management assess how well the objectives are being met.[18] Top management should frequently ask itself: "Is our overall plan and mission realistic?" "Are the needed resources still available?" And, perhaps more important, "Have things turned out as we planned, and if not, why?"

Strategic Planning in Small Businesses

Strategic planning is just as crucial for small organizations as it is for large concerns. Research findings by Richard Robinson and John Pearce clearly show why small firms should develop and implement strategic plans: firms that plan are much more successful than those that don't. Robinson and Pearce's studies measured business success in a number of ways, ranging from growth in sales and profit to "perceived benefits of planning." In virtually every instance, the firms that planned outperformed those that didn't.[19] Even so, small firms typically do not engage in strategic planning. In fact, only about one-fourth of all small organizations develop and implement strategic plans.

Small businesses neglect planning

You may wonder why small firms do not engage in strategic planning. Robinson and Pearce cite four reasons why:

1. Managers of small businesses feel that they simply do not have time to engage in systematic planning.

2. Strategic planning is unfamiliar ground for most managers of small businesses. They are unaccustomed to the planning process. Many even question the worth of long-range planning.

3. Managers of small businesses typically have broad managerial skills, but they lack the specialized expertise required in strategic planning.

4. They are usually reluctant to seek advice or information from others, preferring instead to rely on their own knowledge and skills.[20]

Although managers of small organizations rarely engage in strategic planning, the evidence overwhelmingly suggests that they should. Strategic planning forces managers to develop their reasoning more carefully; it requires them to continually evaluate their surroundings; it helps them establish realistic objectives; and it forces them to keep their objectives in perspective.

Review

✔ *What strategic planning is today.* We view strategic planning as a systematic, ongoing process that attempts to answer two important questions: "Who are we?" and "Where do we want to go?"

✔ *Steps in the strategic planning process.* The sequential steps of strategic planning are to (1) formulate the corporate mission, (2) establish concrete objectives, (3) analyze the environment, (4) pinpoint opportunities and problems based on the environmental analysis, (5) evaluate alternatives, (6) implement the strategy that gives the firm a competitive advantage, and (7) evaluate the success of the strategy.

✔ *Why strategic planning is carried out at two different levels.* An organization that produces a single product or provides a single service develops a strategic plan that covers its entire operation. But an organization that is made up of several diverse operations develops strategic plans for each division. These business-level strategies then are integrated with a corporate-level strategy for the entire organization.

✔ *The importance of the corporate mission.* An organization's mission is comprised of two parts—its philosophy and its purpose. An organization's philosophy establishes its values and beliefs. Its purpose defines the activities that it intends to pursue and the kind of organization that it intends to be.

✔ *How a company's objectives affect its mission.* Objectives transform the company's mission into concrete statements. They identify what the organization hopes to accomplish, and serve as tangible, measurable standards that help management determine whether the company is headed in the right direction.

✔ *The importance of analyzing the environment.* Four external forces help shape an organization's environment: political and legal, social, economic, and technological. Political and legal forces include laws, government regulations, and court decisions. Social concerns affect the way people live and what they value. Economic forces include recessions, the money supply, inflation, and similar economic variables. Technological forces are the innovations developed by firms in an industry.

✔ *What affects a firm's opportunities and problems.* Harvard Professor Michael Porter suggests five major variables that affect a firm's potential for success: (1) the threat of new entrants into the industry, (2) the bargaining power of buyers, (3) the bargaining power of suppliers, (4) the threat of substitute products, and (5) the intensity of rivalry among competitors.

✔ *How to choose the right strategic plan.* A firm has several alternative strategies from which to choose. The options include: (1) producing a product at a low cost, (2) providing a product or service that consumers perceive as different, and (3) serving a specific market niche. The strategy selected should be one that gives a firm a competitive advantage in the marketplace. Some firms can effectively compete on the basis of price, while others compete on the basis of service, the image of their product, their location, or on some other basis.

✔ *The importance of properly implementing a strategy.* The strategy chosen should complement the organization's culture and the skills of its people. The total commitment of top management also is essential.

✔ *Why evaluation and control are necessary.* Since a strategic plan is based on predictions of the future, managers should be prepared to make modifications to the plan whenever unforeseen happenings occur. Any number of variables can cause a firm's strengths to decline. Technological innovations by competitors, the loss of key personnel, curtailment in the supply of raw materials, and escalating energy costs are some of the variables that can drastically alter a firm's competitive position.

✔ *The importance of strategic planning for small businesses.* Most small organizations don't engage in strategic planning although the evidence clearly indicates that they should. Managers of small businesses neglect strategic planning for a number of reasons: they feel they don't have adequate time, they are unaccustomed to planning, they lack the expertise required to plan strategically, and they are uncomfortable seeking advice and information from others, preferring instead to operate on their own knowledge and intuition.

THE MANAGER'S DICTIONARY

As an extra review of the chapter, try defining the following terms. If you have trouble with any of them, refer to the page number listed.

operational planning (117)
business-level strategy (117)
corporate-level (grand)
    strategy (118)
mission (119)
organizational philosophy
    (119)

organizational purpose (119)
vertical integration (125)
horizontal integration (126)
retrenchment (126)
divestiture (126)

liquidation (126)
joint ventures (126)
least-cost strategy (127)
differentiation (127)
niche (127)

REVIEW QUESTIONS

1. Explain the difference between strategic planning and tactical planning.

2. What is the difference between a business-level strategy and a corporate-level strategy?

3. List the steps in the strategic planning process.

4. What are the components of a corporate mission? Explain the importance of a statement of mission or purpose.

5. Is it possible to define a corporate mission too narrowly? Explain.

6. Explain the importance of developing specific objectives associated with the corporate mission.

7. Give examples of each of the following external environmental forces: political and legal, social, economic, technological.

8. How does timing affect the success of a corporate strategy? Give examples of products introduced at the wrong time. At the right time.

9. In your opinion, why do organizations frequently ignore their weaknesses when they assess their competitive position in the marketplace?

10. Michael Porter contends that an industry's environment affects each firm in that industry. List the variables that influence an organization's potential for success.

11. Suggest alternative strategies that are available to business firms. Explain each strategy.

12. In your opinion, should retailers develop strategies, or is strategic planning the domain of manufacturers?

13. Discuss the considerations that are crucial for successfully implementing a corporate strategy.

14. Why do most small businesses neglect strategic planning? Discuss.

MANAGEMENT CHALLENGE

Assume that you recently have been named plant manager for a small carpet manufacturer in northern Georgia. The company has been in business since 1974, but it has never developed a strategic plan of operations. Although pre-vious plant managers didn't see the value in strategic planning, you feel that it is imperative to develop and implement a strategy as soon as possible.

1. Describe the process you would go through in developing and implementing a strategic plan.

2. What kind of mission would a small carpet manufacturer likely formulate?

3. What external forces would affect your operations? Explain.

4. Given the nature of the carpet business, how would you expect to compete in the market-place? How would you determine the basis of competition?

5. In your opinion, how would strategic planning give you an advantage over your compet-itors? Discuss.

CASE 5.1

G.M. Plans to Reorganize Its Product Lines[21]

On January 10, 1984, Roger B. Smith, chair-person of General Motors Corporation, announced a dramatic reorganization of the product lines of America's largest automobile manufacturer. The action was not the first bold decision made by the man who runs GM: his Saturn project was launched to build a 45 MPG model; he reached agreement with Toyota to build 250,000 cars a year in a previously closed Fremont, California, plant; and he had arranged for Nissan to build cars for GM's Australian subsidiary.

The year before Smith took the reins at GM, the company had lost $76 million. But since his arrival, the company has prospered. The turn-around came as a result of plant closings; cost-cutting through consolidations, modernization programs, layoffs, and wage concessions; and a general upturn in the economy.

Smith's reorganization proposal was to con-solidate the five GM car divisions into two groups—one selling small cars and the other selling large models. The plan called for com-bining Chevrolet and Pontiac into a small-car grouping that would sell nothing larger than intermediate-size models. Buick, Oldsmobile, and Cadillac would be combined for large car production. Each group, by itself, would be larger than Ford or Chrysler. The products would continue to be marketed under the exist-ing brand names, but the five car divisions would exist as marketing arms of the two new groups.

Smith's reorganization plan can be attrib-uted to the "blurring" of the company's car lines, which began in the 1970s when GM ordered its divisions to use the same basic models as a cost-saving measure. It didn't take consumers long to realize that they could buy a Buick or Olds-mobile for only a few hundred dollars more than a Chevrolet. Analysts contend that GM's look-alike models confused buyers and contrib-uted to the decrease in GM's market share.

The planned reorganization represents a significant departure from the organization created by Alfred P. Sloan, Jr., who served as president of GM from 1921 to 1956. Smith's radical organizational changes were aimed at several objectives: improving product quality, producing new models on schedule, effectively competing with Japanese imports, and achieving greater cost control.

Questions

1. Do you consider Smith's planned reorganization of GM to be a modification of its basic strategy? Why or why not?

2. Which of the following generic-competitive strategies reflects the approach announced by Smith: least-cost strategy, differentiation, niche strategy? Explain.

CASE 5.2

Apple Computer's Japanese Connection Flops[22]

In 1977, Apple Computer had the Japanese personal computer market all to itself when it became the first manufacturer to sell a personal computer there. Had Apple developed a logical, comprehensive strategy to accomplish its mission in this overseas market, it would likely be No. 1 in Japan today. At least, that's the view of many critics.

Unfortunately for Apple Computer, though, its plans to dominate the personal computer market in Japan didn't materialize. Apple computers arrived with keyboards that didn't work, packaging was shoddy, and Japanese manuals weren't provided. The biggest problem, however, was Apple's refusal to develop a personal computer that processes *kanji,* the complex characters used in writing Japanese. As a result, Apple sales in Japan have been dismal. Few Japanese even recognize the Apple name.

Other faults are cited by the Japanese. Dealers say that Apples are too expensive, often selling for twice the price of similar Japanese models. Promotion is also weak. Apple seldom advertises and frequently fails to display its computers at shows. It even charged software developers for technical information instead of subsidizing software development.

Recognizing its errors, Apple is now attempting to turn things around. For example, it is looking for Japanese nationals to fill its top positions in its Tokyo subsidiary, and it has subsidized a software firm to write programs that will allow existing Macintosh models to handle Japanese. Even so, many observers contend that Apple's first entry into the Japanese market was so bungled that nothing can change the company's bad reputation.

Questions

1. What were the major weaknesses in Apple's strategy to expand into the Japanese market?

2. Critics contend that Apple opted for short-term success at the expense of long-term business ties. Do you agree?

CHAPTER OUTLINE

Types of Decisions

The Decision-Making Process

Is Decision Making a Science or an Art?

Decision Making Under Different Conditions
 Decisions Under Certainty
 Decisions Under Risk
 Decisions Under Uncertainty
 Maximin and Minimax • *Maximax* • *Regret*

Individual versus Group Decision Making

Committees and Decision Making
 How Committees Are Used
 Advantages of Committee Decision Making
 Disadvantages of Committee Decision Making

Creativity in Decision Making
 Personality Traits of Creative People
 The Evolution of Creativity
 Techniques for Enhancing Creative Decision Making
 Brainstorming • *Synectics* • *Delphi Technique* • *Fishbowling* •
 Didactic Interaction

Why Do Managers Make Poor Decisions?

Managerial Decision Making

M A N A G E M E N T   I N   A C T I O N

Which Way to Go?

On a cold winter day in the early 1970s, the chief executive of a large, New England-based electronics company sat with his immediate subordinates around a walnut table in the boardroom. They had a tough decision to make: Should they plunge deeper into the computer industry?

The management of the company's computer division had asked permission to develop, produce, and market a mainframe computer with a capacity larger than anything the company had attempted before. If the plan were approved, the company could wind up with $300 million worth of shipments and an operating profit of $75 million within three years.[1]

Despite the rosy projections, the senior executives had reservations about making the move. There were several problems. First, the economy was in a mild recession. Second, the proposal would bring the company into direct competition with other mainframe producers such as IBM and Honeywell. Because of this, it would require a bigger marketing effort than any they had ever undertaken. Another problem was that encouraging such a project would take the company away from familiar areas. On the other hand, the executives were concerned that killing the project would hurt the morale of the managers who had proposed it.

At about the same time, another chief executive sat with his principal subordinates in an office overlooking Lake Michigan and the Chicago skyline. The top management of a major consumer products company, they faced a different, but equally complex problem. They had just received an offer of $250 million in cash for their one industrial products division. Should they accept?[2]

137

They had been committed to getting out of this business for several years because it did not fit their self-image as a consumer products company. They had even assigned one of their most capable managers the job of improving the division's profits to make it more attractive to potential buyers. The offer was the best they had received, but still not big enough for everyone in the room. Some of the executives pointed to the fact that the division was generating returns comparable to the average of the corporation's other businesses. Others argued that the offer probably was the best they'd get. The sale could finance the company's long-standing goal of acquiring and expanding a small chain of retail outlets. Without the sale, the acquisition would require borrowing or an exchange of stock, which management preferred to avoid.

Regardless of their position, the executives shared a concern for their employees. Would the division's managers and other employees find the buyer a good employer? What would the sale signal to managers and employees in other divisions about top management's commitment to them and to their careers?

Preview

The managers of these two companies were involved in **decision making,** the process of choosing one course of action from all the available alternatives. Because managers are continually confronted with opportunities and problems, they must constantly analyze the effect of different decisions on their organizations and select the alternative that will move the firm toward its stated objectives. The nature of the decision-making process will be analyzed thoroughly in this chapter. After studying it you will understand:

✔ The types of decisions managers must make

✔ The steps in the decision-making process

✔ The debate over whether decision making is a science or an art

✔ Decision making under different conditions

✔ Individual versus group decision making

✔ Committees and decision making

✔ Creativity in decision making

✔ Why managers make poor decisions

Types of Decisions

Decisions like those we just showed you are the kind that executives of large, industrial corporations make every day. Not all decisions are so monumental or time consuming, however. Several authors believe that there are two types of decision situations—"programmed" and "nonprogrammed"[3]—used by managers to solve problems.

Programmed decisions are the kind that managers face again and again. These decisions are "programmable" because a specific procedure can be worked out to resolve them based on experience in similar situations. Once a standard procedure has been established, it can be used to treat all like situations. For example, a retailer may establish a stock reorder point for certain merchandise. When the level of inventory reaches that point, the decision to place an order is routine.

Programmed decisions in repetitive situations

Programmed decisions usually involve an organization's everyday operational and administrative activities. They are found primarily at the middle and lower levels of management. Data used in making a programmed decision usually are complete and well defined. Participants know the details and agree on how to resolve the problem. Senior-level management usually is not involved with particular decisions like this, but may be interested in the results of a series of such decisions over a period of time.

Nonprogrammed decisions are used to resolve nonrecurring problems. No well-established procedure exists for handling them, primarily because managers do not have experience to draw upon. In contrast to programmed decisions, available data are usually incomplete. Moreover, people involved in the decision-making process may disagree on how the situation should be handled. Nonprogrammable decisions are commonly found at the middle and top levels of management and often are related to an organization's policy-making activities. Whether to add a product to the existing product line, to reorganize the company, or to acquire another firm are examples of nonprogrammed decisions.

Examples of nonprogrammed decisions

Such terms may suggest that all decisions fall into one category or the other. Actually, most fall between the two. A continuum of decision situations exists, ranging from those that are highly structured to those that are unstructured. Situations between the two extremes are partially structured.[4] As the name suggests, in a **partially structured situation,** only a part is well structured. Typically, although the manager has a great deal of data available, the final choice is not obvious. Many intangibles are involved in the final choice. Therefore, the manager must base the ultimate decision on the data and supplementary factors, using judgment and experience. For example, a hospital wishing to improve patient care may adjust its patient-staff ratio (a programmable situation), reorganize its staff (a nonprogrammable situation), or both. Table 6.1 illustrates the continuum of decision situations from well-structured to ill-structured.

TABLE 6.1 Continuum of decision situations	WELL-STRUCTURED (PROGRAMMED)	PARTIALLY STRUCTURED	ILL-STRUCTURED (NONPROGRAMMED)
	1. Specification of decision procedure agreed in advance of resolution.	**1.** Only a part of decision process can be completely specified and structured.	**1.** Decision procedure cannot be completely structured in advance of resolution.
	2. Little managerial involvement at time of each resolution.	**2.** Manager makes final resolution from structured portion of his or her experience and from intuition.	**2.** Individuals resolve each situation on the basis of experience and judgment.
	3. Repeated resolutions with same data yield same results.	**3.** Different managers may agree on certain data but reach different conclusions.	**3.** Different managers may reach different conclusions.

Source: Adapted from K. J. Radford, *Modern Managerial Decision Making* © 1981, p. 9. Reprinted by permission of Prentice-Hall, Inc., Englewood Cliffs, New Jersey.

The Decision-Making Process

Management requires decision making

Decision making is part of every aspect of the manager's duties, which include planning, organizing, staffing, leading, and controlling. For example, managers can formulate planning objectives only after making decisions about the organization's basic mission. To accomplish the objectives within some time period, decisions must be made on what resources are required. When pursuing company objectives, management must make decisions on the division of labor and reporting relationships. Prospective staff members are identified and selected according to what the established positions require. The organization pursues its objectives through countless daily decisions required to make or sell the product or service. And decisions about whether to take corrective action when performance does not measure up to standards affect operations.[5] As Herbert Simon said, "Decision making is synonymous with managing."[6]

Managers devote more time to decision making as they move up the corporate ladder. Top executives spend most of their time on decision making, and their performance is judged by how well their decisions turn out. It is not surprising, therefore, that decision making has become a discipline in its own right.

The components of the decision-making process are shown in Figure 6.1.

As this diagram shows, the steps in the process are interrelated and normally in sequence rather than hit-or-miss. The steps are very important.

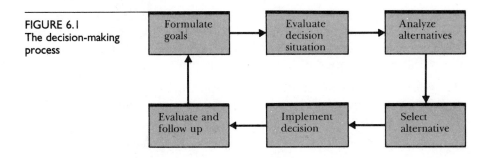

FIGURE 6.1
The decision-making process

Decision making is methodical

Success is measured by whether the objectives have been obtained. For example, without managerial goals, there is no basis for examining alternatives. Without the information obtained through such an evaluation, there are no alternatives to compare. Without a comparison of alternatives, the choice of a particular course of action is unlikely to yield the desired outcome. Without effective implementation of an alternative, it is unlikely that managerial objectives will be met. Finally, successfully implementing a decision is difficult without follow-up and control. Each step in the decision-making process must fall into place if the process is to work. A framework that organizes decision making is very important in formal organizations.[7] Let's take a closer look at each step illustrated in Figure 6.1.

1. *Formulate goals.* The decision-making process begins with the formulation of company goals. These goals may be related to profits, service, sales, costs, or any other measurable standard. For example, one company may state its objectives in terms of return on investment; another in terms of growth in revenues over the previous year.

2. *Evaluate decision situation.* The second step in the decision-making process is determining if the goal can be satisfied objectively, through a programmed decision, or if a nonprogrammed decision requiring the manager's judgment is required. For example, a goal related to minimizing inventory costs can be satisfied by using an inventory-control system that specifies the frequency and quantity of orders to replenish inventory. Other objectives, such as increasing sales or improving customer service, require human judgment.

Steps in the decision-making process

3. *Analyze alternatives.* Alternatives are various courses of action that may achieve the objective. For example, the objective of increasing profits may be achieved by reducing costs, increasing revenues, or a combination of the two. No one knows for certain how all alternatives will turn out, but the manager must be able to predict the results using all available information.

4. *Select alternative.* Based on the expected outcome, the manager must select the alternative that best meets the objective. The choice of alternatives is simple when outcomes can be measured precisely. However, uncertainty surrounds most decisions. It also may be impossible to quantify the expected outcome. In such circumstances, the preferences of the decision maker, intuition, and other variables influence the choice of alternatives.

5. *Implement decision.* Next, the manager puts the decision into operation. Implementation requires making task assignments, developing specific plans, and devising a means for assessing progress.

6. *Evaluate and follow up.* Having implemented the decision, the manager should compare the results of that course of action with the desired outcome and, if necessary, take corrective action to assure desired results.

Is Decision Making a Science or an Art?

There are two different schools of thought on the decision process—*analytical* and *intuitive*. **Analytic, or systematic, decision making** (sometimes called scientific decision making) is based on the theory that problem solving can be reduced to a systematic selection process. Proponents insist that decision theory should construct an ideal procedure for rational choice—a step-by-step, logical sequence for picking the best alternative as a solution to a business problem.

Intuitive decision making is based on the belief that good decision making is an art, not a science. Proponents contend that sound problem solving is largely intuitive and unconscious.[8] They argue that good problem diagnosis and decision making result from an esoteric blend of experience, imagination, intelligence, and feeling joined almost unconsciously.

Contrasting ways of making decisions

Considerable evidence suggests that managers use both approaches in solving problems and in making decisions. The analytical approach is more orderly, logical, and systematic; the intuitive approach is more prone to trial-and-error, or haphazard. McKenney and Keen's studies reveal significant differences in how the two types of decision makers approach problems.

Systematic decision makers tend to:

1. Look for a method and devise a plan for solving a problem.

2. Be very conscious of their approach.

3. Defend the quality of a solution largely in terms of the method.

4. Define the specific constraints of the problem early in the process.

5. Discard alternatives quickly.

6. Move through a process of increasing refinement of analysis.

7. Conduct an orderly search for additional information.

8. Complete any discrete step in analysis that they begin.

Intuitive decision makers tend to:

1. Keep the overall problem continuously in mind.

2. Redefine the problem frequently as they proceed.

3. Rely on hunches.

4. Defend a solution in terms of appropriateness.

5. Consider a number of alternatives at the same time.

6. Jump from one step in the process to another and back again.

7. Explore and abandon alternatives very quickly.[9]

The overriding question is, "Which approach is better?" Neither one is universally appropriate for all managers or all decision situations. The "best" approach depends on the nature of the problem, the type of management system, and a variety of other factors.

Decision Making Under Different Conditions

We have discussed programmed and nonprogrammed decisions. Another labeling scheme for decision making is to classify decisions according to the likelihood of the outcome, which often is determined by existing conditions. This approach distinguishes three different types of decisions:

Types of decisions

1. Decisions under certainty

2. Decisions under risk

3. Decisions under uncertainty

Decisions Under Certainty

Decisions under **certainty** are those in which the external conditions are identified and very predictable. An example of a decision under certainty would be someone investing money in a savings account of a FDIC-insured bank. Under these circumstances, the investor is assured of earning the established interest rate with no risk of losing the investment. Decision making under certainty seldom occurs, however, because external conditions seldom are perfectly predictable and because it is impossible to try to account for all possible influences on any given outcome.

Decisions Under Risk

Decisions under **risk** are those in which probabilities can be assigned to the expected outcomes of each alternative. These probabilities are determined either objectively or subjectively. The assignment of an objective probability is derived through historical data or past experience. Subjective probability is derived through general knowledge of the subject.

A popular approach to decision making under risk is the use of **decision trees,** which are graphic displays of all alternatives available to a manager. They can help the manager analyze alternatives and evaluate potential outcomes. A decision tree depicting decisions and outcomes in sequential order is illustrated in Figure 6.2. Looking at the figure, assume that Company A faces two decision alternatives: (1) work overtime or (2) buy new equipment. Assume that with either there will be: (1) a 60% chance that sales will increase 15% and (2) a 40% chance that sales will decrease as much as 10%.

Based on projected sales revenues and working capital requirements resulting from the choice of either of the decision alternatives, assume the net cash flow shown in Table 6.2 and in the figure. The data in Table 6.2 reveal that if sales increase, the decision to buy new equipment would result in the largest payoff. But if new equipment is purchased and sales decrease, the payoff would be less than if the demand were met by working overtime.[10] Figure 6.2 shows the probabilities associated with the various events.

Decision trees help managers

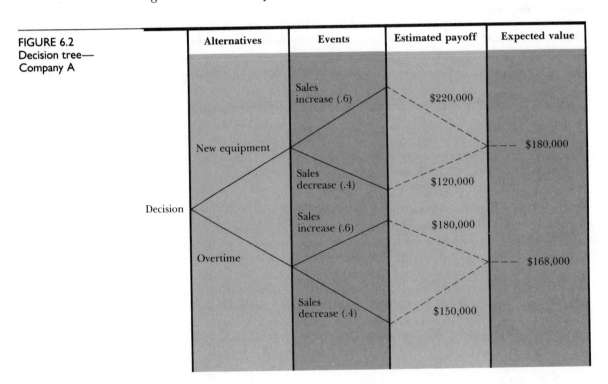

FIGURE 6.2
Decision tree—
Company A

TABLE 6.2
Net cash flow

EVENT	ALTERNATIVE	
	NEW EQUIPMENT	OVERTIME
15% increase in sales	+$220,000	+$180,000
10% decrease in sales	+$120,000	+$150,000

Likelihood of outcome is assessed

The probabilities associated with an increase or decrease in sales with the purchase of new equipment or working overtime are multiplied by the estimated payoff to arrive at an expected value for each alternative. Since the probabilities associated with a sales increase or decrease relate to two mutually exclusive events, they are unconditional and, therefore, additive.[11] That is, the probabilities associated with all possible outcomes must total 100%. The expected value for the purchase of new equipment, regardless of a sales increase or decrease, is:

$$(.6 \times \$220,000) + (.4 \times \$120,000) = \$180,000$$

The expected value for the overtime alternative is:

$$(.6 \times \$180,000) + (.4 \times \$150,000) = \$168,000$$

In conclusion, the purchase of new equipment is clearly a better alternative than the overtime option.

Decisions Under Uncertainty

In decisions under **uncertainty,** probabilities cannot be assigned to surrounding conditions. Some conditions that are uncontrollable by management include competition, government regulations, technological advances, the overall economy, and the social and cultural tendencies of society. To deal with uncertainty, the decision maker must be careful not to focus on a symptom, but must discover root causes. Unless the basic cause is discovered and acted on properly, the solution will not be long lasting. Uncertainty is associated with the consequences of alternatives, not the alternatives themselves. With this in mind, managers must devise a common method of measuring the consequences.

Attitudes influence decision making

Managers' attitudes toward risk influence the way they make decisions under uncertain conditions. A conservative person who is wary of taking risks probably would concentrate on the possible adverse outcomes in choosing alternatives. Someone with a more open risk-taking attitude most likely would stress the possible beneficial outcomes in a decision.

For example, consider a manager of a warehouse that serves a growing market. The manager must make a decision about expanding the warehouse and has three alternatives: (1) build a large extension, (2) build a small extension, and (3) remain in the present facility. The choice among these alternatives is most influenced by the possible future size of the market for the product. Assume that the product's future market can be described as either strong, medium, or soft and that it is possible to assess the profit for each of the three. Table 6.3 shows the profits that would result from building either a small or large warehouse extension, given the possible future states of the market.

Staying with the present warehouse would provide no change in net profit in each possible future market condition. Building a large extension would give a high profit if the market is strong, but a big loss if the market is soft. Building a small extension would bring the biggest profit increase in a medium future market, but also would increase profits in both of the other market situations.[12]

Maximin and Minimax   When a manager determines the minimum payoff for each alternative and then chooses the alternative with the biggest profit, it is called **maximin** decision making. If attempting to minimize cost instead, the manager would determine maximum cost of each alternative and choose the one that would cost less. This is called **minimax** decision making.

Maximin and minimax are highly conservative approaches to decision making that might be selected by a decision maker who dislikes taking risks.

Maximax   A risk-taking manager might opt for another alternative—a **maximax** strategy. This involves determining the maximum payoff for each alternative and choosing the one with the biggest payoff of all. In this approach, the warehouse manager would select Alternative 3 in Table 6.3—the construction of a large extension.

Regret   Another decision-making strategy focuses on the potential losses associated with alternative courses of action. **Regret** represents the loss that a manager suffers because he or she does not know the future at the time the

TABLE 6.3
Changing profit levels for warehouse expansion

ALTERNATIVES	POSSIBLE FUTURE STATES OF THE MARKET		
	SOFT	MEDIUM	STRONG
1. Stay with existing warehouse	0	0	0
2. Build small extension	$100,000	$300,000	$150,000
3. Build large extension	−$400,000	$100,000	$1,000,000

decision is made. In other words, it is the cost of lost opportunity.[13] Table 6.4 shows the "regret" for each alternative in future market states in the warehouse problem.

If the market turns soft, the warehouse manager should have chosen Alternative 2—zero regret—since the small extension could handle such a market's demands. If Alternative 1 had been selected, the regret is the $100,000 profit the company would have made by building the small extension, and so on.

Individual versus Group Decision Making

Whenever a decision must be made, the manager needs to decide whether to make it personally or to involve other people. To a great extent, the nature of the problem and the impact of the decision determine whether a manager will be individualistic (authoritative) or group oriented (participative). Continental Airlines chairperson Frank Lorenzo, a highly authoritative leader, is featured in On the Job on page 149.

The manager's approach to making the decision depends on a number of variables. Some of the questions that shape a manager's decision-making style are these:

- Will the group generate a quality decision?

- Will my decision be accepted by the group?

- Can the group offer information of which I am unaware? For example, does an employee have knowledge of a personal nature of which I am unaware?

- How does the group view its role in decision making?

- How quickly must a decision be made?

- Who is affected by the decision?

- What impact will the decision have on the group?

Group versus individual decision making

The manager leaning toward participative decision making should be aware of both the benefits and shortcomings of group action. A number of studies have compared the performance of individuals and groups in solving problems. The results of these studies show that groups tend to make more "correct" decisions but that individuals make decisions more quickly.[14] There are several reasons for the comparative accuracy of group decision making. First, social interaction provides an error-correcting mechanism and fosters competition among members for respect. Also, groups possess more knowledge than any single individual does; consequently, they can approach prob-

TABLE 6.4
Regret values—
warehouse problem

	POSSIBLE FUTURE STATES OF THE MARKET		
ALTERNATIVES	SOFT	MEDIUM	STRONG
1. Stay with existing warehouse	$100,000	$300,000	$1,000,000
2. Build small extension	0	0	0
3. Build large extension	$500,000	$200,000	0

lems from different directions and bring insights to the problem that otherwise would not come to light.[15] In Figure 6.3, Victor Vroom identifies five approaches in the continuum from individual to group decision making.

Groups, however, may not be as creative as individuals are. Two studies seeking to determine the relative creativity of groups and individuals revealed that individuals produce more ideas than groups do in "brainstorming" sessions. Moreover, the ideas generated by individuals were better and more unique.[16] The reason appears to be that group members feel inhibited in indiscriminately voicing ideas that may seem absurd. Even though brainstorming should encourage all group members to be uninhibited, people are afraid of sounding foolish and tend to censor themselves.[17]

Groups may be more inclined than individuals are to take risks. Many people, especially business managers, contend that groups make more conservative decisions than individuals do. But experiments suggest just the opposite—groups tend to take more risks.[18]

Not all groups perform equally well in decision making. The performance of a group depends on the characteristics of its members and the structure of the group itself. Research studies on group decision making have resulted in some important findings:

1. The sociability of group members appears to be related to performance. For example, group members who interact regularly have higher levels of output than do those who isolate themselves from social interaction.

2. Age and organizational position of group members affects group performance. That is, younger, lower-level managers solve certain types of problems more quickly and accurately than do older, higher-level managers.

3. Medium-sized groups (five to eleven members) tend to produce more accurate decisions than smaller or larger groups.

4. Small groups (two to five members) reach consensus more quickly than do larger groups.[19]

ON THE JOB

Continental Airlines Chairperson Makes Tough Decisions

Frank Lorenzo, chairperson of Continental Airlines, is known in the airline industry as a manager who gets things done. Some say he's doing what is necessary to keep his company aloft in a highly competitive business. Others call him vicious.

Lorenzo broke new ground in 1983 by filing for protection under Chapter 11 of federal bankruptcy laws so that the airline could get out from under labor contracts that Lorenzo believed were oppressive. And while the company's mechanics, flight attendants, and pilots were on strike, he hired people willing to cross the picket lines at less pay than they ordinarily receive. He employed pilots at $43,000 a year— $30,000 less than the average pay they earned before the strike began.

In the first quarter of 1984, Continental reported its first operating profit in five years. Later that year, the airline announced plans to upgrade its service. It added Boston, Dallas–Fort Worth, and San Jose, California, to its domestic flights and initiated flights from Guam to Hong Kong and Taiwan. By 1987, Continental had become successful enough to purchase People Express.

One pilot opposes the Continental chairperson's tactics. He describes Lorenzo as uncompromising and unwilling to work out problems with employees. Others have high praise for Lorenzo. They believe he's willing to make hard decisions that are essential if the airline is to survive.

Source: Michelle Osborn, "He's Tough: Friends and Foes Agree on Continental's Chairman," *USA Today,* June 20, 1984.

Committees and Decision Making

The responsibility for making a decision usually rests with one manager, though he or she very rarely actually makes the decision unaided. Even President Harry Truman, who had an office plaque reading "The Buck Stops Here," did not make all of his decisions without counsel. In the most common method of group decision making, managers draw on the expertise of different elements of the organization. For example, a manager can obtain accounting data from the controller, legal advice from an attorney, and technical advice from

Getting the right information

the engineering department. The successful decision maker must be able to contact the right person for the information needed. That person's ability and position in the organization determine whether he or she is the right person to contact. The wise decision maker not only tries to find out which people have the needed information but also cultivates a personal relationship with

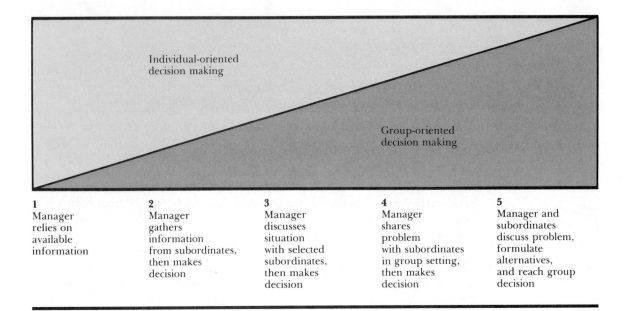

1	2	3	4	5
Manager relies on available information	Manager gathers information from subordinates, then makes decision	Manager discusses situation with selected subordinates, then makes decision	Manager shares problem with subordinates in group setting, then makes decision	Manager and subordinates discuss problem, formulate alternatives, and reach group decision

FIGURE 6.3
Vroom's decision continuum (*Source:* Adapted from Victor H. Vroom, "A New Look at Managerial Decision Making," *Organizational Dynamics*, Spring 1973, p. 67.) Copyright 1973 American Management Association, New York. All rights reserved.

them so that both benefit. Guidance often comes through the formal chain of command; however, the day-to-day information that permits the organization to operate effectively comes from informal contacts and interaction.

Sometimes members of an organization are formally brought together to form committees to advise managers on courses of action or to make decisions. Numerous committees exist within most organizations, ranging from groups that are formal, permanent, and powerful to those that are relatively informal, temporary, and powerless.

Types of committees

Committees generally fall into three categories: (1) formal (standing), (2) ad hoc, and (3) informal (temporary). A **formal (standing) committee** is characterized by regular meeting times, defined goals, and membership created on some systematic basis. The issues it deals with are recurring, are customarily specialized, and usually are significant to the organization. An **ad hoc committee** deals with important but nonrecurring issues requiring high-level problem solving. Such a committee, often called a task force, is created to accomplish specific goals. The committee is dissolved when these goals have been achieved. An **informal (temporary) committee** is formed to deal with relatively unimportant matters that often require no particular resolution. For example, an informal committee might be created to plan the annual Christmas party. The basic difference between an ad hoc committee and an informal committee is the significance of the mission.

How Committees Are Used

Committees and authority

Several studies have examined the use and functions of committees in industry. One study showed that seventy-eight of the ninety-three different companies examined had general management committees. Two-thirds of these committees received authority from the president of the company. The other one-third was appointed by, and received authority from, the board of directors. A quarter of these committees were considered authoritative and another quarter nonauthoritative. The remaining 50% had some authority in specific areas of operations but not enough to warrant being called authoritative.[20]

Uses of committees

Another survey revealed that the existence of a formal, standing, committee to some extent is related to the size of the company. Only 63.5% of firms with fewer than 250 employees had one or more regular standing committees, while 93.8% of firms with more than ten thousand employees reported one or more standing committees. The same study also reported that top executives are on more committees than managers at lower levels are and that these executives are more favorable toward committees than lower-level managers are. The average executive spends nearly three and one-half hours a week in committee meetings, serves on three different committees, and considers committee work appropriate. According to the study, corporations use committees for all kinds of purposes. Two-thirds of the general management committees plan and make policies, and almost as many make decisions. Nearly half of the general management committees advise and review operations as well. Most marketing committees review proposals but do very little policy making. Production committees usually plan, but sometimes make decisions as well. Research and development committees tend to work on major problems, and their contributions are considered highly beneficial to the decision-making process.[21]

Advantages of Committee Decision Making

Committees can be used to achieve a number of organizational goals. The more obvious benefits of committee decision making are similar to those of group decision making:

1. *Broader background.* Perhaps the most compelling reason for using a committee to solve a problem is the fact that a group can bring a variety of opinions on how to solve the problem. Facts related to the problem are analyzed more thoroughly because members with specialized backgrounds tend to ask probing questions in their areas of expertise. If the problem is broad, the expertise of a group can cover a larger area than that of an individual.

2. *Check on authority.* A committee can be used to solve problems when top management does not wish to delegate too much authority to a single person.

3. *Special interest groups.* Another reason to use committees is to include special interest groups so that they will support the resulting decision. This is particularly appropriate when a person or group within the organization finds fault with every decision. Letting them participate in finding the solution makes it difficult for them to criticize the final decision.

4. *Coordination.* Much of the work in an organization flows across department lines. The decisions made by an executive in one department often affect activities in other departments. Committees are one way to approach the problem of coordinating departments. Managers gain insight into problems faced by other departments in this way.

5. *Information exchange.* Information can be exchanged effectively through a committee. All people affected by a particular decision can learn about it at the same time. Decisions and instructions can be given out uniformly and clarified, if necessary. Speaking to someone face to face appears to be a more effective form of communication than writing reports and memoranda. Questions can be answered, and committee members can learn others' attitudes and opinions about particular problems.

6. *Motivation/morale.* Since committees allow many people to participate in decision making, they can be very effective in motivating employees. People who take part in a decision usually are enthusiastic about executing it.[22]

7. *Management development.* Committees can be important in executive development. At committee meetings, younger managers observe more seasoned executives in action and have a chance to develop more reliable judgments. Junior executives can be evaluated for future vacancies at the same time.[23]

Disadvantages of Committee Decision Making

Criticisms of committees and their disadvantages result from their misuse and from weaknesses inherent in the committee system. Some of the weaknesses and disadvantages of committee decision making are as follows:

1. *Cost.* The cost of committees comes not only from each labor-hour spent in committee service but also from losses incurred when timeliness is important. Committees are very time consuming since they are a forum in which all members have a right to express a point of view no matter how trivial. There also may be travel, lodging, clerical, and space costs.

2. *Compromise decisions.* A "yes" by some committee members and a "no" by others comes out as a group "maybe." Discussions often don't settle differences of opinion but, instead, submerge them in compromise. Committee recommendations seem to lean toward the familiar. At times, ideas are accepted because no one can think of an objection at the moment. The conventional procedure for committees is to require a majority vote in favor of a decision to pass it. This may lead to decisions that are watered-down compromises.

3. *Failure to reach a decision.* Despite the high hopes of its members, any committee may find it impossible to agree on a course of action. If a meeting is extremely long, the committee may adjourn without deciding on any course of action at all.

4. *Dominance of a few.* In any group, some people have stronger personalities than others do. If these people dominate a group, its opinion is jeopardized. Any member of a committee—even one on the minority side of an issue—can take a strong leadership role and destroy the committee's purpose. This may occur when a committee wants to come to a unanimous decision.

Disadvantages of committees

5. *Political decisions.* Committees are to some extent political. Members often are chosen to represent certain departments, not for their qualifications. This can be a weakness, since members usually are concerned with what is good for their departments. In such cases, committee decisions on important issues are expressions of politics rather than of merit.

6. *Lack of accountability.* Another disadvantage of committee decision making is that no one person is fully accountable for carrying out the final decision because no one is fully accountable for making it. The individual, though obligated to play an active role in achieving a group consensus, cannot be held personally accountable for the recommendations or decisions made by the group.[24]

7. *Guided decisions.* The chairperson tends to push for a conclusion when a committee appears to be going in circles. When this happens, the rest of the committee members sometimes back off and let the leader make the decision. This destroys the committee concept, and members feel railroaded into submission. In other instances, opposition to the leader's direction develops, and two or more polarized viewpoints emerge. Many members may view themselves in a win-lose position. It then becomes impossible to achieve total team support for the chosen course of action.[25]

Creativity in Decision Making

Most of us associate creativity with brilliant ideas, dramatic discoveries, and original insights—the products of genius. But the evidence overwhelmingly suggests that creativity actually is a relatively common resource that can be harnessed by managers in virtually every phase of decision making. Several methods have been developed to increase the output of good, original ideas by people working both alone and in groups. The Manager's Notebook on page 154 presents one method. New, useful ideas can be readily translated into revenues and profits.

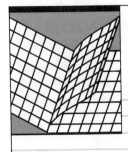

THE MANAGER'S NOTEBOOK

Unlocking Creativity in Employees

No person can have too many creative ideas, and no company has too many creative people.

The trouble is, we've been taught to hide our creativity. Schools, parents, and employers generally reward people who follow the rules and give the "right" answers, not the people who shake things up.

There are ways an employer can train people to bring creativity to problem solving, however. One way is to lead them through a six-step program:

1. Demystify creativity. Help your employees realize that they can be creative if they let themselves. Ask them to list ten personal achievements they consider creative.

2. Teach them never to impose boundaries on themselves, but to go beyond the obvious, trying new ways of thinking, and generating numerous ideas to end up with a few good ideas. Give them the nine-dot exercise shown here and ask them to link the dots with four interconnecting straight lines.

3. Help them learn to differentiate between irritants and problems. Introduce them to the steps in the creative problem-solving process: define the problem, gather relevant information, explore all ways to solve the problem, analyze the advantages and disadvantages of each option, use intuition to help in the process before taking action, make a decision, fantasize the worst and the best that could happen, implement and evaluate the decision. Have them list some irritants or concerns and turn them into a problem statement.

4. Remind your employees that good ideas come from generating many ideas and that they must suspend judgment on their ideas to allow their creativity to flow. Warm them up by asking them to give as many uses as possible for one object in the room; then have them go to work on the problem they defined in the previous step.

5. Encourage them to synthesize and analyze. Take two different objects, such as a pen and a clock, and ask them to combine the strengths of each into a new invention.

6. Give them a way to discover their own creative thinking pattern. One technique is to ask them to fill in a chart identifying every idea, when it came to them, and what they were doing when it came to them. Patterns that spark creativity can be identified this way.

Source: Jerry Conrath, "The Imagination Harvest: Training People to Solve Problems Creatively," *Supervisory Management*, September 1985, pp. 6–10. Copyright © 1985 American Management Association, New York. All rights reserved.

Personality Traits of Creative People

Not all creative people are alike, but most exhibit most of the following characteristics:

1. Independence of judgment

2. Personal complexity

3. Preference for complexity over simplicity

4. Preference for ambiguity over clarity

5. Self-assertiveness

6. Reluctance to control impulses[26]

Creative people also tend to be rebellious, disorderly, and exhibitionists.[27] But the primary feature of creativity appears to be the ability to recall, redefine, and adapt information to unfamiliar uses. The abilities most important for creative thinking can be grouped into two categories—"divergent production" and "transformation."[28] **Divergent production** is the ability to generate numerous alternatives for accomplishing an objective. **Transformation** is the ability to revise what is known in order to produce new forms and patterns; that is, to reinterpret and reorganize information.

The Evolution of Creativity

As shown in Figure 6.4, creativity is the result of a process that has several phases.[29]

Most major discoveries have resulted from the process described in Figure 6.4. But there are exceptions to this process, and the phases sometimes do not fall in this exact order.

Techniques for Enhancing Creative Decision Making

Creativity can be encouraged

How can creativity be encouraged? Does one have to be born creative, or can creativity be learned? Obviously, people differ in their creativity. Many of the traits associated with creativity undoubtedly are innate. Even so, several techniques have successfully demonstrated that creativity can be encouraged dramatically.

Brainstorming Although it has limitations (see page 148), **brainstorming** is a problem-solving technique designed to produce numerous ideas in a short period. The process usually takes place in a classroom-like setting, where the problem and all suggested solutions can be written down. All ideas are welcomed, regardless of their absurdity. None of the ideas can be criticized or evaluated until the brainstorming session is over. The goals are quantity, not quality, and limited inhibition. Participants are encouraged to build on other ideas or to refine or modify other suggestions.

A brainstorming session typically lasts about an hour, but some run only fifteen to twenty minutes. A single session can produce fifty to seventy-five new ideas, although many may not be worth serious consideration. Afterward, the ideas that need further evaluation are separated from those that must be discarded.

Synectics **Synectics,** a Greek word for "joining together," is another free-association method for generating creative solutions to a problem. It is somewhat more structured than brainstorming. Synectics has four basic aspects:

1. The problem is given a thorough, technical review to familiarize each participant with all its aspects before making suggestions.

2. A group leader selects a key part of the problem to focus on.

3. Participants are encouraged to suggest novel ideas.

4. The group must include one technical expert who evaluates the feasibility of ideas and discards those without merit immediately.[30]

Methods for enhancing creativity

When compared with brainstorming, synectics has both strong and weak features. Less time is needed for analysis because ideas are evaluated immediately. Since the group focuses on one segment, a much more complex problem can be evaluated systematically. The major drawback of synectics is that the group's so-called technical expert may reject ideas simply because he or she is unfamiliar with them.

Delphi Technique The Delphi technique (which was first mentioned in Chapter 4) is a relatively complex problem-solving method. It was originated by Dr. Olaf Helmer and Norman Dalkey and first described in 1963.[31] Although primarily intended for use in long-range forecasting, it also can be used to

FIGURE 6.4
The process of
creativity

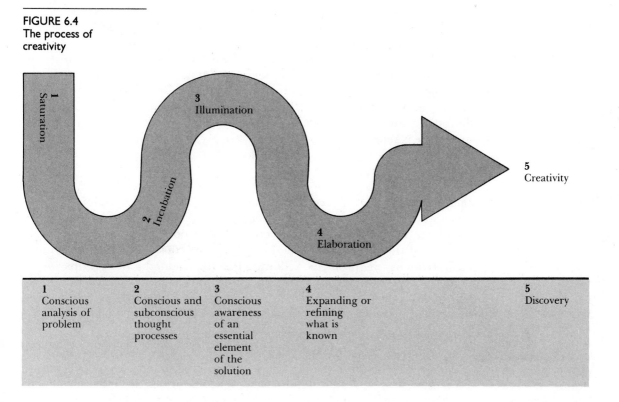

| 1 Saturation | 2 Incubation | 3 Illumination | 4 Elaboration | 5 Creativity |

| 1 Conscious analysis of problem | 2 Conscious and subconscious thought processes | 3 Conscious awareness of an essential element of the solution | 4 Expanding or refining what is known | 5 Discovery |

generate creative solutions to unique problems in an organization. It is designed to develop a range of possible alternatives that reflect the collective judgment of the participants. Perhaps the Delphi technique's most significant feature is that it uses experts without requiring them to be in one place at the same time.

The first step in the process is formulating questions, which the experts must answer in writing. For example, the experts may be asked, "How can this product be modified to make it more convenient to use?" or "What kinds of products will consumers want in twenty years that they don't want now?" Participants are usually given several days to respond.

Next, a summary of the answers is distributed to all participants. Since the answers are anonymous, no one can determine who suggested what. Each participant is asked to submit additional suggestions and to comment on the merit of the suggestions.

In the third phase, the participants' new suggestions and comments are distributed. Again, each participant is allowed to comment on the suggestions and to revise his or her answers.

The final step requires that the program leader give the participants a review of the comments, together with specific answers to the original question. Participants may modify their answers again if they wish.

Fishbowling   **Fishbowling** is a decision-making technique that lets one person present a solution to a problem in a "fishbowl" setting. Participants are seated in a circle—a bowllike configuration. A single chair is in the middle of the circle. First, a person who knows a lot about the problem is invited to sit in the chair. The expert tells the others a solution. Participants may ask the presenter questions but may not speak to anyone else. Thus, all attention is focused on the person in the "fishbowl." Once the presenter's viewpoints are thoroughly understood, he or she leaves, a second expert is called on, and the procedure is repeated. Any number of people can sit in the fishbowl. After all experts have expressed their views, the decision-making group works on choosing a course of action.

Didactic Interaction   **Didactic interaction** is a rarely-used procedure because it is appropriate only in certain situations. The problem must require a go/no-go type of decision—to buy or not, to sell or not. One group must list all the pros of the problem and another group, the cons. Then the two groups meet to discuss the problem. Following the discussion, the two groups switch sides. In a second meeting, the participants find holes in their own original arguments. Through this interchange, mutually accepted facts can be pinpointed and used to solve the problem, and a decision can be made.

Why Do Managers Make Poor Decisions?

All managers recognize the importance of making sound business decisions. Yet most managers readily admit having made poor decisions that hurt their company or their own effectiveness. Why do managers make mistakes? Why don't decisions always result in achieving some desired goal? Making the wrong decision can result from any one of these decision-making errors:

- *Lack of Adequate Time.* Waiting until the last minute to make a decision often prevents considering all alternatives. It also hampers thorough analyses of the alternatives.

- *Failure to Define Goals.* Objectives cannot be attained unless they are clearly defined. They should be explicitly stated so that the manager can see the relationship between a decision and the desired result.

- *Using Unreliable Sources of Information.* A decision is only as good as the information on which it is based. Poor sources of information always result in poor decisions.

Reasons for poor decisions

- *Fear of Consequences.* Managers often are reluctant to make bold, comprehensive decisions because they fear disastrous results. A "play it safe" attitude sometimes limits a manager's effectiveness.

- *Focusing on Symptoms Rather Than on Causes.* Addressing the symptoms of a problem will not solve it. Taking aspirin for a toothache may provide temporary relief, but if an abscess causes the pain, the problem will persist. Business managers too often focus on the results of problems instead of the causes.

- *Reliance on Hunch and Intuition.* Intuition, judgment, and "feel" are important assets to the decision maker. But a manager who permits intuition to outweigh scientific evidence is likely to make a poor decision.

- *Failure to Implement Decision.* Decisions are a means to an end; they are not the end of the process. Having made a decision, a manager must then assign duties, establish timetables, and evaluate results.[32]

Sometimes a manager's decision isn't exactly "poor," but it still doesn't produce optimal results. Less-than-optimal decisions can have three causes: (1) bounded rationality, (2) suboptimization, and (3) unforeseen changes in the business environment.

Bounded rationality imposes limits on a decision, such as that it should be economical or logistically practical, for example. These limits serve as a screening device, eliminating some of the alternatives. The manager must choose from the options that have filtered through the restrictions. The overall optimal decision may no longer be a valid option when using this method. The decision maker simply selects the best alternative, given various specifications that must be met.

Suboptimization is a manager's tendency to operate solely in the interests of his or her department rather than in the interests of the company as a whole. In making a decision, the department manager cannot be so self-centered as to ignore the effects of the action on other areas. The key is to improve the company's performance, not just the performance of one department.

Unforeseen changes in the business environment also cause less-than-optimal decisions. This particular pitfall is difficult to avoid because of the vast number of variables that the manager must consider. Regardless of how thorough a manager is in considering all possibilities, no one can predict the future with absolute certainty. The best way of dealing with unexpected shifts in the business environment is to prepare contingency plans for unforeseen changes. Such planning at least gives the manager a point from which to work and a way to save valuable time.

Review

✓ *The types of decisions managers must make.* Decision making is at the core of everything managers do; consequently, their success depends on their decision-making skills. The decisions that managers make vary greatly. Programmed decisions are repetitive and based solely on objective data, whereas nonprogrammed decisions involve new situations where there is no "hard" data. Most decisions, however, are partially structured; that is, they are based on measurable data, but the manager must use judgment and personal preference in choosing among the alternatives.

✓ *The steps in the decision-making process.* Decision making is a systematic process with six steps: (1) formulating goals, (2) evaluating the decision situation, (3) analyzing alternatives, (4) selecting one alternative from those available, (5) implementing the decision, and (6) evaluating the results and following up. The success of this process is measured by whether the objectives in Step 1 were achieved.

✓ *Is decision making a science or an art?* Not all managers make decisions the same way. Some believe that decision making can be reduced to a systematic process that will yield a rational choice and optimal results. Others contend that effective decision making is partly based on intuition, hunch, and judgment. Because of the uncertainty surrounding a decision, they strive for satisfactory, rather than optimum, results.

✓ *Decision making under different conditions.* Decisions can be classified according to the likelihood of the outcome: (1) decisions under certainty, (2) decisions under risk, and (3) decisions under uncertainty. The outcome of decisions under certainty is known. Decisions under risk are those for which probabilities can be assigned to the expected outcome of each alternative, and decisions under uncertainty are those for which probabilities cannot be assigned to surrounding conditions.

Managers differ in their decision-making behavior. Some are conservative by nature and are unwilling to take huge gambles. Others are basically optimistic and more willing to take chances. Risk-averse managers often opt to minimize their maximum losses, whereas risk takers seek to maximize their potential gains.

✓ *Individual versus group decision making.* The responsibility for making a decision usually rests with one person; nevertheless, most managers consult other people before making a decision. One manager rarely has all the information needed to make an effective decision.

✓ *Committees and decision making.* Because of the advantages of pooling human resources, most organizations use groups or committees to help make decisions. Some committees are strictly advisory; others have decision-making authority. Committees can be broadly classified as formal (standing), ad hoc, and informal (temporary).

✓ *Creativity in decision making.* A number of approaches can be used to encourage creative ideas and decisions: brainstorming, synectics, the Delphi technique, fishbowling, and didactic interaction.

✓ *Why managers make poor decisions.* Poor decisions primarily result from unforeseen changes. In some instances, though, ineffective decisions result from erroneous information, failure to analyze all alternatives fully, total reliance on intuition, and fear of disastrous results.

THE MANAGER'S DICTIONARY

As an extra review of the chapter, try defining the following terms. If you
have trouble with any of them, refer to the page numbers listed.

decision making (138)
programmed decisions (139)
nonprogrammed decisions
   (139)
partially structured situations
   (139)
analytical (systematic) decision
   making (142)
intuitive decision making (142)
certainty (143)
risk (143)

decision trees (144)
uncertainty (145)
maximin (146)
minimax (146)
maximax (146)
regret (146)
formal (standing) committee
   (150)
ad hoc committee (150)
informal (temporary) committee (150)

divergent production (155)
transformation (155)
brainstorming (156)
synectics (156)
fishbowling (158)
didactic interaction (158)
bounded rationality (159)
suboptimization (159)

REVIEW QUESTIONS

1. Differentiate between a programmed decision and a nonprogrammed decision.

2. Why are nonprogrammed decisions more
common at upper levels of management than
at lower levels?

3. List the steps in the decision-making process.

4. How does the decision-making process relate
to planning, organizing, staffing, leading, and
controlling?

5. Why is goal formulation necessarily the first
step in the decision-making process?

6. Which approach do most managers use:
analytical (systematic) or intuitive?

7. How do analytical (systematic) decision
makers differ from intuitive decision makers?

8. Give an example of decision making under
certainty.

9. Explain the difference between decision
making under risk and decision making under
uncertainty.

10. Which type of decision making often incorporates decision trees to analyze alternatives and
outcomes?

11. Why are some managers risk averse while
others are risk takers?

12. What are the primary advantages of group
decision making?

13. Cite some limitations of group decision
making.

14. How can creativity in decision making be
encouraged? Describe one method that can be
effectively used to generate creative ideas and
decisions.

15. Cite specific reasons why managers often
make poor decisions.

MANAGEMENT CHALLENGE

Assume that you are in charge of an engineering division of a company that has secured a contract to provide engineering assistance on a canal dredging project in Central America. In conjunction with this project, four of your fifteen staff members will be required to go to the site for an extended period—probably six to eight months.

1. List as many alternative approaches as you can think of for selecting the four engineers for this assignment.

2. Which alternative would you select? Why?

3. How would you classify your approach to this particular decision?

4. Would your decision be influenced by input from your subordinates, or would your decision be based solely on objective data—seniority, for example?

5. Can you think of any advantages of allowing the group to share in the decision? Any disadvantages?

CASE 6.1

Atari's Turmoil[33]

Thumbing his nose at lagging sales, Atari chief executive James Morgan unveiled his company's third-generation video game player in 1984.

Several factors made Morgan's move questionable. First, the video game market, like the market for home computers, was saturated when the new 7800 was introduced. Fewer game cartridges were sold in 1983 than in 1982. And the company's second-generation video game player, the 5200, had sold only a million units compared to more than 16 million for the first-generation model, the 2600.

Introducing the new model wasn't the only move Morgan was making at Atari. Two new game cartridges were introduced in 1984; plans to add additional products were scrapped; plans to use exclusive distributors were abandoned in some regions because too many were unsuccessful; several thousand employees were laid off, including hundreds of white-collar workers; all manufacturing was moved overseas; and the company management was decentralized.

Atari held 20% of the retail market for low-priced home computers at the same time Morgan was shaking up the company with these decisions. Plans for two higher-priced models were abandoned, along with the other changes made by top management. Efforts were focused on short-term product development rather than on long-term research. Perhaps the motto that best describes the actions taken by Atari's management at that time is: "The Future Is Now."

Questions

1. Based on what you now know, was Atari's decision to introduce the 7800 a sound one? Why or why not?

2. Why did Morgan, Atari's former CEO, make so many major decisions in such a short period of time?

3. Should some of the decisions have been made by committees? Who would have been represented on a committee?

CASE 6.2

American Can Company

Chief executives get paid for making tough decisions. At least that's what Bankers Trust chief executive Alfred Brittain says. And, he adds, no decision is tougher or more fraught with anxiety than the decision to transform a company by selling off old businesses and entering new ones.

In recent years, several major corporations have dramatically altered the nature of their business by acquiring new firms. Gould, Inc., for example, was transformed from a car battery and electrical equipment manufacturer to a high-tech electronics firm after its president, William Ylvisaker, decided the firm should sell its low-tech businesses and concentrate on electronic replacements. Similarly, Warner-Lambert's former chief executive, Ward Hagan, transformed his company from a consumer products outfit into a health-care company by selling off American Optical and Entenmann's bakery and fusing money into health care research. Rolm Corporation, a manufacturer of large-scale computers, changed the nature of its business by entering the telephone switching equipment business.

These transformations are mild compared to the move made by American Can under its chief executive, William Woodside. In the late 1970s, American Can's business was slipping away, mostly because of new containers and overcapacity in the company's can and paper operations. In response to prevailing economic conditions and a bleak outlook for the future, Woodside created a work group of six officers to help him study alternative courses of action. The group discussed the alternatives with members of top management each week. After

several meetings, it became obvious to Woodside that the company's paper division would have to go. Although it was more profitable than the can business, it was also more salable. This was especially important since the company needed substantial funds immediately to invest in other businesses.

Woodside's approach allowed all senior-level managers to get a fair hearing. While he realized that not everyone would agree with the final decision, he felt that those who disagreed would realize that it was in their best interest to help shape the future rather than oppose it. Consequently, he listened patiently to suggestions and challenges that came up during the meetings.

In 1982, Woodside announced his decision to sell the paper unit. But he had not decided what business to enter. Although his choice had been narrowed to three service businesses, it was chance and circumstance that resulted in the acquisition of Associated Madison Insurance Company. Today, General Tsai, former CEO of Associated Madison, is vice chairperson of American Can and is considered a strong candidate to succeed Woodside.

Questions

1. In your opinion, was Woodside systematic in his approach to deciding which corporate division to sell?

2. What are the advantages of involving top-level managers in decisions surrounding divestitures? Discuss.

3. Why did Woodside decide to acquire a service firm rather than a manufacturing firm? Does such a decision appear odd?

PLAN

CONTROL

ORGANIZE

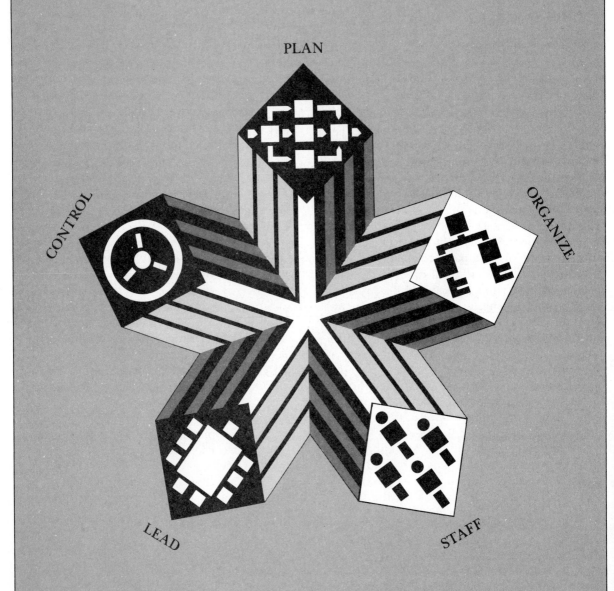

LEAD

STAFF

Organizing and Staffing

What is organizing? It's bringing together and coordinating human and physical resources to accomplish the objectives established in the planning process. Since no one person can do everything needed to achieve an organization's goals, jobs must be created and arranged in a way that gets things done. Organizing involves developing a structure to coordinate the efforts of different people. Part Three will discuss the elements of organizational structure and examine how to match job requirements with people's qualifications. This section also will discuss the need to adapt organizations to their ever-changing environment.

Chapter 7, "Effective Organizing," explains the basic elements of organizational structure. Topics include the advantages of division of labor and the drawbacks of overspecialization, methods of grouping jobs into departments, project management, span of management, authority and responsibility concepts, and distinctions between line and staff positions. Throughout, the chapter emphasizes the relationship between organizational structure and operational efficiency.

Chapter 8, "Human Resource Management," describes what goes into designing jobs and examines the importance of matching qualifications with job requirements. It outlines human resource management and the growing importance of the personnel function in modern organizations. Topics covered include human resource planning, job design and job rating, recruitment, selection procedures, orientation and career pathing, legal constraints on human resource management, and other issues in the developing field of personnel management.

Chapter 9, "Organizational Change and Development," pinpoints internal and external forces that cause change in organizations. The chapter also looks at the manager's role in implementing change and analyzes ways to overcome resistance to change. Several of the most common intervention techniques used in planned organizational development are highlighted.

CHAPTER OUTLINE

From Planning to Organizing: Making the Transition

Defining Tasks: Division of Labor
Advantages of Division of Labor
Disadvantages of Division of Labor

Grouping Specialized Activities: Departmentation
Functional Departmentation
Product Departmentation
Geographic Departmentation
Customer Departmentation
Process Departmentation

Project Management/Matrix Structures
The Project Manager
The Functional Manager
Advantages of the Matrix Structure
Disadvantages of the Matrix Structure

Span of Management
When the Span Is Too Wide
Limits on the Span of Management
Factors Affecting the Span of Management

Authority and Responsibility
Responsibility versus Accountability
Delegating

Line and Staff Positions
Types of Staff Positions
Assistant-to • *General Staff* • *Specialized Staff* • *Operating Services*

Line and Staff Relationships
Line Authority
Staff Authority
Functional Authority

C H A P T E R   7

tive
nizing

G E M E N T   I N   A C T I O N

ng Ma Bell

upreme Court ordered the breakup of American Telephone
veral years ago, it was tampering with what had become an
ion.

stem had operated as a regulated monopoly for more than
providing dependable, affordable service throughout the
150 billion in assets, employed a million people, and had
9 billion. But AT&T had grown too fat and far-reaching for
ment. The U.S. Department of Justice brought an antitrust
T in 1974. As a result, the company was ordered to divest
gs, effective January 1, 1984.

ruling was designed to make the telephone industry more
ners were supposed to benefit, too. It was thought that the
in lower long-distance phone rates, the faster introduction
and services, better access to discount long-distance comment costs for other phone companies, and more equitable
rvices. But even the proponents of divestiture realized that
oblems, including higher costs for equipment installation,
rates, lower overall service quality, and the loss of thousands

loud during the first few months after the breakup. This
people were confused by what the court ruling meant for
any people suddenly were receiving poor telephone ser-

vice. Problems with installations, repairs, and long-distance calls were common. Eventually, the confusion and the problems worked themselves out, and customers began to see that more competition in the telephone industry could mean lower phone bills.

The forced reorganizing proved beneficial for the twenty-two Bell operating companies that were split off AT&T and grouped into seven regional holding companies. They were forced to become more cost-conscious as well as consumer-oriented.

In return for cutting loose the Bell operating companies, AT&T negotiated a deal with the Justice Department. First and foremost, the company was allowed to continue providing long-distance service in the new, competitive environment. Besides that, it could keep Bell Laboratories and Western Electric, which meant that it could continue manufacturing communications equipment. And AT&T was also allowed to enter the data processing industry.

Preview

The breakup of AT&T was the largest single reorganization of a company in our nation's history. Unlike most reorganizations, however, it was not voluntary. Nor was it the result of inefficiency or mismanagement. AT&T was ordered to reorganize simply because the company had grown too big and powerful: it was a monopoly controlling the phone-service industry.

In this chapter, we will analyze the elements of organizing and show how the right organizational structure can help attain company objectives. After studying this chapter, you will understand:

✔ The transition from planning to organizing

✔ Defining tasks and the division of labor

✔ How departmentation groups specialized activities together

✔ The use of project management, or matrix structures

✔ The importance of span of management

✔ Authority and responsibility in management

✔ The difference between line and staff positions

From Planning to Organizing: Making the Transition

A company's organizational chart is a little like the old Abbott and Costello routine "Who's on First?" Only, instead of doubletalking its way through "who's" and "I don't knows," the chart clearly depicts who's in charge and who tells whom what to do. What it doesn't detail is the company's informal organization—the bowling league teams, the grapevine, the people who meet every Wednesday for lunch. These informal organizations usually form for social reasons, but they also help get things done in ways that may cut across the organization chart's formal lines. It is, however, the formal organization that we will be talking about here.

Chapters 4 through 6 examined managerial planning and how it relates to the decision-making process. We pointed out that planning and decision making involve setting objectives and then determining exactly what to do to attain those objectives. Planning is one of a manager's major duties.

Of course, no one person can implement all the plans of a modern organization. Nor can one person do everything necessary to meet the goals set forth in those plans. Planning, consequently, requires organizing the efforts of many people. It forces us to address several basic questions:

1. What specific tasks are required to implement our plans?

2. How many organizational positions are needed to perform all the required tasks?

3. How should these positions be grouped?

4. How can these activities be effectively coordinated?

5. How many layers of management (organizational levels) are needed to coordinate them?

6. How many people should a manager supervise directly?

The answers to these and other questions enable us to create an organizational arrangement, a structure, for putting plans into action.

Organizing arranges resources

Organizing, another of a manager's major duties, involves arranging human and physical resources to help attain organizational objectives. Organizing is the development of jobs and the arrangement of them into a structure that will assure that duties are accomplished in a coordinated way. The process includes the five basic steps shown in Figure 7.1.

Defining Tasks: Division of Labor

In a very small company—made up of only two or three people—the tasks assigned to each employee may be quite varied. For instance, the owner-manager of a small flower shop may employ two people who, together with the owner, prepare floral arrangements, wait on customers, make deliveries, keep records, and perform all the other duties required in the business. But, as a firm

FIGURE 7.1
The organizing process

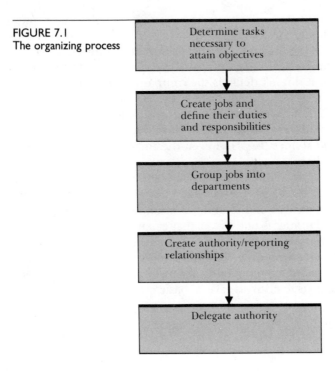

Determine tasks
necessary to
attain objectives

Create jobs and
define their duties
and responsibilities

Group jobs into
departments

Create authority/reporting
relationships

Delegate authority

grows, people must be assigned specific tasks in which they will specialize. This process, called **division of labor,** or **specialization,** is the most fundamental principle of organization. It involves breaking down a task into its most basic elements, training workers in performing specific duties, and sequencing activities so that one person's efforts build on another's. Long before the Industrial Revolution, economists recognized that the division of labor increased worker efficiency and resulted in better performance. In his *Wealth of Nations,* published in 1776, Adam Smith cited the advantages of specialization in the manufacture of pins. "One man draws the wire, another straightens it, a third cuts it, a fourth points it, a fifth grinds it at the top for receiving the head." Ten men working in this manner, Smith said, could produce 48,000 pins in a single day, "but if they had all wrought separately and independently, each might at best have produced twenty pins in a day."[1]

A similar point of view was expressed by Charles Babbage in 1832 in his *On the Economy of Machinery and Manufacturers:*

> Perhaps the most important principle on which the economy of a manufacture depends, is the division of labour amongst the persons who perform the work. The first application of this principle must have been made

Growth leads to specialization

in a very early stage of society; for it must soon have been apparent that a larger number of comforts and conveniences could be acquired by each individual if one man restricted his occupation to the art of making bows, another to that of building houses, a third boats, and so on. This division of labour into trades was not, however, the result of an opinion that the general riches of the community would be increased by such an arrangement; but it must have arisen from the circumstance of each individual so employed discovering that he himself could thus make a greater profit of his labour than by pursuing more varied occupations.[2]

Advantages of Division of Labor

Specialization enhances productivity

The primary advantage of division of labor is that it enables a person performing a task to become highly proficient at it in a relatively short time. As a result, efficiency and productivity increase. Of course, the amount of time required to learn any skill depends on how difficult it is. The more difficult and complex the job, the more time it takes to master the skill required. But the more specialized the task, the less time it takes to learn the required skill.

Another advantage of division of labor is saving the time that is always lost in changing from one job to another. The human body and mind simply can't switch from one task to another without losing some efficiency. In addition, there is less waste of materials in the learning process when division of labor is used.

Disadvantages of Division of Labor

Dangers of overspecialization

Among the disadvantages of division of labor are the boredom and fatigue caused by monotonous, repetitive tasks. Emile Durkheim was among the first writers to warn of the dangers of overspecialization. In his doctoral dissertation in 1893, he cautioned that, besides these demoralizing effects, overspecialization would result in workers' having limited knowledge.[3] Other writers, including Frederick Herzberg, Douglas McGregor, and Chris Argyris, have warned of the dissatisfaction and dependency caused by division of labor. For example, if we make someone's job highly specialized, at first we will most likely see significant increases in productivity—one of the basic advantages of division of labor—and we also may see greater job satisfaction as the person becomes a more effective worker and develops proficiency in skills. But, as specialization continues, productivity may start to decline, and satisfaction may be replaced by dissatisfaction as the work becomes less challenging. Productivity still may be greater, though, because lost motivation, interest, and commitment to the work may be less than the technical efficiencies achieved through greater specialization.

Research on the relationship between specialization and job satisfaction has yielded ambiguous results. Some studies have shown decreased satisfaction with increased specialization; others have found no such relationship. Most research concludes that whether employees with specialized jobs feel dissatisfied depends to a great extent on their personal background.

In addition to the drawbacks of overspecialization just discussed, Lawrence and Lorsch cite four areas in which worker attitudes are affected by increasing specialization:

Specialization affects worker attitudes

1. Specialization sometimes causes workers to think more in terms of their department or function instead of the company. Becoming engrossed in their own tasks, they lose sight of the company's mission. For example, a computer services department may become so preoccupied with its own activities that it may fail to give managers in other departments the information they need to make timely decisions.

2. Specialization leads to time-orientation confusion. Production departments, for instance, are commonly short-run oriented; research and development departments are concerned with the long term. Consequently, production departments typically evaluate their performance in the short run, whereas research and development efforts may go unrecognized for several years.

3. Division of labor creates communication barriers. Specialists develop their own language and customs, which can hamper communication across department lines.

4. Different specialties often formulate rules, policies, and procedures that conflict with those of other operational units.[4]

All things considered, however, specialization is necessary in today's complex organizations. Managers simply need to beware of, and deal with, its pitfalls. Some techniques for doing so will be discussed in Chapter 10.

Grouping Specialized Activities: Departmentation

Departmentation defined

All organizations, regardless of their size or mission, divide their overall operations into subactivities and then combine these subactivities into working groups. This process of grouping specialized activities in a logical manner is called **departmentation.** The operations of the federal government, for example, are divided into three separate divisions—executive, judicial, and legislative. Each of these separate divisions is then further subdivided. The operations of universities are logically grouped into departments, too; for instance, the activities of a regional university may have four divisions—academic, financial, student affairs, and administrative. Similarly, business firms divide their operations into separate activities and then group these activities into departments. Relationships between these groups are depicted in organizational charts. Some of the most common forms of departmentation used by business firms are discussed here.

Functional Departmentation

To understand how and why activities are grouped according to business function, visualize a company that began as a small, family-owned concern and grew into a large, successful corporation.

Paula Ann Nesbitt decided to manufacture and sell Pollyanna dolls. In the beginning, she and two college students, who helped out part time, performed all the duties required in the business. Each student worked fifteen hours a week. They cut material to pattern specifications, sewed, stuffed, and decorated the dolls. Occasionally, they would pick up supplies, make deliveries, and perform routine custodial duties. In other words, they performed a variety of tasks assigned by the owner-manager. Nesbitt developed patterns, created ads for newspapers and magazines, called on area retailers to establish outlets for Pollyanna dolls, and sold directly to customers who dropped by to see her line of dolls. She also devoted considerable time to bookkeeping, organizing the activities of the firm, and supervising the workers. Figure 7.2 illustrates the loose-knit organizational arrangement of this small firm.

As the Pollyanna line of dolls caught on, manufacturing could no longer be performed in the family garage, so Nesbitt leased a medium-sized building and converted it into suitable facilities. And she needed more workers. Sue Crowley, the first full-time employee hired, was placed in charge of all manufacturing operations; Nancy Bramblett was asked to assist in sales and advertising, and a full-time bookkeeper was hired. All personnel activities were handled in a separate department. Other workers were given specific tasks, which they performed repetitively. Thus, the duties of all workers became more specialized, and the organization's structure became more formal. Figure 7.3 illustrates major functional departmentation based on the various business functions of the Pollyanna House of Dolls.

Functional departmentation, such as that illustrated in Figure 7.3, groups together jobs that are similar in function or content. This type of departmentation offers several advantages over other forms:

- The basic functional activities of the firm are given more individual status and prestige.

FIGURE 7.2
Informal organizational structure—Pollyanna House of Dolls

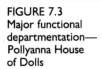

Example of functional departmentation

FIGURE 7.3
Major functional departmentation—Pollyanna House of Dolls

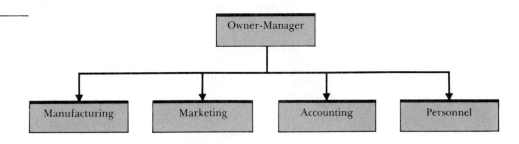

- Efficiency is fostered through specialization of tasks.

- Specialists can work in their fields of training and expertise.

- Tight control of all functional units is assured.

Because of its many advantages, functional departmentation is often used throughout an organization. Figure 7.4 shows primary and also derivative functional departmentation, in which subdepartments are created in support of their primary department.

FIGURE 7.4
Primary and derivative
functional
departmentation

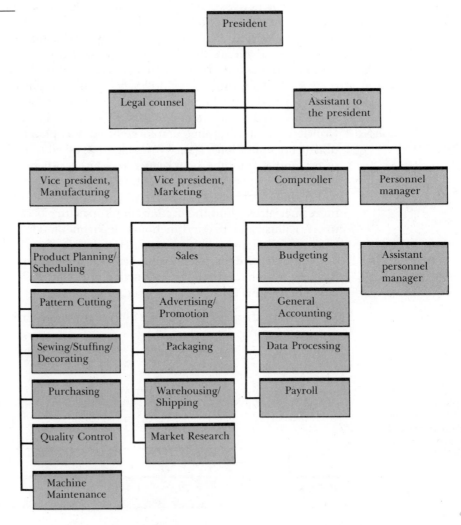

Although functional departmentation has many advantages, it also has obvious shortcomings:

- People in a functional department may lose sight of the overall operations of the business.

- Workers may develop highly specialized skills but no general managerial abilities. Consequently, functional departmentation is not an ideal training ground for top-level managers.

- The geographic area served, or the type of product or product line produced, may require a different type of departmentation.

- Sometimes conflict develops among departments as each unit competes for resources.

Product Departmentation

A firm's activities also can be grouped around its products. Called **product departmentation,** this arrangement is commonly used by manufacturers who produce and sell a number of product lines made up of several different items. For example, in the past General Motors had five passenger-car divisions, but now the company plans to produce and market its passenger cars through large-car and small-car divisions. It also has set up a separate subsidiary to create its new Saturn model, as explained in the In-Box on page 176. Procter & Gamble Company, Sears, Roebuck, and most other companies that manufacture or sell diversified product lines use product departmentation, such as Procter & Gamble's detergents division or Sears's financial services division. If Pollyanna House of Dolls had chosen product departmentation, its organizational arrangement might have looked like that illustrated in Figure 7.5.

Examples of product departmentation

Product departmentation, like functional departmentation, has both advantages and disadvantages. These are its most significant advantages:

- People who manufacture or market a single product or product line come to know a great deal about it.

Advantages of product departmentation

- Economies of scale can be realized if a manufacturing plant produces one product.

- Customers often get better service.

- The use of specialized capital is facilitated.

- The head of a product division can be held accountable for its profitable performance.

- Coordinating functional activities is simpler.

- Expanding products and product lines is easier.

THE IN-BOX

GM's New Auto Division

The Saturn is not only a new car for General Motors. It represents a new way of corporate life for the venerable organization.

GM Chairperson Roger B. Smith plans to establish the company's Saturn subsidiary as a kind of experimental laboratory responsible for creating the new car, which is to be drastically different from other GM cars in styling, engineering, and manufacturing. But, in creating the new division, Smith has other things in mind as well. He hopes that building and selling the cars through a separate organization will require a separate labor contract and possibly concessions from labor. The company is looking for substantially relaxed work rules and hourly wages instead of salaries for blue-collar workers. General Motors also hopes that the new division will free Saturn from the inefficiencies and overstaffing of the old GM bureaucracy.

Although the new Saturn will be introduced to compete with Japanese imports, it will roll up huge costs even before emerging from the factory. Its introduction alone will cost $5 billion, and the division is not expected to show a profit until 1990. The company realizes that for Saturn's price to be competitive, its manufacturing costs will have to be significantly lower than for other GM models. Management hopes to achieve lower costs through the use of "modular construction," which uses a smaller but more flexible labor force. Developed in Europe, this method makes extensive use of automation and few people; it is not tied to the traditional assembly line.

Sources: Amal Nag and Dale D. Buss, "GM Creates Separate Saturn Unit to Compete with Japanese Firms," *Wall Street Journal*, January 9, 1985, p. 3; Melinda Grenier Guiles, "GM's Smith Presses for Sweeping Changes but Questions Arise," *Wall Street Journal*, March 14, 1985, p. 1.

Disadvantages of product departmentation

The disadvantages of product departmentation include the realities that operations are harder to control, that more people with comprehensive managerial skills must be employed, and that efforts and services are duplicated. Walker and Lorsch's study of two firms—one using functional departmentation and the other product departmentation—revealed several significant findings:

1. Efficiency and job satisfaction were higher in the firm with functional departments.

2. Communication flowed better in the plant using product departmentation.

FIGURE 7.5
Product
departmentation

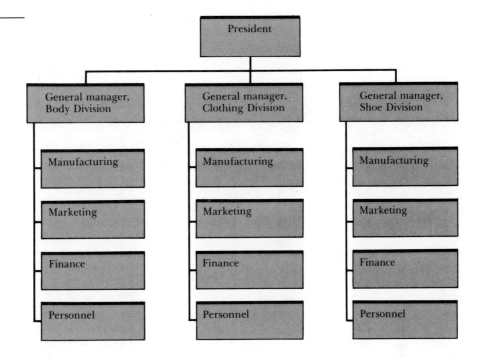

3. The firm using product departmentation adapted to changes more quickly.

4. The plant using product departmentation solved problems more quickly.[5]

Geographic Departmentation

Whenever a company establishes operations in different regions of the country or in different countries, departmentation on the basis of geography may be beneficial. **Geographic departmentation,** often referred to as area or territorial departmentation, groups business activities on the basis of geographic region or territory, enabling a firm to adapt to local customs and laws and to service customers more quickly. It also provides an excellent training ground for managers. Large companies such as A&P, J. C. Penney, and Sears have established retail outlets throughout the United States. Manufacturers and wholesalers also commonly produce and distribute goods in geographic regions. (Firms such as Sears commonly use more than one type of departmentation.) Figure 7.6 illustrates the geographic departmentation of a firm with operations throughout the United States and Canada.

Drawbacks of geographic departmentation

Geographic departmentation suffers from the same drawbacks as product departmentation does—duplication of effort, the need to employ several executives with the skills needed to manage entire corporate divisions, and

FIGURE 7.6
Geographic
departmentation

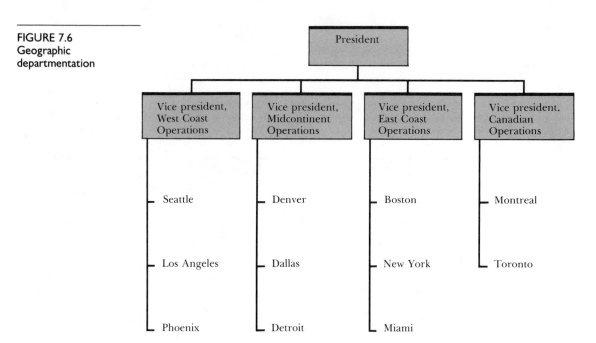

the difficulty of implementing timely changes and of maintaining consistent policies and procedures.

Geographic departmentation also encourages decentralized decision making; that is, not all decisions come out of the home office. A manager who is intimately familiar with the culture, values, and customs of an area usually is in a better position to make decisions than is someone who is removed from the situation. Consequently, geographic departmentation encourages the employment, retention, and promotion of people who are familiar with the traditional values of a particular area. Sales managers, for example, like to hire local salespeople who know the area and can deal with customers there.

In some instances, the decision to set up departments on the basis of geography is based totally on economic considerations. Transportation costs usually are lower when merchandise is shipped from regional factories or warehouses to customers, expenses of route salespeople are less, and increased sales are more likely.

Customer Departmentation

Examples of customer departmentation

Companies that must provide special services to different groups set up departments by types of customers, using **customer departmentation.** For example, a manufacturer may have both an industrial products division for its industrial customers and a consumer products division for other customers.

Or an automobile manufacturer may create a department for fleet buyers such as car rental agencies. Banks, book publishers, and educational institutions also departmentalize according to types of customers. Figure 7.7 illustrates customer departmentation used by a book publisher.

Normally, setting up departments by customers is not a primary form of departmentation. It is used instead within some other framework. For example, a manufacturer of business office equipment (duplicating machines, calculators, cash registers, and so on) may use functional departmentation as its primary type; but within the manufacturing or marketing divisions, it may use customer departmentation. Figure 7.8 illustrates customer departmentation in the marketing division of an office equipment manufacturer that must provide special services to financial and educational institutions.

Retail stores also set up departments on the basis of their customers. A store featuring fashionable wearing apparel, for instance, might operate a bargain basement that sells its merchandise at discount prices. Such an approach shows that it recognizes two different types of customers—one more price-conscious than the other.

Process Departmentation

Manufacturers use process departmentation

Manufacturing firms commonly group activities according to the product's manufacturing processes. Making plywood, for example, involves several sequential processes: poling (removing bark from logs); sawing logs into 8′ lengths; heating; veneer stripping and stamping veneer sheets into 4′ segments; drying and grading according to quality; gluing plies together to form 4′ × 8′ sheets of predetermined thickness; finishing and bundling. The physical layout of a typical manufacturing plant permits raw material to enter the plant, move through the various manufacturing processes, and exit as a finished product. Figure 7.9 illustrates **process departmentation** within the manufacturing division of a functionally departmentalized firm.

Project Management/ Matrix Structures

High-tech firms use project management

Project management is an organizational arrangement that developed because of the need for quick completion of highly technical projects that required significant contributions by two or more functional groups. This concept, born in the U.S. Aerospace Weapons Research and Development Industries, was first used in the Manhattan Project during World War II. Today, several of the most prominent firms in the aerospace industry have adopted matrix structures because they use project management.

As we already pointed out, traditional functional departmentation uses specialists, who work in accounting, finance, engineering, marketing, and so on. In **project management/matrix structures,** these specialists remain in their

FIGURE 7.7
Customer
departmentation—
publishing company

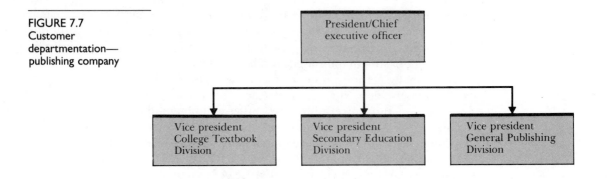

FIGURE 7.8
Customer
departmentation within
a functional division

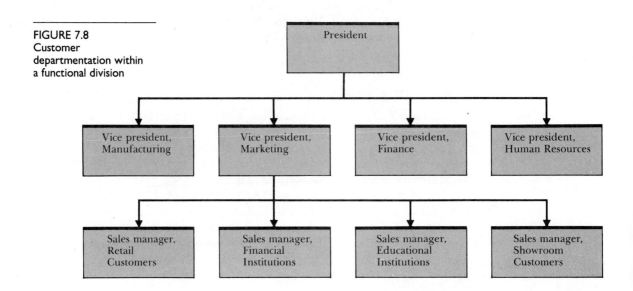

departments but are assigned to special projects elsewhere as needed. Whenever someone is assigned to a project, he or she is accountable to the project manager who directs that project. Figure 7.10 represents the matrix structure of a manufacturing firm that uses project management.

The Project Manager

The project manager is responsible for all phases of a project's life from conceptualization through completion, including planning, engineering, finance, scheduling, cost control, quality control, and customer relations. A project manager's task is complicated by the fact that he or she acts as a junior general

FIGURE 7.9
Process
departmentation—
plywood manufacturer

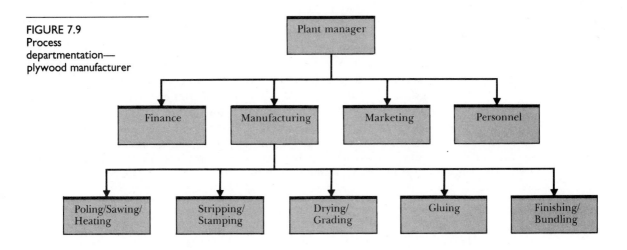

FIGURE 7.10
Project management/
matrix structure

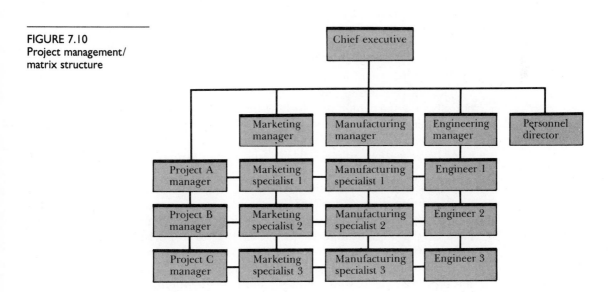

manager with authority only for a particular project. Authority lines are grafted across traditional functional department boundaries. The project manager does not work in the normal superior-subordinate role that a functional manager uses. His or her job is to manage and coordinate the efforts of people who are assigned to the project from various departments throughout the company.

The Functional Manager

Dual authority

In matrix organizations, functional and project managers share subordinates. This dual authority does not present any problems as long as the two managers do not issue conflicting orders. The project manager is concerned with coordination, costs, and time factors, while the functional manager concentrates on technical performance decisions. First, the project manager decides what is to be done and when it is to be done. Next, the functional manager decides who will be responsible for performing each task and controls how it is performed. One superior must be clearly recognized as the one to be obeyed when a conflict arises.

Advantages of the Matrix Structure

The matrix has several advantages over other organizational structures. In a matrix, the project objectives are clear. Everyone assigned to a project can easily see how various duties are connected to achieve a common goal. In addition, resources are used more efficiently in matrix organizations because workers are assigned to different projects as needed and because groups or projects can share machinery and equipment.

Advantages of project management

Because there are more managers in a matrix structure, there are more channels of information. Vertical and horizontal lines of communication improve the flow of information throughout the organization. Horizontal lines permit project information to flow between units, while vertical lines allow information about a particular unit to flow between management and the workers. Communication benefits the total organization—not just one group or area.

Morale is less of a problem in a matrix organization. Workers are motivated because they can see visible results of their efforts. In addition, exposure to more than one working area can give people a clear picture of possible career goals and how to achieve them.

Shutting down a project in a matrix organization isn't nearly as painful as in a single-project organization. When people are employed for only one purpose, they are no longer needed when the purpose is fulfilled; hence, large-scale layoffs can occur. In a matrix organization, however, projects usually are smaller but more numerous. At the end of a project, only a few people in certain areas may have to be fired, and many of them may have known that when they were hired.

Disadvantages of the Matrix Structure

Matrix organizations are built around the concept of dual authority shared by both functional and project managers. The balance of authority and power continually shifts between these managers because human nature tends to create power struggles—one person trying to gain the advantage over others.

The matrix structure lends itself to power struggles that can result in conflict rather than cooperation.[6]

Drawbacks of the
matrix structure

The matrix structure also results in higher overhead because more management positions are created. Normally, each project calls for a full-time project manager even though it may not require all of a manager's time. The structure also may collapse during an economic crunch.

> During boom periods, most organizations are more experimental and even wasteful. Although the matrix structure increases administrative overhead, it also ideally suits the progressive development of new ideas into new products. However, when a slump hits an industry, one common tendency is to discard the matrix in favor of more Spartan and traditional management options. The matrix, in essence, becomes a scapegoat for inefficiency. To overcome these costly cyclical overhauls of organization structure, managers should thoughtfully review the fit between structure and basic task demands. Those who really need a matrix should keep it during the crunch; those who used it to look progressive should discard it and not bring it back.[7]

Because it has so many information channels, the matrix structure is susceptible to what we can call decision strangulation. Sometimes specialists assigned to a project clear all issues with their functional manager and stall the decision-making process. In other cases, conflict between project and functional managers retards the decision-making process.

Span of Management

Spans of
management vary

Span of management, or **span of control,** refers to the number of subordinates that a single manager can effectively supervise. This varies from one situation to another. There is no magical number. As you can see from the preceding organization charts, however, upper-echelon managers usually have fewer immediate subordinates than middle managers do. Likewise, middle managers typically have narrower spans of control than supervisors do. Chief executive officers of medium and large corporations typically have between four and eight immediate subordinates, for example, while supervisors' spans frequently exceed fifteen persons. In part, the variations at different organizational levels result from the complexity and/or diversity of jobs, the need for personal interaction, leadership philosophies, and a host of other variables.

When the Span Is Too Wide

Unfortunately, the need to limit or reduce a span of management usually becomes apparent only after a problem arises. A very good manager typically is assigned more and more duties, greater responsibility, and more subordinates to help with those additional duties. As long as his or her performance level remains high, the manager may be given additional assignments. But at some point the workload becomes too heavy, and the manager's effectiveness declines. Usually, the span of control is reduced and additional organizational levels are created only when the manager's performance is seriously hampered because he or she has too many immediate subordinates.

To understand how the span of control can get too wide, consider how most organizations develop. When someone starts a business, everyone reports directly to the owner-manager. The growing business adds workers, who also report to the owner. Figure 7.11 illustrates the structure of a typical small business in the early stage of its development.

There are advantages and disadvantages in this type of system. Its greatest strengths include the direct access that all employees have to the owner, the speed with which problems can be handled and decisions made, and the one-on-one communication between manager and subordinates. This arrangement is ideal as long as the owner-manager can effectively supervise all the employees.

The shortcomings of the system depicted in Figure 7.11 are apparent if subordinates need to talk to the owner but he or she is busy with other people or problems. The owner-manager may be out of town on business, involved in a community project, or having a conference with vendors, customers, or other employees. The problem is even more acute when the owner-manager makes virtually all the decisions.

When this situation occurs, the owner-manager must reduce his or her span of control by creating additional management levels and delegating authority to those managers. Figure 7.12 depicts the logical organizational arrangement growing out of the chaos created by a span of control that became too wide.

Narrow spans of control permit a manager to have greater interaction with each subordinate; hence, to exercise *close supervision*. But they also result in "taller" organizational structures and communication barriers since information must be transmitted through more people (levels). Conversely, wide spans of control necessitate *general supervision* and result in "flat" organizational structures, like that shown in Figure 7.11.

Limits on the Span of Management

Graicunas's contributions

V. A. Graicunas, a French management consultant, gained considerable notoriety by suggesting that the primary factor limiting a manager's span of control is the possible number of superior-subordinate relationships. This number increases geometrically as the number of subordinates increases arithmetically.[8] Graicunas recognized three types of relationships: (1) single direct, (2) group, and (3) cross. With this rationale, six possible superior-subordinate relationships exist when a manager has two subordinates, as shown in Figure 7.13.

FIGURE 7.11
Developmental
organizational
structure—retail
apparel firm

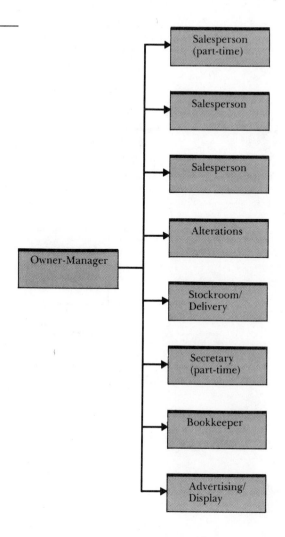

Graicunas's formula

If A's subordinates were increased arithmetically (by adding one additional subordinate, D), the number of possible superior-subordinate relationships would increase geometrically (by more than one), to a total of eighteen. Graicunas's formula for calculating the number of relationships, given any number of subordinates, is

$$n\left(\frac{2^n}{2} + n - 1\right)$$

where n equals the number of subordinates. In this formula, each additional subordinate creates a considerable number of additional relationships, as shown in Table 7.1.

FIGURE 7.12
New organizational
structure—retail
apparel firm

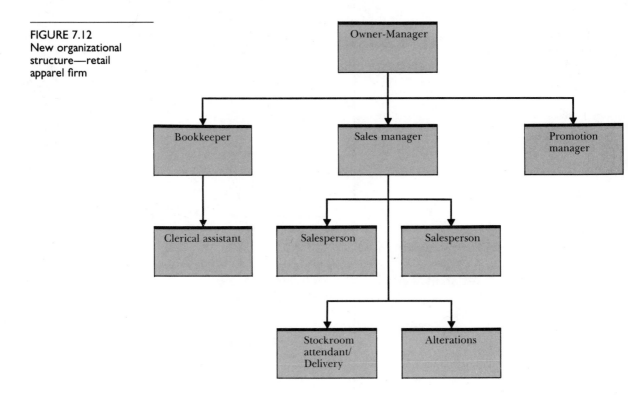

TABLE 7.1
Possible superior-
subordinate relationships

NUMBER OF SUBORDINATES	POSSIBLE NUMBER OF RELATIONSHIPS
2	6
3	18
4	44
5	100
6	222
7	490
8	1080
9	2376
10	5210

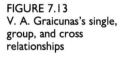

FIGURE 7.13
V. A. Graicunas's single, group, and cross relationships

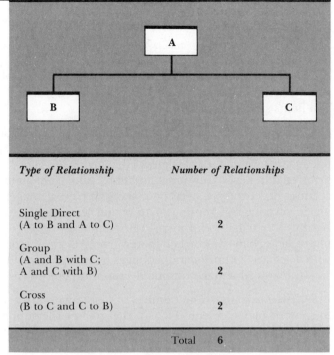

Type of Relationship	Number of Relationships
Single Direct (A to B and A to C)	2
Group (A and B with C; A and C with B)	2
Cross (B to C and C to B)	2
Total	6

What Graicunas failed to recognize is that not all relationships are of equal importance. He also did not realize that *actual* relationships are more limiting than *potential* relationships.

Factors Affecting the Span of Management

For years, academicians have theorized about the factors affecting the span of management. Several variables appear directly related to the number of subordinates that a single manager can supervise effectively.

1. *Routineness and simplicity of work.* Managers supervising people with simple and repetitive jobs are able to manage more immediate subordinates than are those who supervise people with complex, nonrepetitive tasks. Tasks are usually more repetitive at lower levels than at upper levels of an organization. This is a partial explanation of why spans vary at different organizational levels.

2. *Geographic dispersion of subordinates.* Normally, there is an inverse relationship between a manager's span of control and the geographic dispersion of his or her subordinates. For example, a sales manager whose salespeople are scattered over a wide geographic region cannot supervise as many subordinates as a manager can whose subordinates are in one building. This is especially true when the manager and subordinates must meet on a regular basis.

3. *Subordinate training and experience.* The amount of training, experience, and ability that subordinates have is directly related to a manager's span of control. Knowledgeable subordinates who work well on their own require less supervision than inexperienced, poorly trained workers do. Worker turnover also limits span of control.

**Variables affecting
span of management**

4. *Management by exception.* **Management by exception** is a philosophy of supervision that encourages lower-level managers to make decisions on routine matters within set guidelines. The only time higher-level managers become involved is in new, exceptional situations. Management by exception therefore requires decentralized decision making. It frees managers from time-consuming involvement in routine matters and lets them use their time more efficiently. A manager who insists on making all decisions, regardless of their importance, limits his or her span of control. On the other hand, a manager who delegates authority and manages by exception can have more immediate subordinates who make routine decisions on their own.

5. *Use of assistants.* The number of assistants that a manager has is related to span of management. That is, the greater the support given a manager, including the more assistants the manager has to help handle details, the wider the span of management can be.

**Authority and
Responsibility**

As we already have pointed out, **authority** is the right to command subordinates' action. The chain of command that links the organizational levels in a hierarchy is represented in the organizational chart. Most people accept the idea that authority rests in organizational positions. Higher-level positions have greater authority, with ultimate power resting at the top. Authority decreases all the way to the bottom of the chart, where positions have little or none.[9]

**Formal theory
of authority**

In practice, the amount of authority a manager can exercise depends on his or her boss's willingness to let the manager make decisions. For instance, the top-ranking manager of a company may delegate a great deal of authority to subordinate managers, who in turn may delegate considerable authority to their subordinate managers. Or managers may choose not to delegate authority, preferring to make decisions themselves. When authority is dispersed throughout the organization, it is said to be decentralized; when most decisions are made at or near the top, the organization is centralized. Quadram Corporation's success with decentralization is discussed in On-Line Management on page 189.

ON-LINE MANAGEMENT

Quadram Corporation Opts for Decentralization

Many managers would like to have the problems of J. Leland Strange, head of Quadram Corporation. Sales are growing rapidly, the work force is expanding, and profits are increasing. In fact, the company is growing so fast that its new office building outside Atlanta is already too small.

According to Strange, Quadram initially attracted people who were not particularly interested in money but who were vitally concerned with having control over their jobs. Consequently, he embarked on an organizational strategy called radical decentralization. Seven "quads" were created to produce separate products. One quad produces IBM memory boards, for example; another makes disks and tapes for storing data. A third quad produces a personal computer. Each unit works in a different building, and each has its own engineering and manufacturing personnel. In essence, each unit works autonomously, as if it were a separate business altogether.

Such an approach sounds simple, but it is fraught with risk and problems. In a young company, for instance, radical decentralization forces top management to place a lot of trust in relatively inexperienced managers. Moreover, there is waste associated with duplicated effort, excess ordering, and the like. But the advantages are apparent, too. Decisions are made quickly, and all workers can see the fruits of their labors.

Quadram's structure is best suited to firms that make several products and compete in rapidly growing markets, but such an environment makes it difficult to employ seasoned managers. Executives who are accustomed to a bureaucratic structure with several layers of management often flounder in a decentralized environment.

As the company continues to grow, it will probably take on many of the characteristics of a larger organization—slower sales growth, more levels of management, and a move toward greater centralization. But for now, Quadram's primary concern is keeping workers enthusiastic and productive.

Source: Scott Kilman, "Growing Pains," *Wall Street Journal,* May 20, 1985, p. 64-C.

"I like the job—I've got responsibility and the chance to stamp all over somebody now and then."
© Punch-ROTHCO

Responsibility versus Accountability

Responsibility, which complements authority, is a felt obligation. Unlike authority, responsibility cannot be assigned or given away. It must be willingly accepted. For this reason, authority should be given only to managers who are willing to assume an equal amount of responsibility.

Authority linked with responsibility

Although responsibility can't be delegated, a manager certainly can hold subordinates accountable for their actions. For example, a manager who uses authority irresponsibly or who consistently makes poor decisions may be reprimanded, may have the authority taken away, or may even be fired.

Delegating

Advantages of delegating

Delegating is the process of allocating tasks to subordinates, giving them adequate authority to carry out those assignments, and making them obligated to complete the tasks satisfactorily. Delegating is important for several reasons. First, it frees a manager from some time-consuming duties that can be adequately handled by subordinates and lets the manager devote more time to problems requiring his or her full attention. Second, decisions made by lower-level managers usually are more timely than those that go through several layers of management. Third, subordinate managers can reach their full potential only if given the chance to make decisions and to assume responsibility for them.

Managers hesitate to delegate

There are, nevertheless, several reasons why managers hesitate to delegate authority to subordinates. Some managers, like Henry Ford in the early days of Ford Motor Company, feel the need to be in total control of every aspect of an organization. Others lack confidence in their subordinates or fear the consequences of having subordinates make decisions. In some instances, subordinates are reluctant to assume an equal amount of responsibility. According to William Newman, subordinates inhibit the delegation process for a variety of reasons:

- It's easier to let the boss make the decision; subordinates usually feel that making decisions is the boss's job.

- Subordinates fear criticism for making bad decisions.

- Subordinate managers don't have enough factual information on which to base a decision.

- Subordinates are already overworked.

- Subordinates lack self-confidence.

- There is a lack of incentive or reward for assuming a greater workload.[10]

Line and Staff Positions

The manager in most modern organizations has to deal with people in two types of jobs: **line positions** and **staff positions.** The distinction between a line job and a staff job is baffling to most people; even authors of books on management and organization theory cannot agree on the distinguishing characteristics. Some writers include finance as a line function, for instance; others as a staff function. Most authors classify positions as either line or staff. Others contend that the relationships between positions are either line or staff, not the positions themselves. Consider the following statements:

> The term "staff" is typically used to refer to individuals or departments assisting managers in the performance of their basic production, marketing, or financial functions. The latter managers are called line because they form a part of the main line of authority (or chain of command) that flows throughout the organization.[11]

Contradictory views

> Line groupings, represented by manufacturing and marketing, are those units directly involved in producing and selling the product or service. Staff groupings, characterized by personnel and finance, are those units that perform in support of the line functions but are generally not involved in direct production or selling.[12]

> A . . . logically valid concept of line and staff is that they are simply a matter of relationships.[13]

> The line functions contribute directly to accomplishing the firm's objectives, while staff functions facilitate the accomplishment of the major organizational objectives in an indirect manner.[14]

These definitions are no help at all if we want to draw a sharp distinction between line and staff positions. How can we determine whether a position is line or staff? The following distinctions should be helpful:

1. Line positions have authority over a business's operations, such as production and selling in a manufacturing firm. Sales manager and production supervisor, for example, are line jobs. (Note: Not every job in manufacturing and marketing is a line position. Purchasing, advertising, and engineering, for instance, are staff functions within manufacturing and marketing areas.)

Line and staff distinctions

2. People with line positions are responsible for physically producing the product or service and for selling it.

3. Staff people advise and assist line people. That is the only reason these positions exist.

4. All staff positions are advisory. Staff people may make recommendations, but line managers retain formal authority and decide what to do with a staff person's advice.

Using these distinctions, we can classify the organizational positions shown in Figure 7.14 as either line or staff.

FIGURE 7.14
Selected line and staff
positions—
manufacturing
organization

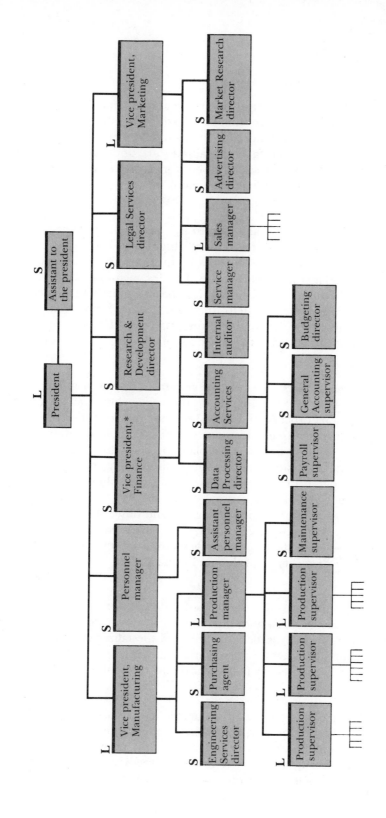

L = line, **S** = staff

*Some experts classify the job of the chief financial officer as a line position, since he or she has ultimate responsibility for the successful operations of a business. Others view the accounting/finance function as a supportive staff function; this author agrees.

Types of Staff Positions

Much of the confusion over line and staff positions occurs because we sometimes fail to realize that there are different types of staff jobs. Many large organizations create as many as four different types of staff positions: assistant-to, general staff, specialized staff, and operating services. First, let's distinguish among these different forms of staff positions and then analyze their relationship with line managers.[15]

Personal assistant

Assistant-to   An **assistant-to** is a personal assistant to someone holding an office or position that is usually high in the organization. The president of the company shown in Figure 7.14, for example, has an assistant. The assistant to a manager has a wide range of duties, including whatever the boss directs him or her to do. The assistant may be a troubleshooter, speech writer, adviser, or anything else that helps the boss. Although the position is powerful because of its ties with a high-ranking manager, it carries no formal authority over other positions in the organization.

Originated in the military

General Staff   The idea of **general staff** was originally conceived by the military as a way to help line officers develop strategic battle plans. No single military officer could possibly gather and analyze all the necessary information and make timely decisions without the help of other people. Consequently, the military began using planning specialists in all areas (personnel, intelligence, operations and training, and supply and logistics). These staff officers prepared plans in their own areas and submitted them to the commanding officer. Today, the general staff assists the general commanding an army, the general commanding a division, and other, lower-ranking officers.[16]

Recently, large corporations have created general staff positions to help develop strategic, long-range plans. But they still are used more in the military and in government than in business.

Special qualifications

Specialized Staff   Specialized staff positions are filled by people with special training, skills, and experience. In most cases, they are hired because they have formal, academic training. A specialized staff includes accountants, computer programmers, personnel managers, engineers, and corporate attorneys. It is this category that we normally think of as "staff."

Operating services indirectly benefit

Operating Services   Most people in operating services have tasks not directly related to the purpose of the business. Their efforts benefit the entire organization indirectly. For example, cafeteria workers, custodians, and groundskeepers at a university are not directly concerned with educating students; nevertheless, their physical contributions to the organization are worthwhile.

FIGURE 7.15
Line, staff, and
functional authority—
selected positions

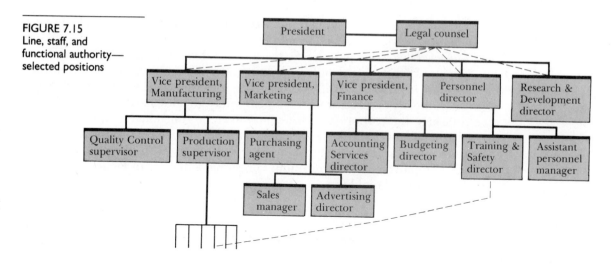

Line and Staff Relationships

Now that we understand the difference between line and staff positions, we need to examine the authority relationships between them more closely. Three distinct types of authority are evident in business organizations—line, staff, and functional.

Chain of command

Line Authority   **Line authority** enables a manager to tell subordinates what to do. Both line and staff managers have line authority over their subordinates. This authority is represented by the chain of command, which links superiors and subordinates from top to bottom in an organization. In Figure 7.15, the president has line authority over the vice presidents and the personnel director. Similarly, the personnel director has line authority over the assistant personnel director, and the vice presidents exercise line authority over their subordinates. Line authority, represented by the chain of command, extends all the way to the lowest level in the organizational structure.

Authority to assist and advise

Staff Authority   As we already pointed out, people in staff positions assist and advise line managers. They relieve some of the line managers' burdens by giving them the information they need to make operational decisions. People in these positions have the authority to offer advice and make recommendations; they have **staff authority.** In Figure 7.15, the legal counsel exercises staff authority by advising the company president. Likewise, the personnel director may advise and assist other managers on personnel matters. For instance, he or she may advise them on federal Equal Employment Opportunity guidelines, give them regional salary information, assist in recruiting, arrange training programs, and so on.

Functional Authority   **Functional authority** is exercised over people or activities in other departments. Usually limited in scope and duration, it is exercised one level below the person who has it. The safety director may be given functional authority over people who work under the production supervisor when it comes to established safety procedures, for instance. He or she may be given the authority to direct workers to wear safety goggles, hard hats, and the like. Similarly, the corporate attorney may exercise functional authority over the vice presidents in hiring. For example, the attorney may insist that they follow prescribed hiring procedures to assure compliance with federal laws prohibiting employment discrimination. Functional authority in Figure 7.15 is designated by a dashed line.

Examples of functional authority

Review

✓ *The transition from planning to organizing.* Organizing is the arranging of human and physical resources into a structure to coordinate and channel everyone's efforts to accomplish the company's strategic plan. Organizing has five basic steps: (1) determining major tasks required, (2) designing jobs, (3) grouping jobs into departments, (4) creating authority and reporting relationships, and (5) delegating authority to subordinate managers.

✓ *Defining tasks and the division of labor.* Division of labor is the most fundamental principle of organization theory. In very small firms, each person usually performs a variety of tasks; but, as a firm grows and becomes more complex, the need for division of labor, or specialization, arises. Each person is assigned specific tasks, at which he or she becomes proficient. Productivity and efficiency can be improved dramatically through division of labor. Adam Smith and Charles Babbage discussed its advantages.

✓ *How departmentation groups specialized activities together.* Once the major activities of a business are divided into specific tasks, these tasks are grouped in a logical manner. This is called departmentation. The most common method for grouping activities is on the basis of business function. Other bases of departmentation are product, geographic, customer, and process. Most firms use a combination of these different types of departmentation. For instance, a company may use customer or product departmentation within its divisions, or it may use geography as its primary type of departmentation and customer departments in each territory.

✓ *The use of project management, or matrix structures.* Project management is an organizational arrangement used by many firms that manufacture highly technical products requiring significant contributions by two or more functional units. People from different functional areas, or departments, are assigned to work on a specific project under the direction of a project manager. When the project is finished, they are reassigned to their department or to another special project. Because authority flows both vertically (from the functional manager) and horizontally (from the project director), the organizational structure is often called a matrix structure.

✓ *The importance of span of management.* Span of management refers to the number of immediate subordinates that a manager can effectively manage. One of the most important factors when designing an effective organization is the number of people that one manager can effectively supervise. There is no exact, magical number because every manager has limitations. Some managers work well with a wide span of management; others perform better with a narrow span. A number of factors affect a manager's span, the most important of which are the type of work done, the geographic dispersion of subordinates, the stability of the work force, the experience and training of subordinates, the use of assistants, and the manager's willingness to delegate authority.

✓ *Authority and responsibility in management.* Authority is an organizational right to command action of subordinates. In formal organizations, it is represented by the scalar chain, which links all positions in the hierarchy. The top position in the organization has ultimate authority. To promote efficiency, however, some authority is usually delegated to lower-level positions. When lower-level positions have significant authority, the organization is said to be decentralized. When most decisions are made at or near the top of the structure, the organization is highly centralized. Responsibility, which goes hand in hand with authority, is a felt obligation that complements authority. People who are given authority must be willing to assume an equal amount of responsibility.

✓ *The difference between line and staff positions.* Organizations have two types of positions—line and staff. Line managers have direct authority over the operations of a business (production and sales); staff managers advise and assist line managers. There are four categories of staff positions in business: assistant-to, general staff, specialized staff, and operating services. Line and staff jobs have different authority relationships. All managers, whether line or staff, have line authority over their immediate subordinates. For instance, a sales manager has line authority over salespersons, and a personnel manager exercises line authority over the assistant personnel manager. However, staff managers have no direct authority over their business's manufacturing and selling activities. Staff managers have the right to advise line managers and to act on matters that are incidental to manufacturing and selling. This is called staff authority.

THE MANAGER'S DICTIONARY

As an extra review of the chapter, try defining the following terms. If you have trouble with any of them, refer to the page numbers listed.

division of labor
   (specialization) (170)
departmentation (172)
functional departmentation
   (173)
product departmentation
   (175)
geographic departmentation
   (177)

customer departmentation
   (178)
process departmentation
   (179)
project management/matrix
   structures (179)
span of management (span
   of control) (183)
management by exception
   (188)

authority (188)
responsibility (190)
delegating (191)
line positions (191)
staff positions (191)
assistant-to (194)
general staff (194)
line authority (195)
staff authority (195)
functional authority (196)

REVIEW QUESTIONS

1. What does organizing entail? Be specific.

2. Pinpoint the advantages and disadvantages of division of labor.

3. On what bases can the activities of a firm be grouped?

4. What is the most commonly used type of departmentation? Why?

5. What are some of the ways in which forms of departmentation can be combined in one firm?

6. Why do some companies use project management?

7. How does the job of a project manager differ from that of a functional manager in a matrix organization?

8. Can you think of any disadvantages of project management?

9. Explain why some managers have wide spans of management whereas others have narrow spans.

10. How do you know when a manager's span of management is too wide?

11. Briefly explain some of the barriers to effective delegation of authority.

12. Do you feel that delegation is important? Why or why not?

13. Distinguish between a line job and a staff job.

14. Name the different types of staff positions and give an example of each.

15. Identify each of the following positions as line or staff (manufacturing firm): production supervisor, secretary, plant guard, personnel manager.

MANAGEMENT CHALLENGE

1. As a manager of subordinates who perform repetitive, boring tasks day after day, what could you do to make their jobs more interesting and challenging? Discuss.

2. What kinds of personnel problems could you anticipate if you were a production supervisor on an assembly line? Why? Inasmuch as specialization leads to improved efficiency and productivity, shouldn't you attempt to make jobs more specialized rather than less specialized? Why or why not?

3. As a management consultant called in to advise the owner of a newly created manufacturing company on proper organization structure, you would focus on what elements? Be specific.

4. Today, more than ever before, workers are demanding greater control over their jobs. How can you allow your subordinates a greater voice in their jobs without losing control? Discuss.

5. Why is it important for a manager to understand the proper relationship between line managers and staff managers? Can you think of any situation in which the relationship between a line manager and a staff manager could result in conflict? Explain.

CASE 7.1

Chrysler's Geographic Departmentation Headaches[17]

Chrysler Corporation has found that setting up operations in different countries can have its drawbacks.

   In 1984 the company began importing the first of its Mexican-made K-cars: the Plymouth Reliant and the Dodge Aries. The cars offered the company substantial savings in labor costs; but, unfortunately for Chrysler, too many Americans consider Mexico a backward country incapable of manufacturing high-quality, technologically advanced products. Dealers were worried about the quality of the Mexican-made cars. Some refused delivery; others ripped off the sticker showing place of origin. Many dealers argued that the cars would have to be discounted substantially if they were to sell. Others doubted that quality could be maintained because the plant in Toluca, Mexico, was less automated than were plants in the United States. To alleviate the fears and anxiety of the dealers, Chrysler had them tour the Toluca plant to observe the manufacturing process first-hand.

The public also was skeptical. Initially, the Mexican-built cars were imported and sold in the southwestern United States where there are many Hispanics. But even some Hispanics wanted U.S.-made cars.

What induced Chrysler to build cars in Mexico and import them into the United States? First, it already had a plant there assembling cars from parts made in the United States. Second, labor costs are lower. Wages and benefits paid Mexican workers average $2 per hour compared to $23 in the United States. Third, the Mexican government demanded that foreign auto makers who sell cars in Mexico also export them from there.

Sales of the Mexican-made cars were helped by the fact that the first three thousand were

imported into the United States when demand for K-cars was strong and Chrysler's St. Louis plant was operating at capacity. Whether the K-cars' quality is high remains to be seen. That will be judged by the American car buyer, not by Chrysler or its dealers.

Questions

1. Undoubtedly, Chrysler's decision to manufacture cars in Mexico was influenced by cost considerations. What other factors should govern geographic departmentation decisions?

2. List the advantages and disadvantages of building cars in Mexico. Consulting your list, do you believe that Chrysler made a wise decision?

CASE 7.2

Hewlett-Packard Centralizes Operations[18]

Since the company started in 1939, Hewlett-Packard has always been a loosely knit federation of highly autonomous divisions. Until recently, the company's two product lines—electronic instruments and computer products—were manufactured and marketed by fifty autonomous divisions around the world while the home office focused on strategic planning. While the autonomy kindled the entrepreneurial spirit, it also created problems for the company. For instance, as more and more of the company's instrument products began to use microprocessors, they became more like computers, and vice versa. It wasn't uncommon for both divisions to attempt to sell their products to the same customer for the same application. Even worse, the organizational arrangement

contributed to product delays. For example, Hewlett-Packard fumbled the ball when the software for the H-P 9000 wasn't produced on time. As a result, other companies captured the lion's share of the market for engineering work stations.

Besides these problems created by decentralization, Hewlett-Packard noticed that companies no longer buy computer equipment piecemeal. They now insist that whatever they buy fit comfortably into a system. As a result, top management of H-P decided that the company could best meet the challenge if its divisions were brought together and closely coordinated. This meant bringing the instrument and computer people together, centralizing operations, and redefining each division's autonomy. In addition, the reorganization called for a companywide marketing effort instead of divisional marketing programs.

Like most organizational shake-ups, Hewlett-Packard's reorganization entailed some casualties. Several key people took jobs with competing firms. But the real test will come in the marketplace, where H-P is striving to increase its market share in the face of stif competition.

Questions

1. Why is decentralization successful for Quadram Corporation (see On-Line Management on page 189) and unsuccessful for Hewlett-Packard? What is different about the two companies?

2. Suggest some alternative organizational structures for Hewlett-Packard that might alleviate its problems. What are some of the drawbacks of centralization for the company?

CHAPTER OUTLINE

Staffing: A Managerial Function

Human Resource Planning

The Job Design Cycle

Step 1: Job Analysis
Job Description • Job Specification
Step 2: Job Evaluation
Step 3: Wage Allocation
Step 4: Implementation
Step 5: Job Modification
Work Simplification • Job Enlargement • Job Rotation • Job Enrichment • The Plan-Do-Control Approach • Telecommuting • Alternative Job-Enrichment Methods
Job-Rating Methods
The Simple Ranking Plan • Grade Description Method • Point System • Factor Comparison System
Handling Pay Differentials

Developing Sources of Applicants

Internal Sources of Applicants
External Sources of Applicants

Receiving Applications

Screening Job Applicants

The Personal Interview
Pitfalls of Interviews
Selection Tests

Induction and Orientation

Career Planning and Career Pathing

What Employers Look For in Prospective Employees

The Legal Environment of Staffing

Equal Employment Opportunity
Affirmative Action

Human Resource Management

M A N A G E M E N T   I N   A C T I O N

Protecting Their Investment in People

The best employees are not inexpensive. Recruiting them and paying their moving, training, and educational expenses can represent a significant chunk of a company's budget.

Some companies, however, have decided to protect their investment. A growing number is now requiring that employees reimburse them for relocation, training, and educational expenses if they quit within a year or two. Many, like Electronic Data Systems (EDS), make new employees sign an agreement to repay the company for relocation and training costs if they quit before a stipulated time. Cheryl Deiter Taylor signed an agreement like this when she joined EDS. When she quit eighteen months later, she had to reimburse the company more than a thousand dollars for moving her from Florida to Dallas. When Ronald Ellison quit EDS in 1983, a court ordered him to pay the company $9,000, plus interest and attorneys' fees, for training expenses incurred by the company.[1]

Government contractors such as EDS have another reason for requiring payback agreements. Because the government pays a share of their employee-relocation costs, they are required to reimburse the government if the employee quits within a year. General Dynamics, McDonnell Douglas, and Northrop, for instance, have similar policies.

The overriding purpose of these repayment agreements is to keep firms from being exploited. Lockheed, for example, has a policy that limits employees from getting company-financed college degrees in their spare time if they then use that training to get other jobs. Its policy stipulates that employees who quit Lockheed within one year after receiving a college degree must pay back the company for its educational assistance. American Airlines takes a similar approach with its pilots. According to one company spokesman, American is only trying to protect its investment: "We feel that if we train a person, we have invested $10,000 in him, and we deserve to get something out of it. It's that simple."[2]

Preview

Payback agreements such as those just discussed are used most often in occupations in which there is a critical shortage of qualified job applicants and in which training costs are high. They are designed to prevent competing companies from pirating employees. Some critics compare these agreements to indentured servitude; others label them a form of blackmail. But regardless of the hostility, one fact remains clear—payback agreements reflect the tremendous investment that companies make in their most important and costly asset—their employees.

In this chapter, we will analyze what managers do in the area of human resources and discuss in detail the tasks that are crucial in the manager's staffing duties. The following areas are covered in this chapter:

✓ Why staffing is a major managerial function

✓ Human resource planning and its different aspects

✓ The five basic steps in the job design cycle

✓ How managers develop sources of applicants

✓ The benefits and dangers of application forms

✓ The various ways of screening job applicants

✓ What induction and orientation mean for the new employee

✓ The importance of career planning and career pathing in human resource management

✓ What employers look for in prospective employees

✓ The legal environment of staffing

Staffing: A Managerial Function

Staffing defined

Staffing is a necessary part of management. And, like some of the manager's other duties, it has become significantly more important over the years. Staffing no longer can be viewed simply as hiring people to fill vacant positions. Today, government is intervening more in the work place, organizations are becoming more complex, and managers are concerned about using all resources efficiently. Because of this, staffing has taken on new dimensions. Broadly speaking, it includes human resource planning and job design, as well as recruiting, selecting, developing, and retaining qualified employees.

Most companies, particularly medium and large ones, consider human resources so important that they create separate departments to handle personnel matters. Personnel or human resources departments are equal in importance to manufacturing, marketing, and finance. Like these other major functional departments, the personnel department employs specialists—experts in all aspects of personnel administration.

The typical personnel manager spends time on wage and salary administration, disciplinary problems, training and employee development, human resource planning, employee benefits, reports to outside agencies, public relations, and a variety of other duties. None of these duties is, however, more important than staffing.

The employee selection procedure, illustrated in Figure 8.1, has five steps: human resource planning, developing sources of applicants, receiving applications, screening applicants, and induction/orientation. Some organizations require, as well, a medical examination before induction.

Human Resource Planning

HRP: the first step

For more than two decades, managers have recognized that staffing involves planning. This **human resource planning (HRP)** reflects the growing importance of people in organizations.

There are two approaches to human resource planning—one specific, the other general. The specific approach emphasizes the technical aspect of planning for labor resources, particularly developing mathematical and statistical models for determining personnel requirements. This approach separates forecasting human resource needs from utilizing them, which emphasizes increasing employees' abilities and skills. As late as the 1970s, virtually all firms used the specific approach. Forecasting and utilization were done in the same department, but they were two separate activities.

The general approach to human resource planning equates it with personnel administration. In this approach, HRP is defined as the strategy for acquiring, using, improving, and preserving a firm's human resources; it covers three distinct activities:

1. Evaluating existing labor resources

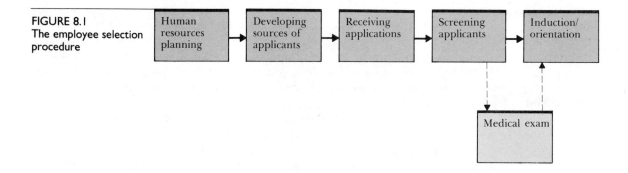

FIGURE 8.1
The employee selection procedure

2. Forecasting future labor needs

3. Ensuring the availability of workers when needed[3]

A firm's success depends on its ability to acquire and use effectively the resources necessary to produce and market its products and services. This involves business planning. In the past, business planning focused on product markets, new materials, and technological advancements. Decisions about allocating scarce resources fell under product development and investments in equipment. Managers did not look at employees the same way as they did other resources. Employees were dealt with on a reactive basis. Managers allowed short-term production requirements to dictate the hiring and firing of personnel. Today, however, the conditions of employment have changed dramatically. Firms no longer have this flexibility in dealing with employees. Legal restrictions, union contracts, the scarcity of skilled labor, and so on may restrict an employer's ability to hire and fire at will.[4] When organizations lose their flexibility in using resources, bottlenecks can occur; thus, resources—including human resources—must be managed very carefully.

Changes in conditions of employment

The ultimate success or failure of a business depends as much on its human resources as on economic, political, or social restrictions and technological problems. The vice president of a large auto parts manufacturer said that his company's 1979 operations were not restricted by its marketing, production, or technological capabilities, but by not having the right people at the right time to take advantage of economic conditions and produce what the market demanded.[5] Such bottlenecks might be avoided if human resources are given the importance they deserve in a firm's strategic business plans.

The Job Design Cycle

Before even beginning to think about selecting employees, a manager must analyze every job in the organization in terms of its duties and requirements. One of the most important aspects of the manager's job is **job design,** the attempt to organize work to require less effort, increase employee satisfaction,

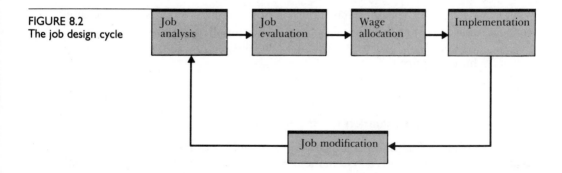

FIGURE 8.2
The job design cycle

reduce costs, and boost efficiency. The cycle of job design has five basic steps, illustrated in Figure 8.2. It should be viewed as continuous, inasmuch as jobs must be analyzed every time they are modified.

Step 1: Job Analysis

Steps in the job design process

Job analysis is the process of gathering, analyzing, and recording facts about each job in a firm. It is performed on three occasions: (1) when an organization is just starting, (2) when a new job is created, and (3) when a job is changed significantly as a result of new technology, additional duties, or new methods and procedures. The data gathered and analyzed in this stage focus on job duties and human qualifications. Job descriptions and specifications are developed from the analysis.

Job Description   A **job description** focuses on the job's duties and responsibilities. It is a series of concise statements about the workers' duties, how they are performed, and the conditions under which they are performed.

Methods of gathering information

The information in a job description can be gathered in a number of ways. The job analyst can watch the job as it is performed, interview the worker who performs it, or have the worker record his or her daily activities on a prepared form. Before gathering the data, however, the analyst tries to learn as much as possible about the job and to develop a feeling of mutual trust and confidence with the worker.

Job Specification   One of the easiest mistakes to make about a job is to assume that its requirements are self-evident. For example, if you were asked what a stenographer does, you most likely would answer that he or she takes dictation, transcribes shorthand, and types. That answer is true, but to fill a stenographer's job, the manager must know more. For example, how fast must the stenographer be able to type? Can someone who is not a stenographer, but who has other skills, fill the position? What skills and training are needed?

A **job specification** indicates how a company answers these questions; that is, it specifies the minimum qualifications needed by the holder of a job. A typical job specification details the training, education, and personal attributes required.

Step 2: Job Evaluation

After thoroughly analyzing each job, a manager can begin the evaluation process. **Job evaluation** is a systematic method of figuring the worth of each job compared to other jobs in the organization and to jobs in similar organizations. It cannot be totally objective, since it depends on the judgments of the evaluators. These judgments, though, are based on a careful examination of the jobs and a direct comparison of their content. That is why this kind of evaluation is likely to be more reliable and acceptable to employees than are haphazard comparisons.

Jobs are compared

Job evaluation methods can be either nonquantitative or quantitative. *Nonquantitative* methods used today are the simple ranking plan and the grade description method, discussed later in the chapter. The more widely used job evaluation methods, however, are the two *quantitative* approaches: the point system and the factor comparison system.

Step 3: Wage Allocation

Wage allocation takes place after all jobs have been evaluated and their relative value has been determined. First, managers must decide whether everyone performing the same job will receive equal pay or whether to establish pay ranges. A pay range includes a minimum and maximum rate with enough space between the two for significant pay differentials. Pay ranges are generally preferred over the equal pay method because they allow employees to be paid according to their experience and performance. Pay can serve as a positive incentive in this method. Many organizations group similar jobs into pay grades to simplify the allocation process. It is easier to price fifteen pay grades, for instance, than to price hundreds of separate jobs.

Pay ranges are preferable

When pay ranges are used, some method must be adopted to advance individuals through the range. People usually are hired at its minimum rate, and its maximum rate is the highest an employee can receive, regardless of how well the job is performed. A person at the top of a pay scale must be promoted to a job in a higher pay scale to receive a raise, unless an across-the-board adjustment is made or unless the job is reevaluated and reclassified to a higher pay grade.

Step 4: Implementation

Once the duties, responsibilities, and procedures of a job are determined, the job is established. Not only should a job help achieve an organization's goals, it also should be satisfying for the worker.

Unfortunately, some jobs fall short on both counts. Jobs in modern, complex organizations generally fail to provide high levels of personal satisfaction.[6] But more and more attention has been given in recent years to modifying jobs to improve the worker's motivation, fulfillment, and sense of accomplishment. Companies also are putting more emphasis on the physical layout of the work area and on technological advancements to improve worker productivity.

Step 5: Job Modification

Jobs can be changed in many ways, through **job modification,** to make them more efficient, more interesting, or less tiring. An increasing number of companies have had success with work simplification, job enlargement, job rotation, job enrichment, the plan-do-control approach, and telecommuting.

Bases of work simplification	***Work Simplification*** **Work simplification** focuses on efficiency rather than on self-fulfillment. Often referred to as the traditional approach to job design, it is based on five points: (1) skills should be specialized, (2) skill requirements should be minimized, (3) training time should be minimized, (4) the number and variety of tasks should be limited, and (5) the job should be made as repetitive as possible.[7] It is a process for limiting the scope of jobs to improve efficiency.
Jobs can be expanded	***Job Enlargement*** **Job enlargement** makes a job richer in variety, interest, and significance. Two ways for enlarging a job are to increase the number of tasks that a worker performs and to allow workers to complete an entire work unit rather than a specialized task. Job enlargement thus increases the content of a job and tries to reduce repetition and monotony. It makes the job structurally bigger by expanding it horizontally.[8]
Alternative job-enlargement methods	***Job Rotation*** An approach to job modification that is closely related to job enlargement is job rotation. In **job rotation,** an employee is moved from one repetitive task to another within the work unit. Learning additional skills and having improved flexibility theoretically increase an employee's interest and knowledge of the job. Job enlargement and job rotation therefore have similar advantages: they relieve boredom through variety and broaden job skills.

Managers also can be rotated from one position to another and from one geographic location to another to test their ability to meet new situations and

"We make early retirement pay here by having remaining workers take on more jobs." Charles Pearson-Knickerbocker News, Albany, NY

solve different problems. But serious questions have been raised about the value of moving managers because of the disruption it causes in their personal lives. More and more, employees are quitting their jobs rather than move to a new area. This is especially true with a two-career couple; in that case, transferring a spouse might force the other to give up a rewarding career.

Job Enrichment   In the 1960s, job enrichment came into fashion. **Job enrichment** refers to "changes in jobs designed to provide increased opportunity for satisfaction of growth needs."[9] It is another element allowing a worker to become more responsible for the total job cycle—from planning and organizing to evaluating results. Frederick Herzberg's two-factor theory of motivation is the basis for most job enrichment projects.[10] He believed that jobs should be designed to provide things that satisfy the worker; namely, achievement, interesting work, recognition, responsibility, advancement, and growth. Herzberg said that "the only way to motivate the employee is to give him challenging work for which he can assume responsibility."[11] Redesigning jobs in a job-enrichment program takes into account the worker's human needs as well as the company's technical production and organizational requirements. Tasks that will increase the worker's motivation get special attention. Jobs are more challenging because they are more complete. As a result, workers feel a greater sense of accomplishment.

Objectives of job enrichment

Herzberg drew a clear distinction between job enrichment and job enlargement. He pointed out the distinct difference between making a job structurally bigger (giving an employee more tasks to perform) and enriching the work by making it more challenging, emotionally meaningful, and rewarding. Job enrichment's purpose is to allow the worker to assume greater responsibility.

Workers participate in decision making

Job enrichment is associated with **vertical expansion,** or enlarging jobs to include the managerial functions of planning and controlling. Employees are encouraged to participate in making decisions about their work and to solve problems and set goals with their supervisor. They also are encouraged to suggest ways to improve efficiency and productivity. Involving the worker in planning and controlling supposedly frees the supervisor from routine decision making and allows him or her to concentrate on higher-level planning; thus, the supervisor's job is enriched, too.[12]

Myers's approach

The Plan-Do-Control Approach   The **plan-do-control approach** to job modification, developed by M. Scott Myers, is a job enrichment method. Myers believed that a job is motivating only if a worker is given considerable influence over all its aspects—planning, doing, and controlling. The "planning" phase includes planning and organizing tasks, solving problems, and setting goals. The "doing" phase includes implementing the plans, and the "controlling" phase covers measuring, evaluating, and correcting the work by comparing it with established goals.[13] In other words, workers assume some of the planning and controlling duties that supervisors normally perform.

Telecommuting   More and more managers are finding that jobs can be made more satisfying by changing the location of the work rather than the job itself. This is especially true with jobs involving computers. **Telecommuting,** a work system of gaining access to an office computer from another location, has become a way of life for a growing number of people. Executives, professors, attorneys, and a host of other people now routinely can use information stored in a central computer from their home, regional office, or other location. All they need is a personal computer, the appropriate software, and a modem that connects their computer terminal to the central computer via telephone.

Advantages of telecommuting

Telecommuting has a number of advantages for employees. The biggest advantage is that it allows them to work when they choose and when they are most productive. Telecommuting also saves the time and expense of driving to the office.

Other ways to enrich jobs

Alternative Job-Enrichment Methods   There are other ways to enrich jobs besides allowing the worker more say in planning and controlling. Workers may be allowed to deal directly with customers who have problems with products, or feedback programs can be set up to give workers immediate information about their job performance. Plans that allow workers some choice of their starting and quitting times are also popular.

Job-Rating Methods

After their duties and requirements are analyzed, jobs must be compared to determine their relative worth. The process of comparing the overall requirements of jobs is called **job rating.** The result of job rating is a wage or salary (or salary range) for each job. This rate or range identifies the level or boundaries at which workers are compensated and serves as a basis for determining overall personnel costs.

As pointed out earlier, job-rating methods can be categorized as nonquantitative and quantitative. The ranking plan and the grade description method are nonquantitative methods used today. The two quantitative approaches—the point system and the factor comparison system—are the more widely used rating methods, however.

The Simple Ranking Plan   Under the **simple ranking plan,** jobs are arranged in order of increasing worth, based on the judgment of the evaluators. This is normally done by a committee of upper-level executives. Committee members review the job descriptions and specifications and grade the jobs in terms of difficulty, responsibility, training and experience required, effort, working conditions, and so forth. After ranking all jobs, the committee groups them into a small number of classes (usually six to ten), and establishes wage rates for each class of jobs.

Although this plan is simple and can be administered quickly, it has many disadvantages. First, the ranking of jobs is based totally on subjective judgments. Because of this, personal bias enters the picture. It also is difficult to maintain consistency over a period of time. In addition, committee members often are inexperienced in evaluating jobs and sometimes lack adequate knowledge of all the jobs in a company. Finally, this method fails to yield a wage rate that reflects overall requirements of individual jobs. That is, though establishing the relative worth of job classes, the plan does not differentiate among jobs within a given class.

Grade Description Method   The **grade description method** is a refinement of the ranking method. Under it, major job classes or grades are established first; then descriptions of jobs within each classification are written, rates of pay (pay ranges and step increases) are determined, and the various jobs are assigned to the major classes. Generally, the classes are differentiated by (1) the nature of the work, (2) the type of supervision required, and (3) the latitude for independent judgment.

Somewhat more objective than the ranking plan, the grade description method still leaves much to be desired. Personal bias enters into assigning jobs to categories. Although the job—not the person—should be evaluated, the grade description method provides no safeguards against this error. This method is best used when an organization is small, when jobs are not too complex or numerous, or when time and resources do not permit another approach.

Point System   Because of its objectivity, the **point system** is by far the most widely used job-rating method in the country. It delivers satisfactory results without undue expense or effort but does not directly produce wage rates. Instead, it yields for each job a number of points that are converted into wages.

Most widely used job-rating method

In order to convert points into dollar values, the job-rating committee members analyze prevailing wage rates for similar jobs in a given geographic region. Using this information, they develop a number of job classes and establish wage ranges for each class of jobs.

Factor Comparison System   The second most popular job-rating method is the **factor comparison system.** A composite of the ranking and point systems, this plan yields a base wage rate, rather than points, for each job evaluated. The plan has these major steps:

Arriving at base wage rates

1. Identify key jobs. A key job is essential to the operation of the company, with well-established content, well-defined procedures, and an existing wage rate that is fair and just.

2. Spread the worth (existing wage) of each key job among factor categories. Assume, for example, that the job of welder meets the requirements of a key job. Its present pay rate—$9.50 per hour—is divided among skill, mental effort, physical effort, responsibility, and working conditions. Continue this procedure for each key job.

3. Compare non-key jobs with key jobs on the bases of skill, effort, responsibility, and conditions. Thus, key jobs become benchmarks with which to compare all other jobs.

4. Calculate the dollar value for non-key jobs.

After the committee has identified and ranked key jobs according to the factor categories (skill, effort, responsibility, and working conditions), it usually adds other jobs to form a comparison table against which to check all jobs. The additional jobs provide enough detail so that all jobs can be "fitted" into the table with little disagreement. As the rating of jobs progresses, the committee may need to make adjustments in the original rankings of key jobs because of finding some, for one reason or another, to be out of line with others.

Handling Pay Differentials

Having rated all jobs and determined each job's relative worth in the company, the evaluators turn to wage allocation. They first must decide whether to give equal pay to everyone performing the same job or to establish pay ranges.

Pay for product or for time

There are essentially two methods of compensating employees: (1) on the basis of work produced and (2) on the basis of time spent. Pay plans based on work produced are called **incentive pay plans.** Salespeople who are paid a commission and factory workers who are paid a piece rate for items they produce are working under incentive pay plans. Under this system, they sometimes can even earn more than their bosses do, as the In-Box on page 215 shows. Workers who are paid an hourly wage or a monthly salary fall into the second category. The wages and salaries of these workers are often determined through job rating.

Developing Sources of Applicants

The second step in the selection procedure (see Figure 8.1) may include advertising in newspapers, journals, and other media; job posting within the company; listing needs with private or public employment agencies; campus and field recruiting; and personal contacts with current and former employees. Sources of applicants thus fall into two categories: (1) sources from within the company and (2) outside sources. Most companies prefer to fill vacancies from within whenever possible. Promoting from within, rather than recruiting externally, offers several advantages:

Promoting from within

1. Morale is boosted.

2. The strengths and weaknesses of applicants inside the company are known.

3. Recruiting from within is less expensive.

A policy of promoting from within has its limitations, too. It inhibits the introduction of new ideas and philosophies and can lead to stagnation; moreover, the promotion of one internal applicant over another may result in jealousy, bitterness, and low morale. The decision to recruit from outside the company or promote from within should be based on one overriding consideration: How will the company's interests best be served? Chrysler Corporation, for example, felt that its long-run interests would be served best by hiring as its president Lee Iacocca, an outsider who came up through the ranks at Ford Motor Company. On the other hand, Roger Smith, chairman of General Motors, joined GM as an accounting clerk and progressed through the ranks during his long and fruitful career.

Internal Sources of Applicants

Job posting

A company can announce job vacancies by placing a notice on a bulletin board or in the company newsletter, or simply by announcing them in staff meetings. The practice of displaying job openings, referred to as **job posting,** encourages all qualified employees to apply. Typically, job posting is limited to nonmanagerial jobs. A notice of vacancy usually includes a description of the job to be filled, the qualifications required, and the salary or salary range.

Job applicants also can be found through employee referral programs that reward employees who refer applicants to their employer. Although the

THE IN-BOX

When Workers Earn More Than the Boss

In 1931, baseball star Babe Ruth was earning an $80,000 salary—$5,000 more than the president of the United States, Herbert Hoover. When asked to justify this salary difference, Ruth quipped, "I had a better year."

It's not uncommon nowadays for professional athletes to earn more than their managers do or for television newscasters to be paid more than their bosses are. But what about other workers? Should real estate agents, insurance salespeople, and other workers paid on commission earn more than the executives of their firms do?

In 1984, eighteen people at Bally Manufacturing outearned the company's top-ranking manager. And at Advest Group, a Hartford, Connecticut, financial services firm, sixty brokers earned more than Chief Executive Anthony LaCroix did. Similarly, Playboy Enterprises pays its financial officer more than it does its chief executive, Hugh Hefner, or its president, Christine Hefner.

Paying employees more than the chief executive often makes good sense. At Mentor Graphics, one of the three firms dominating the field of computer-aided engineering, six salespeople earned more than Chief Executive Thomas Bruggere did in 1984. But Bruggere doesn't mind: "Our goal is to grow quickly. To do that, you can't have a cap on what salespeople earn." Bally Chairman Robert E. Mullane agrees: "This is what's best for the company. I live very nicely. I like my job. Should I be upset when I go to the ballpark and the pitcher is making $2 million?" LaCroix of Advest puts it this way: "It's they who bring in the business, and ultimately that's how I make money too."

Source: John Paul Newport, Jr., "How to Outearn the Boss and Keep Your Job," *Fortune,* May 27, 1985, p. 73.

Employee referral programs

applicants usually come from outside the company, the impetus comes from within. Employee referral programs are most often used to locate highly skilled employees or those in short supply. The reward paid to an employee who serves as the catalyst for finding a qualified employee can range up to five hundred dollars.[14]

External Sources of Applicants

When internal searches fail to produce suitable candidates, a firm has external sources available. These sources of applicants include walk-ins, colleges and universities, business and technical schools, employment agencies, media sources, and labor union hiring halls.

Receiving Applications

The third step in the selection procedure, receiving a formal application, is designed to give the manager personal data, information on work experience and educational background, and other information useful in evaluating an applicant's qualifications. For this purpose, application forms vary from firm to firm, but are used by virtually every organization in the country.

Limits on applications questions

Not only can an application form gather valuable information about work experience, education, and personal interests, it also can serve as a test of an applicant's ability to read and follow directions. Because of the Civil Rights Act, the Age Discrimination in Employment Act, and other equal employment opportunity laws, however, companies must be very cautious in designing their application forms. Essentially, a company is permitted to ask only those questions that are relevant to performing the specific job for which the candidate is applying. Most states now curtail or prohibit questions pertaining to sex, race, religion, marital status, national origin, handicaps, or arrests. Questions about a spouse, child care, pregnancy, military discharge, and home ownership also are generally prohibited or limited. Table 8.1 illustrates the types of questions that can and cannot be included on an application form or in a preemployment interview. Some of this information may, however, be gathered *after* hiring, to meet affirmative action requirements (see page 224).

Screening Job Applicants

The entire selection procedure should be considered a two-way communication process.[15] Companies try to evaluate the qualifications of job applicants, and applicants judge the attractiveness of the company. Although the application form and reference letters provide some valuable information on the qualifications of job applicants, they usually do not provide enough for the company to make an intelligent decision. Consequently, most firms use additional screening methods, especially the selection interview and selection tests.

The Personal Interview

The most widely used screening tool

Managers base personnel decisions on the **personal interview** more than on any other selection device. Most managers feel they can determine the likelihood of an applicant's job success from an interview. Typically, they believe that in this setting they can adequately assess an applicant's character, attitude, personality, and overall abilities to perform the required job duties. This is why many managers either have discarded selection tests and recommendation

TABLE 8.1
Acceptable and
unacceptable
preemployment
inquiries

SUBJECT	ACCEPTABLE INQUIRY	QUESTIONABLE OR UNLAWFUL INQUIRY
Birthplace	After employment, can you provide proof of U.S. citizenship?	Where is your birthplace?
Character	Have you ever been convicted of a crime? Give details.	Have you ever been arrested?
Education	List academic or professional training and school attended	What was the religious or national affiliation of your school?
Language	What languages do you speak fluently?	What is your native language?
Marital Status	(None)	Are you married, single, divorced or separated?
Military	Do you have military training that relates to a particular job?	Type of discharge
Race	(None)	Color of skin or other questions related to color, race, or national origin
Sex	(None)	Please circle: Mr. Mrs. Ms. Miss
Home Ownership	(None)	Do you rent or own your home?

letters in favor of the personal interview or use them merely as complements to the interview.

Selection interviews can be classified according to the type and nature of questions asked. Broadly speaking, they fall into three categories: (1) patterned (structured), (2) planned (nondirective, unstructured), and (3) panel.

Types of interviews

A **patterned (structured) interview** is designed to gather a large amount of factual information in a concise manner. Questions usually require short, factual responses. Often, an interviewer will follow a checklist of items to be certain of gathering all the information that the company needs. Typically, a patterned interview takes place when an application form or data sheet is not required or when the information in them is incomplete.

Because a patterned interview asks the same questions of all applicants and because the responses are recorded, the interviewer can use it to compare one applicant with another directly. Recording responses on a standardized interview evaluation form also provides documentation if anyone, including a federal Equal Employment Opportunity enforcement agency, should question why one applicant was chosen over another.[16]

A **planned (nondirective, unstructured) interview** permits the person being interviewed to respond at length to the interviewer's questions. This type of interview is said to be unstructured because there is no format to be followed. That is, the direction of the discussion is not predetermined; the applicant's responses dictate the direction of the interview.

There are strengths and weaknesses inherent in the format of a planned interview. Because the applicant's response to a question shapes the next inquiry, a particular area of interest can be explored in depth. Some interviewers, however, have trouble staying on job-related matters. The planned interview also suffers from its inability to gather objective data used to evaluate the applicants; it therefore has questionable objectivity and fairness. Because of these limitations, very few interviewers rely solely on a planned approach. A combination of structured and unstructured questions usually is asked.

Another interview format consists of a **panel or board of interviewers** who question the job applicant in a group setting. But because of the costs and difficulty of assembling several executives at the same time, this is not a common practice. Surveys of job applicants who have been subjected to a panel interview report that most applicants feel considerable stress during the questioning.

Pitfalls of Interviews

Selection interview drawbacks

While the selection interview continues to be the most popular of all screening devices, it is riddled with potential weaknesses. Its biggest limitation, of course, is its subjectivity. Interviewers base hiring decisions on their feelings, which are subject to bias and prejudice. Two managers interviewing the same applicant may come to different conclusions about his or her suitability for employment.

Also, interviewers sometimes suffer from inadequate training and preparation. An inadequately trained interviewer may ask leading questions, questions that are not job related, or unlawful questions. Poorly trained interviewers also tend to let one job-related attribute, such as the applicant's speech or grooming, influence their evaluation. This judging of an applicant's total potential for job performance on the basis of a single trait is called the **halo effect.**[17] Studies have shown that some variables influencing interviewers' hiring decisions are body language, interviewer stereotypes of the ideal candidate, racial or sexual prejudice, visual cues by the person being interviewed, and even the order in which applicants are interviewed.[18]

Selection Tests

Because selecting the best applicant for a vacancy is so important, many firms use selection tests as a screening method. The use of testing has declined in recent years, but the number of firms using testing programs remains significant. A survey of 2,500 members of the American Society of Personnel Administration (ASPA) showed that about half of these employers use selection tests.[19]

Types of selection tests

Sometimes a good testing program helps managers make personnel selection decisions. But managers should not fall into the trap of believing that a testing program will automatically solve all personnel problems. The cause of an organization's problems often has little or nothing to do with the selection process. If, nevertheless, a company has concluded that a testing program will benefit the organization, the people responsible for implementing it should become familiar with the different types of tests available. They include **achievement tests,** to measure a person's acquired knowledge or skill; **aptitude tests,** to gauge a person's potential skill or knowledge; **vocational interest tests,** to measure a person's likes and dislikes concerning various occupations, hobbies, and so on; and **personality tests,** to help management pinpoint people who are highly motivated or who have desirable personality characteristics.

Induction and Orientation

Final step in selection procedure

The final phase of the selection procedure is the **induction and orientation** of the new employee. Having made the hiring decision, the manager must establish an environment in which the new employee will feel comfortable and be productive. The induction and orientation phase may include arranging financial aid for travel and moving expenses, completing payroll, insurance, and other forms, explaining the company's policies and practices, making introductions to colleagues, discussing specific job duties, and other activities necessary to integrate the new employee into the company.

Career Planning and Career Pathing

Charting a progression path

Career planning involves matching an individual's career aspirations with opportunities offered by the company. **Career pathing** is stringing together specific jobs in line with these opportunities.[20] In other words, career pathing is mapping out the career steps an employee might take that would lead to a job making the most of his or her potential. Figure 8.3 shows the career path that a salesperson might take toward the position of vice president of marketing.

Career pathing involves assessing the skills and talents necessary at each organization level as well as pinpointing the employee's aspirations. The

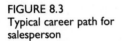

FIGURE 8.3
Typical career path for
salesperson

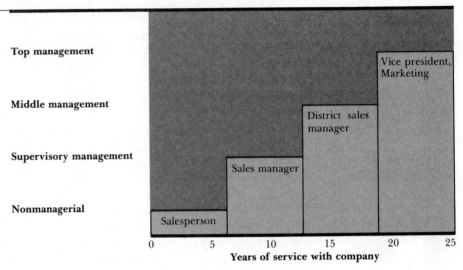

Top management

Middle management

Supervisory management

Nonmanagerial

Salesperson

Sales manager

District sales manager

Vice president, Marketing

0   5   10   15   20   25

Years of service with company

responsibility for career pathing is shared by the organization and the employee. The company should provide counseling, career information, and adequate training to assure that an employee has the knowledge and skills necessary to progress along the chosen career path. The employee must identify his or her aspirations and recognize the training and preparation required at each step.

Career paths do not have to be upward. Lateral movements within the organization may be included, especially for employees who are not "fast-trackers," interested in moving as far and as fast as they can. Lateral moves also can be used to give managers knowledge and experience in other functional areas. This kind of exposure may prove helpful, even essential, in upper-level management positions.

To be of value, career paths must contain four elements. First, they must represent real progression possibilities. Second, they should be flexible enough to respond to changes in job content, organizational structure, and management needs. Third, they should be individualized; that is, they should take into account the individual qualities of everyone involved, especially those of the employees for whom the paths are designed. Finally, they should specify the skills, knowledge, education, training, experience, and other particular attributes required in each position on the path.[21] On-Line Management on page 221 describes how businesses are using computers to chart managers' career paths.

Career paths can be lateral

ON-LINE MANAGEMENT

Computers Aid Promotion Decisions

The career paths of a growing number of corporate managers are now being charted on computers. Just as spreadsheets improved financial planning, software designed to monitor executive talent is improving the quality of personnel planning.

Southland Corporation, for example, has computerized its search for fast-trackers. Twice each year, Southland managers file reports about the promotability of their subordinates. By consolidating the reports on a computer, the company determines if enough people are coming up through the ranks. Southland uses another software package to produce career-development plans, to pinpoint weaknesses of each manager, and to suggest ways of alleviating shortcomings. Other companies using computers to plot managers' careers are Aetna Life & Casualty Company, Northern Telecom, GTE Corporation, and Avon Products. Even the U.S. Army is evaluating computer systems for tracking generals' careers.

To computerize personnel planning, both the skills needed for jobs and the skills possessed by employees must be defined and put into a computer. Then, it is a simple matter to get a list of people who have the qualifications for a particular job. You can do the same thing with pencil and paper, says Edward Ramesh, vice president of human resources for Associates Corporation of North America, but you can't do it as efficiently.

Essentially, promotion planning involves predicting future vacancies caused by retirement or promotion and assessing managers who might fill those vacancies. The computer helps uncover all the ramifications of a change. For instance, when a promotion occurs, the computer forces the manager to deal with the resulting domino effect and to fill the vacancy.

The computer also points out potential problems. For example, the best candidate for one position could be the only candidate for another job likely to become vacant soon. Such information may not be readily apparent if managers are dependent on reams of paper files, three-ring notebooks, and a management-by-crisis philosophy.

Source: William M. Bulkeley, "The Fast Track: Computers Help Firms Decide Whom to Promote," *Wall Street Journal,* September 18, 1985, p. 33.

What Employers Look For in Prospective Employees

College students frequently ask two fundamental questions: "What factors are most important in getting a job?" and "What traits are most important for climbing the corporate ladder?" Some answers to these questions can be found in the results of a nationwide survey of intermediate-size and large businesses, government agencies, and financial institutions appearing in *The Collegiate Forum,* a Dow-Jones publication. Survey respondents were asked to indicate their principal criteria in giving jobs initially, and to rate the relative importance of various factors in succeeding on the job. The results of this study, shown in Tables 8.2 and 8.3, are a guide to what employers look for when they recruit employees and indicate how they will be appraised as prospects for advancement.

Importance of communication skills

This survey clearly shows that oral and written communication skills are the most crucial requirements, both in being hired and in being promoted. Oral skills are more important than writing skills are as a hiring criterion, but writing skills become increasingly important afterward. The grade point average and school attended, though relatively important in the hiring decision, become almost insignificant in a promotion decision. Personality, poise, and appearance are significant criteria both in securing a job and in receiving promotions.

The Legal Environment of Staffing

An organization's employment policies and practices must conform with federal and state laws and with the accepted norms of society. Civil rights legislation and demands to rectify unfair employment practices have made recruitment, selection, promotion, and firing the most important issues in personnel management. To be within the law, human resource plans must conform to the Civil Rights Act, Equal Pay Act, Age Discrimination in Employment Act, and other laws and executive orders designed to prohibit discrimination in employment.

Laws prohibit discrimination

Equal Employment Opportunity

The Equal Pay Act of 1963, as amended in 1972, prohibits wage discrimination on the basis of sex. This law applies to employers engaged in commerce or in manufacturing goods for commerce.

The Civil Rights Act of 1964, as amended in 1972, prohibits employers, unions, employment agencies, and joint labor-management committees controlling apprenticeship or training programs from discriminating on the basis of race, color, sex, or national origin. Title VII of the act prohibits discrimination in any employment condition, including hiring, firing, promotion, transfer, compensation, and admission to training programs. The Equal Employment Opportunity Act of 1972 amended Title VII by expanding its

TABLE 8.2
Factors in obtaining employment—relative importance (in percent)

	VERY IMPORTANT	IMPORTANT	NOT IMPORTANT
Grade Point Average	23.7	64.5	11.8
Oral Communication Skills	69.0	30.0	1.0
Written Communication Skills	38.3	52.2	9.5
Poise	42.9	57.1	0
Appearance	37.9	56.9	5.2
Social Graces	6.8	64.0	29.2
Personality	44.1	51.6	4.3
School Attended	1.1	51.6	47.3
Recommendations	16.9	52.8	30.3

Source: Reprinted with the permission of Allen Blitstein, Southwest State University, from *The Collegiate Forum*, January 1981, p. 6. Published by Dow Jones & Company, Inc., Princeton, N.J. Copyright 1982. All rights reserved.

TABLE 8.3
Factors in job progression—relative importance (in percent)

	VERY IMPORTANT	IMPORTANT	NOT IMPORTANT
Grade Point Average	2.2	32.3	65.5
Oral Communication Skills	75.3	23.7	1.0
Written Communication Skills	61.7	35.1	3.2
Poise	43.0	51.6	5.4
Appearance	29.0	68.8	2.2
Social Graces	8.8	61.2	30.0
Personality	52.7	44.1	3.2
School Attended	0	12.9	87.1
Recommendations	11.3	33.7	55.0

Source: Reprinted with the permission of Allen Blitstein, Southwest State University, from *The Collegiate Forum*, January 1981, p. 6. Published by Dow Jones & Company, Inc., Princeton, N.J. Copyright 1982. All rights reserved.

coverage to include employees of state and local governments and educational institutions. Indian tribes and private-membership clubs are not covered, however, and religious organizations may discriminate on the basis of religion in some cases. Federal government employees are also covered by Title VII, but enforcement for them is carried out by the Civil Service Commission with procedures that are unique to federal workers. The only instance in which an employer is allowed to discriminate on the basis of sex, religion, or national origin is when these attributes are "bona fide occupational qualifications."[22] For example, a women's clothing designer may discriminate on the basis of sex in choosing fashion models to display his or her designs.

The Age Discrimination in Employment Act of 1967, as amended in 1978, prohibits employers from discriminating against persons between forty and seventy years of age unless the employer can show that age is a bona fide occupational qualification for the job.

The Equal Employment Opportunity Act of 1972 prohibits employers from limiting, segregating, or classifying employees or job applicants on the basis of race, color, religion, sex, or national origin to deprive them of employment opportunities. Equal Employment Opportunity Commission guidelines help managers comply with equal employment opportunity legislation.

Under the Privacy Act of 1974, employees have the right to examine reference letters written to employers. The Pregnancy Discrimination Act of 1978 prohibits discrimination in employment based on pregnancy, childbirth, or resulting complications. While pregnant managers have legal protection against such discrimination, they nevertheless face special challenges in keeping their professional standing intact during pregnancy and afterwards (see the Manager's Notebook, p. 225).

Affirmative Action

Rectifying past practices

For more than two decades, managers have struggled to avoid charges of discrimination in their hiring practices. Many, in fact, have instituted **affirmative action programs (AAP)** designed to end discriminatory hiring and promotion practices. These programs first were required of employers who have contracts with the federal government. Through various amendments to the Civil Rights Act and regulatory interpretations, this requirement has been extended to cover any financial institution that uses Federal Deposit Insurance Corporation (FDIC) insurance, issues savings bonds, is a federal depository, or contracts with the federal government.

Objective of Affirmative Action

An Affirmative Action Plan's purpose is to identify and correct any underutilization of women and minorities in a work force. Contrary to popular belief, a company is not required to hire and promote anyone who is not fully qualified to perform a job. Where people are being underutilized, an Affirmative Action Plan sets realistic goals and timetables for corrective action. These are evaluated on the basis of the company's good-faith efforts to rectify discriminatory practices.[23]

Under the regulations of the Office of Federal Contract Compliance Program (OFCCP), a compliance review officer must analyze three specific areas of affirmative action programs: (1) recruiting, hiring, selection, and placement; (2) promotion and transfers; and (3) terminations. In hiring, the officer examines interview procedures and records, reasons for rejections, retention of applications, the ability to retrieve applications later, interviewers' feedback to the Equal Employment Opportunity coordinator, and other areas. The officer also monitors disparate rejection ratios. Once this information has been reviewed, the compliance officer should be able to determine whether

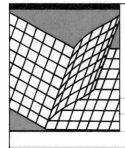

THE MANAGER'S NOTEBOOK

Managing for Maternity

No matter how openminded a company is, top management can get nervous about pregnant workers' or managers' absenteeism and chances of returning to work. The following tips can help women to integrate their pregnancy and their career, avoiding any unspoken concerns or complaints from others in the office.

- Fully explore your company's maternity benefits so that you know all of your options. How much leave time do your state's laws permit you to take and still return to the same or a comparable position? How much pay or disability coverage can you plan on receiving? Talk to other women who have been pregnant about their experiences.

- Try not to announce your pregnancy until the beginning of the fourth month. In the event of a first-trimester miscarriage, you don't want to broadcast your family planning efforts. About 15% of pregnancies end in miscarriages during the first three months.

- Tell your boss before you tell anyone else in the office. Otherwise, he or she is likely to hear through the grapevine, and you will be less likely to get off to a good start—with a well-presented maternity plan.

- When telling your boss, remind him or her of your worth to the organization and express an enthusiasm for returning to work. Reassure your boss that not only will you be back, but that as a parent you will be an even more responsible employee.

- Watch out for power plays for your job. An announced absence can bring out the worst in ambitious peers and subordinates.

- Look especially good on the job, to dispel the notions that pregnant women are easily distracted and function less effectively. If you must slow down from time to time, prepare your staff for that possibility.

- Make sure, during the second and third trimesters, that everyone who will be affected by your absence knows the status of your work and who will be filling in for you while you're on leave.

- Well in advance, begin training the people who will fill in for you. You'll be glad you did if you have an early delivery or are more tired toward the end of your pregnancy.

And remember, according to Susan Stautberg, author of *Pregnancy Nine to Five:*

> If you consider yourself a person on the job who happens to be pregnant, rather than a pregnant woman who happens to have a job, other people will get the message and turn their attention to your work instead of your waistline.

Source: Susan Schiffer Stautberg, "Bringing Career Skills to Bear on Your Pregnancy," *Wall Street Journal,* June 17, 1985, p. 20.

there has been a "differential rate of selection which works to the disadvantage of the covered group."[24] For example, if the selection rate for minorities or women is less than 80% of that of the other applicants, the employer must prove that hiring practices were related to the job requirements.[25]

Areas of analysis

The compliance officer also compares promotion rates of minorities and women to the rates of other employees. In addition, the officer extensively analyzes data on firings to see whether a disproportionate number of minorities and women have been fired from specific kinds of jobs, whether there has been a disproportionate number of firings based on age, and the employer's reasons why. The compliance officer also reviews the representation of minorities and women in supervisory positions, and compares wages of a sampling within selected job titles.

Review

✓ *Why staffing is a major managerial function.* Today more than ever, managers are devoting vast amounts of energy and resources to solicit, recruit, employ, train, and retain highly competent employees. Because of government intervention in the workplace, the increasing complexity of organizations, and the need to use resources more efficiently, employers today consider their employees their most costly and valuable asset.

Staffing is one of the major duties of a manager. To handle personnel activities, most firms have a separate department headed by a personnel director or manager of human resources.

✓ *Human resource planning and its different aspects.* Human resource planning, the first step in the selection procedure, is the strategy for acquiring, utilizing, improving, and preserving a firm's human resources. It includes evaluating existing labor resources, forecasting future needs, and ensuring that workers will be available when needed.

✓ *The five basic steps in the job design cycle.* Job design is the attempt to create and modify jobs in a way that will increase employee output and stimulate their interest in their work. Its objectives are to improve efficiency, organize work to require less effort, reduce costs, and provide workers with challenging, self-fulfilling tasks. Job design has five steps: job analysis, job evaluation, wage allocation, implementation, and job modification.

Job rating is an essential part of job design. Nonquantitative rating methods used today are the simple ranking plan and the grade description method. The more widely used methods, the point system and the factor comparison system, are quantitative approaches.

✔ *How managers develop sources of applicants.* The second step in the selection procedure involves soliciting applications from workers inside and outside the firm. Job posting and employee referral programs are commonly used internal sources. External sources include walk-ins, colleges and universities, media, employment agencies, union halls, and business and technical schools.

✔ *The benefits and dangers of application forms.* The third step in the selection procedure is receiving employment applications. Most firms have special forms designed to gather information on work experience, education, hobbies, interests, and references to help evaluate an applicant's job qualifications. Forms must be carefully designed so that they ask only those questions directly related to the job the applicant is seeking.

✔ *The various ways of screening job applicants.* The personal interview is the most commonly used screening device. Interviews can be classified according to the type and nature of questions asked or the number of people involved. They fall into three categories: patterned, planned, and panel.

The selection test is another widely used screening tool. Selection tests fall into four categories: achievement, aptitude, personality, and vocational interests. In recent years, a growing number of firms have stopped using these tests.

✔ *What induction and orientation mean for the new employee.* The final phase of the selection procedure, induction and orientation, is designed to establish an environment in which the new employee will be comfortable and productive.

✔ *The importance of career planning and career pathing in human resource management.* Career planning involves matching an employee's career aspirations with the opportunities available in the firm. In career pathing, the company maps out the sequential steps that an employee might take throughout his or her career to reach his or her personal goal.

✔ *What employers look for in prospective employees.* Surveys have shown that oral and written communications skills are the most important requirements in being hired and promoted. Oral communication skills, grade point average, and school attended are important in hiring but become less so in promotions.

✔ *The legal environment of staffing.* Recruiting, screening, retaining, and promoting employees must be accomplished within the limits of laws prohibiting discrimination on the basis of race, color, sex, religion, age, or national origin. A few of the laws that govern employment practices are the Civil Rights Act, the Equal Pay Act, the Age Discrimination in Employment Act, and the Equal Employment Opportunity Act. Many employers also must have affirmative action programs designed to eliminate discrimination in hiring and promotion. These plans identify problem areas and evaluate the opportunities for minorities, women, and older workers. Affirmative action plans specify goals and timetables for rectifying existing deficiencies.

THE MANAGER'S DICTIONARY

As an extra review of the chapter, try defining the following terms. If you have trouble with any of them, refer to the page numbers listed.

human resource planning (HRP) (205)
job design (206)
job analysis (207)
job description (207)
job specification (208)
job evaluation (208)
job modification (209)
work simplification (209)
job enlargement (209)
job rotation (209)
job enrichment (210)
vertical expansion (211)
plan-do-control approach (211)

telecommuting (211)
job rating (212)
simple ranking plan (212)
grade description method (212)
point system (213)
factor comparison system (213)
incentive pay plans (213)
job posting (214)
personal interview (216)
patterned (structured) interview (217)
planned (nondirective, unstructured) interview (218)

panel or board of interviewers (218)
halo effect (218)
achievement tests (219)
aptitude tests (219)
vocational interest tests (219)
personality tests (219)
induction and orientation (219)
career planning (219)
career pathing (219)
affirmative action programs (AAP) (224)

REVIEW QUESTIONS

1. What is the role of the personnel manager in selecting people to fill vacancies in a company? Explain.

2. List and describe each step in the employee selection procedure.

3. What are the objectives of job design?

4. List the steps in the job design cycle.

5. Why should job design be considered a continuous process rather than a single program?

6. Cite four ways to enrich jobs. How do they differ?

7. Describe the various methods used to establish wage rates. What advantages do the quantitative methods have over the nonquantitative methods?

8. In your opinion, should a firm practice "promoting from within?" Why or why not?

9. Can you think of any questions that should *not* be included on an application form or in a preemployment interview?

10. In your opinion, why do most managers rely on the personal interview as the basis for making hiring decisions?

11. Discuss the pros and cons of a patterned interview; a planned interview.

12. What does a career path show? Why is career pathing advantageous to the employee? to the employer?

13. Cite four laws that affect the staffing function and explain the primary objective of each.

MANAGEMENT CHALLENGE

Assume you are the comptroller for Northwest Distributing Company, a small regional wholesaler of paper and tobacco products, nonperishable foods, detergents, candy, and other consumer goods. At the present time, all accounting functions, including inventory, are handled manually; but the owner of the business has decided to convert to a computerized management information system. Specifically, she wants a system that will provide information on inventory levels of all items handled and that will help with billing, accounts payable, payroll, and other accounting functions. The owner has asked you to hire someone with an accounting background who can design and implement such a system. She also has informed you that she expects the new system ultimately to replace three or four clerks who now perform most accounting activities.

1. What qualifications would you seek in the new employee? Be specific.

2. How would you locate potential applicants who possess the qualifications needed for the job?

3. Describe the procedure you would follow in hiring the best-qualified applicant.

4. What steps would you take to avoid discriminating against applicants on the basis of sex, race, color, age, or national origin?

5. If the owner prefers to employ a qualified minority, what steps would you take to encourage minority applications?

CASE 8.1

A New Twist at PPG Industries[26]

Manufacturing fiberglass involves converting sand, limestone, and other raw materials into molten glass, which is extruded and wound into a continuous filament to produce the basic fiber. Once the filaments are wound, they are processed almost the same way as natural materials are before the finished yarns are shipped to fabric manufacturers.

PPG's fiberglass plant in Lexington, Kentucky, produces fiberglass yarns this way. The plant is highly automated and equipped with modern technology. It operates around-the-clock in a continuous production process. But in the past, the plant's efficiency dropped in the twisting operation. Twist frames transfer fiber from large tubes onto bobbins at specified degrees of twist to obtain the desired yarn texture, strength, and size. Although the operation is highly automated, the twist-frame machines were running at only 65% of capacity. The machines had to be turned off to clean lint, dust, and other debris from the frames. Periodically, the twist-frame operator signaled for a frame cleaner, whose only job was to clean the frame. The machines needed cleaning at different times, depending on their size and the time required to twist and wind different-sized bobbins.

Frame cleaning was a dirty job. Pay and job status were low, it was boring work, and attempts to increase the frame cleaner's sense of involvement yielded little or no success. Because of the problems encountered, PPG's management chose to make cleaning part of the twist-frame operator's job. The operator was required to clean his or her own frames, and the job of frame cleaner was eliminated. The company gave frame cleaners other jobs instead of laying them off.

As a pilot project, 10% of the total twist-frame operation was selected. Eventually, the entire operation was converted over a ten-week period because of the pilot project's success.

About 15% of an operator's time was spent in frame cleaning in the redesigned approach. Because the frame operators' efficiency was measured by the number of bobbins they filled each day, the less time they spent cleaning the frames, the more bobbins they could fill. No pay raise was given despite the added responsibilities.

Questions

1. Job enlargement for the frame operator resulted in adding an undesirable element—frame cleaning. Did this solve a problem or create a potential problem?

2. In your opinion, is management justified in modifying jobs if it results in layoffs or terminations? Why or why not?

CASE 8.2

One Executive's Search for a High-Level Job[27]

Morton Ehrlich quit his $160,000-a-year job as senior vice president at Eastern Airlines in July 1984, after being passed over for the presidency of the company. Like other executives who suddenly find themselves out of work, Ehrlich found the experience traumatic for himself and his family, even though he didn't face the financial problems normally associated with unemployment. What happened at Eastern Airlines a few months earlier was even more traumatic, however.

In 1983, Ehrlich felt that he was about to reach the pinnacle of his career—the presidency of an airline to which he had devoted seventeen years of his life. A seasoned veteran who had gained an industrywide reputation as a good planner, he felt he was ready for the challenge. His confidence was bolstered in March 1984, when Chairman Frank Borman promised that Ehrlich would be the next Eastern Airlines president. According to Ehrlich, the two men had talked about the office that Ehrlich would occupy, and a party was planned to announce his promotion. But for some reason, which Borman doesn't discuss, Ehrlich was passed over. Ehrlich calls the decision the biggest disappointment of his life; Borman says that Ehrlich left Eastern Airlines as a friend, albeit somewhat disappointed.

Immediately after learning that he would not be named Eastern Airlines president, Ehrlich began his job search. He prepared a two-page résumé, bought a telephone answering machine, contacted a number of associates, and consulted several executive search firms. He even asked friends to make calls on his behalf. Although his experience was limited to the airline industry, Ehrlich expanded his job search to other industries: he was considered for the presidency of a large travel wholesaler, for chief executive of a utility company, and for head of marketing for a health-services firm. But his real desire was to use his talent and experience in the industry he knew best.

Ehrlich's first break came as a result of a phone call from a retired Eastern executive to Frank Lorenzo, head of Texas Air Corporation. In August Lorenzo offered Ehrlich a job as vice president, but, considering the job as a step backward, he turned it down. At the same time, Ehrlich asked his friends to inform TWA investor Carl Icahn that he was interested in a job with TWA. Icahn arranged a luncheon meeting with TWA President Richard Pearson, and two days later Pearson offered Ehrlich the number two position at TWA—executive vice president for planning and government affairs.

During the time that he was out of work, Ehrlich's family suffered along with him. Ehrlich contends that he'll never forgive Borman. Such a reaction was almost identical to that of Lee Iacocca, now heading Chrysler, who was fired by Henry Ford II at Ford Motor Company. According to Ehrlich, the only bright side of an unpleasant situation like this comes from knowing that if it can happen to Lee Iacocca, it can happen to anyone.

Questions

1. How would you describe Ehrlich's approach to finding a job?

2. In your opinion, what was Ehrlich's biggest obstacle to finding a suitable position? What were his greatest assets? Discuss.

CHAPTER OUTLINE

The Nature of Organizational Change
>Forces of Change
>Motivation for Change
>Planned versus Reactive Change

Implementing Planned Change
>The Lewin Model
>An Expanded Change Model
>The Manager's Role as a Change Agent

Managing Resistance to Change
>Sources of Resistance
>Overcoming Resistance

Organizational Development
>OD Assumptions and Values
>A General OD Model

OD Intervention Techniques
>For Individuals
>*Sensitivity Training • Management Training • Role Negotiation • Job Design and Modification • Career Planning*
>For Groups
>*Team Building • Process Consultation • Intergroup Team Building*
>For the Whole Organization
>*Survey Feedback • Confrontation Meeting • Structural Redesign*

Grid Organizational Development

Evaluating the Results of OD: A Final Step

Organizational Change and Development

MANAGEMENT IN ACTION

Changing Levi's

Levi Strauss & Co., a name that has meant quality and durability for more than a hundred years, has discovered that being too stiff doesn't pay.

While fashions came and went in the rest of the clothing industry, Levi Strauss prospered for years on the popularity of a single garment that was worn by construction workers and trend setters alike—blue jeans. Then the trend setters turned away from basic blue jeans to designer jeans. Jordache, Gloria Vanderbilt, and Calvin Klein became household names. Slick promotional campaigns and competitors' ads based on sex appeal grabbed the buyers' attention. The company was caught unprepared.

But consumer tastes weren't the only reason for Levi Strauss's problems. A strong U.S. dollar overseas made American-produced goods relatively expensive. U.S. manufacturers such as Levi Strauss found foreign markets tough to penetrate.

Levi Strauss President Robert D. Hass summed up the situation this way: "This company is guilty of being too rigid and too deliberative in an industry made up of entrepreneurs who hustle. And we're going to have to change."[1]

To halt declining sales and profits, Levi Strauss did go through some huge changes. Managers were relocated from the corporate headquarters in San Francisco to low-rent sections of the city to shake up corporate complacency. There they were given the opportunity—and the financial backing—to start fledgling fashion apparel businesses. The firm also introduced new lines of merchandise, threw lavish parties for the press, spent more money on advertising, and tried to crack new markets that had been dominated by fashion apparel manufacturers. The company's changes were designed to make it more competitive in the marketplace.

Preview

Levi Strauss's problems are typical of those faced by firms that cannot—or will not—adapt to changing market conditions. Demand for designer jeans, advertising based on sex appeal, the strength of the U.S. dollar overseas, and reliance on a single product are to blame for Levi Strauss's problems.

Like most companies, Levi Strauss began to change only when outside pressures forced it to take some kind of action. Such action, known as reactive change, usually is taken only after crises have developed. After studying this chapter, you will understand:

✓ The nature of organizational change

✓ How planned change is implemented

✓ How to manage resistance to change

✓ The elements of organizational development

✓ OD intervention techniques for individuals, groups, and organizations

✓ How grid organizational development tackles management problems

✓ The importance of evaluating the results of organizational development

The Nature of Organizational Change

The effect of change on our society has become a hot news topic. Major magazines, newspapers, books, and television documentaries paint vivid pictures of the profound impact of change on our daily lives. Often, the negative effects—stress, suicide, drug and alcohol abuse—are emphasized. Sometimes, the world of new opportunities—as in computer technology—is stressed.

Change affects society

Like individuals, organizations feel the effect of change, whether for better or worse. And, like individuals, they must try to anticipate and prepare for future events. Managers must constantly cope with change. But they need not merely react to changes happening around them. They can make changes happen themselves. **Organizational change** can be any change that managers make to alter the way things are done—from installing a new copying machine to eliminating an entire level of supervisors.

Forces of Change

Organizational change can take many different forms. It can mean adding a new product line, such as Levi's 501 Blues; creating new departments, such as

Levi's fledgling businesses; consolidating activities by eliminating subgroups; selling a subsidiary; changing manufacturing processes; or modifying employees' behavior through seminars.

Both internal and external forces make organizational change necessary. *External* environmental forces include the social, political, cultural, economic, and technological influences discussed in Chapter 3. Some specific examples are changing societal values, new laws and regulations, changes in interest rates and the money supply, and technologically advanced production methods.

External forces of change

Internal forces of change are a result of how the technological, structural, and human subsystems that make up an organization interact and depend on one another. Historically, management's attempts to change and improve organizations have focused on these organizational subsystems. Too often, though, a change is made to one of them at the expense of the other two. For example, the scientific management movement spearheaded by Taylor, Gantt, and the Gilbreths emphasized the technical ways to improve organizational efficiency. The behavioral school, introduced by Münsterberg, focused on the managerial style and humanistic aspects of organizations. Changes to the subsystems frequently focused on different approaches to departmentation, job design, span of control, compensation systems, appraisal systems, and line-staff relationships.[2] Each of these areas is a valid target for change. But many of an organization's problems stem from dealing with these areas, or subsystems, as if they were independent of one another. They are not. As shown in Table 9.1, a favorable change in one subsystem may have adverse effects on the others.

Internal forces of change

Motivation for Change

Most managers have difficulty initiating change; in fact, people in all organizations suffer from a fundamental inertia that shows up in operations. Sometimes these operations are refined, cherished, and defended even when they are outdated or when they no longer help the organization.[3] For example, some retailers stick to their traditional hours of operation—nine to five, closed on Sunday—even though the public may want longer hours and Sunday openings.

Normally, external and internal forces for change must build to a critical state before managers are willing to change the status quo. In areas where Sunday closing is customary or mandated by so-called blue laws, competitive forces and consumer preference are forcing changes. Although some merchants are digging in their heels about changing their operating hours, others are yielding to consumer preference and competitive pressures and are now open seven days a week. They are changing their customary policy because of the pressure they feel.

Change is usually forced

Before organizational change can begin, someone in the organization (usually top management) must recognize that it is needed. This person sees that something is causing problems and affecting an aspect of the organization

Managers initiate change

TABLE 9.1
Interdependence of
organizational
subsystems

SUBSYSTEM	ORGANIZATIONAL CHANGE	POSSIBLE ADVERSE IMPACT ON OTHER SUBSYSTEMS
Technological	Change in process technology	Retraining of personnel
	Introduction of robotics	Displacement of workers
Structural	Job modification	Loss of status
	Addition of new department	Reallocation of resources
		Reassignment of personnel
Human	Transfer of key executive	Change in reporting relationships
		Loss of technical expertise

that management values. In the case of Sunday operations, for instance, the top management of a retail store may decide to open because of declining revenues and profits.

In studying successful organizational change, Dalton found that one of its most important conditions is a sense of tension or a felt need for change among those who have the authority to initiate it.[4] In the example in the preceding paragraph, the retail store's management may feel that staying open on Sunday is necessary if the store is to maintain or improve its market share. Unfortunately for most organizations, inertia delays the motivation to change until problems are severe. This "pain-induced change" is characterized by considerable external and internal pressure for change long before a need for change is recognized.[5]

Planned versus Reactive Change

Once motivated to change, very few organizations adapt and change in a smooth, orderly manner. The more common process includes a series of sticking points, at which the organization's need to change builds, followed by lurches into change. An organization's behavior at the sticking points may be somewhat inadequate at first; but, as the organization's environment changes and it continues not to adapt, the organization becomes increasingly out of step. A retailer who chooses to stay closed on Sunday, for example, may feel intense pressure from customers to remain open seven days a week. When a business is so out of step that sales and profits start slipping, management grudgingly takes some kind of action. This is the mechanism of **reactive change.**[6]

A proactive approach   **Planned change** is a more proactive approach. Proactive management tries to anticipate the future and to see the organization as it should be if it is to be effective in the future. Management will never be able to anticipate the future with total accuracy, but proactive planning can reduce those out-of-step periods that characterize reactive organizations.

Implementing Planned Change

Once an organization's management concludes that change is necessary, it should be brought about through a systematic process. An established change process serves two functions: it provides a sense of direction, and it assures that no essential element is overlooked.

The Lewin Model

Kurt Lewin suggested a process of planned change. The **Lewin model** has three successive stages: (1) unfreezing the status quo, (2) moving to a new level, and (3) refreezing at the new level.[7]

Stage one

The *unfreezing stage* has three objectives. First, support for the old way of doing things must be removed by recognizing its inadequacies. This first stage is basically a fact-finding process. It is most effective when employees are fully involved—not merely told by management that changes will take place. For instance, an office wants to investigate replacing its typewriters with word processing work stations. The office manager would be wise to ask typists for their opinions of typewriter efficiency, the amount of filing required, and the ease of correcting documents with the typewriters. Second, alternative plans of action should be evaluated and the best plan chosen. Again, employee involvement in evaluation can be valuable in gaining their acceptance of the plan finally chosen. In the office we just mentioned, for example, the typists might be asked to try out one word processing station and then report on its efficiency, filing space, convenience with floppy disks, and ease of correction. The third objective of the unfreezing stage involves gaining commitment to change. To do this, the manager must overcome the natural resistance to change of those who are affected by it. The Manager's Notebook on page 238 has some practical suggestions in this area. In the case of the typists, special training sessions might help to eliminate a fear of computers that some of them might have.

Stage two

The second stage in the Lewin model is movement to a new level—actually *implementing the change*. This movement may result from an order or recommendation, or it may be initiated by the workers. The specific technique used depends on such considerations as the type of change proposed and how quickly the change has to be made. In our example, the typists who saw the advantages of word processing work stations over typewriters may adamantly insist that a change be made.

Stage three

The final stage in the Lewin model, the *refreezing stage,* focuses on reinforcing the behavior patterns brought about by the change. This is done through

THE IN-BOX

Coca-Cola Shakes Up Its Bottlers

In 1979, Coca-Cola management decided to do something about the fact that PepsiCo had taken the lead in grocery-store and diet soft-drink sales.

The answer was a giant upheaval that put Coke back on top within six years. How was it done? The firm replaced two-thirds of its management between 1980 and 1982 and changed its product line, first by introducing Diet Coke and then by marketing an array of other drinks.

But some of the biggest changes had to do with the company's franchised bottlers. The company decided to replace the incompetent and uninterested with intelligent risk takers who had "no holds barred" marketing philosophies. Company executives say that no one was actually forced out. In some cases, Coke urged franchisers to sell, lined up aggressive replacements, and arranged financing. In most cases, the purchase price offered by Coke-backed buyers was so good that the bottlers had no reason to resist the change.

Naturally, some of the bottlers rejected the buy-out offers. After negotiations that dragged on for more than a year, one San Francisco bottler finally gave in and sold out. When asked to explain Coke's success in getting reluctant bottlers to sell, one Coke executive replied, "You persevere, persevere, persevere."

Source: Thomas E. Ricks, "Coca-Cola Celebrates New Success After Restructuring Its Bottlers," *Wall Street Journal*, June 28, 1984, p. 29.

feedback to participants—in effect "proving" the superiority of the new system over the old—and continual reinforcement of the new system. A follow-up survey of the typists, for instance, might dramatically demonstrate increased efficiency, decreased filing time, and easier corrections with word processors.

An Expanded Change Model

Several authors have taken the change process beyond Lewin's three basic steps. The expanded models by Lippett (1958), Greiner (1967), Shirley (1975), Ivancevich (1978), and Marchione and English (1982) are among the best known. These models are not so much departures from Lewin's concept as they are refinements of it. The **Greiner model** has six phases, which were observed in organizations that have made successful changes.[8]

In phase I, called pressure and arousal, a problem is recognized. Pressure on the organization from external and/or internal sources must be strong enough to gain management's attention. The awareness of a problem then becomes the catalyst for change.

Greiner's model

Phase II is intervention and reorientation. Managers become aware of the need for a fresh perspective on the organization, either through new management or through the eyes of an outside consultant. This new view can encourage managers to examine all aspects of the organization, not just the areas where they feel a problem exists.

Phase III is diagnosis and recognition of specific problems. Consulting subordinates is valuable at this stage, not only because they can provide additional information, but also because they will have greater commitment if actively involved.

Phase IV focuses on solutions to identified problems. Naturally, there is a temptation to apply old solutions to new problems, but organizational problems are usually so complex that each requires a unique solution. Solutions are also unique because the elements that go into them—time, financial resources, and management support—vary from one problem to the next. As in Phase III, a shared approach is most effective. Specific goals of the proposed solutions should be defined at this stage. They will act as standards that will make future evaluation easier.

Phase V involves experimenting with the solutions determined in Phase IV. Solutions are tentatively implemented and evaluated. Depending on the evaluation, solutions may be eliminated, refined, further evaluated, or implemented on a full-scale basis. Full-scale implementation often meets less resistance because workers have already seen positive results.

Phase VI, the final phase, reinforces the positive results of the change. Positive reinforcement rewards people for changing and makes future changes easier.

The Manager's Role as a Change Agent

Regardless of the change model used, the manager plays a crucial role in organizational change. As Blake and Mouton point out, it is absolutely essential for managers to lead the way when changing a company.[9] Anything managers do that suggests uncertainty and indecisiveness causes a ripple effect throughout the organization. This results in foot-dragging and also causes employees to question how committed to change top management really is. Effective leadership does not mean that managers cannot use consultants, but it is clearly the duty of top management to be a visible instrument in the change process.

The correct approach

Managers can take any one of three positions when the winds of change begin to blow. Too often, they deny the need for change altogether. This is especially true when other organizational members strongly resist change. An alternative is to try to accommodate the change: this usually involves preserving as much of the status quo as possible while attempting piecemeal, quick-fix solutions. The third and preferable way is for the manager to be truly an agent for change. This means recognizing the need for change and accepting primary responsibility for paving its way. Depending on the problem, facilitating change may involve intervention, development programs, or other activities designed to improve an organization's effectiveness and health.[10] Various intervention techniques and organizational development approaches are discussed later in this chapter.

Managing Resistance to Change

The most-needed and best-planned change carries no guarantee that it will be accepted. The following statement accurately summarizes people's natural resistance to change:

> As common as change is, the people who work in an organization may still not like it. Each of those "routine" changes can be accompanied by tension, stress, squabbling, sabotage, turnover, subtle undermining, behind the scenes foot-dragging, work slowdowns, needless political battles, and a drain on money and time—in short, symptoms of that everpresent bugaboo, resistance to change.[11]

Sources of Resistance

Understanding the sources of resistance to change is the first step in designing a program to help an organization accept change. These are the most common causes for resistance:

1. *Ignorance.* When people have insufficient knowledge, they are uncertain about the causes and effects of change. This uncertainty, in turn, causes stress and resistance. As with walking in the dark, most people would rather stay put than venture into the unknown. Also, when people are uncertain about reality, they try to guess about it, sometimes adding imaginary problems to the real ones. For example, if employees learn via the grapevine that management is considering merging departments to streamline operations and cut costs, they are likely to resist the change because they fear losing their jobs or having new reporting relationships.

Lack of information

2. *Desire for security.* People often want to retain the status quo even when they know it is inferior. The security of the "known" makes them resist change. The faster or more major the change, the more powerful the lure of the comforting status quo. This phenomenon was first discussed extensively by Alvin Toffler in his best-selling *Future Shock.*[12]

Fear of the unknown

Toffler and another futurist, John Naismith, vividly describe our changing society and suggest ways that organizations will adapt to change. Naismith and Toffler think that as America becomes an information society, the results will be widespread use of microcomputers, "listening" word processors, and electronic mail. They predict the emergence of a global economy, which will spawn new industries such as space science and molecular biology. Toffler predicts an end to assembly lines, fewer mass-produced goods, and a move toward customized products. He also foresees the development of new sources of energy, extensive use of robotics in manufacturing, and continued movement toward greater participatory management.[13]

Fear of failure

3. *Fear and lack of ambition.* Another source of resistance to change is people's unwillingness to learn the new skills or behavior that change may require. There are two reasons why. First, workers fear inability to learn the skills or behavior; therefore, change will mean failure. This fear is especially prevalent in older workers who have developed their skills over a long period. Second, some workers simply may not want to exert the energy, time, and mental effort required.

Fear of social changes

4. *Informal group pressure.* Most organizational changes have some impact on informal networks in the formal organization. Breaking up a closely knit work group or changing social relationships can provoke a great deal of resistance. Managers often overlook this source of resistance because the informal network is not the focal point of organizational change. This often unplanned, secondary spillover effect can cause resistance to a change.

Loss of status

5. *Eroding power bases.* The fifth source of resistance to change results from its effect on personal power bases. When people expect their status or power to decline, resistance is inevitable. Besides the direct loss of status or power from a change, there are power and status considerations in the change process itself. That is, change often invites criticism from other employees and causes workers to question their own abilities and self-worth.

Change can be threatening

6. *Potential loss of job security.* Advances in technology have made the concern for job security an especially strong source of resistance. A change that can eliminate jobs is threatening to employees. Two examples are the worker whose job will be taken over by a machine or a middle manager who is afraid that computers will eliminate his or her duties.

Personal disagreements

7. *Personality conflicts.* The last source of resistance is caused by personality clashes. These conflicts often are the result of misunderstandings, lack of trust, or past resentments. For instance, if employees whose personalities conflict must have daily personal contact because of a structural change, they are likely to resist the reorganization. This resistance can be strong enough to override the best of changes. Conflicts among workers, between positions, or with management in general can all inhibit acceptance of change.[14]

Overcoming Resistance

Managers often underestimate both the amount of resistance a proposed change can provoke and the negative effect that this resistance can have on progress. There are certain ways to minimize the resistance, however. Kotter and Schlesinger's approaches, illustrated in Table 9.2 and described below, are among the most effective methods that managers can use in dealing with resistance to change.[15]

Keep employees informed

1. *Proper communication.* One of the best ways to overcome resistance is through education and communication. All the people who may be affected by a change need advance information about the reason for the change, its nature, its planned timing, and the impact it is likely to have on the organization and personnel. When lines of communication are kept open, people can get the information they need as well as communicate their concerns. For communication to effectively reduce resistance, good superior-subordinate relationships are necessary so that people will believe what they are told.

Involvement

2. *Participation.* Basically, participation means involving affected workers in the change process. People affected by a proposed change can be encouraged to provide their opinions and suggestions. If employees participate in an activity, such as collecting performance data, they may be convinced of the need for change. This approach requires that management show a genuine interest in what others have to say and, whenever possible, give credit to the right people for their valuable input. Why is this method so effective? Because change is threatening when done *to* us, but exciting when done *by* us.

Be supportive

3. *Empathy.* Facilitation and support is the third method for overcoming resistance to change. This method recognizes that resistance can come from good and rational concerns. Being supportive may involve extra training in new skills, or simply listening and providing emotional support. Management also can smooth the change process by emphasizing its most personal benefits and giving people time to adjust. A change also can be implemented in phases in an effort to minimize the upheaval.

Inducements

4. *Negotiation and incentives.* Managers can use this approach for specific sources of resistance. For instance, if workers fear losing their jobs, they may be given some guarantee that they won't be fired. Another way to use negotiation and agreement is to offer incentives to those who support the changes even if the change results in the loss of jobs. Exxon Corporation, for example, offered its employees bonuses to take early retirement when it decided to cut its work force by forty thousand in 1986.[16] Coca-Cola Co. offered attractive prices to bottlers it was trying to buy out during its restructuring, as shown in the In-Box on page 244.

TABLE 9.2
Methods for minimizing
resistance to change

SOURCES OF RESISTANCE	POSSIBLE REMEDIES
Ignorance; inadequate information	Complete and accurate communication based on mutual superior-subordinate trust
Loss of job security	Empathy; additional training; gradual change; incentives
Fear; lack of ambition	Incentives; supportive atmosphere; guarantee of job retention; involvement
Personality conflict	Manipulation; coercion
Loss of status	Additional training; incentives
Informal group pressure	Incentives for group leader; co-optation; manipulation; coercion

5. *Manipulation.* Some managers try to reduce resistance by manipulation and co-optation. Manipulation usually involves the select use of information and the conscious structuring of events. For example, when Exxon announced its plans to reduce its work force by one-fourth, it realized that forty thousand people might not want to retire voluntarily, even with the inducements. So Exxon informed its employees as part of its announcement that involuntary retirements and firings—with regular severance pay—would make up the balance. Exxon manipulated its employees by creating uncertain conditions.[17]

Co-optation

Co-optation is a form of manipulation in which potential resisters or leaders of resisting groups are given a role in designing or implementing change. The basic difference between co-optation and the participation referred to earlier is that co-optation looks for help merely to silence potential dissenters, not for the sake of valuable information that may be gained.

6. *Coercion.* The last method for overcoming resistance is explicit and implicit coercion, which forces acceptance. Explicit coercion often takes the form of firing or transferring resisters. Issuing statements designed to create fear of the business going bankrupt is an example of implicit coercion.

Negative incentives

Choosing a method to minimize or eliminate resistance depends on the source of the resistance and the time constraints for implementing the change. The objective of all these methods is to turn resistance into commitment.

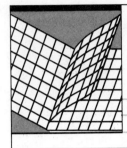

THE MANAGER'S NOTEBOOK

The Energy of Change

The manager about to institute sweeping changes should keep in mind the caveman and the bear.

Like the caveman, employees facing major challenges will feel a burst of energy. The caveman used this so-called hyperenergy to fight with, and kill, the bear, or to run and hide. The manager, likewise, can use the employees' energy to make the change process a success. But the manager with a take-it-or-leave-it attitude can provoke employees so that they use this creative force for serious resistance to change.

Middle managers react to change from on high with their own level of hyperenergy. After adjusting to the change, they must be careful of their impulse to pass it on to subordinates too quickly; instead, they must plan how to approach them. Here are some guidelines:

1. After announcing a change, never expect it to happen instantly. Education is a must. Managers need to explain the benefits of a change and to make fair provisions for employees who will lose as a result of change.

2. Draw up a goal agenda—a flexible, informal set of plans with objectives to be reached for meeting certain critical goals. Compile a list of people on whom to depend. Include, besides supporters of the change, those who may have doubts and even some employees you may dislike.

3. Don't try to assume total control over the change plans. This may create distance between you and the employees.

4. Ask yourself whether the employees will need training. Employees may be resisting the change because they lack the knowledge they need to take part in it.

5. Always ask for employees' worries and reactions. Speaking up reduces the stress that accompanies hyperenergy.

6. Remember that mistakes are an inevitable, intermediate step in the change process.

Source: Dennis J. Gillen, "Harnessing the Energy from Change Anxiety," *Supervisory Management*, March 1986, pp. 40–43. Copyright © 1986 American Management Association, New York. All rights reserved.

Organizational Development

Focuses on changing attitudes

In recent years, organizational development has gained widespread attention as an approach to organizational change. It generally is considered a long-range method for improving an organization's performance by modifying its employees' attitudes and behavior. That is, it tries to identify and correct the reasons for such problems as absenteeism, apathy, low productivity, and turnover. Organizational development differs from organizational change in that it tries to change employees' attitudes and behavior rather than organizational structure and technology.

Based on behavioral science

Begun at MIT in the late 1940s as an application of behavioral science, organizational development has evolved to organizational problem solving. It rests on the theories of several psychologists, including Carl Rogers and Abraham Maslow, and social scientists, especially Kurt Lewin.[18] The term *organizational development* first appeared about 1957, when it was used by a number of theorists, including Blake and Mouton, Shepard, and Beckhard. It drew on the laboratory methods of the National Training Laboratories and the research methods of the Survey Research Center.[19]

Beckhard gives five elements of **organization development (OD)**:

Beckhard's definition

> Organization development is an effort (1) planned, (2) organization-wide, and (3) managed from the top, to (4) increase organization effectiveness and health through (5) planned intervention in the organization's "processes," using behavioral-science knowledge.[20]

Let's examine each of these elements more closely:

1. *Planned.* OD is planned evolution and improvement. This planning includes examining the present and systematically diagnosing the organization's needs, formulating a specific plan for improvement, and mobilizing the organizational resources needed to carry out the change.

2. *Organizationwide.* The goal of OD is to improve the effectiveness of the total organization, although specific aspects may focus on subsystems. The underlying view is that an organization is a system of interrelated parts.

3. *Managed from the top.* In an OD effort, the manager is a key element to success. For the change to work well, commitment is essential at all levels. The commitment and active support of top management is crucial because it serves as a standard for the rest of the organization's members.

Five elements

4. *Increase organizational effectiveness and health.* One of OD's aims is to teach the organization how to improve its problem-solving capabilities. It tries to make the organizational culture more effective at defining its mission, planning its efforts, coping with change, and achieving its goals.[21]

5. *Planned intervention using behavioral-science knowledge.* OD is directed at individual, group, and organizational effectiveness in an effort to change attitudes, values, beliefs, norms, and ways of working and relating to others. It is based on behavioral-science theories on motivation and interpersonal relationships.[22]

OD Assumptions and Values

Its behavioral-science orientation is reflected in OD's assumptions and values. Organizational development's assumptions about human nature are basically the same as those of Douglas McGregor's Theory Y. This theory, discussed in detail in Chapter 10, is based on a trusting, positive view of people and advocates integrating individual needs with overall organizational goals.[23]

Theory Y and OD assumptions

OD looks at people at individuals, as group members, and as members of a wider organization. According to the OD philosophy, people are intelligent, have integrity, and need to achieve and develop. A supportive, challenging environment will motivate them to fulfill these needs; however, most organizational environments only partially tap the human potential of their individual members.[24]

As Maslow's hierarchy of needs shows, people are also social animals who want to be accepted by the group.[25] Since they spend most of their time at work, people consider their work group a very important reference group. As a result, the group's feelings and effort help the individual feel more effective. Cooperative team effort also has a synergistic effect—the group performance is greater than the sum of individual performances.

Work groups in an organization are interdependent parts of a larger system. The larger system, the organization, has a "culture" that reflects the organization's values, degree of trust, freedom of expression, support, and appreciation of individual worth. This organizational culture in turn affects job satisfaction, work-group effectiveness, communication, and general morale.[26]

The values of OD are summarized by French, who believes that organized effort is justified because it is a way to fulfill human needs and aspirations. French also believes that the freedom to express feelings and sentiments is a legitimate part of an organization's culture. He considers satisfactory interpersonal and intergroup relations to be basic to effective, healthy organizations.[27]

Margulies and Raia have compiled a list summing up the specific, action-oriented values of OD. They say that OD:

1. Provides opportunities for people to function as human beings rather than resources in the productive process.

Values

2. Gives each member of the organization opportunities to develop to his or her full potential.

3. Seeks to make the organization more effective in meeting all its goals.

4. Tries to create an environment in which exciting and challenging work can be found.

5. Gives people in organizations the chance to influence how they relate to work, the organization, and the work environment.

6. Treats each human being as a person with a complex set of needs, all of which are important in his or her work and life.[28]

A General OD Model

The OD process is a continuous cycle of (1) evaluating the status quo and diagnosing needs, (2) intervening to achieve the needed changes, and (3) reinforcing both positive results and the process itself.

Three phases

The first phase of OD, evaluation and diagnosis, is an organizationwide effort to answer the fundamental management questions: "Where are we now?" "Where do we want to be?" and "How do we get there?" Answers to these questions help shape the selection of an intervention method.

The intervention phase of OD is the action phase. This is the time when the organization is in transition from where it is to where it wants to be. Intervention is typically characterized by group processes, team effort, and the use of a change agent, usually referred to as a facilitator.

The third phase of the OD model is reinforcement. If a change is to be adopted permanently, people need positive feedback on the results, and they need their changed behavior reinforced. Change often fails at this point because its focal point becomes out of step with the rest of the organization.

OD Intervention Techniques

The types of organizational problems, their sources, and the circumstances surrounding each are virtually unlimited. The OD intervention technique required, therefore, depends on which best fits the organization, the problem, and the situation.

The depth of intervention needed is an important factor in selecting an intervention technique. Sometimes techniques focus on an individual within an organization. Other times, a group or the organization as a whole is the focal point. The survey feedback technique is much less individualized than sensitivity training, for example.

The intervention techniques presented here illustrate these various approaches. Although they are discussed separately for ease of presentation, they usually are used in combinations.

For Individuals

Sensitivity Training   **Sensitivity training** was developed by Leland Bradford, Kenneth Benne, and Ronald Lippett in 1946 when they were studying leaderless discussion groups.[29] This technique, often called T-Group training or

T-group training

laboratory training, grew in popularity and received much public attention in the 1960s but has declined in popularity recently.

The theoretical basis of sensitivity training is the belief that individual values, attitudes, and behavior determine an organization's effectiveness. This approach tries to make people aware of and sensitive to their own behavioral patterns and those of others. This is done face-to-face in groups of people whose status is equal or unknown. This temporary environment teaches people things about others that can be applied at the work site.

Sensitivity training has come under sharp criticism in recent years. The main objection to this approach is the use of unskilled moderators and the emotional danger inherent in breaking down people's defense mechanisms. Also, organizations often failed to achieve the desired results after sensitivity training was used.[30]

Management Training   The underlying assumptions behind **management training** are that managers are a significant factor in an organization's effectiveness and that they can improve their leadership skills. Training usually is conducted in a seminar, either in-house or at a training center. Management training has three objectives: (1) to teach specific behavior to people that they, in turn, can teach others, (2) to develop general diagnostic skills needed by managers, and (3) to help managers solve problems in their own organizations.[31]

Seminars

Role Negotiation   Developed by Roger Harrison as an intervention technique, **role negotiation** is directed at the work relationships among group members. In a series of controlled negotiations, managers candidly discuss what they want from one another and explain why. The typical procedure used in this technique has four stages. In stage one, called contract setting, managers list things that other managers should and should not do. In stage two, issue diagnosis, the lists are consolidated. In stage three, managers actually negotiate one-on-one with other managers about their roles in the organization. The outcome of the first three stages is written down in the final stage, written role assignments.[32]

Candid discussions

Job Design and Modification   As pointed out in Chapter 8, the term *job design* refers to specifying the contents, methods, and relationships of jobs. Three broad approaches to job design and modification are used as OD intervention techniques: job enlargement, job enrichment, and autonomous work-group design.

Job enlargement (see Chapter 8) is an approach that makes jobs bigger by increasing the number of tasks a worker must perform. Advocates believe that job enlargement increases worker motivation because he or she is less bored, has more meaningful tasks, and takes on greater responsibility. Job enrichment (see Chapter 8) expands work by adding planning and controlling duties to a job. The third approach, **autonomous work-group design,** is used extensively in Europe and was developed by the Travestock Institute of Human

Job enlargement and job enrichment

Relations in London.[33] This approach views the organization in two dimensions—the social system made up of interpersonal relationships, and the technological system comprised of tasks, tools, and work activities. The objectives of autonomous work-group design are (1) to develop a sense of accomplishment, (2) to give workers control over their own activities, and (3) to develop satisfactory relationships among people who work together. These goals are achieved through changes in work-flow patterns, superior-subordinate relationships, and communication systems, and through job enrichment and job enlargement.[34]

Management by objectives applied

Career Planning   Career planning is an intervention technique designed to help ease career crises and the stress accompanying them. Essentially, career planning applies management by objectives (MBO) to an individual's career. That is, it identifies attainable career goals and establishes the career path leading to them. Crises and stress are minimized by matching an individual's career aspirations with opportunities offered by the organization.

For Groups

Most managers recognize that an organization's overall effectiveness depends on how well individuals and groups perform. As a result, OD interventions that focus on group effectiveness are getting greater emphasis today. When Heisler surveyed businesses to learn what OD techniques were being used, he found that team building was the most popular group approach.[35]

Planning-commitment process

Team Building   All the basic **team-building** formats begin with a planning-commitment process that is essential to their success. Planning begins by assessing a work unit's needs from information gathered about current conditions. Next, the resources available to meet those needs are assessed. If a problem has to do with the social system of the work group and the necessary resources are available, the next step is commitment. Everyone in the work group must understand what is planned in the team-building program and the rationale for change. Group members also must know what has to be done, and they must agree on time demands. The starting point of team building is the enthusiastic commitment of group members to work toward solutions.

Patten identifies four conditions necessary for the development of effective teams. First, the group must have mutual objectives. Second, group members must depend somewhat on one another's experience, ability, and commitment. Third, group members must be committed to a team effort to achieve synergism. And, finally, the group must be accountable as a unit within the organization.[36]

Ideally, the team-building program becomes a cyclical, ongoing process. The cycle starts when it is felt that a problem exists. This is followed by a planning-commitment stage and team-building format sessions. Actions planned in the team-building sessions become group practices and then are evaluated.

Evaluation becomes a continual practice that leads to new team-building cycles when needed.

Process Consultation   **Process consultation** is defined as "a set of activities on the part of a consultant which help the client to perceive, understand, and act upon process events which occur in the client's environment."[37] Process consultation assumes that an organization's effectiveness depends on how well its people relate to one another. An organization's problems, therefore, often can be traced to the breakdown of critical human processes at key places.

Use of outside consultant

Process consultation has four steps.[38] First, an agenda-setting meeting is held. Next, the group is told how well it functions. Third, individuals and groups of people are coached and counseled. Finally, structural changes are made in the group. This process typically involves a professional consultant from outside the company.

Intergroup Team Building   The previous discussion of team building was concerned with intragroup effectiveness; that is, effectiveness within a work unit that has common tasks and goals. But because organizations are made up of many work units differing from one another but needing to work together, effectiveness within groups does not assure effectiveness between them.

Developing harmonious relations

Whenever work units must collaborate, conflict between them can prevent each from achieving its objectives. An **intergroup team-building** program may be used as a problem-solving process to reduce conflict and improve their future dealings.

Like other intervention techniques, the intergroup process begins with a perceived need, followed by a planning-commitment process, then a team-building session. Sessions can be conducted with individual units followed by mixed-unit sessions, all mixed-unit sessions, or task-force sessions comprised of selected members from both groups.[39]

For the Whole Organization

The following interventions are examples of OD techniques designed to improve overall organizational effectiveness.

Anonymous questionnaires

Survey Feedback   Developed by Floyd Mann at the University of Michigan's Survey Research Center, the **survey feedback** technique is based on the assumption that organizational behavior is a result on how its people perceive reality.[40] Attitudes and opinions are collected through anonymous questionnaires. This information is shared with the employees on a group-by-group basis. The groups use the information to come up with action plans to change the organization's structure and working relationships. The objective of this approach is to solve existing problems and to help groups understand their own behavior so that they can be more effective in the future.

Confrontation Meeting   This intervention technique was developed by Richard Beckhard as a way to generate information rapidly, to identify problems, and to set priorities for future courses of action.[41] A **confrontation meeting** is typically a one-day activity that brings together large segments of an organization drawn primarily from top management. Each session goes through the following six steps: (1) setting ground rules, (2) collecting information, (3) sharing information, (4) setting priorities and planning action, (5) follow-up by top management teams, and (6) reviewing progress.[42]

Top-management meeting

Structural Redesign   Generally, an organization's structure is changed to make it more efficient by redefining the flow of authority. There also can be changes in functional responsibility, such as a move from product to matrix organizational structure.

Organizational structure often reflects the personal desires, needs, and values of the chief executive. Changing structure, therefore, may create resistance and concern because people are worried about their power or status, or how the change will affect their work groups.

Reorganization

Grid Organizational Development

Normally, OD intervention techniques are tailor-made to fit the needs of organizations; however, there are several commercial techniques, available through licensed individuals, that can be adapted to a variety of situations. Probably the best-known packaged technique is that developed by Robert Blake and Jane Mouton, commonly referred to as Grid® OD.[43]

Grid OD is based on Blake and Mouton's model of leadership called the Managerial Grid® (see Figure 12.2). Their model depicts two prevailing concerns found in all organizations—concern for productivity and concern for people. Some managers are high in concern for productivity but low in concern for people; others are high in concern for people but low in concern for productivity. Besides helping managers evaluate their concern for people and productivity, the Managerial Grid® stresses the importance of developing a team-management leadership style.

The Grid OD approach involves six phases that could cover a three-to-five-year period if taken sequentially.[44]

Phases one and two are management-development stages that work together and are the foundation of future phases. Laboratory-seminar training is phase one. This training involves a one-week conference conducted by line managers who have already been through the program. At the conference, groups of twelve to forty-eight people from different departments and levels in an organization serve as problem-solving teams. Members evaluate their own management style and work with their team on problem solving and evaluating team performance.

Six phases of Grid OD

In phase two, participants apply what they have learned at the conference to work units in the organization.

The goal of the next four phases of the Grid OD approach is to help managers meet more complex objectives of OD. Phase three involves intergroup development similar to the intragroup development of phase two. Problems that exist between groups are identified and solved wherever group cooperation is vital to success.

The fourth phase is organizational goal setting. In this phase, special task groups focus on identifying organizationwide problems. Management involvement at this stage helps ensure its commitment to solutions.

Goal attainment is the fifth phase of the Grid approach. In this phase, the problems identified in phase four are refined, corrective steps are agreed on, and areas of accountability are assigned.

The last phase of the Grid OD approach is stabilization. Solutions implemented in phase five are evaluated and reinforced. This assessment phase evaluates progress and identifies problems to be tackled in the future.

Evaluating the Results of OD: A Final Step

Assessing the effect of OD

Even in organizations in which change is recognized as the prerequisite of success, the results of change often are not evaluated. Managers sometimes feel that the success or failure of the change will be obvious, or they may find it difficult to evaluate objectively. For these reasons, they sometimes do not formally evaluate the results of their change efforts.

Evaluations determine whether change efforts achieved their purpose. That is why managers should plan evaluations and make them an integral part of the change process. Four elements in the evaluation procedure require attention. First, the purpose of evaluation should be clearly defined. A total system could be reviewed to evaluate the outcome, or specific interventions could be monitored. Next, management must identify what information is needed and its sources. In the third element of evaluation a data-collection method must be chosen, taking into account accuracy needs, costs, and time. Finally, the timing of data gathering and data analysis must be determined.[45]

Results of change efforts vary from company to company; not all have ideal results. However, organizations that have repeatedly seen positive results through planned change exhibit different characteristics from those with less than satisfactory results. Based on an evaluation of successful and unsuccessful change programs, Greiner and Beckhard noted that successful efforts have the following characteristics:

1. Management is aware of strong pressure to initiate change.

Requirements of a successful program

2. There is intervention from someone new to the organization, possibly an outside consultant.

3. There is a shared approach to diagnosing problems that begins at the top of the organization, then gradually moves down through the hierarchy.

4. New and unique solutions to problems are found.

5. New solutions are implemented on a trial basis.

6. There is strong support for change at all levels of the organization.

7. Management exhibits a realistic, long-term perspective. Changes are not made overnight.

8. People are rewarded for the effort of changing and improving.

9. There is a willingness to take risks to improve.[46]

Review

✓ *The nature of organizational change.* For businesses to survive, they must constantly adapt to changing conditions. Internal and external forces require an organization to make changes. External forces may be social, political, cultural, and technological. Internal forces of change result from the interaction and interdependence of the organization's technological, structural, and human subsystems. Historically, efforts to change or improve an organization's effectiveness have focused on these three areas, which are interdependent.

Most managers are reluctant to initiate change; in fact, all organizations suffer from inertia. Normally, change occurs only when problems become so acute that no other alternative is feasible. Before organizational change can take place, someone in the organization—usually a high-ranking manager—must recognize the need for change.

Change takes two forms—planned and reactive. Reactive change is a response to stimuli. Normally it occurs only when pressures build to a critical point and the organization becomes increasingly "out of sync" with its environment. Planned change, on the other hand, is an attempt to anticipate the future and to prepare for it.

✓ *How planned change is implemented.* Once management concludes that change is needed, a systematic process for bringing it about is necessary. One of the best-known change processes is the Lewin model, developed by Kurt Lewin. This has three successive steps: unfreezing the status quo, moving to a new way of doing things, and refreezing at the new level. Employee involvement in each phase is the key ingredient.

Managers play a crucial role in the change process. Change causes anxiety and stress because of the uncertainty surrounding it. As a result, managers must be change agents—viable leaders of the change process. Managers' failure to assume leadership in this area causes uncertainty and resistance throughout the organization.

✓ *How to manage resistance to change.* Understanding the sources of resistance is the first step in designing a program to help an organization accept change. The most common causes of resistance are lack of information, insecurity, fear of the unknown, peer pressure, loss of power and prestige, and personality conflicts that could result from change.

Resistance to change can be overcome in several ways. Good communication and employees' involvement can help reduce resistance. Managers can also achieve acceptance through incentives, manipulation, and coercion. Choosing a method to minimize resistance depends on the source of resistance and the time constraints for implementing the change.

✓ *The elements of organizational development.* An approach to change that has gained considerable popularity in recent years is organizational development (OD). Initiated by top management, this proactive change affects the entire organization. It is implemented through planned intervention techniques that are based on behavioral science.

✓ *OD techniques for individuals, groups, and organizations.* Intervention techniques used to improve individual effectiveness include sensitivity training, management training, role negotiation, job design and modification, and career planning. Interventions designed to improve group performance include team building, process consultation, and intergroup team building. Techniques to improve overall organizational effectiveness include survey feedback, confrontation meetings, and structural redesign.

✓ *How Grid Organizational Development tackles management problems.* The Grid OD approach, developed by Robert Blake and Jane Mouton, helps managers evaluate their concern for people and productivity; it stresses the importance of developing a team-management style.

✓ *The importance of evaluating the results of organizational development.* Evaluation determines whether the change efforts have succeeded. Managers must define the purpose of the evaluation, identify needed information and its sources, choose a data-collection method, and determine the timing of the data gathering and analysis.

THE MANAGER'S DICTIONARY

As an extra review of the chapter, try defining the following terms. If you have trouble with any of them, refer to the page number listed.

organizational change (234)
reactive change (236)
planned change (236)
Lewin model (237)
Greiner model (238)
organizational development (OD) (245)

sensitivity training (247)
role negotiation (248)
autonomous work-group design (248)
team building (249)
process consultation (250)

intergroup team building (250)
survey feedback (250)
confrontation meeting (251)
Grid OD (251)

REVIEW QUESTIONS

1. Why is organizational change necessary? Explain.

2. Describe the forces that shape an organization's environment. Which are controllable? Which aren't?

3. Cite the targets of organizational change. Can you give examples of ways an organization might institute change in each area?

4. Distinguish between planned and reactive change.

5. Describe the process of planned change. What does each phase encompass?

6. Why are managers reluctant to initiate change? Discuss.

7. In your opinion, why must a situation reach crisis proportions before change is undertaken?

8. What role should managers play in bringing about change?

9. People have a natural resistance to change. Why?

10. Discuss some methods for minimizing resistance to change.

11. Pinpoint the relationship between organizational development and behavioral science.

12. Briefly cite the assumptions and values of organizational development.

13. Why are intervention techniques a critical element in OD?

14. What techniques can be used to improve individual effectiveness? group effectiveness? organizational effectiveness?

15. Does change guarantee ideal results? Why or why not?

MANAGEMENT CHALLENGE

As the recently appointed plant manager of a firm specializing in the development, manufacture, and distribution of computer hardware and software, you are considering replacing most personal secretaries with a word processing department that would perform secretarial and clerical duties for the entire plant. Most personal secretaries would be reassigned to the word processing department, where they would work directly under a word processing supervisor.

1. Discuss the process you would follow in making the change.

2. From what sources would you expect resistance to the proposed change?

3. In your opinion, why would employees affected by the change resist the word processing concept?

4. What steps would you take to minimize resistance? Be specific.

5. Assume that some of the older, more experienced secretaries and managers continued to resist the change, even though you feel that it would greatly improve efficiency. How would you handle the situation?

CASE 9.1

The Picture Changes at Eastman Kodak[47]

Eastman Kodak Company's 1984 annual report signaled some big changes for the company. Foreign competitors had been cutting into the photographic business, and Kodak's dominant position was threatened. Net income in 1983 and 1984 was lower than it had been the previous four years, and sales had leveled off. Kodak President Kay R. Whitmore thought change was inevitable.

As a result, Kodak split its photographic division into seventeen separate units to speed the development of new products and to keep in closer touch with the marketplace. It also entered the diskette and video markets and created divisions to produce electronic parts and biological materials. Its chemical business was kept intact.

Kodak selected young, aggressive—but relatively inexperienced—entrepreneurial-type managers for its seventeen new photographic units. Each unit operates as an independent company, with each manager accountable for its performance.

Traditionally, Eastman Kodak operated as a centralized entity that offered workers lifetime job security and a way to progress through the company ranks. But that image began to fade in 1983 when 8,600 workers were either laid off or induced to accept retirement or severance. At the same time, Kodak's top management set some ambitious goals measured in terms of profit and return on equity. To achieve these goals, the company would need new product lines and new business strategies; introducing a new kind of film or a new camera wouldn't be enough. Besides, technological breakthroughs had enabled manufacturers to develop products that didn't require film patented by Kodak.

Through acquisitions, Kodak has entered a number of new markets, many of which are totally unrelated to the photographic equipment and supply business. Since 1981, the firm has bought electronic-publishing systems, ink-jet printing systems, Verbatim (a diskette manufacturer), and Eikonix Corporation (a manufacturer of digital image-processing equipment). Its big push, however, has been in the areas of information processing and life sciences.

Questions

1. Explain the rationale for Eastman Kodak's changing to broaden its base of operations.

2. How do these changes affect employees of Eastman Kodak? How would you expect them to react to such organizational change and growth?

CASE 9.2

Growing Too Fast at People Express[48]

Rapid growth can be painful. Just ask Donald Burr, cofounder of People Express Airlines. Within five years of its birth, People Express had become the ninth-largest U.S. airline; then, suddenly, it was failing. Unprecedented growth was straining the company's fragile structure and threatening its financial stability.

In September 1986, Texas Air Corporation and its acquisitions-hungry chairperson, Frank A. Lorenzo, agreed to rescue People Express from the brink of bankruptcy for $300 million in stock, notes, and some cash. In early 1987, Continental Airlines purchased People Express from Texas Air.

Deregulation had provided the opportunity to establish and expand People Express, which offered low fares and service to areas not served by other carriers. People's low-cost, no-frills flights appealed to numerous travelers in the East. The young company was able to take advantage of an airplane-glutted market by buying used aircraft at bargain-basement prices.

Burr's management philosophy set People Express apart from other airlines. Every employee below Burr's level was required to spend time working directly with customers, every new employee was required to buy one hundred shares of stock upon joining the company, every employee had a title, and there were no secretaries anywhere in the firm. Because every employee had customer-related tasks and bureaucratic duties, they learned to consider

problems from different perspectives. At the heart of Burr's philosophy was his commitment to avoid building a bureaucracy that he believed would stifle creativity and shift attention away from the customer.

Burr's combination was so successful that by the mid-1980s People Express had grown from 250 employees to 4,000, and its fleet of planes had increased from three to seventy-nine. Its giant competitor—Eastern Airlines—was in financial trouble and couldn't match People's lower fares. (Ironically, Texas Air Corporation acquired Eastern within months of taking over People Express.)

The faster People Express grew, the more money it lost. In its final months, Burr had tried to transform the airline from a budget carrier to a more conventional one with higher fares. The scheme failed.

Some critics believe that People Express could have survived if its management philosophy and structure had been changed. Growth requires decentralization. One person is not capable of running all aspects of such an operation—regardless of his or her dedication.

Questions

1. Does organizational growth and development inevitably lead to bureaucratic structure?

2. In your opinion, could People Express have survived if its management philosophy and structure were different?

PLAN

ORGANIZE

CONTROL

LEAD

STAFF

Leading

In Part Three, we discussed the importance of creating a viable structure to help accomplish organizational goals. We also analyzed the manager's responsibility for recruiting, selecting, and developing the human resources that make up the organization.

Part Four discusses the manager's job of energizing and channeling human effort. It reviews various approaches to motivation, analyzes ways of minimizing organizational conflict among group members, presents the advantages and disadvantages of various leadership styles, and discusses the role of communication in achieving organizational effectiveness.

Chapter 10, "Motivation and Human Behavior," contrasts the traditional, human relations, and human resources models of motivation, discussing the relationship between approaches to motivation and attitudes toward human behavior. The chapter also presents several prominent theories of motivation, illustrating how they can be applied in organizations.

Chapter 11, "Groups and the Management of Conflict," pinpoints the differences between formal and informal organizations and shows how and why informal groups develop. The chapter analyzes the characteristics common to informal organizations and focuses on problems inherent in them. The impact of informal groups on formal organizations is discussed, and the role of the manager in minimizing and resolving conflict is stressed. Finally, the chapter addresses ways of minimizing the stress that may stem from conflict.

Chapter 12, "Leadership," contrasts different leadership styles and provides insight into the development of models of leadership behavior. Studies of leadership styles are presented and evaluated.

Chapter 13, "Effective Communication," describes the communication process and shows how effective communication promotes organizational efficiency. Both formal and informal channels of communication are discussed and illustrated, along with the impact of communication on job performance and employee satisfaction. Various obstacles interfering with effective communication are described, and ways to eliminate them are suggested.

CHAPTER OUTLINE

The Importance of Motivation

Evolving Managerial Approaches to Motivation
    The Traditional Model
    The Human Relations Model
    The Human Resources Model

Selected Theories of Motivation

Need Theories
    Maslow's Hierarchy of Needs
    Application of Needs Theory in Business • Criticisms of Maslow's Theory
    Herzberg's Motivation-Hygiene Theory
    Application of Herzberg's Findings • Criticisms of Herzberg's Theory
    The Achievement Motive

Expectancy Theory

Incentive Theory
    Skinner's Reinforcement Theory
    What Constitutes Reinforcement? • Application of Reinforcement Theory
    Equity Theory

Applying Theory in Organizations
    Work Schedule Changes
    Work Structure Changes
    Task Variety • Work Module • Performance Feedback • Better Use of Worker Abilities • Worker-Controlled Pacing
    Work Enrichment

Motivation and Human Behavior

M A N A G E M E N T   I N   A C T I O N

Motivating the Creative Employee

IBM, Intel, 3M, Borg-Warner, Apple Computer, General Mills, and a host of other companies whose futures depend on the creative genius of their personnel all agree on one thing—innovative people must be managed differently than other workers are.[1]

First, you have to identify the innovators. Whereas some are eccentrics who wear plaid flannel shirts and hand-crafted earrings, others lead lives that seem dull and boring by most standards. The only way to spot the truly creative types, according to David Boucher, president of Interleaf, Inc., is to observe who consistently comes up with good ideas. Once identified, they must be given room to maneuver. Lester Krogh, head of research and development at 3M, describes his approach to managing innovators this way: "We try to keep our mouths shut. Sometimes it is necessary to keep your eyes half-closed too."

IBM insulates its creative people from the corporate bureaucracy by assigning them to a facility where they can be creative in peace. But this approach has its drawbacks. As Intel President Andrew Grove points out, this treatment may lead to the creation of a new class system—one that replaces the elite executive class with its private parking spaces, dining facilities, and the like. Joe Lee, executive vice president for General Mills, sums up the proper superior-subordinate relationship in one word—trust. You trust the creative person to work hard and do his or her best; he or she trusts you to provide plenty of room, necessary resources, and helpful moral support.

Innovators also must be treated as professionals. They don't appreciate harsh criticism. "You never yell at people," says David Litwack, vice president for development at Cullinet Software. But you do have to reward

261

them. Pay is important, but what they really want is to turn their ideas into reality and to have the world—and their colleagues in particular—see their accomplishments.[2]

Preview

Litwack's comments highlight how important understanding human behavior is in motivating employees to higher and higher achievement. More important, they underscore the need for recognizing individual differences. While most creative people prefer a great deal of freedom and little bureaucratic red tape, other workers need closer supervision and a structured environment to be productive.

This chapter discusses the relationship between attitudes toward human behavior and the motivational techniques used to improve productivity. After studying this chapter, you will understand:

✔ The importance of motivation in organizations

✔ How management's approach to motivation has evolved

✔ The thoughts behind selected theories of motivation

✔ Three theories that focus on human needs

✔ The expectancy theory of motivation

✔ Incentive theories

✔ How to apply motivation theories in organizations

The Importance of Motivation

Motivation stimulates action

Motivation is the energizing of human behavior, or, simply stated, the process of stimulating action. Its importance to management is evident in the huge number of books and articles on the subject. Few topics in management literature have gained more attention over the past twenty-five years. Why are businesses and researchers so concerned with motivation? There are four reasons. First, a firm's overall performance depends on the performance of its individuals and groups. Businesses cannot function without these human resources. Second, to understand how an organization functions, we must understand why individuals behave as they do. Unless we understand motivation, we cannot fully comprehend how variations in such things as job design, leadership styles, and compensation systems affect performance, satisfaction, and so on.[3]

Third, because of competitive pressures, higher operating costs, and external demands, firms must do everything they can to remain efficient. Between 1947 and 1966, labor productivity in the United States increased each year by an average of 3.2%. Then the growth rate began to decline: from 1966 to 1973, productivity increases averaged only 2.1% per year. By the 1980s, the annual growth in labor productivity had fallen to 0.8%.[4] Managers hoping to reverse this trend are applying what they have learned about human nature and motivation.

Declining productivity

Finally, organizations have become aware of the importance of developing a talent pool that will be a perpetual reservoir of skills and abilities to keep them competitive on a long-term basis. They now recognize that a well-trained, highly motivated human resource is a prerequisite for developing and utilizing technologically advanced equipment.

Evolving Managerial Approaches to Motivation

Before the Industrial Revolution, most goods were produced in small shops under the direct supervision of the owner-manager. Because of the highly personal owner-worker relationship, the social intimacy of the work environment, and the lack of alternative work, the primary forms of motivation were the long-term relationship between master and apprentice and fear—the threat of being fired. The financial and social implications of being fired were usually enough to motivate employees to work hard. But with the start of the Industrial Revolution, the owner-worker relationship became more impersonal, and maintaining an efficient work force became paramount. There are three reasons why managers became concerned about efficiency:

1. Large investments in plant and equipment made an efficient work force necessary for an adequate return on investment.

2. The sheer size of manufacturing operations and the impersonal nature of owner-worker relationships called for new types of supervision.

3. Social Darwinism came into vogue; that is, every worker was accountable for his or her own performance, but no one was accountable for the performance of others. By a sort of "natural selection," good workers would blossom, while inferior workers would be weeded out.[5]

The Traditional Model

Threats and incentive pay

These forces resulted in the development of a management philosophy that we now call traditional management. Basically, it held that finding the one best way to perform any job would improve efficiency and that incentive pay and threats would motivate workers to perform up to their capabilities. In other

"Folsom, I've been getting complaints as to your handling of personnel."
© Al Ross - ROTHCO

words, workers could be enticed into properly performing repetitive, boring tasks if they were motivated and adequately paid. This philosophy is based on the following assumptions of human nature, which management philosopher Douglas McGregor called **Theory X:**

1. The average person has an inherent dislike of work and will avoid it if possible.

Theory X assumptions

2. Because of this dislike, most people must be coerced, controlled, directed, and threatened with punishment to get them to work hard enough to achieve an organization's objectives.

3. The average person prefers to be directed, wishes to avoid responsibility, has relatively little ambition, and wants security above all.[6]

In summary, McGregor's Theory X view of human nature holds that the dislike of work is so great that even the promise of rewards will not overcome it. "People will accept the rewards and demand continually higher ones, but these alone will not produce the necessary effort. Only the threat of punishment will do the trick."[7]

The Human Relations Model

When the traditional model of motivation became accepted throughout industry as the "correct" approach to motivation, problems began to appear. Some of the problems stemmed from the fact that managers were placing severe restraints on the wage incentive system. Workers realized that their wages were not increasing in proportion to their output. At the same time, workers became worried about job security because new, mechanized production methods required fewer people. Layoffs and firings became common. Workers responded with ingenious methods of restricting output, at the same time protecting their jobs. Unionism became a force, and the unprecedented growth in prosperity began to decline.[8]

Workers viewed differently

Trying to overcome the declining growth rates, managers began examining their assumptions about human nature. Although money was considered the primary tool of motivation, the importance of viewing workers as "whole people" began to emerge. This new approach, called the **human relations model,** emphasized two areas: (1) making workers feel important, and (2) allowing workers to satisfy their social needs through social interaction on the job. Employee morale, adequate communication, and job satisfaction became management concerns, and the importance of individual recognition became apparent. Supervisory training in these areas also took on some importance. The one element that stayed the same was the nature of tasks required in the manufacturing processes.[9] As Miles pointed out, management's overriding goal was much the same as it had been under the traditional model—to make sure workers complied with their authority.[10]

The Human Resources Model

The **human resources model** of motivation recognizes that people are motivated by a complex set of variables, including recognition, social needs, money, achievement, and a host of other factors. Human resources models also recognize individualism. They stress the need to let each worker use his or her personal talents to achieve job satisfaction and to accomplish organizational goals at the same time. These methods are based on the assumptions of human nature that McGregor called **Theory Y.**

1. Expending physical and mental effort in work is as natural as it is in play or rest.

Theory Y assumptions

2. External control and the threat of punishment are not the only ways to make people work to achieve an organization's objectives. People will exercise self-direction and self-control for objectives to which they are committed.

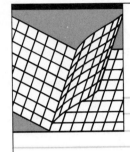

THE MANAGER'S NOTEBOOK

Satisfaction Strategies

Pay raises, overtime, and bonuses may have made their parents happy, but today's workers care about more than cash. To them, job satisfaction is just as, or more, important.

According to Oliver L. Niehouse, president of Niehouse & Associates, Inc., many of today's workers are willing to work fewer or more flexible hours so that they can have more leisure time. They also want to get to the top as fast as possible or feel that somehow they're involved in decision making. Workers also want inside information about what's going on in their organization, Niehouse said. And they're jumping on the "me first" bandwagon, asserting their individuality.

Niehouse urges managers to address these wants by developing several diverse strategies, each centered on one or more of job satisfaction's common points:

1. Make employees your most important asset. Bend minor rules occasionally, listen to workers' complaints and suggestions, and set up little recognition rituals such as choosing the salesperson of the month.

2. Establish solid lines of internal communication. Honestly and accurately tell people what's happening. One company set up a special bulletin board on which workers could post the rumors they'd heard. The company replied to each rumor within twenty-four hours. Within a month, all the rumors had stopped because lines of communication had opened.

3. Improve working conditions when possible. Fixing poor lighting and unsafe conditions will give the employees a better environment and will encourage them to work harder.

4. Involve your best workers in decision making. This rewards capable workers and sets them up as an example.

5. Be the best leader and role model you can—flexible, fair, and aware of what must be done and the people who must do it.

Source: Oliver L. Niehouse, "Job Satisfaction: How to Motivate Today's Workers," *Supervisory Management,* February 1986, pp. 8–11. Copyright © 1986 American Management Association, New York. All rights reserved.

3. Commitment to objectives depends on the rewards associated with achieving them.

4. Under the right conditions, the average person learns not only to accept but also to seek responsibility.

5. Many people have a relatively high degree of imagination, ingenuity, and creativity in the solution of organizational problems.

6. The average person's intellectual potential is only partially utilized under the conditions of modern industrial life.[11]

These assumptions have remarkably different implications for managers than do those of Theory X. Instead of blaming poor performance on basic human nature, Theory Y places squarely on management the responsibility for tapping the reservoir of creativity, hard work, and imagination. The worker's performance is limited only by management's ability to use human resources effectively.

Theory Y also has implications for decision making. Because it recognizes workers' intellectual potential, this philosophy suggests that organizational goals are best achieved if workers have a voice in decisions. Participatory decision making is especially important as it relates to a person's job. Giving workers greater autonomy over their specific job tasks is crucial to the motivational **Managers' role in** process. Finally, a Theory Y view of human nature implies that the manager's **motivation** role is not to manipulate workers; rather, it is to create an atmosphere in which workers can use their commitment and involvement to satisfy their personal needs as well as those of the organization. The Manager's Notebook on page 266 presents one manager's suggestions on how to motivate today's workers, using a Theory Y approach.

Selected Theories of Motivation

In their attempts to explain human motivation, psychologists, theorists, and management philosophers have offered a number of theories that deserve thoughtful consideration. These theories of motivation can be classified as need, expectancy, or incentive theories. **Need theories** focus on internal stimuli or forces that cause people to take action. Such stimuli often are called inner drives, needs, or instincts. **Expectancy theories** try to explain the mental process **Motivation theories** that people go through in deciding whether or not to undertake some action. They recognize that people see and respond to a job's motivational values differently. Instead of focusing on responses to stimuli, expectancy theorists try to explain the thought processes leading to choices of behavior. **Incentive theories** analyze the external influences that shape behavior; they try to show relationships between behavior and its consequences.

The six theories of motivation presented next in this chapter illustrate all three types of theories—need, expectancy, and incentive. They are the most popular and most complete theories of motivation formulated so far.

Need Theories

Maslow's Hierarchy of Needs

Probably the best-known and most widely debated theory of motivation is that proposed by Abraham H. Maslow, a clinical psychologist.[12] From its introduction in the mid-1940s until the late 1950s, Maslow's **hierarchy of needs** was used primarily in clinical psychology. But as more attention focused on the importance of motivation in the workplace, the needs hierarchy emerged in the 1960s as a model of human behavior in organizations. Motivation theory became widely used at that time by both organizational psychologists and managers largely because of the popularity of Douglas McGregor's Theory Y.[13] Maslow's theory says that human needs, arranged in a hierarchy of relative importance, determine human behavior. In other words, Maslow contended that people are motivated to satisfy the need that is most important to them at the time, before they are motivated to satisfy a higher-level need. The needs hierarchy, illustrated in Figure 10.1, has five separate levels of needs.[14]

People's most basic needs, according to motivation theory, are the *physiological* drives: hunger, sex, thirst, and so on. Undoubtedly, these are the most basic and important of all needs. A person who has nothing tries to satisfy his or her physiological needs before any others. As Maslow points out, a person lacking food, love, and esteem wants food more than he or she wants acceptance or prestige. These other needs would be unimportant.

Once a person satisfies his or her physiological needs, they are no longer motivators. Other, higher-level needs emerge and become dominant. When they, too, are satisfied, still higher needs emerge, and so on. This is why Maslow's hierarchy is said to be one of relative *prepotency*, or predominance. A want that is satisfied is no longer a want; a satisfied need is no longer a motivator.

The second level is *safety and security* needs. At this stage, people want freedom from fear and anxiety, and require a sense of stability and order. In other words, people become concerned with their personal safety and security. Earnings from a job, public assistance, or other sources of income can satisfy most people in this area. As with physiological needs, the concern for safety and security dominates how a person looks at the present and the future and also determines his or her value system. Everything else becomes secondary to the desire for safety and security at this stage.

Once these needs are satisfied, a concern for *love, affection, and belonging* takes over. At this point, people feel the need for friendship, family, and loved ones. They hunger for affectionate relations with other people and try to ease the pain of loneliness or rejection.

Motivation in the workplace

Hierarchy of relative importance

Satisfied needs do not motivate

FIGURE 10.1
A. H. Maslow's needs
hierarchy
(*Source:* Data for
diagram based on
Hierarchy of Needs
from "A Theory of
Human Motivation" in
*Motivation and
Personality*, Third
Edition, by Abraham H.
Maslow, revised by
Robert Frager et al.
Copyright © 1954,
1987 by Harper & Row,
Publishers, Inc.
Copyright © 1970 by
Abraham H. Maslow.
Reprinted by permission
of Harper & Row
Publishers, Inc.)

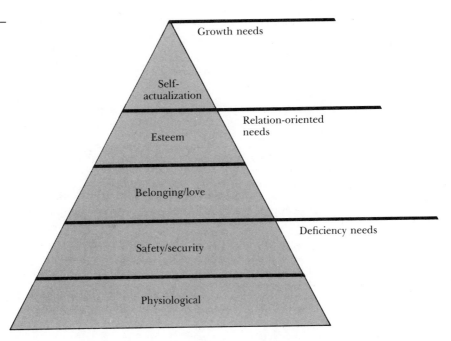

The fourth level, *esteem* needs, includes both self-esteem (self-respect) and public esteem. People want a high self-image as well as the respect and admiration of others. These needs take two different forms. First, we have a need for competency, confidence, and independence. We also want the prestige, status, recognition, and appreciation that others bestow on us. Satisfying the esteem needs produces feelings of self-worth; not satisfying them produces feelings of inability and inadequacy.

Highest-level need

At the apex of the pyramid are *self-actualization* needs. These highly individualized needs are satisfied when a person achieves all that he or she is capable of achieving. For the athlete, it may be breaking a world's record; for the research scientist, it may be finding a cure for cancer; and for the physical therapist, it may be the satisfaction of helping a child walk or laugh for the first time. In other words, these needs differ greatly from person to person. Regardless of the specific form they take, self-actualization needs come into play only after physiological, safety, social, and esteem needs have been satisfied.

Application of Needs Theory in Business   In our industrialized society, physiological needs are rarely motivators. Most Americans are free from hunger. So physiological needs generally cannot be used as inducements for greater effort or improved job performance. People's upper-level needs can be partially satisfied on the job, however. Table 10.1 lists some specific methods that managers can use to satisfy their employees' needs.

TABLE 10.1
Methods for satisfying
various levels of needs

Self-Actualization Needs

1. Use job-enrichment methods to make work more challenging
2. Establish a career path program for employees, enabling them to reach their full potential
3. Encourage employees to solve problems through the use of quality circles or other constructive programs

Esteem Needs

1. Use status symbols to reflect rank and status
2. Formally recognize outstanding performances
3. Reward employees through promotions and pay increases
4. Allow employees to assume greater responsibility
5. Encourage employees to participate in decision making
6. Provide specialized training for teaching employees new skills and abilities

Social/Belonging Needs

1. Provide for social interaction through such external activities as a company bowling team, annual picnic, or Christmas party
2. Arrange offices and work stations to facilitate personal interaction
3. Hold informal departmental meetings and encourage interaction

Security Needs

1. Institute a job tenure system
2. Adopt a guaranteed annual wage plan

Physiological Needs

1. Provide adequate pay

How to satisfy needs

As Figure 10.1 shows, the needs in Maslow's hierarchy can be classified as deficiency, relation-oriented, and growth needs. **Deficiency needs** are at a low level and are usually satisfied by external elements such as pay and job security. To be motivators, however, these external reinforcers must be contingent on work performance.[15] **Relation-oriented needs** can be satisfied on the job through interaction with other workers in work groups and informal social groups. **Growth needs** can be met by taking on interesting and challenging tasks. A sense of accomplishment and self-fulfillment is the goal.

Criticisms of Maslow's Theory Maslow's hierarchy originally drew criticism from several quarters and raised questions that he did not answer to the satisfaction of all his critics. The most basic question concerned the validity of the hierarchy's order. There is some empirical evidence that the two lower-level needs are arranged properly, but no evidence supports Maslow's arrangement of the upper-level needs. Cofer and Appley make this point:

Maslow's formulation that needs or drives arranged in a sort of dominance hierarchy does, we think, receive partial support from various kinds of evidence. That the support is partial is because the evidence concerns only the needs of the two lower levels in his hierarchy, the physiological and anxiety (security) needs. . . . While there is some evidence that intense physiological and safety needs can dominate behavior, evidence for the hierarchical relationship of other needs is wanting.[16]

Altering the hierarchy

Maslow admitted that the hierarchy could be changed through learning and cultural conditioning.[17] For example, people can become preoccupied with one particular level rather than the next step up. They can become wrapped up in gaining more and more satisfaction on the same level. For instance, a person might become almost totally preoccupied with accumulating symbols that reflect public esteem. Or a person might become materialistic, acquiring more automobiles, boats, or appliances than he or she needs. If the hierarchy can be altered horizontally, why not vertically? Critics argue, for instance, that some religious people in India become totally unconcerned with the lower-level needs and devote all their attention to satisfying the higher levels of consciousness. In effect, their hierarchy would reflect a reversal of Maslow's arrangement.

Herzberg's Motivation-Hygiene Theory

Frederick Herzberg's theory of motivation, commonly called the **motivation-hygiene,** or **two-factor, theory,** was developed in the late 1950s. The basis of Herzberg's theory was the responses that his research team received from two hundred accountants and engineers who were asked to recall times when they felt exceptionally good or bad about their jobs and to cite the factors that led to those feelings.

Satisfiers and dissatisfiers

The factors that were mentioned as leading to job satisfaction (**satisfiers**) were found to be unrelated to those resulting in job dissatisfaction (**dissatisfiers).** This suggests that correcting a source of dissatisfaction will not produce feelings of satisfaction. On the other hand, job dissatisfaction is not caused by the absence of a source of job satisfaction. Herzberg noted that the factors leading to satisfaction are tied in with growth needs, which stimulate personal growth and development. Dissatisfiers are primarily associated with a person's social and existence needs and do not prompt long-lasting satisfaction. They relate to the environment in which the job is performed, while satisfiers relate to job content. For these reasons, Herzberg called the job satisfiers "motivators" and the dissatisfiers "hygiene factors." Table 10.2 lists the satisfiers and dissatisfiers recalled by the people taking part in Herzberg's study.[18]

TABLE 10.2 Herzberg's satisfiers and dissatisfiers	**MOTIVATORS**	**HYGIENE FACTORS**
	Responsibility	Company policy
	Achievement	Technical supervision
	Work itself	Interpersonal relations
	Recognition	Salary
	Advancement	Working conditions

Application of Herzberg's Findings   As we have already pointed out, Herzberg's theory assumes that the factors leading to apathy and dissatisfaction are unrelated to those resulting in motivation and satisfaction. Consider, for example, the hygiene factor of salary. An inequitable, insufficient salary causes resentment and disgust among workers. But an equitable salary does not produce feelings of satisfaction. On the other hand, giving workers opportunities to assume greater responsibility produces feelings of self-fulfillment, but giving them no opportunity to assume responsibility does not cause dissatisfaction.

Herzberg recognized that there is a "middle ground," or median, between satisfaction and dissatisfaction. If satisfiers are viewed as positive forces and dissatisfiers as negative forces, then the middle ground represents neutrality. An improvement in poor working conditions will shift feelings from negative (minus) to neutral (zero); similarly, the absence of challenging work will produce neither positive (plus) nor negative (minus) feelings.

In refining his theory, Herzberg made two significant points: (1) the level of hygiene must rise continually to prevent the recurrence of dissatisfaction, and (2) hygiene factors can never serve as motivators. Let's look at each of these points more closely. Turning to the first point, say a manager receives a $3,000 raise one year and only a $2,000 raise the next. He or she will be dissatisfied with the second raise because it's almost like getting a cut in salary. Dissatisfaction also has the same effect regardless of the absolute level of needs. A vice president who feels underpaid will be just as dissatisfied as a sales manager or a supervisor who feels underpaid. In the second point, trying to motivate workers through human relations, pleasant working conditions, and improved benefits doesn't work. The only true way to motivate workers is to upgrade their jobs.[19]

Theory refinements

Criticisms of Herzberg's Theory   A number of research studies have produced results disagreeing with Herzberg's conclusions. Dunnette, Campbell, and Hakel (1967) discovered that Herzberg's dissatisfiers were not related to job dissatisfaction. Friedlander and Margulies (1969) concluded that the satisfiers of

Doubts about Herzberg's theory

social environment and interpersonal relations were important motivational factors for people in research and development.[20] House and Wigdor, who analyzed thirty-one studies of Herzberg's theory, concluded that a given factor can lead to satisfaction for one person and dissatisfaction for another.[21]

Herzberg's research methods have come under attack, too. Information was gathered in interviews using the critical incident technique; that is, participants were asked to recall incidents when they felt *exceptionally* satisfied or dissatisfied about their work. Replications of Herzberg's study that use different data-gathering approaches do not support his theory. To date, more studies fail to support his findings than support them.[22]

The responses of the research participants have also been questioned. Bass and Barrett, for example, contend that the people taking part in Herzberg's study may have been guilty of rationalizing.

> The way a person feels may not be reflected in their performance because of the tendency of individuals to rationalize their actions and feelings. It is so much easier for the individual to claim that success and positive feelings are the result of their own achievements (motivator factors) and that their dissatisfaction does not arise from their own inadequacies but is caused by another person or by environmental conditions.[23]

Perhaps the biggest criticism of Herzberg's theory is its failure to account for individual differences. Basically, it assumes that job enrichment benefits all employees. Research evidence suggests that this is not true. Some workers are content to perform routine tasks and to forego the managerial duties of planning and controlling.

Herzberg's overall contributions

The overall contributions of Herzberg's study do, however, outweigh its limitations. Besides stimulating further research on employee motivation, his efforts called attention to the need for understanding the role of motivation in organizations. Herzberg's study also prompted business managers to look at more than just money as a tool for increasing worker productivity.[24] These contributions often are overlooked in the debates over research methods and the validity of Herzberg's data.

The Achievement Motive

Harvard psychologist David McClelland began studying personality traits in the 1940s in an effort to distinguish among *achievement-oriented, power-oriented,* and *affiliation-oriented* people. His theory of motivation, based on research that used projective personality tests, is now generally referred to as the **achievement motive.**[25]

McClelland used the Thematic Apperception Test (TAT) to pinpoint people who spend their idle time thinking about their family and friends (affiliation oriented) and those who spend it thinking about doing something constructive (achievement oriented).

Achievement-oriented people tend to compare themselves with a standard of excellence, McClelland claimed. They want economic rewards, but their real satisfaction comes in the form of a more intrinsic reward—achievement. Economic rewards are merely a way of keeping a score of achievements.

A trait theory

McClelland's achievement motive is actually a trait theory. It is based on the premise that everyone has a different need for achievement. Research has shown that people who tend to be high achievers respond differently to certain situations than do those with low achievement tendencies. For example, John Atkinson's research indicates that people with high achievement need are willing to take moderate risks, whereas those with low achievement need tend to take either very high or very low risks.[26] The rationale for this is that feelings of achievement are low where there is little risk, and that achievement is not likely at all where the risk is high.

People with high achievement need also want feedback that lets them know whether they are successful. Finally, a person oriented to achievement wants to make certain that he or she gets the credit, not someone else.[27]

People with a high need for power want to exercise authority or influence over others. They prefer individual competition, which lets them assert their dominance. McClelland recognized that power is essential for accomplishing an organization's goals but cautioned against its use for self-gratification, which, he felt, was detrimental to organizational effectiveness.

People with high affiliation needs enjoy social interaction and need close friendships. They are likely to have close friends both on and off the job, and they typically belong to several social organizations.

Achievement need is not innate

Perhaps the most important part of McClelland's theory is his contention that the need for achievement is not necessarily innate, but rather is developed by a person's experiences. McClelland argued that parents could develop a child's need for achievement. Parents who encourage independence and who have high expectations for their children create an atmosphere that nurtures the achievement need. Managerial and professional people instill a higher achievement drive in their children than do other parents, he found.

Expanding the theory

McClelland said that this is why some civilizations and nations are more achievement oriented than others. Civilizations that expect a lot from their youth have high-achieving societies. Those that fail to instill the value of high achievement have successive generations of low achievers.

McClelland believed that people can be trained to think imaginatively and creatively. Once they become creative, they can convert their thoughts into actions. To prove his point, McClelland helped a group of businesspeople in India to develop creative entrepreneurial skills, which they adapted to use on the job. The program's success was measured by promotions, salary increases, and new business startups among the group.[28]

McClelland cautioned that no organization should be totally made up of high achievers, however. Every organization needs some people who dislike taking risks, who are not concerned with responsibility, and who do not need a high degree of independence to be happiest.[29]

Levels of achievement need vary

Of course, all people have achievement, power, and affiliation needs, but different people have different levels of these needs. Outstanding salespeople tend to have a high achievement need and a moderately high need for power. Entrepreneurs, too, are usually high in the need for achievement. The most effective managers, on the other hand, have a high need for power, a moderate need for achievement, and a low need for affiliation.[30]

Expectancy Theory

Three key elements

The expectancy theory of motivation formulated by Victor Vroom in 1964 focused on the thought processes of people who must decide whether to exert some effort to achieve a possible payoff.[31] To understand the theory, you must understand the interrelationship of its three key elements: expectancy, valence, and instrumentality.

Expectancy is the likelihood that some undertaking will produce a particular outcome. This likelihood, or probability, is determined subjectively by the person deciding whether to act and can range from 0 to 1. For example, if a real estate salesperson knows for certain that he or she can sell a given parcel of property, then the expectancy value of the selling effort would be 1. If, however, there is some doubt that the piece of property could be sold at the asking price, the expectancy value would be less than 1.

Valence, or preference, is the degree to which a decision maker wants a particular outcome. Valence can be either positive or negative. Bonuses, recognition, promotions, and support from significant others, for instance, would have positive valences; that is, they would be greatly desired by a rational decision maker. Reprimands, pay cuts, demotions, and disapproval from significant others, on the other hand, would have negative valences. Theoretically, an outcome has a valence because it is related to a personal need that the decision maker wants to satisfy.[32]

Instrumentality refers to how much the decision maker believes that attaining some first-level (organizational) objective will translate into a second-level (personal) payoff. Figure 10.2 shows the interrelationship of these variables.

An example of Vroom's model

To illustrate Vroom's model, consider the decision that a bank auditor must make about working beyond normal hours to account for cash shortages. The auditor has two options: she can stop working at five o'clock and start again the next day, or she can work overtime and continue searching for the reason for the discrepancy. She feels that the error definitely can be detected (expectancy), but it may take four or five hours of overtime. She knows that

FIGURE 10.2
Vroom's expectancy
model (*Source:*
Adapted from *Personnel:
The Management of
People,* Fifth Edition, by
Dale S. Beach, p. 306.
Reprinted with
permission of Macmillan
Publishing Company.
Copyright © 1985 by
Dale S. Beach.)

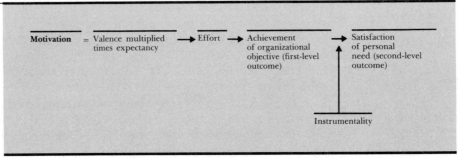

her supervisor will notice her efforts (instrumentality) and that she most likely will be praised for them (positive valence) if she finds the error before the bank opens the next day. On the other hand, her family may disapprove of her working late (negative valence). If she chooses to stop searching at five o'clock to go home, her supervisor also will be aware of that (instrumentality). In that case, the outcome would be a reprimand from the supervisor (negative valence) but approval at home (positive valence). The auditor's decision about whether to continue searching for the error beyond normal quitting time will be determined by the sum of valences and the force of their respective personal payoffs.

Vroom's expectancy theory helps managers understand the relationship between performance and reward: outstanding performance should be rewarded; mediocrity should not. The model also suggests that rewards should have a direct cause-effect relationship; that is, rewards (recognition, praise, bonuses, and so on) should be directly tied to specific individual performance.

Managers also should recognize that because individuals have different needs, they place different values on a given reward. This is why managers should try to match rewards to the workers' needs. Finally, managers should develop high, but realistic expectations for their subordinates' performances, helping them to see that they are capable of performing at that level. As Mescon, Albert, and Khedouri point out, workers' self-perceptions are greatly influenced by their managers' expectations.[33]

Incentive Theory

The theories of motivation we just discussed are often referred to as *cognitive theories* because they are based on inner feelings and thought processes (*cognition*). The major problem with cognitive theories of motivation is that they cannot be physically observed; thus, they cannot be scientifically measured. This is why some researchers feel that more attention should be given to models that are subject to scientific analysis.[34]

Skinner's Reinforcement Theory

Behavior shaped by consequences

One such model, called **reinforcement theory,** was proposed by psychologist B. F. Skinner.[35] Skinner's reinforcement theory is based on the belief that all human behavior is shaped by its consequences. That is, a person behaves a certain way because of a reinforcement or stimulus he or she received in the past for the same behavior. If the outcome of a particular action is pleasant, positive reinforcement occurs and a person is likely to behave the same way again. He or she is likely to change the behavior if the reinforcement is negative.

Types of reinforcement

Skinner recognized three distinct types of reinforcement—positive reinforcement, negative reinforcement, and punishment. In **positive reinforcement,** a favorable consequence encourages repetitive behavior. For example, a worker who is paid on a piece-rate basis may consistently produce at a high level because pay is a positive reinforcer. Prizes and bonuses being offered by some companies are positive reinforcers that are encouraging workers to stay healthy, as described in the In-Box on page 278. **Negative reinforcement** of some behavior occurs when unpleasant consequences are removed. For example, consider a worker whose supervisor complains about the fact that he is always late. If he begins getting to work on time, the supervisor stops complaining. Eliminating the complaining causes the worker to arrive on time consistently.

In **punishment,** behavior is changed because it results in unpleasant consequences. Punishment involves inflicting physical or emotional pain, or withdrawing a desired consequence. Its purpose is to modify certain behavior. To understand the role of punishment as a reinforcer, consider what happens to a baseball player who "misses" a bunt signal from his coach. He may be fined and taken out of the game.

Punishment and negative reinforcement are not the same. Negative reinforcement involves unpleasant outcomes, just as punishment does, but it encourages behavior that *avoids* unpleasant consequences. Punishment, on the other hand, does not encourage action—it suppresses action. This is an important distinction. Punishment is used to control what a person should not do. Instead of motivating a person to take some action, it merely conditions him or her to avoid those actions that should not be taken.[36]

Lack of reinforcement

Learned behavior that is not reinforced will ultimately disappear because of the lack of reinforcement. This is called **extinction.** The behavior is normally replaced by one that wins reinforcement. For example, a worker who receives no response for his or her suggestions on ways to improve efficiency or reduce costs will quit making suggestions at some point. This behavior will be replaced by one that will result in reinforcement, such as working longer hours.

What Constitutes Reinforcement?   By now, you must have asked yourself an important question: "What is reinforcement?" Often, a manager thinks his or

THE IN-BOX

Rewarding Healthy Workers

Johnson & Johnson, the giant health-care corporation, is one of a growing number of companies that has started rewarding its employees for staying healthy.

When they attend smoking or stress workshops, exercise, keep their weight down, wear seat belts in their cars, or install smoke detectors in their homes, Johnson & Johnson employees can earn "Live-for-Life" dollars. These can be exchanged for items such as clocks, fire extinguishers, Frisbees, and sweat suits. The chance to win the prizes motivates Johnson & Johnson employee John Benda to keep his weight under control, he says.

Other companies also offer incentives to encourage their employees to improve their health. Intermatic, Inc., workers who stay off cigarettes for a full year get a trip for two to Las Vegas. The Hospital Corporation of America pays its staff twenty-four cents for every mile they run or walk, for every quarter-mile they swim, or for every four miles they cycle. Other firms reward their employees who keep themselves healthy and don't miss work.

Berol Corporation of Danbury, Connecticut, takes a different approach. Each worker is credited with an extra $500 each year, which is reduced by the amount paid out by the company's insurer for each medical claim made. Whatever is left of the $500 at the end of the year belongs to the worker. While this plan puts money in the healthy workers' pockets, it also saves the company $125,000 in reduced medical insurance premiums annually.

Employees and employers alike benefit from programs that motivate workers to stay healthy. Large Fortune 500 companies lose an average of $88 million a year from employee illness and spend $100 million annually for employee medical coverage. Health promotion efforts can help reduce both types of costs. As one analyst put it, any program that can cut these staggering costs is a terrific investment.

Source: Anastasia Toufexis, "Giving Goodies to the Good," *Time,* November 18, 1985, p. 98.

her rewards are reinforcing, but they fail to gain the desired results. This is because a reinforcer is defined by its effect, not its intent. If a consequence does not have the effect the manager wants, it is not a positive reinforcer even though it may be a pleasant event. We can't determine what a reinforcer is until we see its impact.

We can, however, get an idea of what is positively reinforcing by listening to what people say. Participants in a survey of 1,500 blue-collar and white-collar workers by the U.S. Department of Labor were asked to rate job factors that were "very important" to them. The top ten rankings for each group are shown in Table 10.3.

Twenty-three job factors were listed in this study. Even so, both white-collar and blue-collar workers selected the same top ten factors, with the exception of two items: opportunity to develop special abilities and job security.[37] The results of this survey can, however, be misleading. The rankings that appear in Table 10.3 are average rankings—not the rankings of any one person. It would be incorrect to assume that *all* white-collar workers considered interesting work the most important job factor or that *all* blue-collar workers ranked good pay as the most important factor.

Application of Reinforcement Theory   Punishment is the most widely used but least effective technique for controlling behavior, according to Skinner. Punishment tells a person what not to do, but it doesn't turn his or her behavior

TABLE 10.3 Factors ranked as "very important" by two groups of survey respondents	RANK	WHITE-COLLAR WORKERS	RANK	BLUE-COLLAR WORKERS
	1	Interesting work	1	Good pay
	2	Opportunity to develop special abilities	2	Adequate help and equipment
	3	Adequate information	3	Job security
	4	Adequate authority	4	Adequate information
	5	Adequate help and equipment	5	Interesting work
	6	Friendly and helpful coworkers	6	Friendly and helpful coworkers
	7	Opportunity to see results of effort	7	Clearly defined responsibilities
	8	Competent supervision	8	Opportunity to see results of effort
	9	Clearly defined responsibilities	9	Adequate authority
	10	Good pay	10	Competent supervision

Source: Donald Sanzotta, *Motivational Theories and Applications for Managers*, p. 44. © 1977 AMACOM, a division of American Management Association, New York. All rights reserved.

in the desired direction. Also, the undesirable behavior may surface again when the punishing agent is removed.

Positive reinforcement is the preferred type of behavior modification on the job. Besides increasing the likelihood of a desired response, it creates good relationships between the supervisor and the subordinate. It also avoids the emotional damage that punishment can cause.

Behavior modification used

Behavior modification can be used in a number of situations, including employee training, compensation, supervision, quality assurance, attendance, and job design.[38] Most of the companies that use behavior modification praise it highly. For example, Emery Air Freight credits it with saving the company more than $2 million over a three-year period.[39] B.F. Goodrich management attributes a 300% increase in productivity at one of its Ohio plants to the introduction of positive reinforcement. Essentially, the B.F. Goodrich program provided cost, scheduling, and goal-accomplishment information to first-line supervisors once a week. Daily meetings were held to permit supervisors and workers to discuss how their work groups were doing. Charts were developed comparing achievements to goals. Five years after the program was implemented, productivity had tripled and production costs had decreased. The company attributes its success to giving supervisors and workers information about their performance.[40]

Criticisms

Behavior modification has its critics, too. According to Fry, some of its major drawbacks are that it: (1) is coercive, (2) is a form of bribery, (3) depends on outside reinforcers, and (4) requires continual reinforcement.[41] Skinner's theory, in particular, has been criticized because it denies the existence of free will and the "autonomous man" concept, which are central to the constructs of Maslow and McGregor.[42]

Equity Theory

Equity theory tries to explain the "fairness" of financial incentive plans. According to the equity theory of pay, a person looks at the relationship between what he or she puts into work and what he or she gets out of it in comparison with that of other workers. This comparison is more important to a worker than is the direct relationship between performance and reward. This is the central factor in determining the effectiveness of a pay plan.[43] Equity exists whenever the following formula is in balance:

$$\frac{\text{Individual A's Outcome}}{\text{Individual A's Input}} = \frac{\text{Other Workers' Outcome}}{\text{Other Workers' Input}}$$

If one side of the equation is greater than the other, inequity exists. The worker who sees this imbalance wants to reduce his or her feeling of inequity.

When inequity exists

Equity theory predicts that people who feel overpaid on an incentive plan will increase their input by producing better but fewer items to reduce inequity. Those who feel underpaid will raise their output by producing more, lower-quality items. Under an hourly wage plan, people who feel overpaid will reduce their inequity by increasing their input, but those who feel underpaid will reduce both their input and the quality and quantity of their output.[44]

Several researchers have tried to refute the notion that workers under performance-reward pay systems that pay people for what they produce, for example, work harder than do those under nonperformance-contingent pay plans, such as those that pay people by the hour. A summary of their research findings had these indications:

1. When a task is repetitive and boring, monetary rewards do not have a long-lasting effect on performance.

2. The use of performance-reward pay plans in an intrinsically satisfying job may hurt employee motivation.

3. Money alone will not motivate workers to produce more. The nature of tasks, perceived equity, and perceived ties between performance and pay also determine the effectiveness of a pay plan.

4. Intrinsic rewards are better predictors of performance than extrinsic rewards are.

5. Although an incentive pay plan may temporarily relieve boredom, output under such a plan may suffer if the task is disliked.

6. Workers do not like to feel that they perform their tasks for money.[45]

Applying Theory in Organizations

Workers want satisfying jobs

Work is more than a way to get money. It also can bring about recognition, achievement, and self-fulfillment. When work is boring and unfulfilling, people work only as much as is necessary to satisfy their basic needs. Once they satisfy their biological and security needs, work becomes meaningless. Since today's workers have better educations and higher expectations than their predecessors had, they find little satisfaction in unchallenging jobs that lack opportunity.

Moreover, when jobs fail to satisfy people's higher-level needs in the long run, workers may actively or passively rebel. They may restrict output, become active in their union, develop an indifferent attitude, or show signs of chronic absenteeism. They also may have trouble getting along with their supervisors and coworkers. Because such reactions keep organizations from achieving their potential and may even lead to business failure, organizational objectives can be satisfied best when personal needs are fulfilled. This is why managers must make jobs as interesting and as challenging as possible.

Digital Equipment Corporation, for instance, has instilled new vigor in its Enfield, Connecticut, plant by trying the "bossless" system. Workers set their own hours, plan their own schedules, and check their own work.[46] W. L. Gore & Associates has taken a similar approach. The atmosphere is informal, with every worker free to learn as much as he or she wants and to assume responsibility and leadership.[47]

Several approaches to creating more personally satisfying jobs have yielded considerable success. Among the more promising innovations are changes in work schedules, job enlargement, job enrichment, and a combination of job enlargement and job enrichment.[48]

Work Schedule Changes

The typical five-day, forty-hour workweek can be modified a number of ways, but the three predominant approaches make use of: (1) a four-day workweek, (2) flextime, and (3) double shifts for two or more consecutive days, usually on weekends.

Ways to change the work week

The **four-day workweek,** which compresses forty hours into a four-day schedule, is designed to benefit employees and companies alike. A longer weekend allows workers to devote more time to personal activities, to moonlight if company policy doesn't permit employment elsewhere during the week, and to save in commuting costs, parking fees, and the like. Employers supposedly benefit because it results in lower absenteeism and turnover, higher employee morale, and increased productivity.

Although the four-day workweek became common in the early 1970s, the reaction of both employers and employees was mixed. While most people voiced enthusiasm over the plan, some firms reported declining productivity. A significant number of firms have reinstated the traditional five-day workweek.

Flextime allows employees to determine their own starting and quitting times, as long as all employees are on the job during critical "core" hours and work needs are met. The system is not appropriate, for instance, when employee activities are highly interdependent. Under flextime, one worker may choose to work from 7:00 A.M. until 3:00 P.M., another from 10:00 A.M. until 6:00 P.M. A plan like this lets workers schedule their work around traffic congestion, family responsibilities, and personal preferences. Flextime was first introduced in 1967 at the aerospace research and development facility of Messerschmitt-Bolvok-Blohm in Germany. The first major U.S. corporation to use the plan was the John Hancock Mutual Life Insurance Company in Boston.[49] Organizations using flextime today include Exxon, Hewlett-Packard, Sun Oil, Samsonite, and the federal Social Security Administration.

Firms using flextime

Overall, flextime programs have proved successful from the employer's standpoint. Because less time is lost from tardiness, the ratio of worker-hours worked to worker-hours paid increases. Absenteeism and sick leave used for personal business also are reduced. The hours worked appear to be more productive, and there is less slowing down toward the end of the workday.[50] Studies to assess their acceptance by employees reveal that flextime plans nearly always raise employee morale. Nearly half of the respondents to one survey— 45%—report improved motivation and productivity.[51]

Due to the shortage of health-care personnel in the early 1980s, a number of hospitals and other types of health-care facilities tried getting registered nurses to join their staffs by offering them two **consecutive shifts** for two consecutive days, usually on weekends. The plan was designed to benefit both health-care facilities and employees. Employers would be adequately staffed on critical days that most employees prefer off and employees could earn a week's salary in two days instead of five. Critics of the plan argued that fatigue would result in poor services, but hospital administrators countered by stressing the importance of having enough qualified personnel on hand when there was a shortage of trained workers.

Work Structure Changes

Changing jobs structurally

As pointed out in Chapter 8, when we were discussing job enlargement, a job can be made structurally bigger. Instead of performing a fragmented job, the worker does an entire unit of work. The job is expanded horizontally.

For such job enlargement to be motivating, it must give each worker a variety of tasks that make up a complete work module, or unit. If a job has been enlarged properly, workers also must be given information on how they are performing, their abilities must be put to better use, and people, not machines, must control the work pace.[52]

Task Variety Task variety is just the opposite of the task specialization that scientific management endorsed. While specialization leads to increased productivity and efficiency, those economic benefits may be offset by employee turnover, absenteeism, and other negative factors associated with unfulfilling work. Mechanized, repetitive tasks don't provide opportunities to satisfy workers' higher-level needs. Repetitive jobs also increase boredom and daydreaming, which make people more prone to error and to accidents.

Work Module A complete work module, or unit, can be developed by combining sequential tasks. In this way, a worker can see the interrelationship of various activities, and can have a better sense of accomplishment. When a worker is allowed to complete an entire unit, he or she usually finds the work more challenging and rewarding.

Job rotation

Establishing work modules has the added advantage of introducing job rotation (see Chapter 8) more easily. A worker can be trained to work at several different modules and can be rotated among them. This also reduces boredom and fatigue and allows the worker to think more.

Performance Feedback When a worker performs repetitive, specialized tasks without a meaningful finishing point, providing information on his or her

"We had to do something since McCartie doesn't work well with people."
© Punch - Cotham

performance is meaningless. But if the worker's job is enlarged to encompass all the tasks required in a complete work unit, providing information on his or her accomplishments is important. Not only is the job more psychologically rewarding, but the worker's output can be measured and evaluated for rewards as well. Both internal and external rewards reinforce energized efforts.

Using skills is satisfying

Better Use of Worker Abilities Because people get satisfaction from jobs that make them use their skills, enlarged jobs are more satisfying than repetitive, specialized jobs are. Vroom, Kornhauser, and other researchers found a positive correlation between job satisfaction and the use of skills and abilities.[53] Simplified jobs are less motivating because they require little ability and thought. Enlarged jobs motivate workers because they are more challenging.

Worker-Controlled Pacing Machines typically control the workers' pace in mass-production plants. All workers performing the same job must work at the required speed, regardless of their abilities and work habits. Job enlargement virtually eliminates machine-paced operations because production speeds for complete work modules are difficult to standardize.

Having people control the pacing at which they work has several advantages over machine-controlled pacing. It motivates workers because it allows them partial control of their own work environment. Not only can workers set their own work rhythm, they can also develop their own work habits and methods that suit their personalities. Enlarged jobs built around worker-paced systems also help eliminate turnover and absenteeism. And, finally, a worker-paced system is less vulnerable to equipment failure and shutdowns. Since work modules are individualized, any single shutdown will have little, if any, effect on other aspects of production.[54]

Work Enrichment

A person's work can be enriched—expanded vertically—in a number of ways. Hackman, Oldham, Janson, and Purdy suggest five methods: (1) change the job so that each group is accountable for an identifiable body of work, (2) combine tasks so that one person assembles a product from start to finish instead of having it worked on by several people who each perform a particular task, (3) allow each worker to have direct contact with customers, (4) let workers plan and control—as well as perform—their operations, and (5) design ways for each employee to get immediate feedback on his or her performance.[55]

Alternative enrichment methods

In summary, job enrichment increases motivation because it involves the worker in all aspects of his or her job. It provides greater autonomy and participation, which are vital ingredients for self-management. However, a number of studies show that letting workers participate in decision making alone does not make them highly motivated and productive. They also must be allowed to set high performance goals.[56]

Review

✓ *The importance of motivation in organizations.* Over the past twenty-five years, motivation has become one of the most widely discussed subjects in management literature. There are several reasons why it has become so important to managers and to scholars: (1) business prosperity depends on energized human effort, (2) to understand how an organization functions, managers must understand human behavior, (3) competitive pressures mean that firms must improve how their people perform, and (4) long-term survival depends on developing and maintaining a skilled, motivated work force.

✓ *How management's approach to motivation has evolved.* The traditional approach, based on a Theory X view of human nature, relied on fear and punishment to bring about satisfactory performance. Over time, the traditional approach evolved into a human relations approach, which focuses on the social needs of workers. Although it maintained a Theory X view of human nature, this approach recognized the importance of social interaction, adequate communication, and individual recognition. Manipulating workers to comply with authority remained the core of this approach.

The human resources model of motivation, based on a Theory Y philosophy of human nature, emphasizes the full potential of workers and places the responsibility for motivation on the shoulders of managers. It says that the only limit to the worker's creativity, hard work, and outstanding performance is management's inability to utilize human resources fully. It also stresses the importance of giving employees interesting and challenging work that leads to feelings of accomplishment and satisfaction.

✔ *The thoughts behind selected theories of motivation.* Three theories of human motivation have been devised. Need theories focus on the internal stimuli or forces that cause people to take action, expectancy theories try to explain the mental processes that people go through in deciding whether to undertake some action, and incentive theories analyze the external influences that shape behavior.

✔ *Three theories that focus on human needs.* Abraham H. Maslow's hierarchy of needs theory says that human needs, arranged in a hierarchy of relative importance, determine human behavior. The motivation-hygiene (two-factor) theory of Frederick Herzberg discusses the importance of satisfiers and dissatisfiers in job satisfaction. David McClelland's achievement-motive theory is based on the premise that everyone has a different need for achievement.

✔ *The expectancy theory of motivation.* Victor Vroom's expectancy theory of motivation focuses on the thought processes of people who must decide whether to exert effort to achieve a possible payoff. It involves the interaction of expectancy—the likelihood that some undertaking will result in a particular outcome; valence—the degree to which the decision maker wants a particular outcome; and instrumentality—how much the decision maker believes that attaining an organizational objective will result in a personal payoff.

✔ *Incentive theories.* The reinforcement theory of psychologist B. F. Skinner is based on the belief that all human behavior is shaped by its consequences. Skinner recognized three types of reinforcement—positive reinforcement, negative reinforcement, and punishment. Learned behavior that is not reinforced will disappear; Skinner called this extinction. Equity theory, which concerns the "fairness" of financial incentive plans, explains that workers look at the relationship between what they put into work and what they get out of it in comparison with other workers' input and outcome.

✔ *How to apply motivation theories in organizations.* Work schedule changes, such as a four-day workweek, flextime, and consecutive shifts, have proven satisfactory for some organizations. Both enlarging and enriching a person's job have yielded significant results, too. Enlarging work means making it structurally bigger by giving the worker more tasks. In work enrichment, workers are given more control over their jobs.

THE MANAGER'S DICTIONARY

As an extra review of the chapter, try defining the following terms. If you
have trouble with any of them, refer to the page number listed.

motivation (262)
Theory X (264)
human relations model (265)
human resources model (265)
Theory Y (265)
need theories (267)
expectancy theories (267)
incentive theories (267)
hierarchy of needs (268)
deficiency needs (270)

relation-oriented needs (270)
growth needs (270)
motivation-hygiene (two-factor)
    theory (271)
satisfiers (271)
dissatisfiers (271)
achievement motive (273)
expectancy (275)
valence (275)
instrumentality (275)

reinforcement theory (277)
positive reinforcement (277)
negative reinforcement
    (277)
punishment (277)
extinction (277)
equity theory (280)
four-day workweek (282)
flextime (282)
consecutive shifts (283)

REVIEW QUESTIONS

1. Briefly explain the importance of motivation to business managers.

2. How does modern motivational theory differ from traditional motivational theory? Why have approaches to motivation changed over the years?

3. List the assumptions of the traditional model of motivation.

4. What are the assumptions of the human relations model of motivation?

5. How does the human resources model differ from the human relations model?

6. Differentiate between need, expectancy, and incentive theories of motivation. Which of these categories does Maslow's hierarchy of needs fall into? Skinner's reinforcement theory?

7. What needs constitute Maslow's hierarchy?

8. What is the significance of arranging needs in a hierarchy? Explain.

9. Suggest ways that self-actualization needs can be satisfied.

10. According to Herzberg, why won't the absence of a satisfier cause job dissatisfaction?

11. Explain why the achievement theory of motivation is called a "trait" theory.

12. Give examples of positive valence. Negative valence.

13. Provide examples to illustrate the difference between negative reinforcement and punishment.

14. Under the equity theory of motivation, how do people react when they believe they are underpaid? Overpaid?

15. Discuss some specific methods for making work more challenging and satisfying.

16. Why should managers concern themselves with making work interesting and fulfilling for their employees?

MANAGEMENT CHALLENGE

The four people described below are employed by Apex Manufacturing Company, a large producer of floor coverings, vinyl siding, and cabinet tops. Describe the motivational technique you would use to inspire each worker.

1. Mary Wells, age thirty-nine, married, two children, fifteen years seniority with Apex, present salary $22,000. Supervisory evaluation indicates work is satisfactory but not exceptional. Rate of absenteeism has steadily increased during past two years.

2. Bert Pfeffer, age fifty-five, widowed, production foreman, present salary $34,000. Personnel record indicates that Pfeffer is a very knowledgeable and hard-working manufacturing supervisor but weak in human skills. He has been passed over for a promotion on two occasions because of poor social skills and a limited educational background.

3. Betty Flowers, age twenty-six, single, salesperson, B.A. and M.B.A. from major university; joined Apex immediately after receiving M.B.A. Considered bright, aggressive, and results-oriented. Annual salary averages $40,000. Works on salary plus commission basis. Management's only concern is losing her to a competitor.

4. Paula Brookside, age twenty-eight, divorced, data entry clerk, salary $5.25/hr. Worked two years as bank teller before joining Apex. High school diploma plus data processing certificate from vocational-technical school. High rate of absenteeism. Appears indifferent toward her job.

CASE 10.1

Too Much Talent—Too Few Slots[57]

How do you retain and motivate talented people if you can't promote them? This question is being asked more frequently by top-level managers in all types of industries.

More than seventy-one million people between ages twenty-five and forty-five will swell the labor force by 1995, but the number of management jobs will decline. In 1980, there were three candidates for every two middle-management positions; by 1995, that ratio will be five to one. And the glut will get worse. What's now a problem for middle managers will be a problem for senior-level managers in ten or fifteen years.

It's not simply a problem of too few promotions for too many candidates; it's also one of increased expectations. Except for the high-growth firms, corporate America can't handle the impatient, ambitious expectations of the fast-trackers. The end point of this dilemma is now becoming quite visible—managers of all ages will "plateau" before their energies and desires wane. They will feel stuck in jobs with no way out.

This is a problem that managers cannot ignore. Failing to provide opportunities for advancement may lead to lower morale, less enthusiasm, declining productivity, and firings. Without question, high-growth companies have less of a problem. People who get trapped on a job plateau in rapidly developing companies probably don't have enough talent, anyway. But for companies growing at slower rates, the loss of talented people can be catastrophic.

According to Frank Gaines, Jr., former manager of executive development and compensation at Exxon, companies should plan managers' careers so that they arrive at their ultimate potential ten years before retirement. But that's not always possible. When firms cannot offer deserving managers promotions, they must dangle other carrots in front of them.

Questions

1. Suggest ways that a company can keep its fast-trackers motivated if opportunities for promotion are unavailable.

2. Discuss the role of the supervisor in keeping plateaued workers motivated.

CASE 10.2

Gears Grind at Sullivan Machinery[58]

In 1984, Joy Manufacturing Company sold its machine-tool business in Claremont, New Hampshire, following months of record-setting losses. The new owner, Sullivan Machinery Company, is doing business differently to make the machine-tool business profitable again.

First, new owner Donald Hoodes persuaded local union members to accept a 30% pay cut in return for keeping their jobs. In connection with this move, profit-sharing and pay incentive plans were initiated. The most significant change, however, was Hoodes's approach to motivating workers: trying to light an entrepreneurial spark on the shop floor. According to James L. Koontz, president of the National Machine Tool Builders Association, the whole industry got into financial trouble because managers forgot how to go out onto the shop floor to deal with their employees.

Historically, the machine-tool industry was comprised of small firms employing fewer than one hundred workers. Conglomerates gobbled them up when profits surged in the 1970s. When the recession hit in the early 1980s, sales and profits declined. Workers lost their jobs, foreign competitors made inroads into the industry, and several U.S. plants were closed.

Critics say that many of the problems encountered by firms in the industry were caused by bureaucratic decision making that was both untimely and poor. For example, purchasing a

new piece of equipment took between nine and twelve months under Joy Manufacturing's system of operations, says manufacturing manager Thomas Franklin. Under Sullivan's management structure, new equipment can be purchased and installed in a matter of weeks.

Workers as well as managers are given greater latitude under Sullivan's management philosophy. They are also expected to produce more. For example, operator Henry Barton is expected to run two gear-cutting machines simultaneously. If he runs three, he receives incentive pay. How is he doing? After less than a year under the new management, Barton was running four machines at the same time. According to Sullivan's personnel manager, Barton would have been discouraged from such practices under Joy's management. Barton sums up his feelings this way: "I don't look at it as extra money. That's what I earn from my own efforts."

Questions

1. In your opinion, is Henry Barton motivated by money? Explain.

2. How did Joy Manufacturing Company's "bureaucracy" affect management personnel? workers?

3. According to what you have learned about motivation theory, how can Sullivan Manufacturing Company continue to motivate its employees?

CHAPTER OUTLINE

Differences Between Formal and Informal Organizations

Informal Organizations

Types of Informal Groups

Stages of Informal Group Development

Advantages of Informal Group Membership

Friendship • Security • Work-Related Benefits • Information

Characteristics of Informal Groups

Impact on the Formal Organization

Communication • Productivity • Conduct • Turnover

Conflict: A By-Product of Group Dynamics

The Evolution of Conflict

Forms of Conflict

Intrapersonal Conflict • Interpersonal Conflict • Intergroup Conflict

Causes of Conflict

Organizational Structure

Specialization • The Scalar Principle • Chain of Command

Common Areas of Conflict

Line versus Staff

Informal versus Formal Organization

Worker versus Supervisor

Unionist versus Nonunionist

Union versus Company

Conflict Resolution

Avoid Differences

Repress or Delay Differences

Bring Differences into Conflict

Problem Solving

Filley's Categories

A Strategy for Conflict Resolution

Stress: A By-Product of Conflict

Dysfunctional Stress

Functional Stress

Groups and the Management of Conflict

M A N A G E M E N T   I N   A C T I O N

Fighting Industrial Rumors

In recent years, some of the nation's largest and most prestigious companies have been targets of widespread and potentially damaging rumors. Procter & Gamble, McDonald's, Warner-Lambert, Squibb, and Xerox, for example, have had to wrestle with rumors about tainted food products, cancer-causing substances in their equipment, funneling corporate profits to religious cults, and other tales. The companies have attempted to locate and eliminate their sources, but, as one executive aptly said, squelching rumors is like trying to package fog.[1]

No one knows for certain why rumors originate. Often, they are begun by individuals or groups outside the company, but sometimes they come from within. Tulane University Professor Frederick Koenig contends that most malicious industrial rumors tend to crop up in bad economic times. For the low-income worker trying to make ends meet, starting or spreading a rumor is a means of justifying his or her anxieties and the belief that the world is going to hell. It's the worker's way of saying, "If I'm not making it, everybody who is has got to be lying, cheating, or doing me dirty."[2]

Perhaps a more plausible explanation for rumors is that the bearer of news—good or bad—achieves a certain sense of satisfaction and prestige from his or her peer group for being "in the know." In order to maintain this position of status, the gossip must continually supply the rumor mill with grist.

Preview

The mechanism used to transmit industrial rumors is the proverbial grapevine, an informal device that spreads truths, half-truths, and untruths quickly throughout the company and even beyond its boundaries. In many cases, the grapevine transmits information that arises from conflicts between workers. In most cases, however, it is a harmless outlet for people's imaginations, frustrations, and apprehensions.

The grapevine is only one of several types of groups that directly affect the formal organization. In this chapter, we will identify various types of informal organizations and explain how groups can satisfy certain human needs. We also will explain how group membership affects employees' attitudes toward their employer, their supervisor, their coworkers, and their jobs. Finally, we will show how conflict is a natural by-product of group dynamics and will suggest ways to resolve conflict that otherwise would detract from the success of the formal organization. After studying this chapter, you will understand:

✔ The differences between formal and informal organizations

✔ What informal groups are like and how they affect an organization

✔ Why conflict is a natural outgrowth of group interaction

✔ The causes of conflict

✔ Common areas of conflict

✔ Ways of resolving conflict among individuals and groups

✔ How to deal with stress

Differences Between Formal and Informal Organizations

Characteristics of formal organizations

All the organizations mentioned so far in this book are **formal organizations;** that is, each was created to accomplish some objective through the coordinated efforts of people. Sears, the American Red Cross, Procter & Gamble, and the New York Stock Exchange are examples of formal organizations. Each is characterized by well-defined authority-reporting relationships, job titles, policies and procedures, specific job duties, and a host of other factors necessary to accomplish its respective goals. Typically, the formal structure is represented by a printed chart that appears in organizational manuals and other formal company documents. The basic elements of formal organizations can be found in the following definition by Porter, Lawler, and Hackman: "Organizations are: (1) composed of individuals and groups, (2) created in order to achieve certain goals, (3) operated by means of differentiated functions that are intended to be rationally coordinated and directed, and (4) in existence through time on a continuous basis."[3] The methods that IBM and Procter & Gamble use to indoctrinate workers in their formal organizations are shown in the In-Box on page 294.

In small formal organizations, the right hand always seems to know what the left hand is doing. Employees interact regularly, lines of communication are short, and a common purpose unifies the employees. But as an organization grows, people are added to fill specialized jobs, staff departments are created to advise and assist other units, communication gets bogged down, and employees sometimes feel they are little more than computer numbers.

Informal groups defined

To deal with such changes, workers often seek security and identity through the formation of informal groups. These groups, which operate outside formal authority relationships, are called **informal organizations.**[4]

Informal Organizations

Informal organizations differ from formal organizations in several ways. Chris Argyris identifies four major areas of differentiation:

1. *Interpersonal Relations.* In a formal organization, relationships among people are prescribed, whereas in an informal group, relationships largely depend on people's needs.

2. *Leadership.* Leaders of formal organizations are designated; leaders of informal groups emerge.

3. *Behavioral control.* Formal organizations control employee behavior through reward and punishment. Informal groups control members through group pressure.

4. *Dependency.* Because of the formal leader's capacity to reward and punish, subordinates are more dependent than are members of an informal group.[5]

Yet, despite these differences, it is a mistake to think of the formal and informal organizations as two distinctly separate organizational entities. The two coexist and are inseparable. Every formal organization encompasses numerous informal groups, and every informal organization eventually evolves into some degree of formality.

How informal groups work

Informal organizations develop in response to people's needs for security, belonging, and esteem. Unlike formal organizations, informal groups arise spontaneously out of the activities and interactions of employees. They are an inevitable fact of industrial life. The perceptive manager in any firm

THE IN-BOX

Companies Help Shape Group Behavior

Some of the most successful and profitable corporations in the United States have discovered the importance of establishing loyalty and pride among their employees. To this end, IBM and Procter & Gamble, in particular, are adept at indoctrinating new employees. Seven steps of socialization shape workers' behavior and build solidarity among the work force.

1. These companies are careful not to oversell during interviews; they stress both positive and negative aspects of the job, as well as the heavy demands placed on new employees. This rigorous screening eliminates applicants who would not fit in with the established culture.

2. The companies design situations to humble new employees and force them to question their previous behavior, beliefs, and values. The heavy load assigned during the first few weeks prevents social activities outside the firm, eliminating distractions and compelling new employees to work together and to rely on coworkers for help.

3. The firms closely monitor their workers in the field during their first few months. Promotions at predictable intervals reward good performance. Slow progress through the ranks is the rule; employees cannot expect to cut corners or bypass rungs on the ladder.

4. At every career stage, new employees are evaluated and rewarded accordingly.

5. A "family" consciousness is encouraged so that employees will be willing to make personal sacrifices for the good of the company.

6. Emphasis on significant events in company history confirms the importance of the firms' culture and reinforces a code of conduct for all employees in the organization.

7. Promising new employees meet peers or superiors recognized by the company as winners and with whom they share common qualities. These "role models" serve as impetus for achievement for new workers.

Source: Richard Pascale, "Fitting New Employees into the Company Culture," *Fortune,* May 28, 1984, pp. 28–42.

can observe the countless products of informal organizations. For instance, a group of machine operators may walk off the job because they all feel dissatisfied with their working conditions. Or the rumor of a mass layoff may spread through a plant like wildfire. Workers sensing an emergency, such as a deadline, may show an extraordinary team effort to overcome the crisis. Other workers routinely bypass formal communication channels to get things done. All these activities show how informal groups work.

Types of Informal Groups

Broadly speaking, informal groups can be classified as (1) those that exist within the formal organization, and (2) those that are outside or apart from it. Workers who are on the same shift, who have similar backgrounds and job duties, or who have similar values and philosophies are examples of groups in the first category.

People also belong to friendship groups outside their work environment. For example, a group of neighbors may have common recreational, social, or political interests. Friendship groups outside the company and work groups within the company often overlap. In fact, some employers encourage their workers to develop social and recreational ties with their coworkers because they believe this builds a spirit of teamwork and company loyalty.

Informal groups can thus be classified as organizational unit groups, task groups, friendship groups, and interest groups.

1. *Organizational unit group.* An **organizational unit group** includes all employees under the authority of a single supervisor. It might officially be designated as a department, but because all workers are subjected to the same environmental forces, they develop cohesion and share goals.

2. *Task group.* Closely related to the organizational unit group is the **task group.** Sometimes these two types of groups are synonymous. In many cases, however, three or four people in the same department are assigned to work together as a team. Team members frequently develop a unified sense of accomplishment and a high level of esprit de corps.

Types of informal groups

3. *Friendship group.* A **friendship group** permeates the boundaries of the formal organization. The unifying force may be similarities in age, religion, political beliefs, ethnic background, marital status, educational background, and so on.

4. *Interest group.* An **interest group** seeks to advance the position of its members. Workers who feel threatened by automated equipment, for example, will likely band together to show a unified front. Or employees who feel that their interests can best be served through union representation will unite to promote a common cause. An interest group, then, is often defensive in its actions and is comprised of members who share a single purpose.

Membership in these groups changes over time. New employees are hired, some are reassigned, and others leave for one reason or another. In some cases, a change in technology or work flow by management affects on-the-job relationships. People's interests and attitudes also change from time to time. Any change in the work or social environment affects the makeup of the informal organization and serves to strengthen or weaken the driving force behind the group.

Stages of Informal Group Development

Informal groups arise from the interaction of people. Interaction and communication are preconditions for the emergence of a group. When people come into contact with one another on a regular basis, conditions are ripe for a group to emerge. As potential members repeatedly interact for successive days or weeks, a rudimentary group is created.

Common interests link members

The realization of common interests tends to knit the members of an informal group together and signals further development. When members perform similar tasks, or different tasks within the same department, they are linked by a common interest in the product produced or the service rendered. They often have similar problems or privileges and are subjected to the same working conditions. This linking element not only unites group members but also separates them from other workers with different interests. Group unity is strengthened by the consciousness of being different from others, of having higher or lower status, or of being more or less privileged.

All groups appear to go through the same sequence of development. Bruce Tuckman reviewed various studies of group development that focused on groups engaged in problem solving, production, military operations, and therapy. Tuckman concluded that there are four stages of group development. He calls these stages *forming, storming, norming,* and *performing.* Rodney Napier and Matti Gershenfeld identify four phases similar to Tuckman's, but they add a fifth phase called *reforming.* The characteristics of each phase are shown in Table 11.1.

Advantages of Informal Group Membership

People join groups for a variety of reasons. Sometimes they merely want to satisfy their social needs. Other times, they feel that their economic interests can be served best by being part of a group. Although the reasons for joining an informal organization vary from person to person, most people consciously affiliate because they want friendship or security or because they realize the work-related advantages of group acceptance.

Friendship   We all are social animals. We have social needs that can be satisfied through personal interactions with others; consequently, we tend to join groups

TABLE 11.1 Stages in group development	Phase I	Forming	Members test the boundaries of acceptable behavior, they become familiar with one another and with the requirements for group membership, and they exhibit a high degree of dependence on the group leader or other group members
	Phase II	Storming	Conflict arises, members take stands on issues they deem important, and they vie for power and status
	Phase III	Norming	Hostility is reduced, the group is reorganized into a more effective unit, and harmony prevails
	Phase IV	Performing	Energy channels itself into work, open communication and a relaxed atmosphere are evident, and members feel a sense of shared responsibility
	Phase V	Reforming	Crises cause old behavior patterns to reappear; the group may be recycled through the phases if it cannot cope with the crises

Source: Bruce W. Tuckman, "Developmental Sequences in Small Groups," *Psychological Bulletin* June 1965, pp. 384–399; Rodney W. Napier and Matti K. Gershenfeld, *Groups: Theory and Experience* (Boston: Houghton Mifflin, 1973), pp. 247–255.

Reasons for joining groups

for companionship. Group membership gives us the chance to share experiences and provides us with a sense of belonging. It also offers us a forum when we need to state our opinions, vent our hostility, or simply voice our frustrations. Groups also keep us from getting lonely and figuratively provide us a shoulder to cry on when we need sympathy.

Security   Group membership provides people with some security. Although the members themselves may disagree, the group will rally to defend itself and its members from outside threats. If members get into trouble, they can count on the group to come to their defense. It is common for group members to cover up mistakes made by another member or to "go to bat" for a worker who needs their help.

Work-Related Benefits   Membership in a group can yield immediate job-related benefits. Work situations in which workers need assistance crop up every day. A computer programmer, for example, may need help with a particular program, or a production worker may need assistance in assembling a product. In such situations, fellow workers usually offer help and advice right away.

In addition, group members benefit from actions that one or more members take to make the jobs of all easier or their working conditions better. Acting on behalf of all group members, a group leader may ask the supervisor to relax his or her production expectations or to increase the workers' pay rates. This way, the group members show that they are standing together in their effort to win better benefits. Meanwhile, workers may deliberately restrict output to demonstrate that it is impossible to meet production standards.

Information A work group serves as a good way to disseminate information, keeping members informed of happenings in the workplace. Rumors travel quickly via the grapevine, thereby allowing the informal group to adapt to new developments as they occur.

Characteristics of Informal Groups

As we have already pointed out, groups differ greatly in their makeup and objectives. Even their membership changes from time to time as people come and go. Several characteristics, nevertheless, are common to all informal groups. Beach identified eight elements that characterize most informal organizations.

1. *Interaction.* A characteristic common to all organizations is the interaction and communication of their members. In some cases, interaction takes the form of verbal expression; in other instances, it occurs as a gesture or facial expression. Verbal and nonverbal interaction and communication help people relate to one another, providing a means to experience group identification.

2. *Activities.* All groups do something. Obviously, work groups carry on job-related assignments, but other types of groups carry on activities, too. Informal groups may commute to work, disseminate information to their members, or merely share jokes on coffee breaks. The nature and amount of activity varies from group to group. While some groups are constantly in motion, others may be fairly placid.

3. *Norms.* A norm can be defined as an established standard of behavior or accepted code of conduct. Just as society in general has its common law, its taboos, and its belief about what is morally right and wrong, so does an informal group. Although these standards of behavior are unwritten, they are frequently spoken. A new member often learns of the group's norms by innocently violating the code. Corrective action and compliance are enforced by social pressure, ostracism, or even physical threats.

Code of conduct

4. *Informal leadership.* Informal leadership is evident when a person without formal authority is good at directing the behavior of others. Because the informal leader has no legitimate authority, he or she must rely on personal influence to direct others' actions and behavior.

Role of the informal leader

Sometimes, leadership roles are diffused in the group. One person may be especially adept at being the group's spokesperson before management.

Another, with a wide range of outside contacts, may be seen as the best person to arrange special meetings or to organize social activities. In most cases, however, the group leader assumes a leadership role in all group activities. Reflecting the values of the group, this person is acknowledged by the members as the one in charge.

To management, the informal leader may be viewed as a troublemaker and a malcontent. If he or she is removed from the group, however, another leader will emerge. The new leader, too, will exhibit the predecessor's behavior because the leader simply reflects the group.

Realizing that informal groups are an inevitable part of business life, most formal managers try to work through informal leaders to win the group's cooperation. This does not mean that the formal leader should channel orders through the informal leader. Instead, the formal leader will usually devote a little extra attention to winning the support of the informal leader whenever he or she senses that workers are reluctant to put their full energy into a project.

5. *Cohesion.* Think of cohesion as the "glue" that holds group members together. It is the unifying force that gives meaning to the group.

Cohesion: the unifying force

Many considerations affect the degree of cohesion among group members. Individuals feel strongly attached to a group if they feel that it satisfies their needs; or, if they can see an economic advantage to the functioning of the group, they are likely to feel a strong affinity to it. On the other hand, if members feel that the group does not serve their interests or if they are frustrated by belonging to it, they will show little loyalty toward the group or its members.

Cohesion is enhanced when management creates a climate of cooperation rather than competition among group members. Similar pay, equal treatment of workers, and similar jobs tend to increase cohesion within a work group. Different pay for workers performing similar tasks, preferential treatment of workers, or any conditions that cause rivalry tend to diminish group cohesion. Any threat from an outside force also will unify group members. As we have already pointed out, introducing robotics or other equipment that may displace workers will be considered a threat to job security and will result in workers uniting against the new equipment. In friendship groups, the personal and social characteristics of group members affect cohesion. Similarities in ethnic background, social class, sex, age, and so forth strengthen group cohesion.

6. *Social pressure and conformity.* Group membership provides many benefits for members, but, in return, the group demands conformity to its ways of thinking and acting. Conformity helps the group to maintain its security and to accomplish its goals. Groups characterized by high levels of cohesion are able to demand and enforce rigid conformity; groups with little cohesion cannot. The degree of conformity exhibited by a member is in proportion to

Pressure to conform

the benefits derived from being a part of the group. Likewise, the amount of pressure the group exerts to ensure conformity depends on the group's need for solidarity to attain its goals, the members' certainty that sanctions will be imposed, and how much members depend on the group for personal satisfaction.

7. *Group culture.* Informal groups have their own ways of doing things and their own unique customs and rituals. They coin new words, prescribe appropriate dress, and exert discipline. They also tend to have initiation ceremonies for newcomers; for example, new members often are subjected to hazing or to practical jokes to see how they react. Groups essentially create a new way of life for their members.

Perhaps the most colorful characteristic of any group is the language it develops. Jargon that is meaningless to the outsider conveys messages expediently and accurately to group members. New words may be created for tools, procedures, people, and other facets of the work or social environment. Such language not only enhances cohesion among group members but also creates an atmosphere of exclusiveness and secrecy.

8. *Informal structure.* Like formal organizations, informal groups encompass positions and organizational levels. As shown in Figure 11.1, an informal organization has four status positions: group leader, small group nucleus, fringe shell, and outer shell.

The small group nucleus consists of trusted members whose advice is sought by the group leader before action is taken. Members of this nucleus are subgroup leaders; that is, they have their own followers who look to them for information and guidance. Fringe shell members are the rank and file who support the actions of the group but who provide little, if any, leadership. Outer shell members are rather passive in group activities but go along with the group, thereby displaying solidarity throughout the ranks.[6]

Impact on the Formal Organization

One of the manager's tasks is to define the formal roles of subordinates. These roles and their planned interrelationships make up the formal organizational structure that serves as a guideline for cooperative action. Unfortunately, few organizations enjoy total cooperation from all employees; even with the best organizational structure, they rarely, if ever, achieve total harmony.

There are several reasons for this imperfection in the way that formal organizations operate. First, managers sometimes fail to specify job duties precisely. Jobs change over time, but job descriptions may not be updated to reflect these changes; thus, what the formal organization expects is not the same as the duties listed in job descriptions. A second reason can be found in the activities of informal groups. When these groups' activities are in line with those of the formal organization, cooperation with the formal organization is

FIGURE 11.1
Positions in an informal
organization

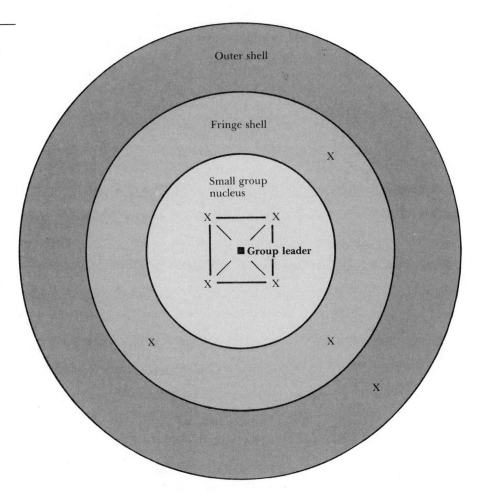

assured. When the group's role conflicts with the expectations of the formal
organization, however, relationships between the two are often strained. Thus,
it becomes apparent that a worker's behavior usually is influenced more by
social-group pressure than by rules, policies, goals, and authority relationships
in the formal organization. The result is called **role incongruency.**[7]

Groups affect formal organizations in a number of ways. Sometimes,
informal groups complement the formal organization; in other cases, the
activities of groups are not helpful. The beneficial and dysfunctional effects
of informal groups can be observed in four areas: communication, employee
productivity, employee conduct, and turnover.

**Conflict with the
formal organization**

Communication   Formal communication channels are represented by an organization's scalar chain (see Chapter 2), which links the various positions in a hierarchy. All official organizational communication is routed through this chain of command. Since formal channels are recognized as official and authoritative, written documents such as letters, memos, directives, and organizational requests normally follow them.

Informal routes of communication

Besides receiving communications through the formal channels, all organizations have informal routes for messages. Although coexisting with the formal channels, these routes frequently diverge from them by bypassing levels of authority and cutting across vertical chains of command. These informal channels of communication serve the workers' interests by providing them with tidbits of information that affect their social and work environment. In many cases, the functioning of this so-called grapevine supplements the formal channel by filling in the gaps or by giving meaning to formal announcements. In too many instances, however, the grapevine circulates inaccurate information and results in misunderstandings and errors.

Productivity   Informal groups can positively or negatively affect employee productivity. Regardless of the production standards that the formal organization sets, the group will establish its own output expectations. If a group decides on high productivity, all members will be pressured to meet those standards. If the group deliberately restricts output, on the other hand, all members also will be expected to conform.

Restriction of output

The tendency of groups to set production norms was first observed during the Hawthorne experiments at Western Electric Company. In one of the experiments, the Bank Wiring Observation Room, the research team learned that output was restricted for two reasons. First, the group felt that greater productivity would imply that fewer workers were needed, resulting in layoffs. In this case, group norms were considered a way to maintain job security. Second, the workers believed that increased output could cause management to set higher piece-rate standards; hence, more work would be expected for the same amount of pay.[8]

Restriction of output is common for other reasons, too. It creates the impression that all workers are equal, thereby enhancing group solidarity. It also stabilizes take-home pay from week to week. Contrary to popular belief, many workers do not seek only to earn the most money possible. They also want to maintain their coworkers' friendship or save their energy for recreational activities at the end of the workday. In short, they value the social ethic as much as the work ethic; they are not necessarily motivated to accumulate more and more money, for money's sake.[9]

Studies show that the production norms established by informal groups are related to the degree of cohesion in the group. If there is a low level of cohesion, production rates among workers will vary significantly. But when the cohesion level is high, groups tend to set higher production standards. Likert contends that groups having a great deal of peer-group pride and loyalty are more productive because members are more cooperative and helpful toward one another. He also found that groups with a high level of peer-group loyalty have lower rates of absenteeism than do low-loyalty groups and that their attitudes toward their jobs are more positive.[10]

Conduct   Most informal organizations have a stabilizing effect on workers. When relations between management and workers are good, the informal group tries to enforce rules and regulations to maintain harmony. But if relations between management and workers are strained or are lacking in trust, the informal organization becomes a vehicle of discord and disorder.

Turnover   Just as the informal organization affects communication, productivity, and conduct, it also has an impact on employee turnover. Workers who become part of closely-knit groups develop loyalties to both their coworkers and their employer. When their roots become entrenched, they are naturally reluctant to sever their ties. The result is a stable work force.

Conversely, workers who are not accepted by the group tend to find themselves "out of sync" with all that is happening around them. Eventually, people who are socially isolated will feel uncomfortable with their surroundings and will seek employment elsewhere.

Conflict: A By-Product of Group Dynamics

The president of one of the country's largest and most successful companies once remarked that life is nothing more than a series of problem-solving ventures—just one conflict after another. A comment like that is typical of the way that most managers react to conflict within the groups in their organizations. Too often, they feel that conflict results from poor management—a weakness on their part that they cannot overcome. In reality, though, conflict in a group or company does not necessarily mean either ineffective management or a breakdown in organizational efficiency. Whenever individuals with varying needs, values, and personalities come together within an organizational structure, conflict is inevitable. It may, in fact, even be desirable for promoting change and growth. Depending on a manager's response to conflict, the outcome may help or stifle group and individual growth. Thus, conflict is not alarming; its mismanagement is.

Conflict can be defined as an emotional or physical struggle arising when two or more persons vie for the same resources, activities, or goals, but when only one can achieve them at the expense of the other. This definition primarily addresses conflict between individuals and between groups. Another form of conflict occurs within a person when experiencing conflicting needs

Group cooperation with management

Social isolation

Conflict is both good and bad

or the inability to control a frustrating situation. We will discuss each of these kinds of conflict, but first let's see how conflict comes about in the first place.

The Evolution of Conflict

According to Louis R. Pondy, conflict can be understood best if it is viewed as a dynamic process composed of five states. Pondy writes:

> In the same sense that a decision can be thought of as a process of gradual commitment to a course of action, a conflict episode can be thought of as a gradual escalation to a state of disorder. If choice is the climax of a decision, then by analogy, open war or aggression is the climax of a conflict episode.[11]

Pondy's first stage, illustrated in Figure 11.2, is called *latent conflict.* For this stage, Pondy identified the underlying causes of conflict as: (1) competition for scarce resources—when the aggregated demands of participants for resources exceed the resources available to the organization, (2) drives for autonomy—when one person seeks to control an activity that another person regards as his or her own province or tries to insulate himself or herself from such controls, and (3) divergence of subunit goals—when two parties must cooperate on some joint activity and are unable to reach consensus on concerted action. When these underlying sources are present, the potential for more obvious conflict is high.

At the second stage—*perceived conflict*—the parties involved become aware of the conflict. Perceived conflict does not necessarily emerge from latent conflict, for some latent conflicts never reach the level of awareness. At the third stage—*felt conflict*—an emotional response to conflict occurs. If nothing is done to resolve the conflict, *manifest conflict* (the fourth stage) emerges. The resulting behavior can range from physical or verbal attack to refusal to work. The final stage—*conflict aftermath*—follows this open conflict. If the parties involved are satisfied with the conflict's resolution, future relationships may be more cooperative. If the conflict was suppressed rather than resolved, however, the first stage will reappear.[12]

Forms of Conflict

Intrapersonal Conflict   Conflict within an individual, or **intrapersonal conflict,** often results from conflicting needs or frustrating situations. A person entering an organization brings along a highly complex system of needs and attitudes. A young sales representative, for example, might have ambitions of becoming vice president of marketing. Achieving this goal might mean sacrificing something equally important, such as time at home with the family. Sometimes a solution seems impossible and the problem persists, unsolved,

Latent conflict

Conflict evolves

FIGURE 11.2
Pondy's stages of
conflict

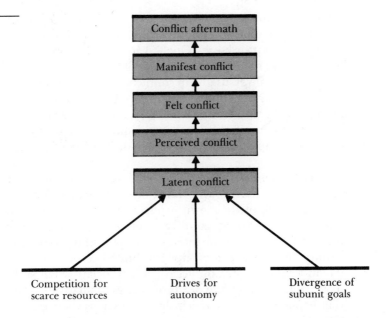

for a long time. The individual's stressful state in this situation is caused by conflicting needs.

Intrapersonal conflict also can arise when people know what they want but are unable to attain it, or when a situation prevents them from behaving according to how they perceive their roles. Another cause of intrapersonal **Role conflict** conflict is role ambiguity, a situation that arises when role demands are not clearly communicated. This form of role conflict often occurs when incompatible demands are placed on a manager by two different groups of people. For example, a manager's boss may expect him or her to reduce the budget and cut spending, while the manager's subordinates want their budgets increased. The manager may be uncertain whether he or she should represent higher management or the people in the department.

An individual in a given situation usually plays one or a few roles, shifting among them when entering situations where he or she has a different position or status. When roles conflict, the individual must work out some system of priority or compromise. If this is impossible, frustration will cause performance or morale problems.

Interpersonal Conflict **Interpersonal conflict** involves confrontations or rivalries in the work environment between individuals or between individuals **Reasons for** and groups. Conflict between individuals most often occurs when two people **interpersonal conflict** compete for the same job or for limited resources. For instance, if two or more salespeople want to be promoted to the position of sales manager, they become rivals in a situation where only one can succeed. Conflict also arises between employees and their bosses. One way to deal with this type of conflict is described in the Manager's Notebook on page 307.

Individual versus group conflict arises whenever a group member resists conforming with group norms in an effort to promote his or her own self-interests. As pointed out earlier, a group member trying to win a promotion or salary increase will likely fall into disfavor with the group if he or she exceeds what the group considers the normal level of production.

Intergroup Conflict   Intergroup relations are vital to the success of large organizations, yet, intergroup conflict often develops. People have a natural tendency to think of their own group as the "good guys" and the other as the "bad guys." **Intergroup conflict** develops for a variety of reasons between two or more departments or interest groups within an organization. One source is competition between groups for limited resources, such as money, personnel, and equipment. Conflict is likely to occur when sufficient resources are unavailable to satisfy the needs or wishes of all groups. For example, consider what happens when a municipality must choose between replacing police squad cars or buying new garbage trucks. The police department and the sanitation department are thrust into a conflict that often results in hurt feelings, charges of favoritism, and so on.

Communication difficulties are another source of intergroup conflict. A particular functional unit in an organization tends to develop its own vocabulary. When this group has to communicate with other groups in the organization, it might encounter semantic problems. For instance, computer systems are being used more widely today in large and small companies alike. Too often, managers have resisted introducing such systems because they do not understand the technical language used. For this reason, there is a push in business to find systems analysts who not only understand the technical aspects of computers but who are also experienced in business administration and can facilitate communication flow.

Sources of intergroup conflict

Sometimes, intergroup conflict arises because groups have different interests and goals: what is paramount to one group may be insignificant to another. For example, a group of young workers may want management to do something about the company's promotion system, which they feel is inadequate. At the same time, older workers may be accusing management of ignoring improvements in the company's pension plan. Management recognizes the two different goals but, believing that the pension issue is the more pressing, addresses that goal. Management may want to solve both problems but is not able to do so within the current budget. As a result, one group becomes hostile because it is ignored.[13]

Overlapping task definitions can be another source of intergroup conflict. Difficulty in assigning credit or blame between two departments increases

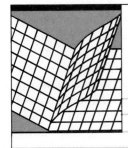

THE MANAGER'S NOTEBOOK

How to Disagree With Your Boss

What should you do when you and your boss disagree over some decision he or she has made? Look for another job? Tell your boss off? Forget about it? One way of dealing with stress that arises from conflict with your boss is to speak up. Of course, that is easier to say than to do, but stress associated with suppressing personal feelings is often worse for you than being told to mind your own business. In fact, a tactful discussion with your boss may be the only way to cope with the harmful effects of stress.

First, you should identify your reasons for your conflict; then put yourself in your boss's shoes. Why did he or she make a decision that adversely affected you? If you still feel that you were mistreated, compare your reasons with the company goals. If your reasons conflict with your company's goals, you may have to change your values or quit.

If, however, your reasons are compatible with your company's goals, you should speak up. Don't write a memo and don't call your boss on the phone. Instead, ask for a personal conference to discuss the reasons you feel that the decision was wrong.

Before you meet with your boss, rehearse what you are going to say. And once you enter the discussion, remember to focus on the facts rather than on emotions. You may find it helpful to suggest that a third party be consulted for advice—someone who is considered knowledgeable about your situation. If you can't change your boss's mind, agree to disagree. A disagreement doesn't mean that you have to quit your job; in fact, if you sat on the U.S. Supreme Court, a part of your job would be reporting a minority opinion.

Whatever happens, thank your boss for allowing you to comment. Let your boss know that the reason you spoke up is because you care about your job. Employees who don't care don't speak out.

Source: Peter A. Reinhardt, "When To Speak Up If You and the Boss Disagree," *Wall Street Journal,* September 9, 1985.

the chance of conflict between them. Who is responsible for losing a talented management trainee—the personnel department that located the trainee or the training department? Who can rightfully take credit for the great interest in a new product line—marketing, advertising, or research and development? This inability to pinpoint both positive and negative contributions causes groups to compete all the more for control over recognized activities.[14]

Causes of Conflict

In the preceding section, we discussed the various types of organizational conflict and pinpointed some of its most common sources. These sources are listed in Table 11.2.

In addition to the sources of conflict listed in Table 11.2, conflict also can be caused by the organizational structure itself. The structure of an organization provides a formal framework within which the organization uses resources to get things done. Since an organization employs individuals with different personalities, however, all aspects of the organization's structure will not be compatible with all its members. As Labovitz said:

> One source of conflict stems from the structure of an organization—the fact that complex institutions expect people who share different goals, time orientations, and management philosophies to integrate their efforts into a cohesive whole directed towards the accomplishment of organizational objectives.[15]

Organizational Structure

A close look at a few structural areas will help you understand how conflict may emerge from the very structure of an organization.

Specialization Although specialization of labor can make a firm more efficient, too much specialization can cause adverse reactions among employees. Tasks that are routine and fail to stimulate or challenge an individual's creativity are likely to cause boredom and frustration.

As specialization increases, departmentation is a natural consequence. Often, members of a particular department become such a cohesive unit and are so involved with achieving their own goals that they either ignore or subordinate larger corporate goals.

The Scalar Principle The scalar principle of organizational structure, discussed in Chapter 2, holds that authority flows in a scalar chain, that is, in a direct line from top to bottom, starting at the top of the organization with the president and progressing down to the lowest levels.

> The pyramid shape of the organization structure, with fewer positions at the top than at lower levels, implies that success results from competition among peers, which forces concentration on task performance rather than organizational goals.[16]

Conflict is the natural outcome of such competition among coworkers.

Chain of Command The chain of command concept is based on the premise that an employee should answer to only one superior. This eliminates the potential for conflict when one person answers to more than one boss. Authority must be well defined if conflict is to be minimized. To avoid confusion and uncertainty, people must clearly understand who has authority over others.

Organizational
structure causes
conflict

TABLE 11.2 Sources of organizational conflict	TYPE OF CONFLICT	PRIMARY SOURCES OF CONFLICT
	Intrapersonal	Conflicting needs Role ambiguity Incompatibility of organizational and personal values
	Interpersonal	Personality differences Power struggles Competition
	Intergroup	Limited resources Communication problems Conflicting interests Overlapping tasks

Common Areas of Conflict

Conflict between individuals and between groups occurs throughout organizations; however, it is particularly acute between certain groups and individuals because of their different values, expectations, and goals. The following discussion pinpoints some of the primary areas for potential conflict.

Line versus Staff

For years, managers have known about the potential for conflict between line and staff managers. One of the first studies to stress this conflict was conducted by Melville Dalton, an industrial sociologist who observed firsthand the relationships between these two groups in a number of industrial settings. According to Dalton, three basic conditions contributed to conflict between line and staff officers.[17] The first dealt with the behavior of the staff personnel. He found that specialized staff managers were significantly younger and better educated than line officers were and wanted more money, power, and prestige. The older line officers disliked receiving what they regarded as instructions from men so much younger than themselves. Staff personnel were clearly aware of this attitude among line officers.

A second problem area was the attempt by staff managers to prove themselves and to gain acceptance.

> They strained to develop new techniques and to get them accepted by the line. But in doing this they frequently became impatient and gave already suspicious line officers the impression of reaching for authority over production.[18]

Line officers resented being guided by the younger, less experienced staff members.

Melville Dalton's studies

Staff managers recognized that a good relationship with line managers was essential to securing a higher staff position. This presented a third problem area. Staff officers frequently compromised staff rules by permitting minor rule-breaking by line managers. At times, line officers hid errors made by lower staff from the upper staff and line management. Line managers resented the younger staff personnel introducing new ideas and techniques, fearing that their own abilities would be questioned. In response, staff managers sometimes would withhold introduction of a new process if it was felt that line officers would not receive the innovation favorably.

Informal versus Formal Organization

As we have pointed out, informal groups have their own leaders, norms, and codes of conduct. To a great extent, the group sets its own production standards and decides how diligently the members will work. It exerts social pressure on any member who fails to comply with the accepted group norm, even if the norm conflicts with company standards.

Examples of group conflict

Two areas of potential conflict thus arise. On one hand, any member who repeatedly deviates from the informal group norm will be ostracized from the group and will become socially isolated, creating conflict with the other group members. On the other hand, if the norms of the informal group conflict with the production expectancy of the formal organization, conflict arises between the group and the organization as a whole.

Worker versus Supervisor

A worker often becomes dissatisfied with a supervisor for a number of reasons. The worker's value system may differ greatly from that of his or her boss; the supervisor may be perceived as unfair, inconsistent, or indifferent to the worker's needs; or the worker may feel that the boss is ineffective or incompetent. While the worker's frustrations may not evolve into open aggression, this attitude is certain to affect the worker's performance and relationship with coworkers.

Unionist versus Nonunionist

Invariably, conflict arises between workers who join a union and those who do not. In states that have enacted right-to-work laws, workers who are eligible to be represented by a bargaining agent (union) can opt not to join without fear of losing their jobs. This often creates deep-seated resentment between those who are "brothers in toil" and so-called free riders, often erupting into open hostility during periods of labor unrest. Nonunion workers are not required to honor picket lines established by their union counterparts; nevertheless, when nonunion workers attempt to cross the picket line, they may be met with personal insults, threats, intimidation, and sometimes physical violence.

Union versus Company

Union-management relations is an area that is always ripe for conflict. First, collective bargaining is usually seen as a win-lose situation; that is, a "gain" for the union is a "concession" by the company. Second, any bargaining issue that is settled through compromise is often considered a lose-lose situation, with neither side emerging as a clear-cut winner. As long as managers and union leaders see themselves as adversaries at the negotiating table, they will continue to act out their conflicting roles.

Conflict Resolution

As pointed out earlier, conflict evolves through various stages. A manager has several alternatives in resolving disputes, but it is important to note that he or she has much greater influence in the early stages of a conflict and significantly less influence in its later stages. Now let's look at the various approaches that can be used.

Avoid Differences

An organization can minimize potential conflict by employing people whose backgrounds, values, and interests are similar. Whenever this is possible, interpersonal conflict can be controlled to reduce high-risk confrontations. On the other hand, however, employing similar people may result in illegal discrimination.

Repress or Delay Differences

There are two methods of repressing differences. First, the manager can emphasize harmony and teamwork or bring disputing parties together only under highly controlled circumstances. A second approach is to punish people guilty of disruptive behavior.

Bring Differences into Conflict

This is a high-risk approach that may result in lifelong scars, financial costs, tensions, embarrassments, and wasted time and effort.

Problem Solving

Perhaps the best approach to conflict resolution is to bring the disputing parties together, giving them a chance to air their differences. With this method, the manager avoids acting as an arbitrator or judge. Instead, he or she acts as a mediator whose function is to encourage communication for helping restore harmonious working relationships.

The traditional
approach

These approaches represent two distinct philosophies regarding conflict resolution. The traditional philosophy, represented by the first three approaches, holds that conflict is caused by personality differences or leadership failures. Because of this, conflict can be resolved by physically separating the conflicting parties or by direct managerial intervention.

The modern approach

The more popular, contemporary approach sees conflict as an inevitable consequence of everyday organizational life caused by the complexities of the internal organization. This theory holds that positive organizational changes may result from using a problem-solving approach to conflict resolution.

Filley's Categories

According to Alan C. Filley, all techniques for resolving conflict can be placed into three categories: win-lose, lose-lose, or win-win methods.[19]

The **win-lose method** is based on force. Personal goals are satisfied at another's expense through the use of authority, intimidation, threats, and so forth.

Win-lose approach

> Win-lose methods, in which the supervisor inevitably wins and the employee inevitably loses, include the use of mental or physical power to bring about compliance. Other win-lose methods involve failing to respond to subordinates' suggestions for change. Majority rule is also a win-lose method as is minority rule when the few are in control.[20]

Lose-lose approach

The second category for resolving conflict, the **lose-lose method,** usually ends up with neither party being truly satisfied with the outcome. Compromise is an example of a lose-lose situation. This can be thought of as a "give and take" exchange with no clear winner or loser. A form of compromise is bargaining. In this situation, both sides realize they have to give a little but want to minimize the loss; thus, both parties lack real commitment to the solution. Another lose-lose strategy involves side-payments—one party agrees to a solution in exchange for a favor from the other party.

Sometimes, differences between two conflicting parties may be minimized while accentuating common interests and goals. This is called **smoothing.** Although parties may come to realize that their differences are not as great as originally thought, this still can be considered a lose-lose method. Eventually, the central issue of the conflict will resurface, and the previous situation may even be aggravated.

Another lose-lose approach in which neither party is satisfied is the use of a third party to settle a dispute. Arbitrators frequently resolve issues at some middle ground between the positions held by the disputers. Although each disputant gains something, the outcome is rarely satisfying to either side.

Win-win approach

The third alternative for resolving conflict is the **win-win method.** Considered the most constructive resolution, it is also the most difficult to reach. The heart of the win-win approach is using participative management techniques to gain consensus and commitment to objectives. With this method, all parties identify goals, consider obstacles to reaching them, regard alternative solutions, and finally settle on the most mutually beneficial solution.

A Strategy for Conflict Resolution

Table 11.3 illustrates both functional and dysfunctional rationales for using the various conflict-resolving approaches. Most managers will find the following guidelines helpful in resolving conflict.

1. Conduct a problem analysis to determine the basic issues.

2. State the problem as a goal or as an obstacle rather than as a solution.

3. Identify the steps to attaining the goal.

4. Depersonalize the problem.

5. Separate the process of defining the problem from the search for solutions and from the evaluation of alternatives.[21]

A high-risk approach

Bringing conflict out into the open involves risks to the organization. There is always the possibility of worsening the situation by making the conflict more widely known. Further, once the conflict is in the open, no one may be able to predict the outcome of its resolutions.

While the problem-solving approach takes a longer time to reach a solution and means full commitment of all parties involved, it generally yields better and longer-lasting results than other approaches do.

Stress: A By-Product of Conflict

Stress can be defined as a person's physical, chemical, or emotional response to tension or pressure in his or her environment. It occurs whenever environmental forces throw bodily or emotional functions out of balance. Consequently, stress is a natural outcome of organizational conflict. Job stress can never be totally eliminated; in fact, a certain amount of it can actually encourage individual growth, development, and achievement.

> It is difficult . . . for those who manage other people to accept the notion that anything other than peace and tranquility can be positive. Managers forget that some conflict is therapeutic . . . they fall into the trap of assuming that it is management's role to reduce tensions and promote harmony and cooperation.[22]

Conflict causes stress

While stress can have positive effects, too much of it may result in a psychological or physiological imbalance within the individual. Because these consequences may severely hamper the achievement of organizational goals, management must be aware of the symptoms of stress.

The typical pattern of a person under stress begins with minor changes in behavior. If stress is not reduced or eliminated, severe health or personality

TABLE 11.3
Conflict management/
resolution continuum

(+)
Functional Reasons

3 One or both parties lack confrontation skills.
2 One party believes the other party cannot face confrontation.
1 Person's head and gut augur disaster if confrontation takes place.

(−)
Dysfunctional Reasons

1 One or both parties lack courage.
2 One or both parties fear taking a risk.
3 One or both parties want to avoid the pain of confrontation.
4 One or both parties refuse to acquire confrontation skills.

(+)
Functional Reasons

4 One or both parties are not psychologically ready for confrontation.
3 The current moment is inauspicious, the time and/or place inappropriate.
2 The parties need to collect more objective data for an accurate perception of problem.
1 Either party or both work to defuse the issue; time provides perspective, and distance reduces "heat."

Delay

(−)
Dysfunctional Reasons

1 Either party or both defuse the issue by delaying; the issue then becomes clouded.
2 The passing of time contaminates and distorts perception of issue; memory fades.
3 The issue will eventually lose priority status; something else will probably supersede it.

(+)
Negotiation Model (Win-win climate)

7 Parties seek satisfaction for both sides.
6 Parties exercise spirit of compromise.
5 Parties seek consensus.
4 Parties lower their defenses.
3 Parties assert their positions responsibly.
2 Parties actively listen to each other.
1 Parties meet on neutral grounds.

Confront → **Resolve**

(−)
Power Model (Win-lose climate)

1 One party uses physical power.
2 One party uses psychological power by withholding money or affection from the other, demoting the other or withholding his or her promotion, or threatening the other's status.

Source: Reprinted by permission of the publisher, from "Strategies for Resolving Conflict: Their Functional and Dysfunctional Sides," by Michele Stimac, *Personnel*, November/December 1982, p. 63, © 1982 American Management Association, New York. All rights reserved.

Recognizing stress

disorders may appear. Given certain characteristic modes of adaptation in the form of personality traits, once a person experiences some kind of emotional stress, he or she is likely to make greater use of those mechanisms that worked best in the past. The first sign of stress is that a person seems to be conspicuously more like he or she always was. For example, highly motivated and achievement-oriented people may become workaholics and strive for even higher output. People who have trouble motivating themselves under normal work conditions may react to stress by producing at a lower capacity or by frequent absences from the job.

If this mechanism does not adequately handle the stress, we will begin to see the appearance of inefficient functioning—vague fears, inability to concentrate, compulsions to do certain things, increasing irritability, and declining work performance. We will also see the effects of psychological defensive mechanisms—tension, inability to sleep, and so on.[23]

If stress continues to build, severe disorders may become apparent, such as radical personality changes or excessive use of alcohol or other drugs. Because individuals respond to the same conditions in different ways, these psychological and physiological consequences vary from person to person.

Dysfunctional Stress

Occupational stress can be either functional or dysfunctional. **Dysfunctional stress,** which can result in decreased job satisfaction and low levels of performance, can be caused by a number of occupational situations, one of which pertains to job duties. This type of stress becomes prevalent when the worker does not clearly understand the duties and responsibilities associated with his or her job. The lack of promotional opportunities also gives rise to dysfunctional stress. Other situations that cause dysfunctional stress include: (1) a sense of having little influence with your boss; (2) your present relationship with your supervisor; (3) lack of authority, lack of control, and slow job progress; (4) feeling unreasonable pressure to improve job performance; and (5) someone else's getting a job that you want.

Causes of dysfunctional stress

Functional Stress

Functional stress, on the other hand, is seen as beneficial to the organization. Studies have indicated that very low levels of stress may be just as detrimental to the individual and the organization as very high levels are. This means that there is an optimum level between the extremes of stress. This level, unique for each individual, is the point at which individual performance and effectiveness are maximized. Basically, four functional stresses are positively related to job satisfaction: (1) excess of responsibility, (2) seeing yourself as less than totally qualified, (3) having an excessively heavy workload, and (4) making decisions that affect the lives of others.[24]

Beneficial stress

A certain amount of interpersonal conflict, too, may actually be beneficial.

> First, it may increase the motivation and energy available to do tasks required by the social system. Second, conflict may increase this innovativeness of individuals and the system because of the greater diversity of the viewpoints

and a heightened sense of necessity. Third, each person may develop increased understanding of his own position, because the conflict forces him to articulate his views and to bring forth all supporting arguments. Fourth, each party may achieve greater awareness of his own identity. Fifth, interpersonal conflict may be a means for managing the participants' own internal conflicts.[25]

Although a limited amount of conflict and stress are positively correlated to job performance, there is a limit to the amount of pressure that the human body and mind can sustain. Whenever a manager's expectations are significantly greater than a subordinate's ability to produce, conflict and stress surface. One study of job stress revealed that nearly half of the survey respondents complained of work overload.[26] A later study of upper- and middle-level managers in Canada indicated that workload was the single most frequently perceived source of job-related stress.[27]

Assigning too much work to people is a managerial tactic intended to increase motivation, effort, and productivity. In the long run, however, this tactic has a less obvious and negative consequence—conflict and stress. It is understandable why managers use such tactics. Undoubtedly, they realize that deadlines motivate people and that optimum levels of conflict maximize job performance. They should not, though, overlook the many negative consequences.

Review

✔ *The differences between formal and informal organizations.* Informal organizations differ from formal organizations in several respects. Unlike formal organizations that are created to achieve specific objectives, informal groups arise spontaneously in response to people's need for security, companionship, and esteem. In formal organizations, relationships among people are prescribed, leaders are appointed, and control is maintained through formal rules and policies. In informal organizations, leaders assume their role, relationships largely depend on people's needs, and behavior is controlled through group pressure.

✔ *What informal groups are like and how they affect an organization.* Groups fall into four categories: organizational unit, task, friendship, and interest groups. Each type of group is an outgrowth of the personal interaction of members who have similar interests and needs. Common interests unify members and separate them from other workers whose interests are different.

Membership in informal groups is advantageous for a number of reasons. Group membership offers friendship, job security, and work-related benefits. In addition, membership in a group is an excellent way of keeping informed about the happenings in the plant or office.

Groups are not static. They differ greatly in terms of their objectives and makeup, and even their membership changes over time. Even so, all informal groups have eight common characteristics: (1) interaction of members, (2) activities, (3) group norms, (4) informal leadership, (5) cohesion, (6) social pressure and conformity, (7) group culture, and (8) informal structure.

Groups affect formal organizations in a number of ways. In some cases, the way that formal groups operate complements the operations of the formal organization; in other cases, the actions of groups are not helpful. The four areas in which group activity are most apparent are communications, productivity, employee turnover, and employee conduct.

✔ *Why conflict is a natural outgrowth of group interaction.* Whenever people with different values, philosophies, and interests are brought together, conflict is inevitable. Conflict is, however, not necessarily destructive; in fact, some conflict may be desirable for promoting change and growth.

✔ *The causes of conflict.* Essentially, there are three types of conflict: intrapersonal conflict, interpersonal conflict, and intergroup conflict. Intrapersonal conflict, or conflict within a person, results from conflicting needs or situational frustrations. Interpersonal conflict involves rivalries between individuals. Intergroup conflict refers to confrontations between groups within an organization.

✔ *Common areas of conflict.* Although conflict between individuals and between groups occurs throughout organizations, some areas are especially conflict-prone. Conflict commonly occurs between line and staff people, between workers and supervisors, between union and nonunion members, and between informal groups and the formal organization.

✔ *Ways of resolving conflict among individuals and groups.* When conflict is not resolved, it evolves through various stages until it reaches open confrontation. While managers have several alternatives to choose from in trying to resolve conflict, they are usually more effective intervening in the early stages of conflict than in later stages. Managers can avoid conflict by employing people with similar backgrounds and values, or they can repress differences and hope that open confrontation never materializes. Other approaches to conflict resolution include direct confrontation and problem solving.

✔ *How to deal with stress.* Conflict produces stress. A limited amount of stress can be beneficial, but too much stress can result in decreased job satisfaction and low levels of job performance. The single greatest source of job-related stress is work overload. Managers often assign too much work in an effort to increase motivation, effort, and productivity. In the long run, however, work overload leads to dysfunctional conflict and stress.

THE MANAGER'S DICTIONARY

As an extra review of the chapter, try defining the following terms. If you have trouble with any of them, refer to the page numbers listed.

formal organizations (292)
informal organizations (293)
organizational unit group (295)
task group (295)
friendship group (295)
interest group (295)

role incongruency (301)
conflict (303)
intrapersonal conflict (304)
interpersonal conflict (305)
intergroup conflict (306)
win-lose method (312)
lose-lose method (312)

smoothing (312)
win-win method (312)
stress (313)
dysfunctional stress (315)
functional stress (315)

REVIEW QUESTIONS

1. Distinguish between formal and informal organizations. What characteristics do they have in common? How do they differ?

2. Why do informal groups emerge? Explain.

3. What type of groups exist within formal organizations? Outside of formal organizations?

4. Differentiate between an organizational unit group and a task group.

5. Why does the membership of a group change over time?

6. Give the stages of group development.

7. List the characteristics of each developmental stage.

8. What are the advantages of joining a group? In your opinion, which reason is most important? Least important?

9. List the common characteristics of groups.

10. How do groups force members to conform to group norms? Give an example.

11. Think of a group to which you belong, and provide examples of your group culture.

12. How do groups affect formal organizations? Be specific.

13. Explain why conflict is considered a natural by-product of group dynamics.

14. What are the various forms of conflict? Give an example of each type.

15. Can you think of areas in an organization where conflict is common? Why are these areas conflict-prone?

16. How does an organization's structure cause conflict? Explain.

17. What alternatives are available to a manager who wishes to resolve interpersonal conflict among his or her subordinates?

18. Give an example of each of the following approaches to conflict resolution: win-lose, lose-lose, win-win.

19. Distinguish between functional and dysfunctional stress. How can dysfunctional stress be minimized?

MANAGEMENT CHALLENGE

Assume that you are the plant manager of a small garment manufacturing facility specializing in the manufacture of shirts that are sold to a major retail firm. Your plant is nonunion, like all other satellite plants in your company, and is located in a small town in southern Georgia. All production workers are paid on a piece-rate basis, permitting the typical worker to earn approximately $5.75 per hour. Compared to the industry average, employee turnover is high. In addition, your plant is not considered by corporate management to be operating as efficiently as other plants in the company are.

Word has spread throughout the plant that very soon the facility will be closed: production equipment will be moved to another plant, some managers will be transferred, and all other workers will lose their jobs. To your knowledge, there are no plans to close your plant. In fact, your division chief has told you that, although the company would like to see improved profit margins, it has no plans to terminate operations.

1. How could this rumor have begun in your plant?

2. As a plant manager, how would you expect your employees to react to the rumor?

3. Would you expect the rumor to unify or to divide your work force? Explain.

4. What action would you take to dispel the uncertainty in the plant? Would you involve informal group leaders? Why or why not?

5. What type of stress would you expect the rumor to cause? Would this stress be beneficial or destructive? Explain.

CASE 11.1

Friendly Takeovers Aren't Always Friendly[28]

Chris Donahue's suicide note warned his family: "Don't go down the cellar." The thirty-eight-year-old economist wrote the note just before hanging himself following R. J. Reynolds's takeover of Heublein Incorporated. A week earlier, he had thought he would be given a job at headquarters; instead, he was told that his services were no longer needed.

Mergers and acquisitions are unsettling to the people involved. Employees get transferred or fired, they are often stripped of status and benefits, and they are drained of their pride and dedication. Moreover, mergers tear friendships apart and pit manager against manager and worker against worker. Yet, shake-ups are viewed as a necessary, if somewhat turbulent, way to keep companies afloat.

Even a merger that results in minimal change can be unnerving. Although DuPont didn't meddle much with Conoco when it bought the oil company in 1981, an ex-Conoco manager reported that it was traumatic to see his company disappear from the stock exchange. When mergers do result in major shake-ups, the effect can be devastating, as evidenced by Donahue's fate.

One company that has earned a reputation for rough mergers is Cooper Industries, a manufacturer of industrial machinery. For example, when Cooper Industries took over Gardner-Denver, a maker of mining, drilling, and construction equipment, observers and insiders alike felt as if a thunderbolt had struck. Cooper shut down the corporate headquarters, cut benefits and working capital, and fired employees. In one instance, Cooper closed an entire plant at which fathers and sons and friends had worked together for years.

Cooper's 1981 takeover of Crouse-Hinds, an electrical-equipment producer, was even rougher. It forced out some key operating managers, demoted others, and instilled fear into employees down the line. Even the furniture and coffee china owned by Crouse-Hinds were appropriated for use in Cooper's new headquarters in Houston.

In the final analysis, the costs associated with Cooper's takeover of Crouse-Hinds may have outweighed the benefits. As one observer put it, the takeover "produced little apparent benefit and eventually frayed the intangible fabric of values, traditions, and morale that binds most well-managed companies together."

Questions

1. How would you expect informal groups to react to an announcement that their company is being taken over by another firm? Explain.

2. What impact did Cooper Industries' takeover of Crouse-Hinds have on informal organizations? Did the takeover unify or break up informal groups? Discuss.

CASE 11.2

Confrontation: A Way of Life at Intel Corporation[29]

Throughout its brief history, Intel Corporation has practiced what many—if not most—managers would call organizational suicide: solving disputes through confrontation. According to the president of the company, "constructive confrontation" accelerates problem solving. It requires those in disagreement to be direct and deal with each other face-to-face.

Many managers believe it is impolite to tackle anyone head-on in business. By contrast, top management at Intel feels that it is the essence of corporate health to bring a problem out into the open, even if this entails a personal confrontation. At Intel, no one is too concerned about protocol and formality.

Performance appraisal often fails, according to President Andrew Grove, because managers are afraid to let go enough to tell subordinates what they really think. Also, they are afraid of the angry response that a candid appraisal might elicit.

Bringing together people who disagree over an issue is the key to resolving conflict, according to Grove. He contends that politicking in the workplace grows in the dark; it cannot stand the light of day. One method of eliminating organizational politics is to have disputing parties confront each other "up front." For instance, when two of Grove's subordinates—one in charge of manufacturing and the other of qual-

ity control—came to dislike each other, each sought to strengthen his own position by gaining the support of the president. The manufacturing manager complained that the quality-control manager didn't know what he was doing. The quality-control manager, on the other hand, contended that the manufacturing manager was unconcerned about quality.

In an effort to eliminate the behind-the-back bickering, the president arranged for a face-to-face confrontation. The next time that one of these managers started to complain, Grove stopped him abruptly and called the other manager into the room so that he could hear the complaint. Although the confrontation was tense and embarrassing, each learned that dealing directly with the other was less awkward and more productive than going individually to the president's office to complain.

Questions

1. The method used for resolving conflict at Intel Corporation is generally regarded as a high-risk approach. Yet, the president contends that it is the speediest avenue to problem solving. Do you agree or disagree? Why?

2. Using Alan C. Filley's classification system discussed in the chapter, would you characterize Grove's approach as win-lose, lose-lose, or win-win? Explain.

C H A P T E R   O U T L I N E

A Historical Perspective

Traits of Successful Leaders

Leadership Styles

Early Studies of Leadership
>   The University of Iowa Studies
>   The Ohio State Studies
>   The Michigan Studies

Contingency Approaches to Leadership
>   Characteristics of Subordinates
>   Tasks
>   Climate of the Work Environment
>   Perceived Power of Leaders
>   Attitude Toward Leaders

Contingency Models of Leadership
>   Continuum of Leadership Behavior
>   Blake and Mouton's Managerial Grid®
>   Fiedler's Contingency Model of Leadership
>   House's Path-Goal Theory
>   Reddin's 3-D Theory
>   Vroom and Yetton's Decision Tree
>   Leadership Styles: A Final Note

Leadership

M A N A G E M E N T   I N   A C T I O N

Corning Managers Sold on Participation

Corning Glass Works recently started a program designed to breed a different kind of management style—one that involves workers in decisions. Corning's top managers opted for the participatory management approach because they believe that workers who are involved in a decision feel a personal obligation to see that it turns out right.[1]

Most managers at Corning Glass Works are sold on participative management. What convinced them were experiences like the one at the company's plant in Erwin, New York, where a die-manufacturing problem needed solving. Supervisors handed over the problem to five machinists. Five hours later, the team of machinists had found a solution that cost the company less than $200.

Under the old-style management system, supervisors and engineers would have wrestled with the problem and the solution would have been an edict. Workers would have been kept in the dark, and managers would have operated on the assumption that only they had all the answers. The new approach at Corning is based on trust and involvement: managers trust workers to reach sound decisions, and workers become emotionally involved in their jobs.

Although changing from an autocratic approach to a participative approach sounds simple, it rarely is. The biggest obstacle seems to be convincing supervisors and middle managers to give it a try. Most supervisors and middle managers jealously guard their old-style authority. Many lack the human relations skills needed to be participative leaders.

A second problem is knowing when to give orders and when to get things done diplomatically. Under participative management, one observer noted:

"You don't go tell anybody to do something. You make them aware of a job that has to be done, make some suggestions, and then let them figure out ways to do it." But another analyst added, "Sometimes you have to call the shots."[2]

Preview

For more than half a century, managers and theorists have tried to answer the question, "What makes a great leader?" At one time, most people believed that great leaders were born with the ability to inspire others. Today, though, we accept the notion that anyone can be a great leader if the circumstances are right. We now believe that effective leadership depends on selecting the right style of management for a particular situation rather than on possessing certain personality traits.

The questions that need answering, then, are: "Is one style of leadership better than all others, and, if not, which style is best for a particular situation?" Some managers are convinced that the most effective style of leadership is one that involves subordinates in decision making. They favor a participative approach. Others, like some of the supervisory and middle-level managers of Corning Glass Works, resist participative management, preferring instead to make decisions independently. They favor an autocratic leadership style rather than a participative style.

In this chapter, we will explore the various approaches to leadership and discuss the forces that govern the selection of a particular approach. After studying this chapter, you will understand:

✔ Leadership in historical perspective

✔ What traits successful leaders are thought to have

✔ The influences that shape leadership style

✔ What studies have found about various leadership styles

✔ What situational factors influence a leader's effectiveness

✔ How contingency models depict leadership

A Historical Perspective

Leadership is the art of influencing others to act in order to accomplish specific objectives. All groups need skilled leaders to accomplish their objectives. This skill has three basic ingredients: (1) the understanding that people's motivation varies at different times, (2) the ability to inspire, and (3) the ability to create a climate for motivation.[3]

The earliest theory of leadership, called the **"great man" theory,** dates from the time of the ancient Greeks but stayed popular into the early twentieth century. It assumed that true leaders had two dissimilar characteristics: (1) they were capable of instrumental behavior, such as planning, organizing, and controlling subordinates' activities; and (2) they showed concern for their subordinates and fostered sound group interrelationships. People with these traits were thought to be effective leaders in any situation.[4]

Early studies of leadership

With the emergence of the behavioral school of psychology in the early 1900s, researchers began to reexamine the "great man" theory and to challenge the concept of universal traits. Studies showed that one set of traits or one leadership style might not be equally appropriate in all situations. These studies, forming the basis of the **behavioral theory of leadership,** suggested that there were two distinct styles of leadership: task-oriented (production centered) and employee-oriented (people centered).[5]

More recent theories are based on the environment, or situation, instead of leadership style. Known as **contingency,** or **situational, models,** these theories argue that effective leadership is really a function of the interaction of several variables, including superior-subordinate relationships, the power distribution between superior and subordinate, and the degree to which the job is structured.

Traits of Successful Leaders

Studies designed to pinpoint the specific character traits of successful leaders often yield conflicting results. Several findings, particularly those of Ralph Stogdill and of Edwin Ghiselli, are worth discussing, however. Stogdill's studies reveal that leaders are somewhat more intelligent than their followers are; they are sensitive to their subordinates' needs; they actively participate in group functions; and they possess a high level of communication skills.[6]

Stogdill and Ghiselli's studies

Ghiselli's studies reveal that intelligence and self-actualization are important for success, but the concept of power over others is not very important. He also found that supervisory ability, occupational achievement, self-assurance, and decisiveness are very important. Moderately important traits are maturity, no need for financial reward, initiative, working-class affinity, and no need for security. Masculinity-femininity and physique were considered unimportant.[7]

Following World War II, the U.S. Army conducted a survey of the lives and careers of successful military officers to identify traits associated with effective leadership. The traits were courage, decisiveness, dependability, endurance, enthusiasm, initiative, integrity, judgment, justice, knowledge, loyalty, tact, unselfishness, physical appearance, and conduct.[8] Another study has added the personality trait of dullness to the portrait of a successful manager, as discussed in the In-Box on page 326.

THE IN-BOX

Are Successful Managers Dull?

Dull managers are likely to climb the corporate ladder faster and farther than fun-loving Goodtime Charlies are. So says a group of researchers at Rush Medical College in Chicago.

The conclusion reached by the research team is based on responses from eighty-eight corporate executives of major U.S. corporations who were asked to rate thirty-six activities that are usually relished by people who love to have fun. Surprisingly, the survey results show that fun-seeking executives tend to have lower salaries and fewer responsibilities; they complain about their jobs more frequently than do executives who have low pleasure capacities. They are so busy having fun that they don't do any real work.

Successful (dull) executives have trouble with small talk, and jokes often pass over their heads. They aren't usually distracted by gusto-type activities, like winning the lottery or fine dining, choosing instead to concentrate on job-related issues.

Naturally, not everyone agrees with the research findings. H. Patrick Parrish, director of the Chief Executives Forum, takes exception to the survey results. He, along with many other executives, believes that it is impossible to judge leadership ability by personality. Good leaders, he says, can work hard and play hard.

Source: Sheila Johnson, "Hey Boss, Did You See This Story About—Oops, Uh, Nothing Boss," *Wall Street Journal,* July 11, 1985, p. 27.

Leadership Styles

Managers are relatively consistent in the way that they try to influence others' behavior. The manager who dominates subordinates in one situation is not likely to use a high degree of consideration and participation in another. The behavior patterns of leaders, called leadership style, can be classified as autocratic, participative, and laissez-faire.

Basic styles of leadership

The **autocratic leadership style** is closely associated with the classical approach to management. Not seeking subordinates' opinions, the autocratic leader holds conflict and creativity to a minimum. This type of leader usually supervises closely and motivates through incentives and fear. Subordinates typically react by doing only what is expected and by suppressing their frustrations. To the autocrat, formal authority is the basis for legitimate leadership; therefore, developing close, interpersonal relationships with subordinates is superfluous. The autocratic leader is task-oriented and places little value on showing consideration to subordinates as a leadership technique.

Managers with **participative leadership style** involve subordinates in making organizational decisions. This style does not imply democratic governance or majority rule. Subordinates take part in the decision-making process through consultation.

Managers who use the **laissez-faire,** or **free-rein, leadership style** do as little supervising as possible. Such leaders maintain a hands-off policy, where each subordinate's work is clearly defined. They make few attempts to increase productivity, to develop their subordinates, or to meet subordinates' psychological needs.

One method for classifying leadership styles was presented by Rensis Likert, former director of the University of Michigan's Institute for Social Research. Likert recognized four distinct leadership styles, or *systems,* ranging from highly autocratic to highly participative. Let's look at each of his four systems.

Likert's leadership classifications

System I: Exploitative Autocratic. In this approach, a manager makes all the decisions and informs subordinates of them. The manager essentially relies on threats and intimidation to get tasks accomplished. The level of trust and confidence between manager and subordinate is extremely low. Since such managers typically rule through fear, subordinates tend to become subservient.

System II: Benevolent Autocratic. This approach to leadership can best be described as paternalistic. The manager makes most decisions and attempts to convince subordinates that he or she is looking out for their interests. Such an approach yields a relatively low level of employee trust, but open hostility is not evident. Employees are expected to be subservient, loyal, compliant, and reasonably productive. In return, management treats them decently. Although the social atmosphere is harmonious, employees are never involved in planning or making decisions.

System III: Consultative. The consultative style of leadership is a drastic departure from the first two styles in that the manager asks subordinates for input in decision making and typically exercises general rather than close supervision. The level of trust between manager and subordinates is fairly high. There is no reliance on threats or intimidation to motivate workers; consequently, two-way communication is not stifled.

System IV: Participative. Emphasizing group participation, this leadership style totally integrates workers in the decision-making process. Subordinates feel comfortable discussing matters with their managers, the level of trust is high, and the manager uses supportive rather than threatening behavior. Likert suggested that the entire organization be designed along these lines, with tasks being performed by a series of overlapping groups. The group leader, then, becomes a linking pin between his or her group and the next higher-level group. Decision making occurs throughout the organization, and the overall level of productivity and job satisfaction is high.[9]

Early Studies of Leadership

The University of Iowa Studies

One of the earliest studies to determine the results of various leadership styles was conducted by Ralph White and Ronald Lippitt at the University of Iowa in 1938.[10] Four groups of ten-year-old boys were exposed to autocratic, participative, and laissez-faire leaders. Each group was assigned specific tasks.

White's and Lippitt's studies

The autocratic group leader formulated policy, dictated how to complete the assigned tasks, and did not get involved in the group activities. He constantly gave commands and openly criticized or praised group members. Under the participative leadership approach, policies were developed through group discussion, and alternative work methods were suggested by the group leader, who tried to participate in all group activities. The participative leader encouraged the group members to make decisions, guiding them through suggestions and informal discussions. The laissez-faire leader, after clearly defining the tasks to be completed, then withdrew from the activity.

In terms of goal accomplishment, all groups fared about the same, but there were significant differences when it came to the boys' attitude and enjoyment. Under the autocratic leadership approach, hostility and aggression were apparent. The participative and laissez-faire styles of leadership, though, produced stronger feelings of friendliness and group-mindedness.

The Ohio State Studies

In the 1940s and 1950s, researchers at Ohio State University conducted a series of studies to determine the impact of different styles of leadership. After studying leadership in various kinds of organizations, they classified leadership behavior in two ways: "consideration" and "initiating structure." Consideration behavior involved two-way communication, mutual trust, close rapport, and friendship between leaders and followers. In initiating-structure behavior, the leader assigned tasks, emphasized production goals, and defined the methods for performing tasks.[11] The researchers discovered that some managers lean toward initiating structure, whereas others are oriented toward consideration behavior. The same manager, however, can demonstrate both types of behavior to different degrees.

The Michigan Studies

Other studies of leadership style

Throughout the 1950s, the University of Michigan's Institute for Social Research studied the leadership behavior of managers in all types of organizations. These researchers also found two types of leadership style: "production-centered" and "employee-centered." Like the Ohio State researchers, they found that managers of high-producing units either closely supervised their workers or were employee-centered in their behavior toward their subordinates.

Other studies at the University of Michigan by Bowers and Seashore revealed that managerial leadership style has a major influence on work-group satisfaction and performance. What was more important was their discovery that other factors, such as power, work patterns, and personal and motivational factors, are also important in managerial effectiveness.[12]

Contingency Approaches to Leadership

Modern theorists believe that a leader's effectiveness is greatly influenced by a host of situational factors that affect all managers. Among the more important are the characteristics of subordinates, the nature of the task to be done, the overall climate of the work environment, the perceived power of the leader, and how much subordinates like and trust their leader.

Characteristics of Subordinates

To a great extent, a leader's effectiveness and leadership style are tied to the characteristics of his or her followers. Their ability to work without close supervision and the confidence they have in their abilities affect a manager's success. Studies have shown that people with a high degree of self-confidence and those who feel that they are in control of their own destiny are more productive under participative management. Those who depend on others and who trust more in fate are more satisfied and productive under authoritarian leadership.[13]

Tasks

The nature of work tasks varies greatly from job to job. Some jobs are highly structured, with carefully defined procedures. This is particularly true of highly repetitive tasks in mass-production plants. Other jobs allow a great deal of flexibility, individual discretion, and freedom for experimentation. Scientists, architects, teachers, and other professionally trained people fall into this category. People who have more freedom in their job performance are more satisfied with participative, rather than autocratic, leaders.

Climate of the Work Environment

The overall work climate directly affects worker productivity. What determines the climate in an organization is interaction among employees, two-way communication with managers, the philosophy of top management, tradition, and the organization's purpose. Businesses that involve their workers in decision making, offer jobs calling for independent judgment, promote close working relationships among associates, and encourage experimentation are likely to find that participative, employee-centered leadership will result in higher productivity and more satisfied employees.

Perceived Power of Leaders

Employee's views of leaders

The amount of enthusiasm that employees put into projects and specific work assignments depends in part on the power, prestige, and influence they believe their managers have. Employees usually are more willing to produce at the expected level if they think that their manager can get special benefits or favors from higher-level management or that the manager can personally grant promotions, salary raises, or other "perks."

Attitude Toward Leaders

A leader who has established good rapport with subordinates, empathizing with their needs and concerns, is likely to win their cooperation without having to become highly autocratic. If the workers feel that a manager is fair, trustworthy, and deserving, they will most likely take on work assignments willingly. But if they view a manager with distrust or disdain, they probably will resist everything he or she attempts to do.

Contingency Models of Leadership

Over the years, a number of contingency models of leadership have been developed. Among the most prominent models are those by Robert Tannenbaum and Warren H. Schmidt, Robert Blake and Jane Mouton, Fred Fiedler, Robert House, William Reddin, and Victor Vroom and Philip Yetton.

Continuum of Leadership Behavior

Figure 12.1 depicts the range of a manager's possible leadership behavior, as presented by Tannenbaum and Schmidt.[14] Each type of action is related to the degree of authority the manager uses and to how much freedom his or her subordinates have in making decisions. The approaches on the extreme left of the continuum characterize the manager who maintains a high degree of control. Those on the extreme right characterize the manager who relinquishes most control.

Let's look more closely at each approach along the continuum.

- *The manager makes the decision and announces it.* In this case, the boss identifies a problem, considers alternative solutions, chooses one, and then informs his or her subordinates of the decision. The boss may or may not consider what those subordinates will think or feel about the decision. They have no direct opportunity to participate in the decision-making process.

- *The manager "sells" a decision.* Again, the manager assumes responsibility for identifying the problem and making a decision. Rather than simply announcing it, however, the manager attempts to persuade subordinates to accept it. Recognizing the possibility of reluctance by those who will be affected by the decision, the manager tries to reduce that resistance by telling the employees what they have to gain from the decision.

Seven contingency approaches

- *The manager presents ideas and invites questions.* Here, subordinates have the chance to get an explanation of the manager's thinking and intentions. After hearing the decision, subordinates are allowed to ask questions so that they can better understand what the manager is trying to accomplish.

FIGURE 12.1
Continuum of leadership behavior (*Source:* Reprinted by permission of the *Harvard Business Review.* An exhibit from "How to Choose a Leadership Pattern" by Robert Tannenbaum and Warren H. Schmidt (May–June 1973). Copyright © 1973 by the President and Fellows of Harvard College; all rights reserved.)

- *The manager presents a tentative decision.* Under this approach, the initiative for identifying and diagnosing the problem remains with the boss. Prior to meeting with the staff, the manager has analyzed the problem and has arrived at a tentative decision. But, before it is made final, the solution is presented so that the people who will be affected can react to it. Their reaction either reinforces the decision or prompts its modification.

- *The manager presents the problem, gets suggestions, and makes the decision.* Up to this point, the manager has come before the group with a solution in mind. Under this approach, the subordinates can voice their opinions and suggest solutions before the decision is made. Thus, final decisions are made only after consideration of all the input.

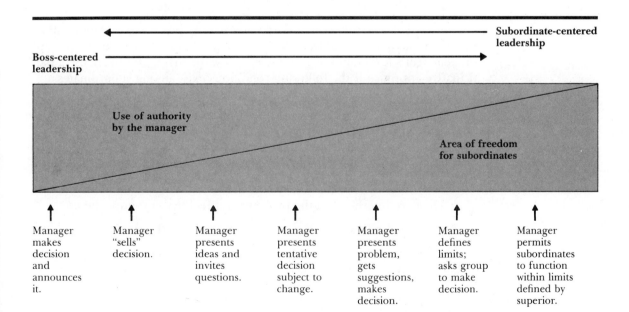

- *The manager defines limits and asks the group to make a decision.* The manager lets the group make decisions, but, before doing so, defines the problem to be solved and the boundaries within which the decision must be made.

- *The manager permits subordinates to make decisions within prescribed limits.* This approach is the ultimate in group freedom and is only occasionally encountered in formal organizations. Subordinates identify and diagnose the problem, develop alternative procedures for its solution, and decide on one or more of these alternatives. The only limits directly imposed on the group are those of higher-level management.

According to Tannenbaum and Schmidt, the leadership style that a manager will use depends on three sets of forces: forces in the manager, forces in the subordinates, and forces in the situation.[15] Let's examine each.

1. *Forces in the manager.* To a great extent, a manager's leadership style is shaped by his or her value system, confidence in subordinates, and ability to tolerate the ambiguity and uncertainty resulting from relinquished control. If a manager believes that his or her role is to make decisions and that the subordinates' role is to carry them out, the manager will most likely choose a style on the left side of the continuum shown in Figure 12.1. Likewise, if a boss has little confidence in subordinates' abilities or cannot tolerate the uncertainty associated with others making decisions, he or she most likely will behave autocratically. But if the boss is concerned with subordinates' development or feels secure with their decision making, then he or she is likely to select an approach that involves a great deal of employee participation. The story of how Becky Roloff used her "people" skills to change the image of Pillsbury's distribution department is told in On The Job on page 333.

2. *Forces in the subordinates.* Subordinates have their own expectations about how their manager should lead. Their value systems are forces that help shape the manager's leadership behavior. Generally, the manager can choose a participative approach if the following conditions exist among subordinates.

Subordinates affect manager's style

- They have relatively high needs for independence.

- They are willing to assume responsibility for decision making.

- They have a relatively high tolerance for ambiguity. (Some employees prefer to have clear-cut directives given to them; others prefer to exercise personal discretion.)

- They are interested in the problem and feel that it is important.

- They understand and identify with the goals of the organization.

- They have the necessary knowledge and experience to deal with the problem, and they are accustomed to participating in decision making.

ON THE JOB

A Corporate Humanist Takes Charge

How do you transform 450 uninspired employees into a gung-ho group of achievers? Just ask Becky Roloff, director of distribution for Pillsbury. In only two years in her job, Roloff changed the image of Pillsbury's distribution department from that of an "elephant's graveyard" to a place where people want to work. No longer is the distribution department tantamount to corporate oblivion. In fact, when a job opens up in Roloff's department, thirty or forty people apply.

Roloff sees herself as a corporate humanist rather than a "numbers jock" and credits her success to intuitive people skills. This, she says, sets her apart from her contemporaries. She believes that if you take care of people, they'll take care of you.

But being a humanist isn't the only thing that sets Roloff apart. She has experience as a grain trader at Cargill, Inc., and has worked in purchasing at Pillsbury. She also was graduated in the top 10% of her class at Harvard and became Pillsbury's first female marketing director in 1985.

Source: Patrick Houston, "She Worked Magic in a Dead-End Job," *Business Week*, November 10, 1986, pp. 94–96.

If these conditions do not exist, greater authority will be exercised by the manager.

3. *Forces in the situation.* Situational forces—such as the type of organization, the ability of employees to work together, the nature of the problem, and the urgency of the decision—also influence a manager's choice of behavior. If members of the organization expect the manager to be decisive, he or she may be pushed to the left side of the continuum. If the prevailing philosophy values a manager's human relations skills, he or she can be expected to be more subordinate-centered. Similarly, if subordinates have similar backgrounds, which permit them to approach problem solving the same way, a participative style can be adopted. But if they are inexperienced in tackling problems on a team basis or if they cannot work together harmoniously, a highly participative approach may not be the most feasible.

The nature of the problem may dictate an authoritative approach. Solving the problem may require knowledge that the subordinates lack. Or the complexity of the problem may require that the manager think it through individually without getting sidetracked by a discussion of peripheral matters.

Finally, the urgency with which a decision must be made has a bearing on the choice of leadership style. Participative decision making consumes more time than authoritarian action does. Thus, if a situation requires a spur-of-the-moment decision, a manager may have no choice but to select a boss-centered approach.

Blake and Mouton's Managerial Grid®

One of the best-known approaches to classifying leadership styles is the **Managerial Grid®,** developed by Robert Blake and Jane Mouton.[16] The Grid dramatizes the importance of a manager having concern for both production and people. As shown in Figure 12.2, the Grid has two dimensions: concern for production and concern for people. Concern for production includes such

FIGURE 12.2
Blake and Mouton's Managerial Grid® (*Source*: The Managerial Grid figure from *The Managerial Grid III: The Key to Leadership Excellence* by Robert R. Blake and Jane Srygley Mouton. Houston: Gulf Publishing Company, Copyright© 1985, page 12. Reproduced by permission.)

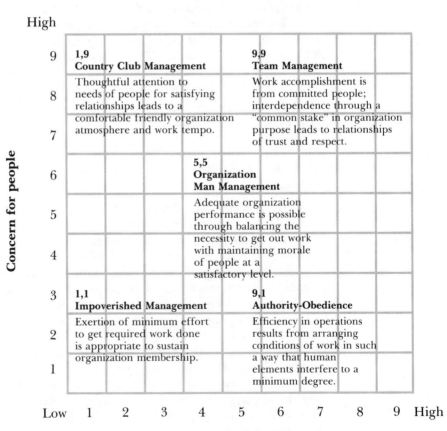

High

1,9
Country Club Management
Thoughtful attention to needs of people for satisfying relationships leads to a comfortable friendly organization atmosphere and work tempo.

9,9
Team Management
Work accomplishment is from committed people; interdependence through a "common stake" in organization purpose leads to relationships of trust and respect.

5,5
Organization Man Management
Adequate organization performance is possible through balancing the necessity to get out work with maintaining morale of people at a satisfactory level.

1,1
Impoverished Management
Exertion of minimum effort to get required work done is appropriate to sustain organization membership.

9,1
Authority-Obedience
Efficiency in operations results from arranging conditions of work in such a way that human elements interfere to a minimum degree.

Concern for people

Low 1 2 3 4 5 6 7 8 9 High

Concern for production

things as procedures and processes, work efficiency, volume of output, and quality of staff services. Concern for people includes such elements as the self-esteem of workers, responsibility based on trust rather than on obedience, and satisfying interpersonal relationships.

The various combinations of concern for productivity and concern for people produce eighty-one different leadership styles. However, only five approaches are highlighted in the figure.

1,1 **Impoverished Management.** The manager has very little concern for either people or productivity.

1,9 **Country Club Management.** The manager has high concern for people but low concern for production. Such managers promote an environment where everyone is relaxed, friendly, and happy.

9,1 **Authority-Obedience Management.** The manager emphasizes production but has little concern for people. His or her primary concern is for operational efficiency.

5,5 **Middle-of-the-Road (Organization Man) Management.** The manager has limited concern for both people and productivity. This approach represents a compromise whereby the manager attempts to keep morale high by lowering production expectations.

Concern for production and people

9,9 **Team Management.** The manager has high concern for both people and productivity. High levels of output are achieved through mutual trust and respect. Team managers are able to mesh the production goals of the company with the personal needs of the employees.[17]

Blake and Mouton recommend the 9,9 team management style as the most desirable. They contend that such an approach results in greater employee satisfaction and improved performance. Others, however, argue that the 9,9 style tends to oversimplify the practice of management. Essentially, they feel that situational forces surrounding the leadership environment have to be more thoroughly considered before a better understanding of leadership can emerge.[18]

Fiedler's Contingency Model of Leadership

Variables affecting leadership style

Fred Fiedler's contingency theory of leadership identified three variables that affect leadership situations: leader-member relationships, task structure, and the leader's position power.[19] Leader-member relationships refers to how well the leader is liked and trusted, task structure refers to the nature of the job itself, and position power pertains to a manager's authority to make individual decisions. Combining these three elements produces the eight different situations shown in Figure 12.3.

Cell	1	2	3	4	5	6	7	8
Leader-member relationship	Good	Good	Good	Good	Poor	Poor	Poor	Poor
Task structure	Structured		Unstructured		Structured		Unstructured	
Leader position power	Strong	Weak	Strong	Weak	Strong	Weak	Strong	Weak
Favorableness of situation	Highly favorable				Moderately favorable		Highly unfavorable	
Appropriate style	T	T	T	E	E	E	E	T

T: task-oriented style
E: employee-oriented style

FIGURE 12.3
Fiedler's contingency model (*Source: From Fred A. Fiedler, A Theory of Leadership Effectiveness*, McGraw-Hill Book Company, 1967, p. 37.)

These eight leadership situations fall along a continuum of situation favorableness, ranging from highly favorable to highly unfavorable. (Favorableness is defined as the degree to which a given situation enables the leader to exert influence over a group.)

Generally speaking, Fiedler found that in "highly favorable" or "highly unfavorable" situations, the task-oriented manager is most effective. That is, when position power is very high, task structure very clear, and leader-member relations very good, the task-oriented leader is most effective. At the other extreme, when position power and task structure are unclear and leader-member relations are poor, the situation is highly unfavorable; thus, a task-oriented approach is best. But when the situation is only moderately favorable, the human-relations-oriented leader is most effective.[20]

Essentially, the model shows that the group's performance depends on the appropriate matching of leadership styles and the degree of favorableness of the group situation for the leader. Because leadership performance depends as much on the organization as on the leader's own attributes, no one can describe a successful leader. A manager might be successful in one situation but unsuccessful in another.

Matching variables with appropriate style

House's Path-Goal Theory

House's four leadership styles

This theory of leadership, introduced by Robert House and advanced by Evans and Mitchell, focuses on identifying and removing obstacles in the path of goal attainment.[21] The theory recognizes four leadership styles: directive (autocratic), supportive, participative, and achievement-oriented leadership. The forces determining the style used are the personal characteristics of the subordinates and environmental factors. Personal characteristics include how employees perceive their own abilities and how much they believe they can control their own destiny. Environmental factors include the nature of the job and the degree of formal authority present.

Directive leadership works best when jobs are highly unstructured or when tasks are unclear. Directive leadership reduces uncertainty, which increases worker satisfaction. However, if the job is highly structured or if the tasks are well known, an authoritative approach would be inappropriate. Supportive leadership is most desirable when the nature of the work is stressful or frustrating. Achievement-oriented leadership is appropriate when tasks are unclear and nonrepetitive.

The path-goal theory is so named because its primary focus is on how a manager influences subordinates' behavior and perceptions of their work, their goals, and their satisfaction. Although using the concepts of consideration (people orientation) and initiating structure (establishing controls), the theory is unique in how it applies expectancy motivation theory to these concepts. (For a review of expectancy theory of motivation, refer to Chapter 10, "Motivation and Human Behavior.") More specifically, the manager's role is to provide subordinates with the "coaching, guidance, support, and rewards" necessary for satisfying performance that otherwise would be lacking.[22]

Reddin's 3-D Theory

William Reddin combined Blake and Mouton's Managerial Grid® with Fiedler's contingency model to produce his three-dimensional theory of leadership.[23] As shown in Figure 12.4, leadership styles and leadership situations can be placed on a grid with task or output orientation (concern for production) on one axis and relationships or human orientation (concern for people) on the other.

The four cells of the grid depict the following managerial situations: (I) the manager is separated from task and human considerations, (II) the manager is highly related to the task, (III) the manager is highly concerned with people, and (IV) the manager is highly concerned with people and tasks. Each cell shows two leadership styles—one that is most appropriate and one that is significantly less effective.

Matching jobs with leadership approaches

In humanistic situations (Situation I), the "missionary" style is less effective than the "developer" style is. In Situation II, typical of upper-level man-

FIGURE 12.4
Reddin's 3-D leadership
model (*Source:* Edwin B.
Flippo, *Personnel
Management*, 1984, p.
398. Reprinted by
permission of McGraw-
Hill Book Company.)

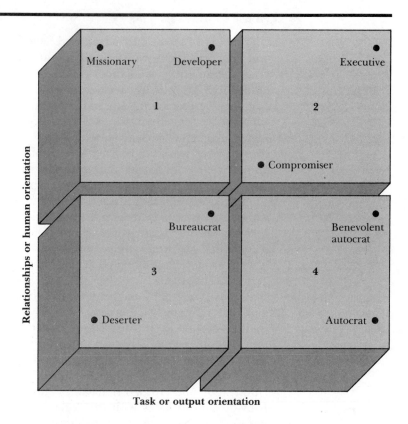

Situation 1	Jobs with humanistic orientations, for example, personnel department
Situation 2	Jobs with integrated orientations, for example, top management
Situation 3	Jobs somewhat separated, for example, data processing, finance
Situation 4	Jobs with heavy task orientation, for example, production

agement jobs, the integration of tasks and human considerations works better than a "compromiser" approach does. Jobs that focus on procedures (data processing, accounting, and the like) are included in Situation III. Here, the most effective style is "bureaucrat"; a less-effective style is "deserter." Situation IV encompasses task-oriented jobs. In situations where productivity is most important, "benevolent autocrat" is more effective than "autocrat" is.[24]

Vroom and Yetton's Decision Tree

Another continuum of leadership behavior is that presented by Victor Vroom and Philip Yetton.[25] This model, often referred to as the Normative Model of

FIGURE 12.5
Vroom and Yetton's
leadership styles

BOSS-CENTERED				SUBORDINATE-CENTERED
AI	AII	CI	CII	G
Manager makes decisions without consulting others	Manager consults with subordinates and then makes decisions	Manager discusses problem with selected subordinates individually; makes decision utilizing input from subordinates	Manager meets with subordinates as a group; solicits input; then makes decision	Manager shares problem with subordinates; encourages active discussion; helps guide subordinates to reach a group decision

Vroom and Yetton's decision tree

Participation in Decision Making, uses five different leadership approaches, as illustrated in Figure 12.5.

Vroom and Yetton propose that, because leadership style develops out of the situation, leaders need to know when to move from one decision-making style to another. Various approaches for making a particular decision range along a continuum from no power sharing—an autocratic leadership style (AI)—to complete power sharing—a participative leadership style (G).

Vroom and Yetton contend that managers selecting a leadership style should be concerned with two variables: the quality of the decision and the acceptance of the decision by subordinates. They can assure a quality decision that is accepted by subordinates if they ask seven questions—three designed for making a quality decision and the remaining four aimed at eliminating subordinates' resistance.[26]

A. Does the problem possess a quality requirement?

B. Do I have sufficient information to make a high-quality decision?

C. Is the problem structured?

D. Is acceptance of the decision by subordinates important for effective implementation?

E. If I were to make the decision by myself, am I reasonably certain that it would be accepted by my subordinates?

F. Do subordinates share the organization goals to be attained in solving this problem?

G. Is conflict among subordinates likely in preferred solutions?

Using a decision-tree flowchart, illustrated in Figure 12.6, the manager can determine which leadership styles are appropriate and which are inappropriate.

FIGURE 12.6
Vroom and Yetton's
decision tree (*Source:*
Adapted from Victor
Vroom, "A New Look
At Managerial Decision
Making," *Organizational
Dynamics*, Spring 1973,
p. 70. Copyright 1973
by American Managerial
Association, New York.
All rights reserved.)

A Is there a quality requirement such that one solution is likely to be more rational than another?	B Do I have sufficient information to make a high-quality decision?	C Is the problem structured?	D Is acceptance of the decision by subordinates critical to implementation?	E If you were to make the decision by yourself, is it reasonably certain that it would be accepted by your subordinates?	F Do subordinates share the organizational goals to be obtained in solving this problem?	G Is conflict among subordinates likely in the preferred solution?

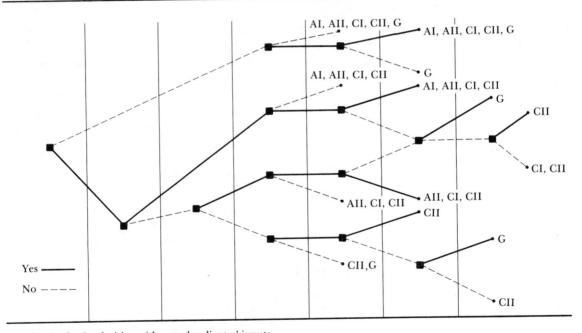

Yes ——
No ————

AI = Authority decision without subordinates' inputs
AII = Authority decision using information gathered from subordinates
CI = Consultative decision with problem discussed individually with each subordinate
CII = Consultative decision with problem discussed with subordinates as a group
G = Group decision

Leadership Styles: A Final Note

Advantages of
participative leadership

A number of studies have shown that a high degree of dictatorial behavior by the manager produces undesirable consequences. Fleishman and Harris found that the more "structure" on the part of production supervisors as perceived by subordinates, the greater the number of grievances filed by employees. Absenteeism also appears to be associated with structure in production groups, although there appears to be no relationship between absenteeism and structure in nonproduction groups.[27] In addition, Seashore and Georgopoulos found a marked inverse relationship between pressure felt by employees and their productivity. Furthermore, punitive methods of correction appear to have a dampening effect on productivity.[28]

Behavior patterns usually associated with participative leadership generally have been found to be related to certain desirable results. Research suggests that democratic behavior on the part of the manager results in more positive attitudes toward the manager, a higher degree of acceptance of change, lower absenteeism, and higher productivity.[29]

Review

✔ *Leadership in historical perspective.* Leadership is the art of influencing other people to act in order to accomplish organizational objectives. Effective leadership has three components: (1) understanding that people's motivation varies from time to time, (2) being able to inspire others, and (3) establishing an environment in which people are motivated to excel. The earliest theory of leadership is the "great man" theory, which said that a great leader was one who could plan, organize, and control subordinates and who showed concern for them. The behavioral theory of leadership and situational or contingency models have challenged the "great man" theory's assumptions.

✔ *What traits successful leaders are thought to have.* Ralph Stogdill and Edwin Ghiselli identified several personality traits associated with successful leadership, including sensitivity, intelligence, and self-actualization.

✔ *The influences that shape leadership style.* Managers are relatively consistent in how they try to influence others. Their behavior patterns generally can be classified as autocratic, participative, and laissez-faire. Rensis Likert grouped leaders into four distinct leadership categories: exploitive autocratic, benevolent autocratic, consultative, and participative.

✔ *What studies have found about various leadership styles.* A study by Ralph White and Ronald Lippitt at the University of Iowa tested the effect of autocratic, participative, and laissez-faire management on a group of ten-year-old boys. Other studies at Ohio State University and the University of Michigan also focused on the impact of different types of management.

✔ *What situational factors influence a leader's effectiveness.* Modern theorists believe that a leader's effectiveness is influenced by situational factors that affect all managers, including the characteristics of subordinates, the nature of the task, the overall climate of the work environment, the perceived power of the leader, and how much subordinates like and trust their leader.

✔ *How contingency models depict leadership.* Theorists have developed several leadership models that attempt to match situational variables with an appropriate leadership style. Among the more prominent models are those of Robert Tannenbaum and Warren H. Schmidt, Robert Blake and Jane Mouton, Fred Fiedler, Robert House, William Reddin, and Victor Vroom and Philip Yetton. Most of the more recent theories argue that an autocratic approach is best in some cases, a participative approach in others. Blake and Mouton hold that a team management (participative) approach is best in all situations. Numerous studies have shown that a participative leadership style yields desirable results, while autocratic leadership produces negative results.

THE MANAGER'S DICTIONARY

As an extra review of the chapter, try defining the following terms. If you have trouble with any of them, refer to the page numbers listed.

leadership (324)
"great man" theory (325)
behavioral theory of
    leadership (325)
contingency (situational)
    models (325)
autocratic leadership style
    (326)

participative leadership style
    (327)
laissez-faire (free-rein)
    leadership style (327)
Managerial Grid® (334)
impoverished management
    (335)

country club management
    (335)
authority-obedience
    management (335)
middle-of-the-road
    (organization man)
    management (335)
team management (335)

REVIEW QUESTIONS

1. Explain the "great man" theory of leadership. What characteristics did a "great" leader possess?

2. How do behavioral and situational theories differ from the "great man" theory?

3. What traits did Stogdill and Ghiselli associate with effective leadership?

4. How do subordinates typically respond to authoritarian leadership?

5. Cite and describe Rensis Likert's system of leadership. Which style does he recommend?

6. Briefly describe the findings of the University of Iowa and Ohio State University leadership studies.

7. What is a contingency leadership approach? Which variables affect leadership effectiveness? Explain.

8. List the various leadership approaches that comprise Tannenbaum and Schmidt's continuum of leadership behavior.

9. Give examples of "forces" that influence the selection of a particular style of leadership.

10. Generally speaking, most leadership models focus on two variables: concern for production and concern for people. Can you offer an explanation?

11. List and describe the five major leadership styles presented by Blake and Mouton. Which approach do they recommend?

12. Name the variables that Fiedler identifies as being important in the selection of an effective leadership style.

13. How does House's path-goal theory differ from Reddin's 3-D theory?

14. Briefly describe Vroom and Yetton's decision tree. Why is their model considered a contingency model of leadership? Explain.

15. In your opinion, is a participative, team-management leadership approach better than an autocratic approach? Why or why not?

MANAGEMENT CHALLENGE

Assume that you are in charge of a construction company that is laying a 30-inch natural gas line from south Texas to the Texas panhandle. Your segment of the line will be tied in with other segments, which extend to the northern tip of Michigan. As construction superintendent, you are continually faced with scheduling decisions. At present, you are confronted with the decision of establishing a pipeyard (including all support equipment) at a site further down the line. Establishing the pipeyard too early will tie up huge amounts of capital and will require security guards. Establishing the yard too late will result in idle workers and needless delays.

Moreover, you have been informed that you and your construction supervisors will be paid a bonus if you can complete this segment of the line in fewer days than originally scheduled.

Given the terrain and the scheduled rate of construction, you will likely need to have the additional pipe and support equipment available in 120 days. In order to obtain the bonus, however, you will need to reach the site within 108 days.

1. Using Tannenbaum and Schmidt's continuum as a guide, how would you make the decision regarding the pipeyard?

2. What are the advantages and drawbacks of involving your subordinates in the decision?

3. Would you inform your supervisors that they will receive a bonus if the planned construction time can be reduced by 10%? Why or why not?

CASE 12.1

Disaster at Non-Linear Systems, Inc.[30]

Non-Linear Systems, Inc., a small electronics manufacturer near San Diego, California, tried to become totally participative in its management philosophy and met disaster as a result. In the 1960s, President Andrew F. Kay eliminated the company's assembly lines and replaced them with independent production units, which were encouraged to organize themselves in whatever way they wanted. He also eliminated time clocks and let workers take breaks whenever they wanted. Salaries were increased over the prevailing area wage rates in an attempt to eliminate the punishment-reward psychology of hourly wages. Workers also were permitted to participate actively in all phases of the decision-making process.

The immediate results were astonishing. Productivity increased, product quality improved to a point that no longer required a quality-control inspector, customer complaints decreased, and sales boomed. Behavioral scientists throughout the country came to witness the remarkable turnaround.

Then something happened. When a recession hit the aerospace industry, inventory piled up, sales plummeted, the company found itself with few controls intact, and losses were heavy. In 1970, management reacted by cutting the work force in half, instituting more controls, and moving back toward centralization. Such measures returned the company back into the black in 1973.

Questions

1. Research the history of Non-Linear Systems and explain what could have caused the company to have experienced disastrous results with "participative" leadership.

2. In your opinion, were the problems caused by the leadership style or by other factors? Discuss.

CASE 12.2

Brunswick Corporation Adopts
New Management Philosophy[31]

In 1982, Brunswick Corporation was repeatedly advised to sell off its sports-products division and to concentrate on its defense and technical operations. Critics claimed such a move could eliminate Brunswick's problems.

But CEO Jack Reichert had other ideas. The company's problems, he contended, were a result of past management practices, not of product lines. Among the changes he instituted were a 59% reduction in corporate staff, the consolidation of eleven divisions into eight, elimination of the company's executive dining room and two corporate airplanes, and a strong movement toward decentralized management. Today, the lowest-ranking employee in the company is only five management levels from Reichert himself.

Most of Brunswick's top and middle-level managers feel that the company's turnaround is a direct result of Reichert's confidence in his people, along with improved efficiency from reducing layers of management. Decisions that previously took weeks now take hours or days. For example, when James Buick, general manager of the company's two hundred bowling centers, asked to spend $400,000 to install automatic scorers, he was immediately advised to go ahead.

Reichert also believes in rewarding managers whose performances are outstanding. Under his leadership, Brunswick's corporate incentive program quadrupled to include the top five hundred managers. Bonuses are related to the financial performance of each manager's division; moreover, managers are evaluated in terms of personal goals specifically related to each manager's job. Today, the company's operations are based on Reichert's philosophy: "Wealth is created at the operation division level, not at the corporate level."

Questions

1. Based on the information presented in this case, how would you classify Reichert's leadership style?

2. Brunswick Corporation has been decentralized under Reichert's leadership. What impact does this have on lower-level managers? Explain.

CHAPTER OUTLINE

The Role of Communication in Management

The Communication Process

Organizational Communication: A Linking Process

Downward Communication

Upward Communication

Horizontal Communication

Informal Communication Channels—The Grapevine

Desirable and Undesirable Characteristics • *Using the Grapevine*

Communication's Effect on Performance and Satisfaction

Obstacles to Effective Communication

Semantic Problems

Varying Perception

Filtering

Poor Listening Habits

Too Many Organizational Levels

Lack of Credibility

Kinetics

Low Readership Level

Impersonal Correspondence

Psychological Communication Barriers

Lack of Empathy

Patterns of Incorrect Evaluation

Defensive Behavior

Communication Problems in International Business

Effective Communication

M A N A G E M E N T   I N   A C T I O N

"You Can Fool Some of the People Some of the Time . . ."

Are you aware that Claude Pepper is known all over Washington as a shameless extrovert? Not only that, but this man is reliably reported to practice nepotism with his sister-in-law, and he has a sister who was once a thespian in wicked New York. Worst of all it is an established fact that Mr. Pepper before his marriage habitually practiced celibacy.[1]

These statements, purposely designed to confuse the voters of Florida, allegedly came from a speech by George Smathers, who was running for a seat in the U.S. Senate in 1950. Perhaps because of statements like this, Pepper lost. Later he was elected to the House of Representatives where he became one of its most respected members and a leading spokesperson for senior citizens' rights.

The efficiency and effectiveness of any group depend on how well the efforts of its members can be coordinated. But coordination doesn't just happen; it results from someone's conscious effort to channel the group's efforts for attaining some goal. George Smathers's objective was to create a negative image of his opponent in the minds of a group (the voters) and to influence their voting behavior so that he would attain his goal of winning the election. More than any other stimulus, communication is the primary tool for influencing human behavior. It comes as no surprise that managers must devote a considerable amount of their time and energy to communicating with other people.

347

Preview   When most people communicate, especially business managers, their objective is just the opposite of Smathers's. Instead of trying to confuse the audience, we go to great lengths to make certain that our thoughts are completely understood. Despite our good intentions, however, we sometimes fail to communicate effectively. This chapter explains why we fail. It describes the interpersonal communication process and how to improve it. When you finish studying this chapter, you will understand:

✓ The role of communication in management

✓ The communication process

✓ How communication links the parts of an organization

✓ The effect of communication on employee performance and satisfaction

✓ Obstacles to effective communication

✓ How to avoid communication problems in international business

The Role of Communication in Management

Communication is one of the manager's most important tools. When used correctly, it embodies the speaker's objectives and helps accomplish tasks that require coordination. Besides important social uses, **communication** has four functions in business: (1) disseminating information, (2) motivating and persuading, (3) promoting understanding, and (4) aiding in decision making.[2]

Purposes of communication

The boundaries between these four categories are not rigid. Naturally, communication can be used to both disseminate information and persuade people, or an effort to promote understanding may be informational as well. The first three purposes of communication are obvious; less apparent is the role of communication in decision making.

Communication is an important part of the decision-making process. Many times, only a unified opinion will get results. Other times, the varying opinions of different organizational members form the basis for a decision. And in some cases, decisions reflect nothing more than the opinion of the most demanding or most articulate participant.

The Communication Process

The ancient Greeks were the first to study the communication process systematically. Their concepts of logic, persuasion, diction, and speaking are not too out-of-date today, twenty-five centuries later. Because public communication was so important in their economic lives—property rights could be gained or lost as a result of the eloquence of a debate—the Greeks had a vital interest in communication.[3]

As does modern communications theory, Aristotle's theories focused on the fundamental elements of the communication process: the speaker, the message, and the audience. Aristotle's model of communication, shown in Figure 13.1, depicts communication as a simple, structured process in which a communicator (sender) transmits a thought, idea, or feeling to another person (receiver).

Aristotle's model

In recent years, the model has been modified to include the findings of behaviorists and other psychologists. Other models reflect technological innovations and intrapersonal communication.[4] Phillip Lewis's model, illustrated in Figure 13.2, shows how communication occurs in a formal organization. This diagram shows that organizational communication is a complex system involving people's feelings, attitudes, relationships, and skills as well as the goals of management and the process of change, adaptation, and growth. Individuals can both send and receive information. Both the receiver and sender have their own personal frame of reference, developed over time. Lewis's model, which is relevant for both formal and informal communication, represents upward, downward, and horizontal transmissions of information.[5]

Each participant in the communication process operates in a *semantic net* that allows him or her to interpret and to relate the message received. Each also uses his or her own *communication skills,* such as reading, writing, and listening abilities, that either strengthen or lessen understanding. Verbal or nonverbal *cues* trigger speaking or action responses.[6]

Verbal and nonverbal feedback

The communication process in Figure 13.2 depicts a manager sending a written or oral message to another organizational member through a channel. The receiver accepts the message and transmits either verbal or nonverbal feedback, thereby becoming the sender. **Verbal feedback** is a written or spoken response. **Nonverbal feedback** is body movement or actions. **Noise** is the interference or the barriers that may occur at any point in the process, distorting understanding. The organizational environment also affects sending, receiving, and interpreting the message. The communication process is successful only when the sender and receiver understand the message to the same degree. Feedback permits clarification and repetition until the message is fully understood.

FIGURE 13.1
Aristotelian model of communication

Communicator *(sender)* — Message → Listener *(receiver)*

Organizational Communication: A Linking Process

The information flow is essential to an organization's effectiveness. Several studies have shown that many work-related problems are caused by poor attitudes rather than by inadequate skills and knowledge. Open communication molds positive attitudes and improves the likelihood of job satisfaction and better job performance. In all organizations, formal and informal information is transmitted through different channels. These channels are categorized as downward, upward, and horizontal.

Downward Communication

FIGURE 13.2
Lewis's organizational communication model (*Source:* Adapted from Phillip V. Lewis, *Organizational Communication: The Essence of Effective Management*, p. 55. Copyright © 1980. Reprinted by permission of John Wiley & Sons, Inc.)

Downward communication occurs when information is transmitted from higher to lower levels in an organization. Directives, policy statements, and memoranda fall into this category. Katz and Kahn identify five major types of downward-flowing information:

1. *Job instructions,* which explain how a task is to be performed. They come from written specifications, training manuals, training sessions, or on-the-job training.

2. *Job rationale statements,* which explain to workers how their tasks relate to other jobs in the company. Specialization in many organizations has made

Organizational environment

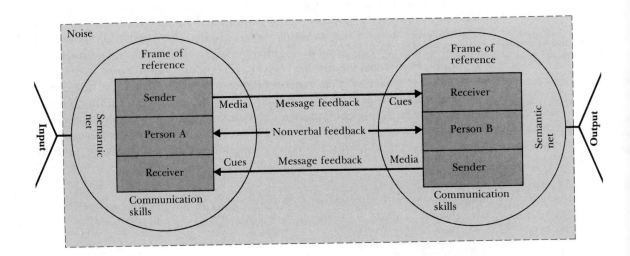

Organizational environment

it difficult for workers to see how their particular tasks fit into the overall operations of the firm. Job rationale communications answer this problem.

3. *Policy and procedure statements,* which explain the employer's regulations and personal benefits provided.

4. *Feedback,* which includes messages that tell employees whether their work is satisfactory. Feedback should be provided daily, as well as in the form of periodic performance appraisal.

5. *Indoctrination communications,* which try to drum up employees' support for a particular organizational goal, such as an area fund-raising drive.[7]

Although downward communication is necessary, it is frequently overemphasized and overused. This creates an authoritative atmosphere that may hurt employee motivation and morale.[8] Downward-flowing information also has a tendency to become lost and distorted. A study of one hundred firms assessing this tendency revealed some startling findings:

1. Employees at the vice presidential level received less than 67% of the information transmitted to them by top management.

2. Employees at the general supervisor level received 56% of the information transmitted to them.

3. Employees at the plant manager level received 40%.

4. Employees at the supervisor level received 30%.

5. Employees on the production line received only 20% of the information transmitted from top management.[9]

In the past, managers placed too much faith in the downward channel, ignoring the benefits that arise when employees fully discuss the company policies. Managers often failed to provide clear channels for funneling information, opinions, and attitudes up through the organization. Managers who assume that the company's supervisory hierarchy provides a sufficient channel for sending messages to subordinates may be in for a big surprise. Too much faith in downward communication may blind the manager to company rumors and only create problems instead of solving them.[10] Upward communication is also vital to successful communication in an organization. More and more executives are discovering the benefits of keeping in touch with their employees, as On the Job on page 352 shows.

Upward Communication

Upward communication is the flow of opinions, ideas, complaints, and other kinds of information from subordinates up to managers. It is generated by suggestion systems, grievance procedures, informal and formal meetings, attitude surveys, and exit interviews. Upward communication is important for

ON THE JOB

Keeping in Touch

Today, more and more chief executives are breaking from the tradition of remaining aloof and are dealing directly with customers and employees. No longer are they content to remain in corporate headquarters, reading financial statements and committee reports. Instead, they are talking directly to the people whose actions affect the bottom line.

John Sculley, chief executive of Apple Computer, for example, listens to customer complaints on Apple's toll-free number. John McCoy, president of Banc One Corporation in Columbus, Ohio, reads exit interviews with employees who quit the firm, and Richard Rogers, president of Syntex Corporation, eats breakfast each morning in the employee cafeteria.

J. Willard Marriott goes a step further. Continuing the tradition his father started, Marriott routinely visits the restaurants in his hotel chain. He also inspects the front desk, loading dock, exercise spa, and several rooms. Everywhere he goes, he chats with workers, calling many of them by name. The edge in the hotel business, he says, is people. As he puts it, he's just trying to communicate that he cares.

Source: Thomas F. O'Boyle and Carol Hymowitz, "More Corporate Chiefs Seek Direct Contact with Staff, Customers," *Wall Street Journal*, February 27, 1985, p. 1+.

several reasons. First, managers need to know how their subordinates feel about their jobs, their working conditions, and the company's policies and procedures. Second, upward communication encourages workers to discuss particular job-related problems that may be hindering productivity and efficiency. Third, it provides managers with feedback on the workers' reactions to policy changes, developments in their departments, and other matters that affect their attitudes and performance. In other words, upward communication supplies management with the information that it needs to make intelligent decisions.

There is another spin-off benefit of upward communication as well. Whenever workers are encouraged to communicate with upper-level managers, downward communication, such as policy changes, meets with less resistance.

Managers who isolate themselves from what is happening below them are asking for trouble. Besides losing touch with reality, they fail to maintain close rapport with their subordinates. In many instances, isolation results when a manager refuses to listen to his or her subordinates or has inadequate personal interaction with them.[11] Workers feel isolated when they think that their boss doesn't want to be bothered with their problems.

Horizontal Communication

Horizontal communication

Horizontal, or lateral, communication refers to the flow of information among workers on the same organizational level. Goldhaber said that horizontal channels can be used for: (1) coordinating tasks, (2) solving problems, (3) sharing information, (4) resolving conflict, and (5) developing rapport among workers.[12]

Horizontal communication is essential for managers and workers alike. Without it, business functions could not be coordinated. Sound decision making also relies on information-sharing among functional units. Several studies have shown that most poor management decisions result from poor communication.

People who work closely together and communicate regularly rarely have difficulty understanding one another. Their interaction also provides emotional support and helps satisfy their social needs. Even so, formal horizontal communication channels often do not give employees all the information they want. As a result, informal channels—commonly called the grapevine—develop.

Informal Communication Channels—The Grapevine

The grapevine is natural

The rumor mill known as the **grapevine** is the informal communication network that is responsible for transmitting an astonishing five out of every six messages in organizations. This network is the informal communication system for the organization and also supplements the formal communication network. The grapevine is a natural phenomenon that can provide social satisfaction, power, and prestige to workers. Messages may be factual or inaccurate.[13] Rumors often start with people who are in a spot for seeing and hearing things but are not necessarily in high organizational positions. For instance, a secretary may overhear a conversation, or a custodian may see a discarded message. From such small seeds, the grapevine grows.

Characteristics of the grapevine

One of the first studies to assess the workings of a grapevine was conducted by Keith Davis, who analyzed the informal communication patterns within a medium-sized manufacturing plant. Based on his interviews with factory workers, Davis concluded that the grapevine: (1) spread information rapidly, (2) was selective in terms of what was transmitted, (3) filled voids left by the formal communication channels, and (4) was confined to the workplace.[14]

Davis identified four different networks for transmitting information via the grapevine—the single strand, the group chain, the probability chain, and the cluster chain. These patterns are diagrammed in Figure 13.3.

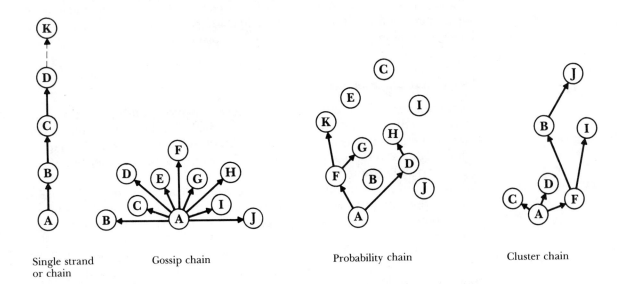

Single strand
or chain

Gossip chain

Probability chain

Cluster chain

In the *single strand,* with one person communicating with only one other, information is often distorted. In the *gossip chain,* every member talks with everyone else, usually about personal matters. Communication is random in the *probability chain,* which might carry a rumor about a promotion. Messages are transmitted selectively in the *cluster chain.* The study also revealed that some grapevine members were much more active than others in transmitting information.

Desirable and Undesirable Characteristics   The grapevine is both good and bad. It is desirable because it gives managers insight into employee attitudes, serves as a safety valve for employee emotions, and helps spread useful information. But the grapevine also can spread incorrect information, and it is uncontrollable.[15]

Most studies show that the information the grapevine transmits is reasonably accurate, although sometimes distorted. Information passing from person to person tends to be modified in three ways. The first change is *leveling,* in which details are dropped or the information is simplified. The second change takes the form of *sharpening,* in which people dramatize selected parts of the data. The last change is *assimilation,* in which information is shaped to serve the needs of the grapevine member.[16]

Using the Grapevine   Because of the large volume of information transmitted via the grapevine, managers need to learn to adapt to, manage, and use it wisely. They must recognize that the existence of a grapevine does not necessarily mean that something is wrong in the organization; it is a normal response to work activity. Since most of the grapevine's information is accurate, managers must learn to listen to it attentively. Because it cannot be suppressed or eliminated, it should be used as a way to disseminate useful information quickly and accurately.

Managers can use the grapevine

Communication's Effect on Performance and Satisfaction

Group communication patterns

Figure 13.4 shows the communication patterns of groups of five people. The patterns were developed by Harold J. Leavitt to assess the effect of communication on work performance and task satisfaction.[17] Each pattern depicts one form of communication that could take place in the group. The chain represents a business hierarchy with a top-level manager and four lower-level managers. The wheel represents communication from a supervisor to four subordinates. The circle shows the communication flow among members of a task force, and the "Y" is similar to an informal communication network.

Except for the circle, the patterns are relatively centralized because all information is channeled through one participant. The wheel proved most efficient in terms of speed and accuracy in problem solving when tasks were simple, but wheel members were less satisfied because of the low degree of communication. The circle provided the most satisfaction but was slow and inaccurate. As the problems became more complex, the wheel was less efficient; the central person became overloaded with communication and feedback.

These experiments have important implications for management. If the task to be performed is simple and employee morale is not a consideration, then a centralized network is preferable. A decentralized network is better if the task is complex. If speed and accuracy are vital in accomplishing a complex task, the chain network is preferable.[18]

Obstacles to Effective Communication

The overriding objective of communication is to make the message understood. Secondary objectives include securing a response (feedback) that is either positive, negative, or noncommittal and maintaining favorable relationships with people with whom we communicate.[19] But we often fail to communicate effectively; our efforts falter because of obstacles and barriers inhibiting the communication process.

Semantic Problems

When we want to communicate with another person, we must symbolize our thoughts or ideas. The most commonly used symbols are words. Hearing or reading the symbols, the receiver translates them into an idea or image. Usually, the message received is very similar to that sent. If the symbols used have no meaning to the receiver, however—such as when an illiterate person is handed a memo—the communication process breaks down. When this happens, understanding cannot take place. Problems caused when the intended audience does not understand the use of words and phrases are called **semantic problems.** Managers must be very careful to gear their communication to the audience they wish to reach.

Failing to understand words and phrases

Varying Perception

Selective perception

Rarely do two people observe, analyze, and react to an event the same way. Ten people who witness an automobile accident will give ten different versions of what happened. Likewise, the same information given to ten people at a meeting will result in ten different interpretations. These differences in interpretations are caused by **selective perception,** in which each person's brain selects the stimuli that seem most important.[20] When listening to a message, people choose the bits of information that they believe are most interesting or relevant. The message can be distorted as a result, just as our perceptions sometimes distort our visual impressions, as Figure 13.5 shows. People of different ages, cultural backgrounds, and national origins do not perceive stimuli the same way. Managers should remember that we all rely on our past experiences to interpret what we see.

FIGURE 13.4 Organizational communication networks (*Source: Harold J. Leavitt, "Some Effects of Certain Communication Patterns on Group Performance," Journal of Abnormal and Social Psychology, January 1951, p. 38. Reprinted by permission of Plenum Publishing Corporation.)*

Filtering

None of us wishes to look foolish in the eyes of our boss. This is why we all tend to filter or screen out upward-flowing information that will discredit us.

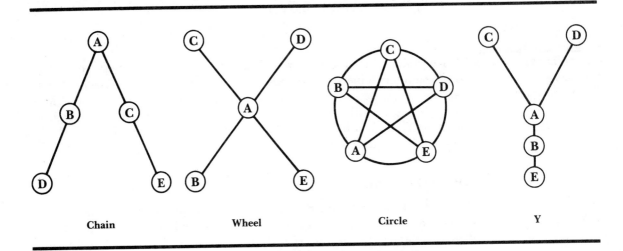

| Chain | Wheel | Circle | Y |

"Mr. Pointman, while you were out, a Miss or a Ms or a Mrs. Valdy or Volney or Balmey left a garbled message for you." © Punch-ROTHCO

Distorted information

Because we all want to look good in our boss's eyes, we overemphasize our own contributions and pinpoint the inadequacy of others' contributions; in either case, we discolor our message. Information is like a weapon or a defense. It can be shaped, molded, and used in a number of ways to achieve our ends, maximize our gains, and weaken our competitors.[21]

Several factors contribute to the filtering of upward communication. Many employees feel that being candid is dangerous to their long-range welfare. Fearing that disagreements with their boss will jeopardize their chances of promotion, they stifle criticism and honest expression. Employees' value systems, personal anxieties, and aspirations also discolor the information they transmit. Managers should, then, be aware of circumstances that lead to filtering information:

1. *The authority structure of the organization.* Arbitrary and inflexible authority tends to increase upward distortion. Vague, conflicting rules, excessive secrecy, and close supervision are conditions that create feelings of anxiety and insecurity among workers.

2. *Severe competitive conditions or intense rivalry among subordinates.* Competition in which people either win or lose is likely to increase subordinates' anxiety and insecurity and, therefore, the likelihood they will distort information.

3. *A climate of cynicism and mistrust in the company.* Such an environment tends to accentuate subordinates' feelings of insecurity. This also leads to further distortion.[22]

Poor Listening Habits

Studies show that most managers spend between 45 and 63% of their time listening.[23] Yet, tests of listening comprehension have shown that, without proper training, they listen at only 25% efficiency.[24] Why are most people poor listeners? How can we improve our listening ability? By recognizing the traits associated with poor listening and focusing on good listening habits. Here are some keys to effective listening:

Keys to effective listening

1. Learn to tolerate silence.

2. Concentrate on the speaker. Maintain eye contact with the speaker and observe body movements and facial expressions.

3. Use your power as a listener. Don't intimidate or disrupt speakers.

4. Ask questions for clarification.

5. Reflect feelings. Show you are sympathetic with, or at least understand, a speaker's point of view. Restate the speaker's message.

6. Use an attentive posture to reinforce listening.

7. Keep emotional biases under control.

8. Avoid judging the speaker. Keep an open mind.[25]

Too Many Organizational Levels

FIGURE 13.5
Perceptual distortions

The more levels a message must travel through, the greater the possibility it will be lost or distorted. A study conducted by Pidgeon Savage Lewis, Inc., a

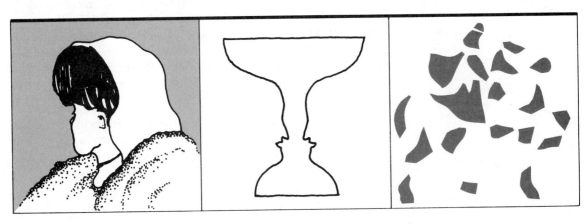

Old woman or young woman?   Two faces or an urn?   What do you see? Concentrate on seeing a knight on a horse.

Minneapolis-based advertising firm, revealed that 80% of the information transmitted through five organizational levels is lost along the way.[26]

Lack of Credibility

Expertness and trustworthiness

Communication is greatly affected by its believability. Messages are more credible when the speaker or writer is considered trustworthy or expert, and less believable when the person is perceived as unreliable or lacking in experience. For example, a manager who must inform employees about new company policy might ensure effective communication of the message by delivering it personally rather than delegating to a less-trusted subordinate.

Kinetics

Body language

Body movements, especially facial expressions, convey meaning as forcefully as the spoken word does. Americans love "people watching" and decoding body language. A wrinkled forehead, a raised eyebrow, a tug on one ear, the tapping of fingers on a desk, or the crossing of arms over the chest all convey messages. When we are uneasy, we perspire or loosen our collar; when we are nervous, we shift our weight or clear our throat repeatedly. Happiness and contentment elicit humming. Nonverbal communication often reveals the emotional side of our communications.[27]

Researchers can relate human body language and other nonverbal behavior to the message being transmitted. The result is a dictionary of body language, with nonverbal messages a part of the total communication process. The sender's nonverbal messages reveal sincerity, honesty, conviction, ability, and qualifications. The body language of the person receiving the message is also revealing. It often can tell the sender whether the receiver accepts or rejects the message.[28]

Low Readership Level

Comprehension problems

The level of a piece of writing and the comprehension level of the audience often conflict. For example, some workers in an industrial plant may not understand the details of the company personnel policy manual, labor agreement, or insurance contract. Consequently, they may depend on their fellow workers to explain their rights and responsibilities. This communication barrier often arises because companies fail to consider their employees' educational backgrounds. They incorrectly assume that all workers are able to read and understand all company documents.

This problem can be partially resolved if managers closely examine the documents they are directing to the general work force.[29] They may need to rewrite the documents in more understandable terms or to hold informal explanatory meetings with small groups of workers.

Impersonal Correspondence

Correspondence needs personalizing

Employees often discard a sizeable portion of written memos simply because they appear impersonal. How many times have you thrown out a letter addressed to *Dear Student, Occupant,* or *Dear Prospective Customer* without opening it? But people do pay special attention to correspondence addressed to them personally—no words are more important to us than our names are. Why do businesses continue to send out millions of pieces of impersonal correspondence annually? It costs less. Fortunately, technology now allows business to personalize business correspondence quickly and cost-effectively. Word processing, in particular, enables an organization to produce personalized correspondence more efficiently than ever before.

Psychological Communication Barriers

Physical objects are significant

Also breaking down communication are psychological barriers, often caused by physical objects. A desk, for example, can be placed so as to discourage communication; the formality of office decor, too, may stifle the communication flow. Rank and job status also affect the communication process, determining what is said and shaping the way it is said.

For a better understanding of how physical objects influence communication, consider the table around which the Paris peace talks were held toward the end of the Vietnam War. Participants rejected a rectangular table because the negotiator at the "head" would have an advantage over the others. Also, the chairs could not be the same height because the North Vietnamese, being shorter than the American negotiators were, would have been placed at a disadvantage. Before all parties agreed on the final design, several months elapsed and several table shapes were proposed and rejected.

Lack of Empathy

Too often, communication is defined as "authority at work." It is the ship's captain yelling down the tube, "Fix the engine!" But is it?

> The essential is not a "command" voice, nor is it the spirit of good cheer in the monthly letter to employees in front of a house magazine, meant to build morale in the plant and urge the sales force to "go get 'em." It is instead the ability to put yourself in the other fellow's shoes, identify what is on his mind, provide him with whatever information there is to help him understand what is going on, and help him do his job better.[30]

The manager who communicates well recognizes others' viewpoints, is sensitive to the pressures they feel, and respects them enough to share the truth as he or she sees it.

Patterns of Incorrect Evaluation

Forms of incorrect evaluation

Often, our communication is distorted because others evaluate it incorrectly. Usually, there are five reasons why: indiscrimination, bypassing, polarization, frozen evaluation, and inference-observation confusion.[31] **Indiscrimination** (stereotyping) occurs when we fail to recognize that everyone is different. **Bypassing** occurs when the sender and the receiver "miss" each other in their communication. The receiver hears the message of the sender but interprets it incorrectly. **Polarization** is the tendency to treat all situations as "either-or" propositions—to neglect intermediate terms. For example, we tend to describe people as either polite or rude, tall or short, shy or boisterous. In reality, though, the polar (extreme) terms often fail to communicate our thoughts adequately and accurately. An apathetic person, for example, is neither rude nor polite; similarly, the majority of people are neither tall nor short, shy nor boisterous. **Frozen evaluation** occurs when we fail to take into account time and its effect. The purchasing power of currency, for instance, is eroded over time; consequently, personal income of one era should not be compared with that of another era without taking into account inflation, taxes, and so on. **Inference-observation confusion** arises whenever we make invalid conclusions based on our limited observations.

Defensive Behavior

People tend to be defensive. They dislike challenges to their self-image and find it hard to tolerate differences in others.[32] When the defense mechanism gets out of control, questions become accusations and replies justifications. Six behavior traits of others appear to bring about defensiveness in people:

1. Passing judgment
2. Trying to manipulate someone
3. Attempting to change someone's behavior or attitude
4. Showing a lack of concern
5. Arousing feelings of inadequacy
6. Assuming a "know-it-all" attitude[33]

Minimizing defensiveness

Managers can minimize subordinates' defensiveness by showing human characteristics opposite to those that bring it about. Questions should be non-judgmental, communication should be honest and straightforward, personal bias should not be forced on others, mutual trust and respect should be demonstrated, and an open-minded attitude should prevail. This approach builds a supportive, rather than a hostile, climate for the effective exchange of thoughts and opinions. The In-Box on page 363 discusses the defensiveness of some companies in dealings with the press and suggests ways to deal with the media.

Communication Problems in International Business

Translations are difficult

Literally hundreds of times American businesspeople have "botched" international dealings because they failed to understand the international environment. Sometimes, political or economic forces were not fully understood; other times, competitive or technological factors were to blame. Most problems, however, stem from communication blunders. Messages may be translated incorrectly, inappropriate media may be used, regulations may be overlooked, or cultural differences may be ignored. Consider the following big-business blunders compiled by David A. Ricks.

> When Pepsi Cola's slogan "Come Alive with Pepsi" was introduced in Germany, the company learned that the literal German translation of "come alive" is "come out of the grave."
>
> A U.S. airline that promoted its "rendezvous lounges" on its Boeing 747s learned that *"rendez-vous"* in Portuguese refers to a room that is rented for prostitution.
>
> Chrysler's "Dart Is Power" slogan, translated in Spanish, suggests that drivers of the car needed sexual vigor.
>
> Pepsodent's slogan "Wonder Where the Yellow Went" was viewed as a racial slur by many people in Southeast Asia.[34]

Nonverbal communication blunders also have hurt American business in international trade. Consider the following foul-ups:

> A U.S. soft-drink manufacturer offended some of its Arab customers because its labels incorporated six-pointed stars that were interpreted as reflecting pro-Israeli sentiments.
>
> General Motors intended to tell the Belgian market that its cars had a "Body by Fisher." The Flemish translation was "Corpse by Fisher."
>
> A refrigerator manufacturer used a picture of its refrigerator, including a ham, in its promotional campaign. Unfortunately, the photo did not go over well in the Middle East, where Moslems do not eat ham.[35]

Cultural differences

Other communication blunders are not so obvious but are just as harmful. Americans expect prompt responses to statements and questions; people of other nationalities prefer a slower response time. Head shakes to the left and right mean "no" to Americans; the same message would be conveyed by waving a hand in front of the face in the Orient. Americans need more "personal space" than do many Asians; close proximity to another person while conversing can be very uncomfortable to Americans. Humor, a natural and accepted aspect of American lifestyle, is almost nonexistent in some cultures. The American gesture to cut one's throat means "I love you" in Swaziland, and our use of the curled index finger to summon another person connotes

THE IN-BOX

What Do You Say When the Media Call?

How can a company communicate its point of view to the public when it thinks the media have been unfair? It can fight back. For example, Mobil Oil withdrew its advertising from the *Wall Street Journal* because of news stories about the company. Bechtel Group persuaded ABC to run a report challenging allegations made in a "20/20" program. And Illinois Power responded to a segment on CBS's "60 Minutes" by disseminating a videotape of its own, showing that the program had edited interviews with a company executive.

Fighting back reflects a new approach in the way that corporations are dealing with the press and television news. More than ever before, companies are looking for ways to use the media to their advantage.

Different companies handle requests from the media differently. Amerada Hess never returns their calls, Winn-Dixie seldom bothers to call back, and Texas Instruments hasn't talked much since it lost $145 million in 1983. IBM says it is candid with the news media, but executives are hesitant to grant interviews.

Procter & Gamble has hit on another approach. It is cooperative in some cases and uncooperative in others. For example, P&G executives don't talk about the company's strategy for developing and promoting new products, but they jumped at the chance to dispel rumors that linked their company with Satanism.

Big companies that refuse to talk with the media seldom succeed in avoiding unwanted stories. Reporters simply talk with employees, creditors, and competitors, and they dig into documents filed with the Securities and Exchange Commission. Consequently, they are able to piece together enough information for a full-blown story. The logical approach, then, seems to be an "open door" policy. In fact, being open and candid with the media and the public can work to a company's advantage. If nothing else, an interview with a news reporter gives the company an opportunity to respond to allegations and to educate the media. In some cases, an effective corporate spokesperson can dramatically sway public opinion and create a favorable image in the minds of the consumers.

Source: Walter Guzzardi, Jr., "How Much Should Companies Talk?" *Fortune*, March 4, 1985, pp. 64–68.

vulgarity in some countries. Although the list of "do's and don'ts" is endless, these cultural differences clearly underscore the difficulties of communicating in international markets. To minimize communication problems, managers can learn local customs by checking with embassies, consulates, or employees who have worked overseas.

Review

✔ *The role of communication in management.* Accomplishing business goals depends on the coordination of human effort. A business uses communication to receive and convey information, to motivate and persuade, to develop understanding, and to make decisions.

✔ *The communication process.* The communication process occurs when a sender transmits a message or idea to a receiver through some channel. The message may be verbal or nonverbal. The receiver accepts the message and transmits either verbal or nonverbal feedback to the sender. Noise is the interference or the barriers that may occur at any point in the process, distorting understanding.

✔ *How communication links the parts of an organization.* In an organization, communication essentially flows in three directions: downward, upward, and horizontal. Downward communication occurs when upper organizational levels transmit information to lower organizational levels. Directives and policy statements are examples of downward communication. Upward channels are established to elicit the opinions, ideas, complaints, and attitudes of workers throughout the company. The grievance procedure and suggestion system are examples of upward communication. Horizontal communication is the flow of information among workers on the same organizational level. By communicating with one another, workers can coordinate their tasks, solve problems, share information, resolve conflicts, and establish personal rapport.

✔ *The effect of communication on employee performance and satisfaction.* A number of studies have shown that communication directly affects workers' job satisfaction and performance. When the task to be performed is simple and employee morale is not a consideration, limited communication among organizational members is preferable. But if the task is complex or employee morale is important, extensive interaction among group members is preferable.

✔ *Obstacles to effective communication.* For communication to occur, understanding must take place. Unfortunately, messages sometimes become garbled and lost, resulting in communication failure. Some obstacles interfering with the communication process are organizational barriers, language problems, and perceptual barriers.

✔ *How to avoid communication problems in international business.* Language problems, in particular, interfere with the communication process required to transact business in international markets. Because of cultural differences and problems in translation, communication is easily distorted. Managers can learn of local customs and minimize these communication obstacles by contacting embassies, consulates, and employees who have worked overseas.

THE MANAGER'S DICTIONARY

As an extra review of the chapter, try defining the following terms. If you have trouble with any of them, refer to the page numbers listed.

communication (348)
verbal feedback (349)
nonverbal feedback (349)
noise (349)
downward communication
   (350)

upward communication (351)
horizontal (lateral)
   communication (353)
grapevine (353)
semantic problems (356)
selective perception (356)

indiscrimination (361)
bypassing (361)
polarization (361)
frozen evaluation (361)
inference-observation
   confusion (361)

REVIEW QUESTIONS

1. What purposes does communication serve? Discuss.

2. Describe the communication process. What are the components of the process?

3. Why is communication referred to as a "linking" process?

4. How does noise affect the communication process? Give examples.

5. Give examples of downward, upward, and horizontal communication.

6. Why is horizontal communication beneficial to both managers and workers? Explain.

7. In your opinion, should managers try to eliminate grapevines? Why or why not?

8. How accurate is the information that is transmitted via the grapevine?

9. How does communication affect workers' job satisfaction?

10. List and briefly describe six obstacles to effective communication.

11. Describe some communication problems that can occur in international business. Can you give examples?

12. Can communication barriers be eliminated? Why or why not?

MANAGEMENT CHALLENGE

Assume that you are the store manager of a retail firm located in a shopping mall in Oklahoma City. Employee morale seems low, and sales have been declining for two years. The rumor mill says that the store will close by the end of the year if conditions don't improve. To your knowledge, the rumor is based on sheer speculation.

1. How would you handle this situation?

2. Would you try to verify the rumor? If so, how?

3. Would you discuss the rumor with your employees? Why or why not?

4. Could the rumor be responsible for employee morale? Explain.

5. If you discussed the rumor with your employees, what communication obstacles would you have to overcome? Explain.

CASE 13.1

Communication at Copperweld: A Number 1 Priority[36]

Employee effectiveness, pride, and productivity are directly tied to communication, according to Robert Loughhead, president of Copperweld Steel in Warren, Ohio. This is why Copperweld instituted a comprehensive communication program designed to ensure two-way communication. Loughhead's philosophy is based on the belief that greater employee awareness enhances pride and can improve product quality and levels of output.

Copperweld uses a variety of communication tools: employee publications, posters, meetings, audio-visual presentations, brochures, and direct mailings to employees' homes. The direct mailings frequently include a candid assessment of a company problem and a request for a solution. Later, a series of progress reports follows up the problem, explaining in detail the recommendations from employees, the action taken by the company, and the results.

In addition, Copperweld uses two employee publications in its program—*The Communicator* and *Link. The Communicator* is sent to all employees, whereas *Link* is for all management personnel. Both publications are geared exclusively to the employees. Neither publishes propaganda or messages from the president, except in a question-and-answer format. An article entitled "Copperwelders Speak Out" is a regular feature. Each month eight workers, randomly chosen as they leave work, are asked their opinion of an issue. Their responses are printed verbatim.

Another element of the communication program is a film designed to acquaint employees and their families with Copperweld's position in the industry, the importance of reinvesting in the company, and areas in which improvement is needed. In addition, various departments hold a "Coffee and Conversation" program at which the president or members of his staff answer questions and listen to suggestions from workers.

What have been the results of the total awareness program? According to Loughhead, morale is high, production records continue to be broken, efficiency has improved, yield is better, reworking operations are fewer, and service to customers has improved.

Questions

1. In your opinion, is the improved performance a result of Copperweld's awareness program, or is it due to other factors? Discuss.

2. Can you think of other elements that could be added to Copperweld's communication program?

CASE 13.2

Safety Comes First at Du Pont[37]

Communicating the importance of safety to workers is the number one communication objective of Du Pont. This goal is not new; it has always been at the top of the company's list.

How is Du Pont doing? Has the message really been communicated? First, consider some facts. The chemical industry as a whole is a relatively safe place to work, despite the potential hazards. Over the years, the chemical industry has had a better safety record than has any other segment of American industry. For every incident resulting in a lost day's work in the chemical industry, there are four such incidents on an all-industry average. In some industries, such as trucking and meat products, the differences in accident rates are even more pronounced.

Du Pont's accident rate is only one-seventeenth of the chemical industry average. In some plants, laboratories, and offices, no Du Pont employee has lost a day of work for more than twenty years because of an on-the-job accident or occupational illness. It is literally safer for Du Pont employees to go to work than to stay home.

Du Pont's safety record has been established with the aid of an effective communica-tion program from the top down. No Du Pont employee can honestly say that he or she is unaware of the importance of safety in the plant, office, or laboratory. Clerical and production workers hold regular safety meetings, staff meetings begin with a discussion of safety, and safety signs are posted everywhere. Du Pont's safety communication program has been called "obsessive in attention to detail." The board of directors long ago established one overriding policy: no product would be made and no process utilized unless it could be done safely; no employee would ever be asked to perform a task unless it could be done without risk to that worker.

Questions

1. Is safety the responsibility of top management or of the safety director? Explain.

2. How are safety procedures communicated to workers in most plants? Why does the chemical industry, and Du Pont in particular, place so much emphasis on safety?

3. What problems do multinational firms have in communicating the importance of safety measures to employees in foreign subsidiaries?

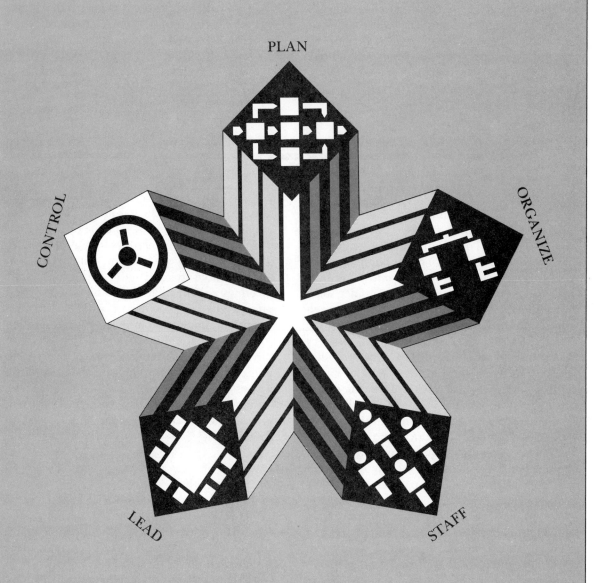

Controlling

*I*n Part Four, we examined the leadership role of managers. We analyzed means for motivating workers, dealing constructively with interpersonal conflict, and communicating effectively. We also reviewed several prominent leadership models and evaluated various styles of leadership behavior.

Part Five discusses the controlling function of managers. It stresses the importance of monitoring business operations and of taking corrective action when necessary. We also will see how quantitative control tools can help managers to be more effective.

Chapter 14, "The Controlling Function," examines the steps in the controlling process: (1) establishing standards, (2) measuring performance, (3) comparing performance against standards, and (4) taking corrective action. Then, it examines three areas: production control, financial control, and work performance control. It explains various methods for ensuring that performance expectations are met in each of these three areas.

Chapter 15, "Management of Production and Information," focuses on ways to ensure efficiency in both manufacturing and service operations. It explains what production-operations management (POM) is, discusses elements of the production-operations process, and looks at five major decision areas: process and product design decisions, capacity planning, materials management, work force decisions, and quality assurance decisions. Finally, we discuss the importance of technology and management information systems as integral parts of the control process.

Chapter 16, "Quantitative Control Tools," examines a number of quantitative tools and techniques that can help managers make cost-effective decisions. These include break-even analysis, models for inventory decisions, linear programming, network analysis, queuing models, and simulation.

CHAPTER OUTLINE

The Control Process

Establishing Standards
   Methods for Setting Standards
   Types of Standards

Measuring Actual Performance
   Timeliness of Information
   Appropriate Units of Measurement
   Reliability of Information
   Validity of Information
   Channeling Information to the Proper Authority

Comparing Performance Against Standards

Taking Corrective Action

Developing a Control System
   Problems with a Control System
   Managing Control System Problems

Production Control
   Scheduling to Avoid Bottlenecks
   Quality Assurance
   Quality Circles
   Inventory Control

Accounting and Financial Control
   Budgeting
   Operating Budget • Budget for Capital Items
   Cost Accounting
   Financial Statement Analysis
   Liquidity Ratios • Leverage Ratios • Activity Ratios • Profitability Ratios

Work Performance Control
   Common Pitfalls of Performance Appraisals
   Feedback and Corrective Action

The Controlling Function

Operating in a Crisis

Ideal Basic Industries, Inc., the Denver-based cement maker, flourished for nearly a century. In the mid-1970s, it looked as though good times would last forever. Business boomed, cement prices rose dramatically, and profits soared.

Today, things are different at Ideal. Instead of expanding operations, Ideal's new chief executive officer is trying to control costs to pull his company out of a quagmire created by an economic slump and poor management decisions. Sales are slipping, and the company is operating in the red. Its biggest problem is trying to unload a new, state-of-the-art cement plant that sits idle on the Gulf Coast because it can't process the limestone it was designed to handle and operated at 100% over budget. In addition, several other plants were not modernized as they should have been.[1]

To survive the crisis, CEO Michael Nelligran is selling off assets, cutting back the work force, and eliminating benefits. He has already sold the company's jets, reduced stock dividends, and moved out of his oak-paneled office. But these actions may be too little too late. Foreign competitors have forced prices down, and Ideal's older plants are inefficient. To remain competitive, Ideal will have to pour tons of money into modernization projects and drastically cut operating costs.[2]

371

Preview

Some of Ideal's problems can be blamed on an economic slump in the cement industry and intense pressures from foreign competition. But many of its woes can be traced to its failure to control costs and its misallocation of resources. The company spent lots of money on frills, including corporate airplanes and plush offices, while failing to modernize plants and building the wrong facilities. Simply stated, Ideal's operations got out of control.

In this chapter, we will examine the controlling process and discuss the proper way to design and implement a control system. We also will analyze three primary areas of control: production, financial, and work performance control. You will learn in this chapter:

✔ The importance of control for an organization

✔ How to establish standards

✔ What to look for when measuring actual performance

✔ Why a manager must have standards for comparing performance

✔ Common errors managers make when taking corrective action

✔ What kinds of controls are needed in an organization

✔ The types of production control

✔ Accounting and financial control methods

✔ How to control work performance

The Control Process

Because organizations seldom function according to plan, managers must continually monitor their firm's performance. Making sure that plans are being carried out and taking corrective action when necessary are the aspects of a manager's job referred to as controlling. Essentially, **control** is concerned with making events conform to plans. According to Henri Fayol, "Control consists in verifying whether everything occurs in conformity with the plan adopted, the instructions issued and principles established. It has for its object to point out weaknesses and errors in order to rectify them and prevent recurrence."[3]

Control defined

The controlling function begins whenever plans are activated. Keeping themselves apprised of such elements as time, quantity, quality, and costs, managers compare these elements against yardsticks (standards). Without systematic control, a manager has no assurance that all elements of the organization will work toward meeting the company's goals.

There are essentially four steps in the control process:

Steps in the control process

1. Establishing standards or targets

2. Measuring actual performance

3. Comparing performance against standards

4. Taking corrective action

Establishing Standards

Ways of expressing standards

The control process begins when standards are set. **Standards** are units of measurement established by management to serve as benchmarks for comparing performance levels. Standards can take different forms: for example, they can be expressed in monetary terms (a salesperson's quota), in units of production (a production manager's expected output), or in measures of acceptable quality (the number of rejects allowed daily). In many cases, determining a quantity can be difficult; hence, an evaluator must sometimes make subjective judgments.

In virtually all cases, standards are attainable, minimum levels of acceptable performance. The 2.0 grade point average required for graduation at most universities is the minimum level of achievement established by administrative officials, for example. It is a criterion for comparing the academic performance of students against a standard established through reasoned judgment, experience, and tradition.

Methods for Setting Standards

Three different methods are used for establishing standards: (1) judgment, (2) statistical or historical data, and (3) observation.

Judgmental standards

A manager arrives at judgmental standards through personal knowledge, experience, and intuition. Industry norms are a useful supplement to the manager's judgment when setting standards concerning profitability, market position, employee attitudes, and social responsibility.[4]

Statistical and historical data

A second method for setting standards uses statistical and historical data. Past performance is used as a benchmark or goal for future performance. When standards are based on an analysis of past performance, however, workers have little motivation to do better than they have in the past.

Engineering techniques

The third method for setting standards utilizes engineering techniques, such as work sampling. Workers are observed in action, and standards are set accordingly. The major drawback to this method is that workers soon learn to slow down the pace when engineers with stopwatches and calculators come around. They realize that they can look better on daily production reports if, later on, they exceed the engineered standards.

Types of Standards

There are three types of standards: performance standards, corollary standards, and standards of conduct. Performance standards deal with quantity, quality, cost, and time. Corollary standards support a given level of performance. These include minimum personnel requirements and adequate physical resources, such as when a company knows it will need at least five hundred workers and a well-equipped factory to produce a certain number of computer terminals. Standards of conduct are moral and ethical criteria that shape the behavioral climate of the workplace. They originate from law, custom, and religious beliefs.

Measuring Actual Performance

The way that standards are expressed may define how they should be measured. Profitability standards, for example, imply that the measuring unit is dollars. Quantity standards are typically defined in terms of physical units of output. To make sure that performance levels are measured accurately and correctly by any standard, managers should pay close attention to:

1. The timeliness of the information
2. The appropriateness of the units of measurement
3. The reliability of the information
4. The validity of the information
5. The channeling of the information to the proper person

Timeliness of Information

Drawbacks of accounting data

Control information is useful only if it is timely. Some managers rely too much on data supplied by the accounting department; as a result, they fail to develop other sources of information. Although accounting data may have historical significance and is necessary for preparing annual reports or for closing books, it is often of little value to the manager responsible for efficient day-to-day activities. Managers must have accurate information during each working day so that they have an adequate basis for taking corrective action.

Appropriate Units of Measurement

Multiple measurements

Occasionally, organizations use several different measurement units to ensure that performance is being gauged adequately. For example, profit can be calculated as a percentage of sales, as a percentage of return on capital invested, or in dollars and cents. Production may be measured as a ratio of output to input or in total units produced. When multiple measures are used, each serves as a check on the information provided by the other measures.

Profits, productivity, and sales usually are based on quantitative assessments. Other measures of performance—such as whether a professor is a good student adviser—rely on a manager's past experiences and value system.

Reliability of Information

Degree of accuracy

The reliability of information is its degree of accuracy. Accurate information has consistent data and measures all aspects of the situation.

Validity of Information

Sampling

Even though information may be reliable, it may be invalid if it does not reflect what it is intended to measure. In some cases, an inadequate sampling of performance results in unreliable, invalid data. In theory, of course, the best approach to measuring performance is to review all performance—to inspect every circuit board a person produces, for example; but practical considerations—such as costs and time limitations—often necessitate sampling instead of total observation. Managers must be careful to make sure that the sample chosen is representative of the total performance.

Channeling Information to the Proper Authority

The timeliness of information, the appropriateness of the unit of measurement, and the reliability and validity of control data are all directed to getting the right information at the right time. But effective control also depends on channeling the information to the right person. The flow of control information varies with each company's organizational structure and with the kind of corrective action required. In general, control information should be channeled to the person who is accountable for the operation and who has authority to take corrective action.

Comparing Performance Against Standards

Actual output or performance that does not precisely conform to standards may still be "in control." A slight departure from standards is normal and expected; however, gross departures from standards signal the need for immediate corrective action. A manager needs to distinguish between acceptable variation and variation indicating that the process is out of control.

Analyzing variance

Accountants and statisticians frequently speak of *variances*. The accountant watches variances of actual costs from budgeted amounts. Applying a tool called "analysis of variance," the statistician can estimate whether variations in sample results result from chance or from some assignable cause. The purpose of a manager's comparing past performance with planned performance is not only to determine when an error has been made but also to predict future outcomes. A good control system, then, will provide quick comparisons so the manager can detect possible trouble while the operation is still under control. Comparisons of actual performance over time often will show a trend that might be a danger signal. The manager cannot change the past, but the knowledge of the past will help him or her make the right decisions today that will affect tomorrow.

Control charts are frequently used to compare actual data with standards. A pictorial presentation of data lets a manager see significant departures from standards. Figure 14.1, an example of a simplified control chart, analyzes thirty samples of newspaper copy. The number of errors in each sample is plotted on a control chart that reflects upper control limits of the individual firm and of the industry as a whole. In addition, the industry average is plotted.

Sample control chart

As evidenced by the chart, the quality requirements of the *Centerville Daily News* are more stringent than those of the industry as a whole. In five

FIGURE 14.1
Control chart—
Centerville Daily News

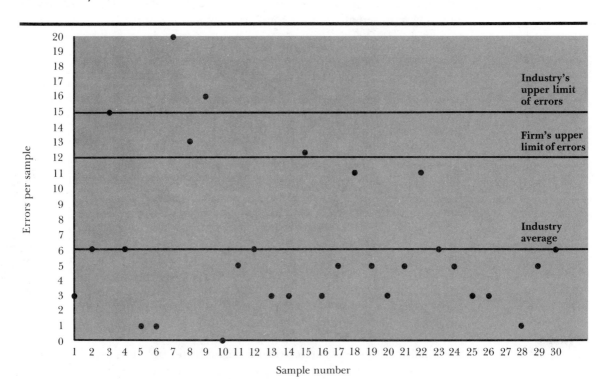

instances, the number of errors exceeds the firm's upper-control limit; in two cases, they exceed the industry's upper-control limit. An investigation leading to corrective action is clearly warranted.

Taking Corrective Action

Deciding about corrective action

The purpose of comparing actual performance against intended performance is, of course, to determine if corrective action is needed. But the manager cannot see the total activity and therefore must carefully avoid two types of errors: taking corrective action when no action is warranted and failing to take corrective action when it is clearly needed.

Developing a Control System

Managers must set up a definite system of control in all areas of operation. They need, essentially, eight kinds of controls:

1. Controls that standardize performance to increase efficiency and to reduce costs. These controls include written procedures and inspections.

2. Controls that safeguard company assets from theft, waste, or misuse, such as a rule for employees to get written permission for taking equipment home with them.

3. Controls that standardize the product's quality, such as blueprints and statistical quality-control procedures.

Types of controls

4. Controls that set limits for delegated authority.

5. Controls that measure on-the-job performance of all employees in the company, including periodic performance reviews.

6. Controls for planning and programming operations, such as production forecasts and sales budgets.

7. Controls that allow top management to keep the firm's plans and programs in balance. Included in this category are the master budget and policy manuals.

8. Controls designed to motivate people to contribute their best efforts. This includes recognizing people's achievements through promotions, suggestion awards, and profit sharing.[5]

To be effective, controls must have accurate and continuous information. They also must be cost effective; that is, the cost of maintaining control over an activity must not exceed the loss that would occur without the control. Controls also should be timely, objective, and simple. The growing importance of on-line information services in the area of control is explained in On-Line Management on page 378.

ON-LINE MANAGEMENT

The Value of On-Line Services

A growing number of managers are beginning to appreciate the value of on-line information services. Managers with a computer and a modem on their desks can easily gain access to virtually any information they want without having to visit a library or dig through tons of reports. For instance, a manager can use Dialog, CompuServe, or a number of other on-line service companies that have compiled and stored millions of bits of information in data banks.

Dow Jones News and Retrieval Service, for instance, provides subscribers access to some forty data bases containing financial and general business information as well as weather and sports information. Users pay a subscription fee of $50, plus hourly fees for on-line access. The hourly fees vary with peak and nonpeak usage, as well as with the specific data bases being used.

Security analysts and money managers who want more detailed information can use services such as CompuStat, Value Line, and Data Resources, Inc., to track companies and finances.

Managers who are sold on information services cite several reasons for their enthusiasm. Access to information gives them a leg up on their competition because they have more information on which to make decisions. Managers who have become accustomed to using the services find that they are cost effective, too. As one executive put it, information services allow him to run his operation on a shoestring budget because he no longer needs a conventional office or library.

Source: David Needle, "Making On-Line Services Pay Off," *Personal Computing*, November 1985, pp. 75–83.

Problems with a Control System

Side effects of control systems

Unfortunately, control systems often have undesirable side effects because of the human reactions of organization members. For example, an incentive pay plan may cause a worker to focus on increasing daily output to the point of losing sight of broader organizational goals, such as improving product quality. Another consequence of a control system is the premium that it places on the short-run at the expense of long-run objectives. For instance, to increase short-term profits, a manager may neglect maintaining machinery; because of this lack of maintenance, it may have to be replaced sooner than ordinarily would be the case.

A person who is rated by the control system may be tempted to "fudge" the figures to look better on paper. The most common methods involve borrowing income or production output from the next period and applying it to the current period or postponing current expenses into the following period.

Morale also can suffer because of control systems. For instance, sales quotas usually are based on the previous year's sales without regard for current economic conditions. Employees can become discouraged if they feel their quota is set arbitrarily high and they know they will be evaluated on whether or not they meet it.

Managing Control System Problems

To minimize these adverse effects, managers should inspect the control system to ensure that it is producing the operational results desired. Managers must recognize that controls are a means to an end, not ends in themselves.

Production Control

Critical elements

Whatever the product, a manager needs a system for planning and controlling its production. **Production planning** is concerned with determining what products will be produced and how, when, and where they will be produced. **Production control** focuses on meeting the production plans efficiently. Scheduling to avoid bottlenecks, quality assurance, and inventory control are by far the most critical elements of a production-control system.

Scheduling to Avoid Bottlenecks

The most common type of production planning and control is called **order control.**[6] It is used in shops that produce custom-made products, such as cabinets. Order control has six basic steps:

1. Receive the order from the customer
2. Develop a list of material required
3. Prepare a routing form
4. Prepare production schedules
5. Give dispatch notices to operators to begin work
6. Follow up[7]

Let's examine each step more closely.

1. *Receive the order from the customer.* The purchase order will indicate the item desired, the quantity, a description of the product, and the model number.

2. *Develop a list of material required.* The next step is to compile a listing of parts and materials necessary to complete the order. For each product they manufacture, most companies develop a form that indicates part numbers, quantities, and descriptions of each component of the item being produced. This step also includes a job-cost sheet, which reflects the total cost of producing the item.

3. *Prepare a routing form.* Routing is the sequence of operations the job passes through on its way to completion. The routing sheet describes the operations to be performed at each step along the way, the time standards, and the machine number that will perform it.

Order control steps

4. *Prepare production schedules.* The production schedule usually is in the form of a chart so that it can be easily read and understood. It shows in detail what manufacturing operations are to be carried out and when they are to be performed. Two widely used scheduling charts are the Gantt chart and the PERT chart. Each is illustrated in Chapter 16, "Quantitative Control Tools."

5. *Give dispatch notices to operators to begin work.* Dispatching is the actual ordering of the work to be done. These orders are contained in written forms called shop orders, job tickets, or manufacturing orders. The materials requisition authorizes release of the materials to be used. A job ticket specifies the work to be done and provides a place for the operator to sign off when completing the task. As each task is completed, the ticket and the product are forwarded to the next point of operation.

6. *Follow up.* This activity involves checking to see whether plans are actually being executed. Its aim is to see that the manufacturing workers are sticking to the production schedule. Control standards include scheduled completion dates, product quality requirements, and required quantities.

Specific control tools

Production supervisors can use several different production-control techniques to make sure that work is progressing according to plan. For example, the supervisor may prepare a report at the end of each day listing orders received, orders processed, and orders remaining. The supervisor also can review actual and planned completion dates on a daily basis. Forms that are sent to production for other purposes are also useful in controlling production. Move orders, which authorize the transfer of partially completed goods from one operation to another, can be helpful in this respect. Inspection reports that summarize the results of operations at different stages of production also can be used for control purposes.

Because a bottleneck is one area of production can have a domino effect on other areas, some companies hire special expediters whose job is to solve production problems by eliminating bottlenecks. The solution may involve working overtime, hiring additional employees, or subcontracting part of the work.

Quality Assurance

The second area of production control is *quality assurance*. Like other areas subject to control, quality assurance is built around the four basic steps in the controlling process—establishing standards, measuring output, comparing output against standards, and taking corrective action as needed.

Product quality is directly related to the firm's strategy. One firm may target a high-income segment of the market that demands high-quality goods, while another may sell to the mass market, which is willing to accept a lower-quality product. Production costs also are related to quality. Higher-quality items typically are more costly to produce.

The product's characteristics may involve quality decisions such as strength, weight, and size. The manufacturer chooses a specific quality level based on its production and marketing objectives.

Inspection defined

Inspection is the task of comparing actual quality to the established standard. Most firms have some type of formal inspection procedure ranging from informal, visual inspections to elaborate statistical methods. Some manufacturers—such as those who make pacemakers, which regulate the pumping of the human heart—inspect each item produced.[8] Sampling techniques are usually used, though. This way, a small proportion of the items is inspected to determine with reasonable accuracy if the batch meets the quality standards. If a deviation exists, its cause must be identified and corrective action taken.

Quality Circles

Quality circles are small groups of workers who volunteer their time and energy to identify, analyze, and solve quality-related problems in their areas of responsibility. Although quality circles originated in Japan, the idea is rooted in motivational theory, which advocates increasing employees' responsibility for their own quality of work.[9] Quality circles, typically used in manufacturing, have been successsfully used in other areas as well. Participants usually are allowed to select their own projects but are restricted to their areas of expertise.

The idea behind quality circles is that a worker with the proper training can discover previously unrecognized quality problems. In a typical quality circle effort, supervisors volunteer for training as circle leaders, and circle members work on solving job-related problems in weekly sessions. The problem-solving technique most commonly used in quality circles include brainstorming, logging problems within the circle's sphere of influence on a check sheet, using charts and diagrams that show problem areas, and inspecting production.[10]

Uses of quality circles

The use of quality circles has spread beyond product quality. Today, circles are used to generate ways for lowering production costs, for improving safety, and for reducing customer complaints. A growing number of companies have found that quality circles let them integrate their employees more creatively into their operations, while upgrading their work force at the same time. The list of companies reporting success with quality circles includes Lockheed, Motorola, American Airlines, International Harvester, General Motors, and many more.

Inventory Control

Inventory control is directed toward maintaining supplies of inventory at adequate levels to meet production and sales requirements. **Inventory** includes both the raw materials or component parts for manufacturing the product and the finished goods from which customer orders are filled.

Avoiding stock outages

The goal of inventory control is to avoid two problems. The first is over-investment in inventories, which ties up the company's working capital and can result in losses from obsolescence. The second problem is underinvest-ment in inventories, which often results in stock outages. Managers use inventory control to maintain an optimum level of supplies or products on hand at all times—enough to meet the needs of both production and sales.

Inventory control methods

Inventory control is usually maintained through one of two systems: the ABC system or the Economic Order Quantity model. With the ABC system, inventory is divided into three dollar-volume categories—A, B, and C—with the A items being the most active and the C items the least active. Inventory control efforts are first focused on the A items, then B, then C.[11] The Economic Order Quantity (EOQ) model can be used to determine what quantity to order to minimize total inventory costs. As the quantity ordered increases, warehouse storage (carrying) costs rise, but ordering costs decrease due to volume discounts; thus, the two expenses tend to offset each other. The problem is finding the optimum point to minimize total inventory costs.

Accounting and Financial Control

Managers cannot maintain overall control without a network of accounting and financial controls that extends into all areas of an organization. These controls, essential to sound fiscal management, help monitor revenue and costs. Three areas of accounting and financial control that deserve special attention are budgeting, cost accounting, and financial statement analysis.

Budgeting

As first mentioned in Chapter 4, "Managerial Planning," a budget is a formal plan expressed in numerical terms. It includes target figures for sales, the cost of materials, and production levels. Actual performance is then compared with these targets as a means of controlling a firm's operations and minimizing any deviations from plans. A budget should be considered a blueprint: it is both a quantitative guide for action and a standard for the evaluation of performance.

Sales forecast

Operating Budget   The budgeting process usually begins with the development of a sales forecast, which shows the quantities of various items to be sold and the revenue that will be generated. Typically, a sales forecast is prepared periodically—quarterly, for example—and by geographic region of operation. It is generally regarded as the most crucial element in the budgeting process. All the firm's budgets must be coordinated with the sales forecast because revenues from sales define the upper limit of expenditures and profits. As On the Job, page 384, shows, a company like H. J. Heinz is cutting costs with an eye on its sales forecast.

The next step is to develop production budgets. These show the expenditures for labor, materials, and overhead to be incurred in producing the goods needed for meeting the sales forecast. Production budgets may not always match sales budgets, however, if a company wants to smooth out seasonal trends. All other units in the organization also prepare their own budgets, specifying targets for expenditures. Taken together, these individual departmental budgets represent the organization's master budget. After preparation of this budget, the chief financial officer administers it, often shifting funds from one department to another or from one line item to another. Sometimes, top administrators must make cutbacks after the budget's implementation because of excessive spending or lower-than-expected revenues.

Performance report

Feeding back budgetary information to operating managers is critical to the control process. Performance data must be gathered, compiled, and sent to the appropriate manager in the form of a performance report. The **performance report** shows budgeted targets, actual performance, and variances. The operating manager has the duty to review the report and to take corrective action when necessary.

Payback method

Budget for Capital Items   At some point, most business firms must replace manufacturing equipment, build new facilities, or purchase additional land. These items, called **capital outlay items,** must be budgeted. Capital budgeting encompasses the following steps: (1) identify alternative projects in which to invest, (2) evaluate the advantages and disadvantages of each, (3) select the best alternative, and (4) implement the decision.

There are a number of capital budgeting methods, the simplest of which is the *payback* method. It ranks alternative projects according to the time each takes for recovering the initial cost. Those for which the payback period is shortest are preferred over those with longer payback periods. Table 14.1 illustrates the payback period for three different machines.

Under the payback method, machine 1 is the best alternative, since its payback period is the shortest. Although it is simple, this method ignores the "time value of money" and gives no importance to the total revenues generated. Other methods are the internal rate of return, average rate of return, and net present value.

ON THE JOB

Heinz Trims Costs

Anthony "Tony" O'Reilly, the chief executive officer of H. J. Heinz, wants to create an "ongoing feeling of desperation" in his company.

O'Reilly's knotted-stomach approach is designed to push the company toward his goal of becoming the lowest-cost producer in the food industry. He doesn't want anyone to get complacent in the quest for lower costs. Once you start thinking you are the low-cost producer, you begin to lose your advantage, he says.

O'Reilly has been fanatical in his search for ways to cut costs. He saved the company $4 million annually by eliminating the back label from large bottles. He also developed a new way to peel potatoes, and designed a system to reuse water from one processing area in another. He's also implemented a program in which hourly workers devise ways to improve efficiency and lower costs.

Top management is convinced that consumers are becoming reluctant to pay more for Heinz products than for other comparable items. The company is thus forced to cut costs rather than raise prices to increase its profits. It can continue to charge premium prices only if it can support its higher cost by offering higher quality. Persuading the consumer that the difference justifies the price takes some slick advertising. But Heinz's advertising budget isn't immune to O'Reilly's cost-conscious approach, either. He's already warned the company's marketing arm that he'll trim their budget, too, if profits begin to drop.

Source: Bill Saporito, "Heinz Pushes to Be the Low-Cost Producer," *Fortune,* June 24, 1985, pp. 44–54.

Cost Accounting

One specialized accounting area important in management control is cost accounting. **Cost accounting** is concerned with the proper recording, reporting, and analyzing of the various costs involved in operating a business. The objective of cost accounting, which is a major part of the financial accounting system of a firm, is to inform management promptly of the cost of producing or selling an item or of providing a particular service.

Cost accounting was first developed and used in determining the unit manufacturing cost of products. Its primary aim was to arrive at inventory values for presentation on financial statements. This is still an important function, but now unit costs are important in budgeting, pricing, and other decision areas as well.

TABLE 14.1
Payback method for
capital budgeting
decisions

	MACHINE		
	1	2	3
Initial cost	$6,000	$8,000	$12,000
Revenues generated:			
First year	2,000	2,500	3,000
Second year	2,000	2,500	3,000
Third year	2,000	2,500	3,000
Fourth year	3,000	2,500	3,000
Fifth year	4,000	2,500	1,000
Payback period	3 years	3.2 years	4 years

Financial Statement Analysis

Financial statements

One of the most widely used methods for evaluating a firm's financial condition and for monitoring its use of resources is financial statement analysis, an approach that makes extensive use of financial ratios. Financial ratios are typically grouped into four categories: liquidity ratios, leverage ratios, activity ratios, and profitability ratios. These ratios, derived from components of a firm's balance sheet and income statement, are compared to industry averages to indicate how the firm is doing relative to other firms in the industry. A firm's **balance sheet** presents its assets (that which it owns), liabilities (that which it owes), and net worth at a given period. Its **income statement** shows its revenues and expenses. Let's first examine two financial statements of the XYZ Company, and then compute specific ratios using the data from these statements. XYZ's balance sheet is represented in Table 14.2; its income statement is in Table 14.3.

Liquidity Ratios   **Liquidity ratios** are designed to measure the ability of a firm to meet its current obligations. The most commonly used liquidity ratios are the current ratio and the acid test (quick) ratio.

Current ratio

The *current ratio* is calculated by dividing current liabilities into current assets. Current assets include cash, marketable securities, accounts receivable, and inventories. Current liabilities are accounts payable, short-term notes payable, current maturities on long-term debt, accrued income taxes and accrued wages. The current ratio for XYZ Company is:

$$\text{Current Ratio} = \frac{\text{Current Assets}}{\text{Current Liabilities}} = \frac{650}{200} = 3.25 \text{ times}$$

Assets			Liabilities		
Current Assets			Current Liabilities		
Cash	50		Accounts Payable	80	
Marketable Securities	150		Notes Payable	80	
Receivables	150		Accruals	40	
Inventory	300		Total Current Liabilities		200
Total Current Assets		650			
			Long-Term Liabilities		
Fixed Assets			Bonds Payable		750
Plant/Equipment	1,500				
Less Depreciation	500		Total Liabilities		950
Net Plant/Equipment		1,000			
			Equity		
			Common Stock	600	
			Retained Earnings	100	
			Total Net Worth		700
			Total Liabilities		
Total Assets		1,650	and Equity		1,650

TABLE 14.2
Balance sheet—XYZ
Company, December
31, 1987 (in thousands
of dollars)

Acid-test ratio

The *acid-test ratio* is calculated by subtracting inventory from current assets and dividing the balance by current liabilities. This ratio measures a firm's ability to pay off short-term obligations without depending on the sale of inventories, which are relatively illiquid, or unsalable. The acid-test ratio for XYZ would be:

$$\text{Acid-Test Ratio} = \frac{\text{Current Assets} - \text{Inventory}}{\text{Current Liabilities}} = \frac{650 - 300}{200} = 1.75$$

Types of leverage ratios

Leverage Ratios   **Leverage ratios** are used to help predict the long-term solvency of a firm. These ratios are of primary interest to bondholders and stockholders because the more debt added to the capital structure, the more risk is involved for creditors and shareholders. The most important leverage ratios are the *debt to equity ratio,* which provides creditors with an idea of the firm's ability to withstand losses without impairing the creditors' interest, and the *coverage of fixed charges ratio,* which stresses the importance of a company's covering all interest charges on its debt. It is computed by dividing net income before interest and taxes by these fixed interest charges. Creditors want this ratio to be high.

TABLE 14.3 Income statement— XYZ Company for year ended December 31, 1987 (in thousands of dollars)			
Sales		$1,500	
Cost of Goods Sold		450	
Gross Profit on Sales			$1,050
Operating Expenses		150	
Depreciation		50	
Interest Expense		85	
Total Expenses			285
Taxable Income			765
Taxes			332
Net Income After Taxes			433

Other ratios

Activity Ratios **Activity ratios** measure how effectively the firm employs the resources at its command. Included in this category are inventory turnover, net working capital turnover, fixed asset turnover, the average collection period ratio, and total asset turnover.

Inventory turnover, for example, measures how quickly inventory is sold. Generally, the higher the inventory turnover, the better the firm is performing. If the ratio is too high, it could signal high "stockout" costs because not enough inventory is available. This ratio also provides a basis for determining whether the firm has obsolete inventory, or if pricing problems exist.

$$\text{Inventory Turnover} = \frac{\text{Cost of Goods Sold}}{\text{Inventory}} = \frac{450}{300} = 1.5$$

Profitability Ratios **Profitability ratios** indicate how well the firm has done during the year in achieving its desired profit level. These ratios measure a firm's overall effectiveness.

Work Performance Control

Another area of control involves employee performance. Its purpose is to ensure that employees contribute to meeting organizational goals. An effective work performance control system includes standards for performance levels and ways of measuring each person's contributions. It also provides for feedback for corrective action and has a recognition and reward system that is tied to evaluation.

In some cases, a manager can use quantifiable and measurable data to evaluate an employee; for instance, in terms of a production worker's quantity of physical output, waste, and so on. In other cases, the rater must use his or

Evaluating employee performance

her own judgment. This is especially true when it comes to management personnel. For example, a financial manager may be evaluated on how promptly he or she reports operating results to higher management. Or a production manager may be appraised on the basis of morale in his or her department. We must realize, though, that performance standards are relative to the group and to the organization. Not only are the needs of each organization different but also the quality of personnel varies from one company to another. The expectations of management also differ from one firm to the next.[12]

Performance appraisal

The key element in the control system is performance appraisal. Performance evaluation serves two purposes: it is a way for a manager to give feedback to subordinates, and it is a basis for salary increases and promotion decisions. A sound employee-appraisal system assesses employee performance on a regular basis. Such systematic appraisals are usually conducted every six months or annually.[13] One study of 244 firms revealed that appraisals are most often conducted once every year, usually near the employee's anniversary date.[14]

Common Pitfalls of Performance Appraisals

Some managers are too strict in their evaluations, others are too lenient, and still others tend to rate all their subordinates average. The last pitfall—commonly called the central tendency effect—has several causes. Managers may not be totally aware of their subordinates' performance, or they may not wish to be forced to account for an unusually poor or unusually outstanding rating. In other cases, managers are guilty of the "halo" effect (see Chapter 8), allowing one outstanding feature to discolor their overall evaluation.

Reasons for inaccuracies

Sometimes, evaluations may be inaccurate through no fault of the rater. The performance may be difficult to measure, goals may be ambiguous, the person's activities may vary from day to day, or the method used may not properly evaluate the critical elements of the job.

Feedback and Corrective Action

An appraisal interview is a common way for a manager to provide a subordinate with feedback as they discuss the specific points in the evaluation. Their discussion focuses on the employee's shortcomings and suggestions for improvement. The success of this type of interview depends, however, on the climate in which it is conducted. When the subordinate senses the boss's support and approval, the appraisal interview can be highly constructive. But when the climate is one of mistrust and skepticism, the subordinate is likely to be defensive.

Appraisal interview

Experienced managers often let their subordinates suggest ways of improving their performance rather than subject them to a "how to do it" session. Self-criticism is usually more palatable than criticism from someone else is. It also provides an opening for an exchange of ideas on how to improve overall job performance.

Review

✔ *The importance of control for an organization.* The purpose of control is to ensure that actual performance conforms to established plans. Managers must keep apprised of such factors as time, quantity, quality, and costs and compare these elements against yardsticks or standards of performance. Without systematic control, a manager has no assurance that all elements of the organization are channeled toward company goals. The establishment of a control process involves four steps: (1) establishing standards, (2) measuring performance, (3) comparing actual performance against standards, and (4) taking corrective action as needed.

✔ *How to establish standards.* Three different methods are used for establishing standards: judgment, statistical or historical data, and observation. Judgmental standards are arrived at through a manager's experience, knowledge, and intuition. Standards also can be arrived at through the use of historical data or through the use of engineering techniques such as work sampling and time and motion study.

✔ *What to look for when measuring actual performance.* To make sure that performance levels are measured accurately, managers should concern themselves with five factors: (1) the timeliness of the information, (2) the appropriateness of the units of measurement, (3) the reliability of the information, (4) the validity of the information, and (5) the channeling of the information to the proper person.

✔ *Why a manager must have standards for comparing performance.* Without standards, managers cannot determine whether actual performance is in control or out of control. Comparing actual performance against standards might identify a dangerous trend, which would signal the need for corrective action.

✔ *Common errors managers make when taking corrective action.* A manager's purpose in comparing actual performance against standards is to determine if he or she should take corrective action. However, because the total activity is not visible, the manager must avoid two types of errors: taking corrective action when none is needed, and failing to take corrective action when it is clearly warranted.

✓ *What kinds of controls are needed in an organization.* Eight types of controls are needed: (1) controls that standardize procedures, (2) controls that safeguard company assets, (3) controls that assure output quality, (4) controls that define authority limits, (5) controls that measure worker performance, (6) controls for planning and programming operations, (7) controls for ensuring that overall company goals are being met, and (8) controls designed to motivate employees.

✓ *The types of production control.* Production control focuses on meeting production plans effectively. The most common type of production control is order control, to carry out manufacturing operations expeditiously to fit a customer's order. The other areas of production control are quality assurance and inventory control.

✓ *Accounting and financial control methods.* Accounting and financial controls help monitor revenue and expenses. As such, they are vital to sound fiscal management. Among the most important financial control tools are budgeting, cost accounting, and financial statement analysis.

✓ *How to control work performance.* Work performance control focuses on the human element of organizations. Employee performance, like other organizational activities, must be monitored and evaluated systematically. Included in this category are quantity and quality of output, attitude, behavior, and other factors for which acceptable standards can be established.

THE MANAGER'S DICTIONARY

As an extra review of the chapter, try defining the following terms. If you have trouble with any of them, refer to the page numbers listed.

control (372)	quality circles (381)	income statement (385)
standards (373)	inventory control (382)	liquidity ratios (385)
control charts (376)	inventory (382)	leverage ratios (386)
production planning (379)	performance report (383)	activity ratios (387)
production control (379)	capital outlay items (383)	profitability ratios (387)
order control (379)	cost accounting (384)	
inspection (381)	balance sheet (385)	

REVIEW QUESTIONS

1. Why is control necessary in organizations? Explain.

2. List the steps in the control process.

3. Differentiate among the various methods for setting standards of performance.

4. Can variations from standards be tolerated? Explain.

5. Explain how a control chart can help a manager determine whether an activity is out of control. Can you give an example?

6. What types of errors can a manager make in taking corrective action? Explain.

7. List the various types of controls needed in organizations. Give an example of each.

8. Do control systems have shortcomings? If so, explain.

9. Name the three major areas of control and explain each.

10. How can a quality circle help management correct problems in manufacturing? Give an example.

11. Why is budgeting considered a control tool?

12. What is the purpose of financial statement analysis? How can financial ratios be used in the control process? Discuss.

13. How can a manager be sure that a worker's performance is acceptable?

14. What kinds of errors can a manager make in evaluating the performance of subordinates? How can these problems be overcome?

MANAGEMENT CHALLENGE

The Morris Company manufactures a limited line of sports equipment, including water skis and skateboards. Historically, the company has priced its products on a cost-plus basis. Because of the strong demand for its products, the company has given little attention to controlling manufacturing costs. They have passed cost increases along to the consumer in the form of higher prices.

In recent months, increased competition and a sluggish economy have made management more conscious of costs. As the production manager for the company, you have been asked to develop a system to ensure that costs are under control.

1. What type of control system would you set up for the Morris Company?

2. Describe in detail the procedure that you would follow in establishing a control system.

3. How could you ensure that manufacturing costs are not excessive? Explain.

CASE 14.1

Union Carbide's Disaster

Monday, December 3, 1984, marked the darkest day in the history of Union Carbide Corporation. On that day, Union Carbide's Bhopal, India, plant emitted a cloud of poisonous methyl isocyanate gas that killed more than two thousand people and injured tens of thousands of nearby residents. The immediate effects of the gas were painfully obvious; long-term effects are still unknown.

What caused the accident? Somehow, a huge quantity of water entered a methyl isocyanate storage tank and started a chemical reaction. Because the cooling system for the tank wasn't working at the time, the chemical reaction occurred swiftly. Immediately after the tragedy, speculation was rampant. Some blamed the leak on equipment failure; others cited human error. Initial reports from India blamed the disaster on design flaws, operating errors, and defective systems. Union Carbide management, blaming faulty safety systems and inadequate safety procedures, contended that company officials in the United States were unaware of these shortcomings. Employees of the Bhopal subsidiary were at fault, they said.

Whatever the exact cause of the leak, Union Carbide suffered great losses. Legal expenses, settlements, and injury to its reputation took a heavy toll on the company. At first, there was speculation that the company would be forced to seek protection under Chapter 11 bankruptcy proceedings, just as Manville Corporation had done in 1982 following asbestos-handling problems.

In a class action suit, attorney Melvin Belli charged that Union Carbide acted "willfully and wantonly," with utter disregard for the safety of Bhopal citizens. The suit contended that the company did not use the same safety systems in the Bhopal plant as it did in its Institute, West Virginia, facility.

Following the Bhopal tragedy, Union Carbide made extensive alterations to the West Virginia plant. They replaced the salt-water cooling system with one that uses chloroform, they increased sampling of tanks for water contamination, and they installed millions of dollars worth of monitoring devices. But these changes were of little consolation to the families of the victims of Bhopal.

Questions

1. How could this accident have been avoided? Discuss.

2. In your opinion, was Union Carbide guilty of failing to maintain adequate control over the operations of its Bhopal subsidiary?

CASE 14.2

Quality from Top to Bottom at Tennant[15]

Tennant Company, a manufacturer of maintenance equipment for industrial floors, has gained an enviable reputation over the past few years for its quality control program. The Minneapolis-based firm's quality assurance program is built on the philosophy that quality is a top management responsibility. The company is convinced that additional quality inspectors and posters encouraging employees to take pride in their work are not enough. An effective program depends on reshaping attitudes from the chief executive officer to the loading-dock employee.

In the 1970s, Tennant was worried about a high level of defects in its products. Customer complaints, the high costs of correcting defects, and concerns about the image of its products prompted Tennant, by 1979, to employ a management consultant to help correct its problems. The company management was particularly concerned about leaking connections in hydraulic lines.

First, Tennant was advised to assign a dollar value to the additional production and service time required to correct defects. Then, small groups of workers and supervisors were formed to identify specific problems. In the case of the leaking hydraulic lines, a study group concluded that assembly workers were not properly trained in the correct way to install the joints. Additional study revealed that Tennant engineers had not kept abreast of the latest technology in hydraulic circuits; moreover, the firm used a number of different joints purchased from sixteen different suppliers.

By the end of 1984, defects were cut in half. In addition, the costs of correcting defects had been reduced from 17% of sales to 8.9% of sales. The company's objective is further reduction—to 2.5% of sales by 1988.

Questions

1. In your opinion, should all firms that institute quality assurance programs expect results similar to those of Tennant Company?

2. What are the "costs" of installing such a program? What are the benefits? Do the benefits outweigh the costs?

CHAPTER OUTLINE

The Development of Production-Operations Management (POM)

The Production-Operations Process

Resource Inputs

Transformation

Outputs

Feedback

Decision Making in POM

Process and Product Design Decisions

Capacity Planning

Forecasting • Facilities Planning • Aggregate Planning • Scheduling

Materials Management

Purchasing • Inventory • Materials Handling • Material Requirements Planning (MRP) • Just-in-Time Scheduling (JIT)

Work Force Decisions

Ergonomics in the Office • Evaluating Worker Performance

Quality Assurance Decisions

The Impact of Technology

Robotics

Computer-Integrated Manufacturing (CIM)

CAD/CAM

MIS: An Important Operational Tool

Management of Production and Information

M A N A G E M E N T   I N   A C T I O N

Pan Am's Terminal Illness

In January 1984, C. Edward Acker, chairperson of Pan American World Airways, got a taste of his company's inefficiency when his flight to Paris left New York's Kennedy Airport an hour and a half late. Immediately after arriving in Paris, Acker angrily called his New York office to relay a message to Martin Shagrue, then Pan Am's senior vice-president of marketing. According to Shagrue, Acker told him to "get your ass out to our Kennedy terminal and fix the damn thing."[1]

Late departures from Kennedy, caused by congestion, had become common for Pan Am. Flights leaving Kennedy within fifteen minutes of schedule dropped from 65% in late 1983 to 40% in January 1984. Because of connecting flight schedules, problems at Kennedy cause problems elsewhere. Delays disrupt flights all over the world. Although Kennedy was built to handle relatively few international flights at a leisurely pace, it is now a Pan Am hub. By 1984, the airport was handling more than 40% of Pan Am's total capacity, up from 28% in 1981. The effect of this is that several planes land almost simultaneously, unload their passengers and cargo, load thousands of other passengers, and then take off again.

Worldport, as Pan Am people call Kennedy, had become a disaster. Operations had bogged down, executives were blaming each other for the problems, and planes were "stolen" from other routes whenever mechanical problems grounded planes destined for Rome, Munich, and Zurich. Some people blamed

Pan Am's problems on its management structure; others cited its heavy losses, with subsequent lack of funds needed to alleviate the congestion. One former Pan Am official blamed the mess on an inadequate number of gates, an inefficient baggage-transfer system, and the design of the terminal.

A day or two after getting Acker's message, Shagrue went to Worldport and had a series of "panic" meetings to improve on-time performance. At about the same time, heads began to roll. In addition to firing several high-ranking officials, the airline began spending $20 million to install new gates, a new baggage system, and new lighting for passenger areas, and to fix a leaky roof. The airline also slightly reduced the number of flights at Kennedy. As a result, Pan Am's on-time performance improved sharply, but it is still short of Acker's goal. As he puts it, he wants the planes moving before passengers have a chance to sit down.[2]

Preview

Pan Am's operational inefficiencies at Kennedy Airport illustrate the problems confronting production-operations managers. These include the design and layout of physical facilities, capacity planning, production logistics, maintenance, service quality, and so on. This chapter describes the nature of production and information management and focuses on the types of decisions that production-operations managers make. It also discusses the importance of ergonomics and technology in the workplace. After studying this chapter, you will understand:

✔ The development of production-operations management

✔ The production-operations process

✔ The kinds of production-operations decisions managers must make

✔ The impact of technology on production-operations management

The Development of Production-Operations Management (POM)

Usually, when we hear the term *production*, we think of a manufacturing plant belching out smoke. But production-operations managers can be found in all types of organizations—insurance agencies, hospitals, government agencies, and restaurants. In factories, they are responsible for producing a physical product; in service industries, a supply of services.

At first glance, manufacturing operations may appear to have little in common with service organizations. But a closer look reveals a common thread—both operations are *transformation processes*. In manufacturing, raw materials, energy, labor, and capital are transformed into finished products. In service firms, they become service outputs. Managing this transformation process efficiently is the job of production-operations managers.

The evolution of POM   Manufacturing management, production management, and operations management all refer to the same general discipline, but the terminology has changed over the years. The traditional view of manufacturing management began in the eighteenth century when Adam Smith recognized the advantages of division of labor in manufacturing operations. The traditional view prevailed until the 1930s; then, production management came into vogue, as Frederick Taylor's work became more widely known. Jobs were carefully analyzed and reorganized to achieve greater efficiency. The human relations movement, born of the Hawthorne experiments, pointed out the importance of superior-subordinate relationships and how to improve worker productivity.[3] The production manager's dual role as a manager of people and production methods is still apparent today.

The term *operations management* reflects the growing importance of service industries, which today employ more than 70% of the American work force.[4] The term **production-operations management (POM)** is now widely used because it encompasses both manufacturing and service firms. We can define it simply as management concerned with the provision of goods and services.

The Production-Operations Process

Components of the process

A **production system** can be defined as a process for converting resources into goods and services, as illustrated in Figure 15.1. The *resource inputs* are converted into goods and services by the process technology, which is the particular technology used to transform the inputs into *outputs*, or products. Changing the technology changes how each input is used in relation to another and may change the outputs. *Feedback* is used to monitor the process technology or inputs to assure that the system produces desired results.[5]

FIGURE 15.1
The production process

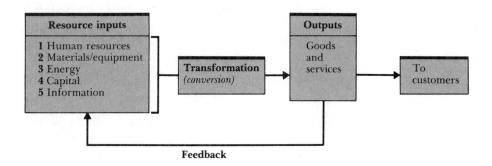

Resource Inputs

Human resources are both physical and mental. Managerial talent, engineering skill, employee cooperation, and similar qualities are crucial to an organization's success. The human values that people bring into an organization become traditions, standards, and ethical guidelines for both internal operations and for relations with the public.[6]

Types of resource inputs

Materials and equipment include the physical plant, manufacturing equipment, tools, raw materials, computers, and other physical resources required in the production process. In an accounting sense, materials and equipment constitute the major assets of a firm.

Energy refers to the physical energy, perhaps electrical and mechanical, used in the operations. *Capital* means the funds that can be spent on human resources, materials and equipment, and energy. Capital is acquired through the sale of stock (equity) or through borrowing (debt). In not-for-profit organizations, taxes or contributions provide a source of funds. *Information* is generated both internally and externally and is used to maintain control over the production process.

Transformation

The objective of combining resource inputs is to transform them into goods or services with a higher value than that of the original inputs. The value of outputs normally is measured by the market prices that they can command. Some outputs—such as those that are social or environmental—are, however, virtually impossible to value. The benefit of transforming a polluted river into a habitat for fish, for instance, cannot be accurately measured. In the past, intangibles and by-products were ignored. Today, we recognize these outputs, and managers are forced to deal with them in terms of different individual and group value systems.[7]

Forms of transformations

Transformations can take various forms.[8] Converting raw materials into finished goods by means of various manufacturing processes involves physical transformations. A locational transformation occurs when goods are transported from one geographic location to another. An exchange transformation takes place when one owner sells goods to another. A storage transformation can occur when goods are put in a warehouse. Curing an illness illustrates a physiological transformation. The gratification that comes from doing well on an examination illustrates attitudinal transformation.

Outputs

The output of a production process can be broken down into two separate categories—volume and standards. Volume of output refers to the physical quantity of output; standards refer to the quality of output. A transformation process may produce the desired quantity of output, but the quality of that

Measuring output

output may be unacceptable. Or the standard of the output may be satisfactory, but the volume may be inadequate. This is why it is important to use different criteria when measuring output. Table 15.1 shows the inputs, transformation process, and outputs for selected organizations.

Feedback

The final element in the production process is feedback. To assure that the output of the system conforms to predetermined plans, the manager compares actual output with desired output. Discrepancies signal the need for corrective action. Think of the system as a continual process in which needed adjustments change the mix of resource inputs.

Decision Making in POM

A convenient way to group production-operations decisions is by the manager's major areas of responsibility—process and product design, capacity, materials, work force, and quality.[9]

Process and Product Design Decisions

Types of production systems

These decisions define how the product or service is made. Basically, there are two types of production systems: intermittent and continuous. **Continuous production systems** are designed to produce a continuous stream of goods, such as in chemical plants or oil refineries. **Intermittent production systems** produce batches of goods, such as those in a custom cabinet shop or an auto repair garage.

Each system has its own characteristics. In a continuous system, the unit cost of the product is usually lower because of economies of scale, storage costs are lower because goods move through the plant rapidly, the production time is usually shorter, and fixed-path handling equipment (conveyors, for example) is common. The investment in equipment usually is greater because it is specialized. Marketing efforts focus on developing distribution channels for a large volume of standardized output.

An intermittent production system has higher unit costs, longer production times, general-purpose equipment, and portable materials-handling equipment. Marketing efforts are directed to getting and filling individual orders for varied products.[10]

Plant location decisions

Where to locate the production facility is one of the manager's major production decisions. Considerations are the location of markets, sources of workers and raw materials, transportation facilities, utilities, taxes, land costs, and a host of other variables.

Having selected the plant location, the manager must next decide on its physical layout. Continuous production systems use product layouts; intermittent production systems use process layouts. In a process layout, people,

TABLE 15.1
Input-transformation-output relationships

SYSTEM	PRIMARY INPUTS	TRANS-FORMATION PROCESS	DESIRED OUTPUT
Auto repair (body) shop)	Autos, workers, equipment	Repairing damaged autos	Restored automobiles
Hospital	Doctors patients, drugs, equipment	Health care	Healthy patients
Barber shop	Barber, tools, customer	Cutting, styling	Well-groomed customer
Chemical plant	Sodium chloride, electricity, electrolytic cells	Electrolysis of brine	Chlorine, caustic soda
University	Faculty, students, buildings, books	Instruction	Educated college graduate
Fast-food restaurant	Food, equipment, workers, customers, energy	Preparation of food	Nourished customer
Oil refinery	Crude oil, equipment, workers	Refining	Refined petroleum products
Garment factory	Cloth, machinery, workers	Cutting, sewing	Wearing apparel
Lumber company	Logs, equipment, workers	Cutting, sawing	Finished wood products

Product and process layouts

machines, materials, and support services are grouped by the functions or processes being used. A product layout focuses on the sequence of operations to be performed. Several devices can help management in solving layout problems. Flow process charts, flow diagrams, and scale models aid in the efficient organization of the manufacturing process.

The issue of materials handling is closely related to plant layout. The type of layout used and the materials-handling system installed are interrelated.

**Product design
decisions**

Product design is another matter affecting the design of the production system. A manager deciding on product design should respond to the following questions:

1. What materials will be most appropriate?

2. How many processes will be required?

3. What quality requirements must be met?

4. Can standardized materials and component parts be used?

5. What does the customer want?

Capacity Planning

**Optimal production
capacity**

Every organization must make decisions about its production capacity. With too little capacity, a firm cannot satisfy the demand for its product or service. Too much capacity results in underutilization of resources and high fixed costs. The objective of the production manager is to determine the optimal production capacity. Forecasting, facilities planning, aggregate planning, and scheduling are all part of capacity planning.

Forecasting   Nearly all functional areas of a business rely on forecasting, which was first defined and discussed in Chapter 4, "Managerial Planning." It is the process of making assumptions about the future that managers use when they plan or make decisions today. Capacity decisions use different kinds of forecasts. For planning the total capacity of production facilities, managers need a long-range forecast. For medium-range capacity decisions affecting employment, subcontracting, and equipment, they require a more detailed forecast by product line. Short-range capacity decisions include the assignment of available people and machines to jobs in the immediate future. As such, they should be highly accurate and quite detailed.[11]

Types of forecasting

Forecasting can be divided into four basic types: qualitative, time series analysis, causal relationships, and simulation. **Qualitative forecasts** usually consist of the opinions of salespeople, or top management personnel, or a combination of both. Some judgmental forecasts are totally intuitive, while others incorporate the opinions in a mathematical or statistical framework. These forecasts have the advantage of incorporating intangible factors and subjective experience; but they may have the disadvantage of including personal bias, overly optimistic feelings, and other human shortcomings.

Time series forecasts use past happenings to predict future events. For example, a firm may use the sales figures for the past ten years to predict sales for the eleventh year. The more commonly used time series models are moving average, exponential smoothing, and regression analysis, which are discussed in Chapter 4.

Causal forecasts try to identify whatever will have a cause-effect relationship on the matter being forecast. For instance, advertising expenditures may directly affect sales of a particular product.

Simulation uses computer-based mathematical models to predict the future. Such models allow the forecaster to determine the effect of various changes without having to institute them. For example, a manager may use simulation to increase a product's selling price by 5% and then by 10%. The effect of these changes on sales can be determined quickly. Chapter 16 has more about simulation.

Location and capacity decisions

Facilities Planning   **Facilities planning** is concerned with both the physical location of the plant and its production capacity. Because investments in the physical plant often are so great, managers must make sound decisions in this area. Before deciding to build a small plant, they should consider that an unexpectedly high demand for the product may require an addition. If demand is unexpectedly low, they may have to eliminate excess capacity. For this reason, accurate forecasts are crucial.

Output requirements

Aggregate Planning   **Aggregate production planning** specifies output requirements by major product groups, either in labor hours required or in units of production for monthly periods up to a year. The process for deriving the aggregate production plan varies from company to company, but one common approach is the corporate annual plan. Typically, a corporate plan specifies how many units in each major product line need to be manufactured during the coming year to meet the sales forecast. The planner uses these data to determine how to satisfy these requirements with the resources available. Other companies may simulate various master production schedules and calculate corresponding capacity requirements to see if adequate labor and equipment are available at each work site.[12]

A number of methods are used for meeting aggregate product demand: (1) the work force can be expanded or contracted through hiring and layoffs as demand fluctuates; (2) a stable work force can be maintained but with adjusted hours; (3) a stable work force and a constant output level can be maintained, with demand fluctuations handled by allowing inventories to vary; and (4) delivery lead times can vary.

Scheduling   Aggregate planning is essential, but it doesn't solve the problem of deciding which job to work on when, or how to assign workers and machines in order to meet the plan. The task of assigning workers and machines to various jobs at given times is called **scheduling**.

Scheduling methods

Several different methods of scheduling are available to the production-operations manager. These methods can be grouped into three classes: (1) charts, boards, and computers; (2) priority decision rules; and (3) mathematical programming methods.[13]

Gantt charts and scheduling boards let production managers schedule work without the aid of a computer. A quick glance at a Gantt chart (see Chapter 16) reveals which jobs are ahead of schedule, which are behind schedule, and the anticipated completion date of all work in progress. The major problem with Gantt charts is keeping them up to date. Because of this, many firms have designed their own computerized scheduling systems.

In effect, scheduling involves resource allocation; that is, it involves assigning limited resources—employees and machines, for example—to different jobs as efficiently as possible. Developments in computer-aided quantitative methods now make scheduling decisions simpler. Linear programming, program evaluation and review technique (PERT), and the critical path method, in particular, have proven to be very useful scheduling tools. These and other management science techniques are illustrated in Chapter 16, "Quantitative Control Tools."

Materials Management

One of the objectives of the production manager is to have the right materials at the right place at the right time. This depends on effective policies of forecasting, inventory, and materials distribution.

Purchasing   **Purchasing** is the procuring of raw materials, components, and services that the organization needs to achieve its goals. It is the link between the company and its suppliers. To a vendor, its customer's purchasing department is the entry way for raw materials and supplies. The company sees its purchasing department as a clearinghouse or pipeline for materials needed to sustain production. This is the step-by-step purchasing procedure:

1. The unit needing the item initiates a requisition

2. The purchasing department reviews the requisition

3. Suppliers are selected

The purchasing procedure

4. An order is placed

5. The order is monitored to determine if goods have been shipped and will be delivered as anticipated

6. The incoming shipment is received, inspected, and accepted[14]

Any functional area of the firm can initiate a purchase requisition. It usually includes the name and description of the item wanted, the quantity desired, and the signature of the preparer. The purchasing agent reviews the requisition to determine if another item costing less can be substituted. Purchasing agents usually are authorized to question requisitions and to suggest alternatives, but they cannot make unauthorized changes. After consulting a list of suppliers, the purchasing agent gathers information on the price and delivery time, selects a vendor, and processes the purchase order. Follow-up uncovers delivery problems and resolves them promptly. When delivered, the person who initiated the purchase requisition inspects the item and authorizes payment.

Maintaining adequate inventory

Inventory As mentioned in Chapter 14, "The Controlling Function," an inventory is a stock of goods held for future production or sale. Raw materials, work in progress, and finished goods all can be classified as items in inventory. Firms maintain inventories for a number of reasons: (1) to offer a wide selection of products for customers, (2) to carry them through interruptions in production, (3) to take advantage of quantity discounts, and (4) to provide a safeguard against uncertain deliveries and lead times.[15]

Unfortunately, there are costs associated with maintaining inventories—they tie up assets, they need storage space, and they make the cost of insurance rise. For these reasons, firms cannot afford to keep unrestricted inventories. Even when closely controlled, inventories of manufacturing firms often account for 25 to 50% of their total assets. The percentage of wholesalers' and retailers' total assets tied up in inventories is even greater.[16]

Several kinds of costs are associated with inventories. **Procurement costs** are those incurred in acquiring the inventories, particularly clerical expenses. **Carrying costs** take several different forms. Capital that is tied up cannot be used elsewhere, resulting in lost opportunities. Carrying costs also include rent, utilities, spoilage, taxes, insurance, and the cost of administering the inventory control system.

Inventory costs

Firms also incur **stockout costs** if inventories are depleted before demand is satisfied. Lost sales and lost goodwill fall into this category. Stockouts also can cause a production line to be shut down, resulting in lost productivity as well as start-up and shutdown expenses.

Setup costs, incurred at the start of a production run, include adjustments to the equipment and clerical expenses. **Production costs** associated with inventory include overtime expenses, labor turnover costs (hiring, training, and layoff costs), and material start-up costs.

There are two basic steps in controlling a firm's inventory. First, an inventory accounting system must be developed. Such a system can be either manual or automated, periodic or continuous. Its purpose is to keep track of all items in inventory. The second step involves deciding when and how much to order. Intelligent decisions in this area depend on accurate information about demand and about the inventory status for each item used in production.

Independent and dependent demand

Demand for a particular item can be either independent or dependent. *Independent* demand exists when it is not influenced by other items. For example, the demand for aspirin is not dependent on anything else. *Dependent* demand is experienced whenever an item is an integral part of something else. The demand for computer chips, for example, is dependent on the demand for computers. Dependence is most obvious in a manufacturing setting that combines components to produce a finished product.

Models have been developed to analyze inventory practices for both independent and dependent demand. Order-quantity (how much) and order-point (when) models are closely associated with independent demand. Material requirements planning (MRP) and just-in-time (JIT) scheduling have been developed for dependent demand. MRP and JIT are discussed later in this chapter.

Materials Handling   Designing and operating a production process requires an efficient materials-handling system for moving materials from one manufacturing stage to another. Materials handling includes moving raw materials from the loading dock through inspection, production, and storage to the distribution system.[18]

Fixed path and variable path

The equipment used can be classified as fixed path or variable path. Fixed-path equipment includes hoists, conveyors, and the like. Variable-path equipment includes trucks, forklifts, railroads, and aircraft. The type of equipment required depends on the nature of the material to be moved, its path, and its volume.

Materials handling also concerns service organizations, such as banks, airlines, and post offices. Instead of moving raw materials through a manufacturing plant, these organizations are concerned with the flow of customers. Regardless of the "material" to be moved, the following principles apply:

1. Keep the transportation distance as short as possible.

2. Eliminate congestion areas by avoiding crossovers, backtracking, and other congestion patterns.

3. Keep the material moving, or minimize the delays at terminal points.

4. Carry payloads both ways (coming and going) whenever possible.

5. Carry full loads.

6. Use gravity if possible; if not, choose another inexpensive and reliable source of energy.[19]

Material Requirements Planning (MRP)   The increasing complexity of manufacturing processes has made better control of inventory and scheduling more important than ever. The computerized data information system called **material requirements planning (MRP)** was designed for this reason. MRP creates a framework for factory management, as Figure 15.2 shows.

How MRP is used

Management and *sales* provide customer orders and orders to produce goods for stock in the MRP system. *Inventory* information comes from regular inventory records. MRP coordinates this information with a *bill of material* prepared by production engineers, indicating how the product is put together

FIGURE 15.2
The role of material requirements planning (MRP) (*Source:* Armine/Ritchey/Moody, *Manufacturing Organization and Management,* 5/e, © 1987, p. 256. Adapted by permission of Prentice-Hall, Inc., Englewood Cliffs, New Jersey.)

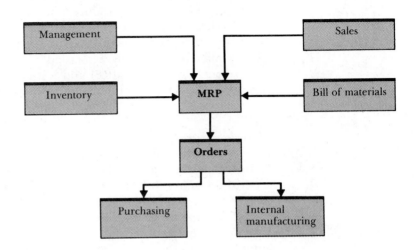

from its parts to the final assembly. The items are made into a master schedule, which is the main tool of MRP. The master schedule can project material and capacity requirements over a period of time. MRP then issues orders for materials either through purchasing or through the internal manufacturing facility.[20]

MRP is commonly used in assembly or fabrication operations. It is best suited for operations that have one or more of the following characteristics: end products produced from many components, assemblies, and materials; dependent demand; or demand for items that is highly variable or discontinuous. MRP has four objectives:

1. *Minimizing inventory.* MRP determines the quantity of an item needed to meet the master schedule. The item can be processed as needed, eliminating the cost of carrying it in inventory for safety's sake.

2. *Reducing production and delivery lead times.* MRP coordinates inventories, procurement, and production, thereby eliminating production delays. It sets up manufacturing activities in priority order by assigning dates to production activities.

Objectives of MRP

3. *Making realistic commitments.* With MRP, production can give marketing timely information on likely completion dates. This is possible because the MRP system contains the bill of materials, inventory status, procurement and production lead times, and a schedule of the workload currently being handled. As potential new orders are added to the system, the production manager can determine how the revised workload can be handled with existing capacity.

4. *Improving efficiency.* Savings result from the fact that components are available when needed. This, in turn, results in optimal inventory levels, the need for fewer workers, fewer production interruptions, and so on.[21]

Just-in-Time Scheduling (JIT)   Developed in Japan, **just-in-time scheduling (JIT)** combines purchasing, materials management, and inventory control. JIT works this way: the manufacturing or assembly operation needing parts tells its parts department or vendor which items it requires. This precise supplying of parts matches the operation's needs, thereby eliminating excessive inventory and streamlining manufacturing costs.[22] JIT differs from material requirements planning in that JIT refers to the exact day or hour that a part is needed; MRP is usually content to provide parts in the right week.[23]

JIT scheduling

Work Force Decisions

Like managers in other areas, production-operations managers are concerned with the human element and its impact on operational performance. An integral part of the operations manager's job is to design systems that consider both the physical and psychological elements of each job. The manager also must develop a way to evaluate the performance of production workers and to take corrective action as needed to improve productivity.

Ergonomics in the Office   For years, designers of production equipment and manufacturing plants have focused on worker comfort, safety, and productivity. Now they are turning their attention to the office, designing office jobs to alleviate eyestrain and back pain, and to improve office workers' productivity. **Ergonomics**, or human engineering, is the science concerned with modifying jobs and job-related tools and equipment to improve job satisfaction without hindering employee efficiency. Figure 15.3 illustrates a work station designed to make the employee more comfortable and efficient.

Human engineering

As the use of microcomputers in offices increases, so does the need to redesign jobs. In a study by T. J. Springer involving a thousand participants, two-thirds of the workers complained of physical discomfort after microcomputers were installed. Participants listed back and neck pains, visual stress, poor seating, inadequate work areas, and uncomfortable furniture as unpleasant aspects of their jobs. But when ergonomically designed furniture was introduced, absenteeism and medical expenses dropped. In addition, employee productivity increased 15%.[24]

There are several problem areas in offices. With the increasing use of personal computers, office workers are becoming more and more sedentary. Ergonomically designed chairs improve support to key body areas and eliminate many of the seating problems cited by workers. Lighting also is a major problem in the modern office. Countless ailments, especially headaches and eyestrain, are being blamed on computer video monitors. Because of this, high-resolution monitors and recessed fixtures that diffuse light and minimize surface brightness are becoming common in the modern office. Some sound is a comfort to workers, but too much noise can cause distractions. Intermittent noise from printers, ringing telephones, and so on should be kept out of the workplace as much as possible.

Ergonomically designed offices

FIGURE 15.3
An ergonomically
designed work station

Companies also are paying more attention to pleasing colors, appropriate textures for fabrics and carpeting, and even the shape of the buildings themselves. In addition, more and more firms are providing workout and social centers, as well as cafeterias.[25] As a result, job satisfaction and productivity are higher, absenteeism is lower, and the overall work environment is improved.

Evaluating Worker Performance   To evaluate a worker's output properly, the manager must be able to compare it with set standards. (See Chapter 14 under the section "Work Performance Control.") Several techniques are used to set standards. First proposed by Frederick W. Taylor, *time and motion study* involves timing the various motions required to perform a repetitive task in a prescribed manner. The times then are added to find the length of an entire work cycle and then the number of cycles in a prescribed period. The manager using *predetermined time standards* defines the basic elements of a job and the time it takes to perform them. The times then are added together to arrive at a total time value for the task being studied.[26] *Work sampling* involves taking random observations of workers to determine the percentage of time spent in productive and nonproductive activities.

Setting output standards

Because wage rates often are tied directly to labor standards, it is essential that standard times and rates be arrived at carefully. Production standards, piece-rate pay, bonus pay, and so on, directly depend on work measurement.

Quality Assurance Decisions

The last major decision area facing production-operations managers involves quality control. Whether an item is a "quality" product depends on personal perception and how well the product conforms to the quality standards in the design specifications.

The production manager's objective is to assure that the product meets the established specifications. To do so, the production manager must be able to measure the output of the transformation process, compare it against standards, analyze variations, and take corrective action as needed.

Achieving quality requires inspecting all goods produced or inspecting a sample of the items. Because total inspection is costly and because a sample can yield reliable results, most companies opt for sampling.

Two types of problems can arise when the production manager uses a sample as a basis for judging an entire batch of output. Both problems are due to incomplete information. First, the manager may make a *Type I error.* This happens when the sample indicates that the manufacturing process is unsatisfactory when, in fact, it is satisfactory. The second problem, a *Type II error,* occurs when the sample suggests that all is well with the process when it isn't. Type I errors result in needless inspection, lost production time, and additional start-up costs. Type II errors cause high levels of rejects, meaning that parts must be reworked and that customer goodwill may be lost.

Type I, Type II errors

We can judge any given product or service on a number of different characteristics, but from the standpoint of quality control, we should concentrate on a few critical characteristics.[27] The product itself generally dictates the inspection procedure. For example, wine and coffee are inspected by taste and smell, engine pistons are measured by calipers, and the quality of an airline's service is judged by its promptness and safety record.

Sampling

Inspection can take place while the production process is going on or after it has been completed. Ongoing inspections are part of *process control,* whereas *acceptance sampling* involves inspecting finished goods. Table 15.2 lists the conditions governing the choice of process control versus acceptance sampling.

TABLE 15.2
Factors affecting the selection of process control versus acceptance sampling

| CONDITIONS | |
PROCESS CONTROL	ACCEPTANCE SAMPLING
Inspection cost per unit is low.	Inspection cost per unit is high.
Consequences of defective output are high.	Consequences of defective output are not serious.
Inspection does not harm the product.	Inspection is harmful to the product.
The cost of adjusting the process is minimal.	Process control is not feasible.

Although inspection can take place at different points in the conversion process, it should, if possible, take place before critical operations are performed.[28] Raw materials and component parts can be inspected on arrival at the plant or even before they are shipped. In the production process, the location of inspection stations depends on the production layout. A *product layout,* such as an automobile assembly line, allows inspection almost anywhere along the line. A *process layout,* such as a custom cabinet shop, requires roving inspectors. A *fixed-position layout*—such as a shipyard, with its stationary product—requires inspection in one place. Inspection and testing also can be done in specialized laboratories with testing equipment, as in the case of pharmaceutical products.

Ways to inspect

The Impact of Technology

Technology in information and production has a significant effect on jobs because it provides information quickly, increases productivity and efficiency, and reduces costs. But it also can cause **technostress**, which is the inability of individuals to adjust to changing technology. People suffering from technostress transfer technology-related stress from work to their personal lives. Not using the new technology well consistently, they may disrupt communication in the organization or make more errors in their work.[29]

Technostress

Improvements in production technology have been quick and sometimes painful. New production technology that means improved efficiency for management can mean job displacement and unemployment for workers. Such technological advances have occurred in robotics, computer-integrated manufacturing (CIM), and other areas.

ON-LINE MANAGEMENT

Robots Perform a Variety of Jobs

Five years ago, the auto industry purchased 90% of all the industrial robots sold in the United States, primarily for welding and painting jobs on assembly lines. But today, nearly half of all robots sold go to customers in other industries. Robots are used to drill and rivet Sikorsky helicopters, unload Tecumseh engine housings, handle radioactive fuel rods for Metaphysics, Inc., and smooth edges on Bendix aircraft parts. The jobs being done by robots, in fact, are as varied as the companies that use them.

No longer do companies want dumb robots that can't be linked with other machines to enhance their power. Virtually every buyer now insists that robots be a part of a computer-based system. But as robots are designed to perform more complex tasks, their price tags go up. Computer hardware and software used to program robots often account for one-third of their total cost. Still, purchasing robots without computers may be unwise. Brian Carlisle, president of Adept Technology, insists that buying a dumb robot is like buying a manual typewriter. A growing number of executives agree. Although the cost of programmable robots is on the rise, their versatility warrants the higher prices.

Source: Doron P. Levin, "Robotics: A Special Report," *Wall Street Journal,* August 8, 1985, p. 1.

Robotics

We often think of robots as an attempt to duplicate human beings. Actually, a robot is by definition a "programmable, multifunctional manipulator designed to move material, parts, tools, or specialized devices through variable programmed motions for the performance of a variety of tasks."[30] Robots not only reduce labor costs but also can take over hazardous or tedious jobs and increase quality and output. On-Line Management on page 411 describes the uses and costs of robots.

Advantages of robots

Introducing robots into a company's production process can mean many changes. Production schedules and material handling requirements may be revised and maintenance requirements increased. So far, introducing robots into the workplace has met little worker resistance when managers take care in selecting sites for initial installations and gradually introduce them to employees. Of course, workers are primarily concerned about possibly losing their jobs to the robots. Experience has shown that if robots are supplements rather than replacements on production lines, employees are more likely to welcome the new technology. Although some robots totally replace employees, robot operators, technicians, engineers, and programmers are still needed.

Robots in the workplace

This creates opportunities for employees who retrain in these areas, as well as for a new generation of engineers, computer scientists, and technicians.

Computer-Integrated Manufacturing (CIM)

A second area where production technology has advanced is **computer-integrated manufacturing (CIM).** According to Harry B. Thompson, a management consultant specializing in manufacturing technology, "CIM is changing the way in which businesses are planned, organized, and managed."[31] CIM consolidates production with a firm's information and control system, linking manufacturing to the operations of the entire organization. Thus, CIM is really a combination of computer-aided design (CAD) and computer-aided manufacturing (CAM): **CAD/CAM.**

CAD/CAM

CAD refers to the use of computers in drafting and design. On the other hand, CAM is the automated machine tools and systems coordinating the drafting and design into actual production. CAD and CAM also can work independently of one another. In addition to designing and producing items, CAD/CAM can generate materials bills, purchase orders, and inventory reports that management uses to evaluate the current and future status of production.[32]

One company benefiting from CAD/CAM is General Electric. Since it began using CAD/CAM to produce industrial and home circuit breakers in its Plainville, Connecticut, plant, production has risen 60%. Instead of lower-level designers' having to do the drafting by hand, higher-level designers work on terminals and store the images in the data base. They can make changes easily until satisfied with their work. After agreeing on a design, they can produce a prototype. It used to take seven to eight weeks to process a prototype because of the many changes, but now the same prototype can be designed in one week and processed in less than an hour.[33]

MIS: An Important Operational Tool

A **management information system (MIS),** commonly called a computer information system, helps managers make decisions. No area of a business benefits from MIS more directly than does the production-operations area.

An information system has several elements.[34] MIS personnel includes both managers who benefit from its use and the technical support staff. The computer hardware an MIS system uses can be either a large mainframe unit or a relatively inexpensive microcomputer. Procedures in the system assure that proper data is put into the computer, processed, and used. In a materials handling system, for example, procedures would be established for ordering, receiving, inspecting, invoicing, storing, costing, counting, and disbursing

ON-LINE MANAGEMENT

MIS at Direct Sales Tire Company

Information technology has changed the way the Direct Sales Tire Company does business.

Several years ago, the Colorado-based company installed an integrated computer system in its headquarters and equipped each of its fifty-five retail stores with a personal computer linked to it by telephone line. The system gives corporate managers and store managers access to the central pool of information about inventory, shipping orders, and financial status. When sales are made, the computer reduces inventory figures immediately. The staff processes daily reports on sales volume, and purchase orders are printed to keep inventory up to date.

The system also evaluates price and purchase agreements for needed items so the best possible purchase can be made. All this information is managed by a staff of less than twenty. The result has been dramatic increases in profits for the company.

Source: Mike Lewis, "Cutting the Automation Giant Down to Your Office Size," *Nation's Business*, September 1984, p. 64.

materials. The heart of a management information system is its data base, which consists of information used in the decision-making process. The size and type of data base used depend on the computer hardware and software of each computer system. Since the reports generated from the data are to be used by managers at various levels, the data base should be as complete and accurate as possible. On-Line Management on page 413 illustrates how the Direct Sales Tire Company used MIS to increase its profits.

Review

✓ *The development of production-operations management.* Production-operations management is concerned with providing goods and services by converting resource inputs into finished products. Manufacturing management, production management, and operations management all refer to the same general discipline, but the terminology has changed over the years. Today, the term *operations management* is widely used to reflect the growing importance of service industries in our economy.

✔ *The production-operations process.* A production system transforms resource inputs into outputs. In a manufacturing plant, raw materials, energy, labor, and capital are transformed into physical goods; in a service firm, these same inputs are converted into service outputs. The job of the production-operations manager is to manage this transformation process.

✔ *The kinds of decisions production-operations managers make.* Production-operations managers make decisions in five areas of responsibility: process and product design, capacity, materials, workforce, and quality.

Process and product design decisions define how the product or service is made. Where to locate the facility is one of the manager's major production decisions. Having chosen the plant location, the manager next decides on the physical layout of the facilities. Product design decisions focus on the type of materials used, quality requirements, and the number of processes required.

Capacity planning decisions are aimed at providing sufficient output capacity for the firm—not too much and not too little. Capacity decisions include developing capacity plans over long-, medium-, and short-term ranges. Forecasting, facilities planning, aggregate planning, and scheduling decisions fall into this category.

Production-operations managers make decisions about when and how much to order. They also manage the logistics system from the purchasing stage through raw materials inventory, work in process, and finished goods inventory. The objective of the production-operations manager is to ensure that adequate raw materials are available when needed and to see that the production process operates efficiently.

Another area of decision responsibility is concerned with managing the work force in the production-operations area. Responsibilities include designing the workplace ergonomically, setting performance standards, and evaluating worker performance.

The last major area of responsibility is that of quality control. Because the objective is to ensure that the product meets the established specifications, the production manager must either inspect all goods produced or inspect a sample of the items. Inspection can take place at different points in the transformation process, but it should be done before critical operations are performed.

✔ *The impact of technology on production-operations management.* Technology is having a profound impact on production-operations management. It provides information quickly, increases productivity and efficiency, and reduces costs. But it can also cause technostress, which is the inability of individuals to adjust to changing technology. Robots, computer-integrated manufacturing, and management information systems have totally changed the production environment.

THE MANAGER'S DICTIONARY

As an extra review of the chapter, try defining the following terms. If you have trouble with any of them, refer to the page numbers listed.

production-operations
   management (POM) (397)
production system (397)
continuous production
   systems (399)
intermittent production
   systems (399)
qualitative forecasts (401)
time series forecasts (401)
causal forecasts (402)
simulation (402)
facilities planning (402)

aggregate production
   planning (402)
scheduling (402)
purchasing (403)
procurement costs (404)
carrying costs (404)
stockout costs (404)
setup costs (404)
production costs (404)
material requirements
   planning (MRP) (405)

just-in-time scheduling (JIT)
   (407)
ergonomics (407)
technostress (410)
computer-integrated
   manufacturing (CIM)
   (412)
CAD/CAM (412)
management information
   system (MIS) (412)

REVIEW QUESTIONS

1. Production is usually referred to as a transformation process. Why?

2. What are the elements of a production process? Give examples to illustrate the process.

3. Name the five major decision areas faced by production-operations managers. What type of decisions fall into each category?

4. What are the characteristics of a continuous production system? an intermittent production system?

5. Discuss the importance of capacity planning. Why is it important for the production manager to determine the "optimal" capacity of a plant?

6. Name and explain the various types of forecasting.

7. Why is scheduling considered a resource allocation problem? Explain.

8. What does materials management encompass? Discuss.

9. What types of costs are associated with maintaining inventory?

10. How is inventory affected by MRP and JIT? Explain.

11. Describe the various methods for determining employee performance standards.

12. How can a production manager ensure that output meets the desired quality specifications?

13. How has technology affected the production process? Give examples.

14. What are the advantages of using robots in manufacturing organizations? the drawbacks?

15. Discuss the importance of MIS in production-operations management.

MANAGEMENT CHALLENGE

1. If you were the manager of a fast-food restaurant, what types of production-operations decisions would you make? Explain.

2. Which of the decision categories listed above would be most important to the success of your business? Why?

3. What are the similarities between a fast-food restaurant and a manufacturing organization? the differences?

4. How would you know if your operation was efficient? What steps would you take to make certain that your restaurant was being run at peak efficiency?

CASE 15.1

Toro Snowed by Poor Control[35]

In the early 1980s, the Minneapolis-based Toro Company—which manufactures yard-maintenance equipment—experienced the most dismal days in its long history. Sales plummeted, inventories piled up, customer complaints about quality skyrocketed, top-level executives left the company, stockholders didn't receive dividends, and one bank "walked out" on the company.

Because of light snowfalls, overzealous forecasts, and a lack of control, Toro had a thirty-month surplus of snowblowers. To liquidate the oversupply of inventory, Toro tried distributing some mowers and snowblowers through mass merchandisers. These merchandisers, who customarily operate on low-profit margins, began selling the equipment at significantly lower prices than the typical hardware store dealer did. As a result, the company lost many dealers.

Product quality suffered, too. Kenneth Melrose, who was promoted to president in 1981, contends that unacceptable quality was the result of bypassing development and testing in the production process. To restore the quality image the company once had, Melrose appointed a vice-president for product excellence.

By 1985 the company had begun to turn things around. The income statement was back

in the black, Toro's work force and inventories had been trimmed, sales had improved considerably, and the firm's debt-equity ratio had been reduced dramatically. The turnaround came as a result of both sacrifice and controls. Incentive compensation for executives was scrapped, salary freezes and wage reductions were imposed, half the work force was fired, Toro's chairperson and nine vice-presidents left, and the plush corporate headquarters was abandoned in favor of Toro's Minneapolis plant.

Although these changes were difficult, Melrose now concludes that they were in the best interest of the company. Stringent controls now keep management aware of inventory buildups. "Now we can go through a year with little snow and still be fairly sold," he says confidently.

Questions

1. Of the five major decision areas discussed in Chapter 15, which area(s) caused management of Toro Company the most problems?

2. Do you feel that such drastic action was called for? Why or why not?

CASE 15.2

Optimized Production Technology:
The Goldratt Approach[36]

The key to production efficiency, according to management consultant Eli Goldratt, is to control the flow of parts into bottlenecks. He says that identifying a plant's bottlenecks in advance and then scheduling the work flow with them in mind will increase manufacturing output dramatically.

Considered a genius by some production managers who have adopted his approach to production scheduling, Goldratt contends that most of the $10 billion spent in the past thirty years to plan the flow of materials through manufacturing processes has been wasted. He also argues that maximizing a firm's output will not lead to maximizing its profit.

Goldratt's optimized production technology (OPT) is a two-pronged tool: a simulated production program and a set of rules governing production operations. His system requires production managers to focus on the flow of materials through manufacturing operations in an effort to detect buildups—bottlenecks—that can have many causes.

The key is to keep potential bottlenecks running at their capacity while carefully controlling the flow of materials into them. Besides minimizing inventory levels, such an approach also reduces overall production costs. In Goldratt's opinion, it is better to permit a worker to stop working temporarily than to allow work efforts to cause inventory to pile up.

OPT computer software simulates a firm's manufacturing process to detect bottlenecks before they occur. Then labor and materials are scheduled so that they flow freely through the system. But the most significant aspect of the system, Goldratt believes, is his management philosophy. He claims that a plant will not necessarily produce the most product at the lowest cost by operating at full throttle. Consequently, a production manager should allow a machine to remain idle if that is what is required to keep goods flowing through bottlenecks.

Some production-operations managers have difficulty adapting to Goldratt's philosophy. Part of their unwillingness to modify their behavior comes from their training. For example, traditional accounting teaches that it is better to produce 500, rather than 5, parts on a machine. But if 450 of those parts are going to sit in inventory, traditional accounting is wrong.

Questions
1. How does Goldratt's OPT system differ from that of JIT? Explain.
2. Why are managers skeptical of Goldratt's system? Is their skepticism justified?

CHAPTER OUTLINE

Break-Even Analysis

Solving a Problem

Drawbacks of Break-Even Analysis

Models for Inventory Decisions

Linear Programming

Elements of Linear Programming

A Maximization Problem

Objective Function • Constraints • Graphing the Constraints • Determining the Optimum Solution

Algebraic Solution

The Simplex Method

Network Analysis

The Gantt Chart: Forerunner of PERT and CPM

Program Evaluation and Review Technique

The PERT Network • Determining Expected Elapsed Times • The Critical Path • Slack Time • A Final Comment

Queuing Models

Simulation

Quantitative Control Tools

Computers in the Casino

Gambling casinos in Las Vegas and Atlantic City are turning to computers to help keep track of their profits and their high rollers.

Many casino owners have become convinced in recent years that an information system that provides them with timely, quantitative data can ease the pinch of competition and tough economic conditions.[1] And, like many businesses, casinos are seeing tough times. Profit margins have slipped from 15% to 7 or 8% in this $5 billion industry.

Once, credit accounts were kept on cards filed manually by cashiers; today, the accounts are stored in a computer data bank. Other tidbits are in the data bank, too—regular players' favorite games and time spent at each game, their betting patterns, and their favorite restaurants, hotels, and entertainers. Information like this provides casino managers with a very effective marketing tool.

Credit limits can be computed with a "ruin factor," which is the probability that a player will lose a certain amount of money based on the way he or she plays. A "complimentary" limit is set, based on probable loss. As much as 20% of a casino's revenue may be spent on gifts ranging from free drinks to air transportation from anywhere in the world. A player who bets an average of $25 in fifteen minutes may be given free parking, for instance. One who bets $1,000 a hand may be given free lodging, a limousine, and free meals at the casino's best restaurants.

Rating customers' gambling patterns and encouraging them to visit your casino is a vital part of a casino's financial success, said Clyde Turner, chief

419

financial officer for the Golden Nugget in Las Vegas. "If you don't understand which of your customers are best," he said, "you're misallocating your resources."[2]

Casinos also use computer surveillance to control costs and to improve efficiency. Bally's in Atlantic City, which monitors each slot machine by computer, has lowered personnel costs and can tell which machines do best in which areas. Computers also provide deviation reports on machines that pay off outside of normal probability curves. These deviations may signal mechanical failure or tampering.[3]

Although they have made great strides, casinos are still considered to be in the early stages of automation. They will probably become more automated as the gaming business becomes more competitive, for it will take more than Lady Luck for casinos to survive.

Preview

Whether they manage gambling casinos, hospitals, or foundries, managers today are finding it harder to rely on intuition and hunches. Today's business environment is so complex and the competition so acute that managers must be sure to make decisions based on the best information available. Quantitative tools specifically designed to solve business problems can be a great help in making cost-effective decisions.

Managers' decisions have always been based on qualitative *and* quantitative information. But in recent years there has been a dramatic shift toward measuring, or quantifying, the variables that affect decisions. This shift is partly the result of newer, more efficient means of gathering data. The primary reason, however, is that more and more quantitative tools and techniques are available that can be widely applied throughout business, either manually or with a computer.

As pointed out in Chapter 2 (see the section headed "The Quantitative School"), quantitative management is the logical extension of scientific management. It is nothing more than management science—a systematic approach to identifying and solving problems through the scientific method. The roots of quantitative management can be traced to Frederick W. Taylor, Henry Gantt, Frank and Lillian Gilbreth, and other pioneers of scientific management. Modern quantitative methods extend and refine their methods.

For the manager, using mathematical models has several advantages when making decisions. First, it forces the manager to think through a problem and all its variables logically. It also gives the manager fast and accurate data, which can lead to alternative solutions. Finally and perhaps most important, using mathematical models yields more precise and accurate results than when the manager relies on intuition alone.

Quantitative tools have proliferated in industry since World War II. In fact, there are so many that no single textbook can adequately explain them all. We will describe the most commonly used quantitative control tools and show how they help managers use resources wisely. This chapter will describe:

✔ The uses of break-even analysis

✔ How managers use models for inventory decisions

✔ How linear programming helps managers use their resources wisely

✔ The use of network analysis in visualizing complex tasks

✔ What queuing models can do for firms that serve customers or for scheduling the flow of materials

✔ How business uses simulation

Break-Even Analysis

Tools to aid managers

A manager's life is full of questions about production, pricing, and inventory. The prudent manager must make decisions that will minimize inventory costs without incurring stock outages, ensure production at the optimum operating level, price goods to assure the best profit, and use all resources effectively. Managers have a number of tools available today that can help them make these decisions, including break-even analysis, models for inventory decisions, linear programming, network analysis, queuing models, and simulation. These quantitative tools not only provide precise answers but also require a manager to think through a problem thoroughly and to envision all the variables affecting the ultimate decision. Let's talk about break-even analysis first.

Break-even analysis, often referred to as **cost-volume-profit analysis,** involves determining the number of items a firm must produce or dollars it must earn to cover exactly the costs of producing those items. When total sales revenues equal total costs, profit is zero. At that point the firm *breaks even.* If revenues fall below that point, the firm loses money. If they rise above that point, the firm makes a profit. Break-even analysis is useful in answering a number of interesting questions:

1. How much will a price change affect profits?

2. What revenues will be generated at a given sales volume?

3. If the product line is expanded, will revenues increase?

4. What increase in sales-promotion expenditures is justified to increase sales volume?

FIGURE 16.1
Traditional break-even
chart

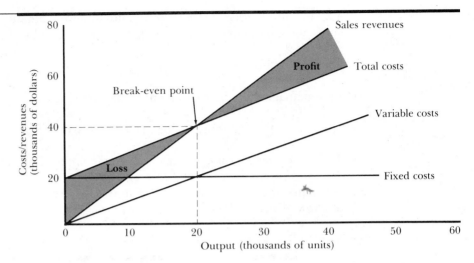

A traditional break-even chart is shown in Figure 16.1. Sales volume in units is shown on the horizontal axis, dollars on the vertical axis. The four lines on the chart represent fixed costs, variable costs, total costs, and sales revenue.

Fixed and variable costs

Fixed costs are represented by a horizontal line because they are expenses remaining constant over a given range of production volume. Included in this category are rent, executive salaries, insurance, taxes, and other costs that do not change as production output changes. **Variable costs** are those that change as volume increases or decreases. Raw materials and labor used in manufacturing the product fall into this category. For purposes of break-even analysis, variable costs per unit are assumed to remain constant. The *total cost* line represents the sum of fixed and variable costs. Hence, at a zero volume of production, total costs are $20,000—the amount of fixed costs. As volume increases, the total cost line reflects both fixed and variable costs. The *revenue* line represents the amount of sales dollars generated by selling some quantity of the product at a constant price. The **break-even point** in Figure 16.1 is 20,000 units. At this point, total costs equal total revenues.

Total cost and revenue lines

The break-even point on a chart (Figure 16.1) is easily visualized. But a precise chart isn't always available or takes too much time to draw; consequently, an algebraic solution is often a more precise starting point and is easier to calculate. The mathematical solution is based on the fact that total revenues and total costs are equal at the break-even point. Use these labels.

$$P = \text{price per unit}$$
$$Q = \text{number of units demanded}$$
$$FC = \text{fixed costs}$$
$$VC = \text{variable costs}$$

The formula for calculating the break-even point in units is

$$Q = \frac{FC}{P - VC}$$

The difference between unit price and variable cost per unit is the contribution to profit and fixed costs, commonly called the **contribution margin.** Therefore, the break-even point (in units) can be determined by dividing the fixed costs by the contribution margin.

Solving a Problem

As the owner-manager of Baseball Enterprises, a firm that manufactures and sells Little League baseballs, you want to determine how many baseballs you must sell before you begin to make a profit. You are given these data.

Calculating the break-even point

Current demand: 40,000 units
Selling price per unit: $3.50
Fixed costs: $100,000
Variable cost per unit: $1.50

Thus,

$$Q = \frac{FC}{P - VC}$$

$$= \frac{\$100,000}{\$3.50 - \$1.50}$$

$$= \frac{\$100,000}{\$2}$$

$$= 50,000 \text{ units (break-even point)}$$

To determine the break-even point in dollars, you can simply multiply the break-even point in units by the selling price.

$$Q \text{ (dollars)} = P(Q)$$
$$= \$3.50(50,000)$$
$$= \$175,000$$

Drawbacks of Break-Even Analysis

Although break-even analysis can be a very useful tool, managers should be aware of its limitations. First, variable costs are not always constant over time, as On the Job on page 424 shows. Increased labor costs resulting from overtime pay, changes in the cost of raw materials, machine maintenance, and so on can cause the unit cost of producing an item to fluctuate significantly.

ON THE JOB

Breaking Even at Mobay Chemical

Mobay Chemical Corporation was struggling through the 1982 recession with some very bad figures. Net income of the Bayer A.G. subsidiary had plummeted from $57.7 million to a loss of $8.3 million. Sales had dropped nearly 10% to $1.1 billion.

Strategic Planning Manager Howard Martin was worried about whether his company's break-even point had changed over the years. He wanted to know whether profits were keeping up with costs. He wanted more history than the company accountants could give him—information about how much the company's fixed costs and break-even point had changed, how the 1982 earnings compared with a time when Mobay was operating at a comparable capacity, and what profits would be at full capacity.

To answer those questions, Martin spent months developing what he called a "profit geometry" analysis of the company's break-even history. He adjusted fixed costs by weight-averaging sales of products per unit of capacity utilization and adjusted for inflation and capacity additions, among other things. The result was adjusted numbers for gross margins and operating results that are consistent over time.

He developed two maximum performance curves for break-even gross margins and operating results at various levels of capacity. Then Martin plotted the company's actual results for the past ten years with the curves.

Martin found that the adjusted 1982 results were even higher than the 50% capacity at which the company was running. He wasn't surprised. "In fact we were doing no worse than we might have expected, given our prior record," Martin said. "Without that historical perspective, we might have taken much more dramatic action than we needed to. We might have laid off a lot of people or sold off businesses or closed down capacity."

Not all managers are as enthusiastic as Martin is about profit geometry. Dennis Piper, director of investment analysis for Pillsbury Company, says that his company uses other successful methods. "We're so diversified, we don't even make an attempt to calculate break-even for the company as a whole. It would be comparing apples and oranges."

But Martin has confidence in his system, especially in tough economic times. "The next time we have a real recession and people get in trouble on utilization of capacity, I think they'll start thinking about break-even analysis," he said. "Financial planners need to figure out how often they make back their cost of capital and how much of their problem relates to utilization of capacity."

Source: Jill Andresky, "Break-dancing in the Dark," *Forbes,* August 12, 1985, p. 68.

Limitations

Second, competition and changes in manufacturing costs may force the product's selling price up or down. Any price change caused by such forces alters the break-even point. Finally, it is often difficult to categorize a cost as either fixed or variable. For example, machinery used to manufacture an item is generally considered a fixed cost. But if a plant is operating at capacity, the cost of leasing or buying additional machinery to increase production is not a fixed cost.

Models for Inventory Decisions

Inventory decisions are very important to managers. As mentioned in Chapter 14 in the section "Inventory Control," too much inventory is costly, while too little inventory can result in lost sales and irate customers. A manager must, therefore, develop an inventory control system that minimizes storage cost and at the same time ensures that stock is not depleted. These problems faced Warner-Lambert executives until they made some changes, as shown in the In-Box on page 426. The inventory control system is built around two questions: When should an order be placed? How much should be ordered?

Types of inventory costs

There are two basic types of inventory costs—the cost of placing an order and the cost of carrying inventory. The optimum order quantity and the optimum order point are functions of these two costs. The **optimum order quantity** is determined by analyzing total cost, which is the sum of the ordering and carrying costs. The **optimum order point** typically is governed by inventory levels; that is, an order is placed when the units on hand reach a certain level. Total costs can be minimized by ordering the right quantity at the right time.

The optimum order quantity and optimum order point can be easily calculated using these formulas (assuming a known and constant demand and lead time).

Let:

C = Incremental cost of placing an order
c_u = Annual cost of carrying one unit of inventory
D = Demand in units (annual)
Q = Optimum order quantity

Calculating optimum quantity

We can obtain the optimum order quantity by using this formula:

$$Q = \sqrt{\frac{2CD}{c_u}}$$

Example

To see how the process works, assume that the Roebuck Distribution Company, a wholesaler of industrial valves, wants to reduce its inventory costs by determining the optimum number of valves to order. The annual demand

THE IN-BOX

Japanese System "Just in Time" for Warner-Lambert

A fast and flexible manufacturing system pioneered by Japanese auto makers is bringing big savings to a company that makes little products.

Warner-Lambert, which manufactures pharmaceuticals and consumer goods ranging from Chiclets to razor blades, is saving about $300 million a year under the program. And it has a cigar-chomping manufacturing management consultant named James Harbour to thank.

The company had been using the costly, large-batch production system, with numerous quality checks of the finished products. But this system can be riddled with damage and delay. Warner-Lambert officials also were concerned about the cost of the large inventories they were carrying. Then Harbour stepped in.

He told Warner-Lambert's aghast executives that quality is the result of tight controls on the production process, not after-the-fact inspections. Material had to flow without interruption through the manufacturing process, and inventory had to be thought of as an expensive liability, Harbour said. The goal, he added, should be the Japanese "just-in-time" inventory system, in which products are manufactured in the least possible time with the least possible inventories. This way, the company wouldn't be stuck with warehouses full of unordered goods or caught short when orders came in. Another advantage would be that executives could dispense with big production runs based on long-range forecasts.

Warner-Lambert executives did what Harbour, former director of manufacturing engineering at Chrysler, told them to do. The company's Adams Brands division in Toronto tightened up tolerances on machines that made the candy-coated gum called Chiclets, and damage fell 60%. Its West German pharmaceutical subsidiary cut the time needed to produce a low-blood-pressure drug from thirty-two to fifteen working days with no loss in quality. At Warner-Lambert Canada, changing the molds on a machine that makes cough-syrup bottles used to take fifty-four hours. Now it takes sixteen.

But perhaps the biggest success story of the program is in its Capsugel division. Before Harbour arrived, Warner-Lambert executives were planning to spend $125 million on new equipment for the division. Now it's getting more than 90% more output from the old machines. By 1986, the company expected to get 13% more from the old machines than it could have from the new equipment.

Source: Steven Flax, "An Auto Man Tunes Up Warner-Lambert," *Fortune*, March 4, 1985, pp. 70–78.

for valves is 600 units, the cost of placing an order is $6, and the average carrying cost per unit is $.50. Using these data, we can calculate the optimum number of units to order.

$$Q = \sqrt{\frac{2CD}{c_u}}$$

$$Q = \sqrt{\frac{2(\$6)(600)}{\$.50}}$$

$$Q = \sqrt{\frac{\$7,200}{\$.50}}$$

$$Q = \sqrt{14,400}$$

$$Q = 120$$

Determining optimum order point

Next, we will determine when to place an order (known as the order point). The order point obviously depends on the daily demand for valves and the amount of time it takes the manufacturer to deliver them. if the Roebuck Distribution Company is open for business 300 days per year, then the daily demand is 2 valves (600 valves/300 days). And if the delivery time is 3 working days, then an order should be placed when the inventory level reaches 6 units.

$$\text{Order Point} = \text{Daily Demand} \times \text{Lead Time}$$
$$= \quad 2 \quad \times \quad 3$$
$$= 6\text{ units}$$

Linear Programming

Linear programming (LP) is a quantitative tool that can be applied to any problem having two essential features: (1) competing uses for limited resources, (2) linear (straight-line) relationships between variables. In other words, linear programming helps managers to determine the best use of their resources as well as how to gain the most profit for the least expense. Simple problems can be solved manually. Complex problems that require working with large amounts of data can be solved with the aid of a computer. Here are a few of the kinds of problems that managers can solve by using linear programming:

- Determining the ideal portfolio mix for an investor to maximize returns

- Determining the best media mix for an advertising campaign to gain the greatest exposure

Types of problems for LP

- Establishing the best route for a salesperson to minimize the cost of covering a sales territory

- Determining the lowest-cost combination of resources in manufacturing fertilizer or other products that must meet certain chemical requirements

- Selecting the best locations for textile-manufacturing plants, bulk gasoline-distribution outlets, or other facilities

- Determining the best combination of food or beverage products to produce and sell to earn the most profits

- Assigning police cars, buses, or taxis to sections of a city in the most efficient manner

Elements of Linear Programming

Elements of LP problems

Linear programming encompasses two types of functions—objective and constraint. The **objective function** is a mathematical expression of the relationship between a dependent variable (profit, cost, and so on) and some other measure of output (quantity of items produced), yielding each item's contribution to profit, for example. The **constraint function** is a mathematical statement that expresses the restrictions on the system under study. For instance, the number of sheets of plywood that a manufacturer can produce is limited by the board feet of timber available. Similarly, the number of mechanical parts that a machinist can produce is limited by the hours available on a turret lathe. Constraints may be in the form of equalities or inequalities. Equalities exist when elements of a mathematical expression are arranged in such a manner that they equal another element or set of elements. Such mathematical expressions are represented by a sign meaning equal to ($=$). Inequalities are mathematical expressions showing that one element or set of elements is less than ($<$), greater than ($>$), less than or equal to ($\leq$), or greater than or equal to ($\geq$) another element or set of elements.

Problems that satisfy the requirements of the linear programming model and involve only two variables can be solved either algebraically or graphically. For example, the optimum combination of manufactured chairs and tables can be determined algebraically or graphically when each makes a different contribution to profit and each requires a different amount of processing in various areas of manufacturing. If the problem encompasses more than two variables—chairs, tables, and lecterns, for instance—the *simplex method* (discussed on page 431) can be used.

A Maximization Problem

LP problem example

The Cypress Manufacturing Company produces two products—boat paddles and birdhouses. Each paddle gives the company $4 of profit, and each birdhouse yields a profit of $8. A paddle requires four hours of processing in machine center A and two hours of processing in machine center B. A birdhouse requires six hours of processing in center A, six hours of processing in center B, and one hour of processing in center C. Machine center A has a maximum daily capacity of 120 hours, machine center B has a capacity of 72 hours, and machine center C has a capacity of 10 hours. Given this information, we want to determine the best combination of producing these two products and the daily profit the company would earn from making them.

Objective Function   The objective of this problem is to make the biggest profit by producing the best combination of boat paddles and birdhouses, each of which contributes to overall profit. Therefore, the objective function can be stated:

$$\text{Maximize profit} = \$4(P) + \$8(H)$$

where

P represents the number of paddles to be produced
H represents the number of houses to be produced

Constraints   The constraints are obvious. Profits are limited by the amount of time available in each processing center. The constraints can be expressed mathematically as follows.

$$4(P) + 6(H) \leq 120$$
$$2(P) + 6(H) \leq 72$$
$$1(H) \leq 10$$

We also need to add nonnegativity constraint statements. Because it is impossible to produce a negative number of paddles and houses, the nonnegativity constraints are:

$$P \geq 0$$
$$H \geq 0$$

Using the linear programming technique, we can now allocate the production capacity to the two products in a manner that will result in the greatest possible profit. The solution requires a graphical representation of all constraint functions as *equalities* for the purpose of determining the area of feasibility. This **area of feasibility**—which is the area of the graph enclosed by the constraint functions—represents all possible combinations of the products that can be physically produced. However, the optimum combination always occurs at a *vertex* of the polygon. Thus, we can find the optimum combination of products by solving the objective function equation, using the various combinations of products identified by each vertex of the polygon.

Graphing the Constraints   Remember that the constraints associated with Sections A, B, and C are

$$4(P) + 6(H) \leq 120$$
$$2(P) + 6(H) \leq 72$$
$$1(H) \leq 10$$

Area of feasibility

FIGURE 16.2
Graphical solution to
linear programming
problem

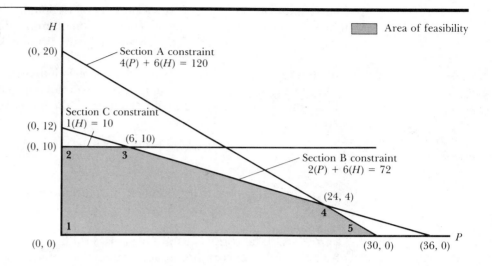

These constraints, graphed in the form of equalities, appear in Figure 16.2.

Determining the Optimum Solution   As we already pointed out, the optimum combination of paddles and houses is at one of the vertices of the area of feasibility. Therefore, we can determine the maximum profit by solving the objective function formula, using the various combinations of paddles and houses shown on the graph in Figure 16.2.

Optimum solution

$$
\begin{aligned}
\text{Vertex 1:} &\quad \$4(0) + \$8(0) = \$ \ 0 \\
\text{Vertex 2:} &\quad \$4(0) + \$8(10) = \$80 \\
\text{Vertex 3:} &\quad \$4(6) + \$8(10) = \$104 \\
\text{Vertex 4:} &\quad \$4(24) + \$8(4) = \$128 \\
\text{Vertex 5:} &\quad \$4(30) + \$8(0) = \$120
\end{aligned}
$$

The optimum combination of boat paddles and birdhouses is 24 and 4, respectively. This combination will yield a profit of $128.

Algebraic Solution

It is sometimes difficult, if not impossible, to read accurately the various combinations of products or resources from a graph. In other instances, a graph may not be readily available. In either situation, the manager can solve the problem algebraically by solving the constraint equations simultaneously. Once the combinations of products or resources are determined in this manner, they can be plugged into the objective function formula to arrive at the maximum profit or minimum cost.

The Simplex Method

Solving complex problems

All methods for solving linear programming problems are *algorithms*; that is, they follow step-by-step procedures for reaching the optimum solution. Algebraic methods can be used to solve problems of varying complexity.[4] The most widely used approach is the **simplex method** developed by George B. Dantzig. Based on matrix algebra, this method yields successively better solutions until the optimal solution is reached. In this procedure, an initial feasible solution is developed and tested. If it isn't the optimal solution, the most favorable terms of the objective function are used for the second feasible solution. This procedure is repeated until the best solution is obtained.[5] The simplex method can be used on a computer to solve complex linear programming problems quickly and efficiently.

Network Analysis

Advantages of network models

Planning and controlling—sometimes called the Siamese twins of management—are basic duties of all managers. Regardless of the nature of a task, the effective manager must think it through to visualize potential problems, risks, and opportunities. When the project is simple, a manager may be able to carry a mental picture of all its phases. This is particularly true if it is routine. When the task is a new, complex endeavor, though, portraying all activities and events as a network is helpful. A network can show the interrelationships of activities and can reveal bottlenecks that may interfere with the project. A diagram of all activities and events can show the manager where to put resources to reduce delays.

In situations where time is most important, the program evaluation and review technique (PERT) is a useful tool. In situations where project costs are important, PERT/cost or the critical path method (CPM) can be very useful techniques.

The Gantt Chart: Forerunner of PERT and CPM

Perhaps the first planning and control diagram that allowed managers to see the interrelationships of all segments of a project was the **Gantt chart,** developed by Henry Gantt. This chart graphically depicts the progress of work activities over time. Figure 16.3 illustrates the use of the Gantt chart in an auto body repair shop.

Illustration of Gantt chart

The figure shows that three different jobs are in progress. For this particular week, the Ford is scheduled for metal work and replacement of parts on Monday and Tuesday, sanding and masking on Wednesday, and painting and baking on Thursday and Friday. The Volkswagen is scheduled for metal work and replacement of parts on Monday, sanding and masking on Tuesday

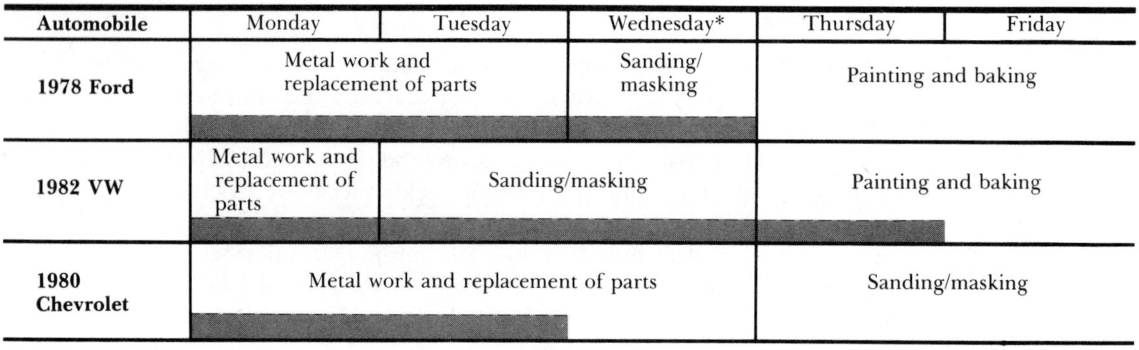

Automobile	Monday	Tuesday	Wednesday*	Thursday	Friday
1978 Ford	Metal work and replacement of parts		Sanding/ masking	Painting and baking	
1982 VW	Metal work and replacement of parts	Sanding/masking		Painting and baking	
1980 Chevrolet	Metal work and replacement of parts			Sanding/masking	

FIGURE 16.3
Gantt chart—auto body repair shop

and Wednesday, and painting and baking on Thursday and Friday. The Chevrolet is scheduled for metal work and parts on Monday, Tuesday, and Wednesday; sanding and masking on Thursday and Friday.

The shaded bars on the chart show current progress on the repair of each vehicle. The asterisk (*) denotes the overall situation at the end of Wednesday. A quick glance at the chart indicates that repair work on the Ford is on schedule, work on the Volkswagen is one day ahead of schedule, and work on the Chevrolet is behind schedule. This information will enable the shop supervisor to assign people working on the Volkswagen to work on the Chevrolet to get that job back on schedule.

The Gantt chart lets the manager evaluate the overall progress of jobs in process and pinpoint and control problems. The principles illustrated by the chart provide the basis for both PERT and CPM.

Program Evaluation and Review Technique

The **program evaluation and review technique (PERT)** was developed in 1957 through the combined efforts of the U.S. Navy and Booz, Allen, and Hamilton, a management consulting firm. Their objective was to expedite the research and development of the Polaris weapons system. At about the same time Du Pont scientists teamed up with computer experts from Remington Rand's Univac division to develop a network model to be used in constructing chemical plants. Known as the **critical path method (CPM),** this network model has gained widespread acceptance throughout the construction industry.[6] The Navy's primary concern was reducing the time to build the Polaris system; Du Pont, on the other hand, was concerned with both time and construction costs.

Methods developed in 1950s

The PERT Network   The first step in developing a PERT network is listing all the activities and events in a project from its start to its finish. Having identified

FIGURE 16.4
Network of events and
activities

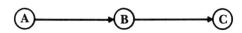

FIGURE 16.5
An expanded network

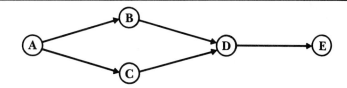

all activities and events, managers can represent them on a diagram. An **event**
is defined as a specific, definable accomplishment in a project, which is recognizable at a particular instant in time. Events are represented on the network
by *nodes* or *bubbles*. An **activity** is an ongoing work effort in a project, represented by an arrow on the network. An activity may represent a process, task,
procurement cycle, waiting time, or simply a connection or interdependency
between two events in the network.

Events and activities

Figure 16.4 illustrates events and activities. Event A might represent the
decision to start a project. Activity AB could represent a time-consuming work
effort of the project. Event B is the culmination of that work effort. Activity
BC depends on the completion of event B; that is, activity BC cannot begin
until event B has been completed. Event C, then, represents the culmination
of activity BC, another work effort of the project.

Obviously, some activities in a project can't begin until preceding events
have been completed. In other cases, two or more activities can be going on
at the same time. Thus, the essence of a PERT network is the arrangement of
events and activities in parallel and sequential format. Figure 16.5 illustrates
these concepts.

As shown in Figure 16.5, activities AB and AC can begin simultaneously
and continue at the same time. Activities BD and CD also can occur at the
same time. Activity DE, however, depends on the completion of event D.

Determining Expected Elapsed Times   Once managers have depicted on a network the interrelationships of all activities and events, they estimate the time
required to complete each activity. Assume that the network in Figure 16.6
represents the following activities associated with a pipeline construction project:

- Clearing the right-of-way

- Stringing the pipe along the right-of-way and bending it to conform to
  the contour of the terrain

FIGURE 16.6
Network, pipeline
construction project

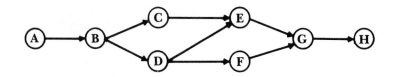

- Digging the trench

- Welding the pipe

- Coating and wrapping the pipe and lowering it into trench

- Testing for "geeps" (uncoated surfaces), repairing if necessary

- Cleanup, including planting grass seed

- Tying in with other segments of the pipeline

- Final testing

Three time estimates

    Managers make three time estimates for each activity in the project—an *optimistic* or best possible time estimate (a), a *most likely* time estimate (m), and a *pessimistic* or worst possible time estimate (b). Naturally, it is uncertain how much time will be required to complete each activity of a project such as pipeline construction. Weather conditions, types of terrain, river and road crossings, and the efficiency of welders are some of the variables directly affecting time needed to complete each phase of construction. Table 16.1 shows the three time estimates, in days, for each activity in this particular problem.

TABLE 16.1
Three time estimates

ACTIVITY	OPTIMISTIC TIME ESTIMATE (a)	MOST LIKELY TIME ESTIMATE (m)	PESSIMISTIC TIME ESTIMATE (b)
AB	6	8	10
BC	4	5	6
BD	7	8	13
CE	3	4	5
DE	1	2	5
DF	3	4	5
EG	8	9	10
FG	8	9	10
GH	4	6	8

FIGURE 16.7
Critical path through
network

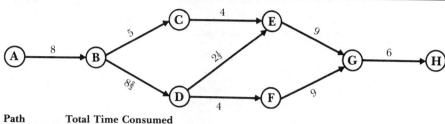

Path	Total Time Consumed
ABCEGH	32 days
ABDEGH	34 days
ABDFGH	$35\frac{2}{3}$ days (critical path)

Calculating expected elapsed time

When it is uncertain how much time is needed to finish an activity, an optimistic and pessimistic estimate should be combined with a most-likely estimate in arriving at a single time estimate for that activity. PERT incorporates these time estimates in the following weighted-average formula in arriving at the **expected elapsed time** (t_e) for each activity:

$$t_e = \frac{a + 4m + b}{6}$$

By substituting the a, m, and b time estimates in this formula, t_e values can be calculated. Thereafter, they are placed on the network itself, which facilitates the determination of the critical path.

The Critical Path   By definition, the **critical path** is the most time-consuming route through a network. A summation of t_e values for each path through the network is presented in Figure 16.7.

Finding the critical path

The critical path, then, is ABDFGH, the longest route through the network. This path is said to be critical because a delay in completing any event on it will delay the completion of the entire project. Events not on the critical path can be delayed without affecting the outcome of the project; consequently, a manager can shift resources from activities that are not critical to those that are. Assigning resources to critical areas makes it more likely that they will be completed faster. For example, activities BC and BD should not begin at the same time, even though it is possible for both to begin simultaneously. Instead, the construction manager should place resources on activity BD until activity BC becomes equally critical. (By allocating resources to activity BD, it will take less time to complete.) At that point, appropriate resources should be reassigned to activity BC.

Determining slack time

Slack Time   Obviously, the construction supervisor needs to know how long all resources should be assigned to activity BD before some are shifted to activity BC. The amount of time that events not on the critical path can be delayed without adversely affecting the project's completion is called **slack.** To determine slack time, we must first calculate earliest time (T_E) and latest time (T_L) values for all events.

- **Earliest expected time (T_E)** is the earliest calendar date on which an event can be expected to occur. The T_E value for a given event is equal to the sum of the expected elapsed time values (t_e) for the activities on the longest path from the beginning of the project to the given event.

Earliest and latest times

- **Latest allowable time (T_L)** is the latest calendar date on which an event can occur without delaying the completion of the project. The T_L value for a given event is calculated by subtracting the sum of the expected elapsed time values (t_e) for the activities on the longest path between the event and the end event of the project from the latest date allowable for completing the project. (If a directed date is not specified, $T_L = T_E$ for the end event.)

Table 16.2 shows the earliest time (T_E), latest time (T_L), and slack for each event in the network.

In this particular case, a directed date was not specified; consequently, $T_L = T_E$ for the end event. There is no slack time associated with events on the critical path. This means these events cannot be delayed without delaying the overall project. There is slack associated with events C and E, which are not on the critical path. Event C can be delayed $3\frac{2}{3}$ days, and event E can be delayed $1\frac{2}{3}$ days.

A Final Comment   Obviously, major projects entail hundreds of activities and events with a staggering number of interrelationships. It is impractical, if not impossible, to calculate manually all the values required. Computer programs are available today to handle the tasks required in PERT and CPM. Such

TABLE 16.2 Time values for each event in the network			
EVENT	**EARLIEST TIME (T_E)**	**LATEST TIME (T_L)**	**SLACK (T_L-T_E)**
A	0	0	0
B	8	8	0
C	13	$16\frac{2}{3}$	$3\frac{2}{3}$
D	$16\frac{2}{3}$	$16\frac{2}{3}$	0
E	19	$20\frac{2}{3}$	$1\frac{2}{3}$
F	$20\frac{2}{3}$	$20\frac{2}{3}$	0
G	$29\frac{2}{3}$	$29\frac{2}{3}$	0
H	$35\frac{2}{3}$	$35\frac{2}{3}$	0

programs can rapidly calculate slack, time-cost tradeoffs, statistical estimates of completing projects in a given period, and other data. The decision to use a computer depends, of course, on the complexity of the project.

Queuing Models

Queuing models, or **waiting line models,** are useful control tools for firms that serve customers or for scheduling the flow of material through various manufacturing processes. For example, queuing models can help determine the number of check-out clerks needed in a supermarket, the number of tellers required in a bank, or the number of salespeople needed in a retail store.

Uses of queuing models

A queuing model helps a manager determine how long customers are likely to have to wait in line for service and the corresponding costs. For example, a supermarket manager knows that customers who must wait too long in the check-out line will leave the store, resulting in a loss of sales. He or she also knows that adding another checker will increase labor costs. The manager therefore seeks to minimize both types of costs—in other words, to minimize the total cost by having the shortest waiting line possible with the minimum number of checkers.

Applying queuing theory

To understand how queuing theory can be applied, assume the supermarket manager has determined that no customers leave during the first five minutes of waiting time. Each additional minute costs the store $10, however, because customers tire of waiting and leave. The manager has estimated the waiting times that would result from having one, two, three, or four checkers on duty and the corresponding labor costs. This data appears in Table 16.3.

TABLE 16.3
Queue and labor costs—supermarket

	NUMBER OF CHECKERS			
	1	2	3	4
Average waiting time (minutes)	12	9	6	3
Costly waiting time in minutes (no loss first 5 minutes)	7	4	1	0
Cost per minute from loss of customers	$10	$10	$10	$10
Total waiting costs from loss of customers	$70	$40	$10	$0
Labor costs (checkers)	$20	$40	$60	$80
Total cost	$90	$80	$70	$80

Source: Adapted slightly by permission from *Management: Concepts and Effective Practices* by Hitt et al. Copyright © 1986 by West Publishing Company. All rights reserved.

TABLE 16.4
Applications of
simulation

Air-traffic control queuing	Maintenance scheduling
Production scheduling	Sales forecasting
Bus scheduling	Truck dispatching
Inventory control	Financial forecasting
Equipment scheduling	Plant layout
Bank-teller scheduling	Energy modeling
Process system design	Distribution system design

As you can see from the total cost figures in Table 16.3, the supermarket manager could minimize total costs by employing three checkers.

This obviously represents the simplest type of problem to which queuing theory can be applied. In fact, the computations become considerably more complex when customer arrival and service patterns are not uniform. This illustration nevertheless shows how valuable queuing models can be in helping managers make decisions.

Simulation

Why managers use simulation

As mentioned in Chapter 15, simulation is a quantitative procedure that develops a model of a process and then conducts trial-and-error experiments to predict its behavior. Managers often simulate a process. There are a number of reasons why. It may be impossible, too expensive, or too disruptive to see the process itself, or there may not be enough time to observe the process operating extensively.[7] Table 16.4 lists several examples of the numerous ways that simulation is applied.

Uses of simulation

Bendix Corporation, Crown Zellerbach, Kimberly-Clark, and 3-M use simulation for inventory control; Southland Corporation, Oscar Mayer, and Procter & Gamble design their plants and physical facilities with the aid of simulation; and Inland Container uses simulation to assess the impact of additional pollution-control equipment on productivity.[8] These and other companies have discovered that simulation is an invaluable tool when the risks and costs of making a particular decision are high.

Review

✓ *The uses of break-even analysis.* In recent years, there has been a dramatic shift toward measuring the variables in the decision-making process. Break-even analysis helps managers determine the units or dollars of output that a firm must produce to cover the cost of producing that amount. It allows managers to assess how a price change will affect profits and to determine the revenue that a given sales volume will generate. Break-even analysis also lets managers see how adding a product to a product line will affect profits.

✓ *How managers use models for inventory decisions.* These models are designed to help managers minimize total inventory costs. Managers are concerned with two kinds of inventory costs—the cost of placing an order and the cost of carrying inventory. These costs can be minimized by ordering the right amount of inventory (optimum order quantity) at the right time (optimum order point).

✓ *How linear programming helps managers use their resources wisely.* The general linear programming model can help a manager determine the most profitable combination of products to produce or the least costly combination of resources to use. When only two products are manufactured or two resources are used, linear programming problems can be solved graphically or algebraically. When there are more than two variables, the simplex method is used.

✓ *The use of network analysis in visualizing complex tasks.* The program evaluation and review technique (PERT) and the critical path method (CPM) are two of the most widely used planning and control tools available to managers. These network models let managers visualize interrelationships among a project's activities and events. They also help pinpoint bottlenecks and the areas where resources can best be allocated. PERT and CPM help managers determine which activities are critical and which can be delayed without affecting the outcome of the project.

✓ *What queuing models can do for firms that serve customers or for scheduling the flow of materials.* Two kinds of costs are important in queuing problems—the cost associated with loss of sales when customers leave a store because of long waiting lines, and the cost of adding additional service. Queuing theory helps managers minimize these costs by having the shortest waiting lines possible with the fewest service facilities.

✓ *How business uses simulation.* Simulation replicates real situations. When the risks of a decision are great, managers often simulate the process to see what would result under different conditions. Simulation lets managers make better decisions because it allows them to see the results of decisions beforehand in an experimental setting.

THE MANAGER'S DICTIONARY

As an extra review of the chapter, try defining the following terms. If you have trouble with any of them, refer to the page numbers listed.

break-even analysis (cost-volume-profit analysis) (421)
fixed costs (422)
variable costs (422)
break-even point (422)
contribution margin (423)
optimum order quantity (425)
optimum order point (425)
linear programming (427)

objective function (428)
constraint function (428)
area of feasibility (429)
simplex method (431)
Gantt chart (431)
program evaluation and review technique (PERT) (432)
critical path method (CPM) (432)
event (433)

activity (433)
expected elapsed time (435)
critical path (435)
slack (436)
earliest expected time (T_E) (436)
latest allowable time (T_L) (436)
queuing (waiting line) models (437)

REVIEW QUESTIONS

1. Why is break-even analysis often referred to as cost-volume-profit analysis?

2. What does a break-even chart show? Be specific.

3. What kinds of questions can be answered by break-even analysis?

4. How is the contribution margin calculated?

5. Can you think of any limitations of break-even analysis? Be specific.

6. Why should managers be concerned with inventory levels?

7. What kinds of costs are associated with inventory?

8. How can inventory costs be minimized?

9. What types of problems can be solved through linear programming?

10. What limitations are inherent in the graphical solution to linear programming problems? Explain.

11. When is the simplex method used for solving linear programming problems?

12. Why is the Gantt chart referred to as the forerunner of PERT and CPM?

13. What are the similarities between a Gantt chart and network models?

14. Cite several uses of PERT and CPM. Why are PERT and CPM considered planning tools? Controlling tools?

15. Explain the significance of slack in PERT and CPM.

16. Explain the different types of costs associated with waiting lines. How can these costs be minimized?

17. Why are processes often simulated before they are placed in operation?

18. Can you think of any applications of simulation? Be specific.

MANAGEMENT CHALLENGE

1. Assume that you are the owner-manager of a firm operating under the following circumstances:

Plant capacity: 80,000 units
Current operating level: 40,000 units
Selling price per unit: $3.50
Fixed costs: $90,000
Variable cost per unit: $1.10

Draw a break-even chart to reflect the information above. What is the break-even point (in units) when the selling price is $3.50?

2. This PERT network shows the activities and events that must be completed to produce a new product. The following information is provided to help you determine the critical path and the amount of time that certain events can be delayed without delaying the entire project.

What is the critical path?

Which events can be delayed without affecting the whole project? How long can each be delayed?

3. Think of a recent situation in which you chose to leave a store because you had to wait in line to be served. What costs did the store incur as a result of your decision? How could the store minimize such losses? Explain.

4. List three processes or systems (other than those mentioned in the chapter) that could be simulated. Why would a manager simulate a process? Explain.

Activity	a	m	b
AB	1	2	6
AC	2	3	4
AE	7	8	9
BD	3	4	9
CE	1	2	4
CF	2	3	5
DG	3	5	7
EG	3	5	7
EH	2	4	6
FH	3	4	5
GI	4	5	8
HI	2	3	4

a = the optimistic or best possible time estimate
m = the most likely time estimate
b = the pessimistic or worst possible time estimate

CASE 16.1

The Sound of Savings at Sturdivant[9]

Sturdivant Sound Systems manufactures and sells stereo and quadraphonic sound systems in both console and component styles. All parts of the sound systems, with the exception of turntables, are produced in the Rochester, New York, plant. Turntables used in the assembly of Sturdivant's systems are purchased from Morris Electronics of Concord, New Hampshire.

Jason Pierce, purchasing agent for Sturdivant Sound Systems, submits a purchase requisition for the multispeed turntables once every four weeks. The company's annual requirements total 5,000 units (20 per working day), and the cost per unit is $60. (Sturdivant does not purchase in greater quantities because Morris Electronics, the supplier, does not offer quantity discounts.) Rarely does a shortage of turntables occur because Morris promises delivery within one week following receipt of a purchase requisition. (Total time between date of order and date of receipt is ten days.)

Associated with the purchase of each shipment are procurement costs. These costs, which amount to $20 per order, include the costs of preparing the requisition, inspecting and storing the delivered goods, updating inventory records, and issuing a voucher and a check for payment. In addition to procurement costs, Sturdivant Sound Systems incurs inventory-carrying costs that include insurance, storage, handling, taxes, and so on. These costs equal $6 per unit per year.

Beginning in August of this year, management of Sturdivant Sound Systems will embark on a companywide cost-control program in an attempt to improve its profits. One of the areas to be closely scrutinized for possible cost savings is inventory procurement.

Questions
1. Compute the optimum order quantity.
2. Determine the optimum order size (in units).
3. Should procurement costs be considered a linear function of the number of orders?

CASE 16.2

Using PERT at Peterson Construction

Sam and Cathy Peterson are building contractors in the San Diego, California, area who specialize in commercial businesses and small residential communities.

Both Sam and Cathy had worked for a number of other contractors for more than fifteen years. But they found themselves out of work for a considerable period during the 1973 recession. That's when they decided to go into business for themselves. They would perform all the carpentry work and would hire subcontractors for other aspects of construction (electrical, plumbing, painting, and so on.)

Their partnership was successful from the beginning. They developed a reputation for quality workmanship and getting their projects done on time. They also earned a reputation in the financial community as hard-working businesspeople who could turn a profit on virtually every job they undertook.

Their philosophy is simple: "Time is money." Construction delays increase the cost of interim financing and postpone the start of other projects. Consequently, they deal with all bottlenecks promptly and avoid delays whenever possible. To minimize the time consumed in a construction project, they use PERT.

The Peterson Construction Company recently won a bid to build an area church. This diagram shows the activities, events, and their relationships for this project. Also included are the optimistic (*a*), most likely (*m*), and pessimistic (*b*) time estimates for each activity (expressed in weeks).

Questions
1. What is the critical path? What is the significance of the critical path?
2. Compute the amount of time that the completion of each event can be delayed without affecting the overall project.

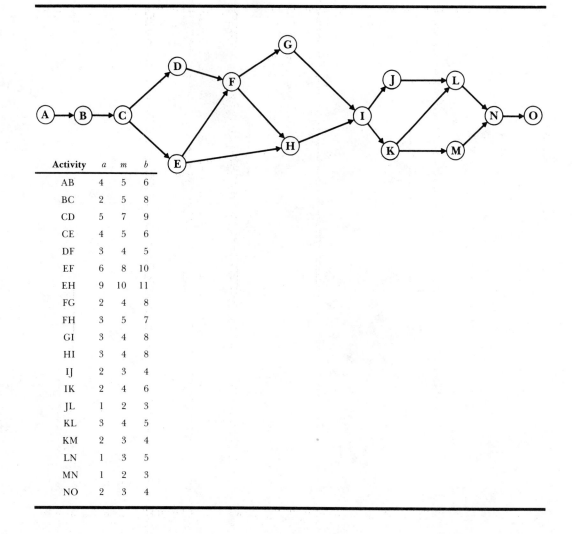

Activity	a	m	b
AB	4	5	6
BC	2	5	8
CD	5	7	9
CE	4	5	6
DF	3	4	5
EF	6	8	10
EH	9	10	11
FG	2	4	8
FH	3	5	7
GI	3	4	8
HI	3	4	8
IJ	2	3	4
IK	2	4	6
JL	1	2	3
KL	3	4	5
KM	2	3	4
LN	1	3	5
MN	1	2	3
NO	2	3	4

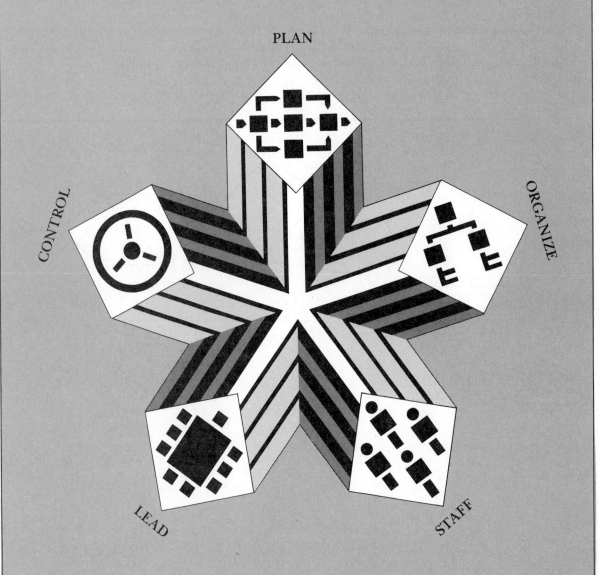

PLAN

ORGANIZE

STAFF

LEAD

CONTROL

Beyond the Management Functions

Parts One through Five focused on the nature and functions of management. In Part Six, we will analyze additional concerns of managers and help you assess your potential for a career in management.

Chapter 17, "Management's Social Responsibility," shows how the idea of business's social responsibility developed, along with opposing views of management's responsibilities to the public. We explain why managers become involved in social issues and discuss ways that business has addressed specific social problems. We also examine the relationship between business ethics and social responsibility.

Chapter 18, "International Management," discusses the growing importance of international trade to the U.S. economy and illustrates various organizational arrangements for producing and marketing products in foreign countries. This chapter also stresses the importance of understanding cultural differences and of overcoming communication barriers that arise in international business. The chapter discusses the economic and financial aspects of international management, including ways that a company can finance overseas operations.

Chapter 19, "Unions and Management," presents a brief history of the labor movement in the United States and reviews the major laws governing union-management relations. It gives special attention to the rights and responsibilities of employers and unions. The chapter tells of the growth of unions in the public sector and examines the collective bargaining process.

Chapter 20, "Your Future in Management," focuses on career opportunities in management. In this chapter, we review the typical career cycle and suggest a systematic approach to selecting a career. Then we present the pros and cons of a career in management and explore growing management opportunities for women. Finally, we analyze the environment in which tomorrow's managers will function and discuss the skills they will need.

CHAPTER OUTLINE

The Changing Social Responsibility Concept

How Society Feels About Business
Public Expectations of Business
Pressures Directed Toward Business
Social Pressure • Economic Pressure

How Business Feels About Social Responsibility
Business and Social Discontent
Social Responsibility and Profits
Criticisms of Social Responsibility
Preservation of Capitalism • Economic Action Doctrine • Lack of Control Objection • Cost Objections • Other Objections
Stockholders versus Society
Helping Society Through Economic Action

Why Managers Assume Social Responsibilities
Preservation of the Free Enterprise System
The Profit Motive
Subsidies and Tax Incentives
Avoidance of "Total Social Accounting"
The Survival Motive
Avoidance of Legal Action
Internal and External Forces

The Role of Ethics in Social Responsibility
Business Leadership in Problem Areas
Environmental Pollution • Unemployment and Discrimination • Inflation • Crime • Urban Problems

Management's Social Responsibility

Business Responds to Society's Needs

Traditionally, corporations have supported worthy causes by writing checks. U.S. firms gave $4.3 billion to charity in 1985. Today, corporations are changing their approach to helping others. Instead of exercising checkbook philanthropy, more and more companies are giving noncash items. Donations of products and services increased 150% between 1983 and 1986.[1]

IBM, for example, pays its employees to teach courses in colleges that enroll large numbers of minorities. Aetna Life & Casualty sponsors a program providing legal help to the elderly. Trailways Corporation gives runaway youngsters free transportation home on its buses. In Lansing, Michigan, General Motors involves employees in a food-collection program for the needy. Du Pont lends employees to the Wilmington, Delaware, Department of Corrections to counsel ex-convicts and to help them find jobs. And General Mills has spent nearly $3 million to help the elderly find decent, low-cost housing.[2]

Why are these corporations helping the disadvantaged? One reason is enlightened self-interest. William Woodside, chairman of American Can, put it this way: "Companies realize that if they want to be part of a viable community with a work force that is reasonably well educated and trained, they're going to have to do something about it themselves." James L. Ketelson, chief executive officer of Tenneco, adds: "We don't think we can solve every problem. We're not even sure that we can solve some of the ones we've chosen to address. But we do know we can make a difference."[3]

Preview   The involvement of business in social problems clearly shows that managers recognize responsibilities extending beyond the corporation. No longer can managers focus solely on maximizing profit at all costs. Today, more than ever before, managers must formulate policies that serve society's needs as well as those of the firm. By helping solve society's problems, business firms create an environment that enhances their chance for success.

In this chapter, we will examine managers' attitudes toward their social responsibilities and pinpoint ways that they meet those obligations. After studying this chapter, you will understand:

✔ How the social responsibility concept has evolved

✔ Society's expectations of business

✔ How managers view their responsibilities to the public

✔ Why managers assume social responsibilities

✔ The role of ethics in social responsibility

✔ How business has addressed specific social problems

The Changing Social Responsibility Concept

Business's corporate conscience

Today's organizations, particularly large corporations, exist in a complex world. Because they are part of a larger community, organizations have obligations to society as a whole. During the first two centuries of this country's existence, managers were more concerned with making their businesses successful than they were with any environmental and social effects. Today, however, because business has such tremendous impact on society, the manager's job has taken on new dimensions. Managers realize that a business should not only be economically efficient but also have a **corporate conscience,** an obligation to the society it serves for humane and constructive policies.

In the past century, our country's economic system has undergone dramatic changes. Among them are people's migration from rural to urban areas, the shift from an agrarian to an industrial economy, the advent of mass-production technologies, intensive government regulation of business, and the growth of large-scale business concerns.

Large firms and social issues

Just as the economy has changed, so has the nature of business. While managers of small businesses may follow their private interests without affecting society as a whole, managers of large firms cannot. The growth of big business brought with it greater social power and, unfortunately, its abuse.

Public anger has led to the passage of laws and regulations aimed at curbing the power that accompanies size. Today, managers in large national firms find themselves having to take stands on social issues that their predecessors would have dismissed as insignificant just a generation before.

Origin of social responsibility

The debate over social responsibility goes back to a 1932 publication, *The Modern Corporation and Private Property* by Adolf A. Berle and Gardiner C. Means. It discussed a development that was increasingly concentrating capital assets in the hands of salaried executives and depriving the stockholders of any effective control over their property. Four years later, Arthur Burns's book *The Decline of Competition* disclosed market controls in mass-production industries that were inconsistent with the traditional concept of free competition.[4] Although neither work specifically touted the responsibilities of business to society, the political and public interest they generated created considerable pressure on business to be more socially responsive.

The concept of business's social responsibility in the United States moved forward in the nineteenth century when the railroads gave financial support to the Young Men's Christian Association (YMCA), which was housing railroad workers. Later, other industries began contributing to social causes as well, and executives of major corporations began stressing the need for social responsibility.

One of the advocates of this philosophy was Elton Mayo, the behaviorist who was a forerunner of the social responsibility school. Mayo urged managers to turn away from the narrow pursuit of economic profits to more responsible and socially acceptable goals. The country that first made this transition, he believed, would outstrip the others in the race for stability, security, and development.[5]

How Society Feels About Business

In the last forty years, five major currents of thought about business's responsibility in American society have evolved. The first is the idea that corporate managers should act as trustees of the public interest, policing themselves and their use of power. Under this concept, managers should deliberately and voluntarily assume public responsibility, even though they may sometimes have to forego immediate profits for the sake of the public good.

Major currents of thought

The most emotional of the five viewpoints is the idea of relating moral principles of conduct to business. It holds that managers need a nobility of purpose that overshadows their daily corporate activities. Managers need "skyhooks" to orient them toward the nobler ideas of ethical conduct.

The third viewpoint is that the answer to concentrated business power is more power. The central theme is that business power is here to stay and that other major groups in society must build up countervailing power. According to this philosophy, the public welfare is served by the balance of interests in the power struggle as all groups pursue their own economic and social interests. This relieves managers of a deliberate, conscious need to promote public interests and responsibility, especially if conflicting with business's private interests.

The fourth philosophy basically states that managers and others will achieve business responsibility only when they recognize the peril to the individual that concentrated power poses.

Finally, the fifth major current of thought is composed of many smaller currents that attempt to reformulate and restate the capitalist ethic. Louis Kelso and Mortimer J. Adler argue in their book *The Capitalist Manifesto* that some of the basic capitalist principles—ownership, for example—must be extended to increasing numbers of citizens. When more people are owners, their stake in the prevailing system will increase; they will then be more interested in, and loyal to, the modified capitalist system.

Public Expectations of Business

People expect and demand far more from business today than they did in the past. As customers, we want better goods at lower prices, convenience, safety, honest advertising, and more product information. As employees, we expect business to provide better and more interesting jobs, better working conditions, and a wider variety of fringe benefits. As citizens, we demand still more, including a sense of responsibility for our physical and social environment and **Involvement in social** an open-handed commitment in helping to cure society's ills. These rising **ills** expectations from all segments of society are one of the most important influences on American business today.

Generally, the public expects business to take the initiative in maintaining the country's economic growth; in creating policies in which business anticipates the need for new rules; in taking a positive approach to problems of the function, structure, and accountability of the large organization; and in having imaginative, sensitive, and courageous corporate executives. The general public also wants business to maintain industrial peace and to stimulate and support community activities without dominating society.

The specific demands growing out of these expectations may differ greatly, but they all have the same roots—public acceptance of the fact that business is the country's economic heart, one of society's major decision centers, and the seat of a powerful, professionally competent, and responsible group of leaders. The public generally demands that business assume social responsibility for what it does in its normal operations.

Pressures Directed Toward Business

It is easy to understand why large corporations are being asked to help alleviate social problems, considering the power and resources they command. The fifty largest U.S. corporations own more than half of all manufacturing assets; the five hundred largest own more than two-thirds.

Business feels both social pressure—the demand that organizations have a conscience—and economic pressure—the need to respond to consumer preferences on what goods to produce to make a profit.

Social Pressure Increasingly, the public is aware that technology has created many problems. A problem like environmental pollution is becoming all too apparent. Other difficulties created by business are less obvious but can be seen in cities and rural areas where decisions to move plants or ill-advised hiring and promotion practices have hurt uneducated and untrained people, especially racial minorities. At the same time, people realize that business has the solutions to some problems, such as pollution and unemployment; they insist that business should train the unemployed who lack specialized skills and should clean up the environment.

Economic Pressure The second form of pressure stems from the needs of a more complex society. Many of the goods we need today are public goods, such as clean air and water. As much as business feels the urgency to respond to these demands, there is little any one business can do to rectify problems of such magnitude as pollution of the Mississippi River, for example. Government, using our tax dollars, must clean up the environment. Further, business has not yet learned how to cope with this new form of group consumer demand, so the market system that works well in the case of the individual consumer demand breaks down. The only channel left open to the public for expressing its demands is the political system. The resulting legislation often forces corporate executives to reevaluate their responsibilities and to reappraise how they deal with the public.

Critics acknowledge that some businesses have made public statements that endorse the social responsibility concept. But they argue that such statements are little more than thinly disguised attempts to make a profit in the long run.

Social pressure	
Economic pressure	

How Business Feels About Social Responsibility

The attitudes and commitments of business executives to society fit these three categories: (1) the laissez-faire, free enterprise philosophy and its variations; (2) the good citizen philosophy; and (3) the government and business cooperation philosophy, which originated in the modern economic order as a mixed public-private market economy.

The **laissez-faire, free enterprise philosophy** can be traced to Adam Smith. In *The Wealth of Nations,* Smith wrote that, motivated by self-interest and led by an "invisible hand," the private interests and "passions of men would lead them to distribute the stock of every society . . . as nearly as possible in the proportion which is most agreeable to the interests of the whole society."[6] This philosophy provides the basis for both an economic system and a moral

Laissez-faire philosophy

society. Managers would meet their social responsibilities through the free market as they tried to maximize profits and competed with one another. When managers followed this practice, the public welfare would be enhanced and business would indirectly meet its social obligations. This philosophy is the basis of the adage, "What's good for General Motors is good for the country."

Good-citizen philosophy

The **good-citizen philosophy** is a practical one maintaining that social welfare can be consciously and effectively pursued. Businesses should be good corporate citizens who do not break the law and who contribute to the community's well-being by paying taxes and by trying to make it a better place to live and work. Its extension in society means that the firm should give to worthwhile causes, encourage its managers to engage in politics, and make whatever commitments it can while assuming its responsibilities to stockholders, suppliers, employees, and customers.

Government-business cooperation

The **government and business cooperation philosophy** maintains that government must establish guidelines and programs so the business community can meet its social responsibilities by complementing government programs, policies, and plans. If business supports government programs, business is indirectly supporting society. Government officials, not business executives, determine which social programs are necessary. People in business need not use their own judgment regarding the kinds of socially desirable programs that should be supported. For example, if the federal government imposed sanctions against firms that conduct business in South Africa, where apartheid is practiced, then individual managers would not be required to make moral judgments on the matter.

Free enterprise creed

The three philosophies just discussed can be summarized in two very different creeds. The **free enterprise creed** holds that the purpose of business is, and should be, to maximize profits. It maintains that the pursuit of self-interest (maximum profits) is today—as in Adam Smith's time, the eighteenth century—the only logical or efficient way to conduct a business and the only way to preserve a free and economically progressive society. The **social**

Social responsibility doctrine

responsibility doctrine considers the free enterprise, maximum-profit philosophy an anachronism. Its proponents point out that in today's society, huge corporations play not only a vital economic role but also important political and social roles. For this reason, they have a significant impact on society. Society can either approve or disapprove, permit or prevent that impact. Proponents of this doctrine hold that business must assume certain social responsibilities to retain its autonomy.

Business and Social Discontent

Because people realize that business is one of society's dominant institutions, they look at it with great expectations. When Alfred North Whitehead observed in 1933 that a "great society is a society in which its men of business think greatly of their functions," he struck a responsive chord among business executives.[7] He was telling managers to look at their jobs in a general social context, advising them that what they do relates to society as a whole and that they should be aware of the role of business in the total social system.

Business's expanded responsibilities

There has been a basic change in the relationship between the values and concepts of society and business. Although still accepting business's traditional economic function, people also believe that business's role must be in harmony with society. More and more people believe that acute social and environmental problems can be solved only if business expands its role to include more than purely economic pursuits. Clearly, Adam Smith's guiding "invisible hand" cannot be relied on to solve the problems of pollution, racial strife, unemployment, overpopulation, and so on.

Social unrest

The past decade has witnessed widespread social discontent among many segments of society. The antinuclear movement is an example. Taking several different forms, this discontent has been directed at many targets, including government, business in general, large corporations, particular industries, and even individual firms. Some observers feel that business avoids or ignores social unrest unless it reaches crisis proportions.

Business has three responses to the pressures of public discontent: public relations, legal, and industrial relations-bargaining responses.

1. *The public relations response.* The philosophy behind this response is that most attacks on a business have selfish interests or are made by people who are ignorant about the organization and how it contributes to the general welfare and economic growth. Electric power companies often take this response to public outrage over nuclear reactors. This philosophy also holds that

How business responds

> if the corporation is to maintain public confidence its image must not be sullied. Direct confrontation with attackers must be avoided, for it may result in unfavorable publicity. Corporations must avoid open engagement in politics in order not to encourage activity by political factions unsympathetic to the cause of corporate business. On the other hand, the public relations response imposes on corporations the duty to inform and educate the populace about the "American way," enterprise democracy, and the vital role played by large corporations in providing material abundance and high standards of living.[8]

2. *The legal response.* When responding to the claims of pressure groups, organizations often use the legal system to interpret their rights. This is a frequent reaction to most social or ethical issues raised by conservation, minority, or consumer groups. Claims that cannot be proved scientifically are often challenged by organizations. Chemical firms, for example, sometimes use the courts in pursuing their right to dispose of chemical waste.

3. *The industrial relations-bargaining response.* Managers who use this approach feel that the issues cannot be avoided. Confrontation often takes the form of bargaining. Often, the process is carried on by making public statements to the news media or by enlisting the help of civic organizations. A business that is pressured by a civil rights group to hire more minorities or to establish an employment office in the urban ghetto might use this response.

Social Responsibility and Profits

In the past, business washed its hands of its social responsibilities simply by making a profit; this meant it was satisfactorily producing goods or services for the public's needs or wants. Today's argument is that making a profit is not enough. Many, including some managers, are convinced that business, as part of society, must help alleviate social problems. If it doesn't, it will be unable to make a profit at all.

Racial strife, proliferating slums, environmental pollution, and other problems scarcely provide a climate favorable to business growth. Therefore, many contend, social responsibility does not conflict with the primacy of profits. The two are complementary.

Modern business has gradually evolved into a social as well as an economic institution. Without losing sight of its need to make a profit, it has developed ideals and responsibilities going beyond the profit motive. The doctrine of socially responsible management generally holds that today's large corporation is so powerful that it would be disastrous to regard it only as a profit-making organization. From this viewpoint, management's duty is to administer the corporation not only for the welfare of stockholders but for other groups as well.

The social responsibility of management is not merely a public relations gesture to protect the firm's profit position. On the contrary, responsible executives sincerely desire to win the respect of the public by using their power for the common good. As pointed out in the In-Box on page 455, the insider-trading scandal that rocked Wall Street in 1986 affected both the securities industry and the public at large. The corporation is considered a multipurpose economic and social entity that is accountable to various groups of claimants.

Opposition to social involvement

Of course, there are those who believe that this social and public affairs involvement conflicts with the traditional, basic profit motive considered essential to the continuation of the system. They believe that corporate dollars should be spent only for obvious corporate purposes. Nevertheless, the legality and the propriety of using corporate resources, including management's time, to help solve social problems is clearly established.

> Profits and physical growth are an indicator of managerial talent and are justified within the accepted rule of the game for the participant and spectator. But they are means to the end of community service, not the end for which management is primarily responsible.[9]

It seems inevitable that business will continue both to make profits and to be socially involved.

Criticisms of Social Responsibility

Criticisms leveled at manager's attempts to assume social obligations take many diverse forms. Four basic objections have been leveled against the social responsibility creed.

THE IN-BOX

Wall Street's Watergate

In the autumn of 1986, Wall Street was rocked with news of the nation's biggest insider-trading scandal. As the news of Ivan Boesky's inside dealings spread across the country, other traders were wondering if they would be caught in the web.

On Wall Street, information is the key to success. Many traders spend much of their time listening to rumors, gossip, and tips. If the information comes from public sources, the traders are earning their money. If it comes from privileged sources, they are stealing it. Ivan Boesky's actions fell into the second category. He paid investment banker Dennis Levine for secret information: the names of companies that were about to become involved in takeovers.

Boesky, the so-called "King of Arbitrageurs," agreed to cooperate with federal investigators in exchange for a light penalty. He would be let off with one felony count and $100 million in fines and restitution. For that, he would implicate others who were involved in the insider-trading scandal. Word quickly spread that for weeks Boesky had been wired with microphones that taped the conversations of other big-time dealers.

The Boesky case has given rise to another round of soul-searching in American industry. Business schools have begun offering courses in ethics, companies are writing codes of conduct for employees, and in the opinion of some observers, a moral wave is sweeping the nation. As one analyst put it, if the nation at large gets another cycle of reform and altruism, it will feel good "until the impulse spends itself and greed comes back into style."

Source: Larry Martz, Bill Powers, John McCormick, Rich Thomas, and Mark Starr, "True Greed," *Newsweek,* December 1, 1986, pp. 48–50; and R. Foster Winans, "The Secret World of Ivan Boesky," *Newsweek,* December 1, 1986, pp. 50–51.

The end of capitalism argument

Preservation of Capitalism Some noted authorities contend that the social responsibility creed undermines and weakens the market mechanism. By giving business noneconomic goals, it may lose sight of what should be the primary purpose of the free-enterprise system—the efficient production of goods. Theodore Levitt, an outspoken critic of the social responsibility doctrine, charges that by making the profit motive secondary to social and welfare activities (which the government should rightfully assume), the corporation is paving the way toward a monolithic society signaling the eventual end of capitalism.

Indeed, as the profit motive becomes increasingly subordinated, capitalism will become only a shadow—and the torpid remains of the creative dynamism which was and might have been. It will thrive in name only, at the convention rostrums and the chambers of commerce—a sort of verbal remains of the real thing, shakily sustained by pomp and ceremony. Like Rome, it will never know that when it believed itself at the height of its glory, it was undergoing its denouement. The incubus of the corporate ministry of man will be completely enthroned while capitalism withers away, a victim of its own halved good intentions.[10]

Economic Action Doctrine   This doctrine holds that the corporation is not a democratic institution; rather, it is built on the authoritarian concept of private property. Such an organization should not extend its influence to the non-economic values of modern life. For democracy to prevail, Levitt said, business must restrict its activity to its economic objectives.

Preservation of democracy argument

Indeed, if there is anything wrong today, it is that the corporation conceives its ambitions and needs much too broadly. The trouble is not that it is too narrowly profit-oriented, but that it is not narrowly profit-oriented enough. In its guilt-driven urge to transcend the narrow limits of derived standards, the modern corporation is reshaping not simply the economic but also the institutional, social, cultural, and political topography of society.

Even if its outlook were the purest kind of good will, that would not recommend the corporation as an arbiter of our lives. What is bad for this or any other country is for society to be consciously and aggressively shaped by a single functional group or a single ideology, whatever it may be.

Sentiment is a corrupting and debilitating influence in business. It fosters leniency, inefficiency, sluggishness, extravagence, and hardens the innovationary arteries.[11]

According to this idea, organizations are not truly being socially responsible when they concern themselves with social problems outside their own sphere of competence and knowledge. Moreover, when a manager pays more attention to social action than to profits, he or she does not necessarily seem more ethical in the eyes of the public. Managers may contend that they are putting society's interest ahead of profit, but the suspicion arises that they are escaping to an area that has no checks on their power. Profits can be measured, and they form a way of measuring efficiency.

Lack of Control Objection   This criticism is related to some people's defense of social responsibility. It holds that the doctrine of social responsibility has no mandatory controls and there is no way of knowing if the doctrine is being followed. There are no sanctions against people who fail to meet its precepts. Even if a system of sanctions were to be worked out, there are no standards against which action and results can be compared. Thus, the doctrine of social responsibility is a collection of generalities that will not work.

Cost of social ills

Cost Objections   The cost of attempting to alleviate social ills has skyrocketed. Critics argue that since money—that is, taxes—will have to be diverted from other projects, the nation will have to give up much of its affluence to deal with its social problems in this way.

Other Objections   Some critics of the social responsibility doctrine fear it will mean higher taxes, greater control by the federal government, and the restricted freedom that sometimes results from federal legislation.

Stockholders versus Society

Although business is increasingly aware of its responsibility to society, most managers in publicly owned organizations maintain that their primary obligation is to their stockholders. A few authors even contend that managers are responsible only to the stockholders.[12] At the other extreme, some people feel that the business community should be the sole dispenser of welfare.

Helping Society Through Economic Action

Lack of social expertise

Some experts believe that business can best help society through economic action. They contend that business has developed tools, techniques, and a philosophy suited to economic goals but unsuited for social goals. All organizations, including business organizations, should do what they can with what they know best.

Economics is fundamental role

While acknowledging that profit making is management's first responsibility, these experts insist on the necessity for growth as only slightly less important. Because business produces society's wealth, management must make adequate profits to offset the risk of economic activity. Business must first increase its own wealth-producing capacity; with it comes the wealth of society.[13]

Leland Doan takes a similar approach in stating what he considers the fundamental role of business:

> Our function is an economic one, and we have a great direct responsibility to carry out that function just as ably as we possibly can. Our social responsibilities are part of the package, but they are indirect. Unless they are properly evaluated in terms of our basic function, they become a sort of hitchhiker. The main point is this: only so long as we do a good job in meeting our economic responsibilities are we going to be able to discharge our social responsibilities. Any activity labeled "social responsibilities" must be judged in terms of whether it is somehow beneficial to the immediate or long-range welfare of the business.[14]

Doan's statements imply that management's responsibility to stockholders conflicts with its responsibility to society. Not everyone agrees. In his book *The Firm: Micro-Economic Planning and Action,* Neil Chamberlain sees no reason why high profits and economic efficiency should be inconsistent with other goals. Instead, profitability usually helps rather than impedes achieving other goals. Low profit usually cannot be blamed on multiple management goals; it is more consistent with poor management than with good management that has other objectives besides profit.[15]

<table>
<tr><td>

Why Managers Assume Social Responsibilities
</td><td>

Aside from the moral obligations that managers may feel toward society, there are other specific reasons why business should take on social responsibilities voluntarily.
</td></tr>
</table>

Preservation of the Free Enterprise System

Social power = social
responsibility

Managers have considerable social power because they are leaders and because they command vast economic resources. Any group, including managers, has social responsibilities equal to its social power. This concept is not new to business. A basic principle of good management is to balance authority and responsibility so that each employee assumes responsibility to the extent of his or her authority.

Keith Davis suggests another reason for managers to assume public responsibility.

> The growing power of government looms on the sidelines waiting to add restrictive controls the moment business becomes lax in any area of responsibility. Businessmen have learned that once a government control is established, it is seldom removed even though conditions change.[16]

Unless business is socially responsible, it cannot keep operating under a free enterprise system.

The Profit Motive

New opportunities

Not all social problems result in losses for private industry. For example, the need to purify air has led to the birth of a multi-billion-dollar-a-year industry manufacturing pollution-control hardware. America's waste-disposal problem has created similar opportunities. Several companies are profiting by transforming garbage and trash into saleable products, such as fertilizer, or by burning it to produce commercial electric power and steam.

Subsidies and Tax Incentives

Tax advantages

In some cases, business needs some kind of government incentive before it can begin making a profit in solving social problems. Often, this takes the form of a federal demonstration grant, such as is available to private firms in the mass-transit field. Partial government subsidies also are available as tax write-downs for projects such as urban renewal and for purchasing pollution-control equipment.

Avoidance of "Total Social Accounting"

Cost-sharing

Many managers fear that unless private enterprise takes direct, forceful action, private business soon may be operating under a **total social accounting system.** Under such a system, the government would determine the cost of a problem, such as pollution, and charge each company for its share of causing that problem. This approach is used in West Germany, where companies are charged a fee for each ton of waste material that they dump into the Rhine River.[17]

The Survival Motive

Industry involvement

In the early twentieth century, industry began research in the natural and physical sciences on a large-scale basis. Chemical firms, in particular, invested heavily in research and development, bringing about today's benefits as well as such problems as toxic waste disposal. If business is to survive and prosper, it must seek solutions to these problems in the same committed way that industry expands and improves its technology.

Avoidance of Legal Action

Today, an ever-increasing number of firms are being prosecuted for violations of either business-related or social laws.

Government becomes involved

History shows that government action involving business is caused by the social changes that result from business's technological innovations. In the 1880s, for example, the oil and railroad industries grew into great power structures contributing greatly to the nation's economic growth. While the net effect was economically good, the social effects of this monopolistic power and its abuse caused Congress to pass the Interstate Commerce Act of 1887 and the Sherman Antitrust Act of 1890. Business's lack of responsibility in packaging and canning food products prompted passage of laws and regulations in this area as well. Because business leaders failed to recognize that they were responsible for the social change caused by such advances as mass production, public pressure caused the federal government to become involved. Laws governing such things as labor relations, child labor, insurance, securities, and other areas have been the result.

Internal and External Forces

The transition from an individualistic to an industrialized economy has been accomplished by extensive changes in all phases of society. As Delbert Miller and William H. Form point out:

> The industrial mode of production has given rise to an economic organization that influences all parts of society. Industrialism as a configuration of technology, economy, and business values emerges as a cultural system. No modern institution can escape the influence of the economic organization of society. The school, the church, the home, and recreation institutions are built upon human values arising from the material framework of modern civilization. Industrial society has become a society in which social relationships tend to be economic relationships.[18]

Impact of public opinion

Several external factors have caused business to become more socially conscious. Managers have to cope with the demands of society on one hand and the strong economic pressures of a powerful labor movement on the other. As big business grows still bigger, managers are forced to look beyond their competition to general business conditions and to the health of the economy and society. The manager must constantly feel the pulse of public opinion and be wary of alienating the public.

Morrell Heald traced the evolution of American management's thinking about its social role. He found that several internal and external factors were influential.

> Primarily, of course, have been the internal factors in industrial growth: the development of large-scale enterprise spanning the nation in its activities and concerns, the unification of the labor force, the application of mass production and the growing awareness of its dependence upon an ever-widening circle of willing and able consumers, and the capital requirements of an expanding economy leading to widespread stock ownership and a redefinition of the role of management. A second group of external factors . . . have been the traditional values of individualism and equality of opportunity which entered into the antitrust movement and the continuing suspicion of the power of collective wealth, the idealism and spirit of service growing out of war-time experience, the growing political power of organized labor and other non-business groups, the acceptance of the principle of the ultimate responsibility of government for social welfare in those areas where private efforts fail, and the involvement of the United States in a world wide struggle for democracy with totalitarianism in its various forms.[19]

Corporate concern with social problems is relatively new, coming about as environmental changes have forced business to look beyond its traditional areas of interest. But because this is a fairly recent concern, many companies still have no formal structure for dealing with these questions, such as a corporate community relations department.

The Role of Ethics in Social Responsibility

The ethics practiced by business managers affect both their organizations and society. Ethical questions arise in every aspect of business and in relation with everyone who is affected, directly or indirectly, by the firm. As the Manager's Notebook on page 461 explains, each individual within a company is responsible for the preservation of the firm's ethics.

Ethical questions

> The moral position of the executive who works for a company that fails in the ethics of social responsibility is ambiguous. The fact that he does not control company policy cannot entirely exonerate him from blame. He is guilty, so to speak, by employment.
>   If he is aware that the company's factories pollute the environment or its products injure the consumer and he does not exert himself to change

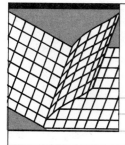

THE MANAGER'S NOTEBOOK

Do You Snitch on Your Boss?

What would you do if you learned that your boss or coworkers are doing something unlawful? Unfortunately, many employees frequently face this question. All kinds of crime occur every day, ranging from kickbacks to false financial disclosure.

Ignore what's going on and you, too, could be breaking the law. According to Harvey Pitt, a former Securities and Exchange Commission legal counsel, you may not be able just to turn your head and look the other way. For example, if you're the head of the sales department and have some salespeople taking bribes or kickbacks, you must report it.

Even if staying silent doesn't result in your being legally charged if action is taken against the violators, you may still have some answering to do. Some companies will fire employees who overlook wrongdoing.

Experts suggest that you see a lawyer if you discover wrongdoing in the company. You may want to consult with the company lawyer or, if you don't trust internal politics, you may prefer outside counsel for guidance.

If you decide to blow the whistle on your company for breaking the law, you may not get much protection. Courts generally uphold a company's right to hire and fire at will unless it is violating specific statutes—antidiscrimination laws, for example.

If you are personally involved in wrongdoing, you should find an attorney who is experienced in handling white-collar crime cases, says Peter Romatowski, an assistant U.S. attorney. The attorney may contact the company for you, preserving your anonymity, or may contact the authorities, trying to negotiate some kind of deal. In nearly every case, the penalty is less when the wrongdoer comes forth and admits wrongdoing as opposed to waiting until the actions are uncovered by someone else.

Source: Janet Bamford, "When Do You Blow the Whistle?" *Forbes*, October 21, 1985, pp. 166–169.

the related company's policies, he becomes morally suspect. If he lends himself to devious evasions of laws against racial discrimination in hiring practices, he adds to the probability of destructive racial confrontations and is in some degree an agent of social disruption. If he knows that his company is involved in the bribery of government officials, or makes under-the-table deals with labor union officials, or uses the services of companies known to be controlled by criminal syndicates, he contributes through his work to disrespect for law and the spread of crime.[20]

Business Leadership in Problem Areas

Environmental Pollution   In many respects, pollution is an offshoot of progress. As the nation becomes more mechanized, more contaminants pour into the environment. Much of our air pollution comes from the conversion of fossil fuels (petroleum, gas, and coal) into energy. Water is polluted when organic, agricultural, inorganic industrial, and synthetic chemical wastes, pesticides, fertilizers, radioactive wastes, and high-temperature water are discharged from power and industrial plants. The largest industrial users and contaminators of water are producers of chemicals, petroleum, pulp and paper, steel, automobiles, textiles, leather, and detergents. Now, attention is focusing on two other problems: noise pollution and solid-waste disposal. Chemical plants that produce industrial chemicals and fertilizers, in particular, have come under close scrutiny because of their waste-disposal practices.

Forms of pollution

The Environmental Protection Agency was established in 1970 to regulate the discharge of pollutants into the nation's air, land, and water. To preserve and enhance the nation's environmental resources, the EPA enforces regulations dealing with clean air and water, noise control, toxic waste, insecticides, and other areas.

Unemployment and Discrimination   Most managers maintain that their companies' policies deal fairly with minorities, women, and older workers, and many feel their social responsibility in this area. Evidence shows, however, that minorities, women, and older workers still experience wide discrimination. There are at least three reasons for management's failure to translate its feelings into action: (1) obligations in this area are relatively low on management's list of priorities, (2) few managers believe they discriminate, and (3) in some cases, top management's policies are not translated into action at lower levels in the organizational structure.

Regulations for equality

The most obvious company motive for undertaking an equal employment effort is the desire to comply with Title VII of the Civil Rights Act of 1964. This section has as its objective eliminating discrimination in employment because of race, color, religion, sex, or national origin in all industries affecting interstate commerce. Other acts, regulations, and executive orders govern discrimination against handicapped and older workers, and other groups. (See Chapter 8.)

There are economic reasons, too, for hiring and training minorities, women, older workers, the handicapped, and the hard-core unemployed. These workers may be trained to become valuable members of an organization, filling the increasing need for skilled workers.

Price stability

Inflation Some people contend that one of the most flagrant mistakes of American business and organized labor is their failure to keep prices stable. Inflation is the price we pay for an expanding economy; this price instability defeats a purpose of free enterprise—the betterment of humankind through a steadily rising standard of living.

For too many Americans, the standard of living is not rising. Inflation devalues fixed incomes, savings in most of the traditional forms, pensions and annuities, public expenditures for education, and so on. When this happens, society's needs are not being adequately served.

Fighting crime

Crime Every form of crime affects business. Robbery, employee theft, drug abuse, the cost of bad checks, shoplifting, vandalism, and burglary cost business billions of dollars annually. With its big stake in reducing the crime rate, business must actively support Crime Stoppers and other programs designed for this purpose.

Urban blight

Urban Problems Most people today realize the magnitude of urban decay, with its crime, delinquency, pollution, inadequate housing, inadequate educational systems, public transportation problems, and poverty. More and more, business is beginning to believe it has an obligation, above and beyond a strictly economic concern, to help solve the urban crisis.

During the past few years, business's concern with the problems of America's cities spawned a number of sizeable new organizations, including Urban America, the Urban Coalition, the National Alliance of Businessmen, and the Urban Institute. Their primary objectives are to encourage business to hire the disadvantaged and to eliminate urban blight.

Review

✓ *How the social responsibility concept has evolved.* In America's early years, managers concentrated on making their businesses successful and were unconcerned with social problems. But as business grew more powerful and its impact on society increased, managers began to recognize a new dimension added to their jobs. They accepted the fact that a business must be more than economically efficient; it must have a corporate conscience as well.

✓ *Society's expectations of business.* The public expects far more from business today than it did in the past. As consumers, we want better goods and services. As employees, we demand better and more interesting jobs and better working conditions. And as citizens, we expect business to help improve the environment and to support community activities designed to alleviate society's ills.

✓ *How managers view their responsibilities to the public.* Managers' attitudes toward social responsibility fall into three categories: (1) the laissez-faire, free enterprise philosophy, (2) the good citizen philosophy, and (3) the government and business cooperation philosophy. The laissez-faire, free enterprise philosophy holds that society's interest will be served as corporations pursue economic efficiency and profit maximization. The good citizen philosophy encourages businesses to contribute to worthwhile causes and to help make their communities a better place to live and work. The government and business cooperation philosophy holds that government must establish social programs that business can support. In this way, business can indirectly assume its social responsibilities.

✓ *Why managers assume social responsibilities.* There are a number of reasons why managers voluntarily assume social obligations. Some believe that social responsibility comes with social power. Others see profit: involvement in solving social problems results in new industries and in tax incentives and subsidies offered by federal and state governments. Still others assume social responsibilities to avoid "total social accounting" or legal action.

✓ *The role of ethics in social responsibility.* The ethics practiced by managers directly affect both their firms and society. Managers who know that their companies are polluting the environment or engaging in unlawful activities are guilty by association. By tolerating such practices, they are contributing to the problem.

✓ *How business has addressed specific social problems.* The approach taken to alleviate social problems depends on the nature of the specific problem. Efforts to clean up the environment have largely come through compliance with federal laws designed to eliminate pollution. Employment of minorities has been brought about in two ways—through legislation passed to eliminate discrimination and through voluntary programs designed to employ and train the disadvantaged. Business has addressed the problem of crime by supporting programs such as Crime Stoppers. It is recognizing the problems of urban decay, inadequate education, and poverty by giving both financial and nonfinancial support to organizations that alleviate these problems.

THE MANAGER'S DICTIONARY

As an extra review of this chapter, try defining the following terms. If you
have trouble with any of them, refer to the page numbers listed.

corporate conscience (448)

laissez-faire, free enterprise
    philosophy (451)

good citizen philosophy (452)

government and business
    cooperation philosophy
    (452)

free enterprise creed (452)

social responsibility doctrine
    (452)

total social accounting system
    (458)

REVIEW QUESTIONS

1. Why are today's managers more concerned
with social responsibilities than were managers
in the past?

2. When did America's managers first become
concerned with social responsibilities? Why?

3. List the five major currents of thought about
business's responsibility in American society.

4. What does the public expect from business?

5. Why does the public expect more from
business today than in the past? Explain.

6. How does the public make its expectations
known? Discuss.

7. Do you consider the "good citizen philosophy" an adequate approach to social responsibility? Why or why not?

8. Give examples of social discontent. What
has led to this discontent?

9. How does business respond to social unrest?
Explain.

10. In your opinion, should business pursue
social as well as economic objectives? Discuss.

11. Why are managers willing to assume social
responsibilities? Explain.

12. What is the relationship between managerial ethics and social responsibility?

13. Cite several social problems and suggest ways
that business can become involved in each
problem area.

MANAGEMENT CHALLENGE

Assume that you are the president and chief executive officer of one of the nation's largest chemical corporations. Historically, your company has tried to be a good corporate citizen, but it has never openly endorsed the concept of social responsibility.

1. Prepare a list of arguments in support of social responsibility.

2. Does the "good corporate citizen" philosophy adequately address these arguments? Why or why not?

3. Can you make a convincing case that opposes the concept of social responsibility?

4. If you were employed by a small company, would your social responsibilities be the same? Explain.

CASE 17.1

American Express Helps Restore Statue of Liberty[21]

In 1983, a national advertising campaign promoting American Express made an interesting announcement: the company would donate a penny to a fund to restore the Statue of Liberty every time one of its charge cards was used and one dollar for every new card issued in the United States.

Card usage increased 28% and new card holders increased 45% as a result. According to Jerry Welsh, an American Express marketing executive, this approach was a blend of corporate marketing and social responsibility. It is a departure from "checkbook giving," which companies practiced in the 1970s.

While contributing to a worthy cause, the firm benefits, too. This kind of corporate philanthrophy is called "enlightened self-interest." It sprang up in the nineteenth century when railroads financially supported the YMCA, which provided inexpensive housing for their workers. Today, companies are applying the

principle with greater sophistication. American Express, in particular, has extensively modernized its contribution program. Using the Statue of Liberty approach, the company directly raised $30,000 for the San Jose (California) Symphony and raised another $205,000 for it out of the publicity. Card usage and new applications increased 25%. Similar tactics have been used successfully in thirty-one markets throughout the country. Instead of engaging in a win-lose situation, American Express has discovered a win-win formula. Its way of supporting worthwhile projects has been dubbed "cause-related marketing."

Questions
1. Why has American Express changed its way of helping charitable causes?
2. Is American Express assuming its social responsibilities by using these tactics? Why or why not?

CASE 17.2

When E.F. Hutton Talks . . .[22]

Try as it may, E.F. Hutton, the nation's fifth-largest brokerage firm, cannot escape an ongoing scandal. In May 1985, Hutton was fined $2 million, plus legal costs, after pleading guilty to two thousand counts of mail and wire fraud involving an elaborate check-kiting operation. In July 1985, the company admitted that it failed to provide eighteen documents subpoenaed by the Justice Department during a three-year investigation of its practices.

Former Hutton President George Ball has maintained his innocence all along, saying that he was unaware of the check-kiting scheme. However, a memo dated May 12, 1981, showed that he praised one branch manager who earned $30,000 a month in interest through check overdrafting.

The controversy has hurt Hutton's profits as well as its reputation. In May 1985, New York City temporarily barred the firm from participating in two municipal-bond offerings. This action alone cost Hutton $500,000 in fees. In addition, New York state's Metropolitan Transportation Authority has indefinitely prohibited Hutton from doing any of its underwriting.

The final blow could come if state officials suspend Hutton's brokerage licenses. But even if they don't, the company is in trouble. Hutton's sales force is demoralized, and its reputation is tarnished. In some industries, that wouldn't matter so much, but in an industry that depends on trust, a company's reputation means a lot.

Questions

1. In your opinion, should E.F. Hutton's brokerage licenses have been suspended? Why or why not?

2. Should individual officers of the firm have been charged with criminal misconduct? Justify your answer.

CHAPTER OUTLINE

International Trade

The United States and International Trade

Organizing for International Trade

World Trade Channels

The Political and Legal Environment

The Foreign Corrupt Practices Act • Political Guidelines for Multinationals

Successful International Management

Communication Problems

Understanding Cultural Differences

Economic and Financial Aspects

The International Monetary Fund • Eurodollars and Eurobonds • Financing International Operations • Free Trade Zones

The Future of International Business

CHAPTER 18

International Management

Kentucky Fried Chicken Doesn't Fly in Brazil

Any way you look at it, Kentucky Fried Chicken has enjoyed remarkable success in the United States. Much of its astonishing growth can be attributed to effective advertising, fast service, and a unique taste—a special blend of herbs and spices, as the ad says. Those ingredients and others have made Colonel Sanders, the chain's founder, a household name for nearly three decades.

Kentucky Fried Chicken's expansion into foreign markets hasn't been as smooth, though. The company ran into numerous problems when it decided to enter the Brazilian market, for instance. Hoping to open one hundred outlets in Brazil eventually, the company began operations in São Paulo. Sales were disappointingly sluggish, however. Further research indicated that a variety of low-priced, charcoal-broiled chicken was available on nearly every street corner of the city. To make matters worse, Brazilians considered charcoal-broiled chicken tastier than the Colonel's recipe. Realizing that it had inadequately researched the Brazilian market, the management of Kentucky Fried Chicken opted to sell hamburgers, Mexican tacos, and enchiladas. Unfortunately, the company only compounded its mistakes. These products were practically unknown in Brazil.[1]

Preview

The blunders made by Kentucky Fried Chicken's management can be traced to inadequate market research. Had the company thoroughly analyzed its competition and the preferences of the Brazilian people, it could have avoided many problems. Before expanding into international markets, companies must evaluate local customs, tastes, and competitive forces. But other considerations are equally important. The political and legal environment of the foreign country, communication problems, a firm's organizational structure, and local economic conditions all affect the success of a firm's venture into international markets. In this chapter, we will explore both the opportunities and problems associated with international trade and management. After studying this chapter, you will understand:

✔ What international trade means for the manager

✔ How to be successful in international management

✔ The future of international business

International Trade

World trade has been part of American history since the days of the Yankee clipper ships. Today, Europe is only hours away by jet, and satellite communication can link remote parts of the world faster than it took a clipper ship to set its sails. Technology has made the world seem smaller.

Multinational corporations

The rise of multinational corporations since World War II has also made the world economy more interdependent. **Multinational corporations (MNCs)** are business firms that produce and market goods and services in more than one country. They include giants such as Coca-Cola, IBM, and Exxon, and smaller companies as well. Whether they are large or small, however, these companies have great economic impact. In economic terms, multinationals produce about $1.25 trillion worth of goods and services annually, or about half of the world's gross product.[2]

International trade

The United States economy depends very much on a strong world economy. American profits are directly affected by economic conditions in other countries, and more than 3.5 million Americans owe their jobs directly or indirectly to world trade.[3] Thus, managers must be aware of the forces that affect **international trade,** which we will define as the flow of goods, services, capital, and intangibles such as technology, patents, and trademarks between one country and other nations. International management involves not only exchanging goods and services but also developing new trade sources.

The United States and International Trade

Competitive advantage

Countries all over the world can produce certain products at an economic advantage and must import others to their economic disadvantage. For example, Brazil has an ideal climate for producing coffee but does not have the technological know-how to develop advanced aircraft. We like to drink coffee, but our climate is not ideal for growing coffee beans; we are, however, highly capable of mass-producing technologically advanced aircraft. Hence, we export our aircraft and import Brazilian coffee. The best solution to the problem is for each country to export the goods it most efficiently produces and to import the goods that other countries best produce.

The United States has an advantage because it produces and exports many different kinds of goods. Its greatest strengths, though, are in producing food products and high-technology items. The United States is the world leader in the export of high-technology goods. Table 18.1 shows a breakdown of these goods and the market share the United States has captured. Agricultural products also represent a large dollar volume of exports for the United States. Soybeans, wheat, and corn alone account for more than $21 billion in annual sales abroad.

Imports and exports

On the other hand, the United States must import large quantities of goods that we cannot produce in sufficient quantities here. In particular, we import huge quantities of oil, certain foods, and manufactured goods. Our dependency on imports sometimes creates problems. During the Arab oil embargo in the 1970s, gas stations were forced to limit their sales—when they had any gasoline at all—to the long line of cars at the pumps.

Our government stockpiles strategic minerals such as uranium so that we will not be dependent on foreign supply sources in case of a national emergency. Table 18.2 shows the percentages of minerals, foods, machinery, and other products that we export and import.

Our trading partners

The bulk of our international trading is done with other North American countries, Asia, and Europe. In North America, we trade primarily with Canada; in Europe, with England, West Germany, France, Italy, Belgium, Sweden, and Switzerland. In Asia, our largest trading partners are Japan, Taiwan, and Korea. Trade with Africa has been rising recently with the importation of oil from several African countries.

Organizing for International Trade

The organizational arrangement for handling international activities varies from firm to firm. Some companies create a separate *international division* through which they channel all international correspondence and trade. Figure 18.1 illustrates such an organizational structure at Dow Jones & Company.

The Dow Jones international division is roughly equal to the five domestic divisions. The international group is further divided along product lines

TABLE 18.1
Leaders in major high-technology markets

CATEGORY	TRADE VOLUME ($ BILLIONS)	TOP FIVE EXPORTERS AND THEIR SHARES (%)			
Aircraft	27.2	USA	54	France	7
		W. Germany	12	Italy	4
		UK	10	TOTAL	87
Telecommunications	19.2	Japan	25	UK	7
		USA	16	France	5
		W. Germany	10	TOTAL	63
Automatic data processing (ADP)	14.1	USA	35	Japan	6
		W. Germany	10	France	6
		UK	9	TOTAL	66
Machine tools	12.0	W. Germany	24	Italy	8
		Japan	15	Switzerland	7
		USA	13	TOTAL	67
ADP & office machines parts & accessories	9.9	USA	43	France	9
		W. Germany	11	Japan	8
		UK	9	TOTAL	80
Office machines	6.1	Japan	43	Netherlands	7
		W. Germany	11	UK	7
		USA	9	TOTAL	77
Microcircuits	3.9	Japan	23	W. Germany	11
		USA	19	South Korea	9
		Singapore	17	TOTAL	79
Medical equipment	2.9	USA	39	Japan	8
		W. Germany	19	France	5
		Netherlands	10	TOTAL	75
Gas turbines	1.7	USA	65	France	4
		UK	11	Italy	4
		W. Germany	7	TOTAL	91
Nuclear reactors	0.8	Belgium	31	Switzerland	12
		W. Germany	23	Sweden	6
		France	20	TOTAL	92

Source: Reprinted with permission, *High Technology* magazine, October 1984, by High Technology Publishing Corporation, 38 Commercial Wharf, Boston, Mass. 02110.

that specifically relate to geographic areas. This international structure, shown in Figure 18.2, is preferred when product-line diversity is limited, when foreign sales are relatively small compared to domestic operations, and when international management resources are limited.[4]

As a company grows in size internationally, a *global area structure,* basing divisions on geography, begins to evolve. In this type of structure, the general

TABLE 18.2
Distribution of U.S. exports and imports (1970–1984) (in percentages)

COMMODITY GROUP	1970	1975	1976	1977	1978	1979	1980	1981	1982	1983	1984
Exports:											
Food and live animals	10.2	14.6	13.9	11.9	13.0	12.5	12.8	13.2	11.6	12.1	11.5
Beverages and tobacco	1.6	1.2	1.3	1.6	1.6	1.3	1.2	1.3	1.5	1.4	1.3
Crude materials, inedible[1]	10.8	9.2	9.6	11.0	11.0	11.6	11.0	9.2	9.3	9.3	9.5
Mineral fuels and related materials	3.7	4.2	3.7	3.5	2.8	3.1	3.7	4.5	6.1	4.7	4.4
Chemicals	9.0	8.2	8.8	9.1	8.9	9.7	9.6	9.3	9.6	9.8	10.5
Machinery and transport equipment	42.0	43.0	43.7	42.2	42.0	39.5	39.1	41.8	42.1	42.1	42.4
Other manufactured goods	17.9	15.6	15.7	16.0	16.1	16.2	17.8	16.3	15.8	15.2	14.5
General imports:											
Food and live animals	13.5	8.8	8.5	8.5	7.9	7.4	6.4	5.8	5.9	6.0	5.5
Beverages and tobacco	2.1	1.5	1.3	1.1	1.3	1.2	1.1	1.2	1.4	1.3	1.1
Crude materials, inedible[1]	8.3	5.8	5.8	5.7	5.4	5.2	4.3	4.3	3.5	3.7	3.4
Mineral fuels and related materials	7.7	27.5	28.2	30.2	24.5	29.1	33.9	31.2	26.8	22.5	18.7
Chemicals	3.6	3.8	4.0	3.4	3.7	3.6	3.5	3.6	3.9	4.2	4.2
Machinery and transport equipment	28.0	24.4	24.7	24.7	27.7	26.0	24.7	26.6	30.1	33.4	36.6
Other manufactured goods	33.3	24.9	25.0	23.8	26.9	24.8	22.9	24.3	25.1	31.7	27.2

Source: Statistical Abstract of the United States (Washington, D.C.: U.S. Department of Commerce, 1986), p. 814.

[1]Excludes fuels.

manager of each geographic unit reports directly to the division head at headquarters. Such an arrangement, illustrated in Figure 18.3, is used by Eastman Kodak and other large multinational corporations.

This type of organizational structure is found mostly in mature and established multinational corporations. Its major advantage is that managers become very knowledgeable about the culture and environment of a certain part of the world; they can grasp the problems and conditions unique to that area. A disadvantage is that coordination and communication across divisions can be complicated.

Organizational structures

A different type of global structure is the *global product structure,* such as General Motors uses. In this type of organizational arrangement, each product

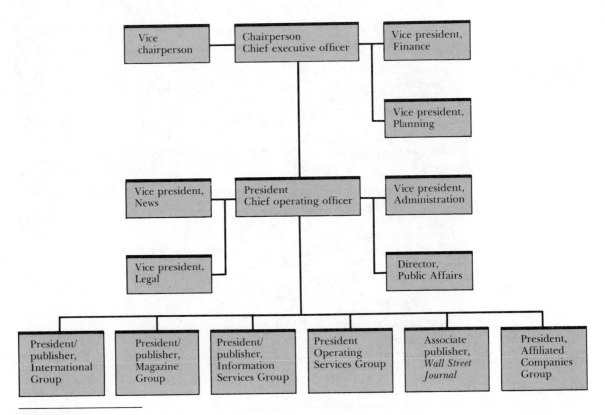

FIGURE 18.1
Organizational structure of Dow Jones & Company (*Source:* Jack Duncan, *Management: Progressive Responsibility in Administration*, p. 474. Copyright © 1983 by Random House, Inc. Reprinted by permission of the publisher.)

division operates like an individual company. It is most effective when divisions are large and relatively autonomous, when unique local conditions are not critical, and when each product requires much technical assistance.[5] But coordination and communication problems arise with this type of structure, too.

In each of these organizational structures, the multinational corporation has directly invested in subsidiaries. These **foreign subsidiaries** are separate companies owned by the American parent corporation and are organized under the laws of the foreign country.[6] Companies prefer to use subsidiaries when conditions permit because the parent company retains all the profits and

FIGURE 18.2
International group of
Dow Jones & Company
(*Source:* Jack Duncan,
*Management: Progressive
Responsibility in
Administration,* p. 474.
Copyright © 1983 by
Random House, Inc.
Reprinted by permission
of the publisher.)

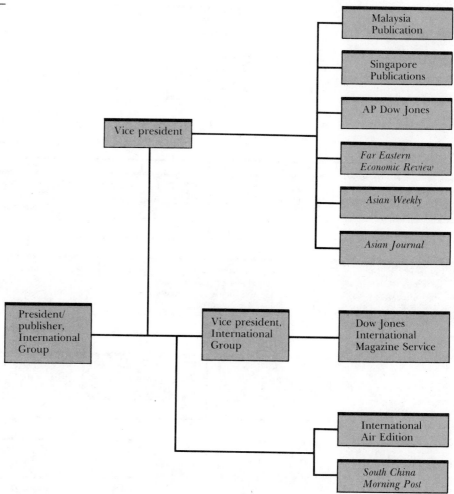

has more freedom in pricing strategies, manufacturing techniques, and research
and development. The subsidiaries must generate a large enough volume of
business to justify their existence, and the host country must be politically
stable for the firm to survive and prosper.

Another type of direct investment is the joint venture, in which a U.S.
firm and a foreign company combine resources to form a new, third company
that usually is located in the foreign country. This type of arrangement is
attractive in countries where potential profits point toward a subsidiary but
local laws and attitudes do not permit it. The American firm typically provides
needed expertise and capital under such an arrangement. Since the foreign
firm has a vested interest in the company, it will help protect the American
firm's interests as well.

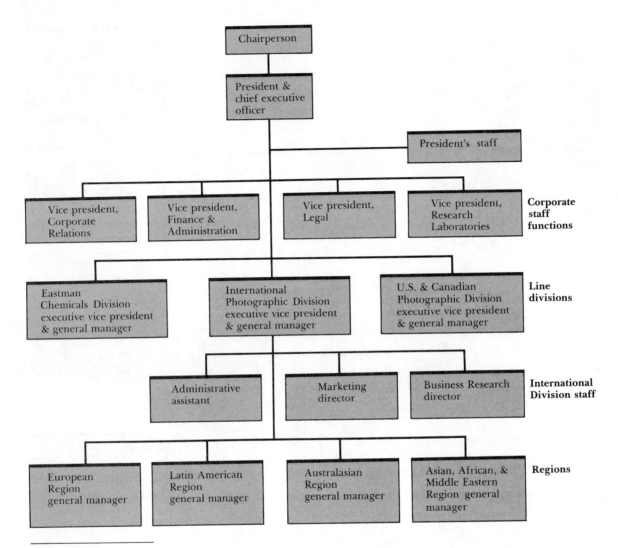

FIGURE 18.3
Eastman Kodak's multinational organizational structure [*Source:* Michael G. Duerr and John M. Roach, *Organization and Control of International Operations* (New York: The Conference Board, 1973), p. 43. Reprinted by permission.]

World Trade Channels

Some firms choose not to invest in subsidiaries abroad. Instead, they transact business through intermediate agents. Export merchants, buyers for export, and export agents are indirect export channels. Import merchants, import commission houses, and import brokers are indirect import channels.

Export merchants are wholesalers who buy directly from a U.S. manufacturing firm to resell in a foreign country. Export merchants handle all details of the sale and bear all the risks in the transaction. The advantage of this type of arrangement is its simplicity and economy. The selling firm sells to the export merchants as if they were a domestic purchaser. It doesn't need to have special personnel trained to deal with overseas buyers or to cultivate demand in foreign countries. Small American manufacturers who would not otherwise sell in foreign markets use this type of arrangement extensively. A major disadvantage is that, without personal contact with the ultimate consumer, the manufacturer has no opportunity to adapt to market changes or to create goodwill for the product.

A **buyer for export** is a commissioned representative of foreign clients who canvasses American markets for items desired by these clients. The advantage of this arrangement is that it involves few marketing expenses for the seller, but it is an unstable market because purchases are irregular and the seller usually must assume shipping costs.

Export agents are to world trade what manufacturer's representatives are to domestic trade. They usually represent several noncompeting manufacturing firms and make sales in the name of the American firm, which then ships the product. Export agents are valuable when there is a need to create a demand through aggressive selling. Since they deal with the same overseas customers repeatedly, they provide feedback about the foreign markets.

Products also can be sold in foreign markets through **licensing agreements.** Under such an agreement, an American firm (the licensor) enters into agreement with a foreign firm (the licensee) for the foreign firm to manufacture or sell on a royalty basis in a specific market for a limited time. The amount of technical assistance and degree of control by the licensor varies with the type of agreement. Although licensing can have the advantage of additional revenue for a small investment of personnel or money, the licensor risks losing control of the product's quality. The licensee also may later decide to go into direct competition with the licensor.

Most American firms import indirectly through intermediaries such as import merchants, import commission houses, and import brokers. **Import merchants** buy foreign goods on their own, assuming all risks, and have a sales force that resells to American business firms. An **import commission house** receives goods on consignment from foreign firms and sells them to American buyers; the importer does not assume title to the goods. **Import brokers** do

Export merchants

Buyer for export

Export agents

Indirect methods of importing

not handle foreign merchandise; instead, for a commission, they bring the American buyer and foreign seller together.

These indirect methods of importing are popular with American firms because they make buying imports as convenient as buying from a domestic firm. Specialized personnel are not needed; and, since the intermediaries usually are American, communication problems are minimal.

The Political and Legal Environment

Firms establishing international operations must weigh many considerations. The political and legal environment, in particular, differs from country to country. Most experts recommend enlisting the help of reputable professionals in foreign countries to ensure compliance with local laws.

Government controls on trade

Legal issues to be considered include trade restrictions, tariffs, and other government controls. The laws of most countries differ from ours with respect to the type and quantities of goods that can be imported and exported. Tariffs also differ. Tariffs levied on imported goods generally range from 10 to 18% of the value of the goods. The tariff may be based on the value of the goods (ad valorum), or it may be a specific amount (such as five cents per pound), or a combination of the two. Elaborate inspection procedures to assess the value of goods often cause extensive delays before the amount of tariff due is finally determined.

Other controls used by governments to limit imports and exports include import licenses that specify the quantity or value of imports, exchange licenses for obtaining foreign currencies with which to buy goods abroad, and import quotas. Our own domestic industries, faced with sharp foreign competition, frequently ask Congress to raise tariffs or to set import quotas.

Managers involved in international commerce must remember that all business transactions are governed by the laws of the country in which they are operating. To avoid legal problems, they need competent assistance from local people familiar with that country's laws.

The Foreign Corrupt Practices Act   Besides having to comply with laws of foreign countries in which they do business, American businesspeople must also comply with U.S. laws governing business transactions abroad. Perhaps the most significant piece of legislation affecting international trade relations is the Foreign Corrupt Practices Act of 1977. The major portion of the law defines "corrupt practices" and lists the civil and criminal penalties imposed for violations.

Major features of FCPA

The Foreign Corrupt Practices Act (FCPA) prohibits any bribery payment, promise of payment, or authorization of payment to a foreign political party, official, or candidate for political office for the purpose of obtaining,

THE IN-BOX

Olin Corporation's Bribery Troubles

Olin Corporation, a multinational company that produces ammunition, chemicals, brass, and paper and cellophane products, is mired in an alleged bribery scandal dating back to the 1970s. On one front, Olin is involved in a long-standing court battle with one of its former executives, who is accused of taking large kickbacks from foreign-based agents of its Winchester ammunition division. At the same time, a five-year investigation of Olin by the Internal Revenue Service alleges that the company had a worldwide policy of funneling bribes through its overseas agents.

The IRS investigators claim that some of Olin's agents paid off officials in Iran, Taiwan, Venezuela, Greece, and the Philippines. They also contend that Olin made direct payments to officials in Nicaragua. Moreover, investigators believe that Olin's top management concealed evidence of payoffs from the Securities and Exchange Commission.

Albert Hakim, former principal agent in Iran for Olin's Winchester division, has testified that he routinely arranged to funnel most of his commission to Iranian military officials who helped Winchester secure contracts. Hakim's company, Multi-Corp, helped arrange $50 million in sales of ammunition and technical-assistance projects to the Iranian military. The payoffs, he said, went to generals and other military officers who were close to the late Shah.

IRS investigators claim that some foreign agents told Winchester employees that payoffs were needed to win contracts. An agent in Venezuela wrote to a Winchester sales executive: "If we want to make business with the VAF (Venezuelan Air Force), we will have to dance to the music they play." Winchester got the contract and paid the agent $124,000 in commissions, most of which was earmarked for military officers. David S. Miller, a former Winchester sales executive, says, "You can't operate without agents in most countries. You need them to hold your hand— to get yourself properly introduced to officials you want to negotiate with."

Source: Edward T. Pound, "Olin Is Still Plagued by Allegations of Bribing Foreign Officials in '70s," *Wall Street Journal,* April 27, 1984, p. 31.

retaining, or directing business to any person. Convictions carry penalties of up to $1 million for the corporation and up to $10,000 and five years' imprisonment for any officer, director, or stockholder of a corporation that breaks the law.[7] The bribery problems of Olin Corporation are explained in the In-Box on this page.

Bribery, a facet of business ethics, must be considered in an international perspective, that is, considering different ethical, religious, cultural, social, economic, and legal settings. Bribing officials may be considered unlawful in virtually every country, but in some countries these payments are still a normal, expected, and customary method of doing business. Even under the Foreign Corrupt Practices Act, some forms of payment are considered legal. For example, payments under threat or duress are permitted; so are gifts or small amounts of cash known as grease payments given to a person "whose duties are essentially ministerial or clerical" for the purpose of expediting routine business transactions.[8]

Adherence to the Foreign Corrupt Practices Act may have cost American business billions of dollars in lost revenue. Consider the following:

> The United States has fallen from first place to seventh during the past three years in the number of overseas construction contracts received. In percentage terms, American firms receive only 4.9 percent of contracts now, versus 16 percent three years ago . . . the FCPA is not the only cause— in fact, . . . the U.S. taxation policy on Americans working overseas is probably the most important factor. But the FCPA ranks . . . a close second.[9]

> Losses have been substantial in the pharmaceutical, engineering and construction industries, which conduct much business with governments of countries that consider political payments normal and necessary.[10]

> When Shaw Mudge & Company of Stamford, Connecticut, recently spent $120,000 retaining an agent to develop sales in India and Sri Lanka, it looked like a successful investment. The maker of essences used in perfume and cosmetics landed a contract worth $350,000 a year from a soap manufacturer in Sri Lanka. Then the buyer asked Shaw Mudge to overinvoice his company by 25 percent and send the difference to a Swiss bank account. Although the procedure wouldn't have cost the company a penny, Shaw Mudge refused to go along because of the Foreign Corrupt Practices Act of 1977, which forbids such payments made to foreign government officials in order to obtain business. The customer company in this case belonged to a government-owned conglomerate, making the buyer a government agent. Without cooperating in the agreement, Shaw Mudge lost the sale.[11]

As these statements indicate, some people feel that the Foreign Corrupt Practices Act puts American firms at a competitive disadvantage. They also believe that the United States should enforce the act only in countries that reciprocate.[12]

Legal payments under FCPA   Some forms of payments used to induce business in foreign countries are clearly illegal. Other types of payments are highly questionable, and still others are legal. Table 18.3 lists the various forms of payments used to gain contracts and conduct business in international markets.

Political Guidelines for Multinationals   The political climate of the foreign country is very important to the success of a business venture. The foreign

TABLE 18.3
Forms of payments to
induce business in
foreign countries

Unlawful Forms of Payment

Mail bribe A voluntary payment involving large sums of cash, with concealed accounting procedures. It seeks unlawful, unethical, or unfair advantage.

Kickback A voluntary payment involving invoicing at an inflated price, with the difference between the actual and inflated price being paid to a local official involved. Concealed accounting procedures are customary.

Political contribution A voluntary, direct payment for political causes involving partially concealed accounting procedures.

Questionable Forms of Payment

Donation A voluntary, direct payment with partially concealed accounting procedures.

Gratuity A voluntary, direct payment involving moderate sums of cash and partially concealed accounting procedures.

Agent's fee A voluntary, direct payment involving moderate sums of cash.

Lawful Forms of Payment

Grease payment A voluntary payment involving small sums of cash.

Extortion payment A payment made under duress or threat.

Bona fide sales commission A percentage of sales paid to a local agent for services performed.

country in which a firm chooses to operate should be politically stable, and the firm should maintain a good working relationship with the government in solving problems related to foreign trade legislation. In the past, some host nations have felt exploited by foreign firms; consequently, they do not regard multinational corporations highly. Local government agencies, the press, and the public closely watch these firms. The governments of twenty-four non-communist countries have proposed a code of ethics for multinational corporations, including the following rules:

1. MNCs cannot meddle in the political processes of countries in which they operate.

Code of ethics

2. No bribes are permissible under any conditions.

3. No donations to political parties are proper unless national laws permit them.

4. MNCs should make full disclosure of local sales and profits, the number of employees, and expenditures for research and development for major regions of the world.

5. MNCs should not participate in cartels and should avoid predatory behavior toward competitors.

6. MNCs should pay the proper amount of taxes in countries in which revenues are earned. They should not attempt to avoid paying taxes by switching money from high-tax to low-tax countries.

7. MNCs should respect the right of their employees to join labor unions.[13]

Managers of international corporations should be a force of goodwill and should strive to be responsible citizens at home as well as abroad. Since multinational corporations bring capital, technology, and experience to developing countries, people in such countries should be made aware of the benefits of hosting a foreign firm. Managers can accomplish this by publicizing the company's good deeds.

Successful International Management

To be successful in international trade, managers must overcome communication problems, respect the cultural differences of foreigners, and develop a thorough understanding of international finance.

Communication Problems

Poor translations

There are more than 2,800 languages in the world, and few Americans can converse in more than one of them. Even though English is widely accepted as the language of commerce, communication problems still arise. Former President Jimmy Carter's speech in Poland will long be remembered for his statement of appreciation for the Polish. His words, literally translated, meant that he "lusted for them." Obviously, this was not his intent. When President John Kennedy spoke in Berlin, he tried to say he was proud to consider himself from Berlin, but he actually said he was a "Berliner"—according to one interpretation, a jelly-filled donut.[14]

Other communication problems

As mentioned in Chapter 13, under the section "Communication Problems in International Business," the translation of product names and slogans can cause problems. Consider the following examples. Ford Motor Company introduced the top-of-the-line Comet Caliente in Mexico, but sales were sluggish. Upon investigation, it was discovered that *caliente* is slang for "street-walker" in Mexico.[15] The Chevrolet Nova literally translated into "star" in Spanish, but Puerto Rican auto dealers were unenthusiastic. When spoken, Nova sounds like *no va,* which in Spanish means "it doesn't go." Sales increased when General Motors changed the name to Caribe.[16] Pepsi Cola's advertising slogan, "Come alive with Pepsi" ran into problems in parts of Asia, where it translated into "Bring your ancestors back from the dead." In Germany, it meant, "Come out of the grave."[17] An American toothpaste manufacturer advertised that using its toothpaste would make one more "interesting." In Latin America, "interesting" is a euphemism for "pregnant."[18]

Company names must also be chosen carefully so as not to be confusing or offensive. An airline trying to gain acceptance in Australia chose the name EMU. Unfortunately, the emu is an Australian bird that is incapable of flight. Esso had difficulties in the Japanese market because phonetically its name meant "stalled car." A trade magazine that promoted giftware worldwide had the word gift in its title. Unfortunately for the company, *gift* is the German word for "poison."[19]

Exxon and Kodak are two company names that were specifically designed for their lack of specific meaning but ease of pronunciation. Kodak used a research team to develop its name, while Exxon was derived by a lengthy and expensive computer-assisted search.

Understanding Cultural Differences

Understanding a foreign country's social and cultural aspects is as important to a company's effectiveness as is understanding its language. Knowing what to do is just as important as knowing what not to say. For example, each nationality views the concept of time differently, and many do not share our concern with time at all. Time is a valuable commodity in America; consequently, people rush to consummate business transactions. Greeks, however, feel time limits are insulting and reveal a lack of finesse. Arabs faced with a deadline feel threatened and backed into a corner.

Understanding different cultures

Nonverbal cues also can offend foreign businesspeople. For instance, a face-to-face position that conveys friendship in one country can mean confrontation in another. South Americans, Greeks, and Japanese feel more comfortable standing or sitting close to strangers than do people of many other nationalities.[20] Some hints for dealing with people from different cultures are presented in the Manager's Notebook on page 484.

Avoiding stereotyping

A stereotype is a mental picture used to identify certain groups of people. It usually contains a label given to the group and a mental list of traits associated with the group. When the label is applied to a national group, it becomes a national stereotype. Because the world is complex, such national stereotypes are used as a mental shortcut in thinking about groups of people. Being sensitive to national stereotypes will help international managers better understand the behavior of certain groups of people they meet but there is a danger in relying on these stereotypes. The international manager must remember that stereotypes are only broad generalizations about groups of people. Each person is an individual and will act and react in his or her own personal way.

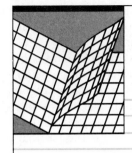

THE MANAGER'S NOTEBOOK

Universally Successful Communication Skills

Several studies have tried to determine which communication skills, if any, are effective with all cultures. The results of these studies are particularly important to American managers engaged in international trade and to those who employ foreign-born employees. Six skills appear to be universally successful, because they minimize defensiveness and build up a supportive climate for effective communication.

1. *Communicate personal respect.* This means to treat others as equals and to use certain titles when addressing others.
2. *Maintain flexibility.* When a manager finds someone behaving in an unexpected manner, the manager needs to camouflage any personal discomfort.
3. *Communicate warmth.* Managers need to show that they care about their employees and that they consider their subordinates vital to the organization.
4. *Remain objective.* A manager shouldn't be judgmental.
5. *Determine facts.* A good manager won't make inferences based on inadequate information and will avoid stereotyping.
6. *Show empathy.* The ability to see things from the other person's point of view is probably the most sensitive cross-cultural skill a manager can possess.

Source: James B. Stull, "Communication in Multinational Companies," *Supervisory Management*, August 1983, pp. 2–9.

Someone traveling to a foreign country, with its different culture and standards, uses a self-reference criterion for interpreting events in the new environment. This means that the person makes decisions and judgments based on standards in the home culture. The effective manager will train himself or herself to balance these assumptions and references with a sensitivity to the viewpoints of the local people.

Economic and Financial Aspects

A firm deciding to venture overseas must consider special aspects of the international economic and financial environment. The manager needs to become familiar with foreign exchange, since the flow of currencies poses unique problems for the firm and its government.

Convertibility of currency

Barter was the widely accepted means of exchange in the past and is still used in some underdeveloped nations and communist countries. For trade to replace barter, purchasers must be able to offer a suitable means of payment to the seller. Gold is widely acceptable but is in short supply and cumbersome; the risk of theft is also high. The only feasible alternative is payment in currency.

Even though the American dollar is widely accepted for trade and investment, there is no "world currency." This is why the American traveler must exchange dollars for French francs, English pounds, or other currencies.

Convertibility refers to the ease with which two currencies can be exchanged. A currency that cannot be readily exchanged is in one of the degrees of inconvertibility; that is, exchange is very difficult, or the currency may have to be sold at a substantial discount.[21]

For both economic and political reasons, governments often institute exchange controls to restrict the convertibility of their currencies. Communist countries use such controls to isolate their economies from outside influences. Even the United States engages in controls by restricting the amount of money that can be invested abroad, primarily in Western Europe.

The most common types of exchange controls that governments use are multiple exchange rates and rationing. *Multiple* exchange rate systems involve using different exchange rates for different types of transactions. For instance, if the item to be imported is high on the government's priority list, the importer will be granted a very favorable exchange rate. If the item is not as desirable, an unfavorable rate may be applied. Alternatively, the government may limit the supply of foreign exchange available and ration it on a first-come first-served basis, or high-priority items may be given the bulk of the exchange that is available.

Exchange rates

Convertibility implies that the appropriate exchange rates have been determined. The ideal situation is one in which an exchange rate is set so that the price of one currency relative to another is at the point where the flow of transactions between the two countries would exactly balance out; this would occur if prices were allowed to fluctuate freely. However, over a period of time instability would result from wide fluctuations. Fixed values of exchange rates protect against the disruptive effects of such instability. These fixed exchange rates, called "par value," are chosen somewhat arbitrarily by each country; at best, they are educated guesses.

The International Monetary Fund   After World War I, international trade and the flow of capital broke down, helping to deepen the Great Depression. This also contributed to the eruption of World War II. Toward the end of this war, in 1944, Allied nations met in Bretton Woods, New Hampshire, to plan to control postwar trading relations between nations. This organization created the **International Monetary Fund (IMF),** designed to perform the following functions:

1. Foster a worldwide system of exchange rates

2. Encourage free currency convertibility

3. Provide for orderly changes in par value when necessary

4. Provide a source of monetary reserves for a currency whose stability is threatened[22]

Functions of IMF

Membership is open to all nations willing to abide by the organization's rules. Most noncommunist countries are members, but the Soviet Union and its satellites are not.

When a country joins the International Monetary Fund, an acceptable par value for that country's currency is set, usually in terms of U.S. dollars. The IMF allows the value to float between 1% above and 1% below its par value. These points are called *intervention points* because IMF regulations require that the nation's government prevent its currency from going beyond these limits. If the demand for the currency exceeds the supply, the price will rise; then, the government must supply more of its own currency by buying up the foreign currency. If more of the currency is being sold than is being bought, the price will fall; then, the government must intervene by buying its own currency, using funds from its own stabilization fund. This fund arises from liquid asset reserves of the government. If a government's assets are inadequate to accomplish stabilization, the country can borrow from the IMF while it takes the necessary steps to end the currency imbalance. The IMF will automatically lend money to a member until its holdings of the borrower's currency equal 100% of the nation's quota.

To provide resources for the fund to lend, all member nations contribute 25% gold and 75% currency based on the relative economic strength of the country, called its *quota*. When a member country borrows from the fund, it exchanges an equivalent amount of its currency. If this amount is not sufficient, there are provisions for additional borrowing, but the IMF's demand for monetary and fiscal action becomes more stringent.

Devaluation and revaluation

The IMF also is instrumental in changing par values of a currency when, in extreme conditions, its support is not sufficient to maintain the prevailing par value of a currency. When the change lowers par value in relationship to all other currencies, it is said that *devaluation* occurs. International managers are directly affected because they will have less international buying power after the devaluation. When par value is increased, *revaluation* is said to occur. Revaluation benefits the international firm by increasing its buying power.

Balance of payments

The IMF also is concerned with the *balance of payments* of countries. The IMF defines balance of payments as "a systematic recording of all transactions during the period, between residents of the reporting country and residents of other countries."[23] Each country engaged in international trade has a balance of payments that normally is examined annually. (The United States reports quarterly and then consolidates to arrive at an annual figure.) This balance of payments is of transactions made between individuals in each country, recorded by a governmental agency. The balance of payments is rarely zero because it would be very unlikely that inflow would exactly equal outflow. Difficulties occur when the outflow is greater than the inflow. This tends to create a balance-of-payments deficit in the country losing the funds and a surplus in the receiving country. If the foreign banks are holding more dollars than they want, they can demand that American Federal Reserve Banks buy back some or all of the dollars, thereby decreasing American reserves of foreign currency.

Balance of trade

The *balance of trade* relates to the balance of payments but has a narrower scope. The balance of trade is simply the merchandise imports and exports of a country. If exports exceed imports, a balance-of-trade surplus exists; if imports are greater than exports, there is a balance-of-trade deficit. Economically speaking, a balance-of-trade surplus is healthier.

Eurodollars and Eurobonds **Eurodollars** are interest-bearing deposits denominated in U.S. dollars in a commercial bank outside the United States.[24] Typically, they come about when foreigners, who receive payments by checks drawn on American banks, deposit the dollars in banks in their own countries. They also are created when Americans or foreigners who hold deposits in American banks transfer those deposits to foreign banks; or when holders of convertible currencies, such as West German marks, exchange them for dollars and deposit them in foreign banks. These original deposits then can be loaned, with most maturities ranging from one to six months. American companies expanding their operations abroad have relied heavily on the Eurodollar market for working capital.

Debt instruments

Eurobonds, an offshoot of Eurodollars, are dollar-denominated debt instruments floated outside the United States.[25] They provide increased financial resources to foreign borrowers and subject both lender and borrower to fewer restrictions than exist in most national markets, including the United States.

Financing International Operations Firms engaged in international trade finance their operations in several different ways. Traditional sources are domestic borrowing, internal cash flows, and stock offerings. A U.S. government agency will offer financial assistance as well. This agency, called the

Government assistance

Export-Import Bank of the United States (Eximbank), facilitates the export of American products and services by offering both financial assistance and business advice. Sometimes, American exporters cannot meet the competition from foreign exporters assisted by their own governments; Eximbank comes to their aid. It also helps small firms in foreign countries to raise funds for buying American products. It has a small-business advisory service that can be used by both American exporters and foreign importers of American products. Eximbank operates under the auspices of the U.S. Department of Commerce.

The Commerce Department also helps U.S. businesspeople who do business abroad through its Bureau of International Commerce. This bureau gathers business and economic information throughout the world, such as lists of buyers, distributors, and agents for various products in each country; living costs and conditions abroad; sources of foreign credit information and financing; and directories of foreign advertising agencies. The Bureau of International Commerce also publishes a monthly publication entitled *Overseas Business Report,* providing information about foreign markets.

Free Trade Zones   A **free trade zone** is an area in a seaport, airport, or some other inland point where goods of foreign origin may be brought in for reexport without payment of customs duty.[26] Goods also may be manufactured,

Advantages of free trade zones

sold, and serviced within free trade zones. There are many advantages in using free trade zones, including tax relief or tax exemption, inexpensive production or storage facilities, access to less-expensive raw materials from neighboring countries, and savings in transportation and financing costs. Transportation savings can be brought about by shipping the product in bulk containers and then breaking it down into the proper size and container for sale from the free trade zone.

There are thirty free trade zones in the United States, primarily located in port cities like New Orleans, New York, and San Francisco. There are more than one hundred free trade zones abroad that American exporters can use. The U.S. Department of Commerce publishes a directory of their locations, listing financial benefits and operating advantages.

The Future of International Business

Conflicting views

There is considerable disagreement over the future of international business and the multinational firm. Some believe that the day of the multinational firm's ascendancy is coming to an end. Instead of continued growth and integration of the world economy, they contend, we are entering an age of disintegration and stagnation, given existing imbalances and growing demands on limited resources.[27] Others disagree with this pessimistic view. They feel that the outcome of activities in five specific areas will strongly influence the future of international business: (1) whether more satisfactory forms of resolving conflicts can be found, (2) the intensity and nature of protectionism, (3) the extent and influence of movements toward internationalism and away from nation-states, (4) the progress of commerce between East and West, and (5) the progress made in developing the poor countries of the world.[28]

The managers of international and multinational firms will want to closely monitor these and other influences that will shape the future of international business.

Review

✓ *What international trade means for the manager.* International management involves developing sources of international trade and transacting business between one country and other countries. International trade is vital to the firms that conduct business on a global basis and has a tremendous impact on our economy as a whole. Today, the jobs of millions of Americans depend on world trade. Besides being part of this worldwide exchange of goods and services, many American firms have heavy investments in overseas operations.

Organizational arrangements for conducting international business vary from firm to firm. In some cases, they create a corporate division through which to channel all international business transactions. Other firms use a global area structure, in which the general manager of the subsidiary reports directly to the division head at headquarters. Others, particularly smaller companies, buy and sell through intermediate agents. Export channels include export merchants, buyers for export, export agents, and licensing agreements. Import channels include import merchants, import commission houses, and import brokers.

The international business environment is significantly different from the domestic environment. Managers engaged in international trade must understand political and legal forces, in particular. They must be especially familiar with the Foreign Corrupt Practices Act of 1977, which regulates payments to foreign officials as inducements for business dealings.

✓ *How to be successful in international management.* To be successful in international business, managers need to overcome communication barriers and to learn the customs of the people of other countries. Special care should be taken in selecting product names and slogans.

Managers engaged in international trade also must understand international finance, especially foreign exchange, and the functions of the International Monetary Fund, which fosters a worldwide system of exchange rates. Firms engaged in international trade finance their operations through traditional sources, such as domestic borrowing and stock offerings, and through financial assistance provided by the Export-Import Bank of the United States.

Some firms engaged in international trade find it advantageous to use free trade zones, which are areas in airports, seaports, and other inland points where goods of foreign origin can be brought in for reexport without payment of customs duty.

✔ *The future of international business.* The future of international trade is uncertain. Some analysts believe that international trade will stagnate; others see continued growth. Forces that will determine the future of international trade include settlement of conflicts, the degree of protectionism exercised by countries, a move toward internationalism, progress in East-West relations, and the development of poor, underdeveloped countries.

THE MANAGER'S DICTIONARY

As an extra review of the chapter, try defining the following terms. If you have trouble with any of them, refer to the page numbers listed.

multinational corporations
   (MNCs) (470)
international trade (470)
foreign subsidiaries (474)
export merchants (477)
buyer for export (477)

export agents (477)
licensing agreements (477)
import merchants (477)
import commission house
   (477)
import brokers (477)

International Monetary
   Fund (485)
Eurodollars (487)
Eurobonds (487)
free trade zone (488)

REVIEW QUESTIONS

1. Discuss the benefits derived by firms that engage in international trade.

2. How can the economy as a whole benefit from international trade? Explain.

3. What goods should the United States import? export? Why?

4. If a firm wishes to engage in international trade but doesn't want to build facilities or locate personnel in foreign countries, what approaches are available to it?

5. How does the political and legal environment of foreign countries differ from that of the United States? Discuss.

6. How can the government of a country limit imports and exports?

7. How does the Foreign Corrupt Practices Act affect managers who engage in international trade?

8. In your opinion, is the Foreign Corrupt Practices Act harmful to U.S. businesses? Explain.

9. Why is it important for Americans engaged in international business to understand the cultures of other nations?

10. How does American culture differ from that of Japan? Latin America? Give examples.

11. Why do governments institute exchange controls to restrict the convertibility of their currencies?

12. What type of exchange controls can governments institute?

13. Explain the functions of the International Monetary Fund.

14. What assistance does the U.S. government offer to businesspeople who wish to expand their operations into foreign markets? Discuss.

15. In your opinion, will international trade increase or decrease in the future? Justify your answer.

MANAGEMENT CHALLENGE

Assume that you are the vice president of marketing for a computer manufacturer that wants to market its personal computers in Europe and Latin America. Your firm does not want to build facilities overseas until the success of the venture can be established.

1. What options are available to your firm? What are the advantages and disadvantages of each alternative?

2. What can you lawfully do to induce potential customers to buy your firm's products? What restrictions are placed on your activities? Explain.

3. What kinds of problems would you anticipate in the overseas venture? How could you minimize these obstacles?

4. What assistance could the U.S. government offer your firm? Discuss.

CASE 18.1

Japanese Businesses Rethink U.S. Locations[29]

Some states in America impose a unitary tax on multinational corporations operating within their boundaries. Such a tax is based on world-wide income rather than on income generated in this country. States that impose such taxes, including California and Florida, are beginning to feel a backlash of opposition from Japanese firms. For example, Fujitsu Ltd., a major computer manufacturer, announced in 1984 that it would not build a plant in California unless the unitary tax were repealed. Kyocera Corporation, another Japanese manufacturer, later blamed the unitary tax for its decision to construct a new $30 million plant in the state of Washington rather than to expand its plant in San Diego, California. Kyocera officials claim that between 1972 and 1983 the company was taxed at an effective rate of 101% on its California profits of $40 million.

Sony Corporation also is pressing for abolition of the unitary tax. Sony's chief executive officer, Akio Morita, unveiled a 1984 survey claiming that more than one hundred Japanese firms were willing to invest nearly $1.5 billion in California if the state repeals the tax. Morita claimed that such an investment would create eleven thousand new jobs.

So far, the reaction of state legislators has been mixed. Some have openly supported abolition of the unitary tax, while others have expressed doubt about its deterring effects. Many Americans seem to feel that the unitary income tax is only one relatively small consideration in plant location decisions.

Questions

1. Can you cite any disadvantages to eliminating a state's unitary income tax?

2. What factors, other than taxes, enter into a multinational corporation's decision to locate a plant in the United States?

CASE 18.2

North and South Korea Talk Trade[30]

November 15, 1984, marked a new beginning for improved relations between North and South Korea. For the first time since the outbreak of the Korean War in 1950, the two countries engaged in trade discussions. North Korea badly needs technology and foreign investment to help develop its natural resources. South Korea needs raw materials from the north; specifically, coal, iron ore, lead, zinc, and farm products. North Korea needs steel, textiles, and other goods from the south. Interested parties have even suggested restoring rail service between the two countries.

Propaganda used by North Koreans in the past may haunt them now. Persistent belittling of South Korea's economy in the past will make it politically difficult for the north to import manufactured goods in exchange for raw materials, since North Korean consumers will believe the goods to be low quality. Moreover, many South Koreans fear that the north will try to exploit the improved relations for subversive purposes.

Actually, each country would benefit from direct trade with the other. South Korea, for instance, wants to broaden its trade with China. North Korea may be the ticket to such trade. North Korea, on the other hand, wishes to attract foreign investment, especially from the United States and Japan. To achieve its goal, North Korea has recently decided to permit joint ventures with foreign investors. Within the next few years, North Korea expects a steady stream of Western businesspeople to fill its new, 1,200-room, high-rise hotel in Pyongyang.

Questions

1. Explain how both North and South Korea could benefit from direct trade. Do economic considerations constitute the only impetus for such trade? Discuss.

2. In your opinion, why does South Korea want to broaden its trade with China? Does the growing protectionism in the United States affect South Korea? Explain.

CHAPTER OUTLINE

What Is Labor Relations?

The History of Organized Labor

Major Federal Labor Laws

The Sherman Antitrust Act

The Clayton Act

The Norris-LaGuardia Act

The National Labor Relations Act (Wagner Act)

The Labor-Management Relations Act (Taft-Hartley Act)
*The Union Shop • Right-to-Work Laws • The Agency Shop •
Circumventing the Law • Other Major Provisions of Taft-Hartley •
Taft-Hartley Amendments*

The Labor-Management Reporting and Disclosure Act (Landrum-Griffin Act)

Public Sector Bargaining

Rights and Responsibilities of Employers

Negotiating the Union Contract

Unions and Management

M A N A G E M E N T   I N   A C T I O N

Companies Resist White-Collar Unions

Historically, unions have not tried very hard to organize technical, professional, and office workers. But shrinking union membership in basic industries has prompted organized labor to take a second look at these white-collar
workers.

Most forecasters anticipate no employment growth over the next decade
in the industries that are the mainstay of the nation's strongest unions. In fact,
they expect the number of unionized workers to drop even lower than its
current level of 20%, which is the lowest it has been since 1942. To remain a
viable economic and political force, labor will have to tap the white-collar
sector, which experts believe will grow by a million workers a year until 1990.[1]

Employers are fighting off organizing efforts because unionization means
they will lose much of their flexibility in managing their employees. Unionization also could result in higher wages, more work rules, and greater fringe
benefits. Unions that try to organize the seventeen million clerical workers,
five million salespeople, and ten million technical-professional workers who
are now unorganized will face formidable obstacles, many of them unique to
white-collar organizing.

One obstacle is the white-collar workers' ignorance of unions and their
purposes. Many white-collar workers think that the primary purpose of unions
is to help lazy workers keep their jobs. Another problem is that white-collar
workers identify more closely with management than do workers on a factory
floor. They also think of themselves as more individualistic, which contradicts

495

the union philosophy. In addition, they fear that they will be branded traitors or troublemakers if they get involved in union activities.[2] Managers, of course, do little or nothing to dispel those feelings and concerns.

Unions' efforts to organize white-collar workers are built around five issues: inadequate pay, lack of job security, inequitable treatment of workers, questionable safety practices, and management's failure to communicate plans to workers. But employers contend that most white-collar workers are satisfied with their jobs. As evidence of workers' satisfaction, employers point to the low success rates of union representation elections, an increasing number of decertification elections that oust unions, and dwindling union membership nationwide.

Preview

Long before American workers received from Congress the right to form and join unions and to engage in collective bargaining, they banded together in an effort to raise their wages, shorten their work hours, and improve their working conditions. But these collective efforts to improve their working conditions were met with strong resistance from employers. Lockouts and court decisions favoring employers made most union efforts ineffective or unlawful in the early days of the labor movement.

Although most employers are now required to recognize labor organizations and engage in good-faith collective bargaining, they still resist organizing efforts. Most managers believe that unions limit their freedom of action and result in higher operations costs. In this chapter, we will examine union-management relations and analyze the environment of collective bargaining. This chapter describes:

✓ The meaning of labor relations

✓ The history of organized labor

✓ How major federal laws affect labor-management relations

✓ What restrictions govern public sector bargaining

✓ The rights and responsibilities of employers regarding unions

✓ The steps in negotiating a union contract and what contracts cover

What Is Labor Relations?

Sooner or later, all managers are affected by labor unions. A strike may shut down your plant. A strike at a supplier could stop the flow of needed resources. A negotiated pay raise at the trucking company that ships your goods could raise their rates and your costs. Or a dockworkers' strike could leave your goods sitting on the pier. All managers should, therefore, be aware of their relationship with unions.

Labor relations defined

Labor relations refers to a continuous relationship between an employer and a group of employees represented by a union. The relationship includes negotiating, interpreting, and administering a written contract covering pay, hours of work, and other employment conditions. Probably no other aspect of a manager's job causes as much anxiety and consumes as much energy as does negotiating and administering the labor agreement.

At the heart of labor relations is power. Workers are aware of the employer's power to fire and discipline them, affecting their lives and needs and those of their families. Most employers use their power fairly, giving their workers reasonable jobs, compensating them adequately, respecting their dignity, and retiring them after rewarding careers. Some employers, however, mistreat their employees by exploiting them economically and crushing their human dignity.[3]

Power in numbers

Although some labor unions are corrupt and violent, most of them represent their members well. They fight hard for improved working conditions, better wages, human dignity, and a share of the fruits of labor. It was what unions considered unfair work conditions that led to the development of the collective bargaining process in the United States. It means that employees join together to negotiate with management so that, as individuals, they do not have to stand alone against the power of a General Electric, a Department of Defense, a Wayne State University, or a Barnes Hospital.[4]

To comprehend the rights and responsibilities of labor and management, you need to know the history of the labor movement and to understand the laws that govern labor-management relations. First, this chapter will present a brief history of the labor movement in the United States. Then, it will discuss major pieces of federal legislation affecting how a manager deals with unions.

The History of Organized Labor

Organized labor is not new to American industry, but the first unions differed greatly from the giant, powerful unions of today. Workers banded together in small guilds in the 1780s to set training, quality, and price standards and to eliminate oppressive working conditions. Their concerns generally benefited workers and employers alike.

Early labor strikes

Craftspeople of this period primarily worked alone or in small shops but sometimes formed organizations to increase their earnings or to restrict their competition. Once in a while, these organizations locked horns with the merchants who bought their goods and with competitors; sometimes, work stoppages resulted. In 1786, for example, the Philadelphia Journeymen Printers stopped work over a wage cut, and the Journeymen Cordwainers (shoemakers) of Philadelphia were locked out by employers in 1799 after collective bargaining failed.[5] Still, for the most part, organized workers presented few problems for employers, and by 1820, unions were virtually extinct or inactive.

Conspiracy doctrine

With the return of economic prosperity in 1824, however, unions sprang up again. Organized workers all over the country began ill-fated efforts to raise their wages and to reduce their working hours. Their strikes seldom were successful. In most cases, the courts ruled that workers' organizations seeking pay raises were illegal because they constituted criminal conspiracies.[6] Employers suffered a severe blow in 1842 when the Massachusetts Supreme Court overturned the conspiracy doctrine and declared that unions were not prima facie, or inherently, illegal.[7] Union activity increased after this, and various national craft federations were formed.

First unions formed

The Civil War, fought between 1861 and 1865, brought significant changes. Advancements in mass-production technology encouraged the development of large factories housing many workers under one roof—a situation that attracted organized labor. The National Labor Union was formed immediately after the war, followed by the Knights of Labor. The Knights were operating on a national basis in 1878 and had opened their membership to all who belonged to the "Brotherhood of Toil." When the American Federation of Labor (AFL) was formed in 1886, however, the Knights had started disintegrating as a result of bad publicity and by association with violent labor unrest.

Goals of AFL

The AFL had two major goals: (1) the economic betterment of its members and (2) the enhancement of the capitalistic system. Under the leadership of its first president, Samuel Gompers, the AFL jumped into the political arena and improved the status and image of organized labor.

Industrial Workers of the World

The Industrial Workers of the World (IWW) was formed in 1905 as an alternative to the AFL. Its goal was to overthrow the capitalist system because it felt that employers and employees had nothing in common.[8] "Big Bill" Haywood, the organizer of the IWW, called the organization's first convention to order with the following comments:

> Fellow workers. . . . We are here to confederate the workers of this country into a working class movement that shall have for its purpose the emancipation of the working class from the slave bondage of capitalism. . . . The aims and objectives of this organization should be to put the working class in possession of the economic power, means of life, in control of the machinery of production and distribution without regard to capitalist masters.[9]

By 1918, the IWW was dead for several reasons, including a lack of permanent, dues-paying members; its association with sabotage and violence; its inability to work through the existing political system; and its failure to appeal to the members' interests. By the beginning of World War I, the AFL was the only federation that had solid economic and political footing. It was the only national, organized labor movement to withstand a severe economic depression, a hostile press, angry employers, and three rival labor organizations.[10]

AFL membership declined from four million to two million workers during the Great Depression, but when the economy bounced back in the 1930s, union membership increased again. The AFL's particular concern was organizing the thousands of industrial workers in mass-production plants across the country. United Mine Workers President John L. Lewis advocated bringing industrial workers under the AFL umbrella. To achieve this objective, the Committee for Industrial Organization (CIO) was formed with Lewis as its chair. While Lewis proposed organizing workers by industry, other labor leaders insisted on organizing them along craft lines. For example, they felt that carpenters working in steel factories should belong to a carpenter's union, electricians who worked in an automobile factory should belong to an electrical union, and so on. Bickering and open hostility over this point came to a head in 1937, when the AFL expelled industrial unions connected to the CIO. The CIO grew stronger that same year, however, organizing auto and steel workers. The CIO was permanently organized in 1938 as the Congress of Industrial Organizations, with John L. Lewis as its first president. In 1941, Ford Motor Company signed its first contract with the United Auto Workers (UAW), a CIO

Formation of CIO

John L. Lewis (1880–1969), first president of the CIO.

George Meany (1894–1980), president of the AFL-CIO for twenty-four years.

member. The AFL and CIO remained separate until their merger in 1955. Conflict among unions has been minimal since then, largely because of the able leadership of George Meany, who presided over the AFL-CIO for twenty-four years.

After 1935, when Congress passed the National Labor Relations Act permitting most workers to organize, union membership grew steadily until the late 1970s, reaching an all-time high of about twenty-three million members. Today, union membership numbers less than twenty million. Gains have been made in the public sector, but membership in the private sector has continued to decline in recent years. The In-Box on page 501 describes how some unions are searching for a new look to attract members.

Major Federal Labor Laws

During the early years of the labor movement, no federal statutes governed unions, which were usually considered conspiracies under common law brought over from England. After the Massachusetts Supreme Court overturned the conspiracy doctrine in 1842, however, judges had to examine union motives and methods in strikes when deciding whether a strike was illegal.

THE IN-BOX

Unions Try to Change Their Image

Realizing that their power has eroded, some unions are trying hard to change their image and organizing tactics. They know that they must make big changes in the way they recruit, educate, and lead if they are to survive and to regain their lost clout.

The labor movement has been battered by the effects of imports, recessions, and nonunion competition. While the total number of civilian jobs rose by 5% between 1980 and 1984, union membership declined 13% during the same period. Unions now lose half of all representation elections (held to determine if nonunionized workers want to be represented) and three-fourths of all decertification elections (held to vote a union out). Moreover, a recent Gallup Poll ranked labor leaders next to last—just ahead of car salespeople—in terms of ethics and honesty.

One avenue to change is finding out what workers really want. Old issues simply aren't important any more. Consequently, unions are now stressing pay equity, day care, advancement for women, health and safety concerns in small firms, and job security for workers in the layoff-ridden, smokestack industries.

Unions also realize that, in confronting employers, they must operate as professional opponents rather than as streetfighters. Some unions, in fact, are hiring younger, better-educated recruiters. And, in some industries, unions even admit that they need a better way of cooperating with employers.

Meanwhile, a number of unions are initiating public-relations campaigns designed to counter their image of being greedy and obstructive. The campaigns try to portray unions as caring members of the community, interested primarily in the welfare and decent treatment of average people. The United Auto Workers, for example, counters Honda Motor Company's ad with a billboard campaign that plays off the company's slogan. The billboard reads: "They make it simple. We make it fair."

Source: Leonard M. Apcar and Cathy Trost, "Realizing Their Power Has Eroded, Unions Try Hard to Change," *Wall Street Journal*, February 21, 1985, p. 1+.

The Sherman Antitrust Act

After Congress passed the Sherman Antitrust Act in 1890, organized workers faced another major obstacle. There is real doubt whether Congress intended to include unions under the act; but, as a result of its passage, strikers found themselves branded combinations and conspiracies in restraint of trade. Federal courts ruled that strikes hurt interstate commerce; therefore, unions and their members taking part in strikes constituted an illegal conspiracy. The

Illegal conspiracy

employer of the striking workers could obtain a court order (injunction) forcing the strikers back on the job and killing their strike. It was not until the Apex Hosiery Company and the Hutcheson cases of 1940 and 1941, respectively, that the U.S. Supreme Court ruled that labor unions are not generally subject to the antitrust provisions of the Sherman Antitrust Act.[11]

The Clayton Act

Prolabor provisions

Because it felt that federal judges had misinterpreted the Sherman Antitrust Act, Congress tried to take them out of labor-management disputes by passing the Clayton Act in 1914. The intention of Congress was to keep employers from getting court injunctions forcing their striking employees back on the job. The Clayton Act also permitted picketing and other prounion activities. It was, however, the courts' interpretation of the Clayton Act that nullified its intended prolabor provisions: judges ruled that the law failed to deny employers the right to secure court injunctions.

The Norris-LaGuardia Act

The legislation that succeeded where the Clayton Act failed was the Norris-LaGuardia Act of 1932. This law effectively neutralized the federal judiciary in labor-management disputes. Essentially, it prohibited employers from using the Sherman Antitrust Act to obtain injunctions.

Yellow-dog contracts

The Norris-LaGuardia Act also made the **yellow-dog contract** unenforceable. When the national unemployment rate was hovering near 20% in the Great Depression, prospective employees willingly signed these contracts, promising that they would not join a union or engage in any union activity as a condition of employment. The ethics of yellow-dog contracts were questionable, but they did give employers tremendous power over their workers.

The National Labor Relations Act (Wagner Act)

The National Labor Relations Act of 1935, called the Wagner Act because its sponsor was New York Senator Robert Wagner, is the Magna Carta of labor. This legislation gave most workers the right to form and join unions and to bargain collectively with their employers. Before the act's passage, fewer than four million people were union members. Ten years later, union membership had tripled.

Wagner Act

Section 7, the heart of the Wagner Act, stipulates that most employees "shall have the right to self-organization, to form, join, or assist labor organizations, to bargain collectively through representatives of their own choosing, and to engage in concerted activities for the purpose of collective bargaining or other mutual aid or protection." The areas subject to collective bargaining are wages, hours of work, and working conditions, including fringe benefits.

To protect workers' rights, Congress placed several restrictions on employers.

1. *They are prohibited from using any form of intimidation, including threatening to fire employees or to close plants, if workers choose to join a union or to become involved in union activities.*

2. *They are prohibited from making financial contributions to support union activities.* Congress gave its blessing to the existence of labor unions, but it stipulated that unions must be economically self-sufficient. In the years before the Wagner Act, company-dominated unions were prevalent. These unions and their officers were mere pawns of management.

3. *Qualified job applicants cannot be rejected by employers simply because they are union members.* Nor can an employer require, as a condition of employment, that a prospective employee refrain from joining a union if one exists in the company. In addition, employees who become active in forming a union cannot be fired, demoted, or coerced for any prounion activity. This includes workers who circulate "showing-of-interest" petitions as well as workers who encourage their coworkers to join.[12]

NLRB

4. *Employers cannot punish employees who testify against them before the National Labor Relations Board.* The **National Labor Relations Board (NLRB)** was created as a part of the act to conduct representation elections and to hear charges of unfair labor practices brought by employees and employers.[13] Workers cannot be fired or harassed for filing unfair labor practice charges or for appearing before the board.

The NLRB administers the act. In addition to conducting elections, the board makes decisions on the makeup of bargaining units;[14] issues cease-and-desist orders; and can order wrongfully discharged employees reinstated, with or without back pay. Although the board can take corrective action, it cannot impose punitive damages.

5. *Employers must bargain in good faith.* The representatives of management and labor usually negotiate wages, hours of work, and other conditions of employment. The process normally begins when labor presents its demands to management, which makes counter offers. Most observers agree that labor initially asks for more than it expects to gain and that management usually offers less than it is willing to give. The compromise that is typically reached is somewhere between the demand and the offer, depending on the relative bargaining strength of the parties.

If management adjusts salaries, working hours, or other basic conditions of employment without first discussing it with the union, it is breaking the law. Management can, however, take the initiative by offering proposals to the union instead of merely reacting to the union's demands. If management makes conscientious offers concerning wages, hours, and fringe benefits that

Boulwarism

are viable alternatives to the union's demands, then management is considered to be bargaining in good faith.

An unbending, "take-it-or-leave-it" approach is not considered good-faith bargaining. Such an approach, first used by General Electric, became known as **Boulwarism** after one of the company's executives. Although this strategy was used quite successfully for several years, it was held to be an unfair labor practice in 1969 by a U.S. Circuit Court of Appeals.[15]

The Wagner Act did not apply to a significant number of workers. Among those excluded were supervisors, government employees, hospital workers, and agricultural workers. Since 1935, amendments to the Wagner Act, presidential orders, and court decisions have allowed more workers to form and join unions. Specific changes are discussed later in this chapter.

The Labor-Management Relations Act (Taft-Hartley Act)

Restoring balance of power

Immediately after its passage, employers all over the country criticized the Wagner Act as unfair. Their main complaint was that they had been saddled with restrictions while unions were allowed to operate freely. Operating in a period of labor unrest, Congress tried to restore the balance of power by passing the far-reaching, comprehensive Labor-Management Relations Act, commonly known as the Taft-Hartley Act of 1947.

The Taft-Hartley Act reaffirmed the rights given workers and the restrictions on employers in the Wagner Act. It also said that employees had the right to refrain from engaging in union organizations and union activities. But, most important, it placed several restrictions on unions. Six unfair labor practices, stated in Section 8 of the Taft-Hartley Act, are described here.

1. *Employees who choose not to join unions or to take part in union activities are protected from union reprisal.* Nonunion workers are not required to honor strikes. (Although not expected to honor a strike call, nonunion workers often fail to report to work during a strike because of peer pressure, their friendship with striking workers, or other reasons.) Strikers who form picket lines cannot legally prevent nonstriking employees from crossing them. Nor can union members verbally abuse nonstrikers or threaten them with personal injury if they try to report to work during a strike.

Strikebreakers often mean violence

It is important to note that mass picketing and picket-line violence are almost always associated with strikes of industrial unions. Picket-line violence generally is directed at **strikebreakers,** people hired to take the place of striking workers. Craft union strikes rarely result in violence; craftspeople's jobs cannot be learned very quickly so strikebreakers are not often used. In industrial union strikes at mass-production plants, managers find it easy to recruit and train strikebreakers for unskilled and semiskilled jobs in a short time. For this reason, the plant can be kept operating.

In particularly hostile strikes, employers may provide transportation, such as a company bus, for strikebreakers willing to cross the picket line. Once inside the plant, they may live in makeshift arrangements for days at a time. Management also may take over the jobs of striking employees.

Closed shop

2. *Unions cannot try to make employers force workers to join or discourage them from joining a union.* This provision specifically prohibits the **closed shop,** in which a person must be a union member to be employed. Although the closed shop is illegal, it is sometimes practiced, as we will explain later.

Below are some conditions of employment not expressly prohibited in Section 8 of the Act.

The Union Shop   Except in states that have right-to-work laws, management and labor can legally negotiate a **union shop** clause in the contract. Such a clause forces eligible workers to join the union. Although employees need not be union members when they are hired, they must join the union on or after the thirtieth day of employment. (In the construction trades, the period is seven days.) Workers who fail to join the union under these conditions are fired.

Union shop

Right-to-Work Laws   Twenty states have so-called **right-to-work laws,** which prohibit union shop contract clauses; in these states, workers cannot be fired for refusing to join the union. Most, though not all, right-to-work states are in the South. The Louisiana state legislature was the last to pass such a bill in 1976.

Right-to-work laws

Arguments for and against compulsory union membership can be powerful. Proponents of a union shop note that a union represents all eligible workers, whether or not they are members. Because nonunion workers have the same wages, hours of work, and fringe benefits as union workers have, union shop supporters argue that all workers should share the costs and responsibilities of union membership.

On the other hand, many feel that people should have the right to work without having to join organized labor groups. They contend that a worker should not be denied the right to bargain individually, on his or her own, if the worker chooses. Freedom of choice is the basic issue: the worker who wants to be represented by a union should have the right to such representation; the worker should not be fired for choosing not to join.

Agency shop

The Agency Shop   In an **agency shop,** workers who refuse to join the union must pay the union for the benefits derived through collective bargaining. In this condition of employment, nonunion workers cannot be criticized for "getting a free ride," yet they are not union members.

Circumventing the Law   The passage of the Labor-Management Reporting and Disclosure Act in 1959 resulted in the revival of closed shop practices. Before 1959, union shop clauses required workers to join the union on or after the thirtieth day of employment. This legislation reduced the time to seven days in the construction industry. Because employers in the construction trades found it impractical to employ workers that they must fire seven days later, they often hired union members only.

In addition, employers sometimes limit their hiring to union members to prevent the problems that occur when nonunion workers are assigned to jobs on which union members are working. Union members have been known to walk off a job when they learn that nonunion workers have been hired. They cite poor-quality workmanship, dangerous working conditions (as in the case of electrical workers, for example), or other reasons for refusing to work alongside nonunion workers. When problems like this occur, employers find it simpler to call the local union hall when skilled craftspeople are needed.

Bargaining in good faith

3. *Unions must bargain in good faith concerning wages, working hours, and employment conditions.* An example of a union's refusal to bargain in good faith is the insistence that the contract include illegal provisions, such as closed shop or union shop clauses in a right-to-work state. This restriction was included to ensure that both parties negotiate within the law.

4(a). *A union cannot coerce an employer or self-employed person to join.* For example, consider the case of a barber in a small, central Tennessee city who is considered both an employer and a self-employed person because he owns his own shop. All other shops in this city are unionized, with uniform prices and working hours. The nonunion barber charges less than the union shops do for haircuts and keeps his shop open on Monday, when unionized shops are closed. Naturally, the union barbers are not happy about the nonunion barber's prices and operating hours. But they can't force him to join the union.

Secondary boycott

4(b). *Secondary boycotts are illegal.* A strike may occur whenever a union fails to settle a dispute or to reach a new agreement with an employer through negotiations. Often, the failure to reach an agreement results not only in a strike but also in a boycott of the employer's products and services. This is designed to put additional pressure on the employer to give in to the union's demands; unless the contract forbids strikes, the boycott is legal.

In some cases, though, the striking union tries to put even more pressure on the employer by boycotting other companies that sell to, or buy from, that employer. Figure 19.1 illustrates this practice, which is called a **secondary boycott.**

In Figure 19.1, the union first establishes a primary boycott of Company A, the employer with whom the union has a dispute. If this proves ineffective, the union may turn to Company B, an "innocent" secondary firm that buys from, or sells to, Company A. A boycott of a secondary company typically involves more than a refusal to buy its products. These boycotts have included harassment and intimidation of customers, picketing, and other activities designed to prod the secondary party (Company B) to pressure Company A to "give in" to the union's demands.

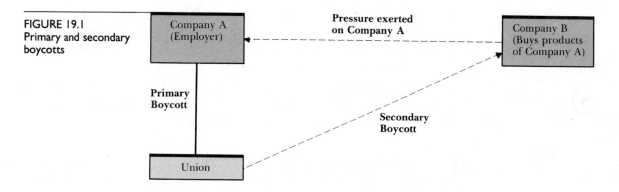

FIGURE 19.1
Primary and secondary
boycotts

4(c). *A union cannot force an employer to recognize it as the bargaining agent for a bargaining unit if another union has been certified by the National Labor Relations Board as the lawfully recognized bargaining agent.* Before the Taft-Hartley Act, several national unions staged "power plays" designed to nullify authorized union elections. These unions advised employers to ignore the results of NLRB-conducted elections and to renegotiate contracts with them.

Jurisdictional disputes

4(d). *Jurisdictional strikes are prohibited.* Before the Taft-Hartley Act, unions were known to force employers to assign jobs to their members that should have been assigned to members of other unions. In some cases, a union would go on strike to obtain the job assignment. Thus, union members sometimes were given jobs outside their jurisdiction. These practices are used almost exclusively by craft unions when work is limited.

Such job assignments raise the issue of craft sovereignty. For example, if wooden doors and door frames on a building are to be replaced with metal doors, a conflict might arise between sheet-metal workers and carpenters. The metal workers may contend that removing the wooden doors is part of the installation of metal doors; carpenters, on the other hand, may contend that removing the wooden doors is exclusively within the jurisdiction of the carpenter's union.

Whenever these disputes occur, the parties involved must try to settle the issue themselves. After charges are filed with the NLRB, ten days must pass before the board can intervene. During this period, the disputing parties must make a valid effort to resolve the dispute. The board will make its decision if they fail.

The National Joint Board of Adjustment in the Building Construction Industry currently serves as mediator and sometimes arbitrator for jurisdictional disputes of the kind we just discussed. Rarely does a dispute go to arbitration by the National Labor Relations Board.

5. *Unions cannot levy excessive and discriminatory initiation fees or membership dues.* Congress did not set a dollar limit on fees and dues; instead, the charges are measured against the prevailing wage rates in the industry. Historically, the fees and dues of craft unions have been considerably higher than those of industrial unions. This is designed to restrict craft-union membership and to encourage membership in industrial unions.

Featherbedding prohibited

6. *Featherbedding is prohibited.* Unions cannot legally force an employer to hire more people than are necessary to perform a task or to hire workers for nonexistent jobs, a practice called **featherbedding.**

Other Major Provisions of Taft-Hartley   In addition to reaffirming employees' rights and restricting union activities, the Taft-Hartley Act has several other important provisions, including Section 14(b) and the National Emergency Dispute provision (Sections 206–210).

National emergencies

Section 14(b) gives individual states the authority to pass right-to-work laws, which prohibit union shops. The National Emergency Dispute provision allows the president of the United States to request a court injunction to end a strike or lockout temporarily if the president believes that it endangers the nation's safety or economy. Such an injunction, which cannot exceed eighty days, is commonly referred to as an "eighty-day cooling off period."

Taft-Hartley Amendments   Employees of nonprofit, private hospitals and nursing homes, who had been excluded from the Wagner Act, were given, in 1974, the right to bargain collectively with their employers. Because of the nature of their work, however, disputes between health-care employees and their employers are settled differently. If the parties are unable to agree on a contract issue, the Federal Mediation and Conciliation Service can issue a thirty-day no-strike, no-lockout order. The service mediates the dispute during this period. Strikes can be called when the thirty days are up if the dispute is not settled.

Health-care organizations

The Labor-Management Reporting and Disclosure Act (Landrum-Griffin Act)

Landrum-Griffin Act

The last major piece of federal legislation governing labor-management relations was the Labor-Management Reporting and Disclosure Act, passed by Congress in 1959. This law, commonly called the Landrum-Griffin Act, was the result of an extensive probe into union activities throughout the 1950s. The late Senator John McClellan was chair of the Senate committee that investigated unions and their officers. Based on the McClellan committee's findings, the Landrum-Griffin Act was passed to ensure the democratic process within organized labor groups. Essentially, the law stipulated the rights of rank-and-file union members and required union officials to file detailed information with the federal government. It also amended the Taft-Hartley Act in several ways, including letting workers who have been on strike for a calendar year or less vote in union representation elections.

Public Sector Bargaining

In 1962, President John Kennedy issued Executive Order 10988, which gave federal government employees the right to collective bargaining. The order also contained procedures governing such bargaining and union restrictions. Seven years later, President Richard Nixon issued an executive order that slightly modified the procedures. The orders placed the following restrictions on unions that sought to represent government workers.

1. **Strikes are prohibited.** Despite the law, though, several strikes have been called. The first nationwide strike of federal employees occurred in 1970, when U.S. Postal Service workers walked off the job. (The National Guard took over the mail service during the strike.) A later nationwide strike of federal employees involved air-traffic controllers, many of whom were fired for participating in the strike and refusing to return to their jobs.

Restrictions on public unions

2. Labor organizations cannot advocate the overthrow of the government.

3. Unions cannot discriminate in their membership on the basis of race, color, creed, or national origin.

4. The operation of these labor organizations must be democratic and free of corruption.

The rights to unionization and collective bargaining filtered down to state and municipal workers. In recent years, strikes by sanitation workers, teachers, police officers, firefighters, and others have become common. For the most part, government agencies have been poorly prepared to deal with these strikes. Strikers often demand (and receive) amnesty as a condition for returning to work.

In 1959, Wisconsin was the first state to pass guidelines governing union-management relations for public employees.[16] Several states had laws prohibiting strikes by public employees, and some prohibited public employee unions; but in 1967, a U.S. Court of Appeals struck down laws prohibiting public employees from joining unions.[17] By 1975, forty states had enacted some form of legislation governing public employee unions. The nature of these laws varies widely from state to state.

Rights and Responsibilities of Employers

The questions that most managers ask about union-management relations are: "What can I legally do to keep a union out of my plant?" "What obligations do I have if a union is voted in?" Here are some of the "do's" and "don'ts".

- Employers can develop a campaign to encourage workers to vote against the union. Such a campaign can and should stress the disadvantages of unionization.

- Don't grant a wage increase immediately before a union election is held; it most likely will be an unfair labor practice.

- Don't question workers about union activities or union membership in a coercive or intimidating manner.

- Don't threaten to close one plant and ship the work to a satellite plant if union talk is apparent.

- Don't discharge or discriminate against workers who are active in forming a union, who join a union, or who file unfair labor practice charges.

- Don't hire permanent replacements for locked-out workers without first consulting the union.

- If a union is voted in, don't engage in surface bargaining, which merely gives the appearance of bargaining. Instead, make a concerted effort to reach agreement with the union on wages, hours, and working conditions.

- Unless the contract prohibits lockouts, you can legally use a lockout to obtain a favorable settlement in a collective bargaining dispute.

- You should insist on a "residual" management rights clause in the contract. Such a clause gives you the right to decide on all issues not covered by the contract.

- Don't cite financial inability to meet the union's demands unless you are prepared to provide financial data to support your claim.

- Prepare for negotiations thoroughly and develop an unswerving negotiating strategy.

Negotiating the Union Contract

If the company fails to keep out a union, it must try to negotiate a contract in good faith. Although negotiations can vary with craft and industrial unions and from industry to industry, the overall process is similar. Generally, the first negotiating session is devoted to a presentation of demands by the union representatives. In the second session, company representatives typically offer counterproposals. Additional sessions are scheduled as needed for haggling over the demands and offers in an attempt to reach an agreement on wages, hours, or whatever else is at issue. Some companies are even giving unions the right to audit their books and have a representative on their boards of directors, as explained in the In-Box on page 511.

THE IN-BOX

Fox in the Henhouse?

Douglas Fraser, former president of the United Auto Workers, was named to Chrysler Corporation's board of directors in 1980 after his union accepted major cuts to help keep Chrysler solvent. Some analysts hailed the move as a long-overdue milestone in labor relations and proclaimed it as a giant step toward full labor-management cooperation. Others criticized the action, saying that Fraser could not serve two masters. No one, they argued, could represent the company, its stockholders, and the union at the same time.

More and more, companies are opening their books to labor. In some cases, independent auditors are allowed to examine confidential data. In other instances, union representatives like Fraser are put on the board of directors. In 1981, for example, United Airlines granted "insider status" to two pilots who were rank-and-file union members. The pilots kept the information confidential and certified to the union that United had correctly reported its financial situation. Similar practices prevail at Uniroyal, where the United Rubber Workers union has the right to audit the company's books.

A number of analysts have cautioned that these inroads into information-sharing will ultimately lead to codetermination. Supporters of the trend say that the more a union knows about a company, the better it is, for both the union and the company. Opponents argue that the notion of opening the books and putting union members on the board "is a cure for which there is no known illness."

Source: "Tasting a New Kind of Power," *Business Week,* February 1, 1982, pp. 16–17.

TABLE 19.1
Makeup of the typical
union contract

Section 1: Recognition of the Union by the Company
This section defines the bargaining unit and recognizes the union as the sole bargaining agent for the workers. Other statements concern the union hiring hall, apprenticeship programs, and the union's control over employment and retention of workers. The length of the contract and its renewal also are included.

Section 2: Management Rights
This section gives the employer the right to direct the work force, to classify, promote, transfer, relieve from duty for lack of work, and discharge workers for just cause. It says that any right not specifically bargained away remains the prerogative of management.

Section 3: Wage and Output Expectancy
Included in this section are base pay rates for all jobs in the bargaining unit; holiday pay, shift differential, overtime pay, and other forms of premium pay; pay for time not worked, such as rest breaks; production quotas; procedures for establishing production standards; and all types of contingency benefits, such as pensions, severance pay, guaranteed annual wage plans, and supplemental unemployment benefits.

Section 4: Means for Assuring Job Security
Seniority provisions affecting layoff, recall, job bidding, and bumping privileges are included here. The procedure for handling employee grievances is clearly delineated. This section also includes no-strike, no-lockout provisions, disciplinary penalties, and the procedure for invoking arbitration.

Section 5: Administration and Enforcement of the Contract
The role of union stewards and the means for selecting arbitrators are defined here.

Negotiating strategies

Two basic negotiating strategies or a combination of the two can be used— the piecemeal approach and the total approach. The piecemeal approach takes one issue at a time and resolves it before the next issue is discussed; that is, each issue is discussed, resolved, and set aside to be included in the contract. The total approach holds that nothing is settled until everything is settled. The two sides discuss each issue but then "hold it in limbo" until they discuss all other issues. Then, trading off begins. Each side typically uses bargaining tactics to gain an advantage or to persuade the opponent to give in. These tactics include bluffing, threatening to strike, making deliberate errors, lying, and so on.

The union contract

One question managers often ask themselves is, "What should be included in the contract?" Obviously, the company does not want to bargain away anything unnecessarily. Yet, it wants to make certain that the contract adequately covers issues that may arise during the period it is to cover. There is no exact list of items to be included. The topics listed in Table 19.1 are minimum requirements.

Review

✓ *The meaning of labor relations.* Labor relations refers to a continuous relationship between an employer and a group of workers represented by a union. The relationship includes negotiating, interpreting, and administering a written contract covering wages, working hours, and other conditions of employment.

✓ *The history of organized labor.* Organized labor in the United States can be traced to the late 1700s, when craftspeople banded together to set quality and training requirements and to eliminate oppressive working conditions. The early unions were little more than autonomous guilds with limited power. Strikes to raise wages or to reduce hours of work were generally considered criminal conspiracies until 1842. Unions gained a foothold in America with the formation of the American Federation of Labor (AFL) in 1886, an organization that improved its members' economic conditions and enhanced the status and image of organized labor. In the twentieth century, industrial workers were organized under the umbrella of the Congress of Industrial Organizations (CIO). The merger of the AFL and CIO in 1955 created a powerful economic and political machine.

✓ *How major federal laws affect labor-management relations.* Before 1932, courts generally favored employers in labor-management disputes. For example, strikes were considered illegal combinations in restraint of trade under the Sherman Antitrust Act of 1890. And the prolabor provisions of the Clayton Act of 1914 were nullified by the courts. The Norris-LaGuardia Act of 1932 was the first effective prolabor law passed by Congress because it neutralized the federal judiciary in labor-management disputes and made "yellow-dog contracts" unenforceable.

The National Labor Relations Act of 1935 is the most significant prolabor law ever passed. Commonly called the Wagner Act, this law gave most workers the right to form and join unions and to engage in collective bargaining with employers. It protected workers' rights by restricting employers.

The Wagner Act prompted growth in union membership, but employers criticized it for being unfair because it hampered them while giving unions free rein. Congress restored the balance of power by passing the Labor-Management Relations Act, also called the Taft-Hartley Act, in 1947. This law prohibited several unfair union practices.

The last major piece of federal legislation passed by Congress was the Labor-Management Reporting and Disclosure Act of 1959, commonly called the Landrum-Griffin Act. It was designed to ensure that labor unions operate democratically.

✓ *What restrictions govern public-sector bargaining.* In 1962, federal government workers were given the right to form and join unions and to engage in collective bargaining. They are not permitted to strike, however. The right to collective bargaining quickly filtered down to state and municipal workers. Legislation governing state and municipal workers varies widely from state to state.

✓ *The rights and responsibilities of employers regarding unions.* Employers cannot legally prevent their employees from forming and joining unions, but they can legally mount antiunion campaigns. Other rights and restrictions concern wage increases, questioning workers about union activities, threatening to close a plant, discriminating against union workers, hiring replacements for locked-out workers, and other areas.

✓ *The steps in negotiating a union contract and what contracts cover.* If a company fails to keep out a union, it must try to negotiate a contract in good faith. In the first negotiating session, the union typically presents its demands. Then, management makes counterproposals. The union and management haggle over the demands and offers in additional sessions. The result is a written contract specifying the rights and responsibilities of the employer and the union for a specified period. The aspects of employment covered in a contract include wages, fringe benefits, work hours, grievance procedures, production standards, job security, and contract enforcement.

THE MANAGER'S DICTIONARY

As an extra review of the chapter, try defining the following terms. If you have trouble with any of them, refer to the page numbers listed.

labor relations (497)
yellow-dog contract (502)
National Labor Relations
    Board (NLRB) (503)

Boulwarism (504)
strikebreakers (504)
closed shop (505)
union shop (505)

right-to-work laws (505)
agency shop (505)
secondary boycott (506)
featherbedding (508)

REVIEW QUESTIONS

1. How do labor unions affect employers? Give examples.

2. Trace the history of the labor movement in America. Why did craftspeople form unions in the early days of our nation's history? Explain.

3. How did early unionists attempt to improve their working conditions? How successful were they? Discuss.

4. Who were the Knights of Labor? What were the objectives of this organization?

5. Why did the Knights of Labor fail? Explain.

6. What were the objectives of the American Federation of Labor? Why did it succeed?

7. Explain why the AFL wanted to organize industrial workers. Describe the controversy surrounding the organizing of industrial workers.

8. Why were CIO unions expelled from the AFL?

9. Why were unions considered unlawful combinations in restraint of trade under the Sherman Antitrust Act?

10. List the unfair labor practices of employers and unions.

11. In your opinion, are the unfair labor practices of employers more or less restrictive than those of unions? Explain.

12. Prepare arguments for and against compulsory union membership.

13. Should government workers have the right to strike? Why or why not?

14. What is included in the typical union contract? Be specific.

MANAGEMENT CHALLENGE

Assume that you are the personnel manager of a medium-size, nonunion manufacturing company that has plants in four different towns. The president of the company has been informed by one of the plant managers that there is strong talk of union organizing. In fact, organizers for the United Auto Workers (UAW) have been pressuring many of the workers to vote the union in.

The president has turned to you for advice. She wants to do everything she can legally do to prevent unionization in her company, but she does not want to break the law.

1. What advice would you offer the company president?

2. If the UAW is successful in its organizing efforts, what responsibilities must the employer assume?

3. What responsibilities must the union assume? Explain.

4. How can the company rid itself of the union?

CASE 19.1

Ingersoll-Rand Fights Off Unions[18]

In 1980, union workers at Ingersoll-Rand Company produced bearings in South Bend, Indiana, hand tools in South Deerfield, Massachusetts, and pneumatic tools in Athens, Pennsylvania. Today, the bearing plant is closed, and the work has been shifted to a nonunion factory. The hand-tool plant has been sold, and workers in Athens, Pennsylvania, have voted to oust their union. Why has all this happened?

During the past few years, Ingersoll-Rand decided to cut its payroll and to move production from unionized plants in the North to non-unionized plants in the South. It also has been encouraging its workers to reject their unions. Today, only 30% of Ingersoll-Rand's workers are union members, down from 60% in 1981.

By law, companies can't close plants, move production, or fire workers to weaken a union, but they can for economic reasons. Ingersoll-Rand's management claims that economic forces, rather than labor problems, forced it to cut its payroll, close some of its plants, and scale back international operations. Management leaves no doubt about its attitude toward unions, however. Robert Ripston, vice president for employee relations, said in a 1981 speech, "Where we don't have unions, we tell workers we want to remain union-free."

Some analysts believe that Ingersoll-Rand has developed and successfully implemented a strategy to eliminate unions. Besides closing plants, the company presses unions to make concessions in plants that are only marginally profitable and openly encourages supervisors to persuade their workers to vote against union representation. For instance, supervisors are asked to tell their subordinates about their bad experiences with unions. They also tell workers that unions are only after their money. In one instance, the company showed a film in which former union members said they were glad to be working in a nonunion plant.

In the past six years, unions have lost five decertification elections and won only one at Ingersoll-Rand plants. Pleased with its success, the company is getting the word to workers in other plants. In Athens, Pennsylvania, for example, supervisors were encouraged to tell their employees that the Teamsters Union apparently let down workers in the company's Tucson and Indianapolis plants because workers threw out the union in both places.

Questions

1. Is Ingersoll-Rand's strategy legal? ethical?

2. In your opinion, why has the percentage of Ingersoll-Rand workers represented by unions been cut in half since 1981? Explain.

CASE 19.2

Arbitrating at Precision Tool Company

In December 1986, both the International Association of Machinists and the Precision Tool Company of Memphis, Tennessee, were awaiting an arbitrator's decision in dispute over the misclassification of four employees.

The story began in January 1985, when Precision Tool decided to build an experimental stamping machine from spare parts on hand and the serviceable portions of discarded stamping machines. Because constructing the stamping machine would be a temporary job, four workers were temporarily hired. The company told these workers they would be let go when the project was completed.

Although all permanent jobs at Precision Tool were classified and had established rates of pay, there was no provision for temporary jobs. The four new employees were called maintenance mechanics, a classification that was closest to their skills and duties. The agreed-on pay rate was six dollars an hour, four dollars less than the established rate for maintenance-mechanic jobs. They were paid less because none had the skills and training required for maintenance-mechanic classification.

Completed after three months of work, the stamping machine became part of the production line and operated perfectly. The cost savings associated with its manufacture were significant. Because of its success and because demand for Precision's products remained unexpectedly strong, management decided to build, repair, and modify other production machinery. The four temporary workers were kept on. Six months after they were hired, their job status was made permanent. Their pay rate, job classification, and job duties were unchanged.

More than a year later, the company's new personnel manager discovered the erroneous classification of the four maintenance department employees. He and the plant manager agreed to establish a new classification paying six dollars an hour—mechanic helper—and to reclassify the workers. The union was notified, as the contract required.

The local union representative then contacted the four maintenance department employees, explained that they had been underpaid for their previous classification, persuaded them to join the union, and processed a formal grievance in their behalf. The grievance asked for a retroactive pay adjustment from the date of employment to the date of reclassification.

The union maintained that all workers should be paid according to their classification. Failing to pay them on this basis constituted a breach of the union contract, the union claimed. Precision Tool contended that the union overlooked the erroneous classification when the employees were initially hired and that it shared the responsibility of proper classification.

Questions

1. If you were the arbitrator, what award would you render? Justify your decision.

2. Who should assume the responsibility for proper classification?

CHAPTER OUTLINE

Your Career Stages
    Beginning Stage
    Decision Stage
    Stabilization Stage
    Maintenance Stage
    Decline/Retirement Stage

Systematic Career Planning

Careers in Management: Pros and Cons

Thinking Like a Successful Manager
    Left-Brain Dominance
    Left Brain versus Right Brain

Luck and Management Success

The Entrepreneurial Firm: An Alternative

Women in Management: Challenges and Opportunities
    Profile of the Successful Female Executive
    Levels of Satisfaction
    Personal Sacrifices • Younger versus Older Female Managers
    Obstacles Facing Female Managers
    Stereotypes • Family Demands • Age Discrepancies • Pay Differential
    A Look to the Future

Adapting to Changing Conditions

The Personal Computer: A Must for Tomorrow's Manager
    Who Uses Computers?
    Advantages of Microcomputers
    Computers and Management Skills

Your Future in Management

One Man's Philosophy

"If I had to sum up in one word the qualities that make a good manager, I'd say it comes down to decisiveness."

"The key to success is not information. It's people."

"The most important thing a manager can do is hire the right people."

". . . managers also have to be good motivators."

"The ability to concentrate and to use your time well is everything if you want to succeed in business."

"You don't succeed for very long by kicking people around."

"Leadership means setting an example."

These quotations, taken from *Iacocca: An Autobiography,* pinpoint some of the keys to managerial success.[1] Taken together, they constitute a philosophy that has served as the springboard to success for Lee Iacocca, chairperson of Chrysler Corporation and former president of Ford Motor Company.

The road to the top of two of America's largest corporations had its potholes, however. Like all other successful managers, Iacocca tasted bitter frustrations and disappointments in his career. He would certainly agree that being fired as president of Ford Motor Company was the low point in his career. But, like other successsful business executives, he also has been exhilarated by his accomplishments. For instance, he is credited with transforming a near-bankrupt Chrysler Corporation into a viable, profitable organization. This feat alone earned him the reputation of being the superhero of the corporate world.

Preview

Managerial success doesn't just happen. It is the culmination of adequate training, a positive attitude, on-the-job experiences, hard work, the combined efforts of lots of good people, and—to some extent—luck. It is, in fact, the result of the day-in, day-out struggle to do the best job that can be done in whatever position the manager holds.

Choosing a career is one of the most important decisions you will ever make. A poor selection will most likely result in frustration and disappointment; a good decision can provide years of accomplishment and happinesss. The objectives of this chapter are to help you approach your career decision in a logical manner and to help you decide whether your personal and professional needs and aspirations can be satisfied best in management. This chapter will explain:

✔ The stages of a career

✔ How to plan your career systematically

✔ The pros and cons of a management career

✔ How successful managers think

✔ The role luck plays in a manager's success

✔ Whether you should consider entrepreneurship

✔ The challenges and opportunities facing women in management

✔ How change will affect tomorrow's managers

✔ The importance of personal computers for managers

Your Career Stages

Coming to grips with what you want to do with your life can be hard work. It involves assessing your opportunities and wants, as well as your abilities and skills. It takes much time and effort, and there is no guarantee that your plans will materialize. Even the best-laid plans sometimes go awry, but failing to plan your career is even more of a risk.

Career planning offers several advantages over letting life take its own course. First, planning gives order to your life's direction because it includes reference points with which to compare your performance. That is, it lets you compare where you are with where you planned to be at different points in your career, and possibly indicates that adjustments are needed. Career planning also provides the satisfaction that comes from knowing that you are in control of your life. Reaching the milestones in your plans reinforces your sense of self-direction. Finally, career planning can be financially rewarding. People who set goals, qualify themselves for attaining those goals, and consistently make decisions that move them toward their goals usually fare better financially than people do who let the winds of chance blow them here and there.

The careers of most people do not move in a straight line and do not maintain the same growth rate. In addition, people sometimes get sidetracked—at least temporarily—along the way. A person's career is made up of several stages:

1. Beginning

2. Decision

3. Stabilization

4. Maintenance

5. Decline/Retirement

Beginning Stage

The choice of a career is indirectly affected by a person's early life experiences. A person's personality, interests, and behavior patterns are shaped in preteen and teenage years by how he or she deals with people and situations and by parental guidance. A person develops a self-image and a value system during this time.

Near the end of their midteens, people begin to think seriously about alternative occupations and to pay more attention to developing the skills and abilities they will need later in life. Natural and learned skills become readily apparent, too. For example, some students will exhibit strong interest in the physical and natural sciences or mathematics, while others will show an interest in art, music, and the social sciences. Once they are old enough to work, many young people gain a limited and somewhat superficial understanding of the business world through their part-time jobs.

Decision Stage

The second career stage, the decision stage, begins around the midteen years and lasts until maturity for most people. It is characterized by part-time jobs, decisions about college and marriage, and a host of other variables that, taken together, force people to think seriously about their future.

Unfortunately, limited experience and immaturity often result in poor career decisions at this point. The high percentage of workers who are dissatisfied with their jobs and the large number of college students who change their majors are evidence of the mismatching of occupational choices and personal wants and abilities.

This stage actually is one of continual refinement. In the beginning, we develop broad, general occupational interests, such as science, business, and so on. In the middle, we sharpen our focus to medicine or marketing, for example, and near the end we decide on what we hope will be a lifetime occupation, such as pharmacy or sales, for instance.

Stabilization Stage

The third stage, stabilization, is characterized by the selection of a specific occupation and the proving of oneself in it. Sometimes, the choice of a particular occupation is made early, as is the case with most professions. But in other cases, a career choice is not settled on until several occupations are tried.

People often seek additional education during this phase to revamp or learn new skills, especially as technological advances necessitate further training. Changing employers is common too, especially in the early years of the stabilization stage. In the latter years, however, mobility is limited because of concern for retirement income, the security that comes with seniority, the desire for continuity, and the risks associated with making midlife career changes.

Toward the end of this stage, most people are able to determine whether they will reach their ultimate goal. Between the ages of fifty and fifty-five, the typical executive most likely will be at, or in line for, the highest position he or she will attain. If the executive feels blocked or stuck on a plateau, yet full of energy and ambition, he or she may be inclined to make a major career move. Such changes, often attributed to midlife crisis syndrome, frequently prove disastrous.

Most people also reassess their priorities near the end of this stage. They weigh the importance of their jobs against the worth of other facets of life and reevaluate the quality of their life. Most managers at this point recognize that their abilities and energies will not take them too much further, so they prepare to enter the maintenance stage of their careers.

Maintenance Stage

The fourth stage in the career cycle is called maintenance. For most people, it begins around fifty to fifty-five years of age and lasts for about ten years. Except for the few who appear to be tireless in their efforts to climb still higher on the corporate ladder, managers at this stage are concerned with securing their positions.

An overwhelming majority of managers at this stage realize that they have peaked. They can rise no higher. A few will be promoted, primarily as a reward for their past contributions rather than for their future promise.

Decline/Retirement Stage

The final stage in the career cycle often is the most unsettling. Older managers lose their influence; they become increasingly out of step with the way the company is moving; and their thoughts turn to retirement. For the most part, they hang on until they reach the mandatory retirement age or until they satisfy their company's retirement guidelines.

Systematic Career Planning

Career planning involves assessing where you are and where you want to be in fifteen or twenty years. It includes a systematic program designed to allow you to reach your potential. Unfortunately, most people don't plan their careers; they simply let them develop (or digress) by chance. The good executives, though, give a great deal of thought to getting that next job—and the one after that. They plan their careers. For example, in her first months at Bendix Corporation, Mary Cunningham prepared a 200-page career plan. She wanted, in her twenties, to develop her abilities; in her thirties, to maximize her financial independence; and in her forties, to position herself for real power.[2]

The value of detailed, long-range planning is that it forces you to think about your career path and to lay out a step-by-step sequence for reaching your ultimate goal. Good career planning involves three assessments: (1) evaluating careers in general, (2) determining the setting in which you wish to pursue your career, and (3) evaluating yourself.

To evaluate careers in general, you must first identify your career concept. You can do this by asking yourself several basic questions: "Do I want job security?" "Will this career allow me to continue developing my skills?" "Do I want to head a major corporation?" The answers to these types of questions help define your concept of a career. Michael Driver, professor of management and organizational behavior at the University of Southern California, identifies four different career concepts: (1) steady-state, (2) linear, (3) transitory, and (4) spiral.[3]

The *steady-state concept* focuses on a lifelong commitment to a particular profession or trade—medicine, law, teaching, carpentry, and so on. People are attracted to steady-state careers out of a desire for security or because they want to develop and refine their skills throughout their lives. A steady-state career must be chosen early in life. Additional training likely will be required along the way.

The *linear career concept* assumes continued upward movement through the hierarchy of a firm. The basis of this concept is the philosophy that hard work and loyalty will be recognized and rewarded in the form of promotions. Power, status, influence, monetary gain, and a sense of accomplishment are the forces that motivate individuals to climb the corporate ladder. But there are risks associated with this career concept, too. Good, deserving managers may get passed over, internal politics may prove detrimental, or the number of openings at upper levels may be inadequate to reward all deserving people who are qualified for advancement.

A *transitory career concept* assumes that a career is comprised of many minicareers. People who embrace this concept expect to change jobs and employers frequently. They appear to enjoy the variety and time off that this concept affords.

In the *spiral career concept,* a person embarks on a new career after devoting years to something else. For instance, a college professor may decide to enter management consulting on a full-time basis after having spent fifteen or more years in the classroom. Or a veteran military officer may choose to return to civilian life and to enter the insurance business. People who pursue the spiral concept generally are bored with their routine and long for something that will let them grow and develop along other lines.

The second important assessment you must make in career planning is whether the organization you plan to work for embraces your career concept. You can become frustrated if there is a mismatch. For example, a steady-state type employed by a company with a "survival of the fittest, dog-eat-dog" atmosphere is likely to experience anxiety and turmoil.

The final career-planning step is self-assessment. This means analyzing your wants, skills, and style. Of the three, wants are usually the most difficult to specify; for this reason, career counselors try to identify wants by focusing on interests and values. Because skills are more readily identified, there is little need for people to spend years performing tasks for which they have little skill. Style refers both to the leadership approach that a person takes in resolving problems and to his or her approaches to decision making. Are you analytical? Are you concerned with how well people get along? Do you think five or ten years ahead? Do you prefer working with people or numbers? Answering these types of questions can help you determine your style.

Once you have identified your career concept, analyzed the setting that best embodies your concept, and evaluated your wants, skills, and style, the choice of a career is much simpler.

Careers in Management: Pros and Cons

Choosing the right occupation *and* the right employer is doubly difficult. Even so, it is crucial to job satisfaction and a positive attitude. Too many employees, especially young managers, are frustrated and dislike both the companies they work for and their managers.

Part of the problem can be attributed to unusually high expectations. Young managers, who are usually better educated than older employees are, have higher job expectations and are likely to feel more dissatisfied when their ambitions aren't met. As a result, many put their personal lives ahead of their jobs. Employees' negative feelings can manifest themselves in poor performance, absenteeism, turnover, and cynicism, all of which have serious ramifications for employers.

According to some observers, recessions and corporate shake-ups in recent years have done more to destroy employees' company loyalty than anything else has. This lessening of loyalty, an offshoot of disillusionment, can be traced to other reasons, too, including decreasing job security. Mergers and cutbacks, for example, have resulted in a net decrease of nearly 500,000 managerial and professional jobs since 1979, and the idea of lifetime employment is dead.[4] In addition, more and more workers believe they are being treated unfairly by their employers. What is surprising is that managers are becoming more disillusioned than either hourly or clerical workers are. Figure 20.1 depicts the levels of dissatisfaction among different groups of workers in the United States, based on research data compiled by Opinion Research Corporation.

Feelings of dissatisfaction among workers are not uniform from industry to industry or from firm to firm, of course. Some industries and companies appear to be suffering more than others are. In California's "silicon valley," for example, turnover at 231 electronics firms averaged 27% in 1984. But companies known for their "womb to tomb" philosophy are seeing the effect, too. Annual turnover at AT&T has more than tripled, for example. And when Du Pont offered an early retirement incentive plan to its employees in 1985, more than eleven thousand workers took advantage of it, more than twice the number the company expected.[5]

On the positive side, a career in management can be highly rewarding—both emotionally and financially. Management can be exciting and challenging, and it can provide status, power, esteem, respect, and wealth. The higher a person's position in an organization, the more influence he or she has over its direction. This in itself motivates many managers to aspire to the highest levels they can attain.

The financial rewards for the successful executive can be enormous. In recent years, all types of financial incentives have been offered by major corporations in an attempt to retain successful executives or to lure them away from other companies. Among the inducements commonly offered are high salaries, deferred compensation plans, front-end bonuses, paid legal and accounting services, insurance, stock and stock options, relocation expenses, management contracts, and a host of other incentives.

These forms of inducements are, of course, reserved for managers who have proven themselves on a long-term basis and whose accomplishments deserve such rewards. When deciding whether to pursue management as a career, remember that the challenges are many but that the rewards are equally great.

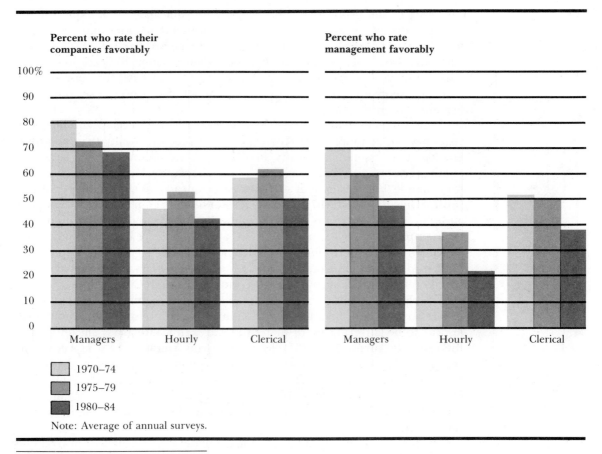

Percent who rate their companies favorably

Percent who rate management favorably

1970–74

1975–79

1980–84

Note: Average of annual surveys.

FIGURE 20.1
Levels of dissatisfaction among American workers (*Source:* Thomas F. O'Boyle, "Loyalty Ebbs at Many Companies as Employees Grow Disillusioned," *Wall Street Journal*, July 11, 1985, p. 25.)

Thinking Like a Successful Manager

Because the variables affecting a manager's career are so numerous, it is impossible to predict how successful any one person will be. Nevertheless, it is a good idea to compare yourself with successful managers to see similarities and differences. Personality traits and leadership styles vary greatly among successful managers, but the one thing they seem to have in common is the way they think.

All available evidence suggests that managers do indeed think differently—or at least they think in longer time frames than other people do. Elliott Jaques, who holds a Ph.D. in social relations from Harvard and an M.D. from Johns Hopkins, probably has done the most research on how managers think. He spent about thirty years conducting research in England's Glacier Metal Company and today works with other clients, including the U.S. Army.[6]

Jaques's research indicates that the time frames of people's thinking differ greatly. In business organizations, people who have short time frames—one day or so—usually are found at the lowest levels of the hierarchy. Those who think in the longest time frames—five years or more—are found at the top of the hierarchy. Jaques contends that the time frame in which a person thinks is the best indicator of cognitive power, which is the ability to perceive things clearly and orderly. People who think a year ahead have less cognitive power than those who think two years ahead.

Other researchers who have attempted to differentiate between the thought processes of top-level executives and other, less successful managers have concluded that executives differ from other people in three ways:

1. Executives show a talent for *integration,* which is the ability to see the interrelationships among variables. Thus, they can draw inferences based on limited information while other people are asking for more data. Executives also have a better ability to recall solutions to past problems in helping to solve current ones. They also have the knack of moving from the particular to the abstract and back again. Lower-level managers have greater difficulty thinking in abstract terms and in moving back and forth.

2. Top-level managers are more adept than other people are at *differentiating* among phenomena that appear similar. They also have the ability to look at things from different perspectives; so they exhibit greater empathy than lower-level managers do. Executives also tend to sort out the relevant information from the irrevelant more quickly than others do.

3. Executives are more *flexible* in their thinking than are other people. That is, they tend to refine their thinking—and decision making—as more and more information is made available. Like a good poker player, they don't bet their entire stake on the first card. Instead, their betting decisions are based on unfolding events as the hand is played out.[7]

Left-Brain Dominance

Research on the workings of the human brain in the past several years has revealed that the left and right hemispheres are profoundly different. Nobel Prize winner Roger Sperry has concluded that the left side of the brain is better at verbal and quantitative skills and logical thinking, whereas the right side is more artistic, musical, emotional, and creative.[8]

What implications does this have for choosing a career in management? Simply this: successful executives are usually left-brained decision makers; they base their decisions on logic and reason rather than on emotions. Moreover, different patterns of brain dominance lead to distinctly different skills and thus to different career choices. As Ned Herrmann points out, a person who winds up in a job that is ill suited for his or her brain can be miserable.[9]

Some critics argue that American industry needs an infusion of "right-brained" people. This would boost creativity and would lead to more balanced organizations. In fact, some analysts are now proposing that corporations screen their job applicants to ensure a proper balance of "creative" and "analytical" employees. The corporate cards appear to be stacked against right-brain-dominated people at this time, however. Logical, verbal, and analytical skills are the desirable traits in corporate settings. Those skills usually are found in accountants, scientists, engineers, and business executives. Right-brained people—those who make decisions on gut feelings—are not in demand. Most corporations are not looking for poetic, artistic types when they search for executive talent.

What American corporations really need, some observers say, is a way to get left-brained executives to develop their creative side; that would be the best of both worlds. Herrmann, who is both a physicist and a musician, agrees. He feels that the best executives are those who use both hemispheres of their brain equally. The typical chief executive must interact with all kinds of people—financial analysts, civic leaders, environmental activists, research and development engineers, and so on. Balanced-brain activity would enable the executive to see things from different perspectives more adroitly.

Left Brain versus Right Brain

The differences between the two hemispheres of the brain are not well understood. Because it is impossible to observe the brain as it functions, we can expect to see even more theories on its workings. To date, there are more than a dozen books and countless articles on the subject. The true test of the quality of decisions made by executives, whether they are right- or left-brain dominant, is reflected on the bottom line, not in an experimental laboratory. Even so, the research into this area offers us food for thought.

Is your thinking and decision making dominated by the left or right side of your brain? To find out, take the test in Table 20.1.

Luck and Management Success

No one can dispute that hard work, talent, and education are the bricks and mortar of managerial success. But luck or chance plays a role in careers, too. To appreciate the impact of chance, consider the following circumstances:

Nate Cummings was able to expand his fledgling business following a chance encounter with Henry Crown, a businessman who used his influence to

TABLE 20.1
Test your brain
dominance

1. When you walk into a theatre, classroom, or auditorium, if there are no other influential factors, which side do you prefer to sit on? right _____ left _____.

2. When you have hunches, do you usually follow them? yes _____ no _____.

3. Do you have a place for everything and everything in its place? yes _____ no _____.

4. In learning a physical activity (such as a dance step or a golf stroke) is it easier for you to: A. learn by imitation and getting the feel of the music or game _____ or B. learn the sequence of steps involved and then talk your way through them _____.

5. Do you like to change pictures and decorations in your office, room, or home several times a year or do you like to keep things pretty much the same? change _____ or same _____.

6. Can you tell approximately how much time has passed without a watch? yes _____ no _____.

7. Speaking in relative terms, is it easier for you to understand geometry _____ or algebra _____?

8. In a communication situation, are you more comfortable as a speaker _____ or listener _____?

9. Regarding your social life, do you prefer to plan your activities in advance _____ or do things spontaneously _____?

Scoring Circle these answers: right for number 1; yes for 2; no for 3; A. for 4; change for 5; no for 6; geometry for 7; listener for 8; and spontaneously for 9. Now add the number of circled answers and that is your BPI, Brain Preference Indicator.

Key 0–3 circled answers means that you are left-brained. 6–9 indicates that you are right-brained. A score of 4 or 5 denotes a mixed-dominant, that is, a person who has skills on both sides of the brain and no clear preference for either.

Source: Priscilla Donovan, "Selling Right and Left," *Sales and Marketing Management,* June 3, 1985, p. 64. Reprinted by permission.

help Cummings acquire Sprague Warner & Company, a food company. Following the acquisition of Sprague Warner, Cummings developed his business into Consolidated Foods, a multi-billion dollar operation.

Theodore Cohen's interest in Japan, his writings on Japanese nationalism, and his service under General Douglas MacArthur would never have happened if another student at New York's City College hadn't pre-empted Cohen's choice of a thesis topic. Cohen had planned to propose German anti-Semitism as his topic, but the student ahead of him forced him to select Japanese nationalism as an alternative.

Movie producer Sam Goldwyn employed George Weissman after Goldwyn read Weissman's review of a movie. From there, Weissman joined an advertising firm that handled the Philip Morris account. Later, he was hired by

Philip Morris and became chairman of the board in 1978. Had Weissman never seen the movie, his career would have taken a different turn.

While in prison for violating Swiss banking laws, international banker Paul Erdman was given a typewriter, which he used to write his best-seller, *The Billion Dollar Sure Thing*. Today, his fictional works make him more money and bring him greater recognition than he would have received as a bank executive.[10]

Some people argue that success comes from factors other than luck, but, in truth, these factors are not the only determinants of success. As a result of his research, Daniel Seligman contends that luck definitely influences careers, but it affects some more than others. Seligman concludes:

1. Luck is important.

2. It affects the careers of the less fortunate more strongly.

3. Luck is more significant in a person's early career than in the latter stages of life.[11]

Career success cannot be fully explained by factors other than luck. While there is a relationship between income and intelligence, for example, all variations in income cannot be explained by variations in intelligence or other variables. Hence, luck comes into play.

The importance of luck in the career of an affluent person is not nearly as obvious as in the career of a less-fortunate individual. An affluent person is expected to be successful. Parental guidance, access to a better education, a more stimulating environment, and the right connections all add to the likelihood of success. But what about the person who doesn't have these advantages? If he or she is successful in a career, doesn't luck play a greater role?

The reason that luck has more influence in a person's early career than in its latter stages is because young people generally have more options than older people do. Even though the importance of luck diminishes with time, it never ceases to exist.

The Entrepreneurial Firm: An Alternative

Every college student asks this important question: "Do I want to work for a large, solidly established corporation or for a young, aggressive firm that may not be around in five or ten years?"

The entrepreneurial spirit is thriving, as evidenced by the number of new firms emerging in all types of business, especially in computer hardware and software. But not everyone has the entrepreneurial spirit or would be happy working in that kind of environment.

Arthur Lipper, who publishes *Venture* magazine, describes an entrepreneur this way:

The entrepreneur is typically the first born or only child. He is an individual who wishes to have more control over his own life than the person who is working for someone else. He is the person who held three or four or five jobs by the time he was midway through high school, he really was the kind out there with the paper route and lemonade stand. He thought of himself as a child as being different—tall, fat, thin, ugly, handsome, whatever. He is proving something to someone. That someone in the male entrepreneur is the father, and in the female entrepreneur it is the mother. He is a morning person rather than a night person, and has enormous energy. I know of no sickly entrepreneurs. Tenacity is their single most important characteristic. He becomes successful in the face of all sorts of people telling him it can't be done.[12]

Being an entrepreneur is one thing; working for one is another. Undoubtedly, the way an entrepreneurial organization is run differs greatly from the structured approach found in most traditional organizations. First, seniority is not important because the firm is new. Consequently, lines of communication are more open and the trappings of bureaucracy are virtually nonexistent. The prevailing attitude is: "Let's work hard, have fun, and make some money at the same time."

Companies founded on entrepreneurship have their limitations, too. According to Lipper, most entrepreneurs are poor managers who are not detail people. They are more interested in what's new, different, and better.[13] Their firms also tend to be here today and gone tomorrow. This is especially true for firms in high-tech fields where the cutting edge of knowledge is constantly changing. College graduates should seriously question their wants and needs before joining a new firm founded on an entrepreneurial spirit. If job security and vertical progression through the managerial ranks are appealing, as opposed to a "let's do it and see what happens" attitude, then joining an established firm seems to be a wiser choice.

Women in Management: Challenges and Opportunities

Traditionally, management has been dominated by men. Except for clerical workers and secretaries, American corporations were almost totally staffed with men twenty years ago. Other areas were devoid of women, too. There were almost no anchorwomen on the television news, almost no female partners in accounting and law firms, and almost no women on stock exchanges, in route sales, and in major financial institutions.[14]

Today the American scene has changed. Spurred on by the Equal Pay Act of 1963, Title VII of the Civil Rights Act of 1964, and the Equal Employment Opportunity Act of 1972, women are pursuing business careers in unprecedented numbers. How are they doing? Given the obstacles that stood in their path, women have made tremendous inroads into the managerial ranks of American corporations. But, unfortunately, many of the same barriers that blocked their progress in the mid-1960s are still evident today.

Women are definitely having trouble breaking into senior-level management. As pointed out by Janet Jones Parker, executive director of the Association of Executive Search Consultants, Inc., there is an invisible ceiling for women at the policy-making level. The problem begins at about the $75,000 range and gets progressively worse. Only one company on *Fortune* magazine's list of the top five hundred corporations, for example, is headed by a female.[15] The In-Box on page 533 indicates that this situation is due for change within the next two decades.

According to one survey of female managers across the country, *overt* discrimination and most of the social customs that went with it have virtually disappeared. But the real gains in hiring and promotion appear to have leveled off. Approximately half of the entry-level managers and one-fourth of the middle managers today are women, but upper management is still almost exclusively male. Roughly 1,000 women hold top management positions in major U.S. corporations, as compared to 49,000 men. And fewer than 400 women sit on the boards of the country's top 1,300 public companies, as compared to 15,000 men.[16]

Black women face even greater difficulty than their white contemporaries do. They must cope with racial as well as sexual discrimination. To add to the problem, some analysts contend that black men have difficulty working for black female managers because they feel mothered and nurtured.[17]

A significant number of black women are aware of what is referred to as the "twofer" concept—the filling of sex and race quotas through the hiring or promoting of black women. This practice leads to hostility because it promotes a feeling of being hired because of sex or race, rather than for the qualifications needed to handle the job.

In 1981, roughly one-fourth of all black managers, especially women, worked in personnel and public relations. Statistics show that despite affirmative action plans, white women are progressing into management positions at a faster rate than black women are. Even so, more black women than ever before are moving into managerial jobs.

Profile of the Successful Female Executive

The successful female executive, like other professionals, is independent, achievement-oriented, and exhibits high self-esteem. And, contrary to the stereotyped image, she is not handicapped intellectually. In fact, research comparing men and women on a variety of aptitudes shows that women surpass men in verbal aptitude and tend to excel on tests of memory and scholastic achievement.[18]

Another common belief is that women are more vulnerable to drastic swings of mood. Again, research fails to support such a conclusion. In all likelihood, this image of female instability is due to society's acceptance of female expressions of fear, grief, disappointment, and other emotions. Because women express, without fear of disapproval, a greater variety of emotions than men do, they are judged to be temperamentally unstable.

THE IN-BOX

Female Managers
Set High Goals

Katherine Graham, chairperson of the *Washington Post* Co., is currently the only woman who heads a Fortune 500 company. But things may be different in the not-too-distant future. Women are now setting their corporate goals high, and more and more are achieving their ambitions. Between 1972 and 1983, the number of executive women in the United States increased from 1.4 million to 3.5 million. Most now occupy lower- and middle-level management positions. But within twenty years, a good number of them will be at the top.

One reason that women are making strides is because companies now realize that females account for half of all prospective managerial talent in the country. They also know that many of the best college graduates are women. The attitude of men toward female managers seems to be changing, too. According to a 1985 *Harvard Business Review* survey, the percentage of men who thought women were temperamentally unfit for management declined from 51% in 1965 to 18% in 1985. Perhaps more important, 47% of the male respondents said they would feel comfortable working for a woman, compared with 27% in 1965.

At a time when companies are facing stiff competition from foreign firms, American corporations are learning that they must reach out for talent and ignore gender. According to Thomas Peters, coauthor of the best-selling book, *In Search of Excellence*, it is competition in the marketplace, not women, that is changing the attitudes of corporations.

Source: Janice Castro, "More and More, She's the Boss," *Time*, December 2, 1985, pp. 64–66.

A third stereotype is that men place greater value on achievement, promotion, and meaningful work than women do. Women, on the other hand, value money, security, social relations, and such. This image, too, is a myth. All available evidence points out that both women and men place greater importance on intrinsic job factors than on extrinsic job factors. Moreover, there is no difference in the degree of importance they attach to these intrinsic variables.[19] Research also shows that women are just as dissatisfied as men are with work that fails to utilize their skills; and they are just as motivated as men are to serve in managerial capacities.[20]

Female managers are no less assertive than male managers, according to research. Although women tend to score lower on personality measures of dominance, this difference is attributed to cultural values. Current research shows that women can assimilate to roles requiring the assertion of influence and leadership as effectively as men can. One survey comparing the leadership styles of seventy male and seventy female managers who were matched on occupational level, seniority, and other relevant factors, revealed that women adopted active, effective leadership styles and were actually more diverse in their management styles than were the male managers.[21]

Levels of Satisfaction

Although women have more difficulty progressing through the corporate ranks than men do, those who are successful appear to be more satisfied with their careers than their male counterparts are. In a nationwide *Wall Street Journal/ Gallup* poll of 722 female executives, 82% of the respondents expressed high levels of satisfaction with their careers. And most—78%—are happy with their personal lives, too. This survey, which was of high-ranking female managers who are employed by firms with sales of $100 million or more, also revealed that older female executives tend to be more satisfied than their younger counterparts are.[22]

In terms of their personal lives, marital status seems to play an important role: married women are more satisfied than unmarried women. Overall, the happiest female executives are those who are married, over the age of forty-five, and have no children living at home. The least satisfied—those who are unmarried and under forty-five—tend to be better educated and are the most likely to leave their employers to start their own businesses.[23]

Personal Sacrifices   Like their male counterparts, female executives can expect to work long hours. They can also expect to make personal and family sacrifices for their careers. Career-oriented female managers usually feel that their jobs deprive them of personal time and prevent them from pursuing hobbies or time-consuming friendships.

About one-fourth of the women studied state that they have achieved their success at the expense of their family life. In some cases, they chose to postpone having children or decided to forego motherhood altogether. A significant number cite their commitment to their careers as the primary cause of the breakup of their marriages.

Younger versus Older Female Managers   When younger female executives are compared with older female executives, significant differences appear. First, many of today's executives were older than their younger counterparts were when they decided to pursue a career. Typically, the older managers worked for a number of years before deciding to make a career out of their jobs. Younger female executives, on the other hand, tend to make career decisions early in life and to map out plans for advancement; consequently, they progress farther and faster than their predecessors.

Most of today's older female executives worked their way up through the corporation from nonmanagement positions. In contrast, only about 40% of the younger executives say they reached their positions through promotions within their company. One study of female executives revealed that higher-level female managers tend to enter their companies in managerial capacities rather than to be promoted through the ranks from nonmanagement slots.[24] Finally, younger female managers take few breaks from their careers. Of the women surveyed, only one-fourth have taken a break for family reasons, and a majority of these were older executives.[25]

Obstacles Facing Female Managers

Women managers can expect to confront a number of barriers as they struggle up the corporate ladder. Several surveys of female managers in all types of industries show that the one obstacle standing out above all others is male prejudice.

Stereotypes   Actually, such prejudice is manifested in a number of ways. Women managers may be excluded from social activities: golf on Saturday mornings, for instance. Or male executives may not take female managers seriously. And, of course, there is the problem of stereotyping. As discussed previously, too many males still view women as being overly emotional and temperamental. Such attitudes can hurt the chances of promotion and virtually eliminate the acceptance of females in policy-making circles.

But men can prove helpful to women in their careers, too. Women managers readily acknowledge that men have been instrumental in helping them perform well and in getting them recognition. An overwhelming majority of survey respondents say that the single person who has been most helpful to them in their careers has been a man.[26] Many female executives, in fact, blame other women for many of their problems. Women, they say, can be jealous, petty, and too critical. While acknowledging that male chauvinism can hinder their progress, they maintain that female jealousy can be just as detrimental. This partly explains why a majority of female managers prefer their senior executives to be male.[27]

Family Demands   Contrary to popular belief, female managers do not view family responsibilities and a lack of formal education as major stumbling blocks.

In one study, only 3% of the female respondents cited family obligations as their most serious obstacle, and only 12% mentioned the lack of formal training.[28] To make certain that family responsibilities don't interfere with their careers, many families of female executives employ part-time domestic workers to help with family and household chores. Although the costs of employing maids and housekeepers can greatly cut into take-home pay, many female managers feel that this is the only way that they can balance both spheres.

Age Discrepancies   Older female managers are finding that working under the supervision of younger female managers can be particularly frustrating. While older women generally have long accepted the inevitability of working for younger men, some are having difficulty coming to grips with the idea that younger women are occupying more and more managerial positions.

Today, nearly 1.5 million women under the age of thirty-five hold managerial jobs, up from 322,000 in the early 1970s.[29] On one hand, this trend signals improvement in the status of career-minded women. On the other, it can stifle progression and lead to dissatisfaction.

Older women tend to be deferential with coworkers and maternal with supervisors.[30] Such behavior can infuriate young female executives and can cause stressful working conditions. Conflict often arises because older workers frequently feel that they know how things ought to be done. Their advice is sought in some cases, but most of the time they are perceived as a source of the "problem" by younger, career-oriented female managers.

Pay Differential   On the average, women earn about two-thirds of what men do for similar work.[31] In the past, this differential has been explained away by citing seniority and educational differences. But things may be changing in the private sector, just as they changed in government a few years ago. Business firms may be charged with the responsibility of developing "comparable pay" guidelines.

For years, women struggled to achieve "equal pay for equal work." Federal law now mandates such practices. But now there is a move on to establish "equal pay for comparable work." Essentially, this means that companies will have to determine which jobs are comparable in skill, effort, responsibility, and conditions; they will then group comparable jobs into pay categories. Thus, jobs that traditionally have been filled by women may be judged as being comparable to those traditionally filled by men.

Most employers insist that their salary programs are already fair and equitable and that federal law does not apply to "comparable" jobs. The Equal Employment Opportunities Commission (EEOC) seems to agree. In its first ruling on the subject, the EEOC said that unequal pay for work of comparable value does not in itself constitute pay discrimination.[32]

Fearful that the government will ultimately require equal pay for comparable work, some firms are beginning to devise their own comparable work plans. For example, AT&T has developed its own plan using fourteen measurements of job-related factors for twenty major categories of employment. For the most part, the company is pleased with what it found when jobs were surveyed. Although a few jobs were found to be undervalued, the company discovered that just as many male-held jobs were underpaid as female-held jobs.[33]

A Look to the Future

Although female managers will be required to overcome a host of barriers as they pursue their corporate careers, the payoffs appear to justify the effort. Salaries for young, aggressive, career-oriented women are on the rise; and pay discrimination is not as blatant as it once was, thanks in part to government intervention and to an awareness of the value of excellent female managerial talent. In addition, their personal satisfaction and achievement are at an all-time high. While job-related stress affects women just as it does men, the majority of female managers contend that the positive aspects of their jobs outweigh the negative.

Most female managers plan to continue their climb up the corporate ladder. Younger female managers will find a more favorable environment than their predecessors simply because their presence has been accepted. Surveys conducted to assess the opportunities for female managers in the future reveal that the opportunities are increasing. In one survey, 75% of the respondents stated that they believed the opportunities for women starting out today are better than they have ever been. Even so, the road will be bumpy. Unfortunately, perhaps the best advice that could be offered is that given by a lower-level female bank executive: "Work twice as hard and three times as long as a man in the same position."[34]

Adapting to Changing Conditions	Future managers, both men and women, will have to be even more flexible than today's managers. Change, a constant in our social and industrial lives, is occurring at such a hectic pace that even the most adaptable individuals will have to struggle to keep up. Some of the forces that will shape the environment in which future managers will operate are these:

1. New laws and regulations/governmental involvement

2. Environmental concerns

3. Ethical considerations

4. Social obligations

5. Demands for challenging jobs

6. International trade

7. Demands for privacy

8. Involvement of workers in decision making

9. Production technology

10. Consumerism

11. Organizational change, mergers, acquisitions

12. Information technology

Many business managers feel that there has been too much government regulation in the past, resulting in needless expenditures of time, effort, and money. They criticize, in particular, the Occupational Safety and Health Act (OSHA) and the Environmental Protection Agency (EPA) for imposing too many rules too quickly. Under the Reagan administration, enforcement has not been as rigid and a noticeable improvement in the outlook for business—especially for small business—is evident. Even so, managers of the future will find that complying with constraints imposed by regulatory agencies will take up a great deal of their time and energy.

Social, cultural, and economic forces will continue to affect business. Growing concern over environmental pollution and other social ills will necessitate unprecedented efforts to clean up the physical environment and to alleviate conditions detrimental to growth and prosperity. In addition, the growing importance of international trade will provide both opportunities and problems for tomorrow's managers.

The demands of employees and customers alike will force tomorrow's managers to be more responsive to these needs. Workers will expect more challenging work, greater involvement in decision making, and more privacy. They also are likely to place personal concerns and interests ahead of their jobs. Demanding high-quality, safe products, consumers will continue to turn to the courts when they feel they have been wronged by business.

Retraining managers will be common in the future. Advances in manufacturing and information technology, the need to motivate workers to higher levels of performance, and organizational change will serve as the impetus for further management development. The skills and tools that managers learn in college and on the job will become obsolete at an alarming rate. As a result, tomorrow's managers will need to upgrade their skills continually to adapt to changing conditions.

Probably the most significant change affecting tomorrow's managers is the improvement in information technology. The sheer volume of information that managers will have at their disposal will dramatically alter the decision-making process. Recent developments in computer hardware and software will give managers access to timely, accurate information. Intuition and judgment will be largely replaced by hard data that can be stored, retrieved, and manipulated instantaneously. Computers will no longer be the domain of financial analysts. Personal computers, which are already becoming common in large and small businesses alike, will be considered absolutely essential tools by managers at all organizational levels.

The Personal Computer: A Must for Tomorrow's Manager

No tool has changed the lives of managers as profoundly as the personal computer has. Its most obvious advantage is its speed. Managers get answers to complex questions almost immediately; letters are composed, reworked, and typed in a fraction of the normal time; and information can be stored and retrieved in fractions of a second.

© Punch-ROTHCO

ON-LINE MANAGEMENT

The Computer Revolution

The personal computer is quietly but profoundly changing managers' lives.

Through the computer, managers are finding the answers to complicated problems no one had time to solve before. Now, managers can dig into problems that used to be handled by teams of experts. One manager said it makes him feel "master of my own destiny."

Personal computers also are changing people's workplaces and the kinds of things that they do on the job. Some executives are using their computers in airplanes, hotel rooms, or at home to do office work. The distinction between time for labor and time for leisure is becoming increasingly blurred.

The most significant impact of personal computers may be on the office power structure: flattening the hierarchy and making it more difficult to hoard authority. Managers with computers delegate fewer typing tasks and less statistical analysis. Secretarial and staff positions often are eliminated or restructured as a result.

Some analysts fear that the growing use of personal computers will lead to greater individualism and away from teamwork, creating prima donnas. As a consequence, managers may become more dependent than ever on their people skills to keep things in order.

Source: Peter Nulty, "How Personal Computers Change Managers' Lives," *Fortune*, September 3, 1984, pp. 38–48.

Personal computers also are changing work habits. Managers are discovering that they can take their work home with them and spend less time behind their desks. Information can be put into the computer at home or on business trips and retrieved at the office. Because the cost has steadily declined, many managers now own one themselves. For a look at how computers are changing managers' lives, see On-Line Management on this page.

No one knows for sure how many managers have access to a personal computer, but the list is growing daily. In 1984, Fortune 500 corporations with sales of $1 billion or more were estimated to have had between two hundred and five hundred personal computers in operation. Those firms were expected to increase their number of personal computers tenfold by 1990.[35] Today, that estimate appears low.

Who Uses Computers?

One-third of the respondents in a 1985 survey of one hundred top-level corporate executives in Fortune 500 companies reported using computers when making important decisions. The respondents, each of whom was one of the top five officers in the corporation, revealed that computers are used primarily by executives under fifty years of age who are required to make financial, budgeting, and marketing decisions.[36] The results of this survey appear in Table 20.2.

More than one-third of the respondents to this survey acknowledged using personal computers in their offices, and nearly one-fourth used them in their homes. According to the survey, 77% of the respondents had been using computers for two years or less; about half (51%) of the executives under fifty years of age used them, compared to only 21% of those over fifty.

Chief executives use personal computers, too. In a December 1984 survey of chief executives of the five hundred largest corporations in the country, 59% reported using a computer in their businesses.

Advantages of Microcomputers

The uses of microcomputers are as varied as the managers who depend on them. Data bases, spreadsheets, and word processing programs enable managers to use their personal computers with a minimum of training. Listed here are some of the more common ways that a personal computer can assist managers at different levels and in different areas of a company.

1. Sales presentations that show prices of competitors' products and other relevant information

2. Budgeting and financial planning

3. Letters, memoranda, and other forms of correspondence

TABLE 20.2
Users of computers in Fortune 500 companies

	AGE OF RESPONDENT	
DECISION-MAKING AREA	UNDER 50	50 AND OLDER
Financial analysis	58%	58%
Current budget planning	54%	47%
Market intelligence	38%	25%
Long-range planning	21%	45%
Public affairs	17%	25%
Personnel	8%	33%

Source: "Top Executives Use Personal Computers," *Spring High-Tech, A Supplement to the Washington Post,* May 5, 1985.

4. In-house mail service

5. Accounting and financial statement preparation

6. "What if" questions that permit the user to change variables in equations

7. Filing, retrieval of data

8. Statistical analyses

9. Forecasting

10. Financial model building

11. Resource-allocation decisions

12. Data bases outside the company (stock quotations, financial news, newspaper and journal articles, and the like)

13. Management training through self-instruction

Computers and Management Skills

One of the uses of a personal computer—management training—deserves additional comment because it is changing the way companies handle management development. In the future, many firms will replace seminars on leadership, communication, and human relations with computer software that teaches these and other matters to managers. A problem with seminars is that they are not tailor-made; they gear their instruction to the entire group, not to the specific needs of an individual. This can be a waste of time and money, and the training may be only slightly beneficial. The right software in a manager's personal computer can solve this problem.

One type of software package that is becoming increasingly popular is a data bank comprised of thousands of responses business managers made to specific problems. When obliged to make a specific decision, a manager can tell the computer what he or she would do and then compare that decision to the responses made by thousands of other managers.

Another software program based on the same concept is one that helps managers deal with people problems. The Management Edge, for example, is a program that asks a manager about an employee's personality and then offers tips on everything from improving performance to firing him or her.[37] The computer responses are based on information about behavioral science and psychology. This practice is also helpful in personal selling. Information about a potential purchaser can be put into the computer, which will match the best sales approach to the personality traits of the customer.

Using computers for management training offers other advantages as well. First, the software costs less than a seminar does. A typical program on a diskette normally costs less than $500. Not only is this less than the registration fee for most management-training seminars but also the program is useful for any number of managers in a firm. Because software programs focusing on specific problem areas are available, managers can concentrate on the areas in which they need help. Finally, timing is important. Software can be used on a personal computer at home or in the office—whichever is more convenient for the user; thus, training programs do not interrupt the normal routine.

Review

✓ *The stages of a manager's career.* Career planning forces you to think about the future and to assess your needs and aspirations, the type of occupations and organizations that can best satisfy those needs, and your personal skills and abilities. Career planning is the development of a program that will let you reach your potential in whatever occupation you choose. All careers have five stages: (1) beginning, (2) decision, (3) stabilization, (4) maintenance, and (5) decline/retirement. Each is influenced by events and accomplishments in previous stages, and each lays the groundwork for successive stages.

✓ *How to plan your career systematically.* Good career planning involves three assessments: (1) evaluating careers in general, (2) determining the environment in which you want to pursue your career, and (3) evaluating your wants, needs, and abilities.

✓ *The pros and cons of a management career.* A growing number of managers, especially young managers, are unhappy in their jobs. Part of the dissatisfaction can be attributed to unusually high expectations. Much of it, however, stems from choosing the wrong career or the wrong employer. On the positive side, a career in management can be both emotionally and financially rewarding; it provides status, power, esteem, and wealth.

✓ *How successful managers think.* Successful managers differ from other people in several respects. Evidence suggests that they think in longer time frames and can see the interrelationships among variables more readily than other people can. They also can distinguish between important and unimportant information in decision making, and they tend to refine their decisions as additional information becomes available. Recent studies show that most executives exhibit left-brain dominance. That is, their decisions are primarily influenced by the left hemisphere of the brain, which governs logic, verbal skills, and quantitative abilities. In contrast, people whose decisions are based on emotions and who are more artistic and creative—right-brain types—are typically less successful in reaching the top rungs of the corporate hierarchy.

✔ *The role luck plays in a manager's success.* Hard work, talent, and education increase the likelihood of managerial success, but luck plays a role, too. It affects the careers of the less fortunate more strongly than the careers of the affluent, and it is more significant in the early stages of a manager's career than in the latter stages.

✔ *Whether you should consider an entrepreneurial firm.* Some managers are happier working for a young, aggressive firm than for a solidly established organization. In a new firm, seniority is not important, communication lines are open, and the trappings of bureaucracy are nonexistent. But entrepreneurships have their limitations as well. Most entrepreneurs are poor managers who are interested in doing things differently. Entrepreneurial companies also tend to have short life spans.

✔ *The challenges and opportunities facing women in management.* Traditionally, men have dominated management; women have found it difficult, if not impossible, to move into management circles. But the future appears to be brighter than the past. Aided by legislation designed to prohibit discrimination, women are now moving up the corporate ladder in unprecedented numbers. Like her male counterpart, the successful female executive is achievement-oriented, intelligent, and industrious. Nevertheless, tomorrow's female managers still have to struggle to dispel the myths that have inhibited their progress and have kept them out of policy-making positions.

✔ *How change will affect tomorrow's managers.* Tomorrow's managers will function in an environment considerably different from today's. Innovations in production technology will require new learning; international trade will become a way of life for more and more companies; social responsibility will take on new dimensions; and environmental, political, legal, and ethical considerations will become increasingly important. Greater emphasis will also be placed on involving workers in decision making. In addition, advancements in information technology will provide both challenges and opportunities for tomorrow's managers.

✔ *The importance of personal computers for managers.* The personal computer, more than any other single tool, is affecting managers at all levels. Because of its versatility, speed, low cost, and ease of operation, the microcomputer is now an essential tool for managers from the front-line supervisor to the chief executive.

REVIEW QUESTIONS

1. What are the advantages of career planning?

2. Briefly describe the phases of a career cycle. In which phase do most managers' careers peak?

3. How can you, as a college student, systematically select a career? What assessments should you make?

4. In your opinion, what are the major advantages of pursuing a career in management? The major drawbacks?

5. Why are many managers dissatisfied with their careers?

6. Discuss some of the differences between successful and unsuccessful managers.

7. Do all successful managers possess the same traits? Explain.

8. Discuss the differences between an entrepreneurial firm and an established company. Where do you belong?

9. What obstacles do female managers face in their efforts to climb the corporate ladder? Which barriers appear to be the greatest? Why?

10. Do you believe female managers are generally satisfied with their progress? Why or why not?

11. List some of the uses of a personal computer by supervisors, middle managers, and senior-level managers.

MANAGEMENT CHALLENGE

1. Using the information presented in this chapter, identify your career concept.

2. What type of organization will let you use your career concept? Name some companies that can offer you an opportunity to pursue your career concept.

3. Make a candid assessment of your needs and aspirations. Now make a list of your strengths and weaknesses. Will you be able to satisfy your needs and reach your potential? If not, what specific action will you take?

4. In your opinion, do you possess the traits associated with managerial success?

5. Do you want a career in management? Why or why not? Be specific.

CASE 20.1

PepsiCo: Where Results-Oriented Management Is a Way of Life[38]

PepsiCo, Inc., has developed a reputation over the years for being tough on managers. Its image is partially shaped by the high turnover rate among senior-level executives and the emphasis placed on short-term profits. For example, people stay in the top 470 jobs an average of only eighteen months. Each year, 4% of the company's top managers leave voluntarily, and at least as many are fired. Internal competition is fierce, quotas are demanding, and individual achievement is rewarded. In general, the pressure placed on managers to produce is tremendous; as a result, many managers opt for what they consider to be better working conditions elsewhere. As one observer pointed out, PepsiCo is not a career company.

Two surveys of PepsiCo's senior-level managers revealed some startling results: a majority felt they weren't cared about as people, many felt alienated, and some believed that feedback on their performances was inadequate. Motivated by these findings, top management of the company is determined to improve working conditions for its managers without becoming too soft. From now on, managers are to be informed of specific career paths to promotion, and job changes will be limited to those that are absolutely necessary. In addition, greater emphasis will be placed on the development of subordinates. For example, pay and promotions will be based partially on how well an executive furthers the development of his or her subordinate managers.

To ensure that managers devote serious attention to these matters, annual merit reviews will incorporate factors stressing the importance of developing managerial talent. Moreover, senior-level managers are expected to do some soul-searching for self-improvement. Behavior desired by top management will be reinforced in the form of bonuses; undesirable behavior will not be rewarded.

The overriding objective of PepsiCo's new philosophy is to make work nicer for management. The loss of too many good people, coupled with feelings of alienation among middle managers, are taking their toll. Even the company's president, Andrall Pearson, acknowledges that change is in order. PepsiCo, however, is still not a career company where employees start young and stay until retirement. As one former executive points out, "There are a lot of great jobs at Pepsi, but very few careers."

Questions

1. What type of individual would be attracted to PepsiCo? Explain.
2. Given the fact that PepsiCo is thriving in the marketplace, why would top management want to change? Discuss.

CASE 20.2

Coca-Cola's "International" Flavor[39]

When Roberto Goizueta became chief executive officer of Coca-Cola in 1982, the huge soft-drink bottler's market share was slipping. Pepsi and Seven-Up were making inroads into the niche that Coke had seized, partially because of successful advertising campaigns and the introduction of new products. Prior to Goizueta's promotion, Coke appeared to be a complacent, sleeping giant, destined to become number two in sales.

Immediately after Goizueta's appointment, things began to change at Coca-Cola. First, in the face of opposition, he introduced Diet Coke to compete with other sugarless soft drinks, including the company's own Tab. Then the company expanded outside the manufacturing business by buying Columbia Pictures. The most noticeable change, however, is evident in the makeup of senior management and the leadership style that now permeates the company. Six of the top sixteen officers are foreign-born, and the management approach is more open and participatory. Today, performance is more important than personality; cronyism, which some thought was rampant under Goizueta's predecessor, has been displaced by individual accountability.

Major decisions at Coke are now made in consultation with top managers. Previously, they were made individually by Goizueta's predecessor, J. Paul Austin, regarded by most people as autocratic and aloof. Goizueta tends to be more active in those areas where his expertise lies—finance, for example—but he delegates his weak areas—marketing and public appearances—to Donald Keogh, president of Coca-Cola.

Unlike most managers, Goizueta has demonstrated a willingness to surround himself with people who are different from himself. He believes that people with the same backgrounds and training tend to think alike; that can lead to stagnation. "If you have two people who give you the same answer," he says, "then you have one person too many."

Questions

1. When a change is made at the top, is personnel turnover inevitable? Discuss.

2. Based on what you now know about Coca-Cola's success in the marketplace, does Goizueta appear to have been a wise choice for chief executive officer?

3. Goizueta clearly is a successful manager. In his approach to revitalizing Coca-Cola, in what ways does his thinking appear "right-brained," and in what ways "left-brained"?

Notes

Chapter 1

1. Lucien Rhodes, "The Un-manager," *Inc.,* August 1982, p. 37.
2. Ibid., p. 36.
3. Irving S. Shapiro, "Executive Forum—Managerial Communication: The View from Inside," *California Management Review,* Fall 1984, p. 166.
4. "A Company Where Everybody Is the Boss," *Business Week,* April 15, 1985, p. 98.
5. Bernard Wysocki, Jr., "The Chief's Personality Can Have a Big Impact—For Better or Worse," *Wall Street Journal,* September 11, 1984, p. 1.
6. Campbell R. McConnell, *Economics: Principles, Problems, and Policies* (New York: McGraw-Hill, 1981), p. 24.
7. Lawrence A. Appley, "New Directions for Management," *Supervisory Management,* February 1981, p. 12.
8. Reprinted by permission of the publisher, from *Leadership: Strategies for Organizational Effectiveness* by James J. Cribbin, pp. 32–33. © 1981 AMACOM, a division of American Management Association, New York. All rights reserved.
9. Ibid.
10. Henry Mintzberg, *The Nature of Managerial Work* (New York: Harper & Row, 1973), pp. 54–94.
11. *Webster's New Collegiate Dictionary* (Springfield, Mass.: G. & C. Merriam Company, 1977).
12. Peter Drucker, *Management: Tasks, Responsibilities, Practices* (New York: Harper & Row, 1974), p. 14.
13. Ibid., pp. 12–13.
14. Herman Wouk, *War and Remembrance* (New York: Simon and Schuster, 1979), pp. 774–775.
15. Gordon L. Weil, *Sears, Roebuck, U.S.A.* (New York: Stein and Day, 1977).
16. Booton Herndon, *Satisfaction Guaranteed: An Unconventional Report to Today's Consumer* (New York: McGraw-Hill, 1972).
17. "GM Eyes Leaner Management Style," by Ann Job Woolley, Associated Press, June 9, 1982. Reprinted by permission of Associated Press.

18. "The Five Best-Managed Companies," *Dun's Business Month,* December 1984, pp. 35–37.

Chapter 2

1. Lee Smith, "Japan's Autocratic Managers," *Fortune,* January 7, 1984, p. 56.

2. Ibid.

3. Ibid., pp. 56–65.

4. Daniel A. Wren, *The Evolution of Management Thought* (New York: John Wiley & Sons, 1979), pp. 152–153.

5. Henri Fayol, *General and Industrial Management* (London: Sir Isaac Pitman and Sons, 1967), p. 6.

6. Ibid.

7. Ibid., p. 22.

8. Ibid., p. 40.

9. Wren, *Evolution,* p. 341.

10. Chester I. Barnard, *The Functions of the Executive* (Cambridge, Mass.: Harvard University Press, 1938), pp. 215–216.

11. Hugo Münsterberg, *Psychology and Industrial Efficiency* (Boston: Houghton Mifflin, 1913).

12. The time period usually associated with the Hawthorne experiments is 1927–1932. However, the Hawthorne Works, in collaboration with the National Research Council, began a series of studies to determine the effect of illumination on worker productivity as early as 1924. Working with Mayo was his protégé, Fritz Roethlisberger, who was another industrial psychologist at Harvard, and William Dickson, a Western Electric engineer.

13. See D. Bramel and R. Friend, "Hawthorne, the Myth of the Docile Worker, and Class Bias in Psychology," *American Psychologist,* Vol. 36, 1981, pp. 867–878; Berkeley Rice, "The Hawthorne Defect: Persistence of a Flawed Theory," *Psychology Today,* February 1982, pp. 70–74; and B. L. Pitcher, "The Hawthorne Experiments: Statistical Evidence for a Learning Hypothesis," *Social Forces,* Vol. 60, 1981, pp. 133–149.

14. *The Gold and the Garbage in Management Theories and Prescriptions* by James A. Lee, 1980, pp. 52–53. Reprinted with the permission of the Ohio University Press, Athens.

15. Interviews with these three participants were conducted by Ronald Greenwood, Alfred Bolton, and Regina Greenwood in 1981. Findings appear in their article "Hawthorne a Half Century Later: Relay Asembly Participants Remember," *Journal of Management,* Fall/Winter 1983, pp. 217–231.

16. Rice, "The Hawthorne Defect," p. 72.

17. Barry Render and Ralph Stair, *Quantitative Analysis for Management* (Boston: Allyn and Bacon, 1982), p. 3.

18. William G. Ouchi, *Theory Z* (Reading, Mass.: Addison-Wesley, 1981).

19. John Merwin, "The Most Valuable Executive in Either League," *Forbes,* April 12, 1982, pp. 129–138.

20. John M. Roach, "Why Volvo Abolished the Assembly Line," *Management Review,* September 1977, pp. 48–52; and Pehr Gyllenhammar, "How Volvo Adapts Work to People," *Harvard Business Review,* July/August 1977, pp. 102–113.

Chapter 3

1. "Small Is Beautiful Now in Manufacturing," *Business Week,* October 22, 1984, p. 152.

2. Ibid., pp. 153–154.

3. Allyn Douglas Strickland, *Government Regulation and Business* (Boston: Houghton Mifflin, 1980), pp. 4–6.

4. Marcia B. Wallace and Ronald J. Penoyer, *Directory of Federal Regulatory Agencies* (St. Louis: Center for the Study of American Business), Working Paper No. 36, September 1978.

5. Strickland, *Government*, p. 12.

6. Willard Marcy, "Enhancements and Impediments to the Innovative Process," in *Technological Innovation in the '80s*, edited by James S. Coles (Englewood Cliffs, N.J.: Prentice-Hall, 1984), pp. 104–106.

7. Ibid., p. 104.

8. Ibid.

9. "U.S. Steel's Debt-Shrouded Future," *Business Week,* October 18, 1982, p. 154.

10. Stephen J. Sansweet, "How Team at Wickes Schemed and Cajoled to Restore Its Health," *Wall Street Journal,* August 2, 1985, p. 1.

11. G. Allport, P. Vernon, and G. Lindzey, *Study of Values* (Boston: Houghton Mifflin, 1960).

12. James S. Coles, *Technological Innovations in the '80s* (Englewood Cliffs, N.J.: Prentice-Hall, 1984), pp. 1–3.

13. Ellen Hume, "Furor on South Africa Makes Firms Question Value of Staying There," *Wall Street Journal,* March 11, 1985, pp. 1+.

Chapter 4

1. John Greenwald, "Coca-Cola's Big Fizzle," *Time,* July 22, 1985, pp. 48–49.

2. Ibid., p. 49.

3. Darryl J. Ellis and Peter P. Pekar, Jr., *Planning Basics for Managers* (New York: AMACOM, 1980), pp. 14–22.

4. Leon Reinharth, H. Jack Shapiro, and Ernest A. Kallman, *The Practice of Planning* (New York: Van Nostrand Reinhold, 1981), p. 6.

5. Louis A. Allen, *Making Managerial Planning More Effective* (New York: McGraw-Hill, 1982), pp. 21–28.

6. Reinharth, Shapiro, and Kallman, *Practice of Planning,* p. 5.

7. S. S. Thune and R. J. House, "Where Long-Range Planning Pays Off," *Business Horizons,* August 1970, pp. 81–87.

8. R. M. Fulmer and L. W. Rue, *The Practice and Profitability of Long-Range Planning,* (Oxford, Ohio: The Planning Executives Institute, 1973).

9. D. W. Karger and C. A. Malik, "Long Range Planning and Organizational Performance," *Long Range Planning,* December 1975.

10. R. C. Davis, *The Fundamentals of Top Management* (New York: Harper & Row, 1951), pp. 46–51.

11. Louis Boone and David L. Kurtz, *Principles of Management* (New York: Random House, 1984), p. 108.

12. Reinharth, Shapiro, and Kallman, *Practice of Planning,* pp. 66–67.

13. Russell L. Ackoff, *A Concept of Corporate Planning* (New York: Wiley-Interscience, 1970), pp. 4–5.

14. Robert J. Mockler, *Business Planning and Policy Formulation* (New York: Appleton-Century-Crofts, 1972), pp. 46–47.

15. David Hussey, *Corporate Planning: Theory and Practice* (Oxford: Pergamon Press, 1982), pp. 64–75.

16. William C. Giegold, *Management by Objectives: A Self-Instructional Approach,* (New York: McGraw-Hill, 1978), p. 1.

17. George S. Odiorne, *Management by Objectives: A System of Managerial Leadership* (New York: Pitman Publishing Company, 1965), pp. 55–56.

18. Gary Dessler, *Applied Human Relations* (Reston, Va.: Reston Publishing Company, 1983), p. 347.

19. Gieold, *Management by Objectives,* pp. 5–6.

20. Steven Kerr, "Some Modifications in MBO as an OD Strategy," *Proceedings of the Thirty-Second Annual Meeting of the Academy of Management,* edited by Vance F. Mitchell, Richard T. Barth, and Frances H. Mitchell (Minneapolis, August 1972), p. 41.

21. Dorothy Schaeffer, "M.B.O. Pitfalls," *Supervision,* August 1983, pp. 9–10; and William Glueck and John Ivancevich, *Foundations of Personnel/Human Resource Management,* Revised Edition, (Plano, Tex.: Business Publications, 1983), p. 256.

22. "British Companies Plan by Hunch," *The Economist,* May 21, 1983, p. 81.

23. Ronald Alsop, "Liggett Tests a New Cigarette Development for Hispanic Tastes," *Wall Street Journal,* July 12, 1984, p. 29.

Chapter 5

1. Steve Lawrence, "The Green in Blue-Collar Retailing," *Fortune,* May 27, 1985, p. 74.

2. Ibid., pp. 74–77.

3. James M. Higgins, *Strategy: Formulation, Implementation, and Control* (New York: CBS College Publishing, 1985), p. 2.

4. Lloyd L. Byars, *Concepts of Strategic Management* (New York: Harper & Row, 1984), pp. 9–10.

5. Ibid.

6. "Living Without Shackles," *Time,* December 12, 1983, p. 51.

7. "Airlines Learning to Adapt to Decontrol," *The New York Times,* December 8, 1983, p. 1.

8. Byars, *Concepts,* p. 12.

9. Michael A. Hitt and R. Dennis Middlemist, *Management: Concepts and Effective Practice,* (St. Paul: West Publishing Company, 1986), p. 151.

10. Kenichi Ohmae, "The Secret of Strategic Vision," *Management Review,* April 1982, pp. 10–11.

11. Subhash C. Jain, *Marketing Planning and Strategy* (Cincinnati: South-Western Publishing Company, 1985), p. 250.

12. Higgins, *Strategy,* p. 48.

13. Michael E. Porter, *Competitive Strategy: Techniques for Analyzing Industries and Competitors* (New York: Free Press, 1980).

14. Alan J. Rowe and Richard O. Mason, *Strategic Management and Business Policy* (Reading, Mass.: Addison-Wesley, 1984), p. 81.

15. Peter Wright, "The Strategic Options of Least Cost, Differentiation, and Niche," *Business Horizons*, March/April 1986, pp. 22–26.

16. Ibid.

17. Thomas A. Staudt, Donald A. Taylor, and Donald J. Bowersox, *A Managerial Introduction to Marketing* (Englewood Cliffs, N.J.: Prentice-Hall, 1976), pp. 134–135.

18. Robert Kreitner, *Management* (Boston: Houghton Mifflin, 1986), p. 182.

19. Richard B. Robinson, Jr., and John A. Pearce, II, "Research Thrusts in Small Firm Strategic Planning," *Academy of Management Review,* January 1984, pp. 128–137.

20. Ibid.

21. Alexander L. Taylor, "Mr. Smith Shakes Up Detroit," *Time,* January 16, 1984, p. 59.

22. Stephen Kreider Yoder, "Apple, Loser in Japanese Computer Market, Tries to Recoup by Redesigning Its Models," *Wall Street Journal,* June 21, 1985, p. 26.

Chapter 6

1. Gordon Donaldson and Jay W. Lorsch, *Decision Making at the Top* (New York: Basic Books, 1983), p. 3.

2. Ibid., p. 4.

3. Herbert A. Simon, *The New Science of Management Decision* (New York: Harper & Row, 1960), Chapter 2.

4. K. J. Radford, *Modern Managerial Decision Making* (Reston, Va.: Reston Publishing Company, 1981), pp. 7–8.

5. E. Frank Harrison, *The Managerial Decision Making Process* (Boston: Houghton Mifflin, 1981), p. 8.

6. Simon, *New Science,* p. 1.

7. Harrison, *Managerial Decision,* pp. 25–26.

8. Edward Sanford and Harvey Adelman, *Management Decisions: A Behavioral Approach* (Cambridge, Mass.: Winthrop Publishers, 1977), pp. 16–17.

9. James L. McKenney and Peter G. W. Keen, "How Managers' Minds Work," *Harvard Business Review,* May/June 1974, p. 84.

10. Harrison, *Managerial Decision,* pp. 283–285.

11. Ibid., p. 284.

12. Ibid., p. 104.

13. Radford, *Modern Managerial,* pp. 106–107.

14. J. Hall, "Decisions," *Psychology Today,* November 1971, pp. 51+.

15. David R. Hampton, Charles E. Summer, and Ross A. Webber, *Organizational Behavior and the Practice of Management* (Glenview, Ill.: Scott, Foresman, 1982), p. 254.

16. D. Taylor, P. C. Berry, and C. H. Block, "Does Group Participation When Using Brainstorming Facilitate or Inhibit Creative Thinking?" *Administrative Science Quarterly,* Vol. 23, 1958, pp. 23–47.

17. Hampton, Summer, and Webber, *Organizational Behavior,* p. 254.

18. M. A. Wallach, N. Kogan, and D. J. Bem, "Group Influences on Individual Risk Taking," *Journal of Abnormal and Social Psychology,* Vol. 65, 1962, pp. 75–86.

19. Hampton, Summer, and Webber, *Organizational Behavior,* pp. 255–257.

20. M. R. Lohman, "Top Management Committees," Research Study No. 48 (New York: American Management Association, 1961).

21. Rollie Tillman, Jr., "Committees on Trial," *Harvard Business Review,* May/June 1960, pp. 6–12+.

22. Paul E. Moody, *Decision Making: Proven Methods for Better Decisions* (New York: McGraw-Hill, 1983), pp. 30–32.

23. Clayton Resser and Marvin Loper, *Management: The Key to Organizational Effectiveness* (Glenview, Ill.: Scott, Foresman, 1978), pp. 190–192.

24. Ibid., pp. 192–194.

25. Moody, *Decision Making,* p. 33.

26. Alfred R. Oxenfeldt, David W. Miller, and Roger A. Dickinson, *A Basic Approach to Executive Decision Making* (New York: AMACOM, 1978), p. 155.

27. George S. Welsh, "Perspectives in the Study of Creativity," *Journal of Creative Behavior,* Winter 1973, p. 235.

28. J. P. Guilford, "Creativity: Yesterday, Today, and Tomorrow," *Journal of Creative Behavior,* Winter 1967, pp. 3–14.

29. This process was first proposed by Graham Wallas, *The Art of Thought* (London: C. A. Watts, 1945).

30. Moody, *Decision Making,* p. 53.

31. Oxenfeldt, Miller, and Dickinson, *Basic Approach,* pp. 167–168.

32. Charles H. Ford, "Manage by Decisions, Not by Objectives," *Business Horizons,* February 1980, pp. 7–18.

33. Laura Landro, "Warner's Atari Tries to End Slump with New Products and Marketing," *Wall Street Journal,* May 21, 1984.

34. Myron Magnet, "How Top Managers Make Company's Toughest Decision," *Fortune,* March 18, 1985, pp. 52–57.

Chapter 7

1. Adam Smith, *Wealth of Nations* (New York: Modern Library, 1937), pp. 3–4.

2. Charles Babbage, *On the Economy of Machinery and Manufacturers* (London: Charles Knight, 1832), p. 169.

3. Emile Durkheim, *The Division of Labor in Society* (New York: Macmillan, 1953).

4. P. R. Lawrence and J. W. Lorsch, *Organization and Environment: Managing Differentiation and Integration* (Homewood, Ill.: Irwin, 1967).

5. Arthur H. Walker and Jay W. Lorsch, "Organizational Choice: Product vs. Function," *Harvard Business Review,* November/December 1968, pp. 129–138.

6. Stanley M. Davis and Paul R. Lawrence, *Matrix* (Reading, Mass.: Addison-Wesley, 1977), pp. 129–144.

7. David Robey, *Designing Organizations: A Macro Perspective* (Homewood, Ill.: Irwin, 1982), p. 357.

8. V. A. Graicunas, "Relationship in Organization," in *Papers on the Science of Administration,* ed. L. Gulick and L. Urwick (New York: Institute of Public Administration, 1937), pp. 181–187.

9. This view of authority is generally referred to as the formal theory of authority. Chester Barnard, however, argued that authority actually originates at the bottom of a structure, since no one can exercise authority unless subordinates accept directives.

10. William Newman, "Overcoming Obstacles to Effective Delegation," *Management Review,* January 1956, pp. 36–41.

11. Louis E. Boone and David L. Kurtz, *Principles of Management* (New York: Random House, 1984), pp. 233–234.

12. Andrew D. Szilagyi, Jr., *Management and Performance* (Glenview, Ill.: Scott, Foresman, 1984), p. 259.

13. Harold Koontz, Cyril O'Donnell, and Heinz Weihrich, *Management* (New York: McGraw-Hill, 1984), p. 285.

14. James H. Donnelly, Jr., James L. Gibson, and John M. Ivancevich, *Fundamentals of Management* (Plano, Tex.: Business Publications, 1984), p. 174.

15. Joseph Litterer, *The Analysis of Organizations* (New York: John Wiley & Sons, 1973), pp. 591–595.

16. Ibid.

17. Amal Nag, "Chrysler Tests Consumer Reaction to Mexican-Made Cars Sold in U.S.," *Wall Street Journal,* July 23, 1984, p. 15.

18. Kathleen K. Wiegner, "John Young's New Jogging Shoes," *Forbes,* November 4, 1985, pp. 42–44.

Chapter 8

1. Judy L. Ward, "Firms Forcing Employees to Repay Some Costs if They Quit Too Soon," *Wall Street Journal,* July 16, 1985, p. 35.

2. Ibid.

3. Guvenc G. Alpander, *Human Resources Management Planning* (New York: AMACOM, 1982), p. 10.

4. Ibid., pp. 17–18.

5. Donald G. Revelle, "Human Resource Planning: Who Is in Charge?" *Human Resource Planning,* Vol. 2, No. 3, 1979, p. 119.

6. Robert H. Guest, "Review of Work Design," *Harvard Business Review,* January/February 1981, pp. 46–47 +.

7. Ralph W. Reber and Gloria E. Terry, *Behavioral Insights for Supervision* (Englewood Cliffs, N.J.: Prentice-Hall, 1975), p. 69.

8. Ramon J. Aldag and Arthur P. Brief, *Task Design and Employee Motivation* (Glenview, Ill.: Scott, Foresman, 1979).

9. Marvin Loper and Clayton Reeser, *Management: A Key to Organizational Effectiveness* (Glenview, Ill.: Scott, Foresman, 1978), p. 5.

10. Herzberg's two-factor theory of motivaiton is discussed in detail in Chapter 10, "Motivation and Human Behavior."

11. Frederick Herzberg, "One More Time: How Do You Motivate Employees?" *Harvard Business Review,* January/February 1968, p. 53.

12. Reber and Terry, *Behavioral Insights,* p. 73.

13. M. Scott Myers, *Every Employee a Manager* (New York: McGraw-Hill, 1981), p. 102.

14. Randall S. Schuler and Stuart A. Youngblood, *Effective Personnel Management* (St. Paul: West Publishing Company, 1986), p. 127.

15. Paul S. Greenlaw and John P. Kohl, *Personnel Management: Managing Human Resources* (New York: Harper & Row, 1986), p. 94.

16. Robert L. Mathis and John H. Jackson, *Personnel: Human Resource Management* (St. Paul: West Publishing Company, 1985), p. 252.

17. Schuler and Youngblood, *Effective Personnel Management,* p. 175.

18. Greenlaw and Kohl, *Personnel Management,* p. 105.

19. John M. Ivancevich and William F. Glueck, *Foundations of Personnel/ Human Resource Management*, Revised Edition, (Plano, Tex.: Business Publications, 1983), pp. 202–203.

20. John M. Ivancevich and William F. Glueck, *Foundations of Personnel/ Human Resource Management*, Third Edition (Plano, Tex.: Business Publications, 1986), p. 541.

21. Judith Gordon, *Human Resource Management* (Boston: Allyn and Bacon, 1986), p. 332.

22. Ivancevich and Glueck, *Foundations,* Revised Edition, pp. 63–65.

23. William Simon, Jr., "Voluntary Affirmative Action After Weber," *Labor Law Journal,* March 1983, p. 138.

24. Antonio Sisneros, "Revisiting Affirmative Action Case Law," *Labor Law Journal,* June 1983, p. 352.

25. William Wang, "Bakke May Prohibit Voluntary Affirmative Action by Universities," *Case and Comment,* May/June 1979, pp. 39–40.

26. "Job Enlargement for Better Utilization of Resources," *Job Design for Motivation* (New York: The Conference Board, 1971), pp. 67–70.

27. Gary Cohn, "An Executive's Quest for a New Job Is a Lesson in Coolness and Strategy," *Wall Street Journal,* November 19, 1985, p. 37.

Chapter 9

1. Patricia A. Bellew, "Levi Is Promoting New Fashions in a Campaign to Become More Entrepreneurial, Competitive," *Wall Street Journal,* January 31, 1985, p. 4.

2. Harold J. Leavitt, "Applied Organizational Change in Industry: Structural, Technological, and Humanistic Approaches," in *Handbook of Organization,* ed. J. March (Chicago: Rand McNally, 1965).

3. Thomas H. Patten, *Organizational Development Through Teambuilding* (New York: John Wiley & Sons, 1981), p. 2.

4. Gene Dalton, *Organizational Change and Development* (Homewood, Ill.: Irwin, 1970), p. 29.

5. Larry E. Greiner, "Patterns of Organization Change," *Harvard Business Review,* May/June 1967, p. 122.

6. Patten, *Organizational Development.*

7. Kurt Lewin, "Frontiers in Group Dynamics," *Human Relations* 1, 1947, p. 34.

8. Greiner, "Patterns," pp. 126–128.

9. Robert Blake and Jane Mouton, *Building a Dynamic Organization Through Grid Organization Development* (Reading, Mass.: Addison-Wesley, 1969), p. 11.

10. Richard Beckhard, *Organization Development: Strategies and Models* (Reading, Mass.: Addison-Wesley, 1969), p. 20.

11. Rosabeth Moss Kanter, "Managing the Human Side of Change," *Management Review,* April 1985, p. 52.

12. Alvin Toffler, *Future Shock* (New York: Random House, 1970).

13. J. G. Wissema, "The Modern Prophets—How Can They Help Us?" *Long Range Planning,* August 1982, pp. 126–134.

14. John P. Kotter and Leonard A. Schlesinger, "Choosing Strategies for Change," *Organizational Behavior and the Practice of Management,* ed. David Hampton, Charles Summer, and Ross Webber (Glenview, Ill.: Scott, Foresman, 1982), p. 736.

15. Ibid., pp. 738–741.

16. "Exxon Asks 40,000 To Retire," *Morning Advocate,* Baton Rouge, La., April 25, 1986, p. 1.

17. Ibid.

18. Donald F. Harvey and Dale R. Brown, *An Experimental Approach to Organization Development* (Englewood Cliffs, N.J.: Prentice-Hall, 1982), p. 10.

19. Ibid.

20. Beckhard, *Organization Development,* p. 9.

21. Dan L. Costley and Ralph Todd, *Human Relations in Organizations* (New York: West Publishing Company, 1978), p. 456.

22. Beckhard, *Organization Development,* p. 13.

23. Douglas McGregor, *The Human Side of Enterprise* (New York: McGraw-Hill, 1960).

24. Ibid.

25. A. H. Maslow, *Motivaiton and Personality* (New York: Harper & Row, 1954), p. 43.

26. McGregor, *Human Side,* p. 54.

27. Wendell French, "Organizational Development Objectives, Assumptions, and Strategies," *California Management Review* 12, 1969, p. 24.

28. Newton Margulies and Anthony Raia, *Organizational Development Values, Process, and Technology* (New York: McGraw-Hill, 1972), p. 3.

29. Michael E. McGill, *Organization Development for Operating Managers* (New York: American Management, 1977), p. 89.

30. Edwin Flippo and Gary Munsinger, *Management* (Boston: Allyn and Bacon, 1978), p. 533.

31. William G. Dyer, *Contemporary Issues in Management and Organization Development* (Reading, Mass.: Addison-Wesley, 1983), p. 179.

32. Harvey and Brown, *Experimental Approach,* p. 356.

33. McGill, *Organization Development,* p. 101.

34. Ibid.

35. W. J. Heisler, "Patterns of OD in Practice," *Business Horizons,* February 1975, p. 82.

36. Thomas H. Patten, "Team Building Part 1: Designing the Intervention," *Personnel,* January/February 1979, p. 13.

37. Edgar Shein, *Process Consultation: Its Role in Organization Development* (Reading, Mass.: Addison-Wesley, 1969), p. 9.

38. Harvey and Brown, *Experimental Approach,* p. 358.

39. Kail Albrecht, *Organization Development* (Englewood Cliffs, N.J.: Prentice-Hall, 1983), p. 181.

40. Harvey and Brown, *Experimental Approach,* p. 400.

41. Richard Beckhard, "The Confrontation Meeting," *Harvard Business Review,* March/April 1967, p. 153.

42. Ibid.

43. Robert R. Blake and Jane S. Mouton, "Management by Grid Principles or Situationalism: Which?" *Group & Organization Studies,* December 1981, pp. 439–455.

44. Robert Blake and Jane Mouton, "Breakthroughs in Organization Development," *Harvard Business Review,* November/December 1964, pp. 134–138.

45. Richard Beckhard and Reuben T. Harris, *Organizational Transition: Managing Complex Change* (Reading, Mass.: Addison-Wesley, 1977), p. 87.

46. Greiner, "Patterns," pp. 126–129; and Beckhard, *Organization Development,* p. 97.

47. Elaine Johnson, "Kodak Facing Big Challenges in Bid to Change," *Wall Street Journal,* May 22, 1985, p. 6.

48. Reggie Ann Dubin, "Growing Pains at People Express," *Business Week,* January 28, 1985, pp. 90–91; "People Express Grows Bigger Without Getting Fat," *Wall Street Journal,* January 7, 1985, p. 2; James R. Norman, "Nice Going, Frank, But Will It Fly?" *Business Week,* September 29, 1986, pp. 34–35.

Chapter 10

1. Walter Kiechel, III, "Managing Innovators," *Fortune,* March 4, 1985, pp. 181–182.

2. Ibid., p. 182.

3. Richard Steers and Lyman Porter, *Motivation and Work Behavior* (New York: McGraw-Hill, 1979), pp. 4–5.

4. Robert A. Ullrich, *Motivation Methods That Work* (Englewood Cliffs, N.J.: Prentice-Hall, 1981), p. 3.

5. Steers and Porter, *Motivation,* p. 15.

6. Douglas McGregor, *The Human Side of Enterprise* (New York: McGraw-Hill, 1960), pp. 33–34.

7. Ibid., p. 34.

8. Steers and Porter, *Motivation,* p. 16.

9. Ibid., p. 18.

10. R. E. Miles, "Human Relations or Human Resources," *Harvard Business Review,* July/August 1965, pp. 148–163.

11. McGregor, *Human Side,* pp. 47–48.

12. A. H. Maslow, *Motivation and Personality* (New York: Harper & Row, 1954).

13. Steers and Porter, *Motivation*, p. 32.

14. In his earlier writings, Maslow recognized two additional needs—cognitive and aesthetic. Both were later dropped from his discussions.

15. Kae H. Chung, *Motivational Theories and Practices* (Columbus: Grid Publishing Company, 1977), p. 55.

16. C. N. Cofer and M. H. Appley, *Motivation: Theory and Research* (New York: John Wiley & Sons, 1964), pp. 684, 691.

17. Donald Sanzotta, *Motivational Theories and Applicaitons for Managers* (New York: AMACOM, 1977), p. 51.

18. Frederick Herzberg, Bernard Mausner, and Barbara Snyderman, *The Motivation to Work* (New York: John Wiley & Sons, 1959), p. 81.

19. Sanzotta, *Motivational Theories and Applications*, p. 27.

20. Chung, *Motivational Theories and Practices*, p. 115.

21. Robert House and L. A. Wigdor, "Herzberg's Dual Factor Theory of Job Satisfaction and Motivation: A Review of the Evidence and a Criticism," *Personnel Psychology*, Winter 1967, pp. 369–389.

22. Sanzotta, *Motivational Theories and Applications*, p. 49.

23. Bernard Bass and Gerald V. Barrett, *Man, Work and Organization* (Boston: Allyn and Bacon, 1972), p. 69.

24. Steers and Porter, *Motivation*, p. 394–395.

25. David C. McClelland, *The Achieving Society* (Princeton: D. Van Nostrand, 1961).

26. Frederick M. Levine, *Theoretical Readings in Motivation: Perspectives on Human Behavior* (Chicago: Rand McNally College Publishing, 1976), p. 380.

27. Sanzotta, *Motivational Theories and Applications*, p. 24.

28. Levine, *Theoretical Readings*.

29. Sanzotta, *Motivational Theories and Applications*, p. 25.

30. R. Wayne Mondy, Robert E. Holmes, and Edwin B. Flippo, *Management: Concepts and Practices* (Boston: Allyn and Bacon, 1983), p. 328.

31. Victor H. Vroom, *Work and Motivation* (New York: John Wiley & Sons, 1964).

32. Andrew D. Szilagyi, Jr., *Management and Performance* (Glenview, Ill.: Scott, Foresman, 1984), p. 407.

33. Michael H. Mescon, Michael Albert, and Franklin Khedouri, *Management: Individual and Organizational Effectiveness* (New York: Harper & Row, 1985), p. 363.

34. Keith Davis, *Human Behavior at Work: Organizational Behavior* (New York: McGraw-Hill, 1981), p. 69.

35. B. F. Skinner, *Science and Human Behavior* (New York: Free Press, 1953) and *Contingencies of Reinforcement* (New York: Appleton-Century-Crofts, 1969).

36. Sanzotta, *Motivational Theories and Applications*, p. 35.

37. Ibid., pp. 43–44.

38. Dale S. Beach, *Personnel: The Management of People at Work* (New York: Macmillan, 1980), p. 441.

39. W. C. Hamner and E. P. Hamner, "Behavior Modification on the Bottom Line," *Organizational Dynamics,* Spring 1976, pp. 3–21.

40. John M. Ivancevich and William F. Glueck, *Foundations of Personnel/ Human Resource Management* (Plano, Tex.: Business Publications, 1983), p. 396.

41. Fred Fry, "Operant Conditioning in Organizational Settings: Of Mice or Men?" *Personnel,* July/August 1974, pp. 17–24.

42. Beach, *Personnel,* pp. 441–442.

43. J. S. Adams, "Injustice in Social Exchange," in *Advances in Experimental Social Psychology,* ed. L. Berkowitz (New York: Academic Press, 1965).

44. Chung, *Motivational Theories and Practices,* pp. 143–144.

45. Ibid.

46. Wendy Fox, "Digital Trying the Bossless System," *Boston Sunday Globe,* October 14, 1984, p. A-89.

47. "A Company Where Everybody Is Boss," *Business Week,* April 15, 1985, p. 100.

48. Chung, *Motivational Theories and Practices,* pp. 189–213.

49. Ibid., p. 190.

50. Gary Dessler, *Applied Human Relations* (Reston, Va.: Reston Publishing Company, 1983), p. 132.

51. Stanley Nollen, "Does Flextime Improve Productivity?" *Harvard Business Review,* September/October 1979, pp. 12–22.

52. Chung, *Motivational Theories and Practices,* pp. 192–196.

53. Ibid., p. 195.

54. Ibid., p. 196.

55. J. R. Hackman, Greg Oldham, Robert Janson, and Kenneth Purdy, "A New Strategy for Job Enrichment," *California Management Review,* Summer 1975, pp. 57–71.

56. Chung, *Motivational Theories and Practices,* p. 202.

57. Judy Linscott, "How to Keep Good People When You Can't Promote Them All," *Working Woman,* February 1985, pp. 24–26.

58. John Milne, "Entrepreneurs in Torn T-shirts," *Boston Globe,* June 4, 1985, pp. 25, 34.

Chapter 11

1. "Tilting at the Rumor Mill," *Dun's Review,* September 6, 1984, p. 52.

2. Ibid., p. 53.

3. John Grant Rhode and Edward E. Lawler, *Information and Control in Organizations* (Pacific Palisades, Calif.: Goodyear Publishing Company, 1976), p. 32.

4. Robert L. Trewatha and M. Gene Newport, *Management* (Plano, Tex.: Business Publications, 1982), p. 216.

5. Chris Argyris, *Leadership and Interpersonal Behavior* (New York: Holt, Rinehart, and Winston, 1961), p. 331.

6. From *Personnel: The Management People*, Third Edition, by Dale S. Beach, pp. 492–497. Reprinted with permission of Macmillan Publishing Company. Copyright © 1975 by Dale S. Beach.

7. Trewatha and Newport, *Management*, p. 297.

8. F. J. Roethlisberger and William J. Dickson, *Management and the Worker* (Cambridge, Mass.: Harvard University Press, 1938), p. 518.

9. Beach, *Personnel*, p. 499.

10. Rensis Likert, *New Patterns of Management* (New York: McGraw-Hill, 1961), pp. 34–36.

11. Louis R. Pondy, "Organizational Conflict: Concepts and Models," in *Contemporary Readings in Organizational Behavior*, ed. Fred Luthans (New York: McGraw-Hill, 1977), pp. 232–249.

12. Ibid., pp. 234–238.

13. James H. Donnelly, Jr., James L. Gibson, and John M. Ivancevich, *Fundamentals of Management* (Plano, Tex.: Business Publications, 1978), pp. 236–237.

14. Ibid., p. 402.

15. George H. Labovitz, "Managing Conflict," *Business Horizons*, June 1980, pp. 31, 32, 35. Reprinted by permission.

16. George H. Labovitz, "The Individual versus the Organization," in *Contemporary Readings in Organizational Behavior*, ed. Fred Luthans (New York: McGraw-Hill, 1972), p. 285.

17. Melville Dalton, "Conflicts Between Staff and Line Managerial Officers," in *Organizations: Structure and Behavior*, ed. Joseph A. Litterer (New York: John Wiley & Sons, 1980), pp. 397–406.

18. Ibid., p. 402.

19. Labovitz, "Managing Conflict," p. 32.

20. Ibid.

21. Ibid., p. 35.

22. Ibid.

23. Harry Levinson, "What Killed Bob Lyons?" *Harvard Business Review: On Human Relations*, 1979, pp. 306–333.

24. R. Douglas Allen, Michael A. Hitt, and Charles R. Greer, "Occupational Stress and Perceived Organizational Effectiveness in Formal Groups: An Examination of Stress Level and Stress Type," *Personnel Psychology*, Summer 1982, p. 361.

25. Richard E. Walton, "Some Benefits of Interpersonal Conflict," in *Organizational Behavior: A Book of Readings*, ed. Keith Davis (New York: McGraw-Hill, 1977), p. 107.

26. Robert L. Kahn, Donald M. Wolfe, Robert P. Quinn, and J. Diedrick Snoek, *Organizational Stress: Studies in Role Conflict and Ambiguities* (New York: John Wiley & Sons, 1964), p. 59.

27. Rolf E. Rogers, "Components of Organizational Stress Among Canadian Managers," *Journal of Psychology*, March 1977, pp. 265–275.

28. Myron Magnet, "Help! My Company Has Just Been Taken Over," *Fortune,* July 9, 1984, pp. 44–51.

29. Andrew S. Grove, "How to Make Confrontation Work for You," *Fortune,* July 23, 1984, pp. 73–75.

Chapter 12

1. Leonard M. Apcar, "Middle Managers and Supervisors Resist Moves to More Participatory Management," *Wall Street Journal,* September 16, 1985.

2. Ibid.

3. Harold Koontz, Cyril O'Donnell, and Heinz Weihrich, *Management* (New York: McGraw-Hill, 1984), p. 506.

4. Richard M. Steers and Lyman Porter, *Motivation and Work Behavior* (New York: McGraw-Hill, 1978), p. 350.

5. Ibid., p. 351.

6. Ralph M. Stogdill, "Personal Factors Associated with Leadership: A Survey of the Literature," *The Journal of Psychology,* January 1948, pp. 35–71.

7. John Ivancevich, James Donnelly, and James Gibson, *Managing for Performance* (Dallas: Business Publications, 1980), p. 287.

8. W. Richard Plunkett, *Supervision: The Direction of People at Work* (Dubuque, Iowa: W. C. Brown Company, 1975), p. 142.

9. Rensis Likert, *The Human Organization* (New York: McGraw-Hill, 1967), pp. 14–24.

10. Ralph K. White and Ronald Lippitt, *Autocracy and Democracy: An Experimental Inquiry* (New York: Harper & Row, 1960).

11. Dale Beach, *Personnel: The Management of People at Work* (New York: Macmillan, 1980), p. 479.

12. David G. Bowers and Stanley E. Seashore, "Predicting Organizational Effectiveness with a Four-Factor Theory of Leadership," *Administrative Science Quarterly,* Vol. 11, No. 2, 1966, pp. 238–263.

13. Victor Vroom, "Some Personality Determinants of the Effects of Participation," *Journal of Abnormal and Social Psychology,* November 1959, pp. 322–327.

14. Robert Tannenbaum and Warren H. Schmidt, "How to Choose a Leadership Pattern," *Harvard Business Review,* May/June 1973, pp. 162–181.

15. Ibid., p. 173.

16. Robert R. Blake and Jane Srygley Mouton, *The Managerial Grid III: The Key to Leadership Excellence* (Houston: Gulf Publishing Company, 1985), p. 12.

17. Ibid., p. 13.

18. Andrew D. Szilagyi, *Management and Performance* (Glenview, Ill.: Scott, Foresman, 1984), p. 441.

19. Fred E. Fiedler, *A Theory of Leadership Effectiveness* (New York: McGraw-Hill, 1967).

20. Ibid.

21. Reprinted from "A Path-Goal Theory of Leadership Effectiveness" by Robert J. House, published in *Administrative Science Quarterly* Volume 16, #3, September 1971, pp. 321–338, by permission of *Administrative Science Quarterly*.

22. Ibid.

23. William J. Reddin, *Managerial Effectiveness* (New York: McGraw-Hill, 1970).

24. Ibid.

25. Victor Vroom and Philip Yetton, *Leadership and Decision Making* (Pittsburgh: University of Pittsburgh Press, 1973).

26. Victor Vroom, "Can Leaders Learn to Lead?" *Organizational Dynamics,* Winter 1976.

27. Edwin A. Fleishman and Edwin F. Harris, "Patterns of Leadership Behavior Related to Employee Grievances and Turnover," *Personnel Psychology,* Spring 1962, pp. 48–50.

28. Rensis Likert, *New Patterns of Management* (New York: McGraw-Hill, 1961), pp. 8–9.

29. Wendell French, *The Personnel Management Process* (Boston: Houghton Mifflin Company, 1978), pp. 106–107.

30. Arthur H. Kuriloff, "An Experiment in Management—Putting Theory Y to the Test," *Personnel,* November 1963, pp. 9–17; Vance Packard, "A Chance for Everyone to Grow," *Reader's Digest,* November 1963, pp. 114–118; "Where Being Nice to Workers Didn't Work," *Business Week,* January 20, 1973, pp. 98+.

31. "A Slimmed-Down Brunswick Is Proving Wall Street Wrong," *Business Week,* May 28, 1984, pp. 90+.

Chapter 13

1. "Florida—Anything Goes," *Time,* April 17, 1950, p. 28.

2. Jerry W. Koehler and John I. Sisco, *Public Communication in Business and the Professions* (St. Paul: West Publishing Company, 1981), p. 16.

3. Ibid., p. 13.

4. Among the more popular models are those developed by Claude Shannon, Wilbur Schramm, John Wenburg and William Wilmot, Lee Thayer, David Berlo, Dean Barnlund, and Gordon Peterson.

5. Phillip V. Lewis, *Organizational Communication: The Essence of Effective Management* (New York: John Wiley & Sons, 1980), p. 54.

6. Ibid., pp. 55–56.

7. Daniel Katz and Robert Kahn, *The Social Psychology of Organizations* (New York: John Wiley & Sons, 1966), p. 226.

8. Jitendra M. Sharma, "Organizational Communications: A Linking Process," in *Communication for Management and Business,* ed. Norman B. Sigband (Glenview, Ill: Scott, Foresman, 1982), p. 590.

9. Ray Killian, *Managing by Design . . . For Executive Effectiveness* (New York: American Management Association, 1968), p. 254.

10. Lewis, *Organizational Communication,* p. 63.

11. Ibid., pp. 66–67.

12. Gerald M. Goldhaber, *Organizational Communication* (Dubuque, Iowa: W. C. Brown Company, 1979), pp. 141–142.

13. S. Bernard Rosenblatt, T. Richard Cheatham, and James T. Watt, *Communication in Business* (Englewood Cliffs, N.J.: Prentice-Hall, 1977), p. 44.

14. Keith Davis, "Management Communication and the Grapevine," *Harvard Business Review,* January/February 1953, pp. 31, 43–49.

15. Lewis, *Organizational Communication,* p. 69.

16. Ibid., pp. 69–70.

17. Harold J. Leavitt, "Some Effects of Certain Communication Patterns on Group Performance," *Journal of Abnormal and Social Psychology,* January 1951, pp. 38–50.

18. Andrew D. Szilagyi, *Management and Performance* (Glenview, Ill.: Scott, Foresman, 1984), p. 376.

19. Norman B. Sigband, *Communication for Management and Business* (Glenview, Ill.: Scott, Foresman, 1982), p. 9.

20. Susan Dellinger and Barbara Deane, *Communicating Effectively: A Complete Guide for Better Managing* (Radner, Pa.: Chilton Book Company, 1980), pp. 9–10.

21. W. H. Read, "Communication in Organizations: Some Problems and Misconceptions," *Personnel Administration,* September/October 1963, p. 8.

22. John C. Athanassiades, "The Sounds and Silences of Employee Communication," *Journal of Business Communication,* Summer 1973, pp. 43–50.

23. William Ford Keefe, *Listen, Management* (New York: McGraw-Hill, 1971), p. 10.

24. Ralph Nichols, "Listening Is a 10-Part Skill," in *Communication for Management and Business,* ed. Norman B. Sigband (Glenview, Ill.: Scott, Foresman, 1982), p. 617.

25. John DiGaetani, "The Business of Listening," *Business Horizons,* October 1980, p. 24.

26. Ralph Nichols, "Listening Is Good Business," in *Readings in Management,* ed. Max Richards and William A. Nielander (Cincinnati: South-Western Publishing Company, 1974), pp. 101–102.

27. Rosenblatt, Cheatham, and Watt, *Communication in Business,* p. 147.

28. Julius Fast, *Body Language* (New York: Pocket Books, 1970), p. 5.

29. Rudolf Flesch's *How to Test Readability* and Robert Gunning's "Fog Index" are perhaps the most widely used guides to testing readership difficulty.

30. Irving S. Shapiro, "Managerial Communication: The View from Inside," *California Management Review,* Fall 1984, p. 167.

31. William V. Haney, *Communication and Organizational Behavior,* Homewood, Ill.: Irwin, 1967.

32. Lewis, *Organizational Communication,* p. 135.

33. Jack R. Gibb, "Defensive Communication," *The Journal of Communication,* September 1961, pp. 141–148.

34. David A. Ricks, *Big Business Blunders: Mistakes in International Marketing* (Homewood, Ill.: Dow Jones-Irwin, 1983).

35. Ibid.

36. George A. Weimer, "Copperweld Speaks and Listens to Its Workers," *Iron Age,* September 7, 1981, pp. 46+.

37. Shapiro, "Managerial Communciation," pp. 157–172.

Chapter 14

1. Mark Ivey, "A Cement Maker That May Be Selling Its Future," *Business Week,* November 18, 1985, p. 87.

2. Ibid., p. 88.

3. Henri Fayol, *General and Industrial Management* (London: Sir Isaac Pitman and Sons, 1949), p. 107.

4. Robert Fulmer, *The New Management* (New York: Macmillan, 1974), p. 257.

5. Justin G. Longenecker, *Principles of Management and Organizational Behavior* (Columbus: Charles E. Merrill, 1964), pp. 511–512.

6. Gary Dessler, *Management Fundamentals: A Framework* (Reston, Va.: Reston Publishing Company, 1977), p. 346.

7. Ibid.

8. Ibid.

9. George Munchus, III, "Employer-Employee Based Quality Circles in Japan: Human Resource Policy Implications for American Firms," *Academy of Management Review,* April 1983, p. 255.

10. Ibid., p. 257.

11. Dessler, *Management Fundamentals,* p. 355.

12. Dale S. Beach, *Personnel: The Management of People at Work* (New York: Macmillan, 1980), pp. 292–293.

13. Robert Mathis and John H. Jackson, *Personnel: Human Resource Management* (St. Paul: West Publishing Company, 1985), p. 341.

14. "HRM Update," *Personnel Administrator,* June 1983, p. 16.

15. Ed Bean, "Cause of Quality-Control Problems Might Be Managers—Not Workers," *Wall Street Journal,* April 10, 1985, p. 27.

Chapter 15

1. William M. Carley, "Pan Am Conducts Major Shake-Up to Improve Its Weak Performance," *Wall Street Journal,* April 26, 1984, p. 31.

2. Ibid., p. 41.

3. Everett E. Adam, Jr., and Ronald J. Ebert, *Production and Operations*

Management: Concepts, Models, and Behavior (Englewood Cliffs, N.J.: Prentice-Hall, 1982), p. 18.

4. *Statistical Abstract of the United States* (Washington, D.C.: Bureau of the Census, 1984), p. 421.

5. Roger G. Schroeder, *Operations Management: Decision Making in the Operations Function* (New York: McGraw-Hill, 1981), p. 10.

6. Joseph G. Monks, *Operations Management: Theory and Problems* (New York: McGraw-Hill, 1977), pp. 6–7.

7. Ibid., p. 11.

8. Richard B. Chase and Nicholas J. Acquilano, *Production and Operations Management: A Life Cycle Approach* (Homewood, Ill.: Irwin, 1981), p. 11.

9. Schroeder, *Operations Management*, p. 12.

10. Richard J. Hopeman, *Production: Concepts, Analysis, and Control* (Columbus: Charles E. Merrill, 1976), pp. 7–8.

11. Schroeder, *Operations Management*, p. 90.

12. Chase and Acquilano, *Production and Operations Management*, pp. 397–398.

13. Monks, *Operations Management*, pp. 439–451.

14. James L. Riggs, *Production Systems: Planning, Analysis, and Control* (New York: John Wiley & Sons, 1981), pp. 403–406.

15. Thomas M. Cook and Robert A. Russell, *Contemporary Operations Management: Text and Cases* (Englewood Cliffs, N.J.: Prentice-Hall, 1984), p. 335.

16. Richard A. Johnson, William T. Newell, and Roger C. Vergin, *Production and Operations Management: A Systems Approach* (Boston: Houghton Mifflin, 1974), p. 359.

17. Riggs, *Production Systems*, p. 412.

18. Leonard J. Garrett and Milton Silver, *Production Management Analysis* (New York: Harcourt Brace Jovanovich, 1975), p. 516.

19. Riggs, *Production Systems*, p. 440.

20. Harold T. Amrine, John A. Ritchey, and Oliver S. Hulley, *Manufacturing Organization and Management* (Englewood Cliffs, N.J.: Prentice-Hall, 1982), p. 244.

21. Adam and Ebert, *Production and Operations Management*, pp. 521–523.

22. El Hoeffer, "GM Tries Just-In-Time American Style," *Purchasing*, August 19, 1982, pp. 67–72.

23. Richard J. Schonberger, "The Transfer of Japanese Manufacturing Management Approaches to U.S. Industry," *Academy of Management Review*, July 1982, p. 480.

24. "Designing the Office Around the Computer," *Personal Computing*, November 1984, p. 66.

25. "Offices in the Future," *Newsweek*, May 14, 1984, p. 72.

26. Monks, *Operations Management*, p. 212.

27. Kostas N. Dervitsiotis, *Operations Management* (New York: McGraw-Hill, 1981), pp. 651–656.

28. Ibid., p. 654.

29. Craig Brod, "How to Deal with Technostress," *Office Administration and Automation,* August 1984, p. 30.

30. Romesh T. Wadhwani, "Integrating Robot Power into Automated Factory Systems," *Management Review,* June 1984, p. 8.

31. Harry B. Thompson, "CAD/CAM and the Factory of the Future," *Management Review,* May 1983, p. 27.

32. "Manufacturing Technology: A Report to Management," *Dun's Business Month,* February 1984, pp. D–J.

33. Ibid., p. G.

34. Adam and Ebert, *Production and Operations Management,* pp. 536–540.

35. Richard Gibson, "Toro Breaks Out of Slump After Taking Drastic Action," *Wall Street Journal,* January 23, 1985, p. 8.

36. Bill Powell, "Boosting Shop-Floor Productivity by Breaking All the Rules," *Business Week,* November 26, 1984, pp. 100+.

Chapter 16

1. "How Casino Computers Stretch the House Odds," *Business Week,* July 30, 1984, pp. 112–114.

2. Ibid.

3. Ibid.

4. Edwin B. Flippo and Gary Munsinger, *Management* (Boston: Allyn and Bacon, 1978), p. 497.

5. For a complete description of the simplex method, see Elwood Buffa and James S. Dyer, *Essentials of Management Science/Operations Research* (New York: John Wiley & Sons, 1978), pp. 369–403.

6. C. William Emory and Powell Niland, *Making Management Decisions* (Boston: Houghton Mifflin, 1968), p. 184.

7. Richard I. Levin, Charles A. Kirkpatrick, and David Rubin, *Quantitative Approaches to Management* (New York: McGraw-Hill, 1982), pp. 540–541.

8. R. Wayne Mondy, Robert E. Holmes, and Edwin B. Flippo; *Management: Concepts and Practices* (Boston: Allyn and Bacon, 1983), p. 540.

9. Joe C. Iverstine and Jerry Kinard, *Cases in Production and Operations Management* (Columbus: Charles E. Merrill, 1977), p. 126.

Chapter 17

1. Trevor Armbrister, "The Helping Hands of American Business," *Reader's Digest,* November 1986, p. 142.

2. Ibid. pp. 141–142.

3. Ibid. pp. 142–144.

4. Arthur Burns, *The Decline of Competition* (New York: McGraw-Hill, 1936).

5. Elton Mayo, *The Human Problems of an Industrial Civilization* (New York: Macmillan, 1933), p. 188.

6. Adam Smith, *An Inquiry into the Nature and Causes of the Wealth of Nations* (New York: Modern Library, 1937), pp. 594–595.

7. Alfred North Whitehead, *Adventures of Ideas* (New York: Macmillan, 1933), p. 124.

8. Don Votaw and S. Prakash Sethi, "Do We Need a New Corporate Response to a Changing Social Environment?" *California Management Review,* Fall 1969, p. 19.

9. A. M. Sullivan, "Moral Responsibility in Management," *Advanced Management-Office Executive,* April 1963, p. 13.

10. Theodore Levitt, "The Dangers of Social Responsibility," *Harvard Business Review,* September/October 1958, p. 46.

11. Ibid., pp. 44–48.

12. Milton Friedman, *Capitalism and Freedom* (Chicago: University of Chicago Press, 1962), p. 133.

13. Peter F. Drucker, *The Practice of Management* (New York: Harper & Row, 1954), p. 386.

14. Leland I. Doan, "Fundamental Role of Business is to Operate Profitably," *Commercial and Financial Chronicle,* July 18, 1957, p. 286.

15. Neil W. Chamberlain, *The Firm: Micro-Economic Planning and Action* (New York: McGraw-Hill, 1962), p. 75.

16. Keith Davis, "Understanding the Social Responsibility Puzzle," *Business Horizons,* Winter 1967, p. 47.

17. Hazel Henderson, "Should Business Tackle Society's Problems?" *Harvard Business Review,* July/August 1968, p. 84.

18. Delbert C. Miller and William H. Form, *Industrial Sociology: An Introduction to the Sociology of Work Relations* (New York: Harper & Brothers, 1951), pp. 829–830.

19. Morrell Heald, "Management's Responsibility to Society: The Growth of an Idea," *Business History Review,* Winter 1957, pp. 383–384.

20. Albert Z. Carr, "Can an Executive Afford a Conscience?" *Harvard Business Review,* July/August 1970, p. 60.

21. Wendy Wall, "Companies Change the Way They Make Charitable Donations," *Wall Street Journal,* June 21, 1984, p. 1.

22. Barbara Rudolph, "E. F. Hutton's Simmering Scandal." *Time,* July 22, 1985, p. 53.

Chapter 18

1. Jose Penteado, Jr., "U.S. Fast Foods Move Slowly," *Advertising Age,* May 25, 1981, pp. 5–8.

2. Jack Duncan, *Management: Progressive Responsibility in Administration* (New York: Random House, 1983), p. 469.

3. Ferdinand P. Mauser and David J. Schwartz, *American Business* (New York: Harcourt, Brace, Jovanovich, 1978), p. 577.

4. Duncan, *Management,* p. 473.

5. Ibid., p. 477.

6. Mauser and Schwartz, *American Business,* p. 586.

7. *United States Code: Congressional and Administrative News,* 95th Congress, First Session, 1977, Vol. 1, 91 (Public Law 95-213), "Foreign Corrupt Practices Act of 1977," pp. 1495–1496.

8. Ibid., p. 1498.

9. "Foreign Corrupt Practices: Can American Afford to Moralize?" *New England Business,* October 1, 1980, p. 22.

10. Neil H. Jacoby, Peter Nehemkis, and Richard Eells, "Naivete: Foreign Payoffs Law," *California Management Review,* Fall 1979, p. 86.

11. "Foreign Corrupt Practices" p. 22.

12. Duncan, *Management,* p. 487.

13. Edwin Flippo, *Management* (Boston: Allyn and Bacon, 1978), p. 581.

14. David A. Ricks, *Big Business Blunders: Mistakes in Multinational Marketing* (Homewood, Ill.: Dow Jones-Irwin, 1983), p. 14.

15. Ibid., p. 39.

16. Ibid.

17. Ibid., p. 84.

18. Ibid., p. 81.

19. Ibid., p. 46.

20. Ibid., p. 16.

21. Richard D. Hays, Christopher M. Korth, and Manucher Roudiani, *International Business: An Introduction to the World of the Multinational Firm* (Englewood Cliffs, N.J.: Prentice-Hall, 1972), p. 149.

22. Ibid.

23. Ibid., p. 155.

24. Ibid., p. 161.

25. Ibid.

26. Mauser and Schwartz, *American Business,* p. 592.

27. R. Hal Mason, Robert R. Miller, and Dale R. Weigel, *International Business* (New York: John Wiley & Sons, 1981), p. 419.

28. Hays, Korth, and Roudiani, *International Business,* p. 392.

29. "Japanese Companies Start to Flee the Unitary Tax," *Business Week,* August 27, 1984, pp. 30–31.

30. David Manasian and Charles Gaffney, "Two Bitter Enemies Are Starting to Talk Trade," *Business Week,* December 3, 1984, p. 56.

Chapter 19

1. "Unions Move Into the Office," *Business Week,* January 25, 1982, p. 90.

2. Ibid., p. 92.

3. John M. Ivancevich and William F. Glueck, *Foundations of Personnel/Human Resource Management* (Plano, Tex.: Business Publications, 1983), p. 530.

4. Ibid.

5. Edwin F. Beal and James P. Begin, *The Practice of Collective Bargaining*, Sixth Edition (Homewood, Ill.: Irwin, 1982), p. 76.

6. In 1806, employers filed a criminal conspiracy charge against the Philadelphia Cordwainers, who were found guilty of combining to raise wages. This ruling, known as the conspiracy doctrine, was overturned by the Massachusetts Supreme Court in 1842.

7. Beal and Begin, *Collective Bargaining*, p. 77.

8. William H. Holley and Kenneth Jennings, *The Labor Relations Process* (Homewood, Ill.: Irwin, 1984), p. 43.

9. Proceedings of the First Convention of the Industrial Workers of the World (New York: Labor News Company, 1905), p. 1.

10. Holley and Jennings, *Labor Relations Process,* p. 45.

11. The Labor-Management Relations Act of 1947 included a provision whereby the president of the United States, under unusual circumstances, can request a court injunction forcing strikers back on the job. Such a request should not be confused with that of an employer who, prior to 1932, could take such action.

12. To get an election conducted by the National Labor Relations Board, a "showing of interest" petition is filed with the district director of a regional office of the board. As a general rule, the petition must contain the signatures of approximately one-third of the workers eligible for representation by a union.

13. Originally, the NLRB was comprised of three members selected by the president of the United States with the consent of the Senate. Later, the Wagner Act was amended to increase the number of members to five. Membership on the board is for five years.

14. A bargaining unit is made up of the workers in a particular company who are represented by a union in the collective bargaining process. Technical and professional employees can be included in the same bargaining unit as other workers only if a majority of such workers vote to be included. An alternative is for technical and professional employees to have a separate unit altogether.

15. Beal and Begin, *Collective Bargaining*, p. 224.

16. The Wisconsin law required employers of local government employees to bargain with unions. State employees were excluded until 1967.

17. In the case of *McLaughlin et al.* v. *Tilendis et al.,* the court ruled that a person's right to form and join a labor organization is protected under the First Amendment of the Constitution.

18. David Wessel, "Fighting Off Unions, Ingersoll-Rand Uses Wide Range of Tactics," *Wall Street Journal,* June 13, 1985, p. 1+.

Chapter 20

1. Lee Iacocca, *Iacocca: An Autobiography* (New York: Bantam Books, 1984).

2. Walter Kiechel, III, "The Neglected Art of Career Planning," *Fortune,* June 27, 1983, p. 153.

3. Ibid., p. 154.

4. Thomas F. O'Boyle, "Loyalty Ebbs at Many Companies as Employees Grow Disillusioned," *Wall Street Journal,* July 11, 1985, p. 25.

5. Ibid.

6. Walter Kiechel, III, "How Executives Think," *Fortune,* February 4, 1985, p. 127.

7. Ibid., p. 128.

8. Kevin McKean, "Of Two Minds: Selling the Right Brain," *Discover,* April 1985, p. 30.

9. Ibid., p. 36.

10. Daniel Seligman, "Luck and Careers," *Fortune,* November 16, 1981, pp. 60–66+.

11. Ibid., p. 64.

12. Jacqueline Kaufman, "New Age Business: Two Approaches," *Management Review,* May 1985, pp. 17–18.

13. Ibid., p. 18.

14. Jennie Farley, *The Woman in Management: Career and Family Issues* (Ithaca: Cornell University Press, 1983), p. 13.

15. Susan Fraker, "Why Women Aren't Getting to the Top," *Fortune,* April 16, 1984, p. 40.

16. "You've Come A Long Way Baby, But Not as Far as You Thought," *Business Week,* October 1, 1984, p. 130.

17. Richard F. America and Bernard E. Anderson, *Moving Ahead: Black Managers in American Business* (New York: McGraw-Hill, 1978), p. 173.

18. Rosalind Loring and Theodore Wells, *Breakthrough: Women into Management* (New York: Van Nostrand Reinhold, 1972), p. 131.

19. Bette Ann Stead, *Women in Management* (Englewood Cliffs, N.J.: Prentice-Hall, 1978), p. 4.

20. Ibid.

21. Ibid., p. 5.

22. Helen Rogan, "Executive Women Find It Difficult to Balance Demands of Job, Home," *Wall Street Journal,* October 30, 1984, p. 33.

23. Ibid.

24. Helen Rogan, "Young Executive Women Advance Farther, Faster than Predecessors," *Wall Street Journal,* October 26, 1984, p. 33.

25. Ibid.

26. Helen Rogan, "Women Executives Feel That Men Both Aid and Hinder Their Careers," *Wall Street Journal,* October 29, 1984, p. 35.

27. Ibid.

28. Rogan, "Young Executive Women."

29. Amy Glickman, "Women Clash: Older Worker vs. Young Boss," *Wall Street Journal,* February 19, 1985, p. 31.

30. Ibid.

31. Cathy Trost, "Pay Equity, Born in Public Sector, Emerges as an Issue in Private Firms," *Wall Street Journal,* July 8, 1985, p. 15.

32. Ibid.

33. Ibid.

34. Rogan, "Young Executive Women," p. 36.

35. Peter Nulty, "How Personal Computers Change Managers' Lives," *Fortune,* September 3, 1984, p. 38.

36. "Top Executives Use Personal Computers," *Spring High-Tech, A Supplement to the Washington Post,* May 5, 1985.

37. Craig Zarley, "Software That Hones Your Management Skills," *Personal Computing,* April 1984, pp. 109–110.

38. Trish Hall, "Demanding PepsiCo Is Attempting to Make Work Nicer for Managers," *Wall Street Journal,* October 23, 1984, p. 33.

39. Damon Darlin, "Road Can Be Bumpy When New Chief Acts to Enliven His Firm," *Wall Street Journal,* September 17, 1984, p. 22.

Glossary

Achievement motive A theory of motivation developed by David McClelland that distinguishes among people who are achievement-oriented, power-oriented, and affiliation-oriented.

Achievement test A selection test designed to measure a person's acquired knowledge or skill.

Activity An ongoing work effort in a project.

Activity ratio Measurement of how effectively a firm employs the resources at its command.

Ad hoc committee Committee that deals with important but nonrecurring issues requiring high-level problem solving.

Administrative planning The process of planning that structures a firm's resources to achieve maximum performance, focusing on policies that govern the major functions of the organization.

Affirmative action program (AAP) Policies and procedures designed to rectify past discriminatory hiring and promotion practices.

Agency shop A labor-management agreement that requires workers to pay a service fee to a union, even though the workers don't have to join the union.

Aggregate production planning Production planning technique that specifies output requirements by major product groups, either in labor hours required or in units of production.

Analytical (systematic) decision making Decision making based on the theory that problem solving can be reduced to a systematic selection process.

Aptitude test A selection test designed to measure a person's potential skill or knowledge.

Area of feasibility Graphical representation of all possible combinations of products.

Assistant-to Personal assistant to someone holding an office or position that is usually high in the organization.

Authority The right to command subordinates' action.

Authority-obedience management Style of a manager who emphasizes production but has little concern for people.

Autocratic leadership style A task-oriented style in which the leader supervises closely, motivates through incentives and fear, and does not seek subordinates' opinions.

Autonomous work-group design An OD intervention technique designed to give workers a sense of accomplishment, control over their own activities, and satisfactory relationships with one another.

Balance sheet Presentation of a firm's assets, liabilities, and net worth at a given period.

Behavioral school School of management thought that emphasizes the interactions of people in organizations in order to understand the practice of management.

Behavioral theory of leadership Theory that there are two distinct styles of leadership: task-oriented (production-centered) and employee-oriented (people-centered).

Bottom-line management Measurement of performance based on meeting short-term goals.

Boulwarism A "take-it-or-leave-it" approach to collective bargaining. This approach, first used by General Electric, is not considered good-faith bargaining.

Bounded rationality One cause of less-than-optimal decision; it imposes limits on a decision that eliminate some alternatives.

Brainstorming A problem-solving technique designed to produce numerous ideas in a short period.

Break-even analysis (cost-volume-profit analysis) Determining the number of items that a firm must produce or dollars it must earn to cover exactly the costs of producing those items.

Break-even point Point at which total costs equal total revenues.

Budget Single-use plan that commits resources to an activity over a given period.

Business-level strategy Long-term, comprehensive strategy of firms that produce a single product or provide a single service.

Buyer for export A commissioned representative of foreign clients who canvasses American markets for items desired by these clients.

Bypassing Failure of receiver to interpret sender's message correctly.

CAD/CAM The use of computers in drafting and design.

Capital outlay items Items that must be budgeted for, such as replacing equipment, building new facilities, or buying additional land.

Career pathing The mapping out of specific jobs in an organization so that an employee can make the most of his or her potential.

Career planning Matching an individual's career aspirations with opportunities offered by the company.

Carrying costs Expenses incurred in maintaining inventories. Carrying costs include rent, utilities, spoilage, taxes, and insurance.

Causal forecast A forecast that tries to identify whatever will have a cause-effect relationship on the matter being forecast.

Certainty Decisions in which the external conditions are identified and very predictable.

Classical (traditional) school School of management thought that focuses on management functions and principles of scientific management in order to understand the practice of management. Using the principles of scientific management, traditional managers emphasized the methodology of performing tasks in order to enhance worker efficiency and productivity.

Closed shop A labor-management agreement that requires a person to be a union member before being hired.

Communication In business, a two-way process of sending and receiving information, motivating and persuading, promoting understanding, and aiding in decision making.

Competitive industry Market structure in which the seller has absolutely no control over the price of the product.

Computer-integrated manufacturing (CIM) A form of production technology that links manufacturing to other business operations, thereby consolidating production, information, and control.

Conceptual skills The abilities needed to view the organization from a broad perspective and to see the interrelationships among its components.

Conflict An emotional or physical struggle arising when two or more persons vie for the same resources, activities, or goals.

Confrontation meeting An organizational technique that brings managers together to collect and share information, set priorities, and plan action, which is then followed up for progress review.

Consecutive shift Work schedule that compresses five days of work into two, without interruption.

Constraint function A mathematical statement that expresses the restrictions on the system under study.

Contingency (situational) model Theory that effective leadership comes out of the situation rather than being part of the leader's style.

Contingency theory Theory based on the premise that situations dictate managerial action, and that no single way of solving problems is best for all situations. It meshes the ideas and concepts of the classical, behavioral, and quantitative schools of management thought and then applies the concepts as appropriate to individual situations.

Continuous production system A system designed to produce a continuous stream of goods.

Contribution margin The difference between unit price and variable cost per unit.

Control Making events conform to plans.

Control charts Pictorial presentations of data that managers use to compare actual performance with standards.

Controlling The managerial function of comparing the organization's performance with its goals and taking corrective action if needed.

Corporate conscience An organization's obligation to society for humane and constructive policies.

Corporate-level (grand) strategy Long-term, comprehensive strategy of firms that offer diverse product lines or are comprised of several unrelated operations.

Cost accounting The proper recording, reporting, and analyzing of the various costs involved in operating a business.

Country club management Style of a manager who has high concern for people but low concern for production.

Critical path The most time-consuming route through a CPM or PERT network.

Critical path method (CPM) A network-modeling technique that breaks a project into activities and events in order to determine where and when resources should be allocated.

Customer departmentation Grouping business activities by types of customers.

Decision making The management function that consists of choosing one course of action from all the available alternatives.

Decision tree Graphic display of all alternatives available to a manager.

Decisional role Role in which a manager makes decisions.

Deficiency need Lower-level need that is satisfied by external elements.

Delegating The process of assigning tasks to subordinates, giving them authority to carry out those assignments.

Delphi technique Forecasting method using a panel of experts to predict the future.

Departmentation The process of grouping specialized activities in a logical manner.

Didactic interaction A rarely used problem-solving procedure appropriate only in situations that require a go/no-go decision.

Differentiation A business strategy that focuses on providing a product or service that customers consider unique.

Dissatisfier Factor contributing to job dissatisfaction as mentioned by workers responding to a study by Frederick Herzberg, who called these dissatisfiers "hygiene factors."

Divergent production The ability to generate numerous alternatives for accomplishing an objective.

Divestiture Strategy in which a firm sells one of its major divisions.

Division of labor (specialization) The most fundamental principle of organization which involves breaking down a task into its most basic elements, training workers to perform specific duties, and sequencing activities so that one person's efforts build on another's.

Downward communication Information transmitted from higher to lower levels in an organization.

Dysfunctional stress Lowered performance by a worker who feels bewilderment, powerlessness, pressure, or unfair competition.

Earliest expected time (T_E) The earliest calendar date on which an event can be expected to occur.

Environmental determinism A school of thought that argues that business performance is only affected by competition in the industry, and that the firm cannot influence its environment. It is based on the proposition that the success of any business depends on how an organization fits with its environment.

Equity theory A theory of motivation that tries to explain the fairness of incentive pay plans.

Ergonomics The science, also referred to as human engineering, concerned with modifying jobs and job-related tools and equipment to enhance worker comfort and efficiency.

Eurobonds Dollar-denominated debt instruments floated outside the United States.

Eurodollars Interest-bearing deposits in U.S. dollars in a foreign bank.

Event A specific, definable accomplishment in a project, which is recognizable at a particular instant.

Expectancy The likelihood that some undertaking will produce a particular outcome.

Expectancy theory Theory trying to explain the mental process that individuals go through in deciding whether to undertake some action. One of the best-known expectancy theories is that developed by Victor Vroom.

Expected elapsed time Formula used by program evaluation and review technique (PERT) to arrive at a time estimate for an activity.

Exponential smoothing Forecasting method based on a moving average that is exponentially weighted so that the more recent data are given greater importance, and the past forecasting error is taken into account in each successive forecast.

Export agent Individual who sells American-made goods to foreign customers in the name of the American manufacturer.

Export merchant Wholesaler who buys directly from a U.S. manufacturer to resell in a foreign country.

Extinction Skinner's theory that learned behavior not reinforced will disappear because of the lack of reinforcement.

Facilities planning Planning for the physical location of a plant and its production capacity.

Factor comparison system Evaluation of jobs by identifying key jobs and spreading their worth among factor categories, then determining the dollar value for non-key jobs by comparing them with key jobs.

Featherbedding The practice of forcing an employer to employ more workers than are needed to perform a job.

Fishbowling A decision-making technique that lets one person present a solution to a problem in a "fishbowl" setting.

Fixed costs Expenses remaining constant over a range of production volume.

Flextime Work schedules that allow workers to determine their own starting and quitting times.

Forecasting Predicting or projecting what will happen under a given set of circumstances in the future.

Foreign subsidiary A company owned by a domestic parent company and organized under the laws of a foreign country.

Formal (standing) committee Committee characterized by regular meeting times, defined goals, and membership created on a systematic basis.

Formal organization Organization created to accomplish specific objectives. It is characterized by authority-reporting relationships, job titles, policies and procedures, specific job duties, and other factors necessary to accomplish its goals.

Four-day workweek Compressing forty hours into a four-day schedule.

Free enterprise creed A business philosophy holding that the purpose of business is, and should be, to maximize profits.

Free trade zone Area in seaports and airports where goods of foreign countries may be brought in for reexport without payment of customs duty.

Friendship group An informal group of people who have similar backgrounds, values, and interests.

Frozen evaluation Communication that fails to take into account the effect of time.

Functional authority Authority exercised over people or activities in other departments.

Functional departmentation Grouping together jobs that are similar in function or content.

Functional stress A healthy level of individual stress that benefits the organization.

Gantt chart A production chart that graphically depicts the progress of work activities over time.

General staff Personnel used primarily in the military, in government and in some large corporations to help develop strategic, long-range plans.

Geographic departmentation Grouping business activities on the basis of geographic region or territory.

Good citizen philosophy Theory that business fulfills its social responsibility by paying taxes, improving the community, and encouraging worthwhile causes.

Government and business cooperation philosophy Theory that government must establish guidelines and programs if business is to meet its social responsibilities by complementing government programs.

Grade description method Evaluation of jobs by establishing classes or grades and describing jobs within each; determining rates of pay; and assigning jobs to the major classes.

Grapevine The informal communication network that is responsible for transmitting most messages in organizations.

"Great man" theory An early theory of leadership assuming that true leaders possess certain traits that make them effective in any situation.

Greiner model A process of organizational change built on six explicit phases.

Grid OD A long-range plan based on Blake and Mouton's Managerial Grid® to help managers develop a team-management leadership style.

Growth need Need that workers can meet by taking on interesting and challenging tasks.

Halo effect The tendency of an interviewer to let one job-related attribute influence his or her overall evaluation of a job applicant.

Hawthorne effect A phenomenon that causes workers to work harder and produce more when they know they are being observed. This so-called effect, which grew out of the Hawthorne experiments, has been criticized in recent years.

Hawthorne experiments A series of behavioral studies conducted at Western Electric's Hawthorne, Illinois, plant between 1924 and 1932.

Hierarchy of needs A theory of motivation, developed by Abraham Maslow, based on five ascending levels of needs: physiological, security, social, esteem, and self-actualization.

Horizontal (lateral) communication The flow of information among workers on the same organizational level.

Horizontal integration Business expansion into related or similar lines.

Human relations model An approach to motivating workers based on making them feel important and allowing them social interaction on the job.

Human relations skills The managerial abilities needed to resolve conflict, motivate, lead, and communicate effectively with other workers.

Human resource planning The planning for hiring and making the best use of people.

Human resources model Recognition, based on Theory Y, that workers have complex motivation and the need for individual expression.

Impact analysis Forecasting method designed to predict the effect of technological breakthroughs on specific industries.

Import broker Individual, operating on a commission, who brings together American buyers and foreign sellers.

Import commission house Firm that receives foreign goods on consignment for resale to American firms.

Import merchant Individual who buys foreign goods for resale to American businesses.

Impoverished management Style of a manager who has little concern for either people or productivity.

Incentive pay plan A pay plan based on work produced.

Incentive theory Theory that analyzes external influences shaping human behavior.

Income statement Presentation of a firm's revenues and expenses for a given period.

Indiscrimination Incorrect evaluation because of stereotyping.

Induction and orientation The manager's establishing of a comfortable, productive environment for a new employee.

Inference-observation confusion Communication problem resulting from limited observations.

Informal (temporary) committee Committee formed to deal with relatively unimportant matters that often require no particular resolution.

Informal organization Group that functions outside formal authority relationships.

Informational role Role in which a manager serves as monitor, disseminator, or spokesperson.

Inspection The process of evaluating the services, processes, or finished goods of a firm to ensure that they conform to standards.

Instrumentality How much a decision maker believes that attaining some organizational objective will be translated into a personal payoff.

Intention-to-buy survey Market research method designed to gather information on what the consumer will buy.

Interest group An informal group of people whose primary purpose is to advance the position of their members.

Intergroup conflict Disagreements or confrontations between departments or other formal groups within an organization.

Intergroup team building A problem-solving process to reduce conflict and improve relations between groups who must work together.

Intermittent production system A system designed to produce batches of goods rather than a continuous stream of products.

International Monetary Fund (IMF) Institution created in 1944 to facilitate postwar international investment and trade.

International trade The flow of goods, services, capital, and intangibles such as technology, patents, and trademarks between one country and other nations.

Interpersonal conflict Work confrontations or rivalries between individuals or between individuals and groups.

Interpersonal role Role in which a manager interacts with others.

Intrapersonal conflict Emotional frustration arising when an employee's job duties clash with his or her values or needs.

Intuitive decision making Decision making based on the belief that good decision making is an art, not a science.

Inventory A stock of goods for making a product and the finished goods for filling customer orders.

Inventory control Maintaining supplies of inventory at adequate levels to meet production and sales requirements.

Job analysis The process of gathering, analyzing, and recording facts about each job in a firm.

Job description A series of concise statements about a job's duties and responsibilities.

Job design The process of organizing work so as to reduce effort, enhance worker satisfaction, reduce costs, and boost efficiency.

Job enlargement Expanding a job horizontally so as to reduce repetitiveness and monotony.

Job enrichment Modifying jobs in order to make them more satisfying. Job enrichment normally allows workers to plan and control their activities.

Job evaluation A systematic method of appraising the worth of a job compared to other jobs in the organization and to jobs in similar organizations.

Job modification An adjustment to a job to make it more efficient, more interesting, or less tiring.

Job posting The practice of displaying job openings on bulletin boards and in company publications.

Job rating The process of comparing jobs on the bases of skill, effort, responsibility, and conditions.

Job rotation The moving of a worker from one job to another to relieve boredom and to broaden job skills.

Job specification A statement specifying the human qualifications needed for a particular job.

Joint venture A company created by merging two or more firms in order to take advantage of each firm's strengths.

Just-in-time scheduling (JIT) A technique that combines purchasing, materials management, and inventory control in order to minimize inventory and costs in the production process.

Labor relations A continuous relationship between an employer and a group of employees represented by a union. The relationship includes negotiating, interpreting, and administering a written labor agreement covering pay, hours of work, and general working conditions.

Laissez-faire, free enterprise philosophy Theory that a free, competitive market aiming at maximum profits enhances the public welfare and enables business to meet its social obligation.

Laissez-faire (free-rein) leadership style A leadership approach in which managers do as little supervising as possible.

Latest allowable time (T_L) The latest calendar date on which an event can occur without delaying a project's completion.

Leadership Skill that has three basic ingredients: the understanding that people's motivation varies at different times, the ability to inspire, and the ability to create a climate for motivation.

Leading The management function that involves influencing others in order to accomplish specific objectives.

Leading indicator An event that always precedes another event, thereby giving advance warning of change.

Least-cost strategy A plan that emphasizes producing a standardized product at a low cost.

Leverage ratio Measurement of the long-term solvency of a firm.

Lewin model A process of planned change in three stages: unfreezing the status quo, moving to a new level, and refreezing at the new level.

Licensing agreement Contract between a U.S. firm and a foreign firm whereby the foreign firm agrees to manufacture or sell on a royalty basis in a specific market for a limited time.

Line authority Authority that enables a manager to tell subordinates what to do.

Line position Position with authority over a business's operations, and with responsibility for physically producing or selling the product or service.

Linear programming (LP) A quantitative technique allowing managers to determine the best use of their resources. Application of linear programming helps managers maximize profit, minimize costs, or satisfy some other business objective.

Liquidation Strategy in which a business is sold to avoid bankruptcy.

Liquidity ratio Measurement of a firm's ability to meet its current obligations.

Lose-lose method Conflict resolution satisfying neither party.

Management The process of maximizing the potential of people and coordinating their efforts to attain some predetermined goal.

Management by exception A philosophy of supervision that encourages lower-level managers to make decisions on routine matters within set guidelines.

Management by objectives (MBO) A process whereby a manager and a subordinate jointly set objectives for the subordinate and identify the results expected of the subordinate.

Management information system (MIS) A computer-assisted system that collects, organizes, and disseminates data to managers for decision-making purposes.

Managerial Grid® An approach developed by Robert Blake and Jane Mouton to classifying leadership styles. The grid shows various combinations of a manager's concern for production and concern for people.

Material requirements planning (MRP) A computerized information system that integrates inventory and production scheduling.

Maximax Strategy that involves determining the maximum payoff for each alternative and choosing the one with the biggest payoff of all.

Maximin Strategy that involves determining the minimum payoff for each alternative and then choosing the alternative with the biggest profit.

Middle management The level of management that includes all managers above the supervisory level but below the level where overall company policy is determined.

Middle-of-the-road (organization man) management Style of a manager who has limited concern for both people and productivity.

Minimax Strategy that involves determining the maximum cost of each alternative and choosing the one that would cost the least.

Mission The philosophy and purpose of an organization on which its objectives, policies, and strategy are based.

Monopolistic competition Market structure that allows each firm considerable discretion in its pricing policies.

Monopoly Market structure in which seller offers a product or service for which there are no good substitutes.

Motivation The energizing of human effort.

Motivation-hygiene (two-factor) theory A theory, developed by Frederick Herzberg, that focuses on factors leading to job satisfaction and dissatisfaction.

Moving average Method of eliminating regular seasonal or cyclical patterns from data to indicate the underlying trend.

Multinational corporation (MNC) Business firm that produces and markets goods and services in more than one country.

National Labor Relations Board (NLRB) The agency created as a part of the National Labor Relations Act to administer the provisions of the act.

Need theory Motivational theory focusing on the internal stimuli that cause people to take action.

Negative reinforcement Skinner's theory that behavior changes when unpleasant consequences are removed.

Niche Marketing strategy in which the product is targeted to a particular group of customers.

Noise Any interference with the communication process.

Nonprogrammed decisions Decisions used to resolve nonrecurring problems. These decisions often are related to an organization's policy-making activities.

Nonverbal feedback Body movement or actions made in response to communication.

Objective Statement of what an organization seeks to accomplish. A single-use plan.

Objective function A mathematical expression of the relationship between a dependable variable and some other measure of output.

Oligopolistic industry Market structure characterized by a few very large sellers and by "interdependency." The pricing policies of one or more firms prompt reactions from other firms in the industry.

Operational planning Planning that is directed toward the fulfillment of departmental goals; carries out a tactical plan.

Optimum order point The level of inventory at which an order should be placed in order to minimize costs associated with procurement.

Optimum order quantity The quantity of an item that should be purchased in order to minimize procurement costs.

Order control A method of production planning and control involving receiving the customer's order to following up.

Organizational change Any adjustment made by an organization in responding to environmental forces or anticipating future events.

Organizational determinism A school of thought that argues that an organization not only adapts to its environment, but that the success of a business depends on how well it can influence environmental forces in its favor.

Organizational development (OD) A long-range program designed to improve organizational performance through modifying employees' attitudes and behavior.

Organizational philosophy A firm's values, beliefs, and guidelines that channel its business conduct.

Organizational purpose A goal that defines the activities an organization intends to perform and the kind of an organization it intends to be.

Organizational unit group All employees who report to the same supervisor.

Organizing The management function of developing a system in which people can perform tasks that lead to the desired results.

Panel or board of interviewers Interviewers who, in a group setting, question a job applicant.

Partially structured situation A decision-making situation on the decision-situation continuum between the two extremes of structured and unstructured.

Participative leadership style Managers' involvement of subordinates in organizational decisions.

Patterned (structured) interview An interview comprised of questions designed to gather a large amount of information in a concise manner.

Performance report Data showing budgeted targets, actual performance, and variances.

Personal interview The meeting, in a particular setting, of interviewer and job applicant so as to assess the applicant's personal qualities and abilities for the job.

Personality test Selection test designed to evaluate various personality traits of job applicants.

Plan-do-control approach Motivating workers by letting them influence all aspects of their work—planning, doing, and controlling.

Planned change A proactive approach to planning that tries to see the organization as it should be in the future.

Planned (nondirective, unstructured) interview An interview that permits the person being interviewed to respond at length to the interviewer's questions.

Planning Determining specific objectives and how to accomplish them.

Planning gap The difference between where a firm would like to be and where it will be if it does nothing.

Point system Evaluation of jobs by assigning points to each job and converting these points to wages.

Polarization Communication terms too extreme to convey thoughts accurately.

Policy General guideline that channels decision making of subordinates. It is a standing plan.

Positive reinforcement Skinner's theory that a favorable consequence encourages repetitive behavior.

Procedure Standing plan that establishes specific methods for handling activities and details the exact sequence in which action must be taken.

Process consultation A group organizational technique in which, typically, a professional consultant helps an organization to perceive, understand, and act on problems in its human processes.

Process departmentation Grouping activities according to the manufacturing processes.

Procurement costs Clerical and other costs incurred in acquiring inventories.

Product departmentation Grouping a business's activities around its products.

Product life cycle A concept that suggests that all products pass through a series of growth curves until they reach a point where demand either levels out or begins to decline.

Production control Meeting production plans efficiently through scheduling, quality assurance, and inventory control.

Production costs Expenses associated with inventory, including overtime, labor turnover, and material start-up costs.

Production-operations management (POM) Management concerned with the provision of goods and services.

Production planning Determining what products will be produced and how, when, and where they will be produced.

Production system Process for converting resources into goods and services.

Profitability ratio Indication of how well a firm has done during the year in achieving its desired profit level.

Program A standing plan that is a composite of policies, procedures, rules, and task assignments necessary to carry out capital and operating budgets.

Program evaluation and review technique (PERT) A network modeling technique that breaks down a project's activities and events in order to determine where and when to allocate resources.

Programmed decisions Decisions that managers face again and again. These decisions usually involve an organization's everyday activities.

Project management/matrix structures An organizational arrangement whereby specialists from functional departments are assigned to special projects under the direction of a project manager.

Punishment Skinner's theory that unpleasant consequences change behavior.

Purchasing The procuring of raw materials, components, and services that the organization needs to achieve its goals.

Qualitative forecast A forecast based on opinions, sometimes combined with statistics.

Quality circles Small groups of workers who volunteer their time and energy to identify, analyze, and solve quality-related problems in their areas of responsibility.

Quantitative school School of management thought that focuses on the use of mathematical models to simulate business problems, letting managers make decisions based on predictable outcomes.

Queuing (waiting line) model Quantitative control tool used by firms to determine the optimal methods for serving customers or for scheduling the flow of material through various manufacturing processes.

Reactive change An organization's adapting and changing, sometimes grudgingly, because it can no longer ignore external or internal pressure.

Regression analysis Forecasting technique that measures the mathematical relationship of one or more variables to the item under study.

Regret The loss that a manager suffers because he or she does not know the future at the time a decision is made.

Reinforcement theory A theory of motivation, developed by B. F. Skinner, holding that all human behavior is shaped by its consequences.

Relation-oriented need Need that can be satisfied on the job through interaction with other workers.

Responsibility A feeling of obligation that complements authority.

Retrenchment Significant change in strategy brought about by poor performance.

Right-to-work law State statute that makes union shop contract clauses illegal.

Risk Decisions for which probabilities can be assigned to the expected outcomes of each alternative.

Role incongruency Conflict experienced within a worker when social pressures on the worker are at odds with the organization's goals.

Role negotiation A technique in which managers discuss what they want from one another and explain why.

Rule Simple standing plan that dictates action that must or must not be taken in a given situation.

Satisfier Factor contributing to job satisfaction as mentioned by workers responding to a study by Frederick Herzberg, who called these satisfiers "motivators."

Scenario Forecasting method that attempts to describe a series of happenings that demonstrate how to obtain a particular goal.

Schedule Single-use plan that commits resources to a given activity.

Scheduling The task of assigning workers and machines to various jobs at a given time.

Scientific management A systematic, analytical study of work. Its objective was to find the most efficient method for performing a task and to train workers in that method.

Secondary boycott Boycott by striking union on companies dealing with the employer.

Selective perception Differences in interpretation because of individuals' varying reception of stimuli.

Semantic problem A communication problem arising when readers or listeners do not understand the use of words or phrases.

Sensitivity training A management development technique holding that individual values, attitudes, and behavior determine an organization's effectiveness.

Setup costs Expenses incurred at the start of a production run, including adjustments to the equipment and clerical costs.

Simple ranking plan Evaluation of jobs by arranging them in order of increasing worth.

Simplex method A linear programming algorithm that can be used to solve complex business problems.

Simulation A quantitative procedure that develops a model of a process and then conducts a series of trial-and-error experiments to predict its behavior.

Single-use plan A predetermined course of action developed for unique, nonrecurring situations.

Slack The amount of time that events of a project can be delayed without affecting the outcome of the project.

Smoothing Reducing conflict by accentuating common goals.

Social responsibility doctrine Theory emphasizing the obligations that businesses have to the general public, including responsibilities to improve the social and physical environment and to alleviate social ills.

Span of management (span of control) The number of subordinates that a single manager can effectively supervise.

Staff authority Authority of staff managers to offer advice and make recommendations to other managers.

Staff position Position that is advisory to those in line positions.

Staffing The managerial function that involves the recruitment, selection, development, and retention of employees with appropriate qualifications for positions created by the manager.

Standard Management's unit of measurement for comparing performance levels. Standards are normally established for output quality and quantity, costs of operations, and employee performance.

Standing plan A predetermined course of action developed for repetitive situations.

Stockout costs Losses that a firm incurs when inventories are depleted before demand is satisfied.

Strategic planning Long-range planning carried out by top management. It includes the development of overall company objectives, and is primarily concerned with solving long-term problems associated with external environmental forces.

Strategy Single-use plan formulated in contemplation of actions that competitors may undertake.

Stress A person's physical, chemical, or emotional response to tension or pressure in the work environment.

Strikebreaker Person hired to take the place of a striking worker.

Suboptimization A manager's tendency to operate solely in the interests of his or her department rather than in the interests of the company as a whole.

Supervisory management The lowest level of management. Supervisors manage workers who perform the most basic job duties required in the business.

Survey feedback An organizational technique that collects and shares workers' opinions in order to solve existing problems and to help groups understand their own behavior.

Synectics A free-association method for generating creative solutions to a problem.

Systems theory This theory holds that a manager must be able to see the interrelationships of the different parts of his or her organization and understand how the organization fits into its larger environment.

Tactical planning Planning that is concerned with the efficient, day-to-day use of resources allocated to a department manager's area of responsibility.

Task group Several workers from the same department who are assigned common tasks.

Team building A management development approach that encourages managers to solve business problems through collective effort.

Team management Style of a manager with high concern for both people and productivity.

Technical skills Specialized knowledge and abilities that can be applied to specific tasks.

Technological forecasting Term applied to various forecasting tools developed in recent years to forecast economic activity and project future technological advances.

Technostress The inability of individuals to adjust to changing technology.

Telecommuting A work system of gaining access to an office computer from another location.

Theory X A theory of human behavior holding that the average human being is lazy and irresponsible and must be coerced into exerting effort.

Theory Y A theory of human behavior holding that the average human being is industrious, intelligent, and responsible.

Theory Z Term used to characterize the Japanese approach to managing a business that has also been adopted by some American firms. It entails security of employment, slow progression through the managerial ranks, collective decision making, and control through cultural pressure.

Time series forecast A forecast that uses a firm's past happenings to predict future events.

Top management The level of management comprised of individuals who have responsibility for making decisions and formulating policies that affect all aspects of a firm's operations.

Total social accounting system Government's determination of business's share of the cost of a problem.

Traditional school *See* Classical school

Transformation The ability to revise what is known in order to produce new forms and patterns; that is, to reinterpret and reorganize information.

Trend line A hypothetical projection of a previous pattern of past events into the future.

Uncertainty Decisions for which probabilities cannot be assigned to surrounding conditions.

Union shop Clause in a labor contract stipulating that eligible workers are required to join a union within a stipulated time.

Upward communication The flow of opinions, ideas, complaints, and other kinds of information from subordinates to managers.

Valence The degree to which a decision maker wants a particular outcome.

Variable costs Expenses that change as volume of production increases or decreases.

Verbal feedback A written or spoken response to communication.

Vertical expansion Enlarging a job to include the managerial functions of planning and controlling.

Vertical integration The ownership of sources of raw materials or component parts, or the distribution outlets.

Vocational interests test A selection test designed to measure a person's likes and dislikes concerning various occupations, hobbies, and so on.

Win-lose method Conflict resolution at the expense of one party.

Win-win method Conflict resolution beneficial to all concerned.

Work simplification A traditional approach to job design based on specialized skills, minimal skill requirements and training time, limited number and variety of tasks, and repetition.

Yellow dog contract Illegal document signed by workers stipulating that they will not join a union.

Name Index

Subject Index